EFFECTIVE TEACHING IN ELEMENTARY SOCIAL STUDIES

Third Edition

Tom V. Savage
California State University, Fullerton
David G. Armstrong
Texas A & M University

Merrill, an imprint of
Prentice Hall
Englewood Cliffs, New Jersey   *Columbus, Ohio*

Library of Congress Cataloging-in-Publication Data

Savage, Tom V.
    Effective teaching in elementary social studies / Tom V. Savage,
David G. Armstrong—3rd ed.
       p. cm.
    Includes bibliographical references and index.
    ISBN 0-13-370826-8
    1. Social sciences—Study and teaching (Elementary)—United
States. I. Armstrong, David G. II. Title.
LB1584.S354 1996
372.83′044—dc20   95-3587
                                     CIP

Cover photo: © Unicorn Stock
Editor: Bradley J. Potthoff
Production Editor: Stephen C. Robb
Photo Editor: Anne Vega
Design Coordinator: Jill E. Bonar
Text Designer: STELLARViSIONs
Cover Designer: Proof Positive/Farrowlyne Associates, Inc.
Production Manager: Patricia A. Tonneman
Electronic Text Management: Marilyn Wilson Phelps, Matthew Williams, Karen L. Bretz,
    Tracey B. Ward
Illustrations: Karen L. Bretz; STELLARViSIONs

This book was set in Transitional 511 and Swiss 721 by Prentice Hall and was printed and bound
by R. R. Donnelley & Sons Company. The cover was printed by Phoenix Color Corp.

© 1996 by Prentice-Hall, Inc.
A Simon & Schuster Company
Englewood Cliffs, New Jersey 07632

Earlier editions © 1992 and 1987 by Macmillan Publishing Company.

Photo credits: AP/Worldwide Photos, pp. 26, 42, 85, 332; The Bettmann Archive, p. 10; Jim
Cronk, p. 390; Scott Cunningham, Merrill/Prentice Hall, pp. 45, 68, 141, 153, 176, 195, 198, 238,
281, 320, 321, 362, 466, 473; Jean-Claude Lejeune, p. 55; Christopher Holstein, p. 14; Mark
Madden, K.S. Studios, Merrill/Prentice Hall, pp. 385, 500, 529; Frances Roberts, p. 84; Barbara
Schwartz, Merrill/Prentice Hall, pp. 93, 166, 179, 277, 440; Michael Siluk, p. 356; Anne Vega,
Merrill/Prentice Hall, pp. 105, 197, 233, 305, 337, 363, 408, 450, 459, 506, 524; Todd Yarrington,
Merrill/Prentice Hall, p. 417.

Printed in the United States of America

10 9 8 7 6 5 4 3 2 1

ISBN: 0-13-370826-8

Prentice-Hall International (UK) Limited, *London*
Prentice-Hall of Australia Pty. Limited, *Sydney*
Prentice-Hall Canada, Inc., *Toronto*
Prentice-Hall Hispanoamericana, S. A., *Mexico*
Prentice-Hall of India Private Limited, *New Delhi*
Prentice-Hall of Japan, Inc., *Tokyo*
Simon & Schuster Asia Pte. Ltd., *Singapore*
Editora Prentice-Hall do Brasil, Ltda., *Rio de Janeiro*

PREFACE

Citizens' roles become more difficult with each advancing year. Complex social problems grow more rapidly than our capacity to respond to them. Who has answers to such intractable difficulties as war, world hunger, and the hatreds that pit neighbor against neighbor in many parts of the world? Closer to home, where are the solutions to social strains caused by youth gangs, lingering racial prejudice, hostility toward immigrants, and growing crime rates? Today, we often feel overwhelmed by conflicting claims of individuals and groups who assert they have the answers. Choosing among competing recipes for change is not easy, but we *must* choose and act.

Young people in school must prepare to be sophisticated, tough-minded adults who can cope with a changing and challenging world. They must understand that there are no easy answers to difficult problems. Good social studies instruction provides this perspective. We believe that the social studies program, even in the early primary grades, needs to help young people develop sophisticated thinking skills. Simplistic instruction that demands little of children other than a repetition of arid "facts" will not do. We need to help young people develop confidence in their abilities to view problems from multiple perspectives, apply rational thinking powers, and above all, make hard decisions.

Social studies is, by nature, controversial. Because of this nature and because social studies is viewed as such a vital subject by knowledgeable individuals, social studies teachers face enormous pressures. Special interest groups ranging across the political spectrum want to "reform" education by gaining control of the content of the curriculum and the methods of instruction. It is important that social studies teachers from kindergarten through grade 12 have a solid knowledge of the purposes of social studies and of the methods most likely to promote growth toward informed and responsible citizenship. This task cannot be delayed until students reach secondary school. It must begin with the first days of the school experience.

It is for these purposes that we have written *Effective Teaching in Elementary Social Studies, Third Edition.* It is our desire that elementary teachers confront and clarify their views of the meaning and purpose of social studies. We hope that this text will contribute to their understanding and assist them in developing a set of beliefs and instructional skills that will help them face difficult choices and implement meaningful instruction.

Because of the interrelated nature of knowledge needed to make decisions, the content of the social studies can no longer be identified as simply history and geography. Definitions of the curriculum need to be expanded to include important multicultural and gender equity issues, environmental issues, and issues relating to global understanding.

New demands are being placed on the instructional role of teachers. Instruction must help pupils learn how to develop thinking skills and must challenge pupils to go beyond merely acquiring knowledge to formulating values and beliefs. Teachers must be aware of new technologies and the exciting possibilities of infusing them into the social studies program. The needs of an increasingly diverse student population must be accommodated, including a large number of pupils who have a primary language other than English. These students must not miss important social studies lessons simply because of language barriers. This text prepares teachers for these challenges.

Effective Teaching in Elementary Social Studies has been used successfully in undergraduate and graduate social studies courses. It is designed for use in elementary social studies methods classes, as a source for discussion in advanced curriculum classes, and as a personal reference for elementary social studies teachers. Users of earlier editions have labeled it as "practical," "readable," and "user friendly." We hope you find the third edition consistent with this tradition.

New to This Edition

The third edition features much new content:

- Up-to-date information about elementary social studies curricula
- A new chapter on integrating the social studies with other subjects
- A new chapter on teaching social studies to limited English proficient pupils
- Updated information on authentic assessment
- Graphic organizers for every chapter to provide the reader with a scaffold or organizing framework for the chapter content
- A wide selection of current children's literature that can be used to teach important ideas and concepts
- A case study to prompt thinking before reading each chapter and for reflection at completion
- More than 60 practical teaching lessons that are ready for classroom use (Some of these lessons are contributions from teachers who used earlier editions.)

Text Features

Each chapter of the third edition of *Effective Teaching in Elementary Social Studies* includes the following:

- **Chapter Goals** to help focus attention on key content in the chapter
- **Graphic Organizers** that show the relationship among items in the chapter
- An **Introduction** to provide a meaningful context for the information to follow
- A **Case Study** that prompts readers to think about a significant issue discussed in the chapter
- **Special Features** including (1) boxed items that pose questions and challenge readers to think about issues and (2) other figures and activities to enrich understanding
- **Key Ideas in Summary** to pull together and reinforce the chapter's important content

- **Chapter Reflections** that prompt readers to return to the case study and review changes that might have occurred in their thinking as a result of reading the chapter
- **Activities** that help readers extend and enrich their understanding
- **References** that direct readers to sources of information used in the preparation of the manuscript

Organization

Content has been organized for flexible use. Some individuals may wish to reorder the material. To accommodate this possibility, the information in each chapter can be used independently of that in other chapters.

The text's four major divisions suggest the general flavor of information in related chapters. The first four chapters, under the heading "Contexts for the Social Studies," set the stage. The focus is on the purposes of the social studies, the social studies curriculum, an overview of history and the social science that form the core of social studies content, and general approaches to planning for instruction.

Part II, "Fundamental Approaches to Instruction," features chapters that respond to the need to implement different types of plans. These chapters present strategies for teaching concepts and generalizations, using learning groups, developing thinking skills, and recognizing the important role of values in arriving at conclusions and taking action.

The third part, "A Selection of Themes," highlights four critical areas that cross subject matter boundaries: (1) law-related lessons, (2) global education lessons, (3) multicultural and gender-equity lessons, and (4) environmental and energy lessons.

Part IV, "Supporting and Assessing Social Studies Learning," provides practical information on using new technologies to further social studies learning and on teaching important map and globe skills. A new chapter focuses on the important trend toward thematic instruction and integration across the curriculum. Another chapter new to this edition deals with ways teachers can support social studies learning for limited English proficient (LEP) pupils. The final chapter explores alternative ways to assess what pupils have learned and includes a section on "authentic assessment."

Effective Teaching in Elementary Social Studies, Third Edition, is a practical book. It goes beyond telling what should be done. The emphasis is on "how to do it." Content builds on years of experience of successful elementary teachers. A number of experienced elementary and middle school teachers teaching kindergarten through grade eight have contributed ideas and have implemented some of the lesson plans. Try the ideas. They work.

Acknowledgments

No work is an independent project. A number of individuals have been patient and have contributed to the development of *Effective Teaching in Elementary Social*

Studies, Third Edition. We would like to give special thanks to teachers enrolled in the master's program at California State University, Fullerton, who provided suggestions and ideas. We are grateful to Carmen Zuniga-Hill, associate professor, California State University, Fullerton, who provided helpful assistance and an insightful review of the chapter on teaching limited English proficient pupils. We also want to recognize the helpful staff at Merrill/Prentice Hall Publishing for assisting in the development and the publication of the text. Finally, we want to recognize the contributions of our wives, Marsha and Nancy, not only for their patience while we worked on the revision, but for their professional suggestions and assistance.

T.V.S.
D.G.A.

CONTENTS

PART I   CONTEXTS FOR THE SOCIAL STUDIES   1

CHAPTER 1   DEFINING THE SOCIAL STUDIES   3

Introduction   6
Defining Social Studies   9
Citizenship Education   9
History and Social Science Education   10
Reflective Thinking and Problem-solving Education   11
Common Emphases within Social Studies Programs   11
Emphases within Citizenship Education   11
Emphases within History and Social Science Education   12
Emphases within Reflective Thinking and Problem-solving Education   13
Establishing Standards for Pupil Performance   14
The Grades K to 8 Social Studies Curriculum   16
Kindergarten: Awareness of Self in a Social Setting   16
Grade 1: The Individual in Primary and Social
*   Groups—Understanding School and Family Life   16*
Grade 2: Meeting Basic Needs in Nearby Social
*   Groups—The Neighborhood   17*
Grade 3: Sharing Earth and Space with Others—The Community   18
Grade 4: Human Life in Varied Environments—The Region   18
Grade 5: People of the Americas—The United States
*   and Its Close Neighbors   18*
Grade 6: People and Cultures—Representative World Regions   18
Grade 7: A Changing World of Many Nations—A Global View   18
Grade 8: Building a Strong and Free Nation—The United States   19
Relating Basic Social Studies Purposes to Subject
    Matter Covered at Each Grade Level   19
The Structure of Knowledge   23
Facts   24
Concepts   25
Generalizations   26
The Motivation Problem   27

CHAPTER 2   THE CONTENT SOURCES: HISTORY,
**   GEOGRAPHY, AND ECONOMICS   33**

Introduction   37
History   38
History of the Curriculum   41

History-related Classroom Activities   43
How Historians Judge the Truth   50
A Selection of Information Sources   51
Geography   52
The Geography Curriculum   53
Geography-related Classroom Activities   58
A Selection of Information Sources   62
Economics   63
Categories of Economic Systems   63
Economics-related Classroom Activities   64
A Selection of Information Sources   73

**CHAPTER   3   THE CONTENT SOURCES: POLITICAL SCIENCE,
SOCIOLOGY, ANTHROPOLOGY, AND PSYCHOLOGY   77**

Introduction   81
Political Science   81
Political Science in the Curriculum   82
Political Science-related Classroom Activities   85
Sociology   91
Institutions   92
Primary Groups   92
Secondary Groups   93
Stratified Groups   93
Relationships within and among Groups   94
Social Change   94
Communication   94
Social Problems   94
Sociology-related Classroom Activities   95
Anthropology   102
Archaeology and Prehistory   103
Human Evolution   103
Culture   104
Cultural Change   105
Anthropology-related Classroom Activities   106
Psychology   111
Individual Differences   112
Perception   112
Fears   114
Aggression   114
Psychology-related Classroom Activities   114

CHAPTER   4   PLANNING FOR INSTRUCTION   123

Introduction   126
Aims, Goals, Intended Learning Outcomes, and Instructional Objectives   127
Aims   128
Goals   128

       Intended Learning Outcomes   129
       Instructional Objectives   130
    Information Needed in Making Instructional Planning Decisions   **138**
       Knowledge about Learners   138
       Pupil Expectations and Prior Experience   139
       Knowledge about Content   139
       Knowledge of Teaching Methods   140
       Knowledge about Available Resources   140
    Organizing Planning Information   **141**
       Unit Plans   142
       Lesson Plans   152

PART II   FUNDAMENTAL APPROACHES TO INSTRUCTION   159

CHAPTER 5 CONCEPTS, GENERALIZATIONS, AND INDIVIDUALIZED LEARNING   161

  Introduction   **165**
  Concepts   **166**
    Types of Concepts   167
    Teaching Concepts   168
  Inducing Generalizations   **171**
  Individualized Learning: Basic Features   **175**
    Altering the Rate of Learning   175
    Altering the Content of Learning   176
    Altering the Method of Learning   177
    Altering the Goals of Learning   177
  Examples of Formal Approaches for Individualizing Learning   **177**
    Learning Centers   179
    Learning Activity Packages   181
    Activity Cards   182
    Learning Contracts   186

CHAPTER 6 GROUP LEARNING   191

  Introduction   **195**
  Basic Group Types   **198**
    The Tutoring Group   199
    The Equal Roles Group   199
    The Assigned Roles Group   201
  Preparing Pupils to Work in Groups   **202**
    Two-By-Two   203
    Think-Pair-Share   205
    Inside-Outside   205
    Numbered Heads Together   207

Buzz Session   208
**Three Popular Group Techniques: Classroom
Debate, Role Playing, and Simulation**   210
Classroom Debate   210
Role Playing   212
Simulations   215
Cooperative Learning Techniques   217
Jigsaw   218
Learning Together   220
Teams Achievement Divisions   221

CHAPTER   7   DEVELOPING THINKING SKILLS   227
Introduction   232
Teaching Pupils to Monitor Their Thinking   232
Thinking Aloud   233
Visualizing Thinking   234
Inquiry Approaches   237
Inquiry Teaching: Basic Steps   238
Using Data Charts to Compare, Contrast, and Generalize   241
Delimiting and Focusing Pupils' Thinking   243
Creative Thinking   244
Critical Thinking   246
Problem Solving   246
Decision Making   250
Finding More Information   254

CHAPTER   8   DEVELOPING PROSOCIAL BEHAVIOR   259
Introduction   265
Values, Morality, and Prosocial Behavior   266
Aesthetic Values   266
Moral Values   267
James Rest's Framework   267
Dealing with Values, Morality, and Prosocial Behavior in the Classroom   268
Clarifying Personal and Aesthetic Values   269
Values-Situation Role Playing   272
Kohlberg's Approach to Developing Moral Judgment   277
Moral Dilemma Discussions   279
*Teaching for Moral Decision Making: Issues, Values, and Consequences
Analysis*   282

PART III   A SELECTION OF THEMES   295

CHAPTER   9   LAW-RELATED EDUCATION   297
Introduction   301

What is Law-Related Education?   301
Goals of Law-Related Education   302
Law-Related Education Topics   304
   Basic Legal Concepts   304
   The Constitution and Bill of Rights   304
   The Legal System   305
   Criminal Law   306
   Consumer Law   306
   Family Law   307
Sources of Information   307
   Special Committee on Youth Education for Citizenship   308
   Constitutional Rights Foundation   308
   Law in a Free Society   308
   Center for Civic Education   308
   Consumer Law Resource Kit   308
   Opposing Viewpoints Series   309
   National Institute for Citizen Education in the Law   309
   Public Affairs Pamphlet Series   309
   Law in Action Units   309
   Cases: A Resource Guide for Teaching about the Law   309
Classroom Approaches to Law-Related Education   310
   Using Case Studies   310
   Storyline   315
   Children's Literature   317
   Mock Trials   317
Community Resources   319

CHAPTER 10   GLOBAL EDUCATION   327

Introduction   331
What is Global Education?   332
Global Education: Issues   333
Organizing Global Education Learning Experiences   334
   Monocultural Emphasis   335
   Experience Emphasis   336
   Contributions Emphasis   337
   Intercultural Emphasis   338
   Personal Emphasis   340

CHAPTER 11   MULTICULTURAL AND GENDER-EQUITY EDUCATION   349

Introduction   353
Multicultural Education's Many Faces   354
Gender-Equity Education: Purposes   357
Basic Goals of Multicultural and Gender-Equity Education   357
Monitoring Teaching Procedures   359
Classroom Approaches to Multicultural and Gender-Equity Studies   361

Single-Group Studies: General Characteristics   *361*
Single-Group Studies: Examples of Classroom Approaches   *362*
Multiple-Perspectives Approach: General Characteristics   *368*
Multiple-Perspectives Approach: A Classroom Example   *368*
Sources of Information   **371**
Multicultural Lessons   *371*
Gender-Equity Lessons   *371*

CHAPTER 12   ENVIRONMENTAL AND ENERGY EDUCATION   377
Introduction   380
Pressing Environmental and Energy Challenges   381
Global Warming   *381*
Deforestation   *381*
Toxic Waste   *382*
Ozone Depletion   *383*
Issues Associated with Energy   *384*
**Classroom Approaches to Building
Environmental and Energy Awareness   387**
Sensitizing Learners to the Problem of Unnecessary Waste   *387*
Developing Environmental Sensitivity through Children's Literature   *390*
Learning What Is Biodegradable   *391*

PART IV   SUPPORTING AND ASSESSING
SOCIAL STUDIES LEARNING   401

CHAPTER 13   TECHNOLOGY AND THE SOCIAL STUDIES   403
Introduction   407
Computers in the Schools   409
Traditional Computer Programs   *410*
CD-ROM   *412*
Internet   *414*
Integrating Computer-based Instruction   *416*
Some "Pros" and "Cons" Related to Computers and Schools   *416*
Videocassettes   418
Videodiscs   418
Personal Digital Assistants (PDAs)   419

CHAPTER 14   UNDERSTANDING MAP AND GLOBE SKILLS   425
Introduction   429
Globes   430
Kinds of Globes   *431*
Parts of the Globe That Need to Be Emphasized   *433*
Maps   433
Conformal Maps   *435*

Equal Area Maps   *436*
Basic Map and Globe Skills   **437**
Recognizing Shapes   *438*
Utilizing Scale   *438*
Recognizing Symbols   *439*
Utilizing Direction   *442*
Determining Absolute Location   *444*
Pointing Out Relative Location   *444*
Describing Earth–Sun Relationships   *447*
Interpreting Information on Maps and Globes   *447*
Teaching All of the Skills at Each Grade Level   **448**

CHAPTER 15   **SOCIAL STUDIES AND THE INTEGRATED CURRICULUM**   **455**

Introduction   **459**
Choosing Appropriate Themes   **460**
Feasible   *461*
Worthwhile   *461*
Contextualized   *462*
Meaningful   *462*
Mapping the Integration   **463**
Integrating Units around Selections of Children's Literature   **464**
The Arts   **465**
Music   **465**
Mathematics   **466**
Science and Technology   **470**
Language Arts   **471**
Readers' Theater   *472*
Reading Study Skills   *472*
Prereading Techniques   *474*
During-Reading Techniques   *475*
Postreading Techniques   *479*
Writing and the Social Studies   *481*

CHAPTER 16   **SOCIAL STUDIES FOR LIMITED ENGLISH PROFICIENT LEARNERS**   **489**

Introduction   **493**
Potential Problems for Limited English Proficient Learners in Social Studies   **494**
Cultural Conflict   *495*
Lack of Social Studies Background   *496*
Sequential Nature of the Curriculum   *496*
Difficulty of Social Studies Materials   *497*
Sheltered Instruction in the Social Studies   **497**
Principles of Second Language Learning in Content Fields   **498**
The Affective Filter   *499*

Meaningful and Comprehensible Input   *499*
Stages of Language Acquisition   *500*
Context and Cognitive Load   *502*
Learning Types of Knowledge Structures   *504*
**Successful Instructional Practices for Teaching
Limited English Proficient Learners**   **506**
Cooperative Learning   *506*
Multimedia and Concrete Experiences   *507*
Language Experiences   *509*

CHAPTER 17   EVALUATING LEARNING   515

Introduction   519
Authentic Assessment   519
Problems in Implementing Authentic Assessment   *520*
Informal Evaluation   521
Teacher Observation   *523*
Teacher–Pupil Discussion   *523*
Pupil-Produced Tests   *524*
My Favorite Idea   *524*
Headlines   *525*
Newspaper Articles   *525*
Word Pairs   *525*
Alphabet Review Game   *526*
Mystery Word Scramble   *526*
Anagrams   *527*
Other Informal Techniques   *528*
Recordkeeping and Informal Evaluation   *528*
Formal Evaluation   530
Rating Scales   *530*
Learning Checklists   *533*
Attitude Inventories   *535*
Essay Tests   *535*
True/False Tests   *537*
Multiple-Choice Tests   *538*
Matching Tests   *541*
Completion Tests   *542*
Using Evaluation Results to Improve Instruction   544

SUBJECT INDEX   549

NAME INDEX   555

LESSON IDEAS

PART I   CONTEXTS FOR THE SOCIAL STUDIES

LESSON IDEA 2–1   RESOLVING CONFLICTING ACCOUNTS OF EVENTS   39
LESSON IDEA 2–2   YESTERDAY ON THE PLAYGROUND   44
LESSON IDEA 2–3   FAMILY ORIGINS AND TRADITIONS   47
LESSON IDEA 2–4   GOD SAVE THE SOUTH   48
LESSON IDEA 2–5   ENVIRONMENTAL PERCEPTION   54
LESSON IDEA 2–6   MIGRATION   56
LESSON IDEA 2–7   REGIONS   57
LESSON IDEA 2–8   MAKING CHOICES   66
LESSON IDEA 2–9   ECONOMIC INCENTIVES   69
LESSON IDEA 2–10   ECONOMIC SYSTEMS   71
LESSON IDEA 3–1   RULE MAKING   86
LESSON IDEA 3–2   CONFLICT RESOLUTION   88
LESSON IDEA 3–3   LEARNING ROLES   96
LESSON IDEA 3–4   IDENTIFYING ISSUES IN THE NEWSPAPER   98
LESSON IDEA 3–5   THE BENEFITS OF COOPERATION   101
LESSON IDEA 3–6   LEARNING FROM AN ARTIFACT   107
LESSON IDEA 3–7   INVENTIONS AND TOOLMAKING   110
LESSON IDEA 3–8   OBSERVING HUMAN BEHAVIOR   115
LESSON IDEA 3–9   UNDERSTANDING PERCEPTION   117

PART II   FUNDAMENTAL APPROACHES TO INSTRUCTION

LESSON IDEA 5–1   COMPARING TWO COLONIES   173
LESSON IDEA 6–1   WORKING IN GROUPS: TWO-BY-TWO   203
LESSON IDEA 6–2   WORKING TOGETHER: INSIDE-OUTSIDE   206
LESSON IDEA 6–3   BUZZ SESSION: MOVING TO AMERICA   209
LESSON IDEA 6–4   ROLE PLAYING: HOW CAN NEEDS BE MET?   212
LESSON IDEA 6–5   JIGSAW: SOUTH AMERICA   219
LESSON IDEA 7–1   FINDING DISTANCES   233
LESSON IDEA 7–2   THE UNHAPPY TALE OF THE MONGOOSE   235
LESSON IDEA 7–3   INQUIRY LESSON: MAPS AND GLOBES   239
LESSON IDEA 7–4   NATIONS OF LATIN AMERICA   241
LESSON IDEA 7–5   WEATHER PATTERNS   247
LESSON IDEA 7–6   DECISION MAKING: ELECTING SCHOOL OFFICERS   251
LESSON IDEA 8–1   WHAT WOULD YOU DO WITH YOUR TIME?   269
LESSON IDEA 8–2   UNFINISHED SENTENCES   270

LESSON IDEA 8–3   VALUES-SITUATION ROLE PLAYING:
SELF–UNDERSTANDING   272

LESSON IDEA 8–4   VALUES-SITUATION ROLE PLAYING:
USING CONTENT FROM HISTORY   275

LESSON IDEA 8–5   ISSUES, VALUES, AND CONSEQUENCES:
SELF-UNDERSTANDING—WORRY ABOUT
THE FUTURE   284

LESSON IDEA 8–6   ISSUES, VALUES, AND CONSEQUENCES:
APPRECIATING DECISIONS MADE BY
OTHERS   287

PART III   A SELECTION OF THEMES

LESSON IDEA 9–1   APPLYING THE BILL OF RIGHTS   304

LESSON IDEA 9–2   A CASE STUDY: POLICE SEARCH   312

LESSON IDEA 9–3   A CASE STUDY: HURT ON THE JOB   313

LESSON IDEA 9–4   WHAT ARE YOUR RIGHTS?   321

LESSON IDEA 10–1   INTERCULTURAL EMPHASIS:
HIDE AND SEEK   339

LESSON IDEA 10–2   THE PARKING LOT SURVEY   341

LESSON IDEA 10–3   WHERE CLOTHING IS MANUFACTURED   342

LESSON IDEA 10–4   WHERE DO DIFFERENT DOG
BREEDS COME FROM?   343

LESSON IDEA 11–1   WHAT DOES A NATIONAL ANTHEM
TELL US ABOUT PEOPLE?   363

LESSON IDEA 11–2   HOW DO LEGENDS HELP US
UNDERSTAND PEOPLE?   365

LESSON IDEA 11–3   WHAT JOBS CAN A WOMAN HAVE?   366

LESSON IDEA 11–4   MOVING WESTWARD   368

LESSON IDEA 12–1   CONTENTS OF THE WASTEBASKET   387

LESSON IDEA 12–2   THE DREADED LITTER CREATURE   389

LESSON IDEA 12–3   BIODEGRADABLE LITTER   391

LESSON IDEA 12–4   POLLUTION   394

LESSON IDEA 12–5   ELECTRIC APPLIANCE SURVEY   394

LESSON IDEA 12–6   MAKING ENERGY-COLLAGE POSTERS   396

PART IV   SUPPORTING AND ASSESSING SOCIAL STUDIES LEARNING

LESSON IDEA 14–1   LEARNING ABOUT MAP SYMBOLS   439

LESSON IDEA 14–2   LEARNING ABOUT ABSOLUTE LOCATION   445

LESSON IDEA 15–1   SEWARD'S FOLLY   467

LESSON IDEA 15–2   SPANISH COLONIZERS AND THE
CARIBBEAN   476

LESSON IDEA 16–1   ALTERING A LESSON TO ACCOMMODATE LEP
PUPILS   508

CONTEXTS FOR THE SOCIAL STUDIES

DEFINING THE SOCIAL STUDIES

CHAPTER GOALS

This chapter provides information to help the reader:

- point out the importance of the social studies component of the elementary curriculum,
- describe and explain the three basic purposes of social studies,
- explain what is meant by "citizenship education,"
- list some topics that are typically covered in the K–8 social studies curriculum,
- identify relationships between the purposes of social studies and topics often taught at each grade level,
- identify and describe characteristics of each level in the "structure of knowledge," and
- explain how teacher attitudes affect pupils' motivation.

CHAPTER STRUCTURE

Introduction
Defining Social Studies
    Citizenship Education
    History and Social Sciences Education
    Reflective Thinking and Problem-Solving Education
Common Emphases within Social Studies Programs
    Emphases within Citizenship Education
    Knowledge / Skills / Values
    Emphases within History and Social Sciences Education
    Knowledge / Skills / Values
    Emphases within Reflective Thinking and Problem-Solving Education
    Knowledge / Skills / Values
Establishing Standards for Pupil Performance
The Grades K to 8 Social Studies Curriculum
    Kindergarten: Awareness of Self in a Social Setting
    Grade 1: The Individual in Primary and Social Groups—Understanding School and Family Life
    Grade 2: Meeting Basic Needs in Nearby Social Groups—The Neighborhood
    Grade 3: Sharing Earth and Space with Others—The Community
    Grade 4: Human Life in Varied Environments—The Region
    Grade 5: People of the Americas—The United States and Its Close Neighbors
    Grade 6: People and Cultures—Representative World Regions
    Grade 7: A Changing World of Many Nations—A Global View
    Grade 8: Building a Strong and Free Nation—The United States
Relating Basic Social Studies Purposes to Subject Matter Covered at Each Grade Level
The Structure of Knowledge
    Facts
    Concepts
    Generalizations
The Motivation Problem
Key Ideas in Summary
Chapter Reflections
Extending Understanding and Skill
References

Figure 1–1
Defining the social studies.

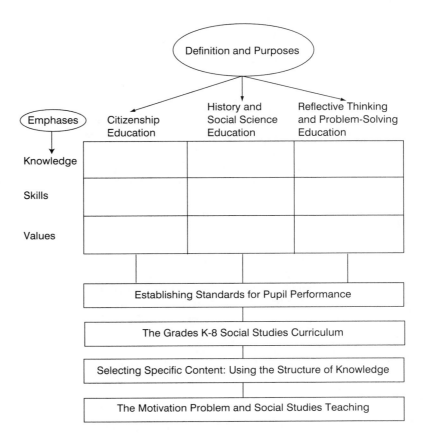

Chapter 1

Case Study

WHAT IS THE RELEVANCE?

Pat Taylor was a new sixth-grade teacher. It was the first week of school and time for the first social studies lesson of the year. She announced that morning, "Today we are starting our study of social studies." She heard an audible groan from the class. Pat persisted. "Who can tell us what we learn in social studies? Susan?"

"Well, we learn about things that happened a long time ago."

"Good. Billy?"

"We have to memorize names, dates, capital cities, lots of boring stuff like that."

"So you think social studies is boring?" Pat asked.

Several heads nodded is agreement. "Sure, who cares about that stuff? Why do we need to know when the battle of the 'Little Big Horn' was fought?" Janelle said.

"Yeah," Mary added. "Why do we need to know that corn is grown in Iowa or that Helena is the capital of Montana? We don't live in those states."

It was obvious that there was widespread agreement that social studies was a boring and not especially important subject. The stress level began to rise. Pat had not enjoyed social studies as a student and generally agreed with what her students were saying. She thought to herself, "What do I tell them? How do I motivate them? What is the purpose of social studies? They must be convinced that it is important or they will create problems all year."

What Is Your Response?

Take a couple of minutes to jot down your response to the following questions.

1. What do you think is the purpose of social studies? How would you respond to these students' questions?
2. Why should students be learning social studies?
3. Is social studies relevant to the lives of students? How can it be made relevant and important?
4. To what extent do you agree with the students in this case?
5. What do you think will happen if a teacher does not believe that the subject is important?

INTRODUCTION

Incredibly complex problems strain the world's social fabric. Pick up any newspaper. Listen to any news broadcast. Reports of mass starvation, epidemics, conflicts between racial groups, religious strife, random acts of violence, and bitterly intolerant debates about what constitutes morality are everywhere. Where is all this leading? Some evidence suggests that it is making us more cynical and frustrated than we have ever been before. One recent poll found that Americans were becoming increasingly indifferent toward problems of minorities and the poor and more and more resentful of immigrants. Fewer than half of the people polled believed that the government was looking after the interests of all of the people. Indeed, only about one-third of the respondents were convinced that elected officials had any interest at all in their constituents' concerns ("Poll Finds Nation of Cynics," 1994).

Clearly there is distrust with many institutions . . . but, not with all. Amazingly, despite the concern we have heard voiced over the past decade about the quality of public education, people in this country continue to place great faith in the schools as one institution that can "make a difference." The social studies component of the school curriculum focuses specifically on kinds of issues that are now challenging the integrity of our national social fabric. It is in their social studies classes that young people encounter human aspirations, problems, and potentials most directly. As social studies specialist Walter Parker (1991) has noted, the subject of the social studies is the great human adventure.

Social studies programs often are guided by important human dilemmas. Table 1–1 presents examples of these, together with related focus questions.

How should social studies lessons address issues such as those listed in Table 1–1? There are competing ideas as to how this task should be approached. Some people believe that social studies lessons should draw most of their content from traditional academic disciplines, most especially from history. A vigorous proponent of this view is E. D. Hirsch (1987), who has put forward proposals designed to promote broader development of what he styles "cultural literacy."

Others reject this approach. They suggest that social studies has obligations that go beyond teaching pupils contents of formal academic disciplines such as history. Many of these individuals believe social studies lessons must be designed for the purpose of helping young people to become socially responsible adults who can adapt to changing social conditions (Cherryholmes, 1992). This suggests the need for social studies instruction that requires young people to develop attitudes and skills that will allow them to adapt and construct the kinds of new knowledge necessary to cope with a future that may be quite different from today's world.

Some authorities who favor a social studies program that will prepare young people for changed future conditions acknowledge that much present social studies instruction does not reflect this orientation. It has been alleged that many teachers are more comfortable with a social studies program that seeks to pass on a conventional wisdom based largely on unexamined beliefs (Thornton, 1994). Those who hold this view suspect that young people soon discover a discontinuity between what is taught in their social studies classes and what they observe in the "real world." A lack of perceived relevance of this kind of instruction has been put forward as an explanation for the relatively low esteem many pupils have for social studies instruction. For educators favoring a more future-oriented social studies instruction, the antidote to pupil apathy is a program that encourages reflective inquiry and active challenges to the status quo.

Is this kind of instruction appropriate for elementary school learners? Some research suggests that even quite young pupils are quite aware of important social

Table 1–1
Common human dilemmas and social studies focus questions.

Dilemmas	Selected Focus Questions
Stability vs. Change	What is worth preserving in society? What needs to be changed? How do we adapt to change while preserving what is good?
Individual freedom vs. Community rights	When do the rights of individuals conflict with the needs of society? How do we decide when individual rights or societal needs should be given priority? What is the proper relationship between an individual and government? What is the role of laws and rules?
Reacting to diversity	How can we live in harmony with people who are different? When should diversity be encouraged? When should conformity be encouraged? How can we overcome irrational prejudice and discrimination?
Providing for wants and needs	How can we organize economic production to meet the most needs and wants? Who should decide what is produced? What is the role of government in controlling the marketplace?
Controlling population growth	What are the implications of continued population growth? What can be done to reduce the rates of population growth? How does one reconcile personal choice, religious freedom, and views of morality with population control? What places in the world are most in need of population control?
Using the environment	Who should decide how the environment and resources are to be used? How can we utilize resources of the earth wisely? How do we assure that future generations will enjoy a quality of life at least equal to our own?
Technological change	How do we use technological changes to our advantage? What happens when ethics and morality conflict with technological advances? Who should control the application of technology to our lives?

problems (Berman & La Farge, 1993). These young people are much more aware of "what is really going on" than many adults suppose. Some authorities believe that elementary social studies teachers need to take advantage of this sensitivity. Pupils need to be taught cooperation and conflict resolution, respect for diversity, and the importance of attacking issues in ways that will make a difference (Berman & La Farge, 1993).

Teaching social studies is not for cowards. Sometimes feelings about important issues run deep. Controversies abound over such issues as program goals, specific lesson content, and alternative teaching methodologies. Effective social studies teachers recognize that conflict and change are among life's constant companions. They tend to be thoughtful people who have a point of view and who are willing to stand up for their commitments. This book is designed to help prospective teachers who seek this kind of active engagement with their profession . . . and with life.

DEFINING SOCIAL STUDIES

"What is included in the social studies?" People give a number of answers to this question. Although the subject has been taught in school for decades, there still is no consensus about what should be included in the social studies (Barr, Barth, & Shermis, 1977). Sometimes this lack of definitional consensus has led to proposals to abandon the term *social studies* altogether and to replace it with more familiar academic labels, such as *history, geography,* or *civics*. Others reject this idea, believing that these labels are too narrow to embrace the kinds of learning that should go on in social studies classes.

Citizenship Education

The leading national association of social studies education professionals is the National Council for the Social Studies (NCSS). In November 1992 the House of Delegates of the NCSS adopted this definition of the field ("Minutes of the 36th Delegate Assembly," 1993):

> Social studies is the integrated study of the social sciences and humanities to promote civic competence. Within the school program, social studies provides coordinated, systematic study drawing upon such disciplines as anthropology, archaeology, economics, geography, history, law, philosophy, political science, psychology, religion, and sociology, as well as appropriate content from the humanities, mathematics, and natural sciences. The primary purpose of social studies is to help young people develop the ability to make informed and reasoned decisions for the public good as citizens of a culturally diverse, democratic society in an interdependent world. (p. 194)

This statement clearly indicates that an important objective of the social studies program is the promotion of "civic competence," or what we have chosen to call *citizenship*. The Task Force on Curriculum Standards for the Social Studies commented about the need for a strong programmatic focus on citizenship: "The United States and its democracy are constantly evolving and in continuous need of citizens who can adapt its enduring traditions and values to meet changing circumstances" (NCSS Task Force on Curriculum Standards for the Social Studies, 1994, p. vii). Few individuals dispute that there should be some emphasis on citizenship in the social studies, but there are disagreements over what the purpose of citizenship education is. Is it the inculcation of patriotism? Is it unquestioned obedience to the laws of society? Is it acceptance of the status quo? Is it voting in elections? Is it active involvement in public affairs?

Though views about the functions of citizenship education vary, three common threads run through many discussions of this issue. First, there is general agreement that

The human adventure is the subject of the social studies.

young people need to be encouraged to commit to such core American values as democratic decision making. Second, it is widely acknowledged that citizenship education lessons should encourage pupils to critique present ways of doing things (Leming, 1989). Third, it is expected that good citizenship education programs will produce young people who will leave school with a predisposition to become actively involved in public affairs.

Sanford Horwitt, a director of a national citizenship education project, is concerned that many young people view citizenship obligations too narrowly. Regarding this issue, he commented, "Young people have an impoverished notion of citizenship. . . . Basically, they think it's not breaking the law, and that's all" (Taylor, 1990, p. 7).

History and Social Science Education

In addition to citizenship, the 1992 NCSS definition of *social studies* states an important emphasis on content from academic disciplines. Though some content in social studies programs is drawn from many fields, programs today continue to place particularly heavy emphases on information drawn from history and such social science disciplines as geography, political science, economics, sociology, anthropology, psychology, archaeology, and law. For this text, we have chosen to label the academic content component of the social studies program *history and social science education.*

Effective citizenship rests on a solid knowledge base. History and the social sciences (and some other subjects that sometimes provide social studies content) have developed information and successful methods of investigation. These have the potential to enrich lives and to help pupils increase their abilities to make the kinds of rational decisions expected of good citizens.

Though we have chosen the term, "history and social science education," the academic content component of the social studies program is not limited to history and the social sciences. Any subject that deals with human behavior can provide good content for social studies lessons. When we look for lesson content, our object is to find information that can help pupils understand their world. We are not guided to select content because it is associated with a particular academic subject, such as history or geography, but rather because it may have potential to help our learners learn significant things about the world "as it is" and "as it might be."

Reflective Thinking and Problem-solving Education

Citizens in democratic societies need to be good thinkers. Adults are called on to respond to pressing problems of all kinds. Decisions they make influence their own lives and those of others in the community, state, and nation. Hence, reflective thinking and problem-solving education is another key component of the elementary social studies program. Lessons associated with this focus help pupils master techniques that are useful to them as they attempt to solve problems. (Specific problem-solving approaches are introduced in Chapter 7, "Thinking Skills Instruction.")

In summary, the social studies has a specific responsibility to promote citizenship education. This is exercised through lessons drawing content from history and the social sciences. This content often is organized and presented so as to facilitate development of learners' reflective thinking and problem-solving abilities.

COMMON EMPHASES WITHIN SOCIAL STUDIES PROGRAMS

For each broad social studies purpose there are three emphases that need to be identified (see Figure 1–2): knowledge, skills, and values. *Knowledge* refers to specific facts and understandings a person needs to know. *Skills* refer to processes of gathering and using knowledge. *Values* are attitudes and beliefs individuals use to justify their actions. When these three areas are combined with (1) citizenship education, (2) history and social science education, and (3) reflective thinking and problem solving, a clearer picture of the content of the social studies emerges.

Emphases within Citizenship Education

Knowledge
Young people should be exposed to knowledge related to the American heritage; the Constitution; the Bill of Rights; political processes followed at the local, state, and national levels; and other basic information an educated adult citizen is expected to know.

The social studies puposes matrix illustrates the major components of a comprehensive elementary social studies program. Each cell of the matrix indicates an important emphasis. All of these components should be addressed somewhere during the total elementary social studies program. However, all of them may not be addressed during any given year. Also, conditions in individual places will result in various degrees of emphasis being accorded to each component of the matrix.

	Citizenship Education	History and Social Science Education	Reflective Thinking and Problem Solving
Knowledge			
Skills			
Values and attitudes			

Figure 1–2
Matrix of social studies purposes.

Skills

Elementary school pupils need to be taught processes associated with rational decision making. They need to learn how to negotiate and compromise, to express their views clearly, and to work productively with others.

Values

Citizens do not make decisions only on the basis of information. They also consider social and personal values. Learners need to be exposed to the values associated with democratic decision making and with values that collectively support the operation of our nation's local, state, and national governments.

Emphases within History and Social Science Education

Knowledge

The academic disciplines, including history and the social sciences, are repositories of information that give us powerful insights into human behavior. This kind of information comprises an important part of the elementary social studies program.

Skills

Elementary social studies programs introduce skills academic content specialists use as they gather and assess the importance of information. Many of them use variants of the scientific method as they seek to verify and modify hypotheses. These same skills often are useful to learners as they begin to confront the kinds of personal and public dilemmas that adults face in their daily lives.

Values

Certain values are implicit in how academic content specialists go about their work. For example, they are predisposed to prize knowledge based on data more than knowledge based on intuition or feeling. Learners in the elementary program need to understand how values affect what individuals believe to be "real" or "important."

Emphases within Reflective Thinking and Problem-solving Education

Knowledge

Young people need to learn basic information about how rational decisions are made. Introducing them to procedures useful for bringing problems into focus and attacking them in a systematic, step-by-step way are important concerns of this part of the social studies program. As they learn how to identify relevant information and to use it to solve problems, pupils acquire techniques for organizing and evaluating data and for formulating and testing hypotheses.

Skills

Pupils' capacity for engaging in serious reflection and problem solving improves when they have opportunities to make decisions about real issues and to experience the consequences of these decisions. In the lower grades, problem-solving skills are developed as learners work with issues important to individuals and families. More mature elementary learners use these skills to work with a broader range of social and political problems affecting communities, states, the nation, and the world.

Many problems in a democratic society require collective decision making. Hence, part of the elementary social studies' skill-development program focuses on helping pupils to work productively in groups. This allows learners opportunities to engage in the kinds of give-and-take discussion that characterizes adult group decision making.

Values

Instruction in this area is designed to help pupils develop a commitment to approaches to reflection and problem solving that are based on rational thinking. It is hoped they will come to prize decisions that rest on evidence and logic and that they will resist jumping to conclusions based on unexamined assumptions or restrictive biases. Helping pupils develop a tolerance for diverse views is another important part of the values dimension of reflective thinking and problem-solving instruction.

The major social studies purposes of (1) citizenship education, (2) history and social science education, and (3) reflective thinking and problem-solving education and the subcategories under each of (a) knowledge, (b) skills, and (c) values frame the overall elementary social studies program. Well-balanced programs provide some learning experiences directed to each of these areas. However, it is not likely that each will receive equal attention at each grade level. At some grade levels it is usual for some areas to receive more emphasis than others. Similarly, there often are differences in

Effective thinking and problem solving are important components of social studies instruc-tion.

program emphasis from school district to school district. Despite such district-to-district variations in relative emphases given to specific areas, there is a general pattern of learning experiences common to many schools. This curriculum sequence is introduced in the next section.

ESTABLISHING STANDARDS FOR PUPIL PERFORMANCE

The best available source of information related to performance standards for school social studies programs is a publication entitled *Curriculum Standards for Social Studies*, prepared by the National Council for the Social Studies Task Force on Curriculum Standards for the Social Studies (1994). It lays out suggested performance standards for key themes or concepts that often provide a focus for social studies lessons.

Curriculum Standards provides lists of performance expectations for learners in the early grades, middle grades, and high school. An example of the information given for the early and middle grades relating to the concept "culture" is provided in Figure 1–3.

Curriculum Standards also provides outstanding examples of kinds of behaviors we can look at to determine the adequacy of learner performances. This material should be on the professional shelf of any teacher interested in social studies curriculum development. For ordering information, write to the National Council for the Social Studies,

Performance Expectations

1. **Culture**

   Social studies programs should include experiences that provide for the study of *culture and cultural diversity*, so that the learner can:

Early Grades	Middle Grades	High School
a. explore and describe similarities and differences in the ways groups, societies, and cultures address similar human needs and concerns;	a. compare similarities and differences in the ways groups, societies, and cultures meet human needs and concerns;	a. analyze and explain the ways groups, societies, and cultures address human needs and concerns;
b. give examples of how experiences may be interpreted differently by people from diverse cultural perspectives and frames of reference;	b. explain how information and experiences may be interpreted by people from diverse cultural perspectives and frames of reference;	b. predict how data and experiences may be interpreted by people from diverse cultural perspectives and frames of reference;
c. describe ways in which language, stories, folktales, music, and artistic creations serve as expressions of culture and influence behavior of people living in a particular culture;	c. explain and give examples of how language, literature, the arts, architecture, other artifacts, traditions, beliefs, values, and behaviors contribute to the development and transmission of culture;	c. apply an understanding of culture as an integrated whole that explains the functions and interactions of language, literature, the arts, traditions, beliefs and values, and behavior patterns;
d. compare ways in which people from different cultures think about and deal with their physical environment and social conditions;	d. explain why individuals and groups respond differently to their physical and social environments and/or changes to them on the basis of shared assumptions, values, and beliefs;	d. compare and analyze societal patterns for preserving and transmitting culture while adapting to environmental or social change;
e. give examples and describe the importance of cultural unity and diversity within and across groups.	e. articulate the implications of cultural diversity, as well as cohesion, within and across groups.	e. demonstrate the value of cultural diversity, as well as cohesion, within and across groups;
		f. interpret patterns of behavior reflecting values and attitudes that contribute or pose obstacles to cross-cultural understanding;
		g. construct reasoned judgments about specific cultural responses to persistent human issues;
		h. explain and apply ideas, theories, and modes of inquiry drawn from anthropology and sociology in the examination of persistent issues and social problems.

Figure 1–3

Example of performance standards.

Source: From *Curriculum Standards for Social Studies: Expectations of Excellence*. Washington, DC: National Council for the Social Studies, 1994. © National Council for the Social Studies. Reprinted by permission.

3501 Newark Street, NW, Washington, DC 20016. Ask about *Curriculum Standards for Social Studies* (Bulletin 89).

THE GRADES K TO 8 SOCIAL STUDIES CURRICULUM

Traditionally, the elementary social studies program was organized around the idea of "expanding horizons." In this pattern, pupils first studied topics that were familiar to them in their daily lives. For example, in the primary grades, programs focused on families, schools, neighborhoods, and local communities. In the middle and upper grades, topics expanded to include emphases on the state, nation, and world. This basic sequence, with important local variations, continues even now.

Children today are much more aware of patterns of life beyond their own communities than were children who grew up before the television age. From their earliest years, television brings images into their homes of patterns of living that may be quite different from their own. Films, too, expose young people to different places and cultures. Information young people glean from their exposure to the media and the growing interdependence of the world's peoples have influenced the organization of the school social studies program.

Today, children do not simply study their own schools, families, communities, and neighborhoods. As the National Council for the Social Studies Task Force on Scope and Sequence (1989) reported, "Social studies programs have a responsibility to prepare young people to identify, understand, and work to solve the problems that face our increasingly diverse nation and interdependent world" (p. 377).

In its report, the NCSS Task Force on Scope and Sequence (1989) identified titles of courses that are common in many school districts throughout the United States. The group found a number of different patterns in grades six, seven, and eight. As a result, the report identified three alternative sequences for these grade levels, which are illustrated in Box 1–1.

Subsections that follow discuss grade-level offerings in the social studies as described in the report of the Task Force on Scope and Sequence (1989).

Kindergarten: Awareness of Self in a Social Setting

The purpose of social studies instruction in kindergarten can be summed up in one word: *socialization*. Lessons teach young children about themselves and about patterns of behavior that are expected at home and at school. Pupils are encouraged to master basic rules governing social relationships.

Grade 1: The Individual in Primary and Social Groups— Understanding School and Family Life

In grade one, socialization experiences begun in kindergarten continue. Some basic social studies concepts are introduced. For example, different categories of people who

---

BOX 1–1   **Alternative Curriculum Sequences for Grades 6, 7, and 8**

The National Council for the Social Studies Task Force on Scope and Sequence (1989) identified three alternative sequences for grades six, seven, and eight.

Alternative One

Grade 6: People and Cultures: Representative World Regions

Grade 7: A Changing World of Many Nations: A Global View

Grade 8: Building a Strong and Free Nation: The United States

Alternative Two

Grade 6: European Cultures with their Extension into the Western Hemisphere

Grade 7: A Changing World of Many Nations: A Global View

Grade 8: Economics and Law-Related Studies (one semester of each)

Alternative Three

Grade 6: Land and People of Latin America

Grade 7: People and Cultures: Representative World Regions

Grade 8: Interdisciplinary Study of the Local Region

Think About This

1. What do you see as the advantages and disadvantages of each option?
2. Which option do you prefer? Why?
3. Which option seems to be the best "fit" with the K–5 social studies program? Why do you think so?
4. What is the curriculum sequence in your area? How does it compare with the curriculum described in this chapter?

---

work in the school can be used to provide pupils with a rudimentary understanding of the idea of "division of labor" (NCSS Task Force on Scope and Sequence, 1989). Pupils might be asked to find out where their grandparents live. This information could be used to help build an initial understanding of concepts such as "urban" and "rural."

Grade 2: Meeting Basic Needs in Nearby Social Groups—The Neighborhood

Using the neighborhood around the school as a context, the second-grade program introduces the study of communication, transportation, production, consumption, and exchange of goods and services. These topics typically are introduced in lessons that help pupils understand how people in neighborhoods and local social groups in other countries go about meeting their needs.

Grade 3: Sharing Earth and Space with Others—The Community

The social studies program in grade three concentrates on the learner's local community. Lessons emphasize the interdependence of cities and communities in the state, nation, and world. Among issues considered are change and growth in communities, and the governments, history, and locations of communities.

Grade 4: Human Life in Varied Environments—The Region

In grade four, pupils are introduced to the concept of "region." Frequently lessons feature an in-depth study of the home state as an example of a region. World geographic regions often are introduced. Lessons afford opportunities to compare and contrast these world regions with characteristics of the home state and with one another.

Grade 5: People of the Americas—The United States and Its Close Neighbors

The title of this course, particularly as it pertains to the "close neighbors" of the United States, reflects more a hope of the NCSS Task Force on Scope and Sequence than an accurate reflection of present practices. Today, most grade-five programs are heavily oriented to the study of the history and geography of the United States. Often, coverage of Canada and Latin America receives sparse attention. It is hoped that as time goes by more and more fifth-grade programs will spend more time on Canada and Latin America, particularly in terms of how these areas interact with the United States.

Grade 6: People and Cultures—Representative World Regions

The focus of instruction at grade six is on representative peoples and cultures of both Latin America and the Eastern hemisphere. Learners are encouraged to become familiar with important cultural contributions of people in these areas of the world. Interdependence among nations is a frequent theme in lessons. A persistent problem at grade six has been the tendency of some teachers to cover too many topics without developing any in depth. Better programs focus on a small group of nations that are presented as examples of particular world areas. This allows for a more detailed study of topics related to the selected nations. This kind of arrangement produces more substantive learning than a more general, "cover everything" approach.

Alternative emphases at grade six include the following:

- European Cultures and their Extension into the Western Hemisphere
- Land and People of Latin America

Grade 7: A Changing World of Many Nations—A Global View

The content of the grade-seven program often ties closely to what is taught in grade six. (However, there are important local variations. For example, in some places, a state history course is taught in grade seven.) The major intent is to increase learners' awareness of the world, especially the world outside the Western hemisphere. Physical geography and place location receive considerable attention. Learners are introduced to historical information about certain places to grasp the idea that conditions change over time. Distinctions are drawn between nations of the developed and developing world.

An alternate emphasis at grade seven is "People and Cultures: Representative World Regions." This emphasis tends to be favored in school districts where the grade-six program has been restricted to a study of Latin America.

Grade 8: Building a Strong and Free Nation—The United States

The primary objective of the grade-eight program is to introduce students to the economic and social history of the United States. Political history receives less attention. The idea is to engender interest in our country's history by focusing on lives of people, especially ordinary people. Lessons also often emphasize the role of the United States in world affairs and the idea of interdependency among nations.

Alternative emphases at grade eight include the following:

* Economics and Law-Related Studies
* Interdisciplinary Studies of the Local Region

RELATING BASIC SOCIAL STUDIES PURPOSES TO SUBJECT MATTER COVERED AT EACH GRADE LEVEL

In planning for instruction at each grade level, it is easy to lose sight of the three basic purposes of the elementary social studies program. Recall that this part of the elementary curriculum has three specific responsibilities:

* Citizenship education
* History and social science education
* Reflective thinking and problem-solving education

As we plan learning experiences at each grade level, we need to think about how to allocate instruction among these three basic program focuses. Once we decide on the relative emphasis, it is useful to develop focus questions to guide instruction. carefully cross-reference each question to its particular focus, we can assure th paying at least some attention to each of the three basic social studies em 1–2 lists sample focus questions for each grade level. Note that Table same number of questions for each major social studies focus. In unlikely to work out quite so neatly; we will probably not e

Table 1–2
Sample focus questions by grade level.

The following chart shows how the topics of the social studies at each grade can be synthesized with the development of questions and the three major purposes of the social studies. Some questions used as a focus for some lessons at each grade level are listed, and a check mark indicates the social studies program where the focus would best fit.

Focus Questions	Citizenship	Social Science and History	Reflective Thinking Problem Solving
Kindergarten: Awareness of Self in a Social Setting			
What is our national flag like? Our state flag?	x		
What are our classroom rules? Our school rules? Why do we have rules?	x		
What are the names of our community, state, and nation?	x		
What are the basic directions (up, down, right, left)?		x	
What are the basic time concepts (minutes, hours, days)?		x	
What do the basic symbols and signs mean (road signs, etc.)?		x	
How do we make choices?			x
How do we know when a problem exists?			x
What kind of class rules do we need?			x
Grade 1: The Individual in Primary and Social Groups— Understanding School and Family Life			
Why do communities need rules?	x		
How can we work cooperatively in groups?	x		
What are some of our patriotic customs?	x		
How do different family members contribute to the family as a whole?		x	
How is the calendar divided into days, months, and years?		x	
How can we make a simple map of the classroom and school?		x	
What specific steps should be taken in solving a problem?			x
What kinds of problems do family members face?			x
How do family members work together to solve problems?			x
Grade 2: Meeting Basic Needs in Nearby Social Groups— The Neighborhood			
How are rules made for people in the neighborhood?	x		
What happens when people break rules?	x		
What are fair rules like?	x		
How can timelines be used to depict a sequence?		x	
What important kinds of transportation and communication are there?		x	
How does the social environment change with time?		x	
What problems do neighborhoods face?			x

Focus Questions	Citizenship	Social Science and History	Reflective Thinking Problem Solving
How can groups work to solve problems?			x
What categories of information are needed to solve a problem?			x

Grade 3: Sharing Earth Space with Others—
The Community

Focus Questions	Citizenship	Social Science and History	Reflective Thinking Problem Solving
What is a person's responsibility to the community?	x		
What are the basic functions of local government?	x		
Who enforces laws in the community?	x		
How does the work of people in one community help people in other communities?		x	
What are the contributions of various ethnic and cultural groups to the community?		x	
What kinds of maps display information about the community?		x	
What are some problems that the community must face?			x
What are some causes of the events in the community?			x
How can information best be arranged for problem solving?			x

Grade 4: Human Life in Varied Environments—
The Region

Focus Questions	Citizenship	Social Science and History	Reflective Thinking Problem Solving
What are the basic functions of state government?	x		
How do groups help governments to make decisions?	x		
How can a person develop group leadership skills?	x		
What economic ties are there between the state and other parts of the United States?		x	
How have people of the state used their environment in different ways at different times?		x	
How do landforms influence climate?		x	
What kinds of information do people need to arrive at solutions to problems facing the state?			x
How can a person tell the difference between statements of fact and of opinion?			x
What might be the consequences of different approaches to solving a problem facing the state?			x

Grade 5: People of the Americas—
The United States and Its Close Neighbors

Focus Questions	Citizenship	Social Science and History	Reflective Thinking Problem Solving
What are the basic rights and responsibilities of citizens?	x		
What are the major political parties? What are their symbols?	x		
What qualities do people seek in national leaders?	x		
How are regions of the United States interdependent?		x	

Table 1–2, *continued*

Focus Questions	Citizenship	Social Science and History	Reflective Thinking Problem Solving
What were the major historical events in the development of the United States?		x	
How do innovations change the economy of the United States?		x	
What criteria should the United States' citizens apply as they attempt to solve problems facing the country?			x
How can we develop and test hypotheses about complex problems?			x
What role do personal values play in decisions people make?			x
Grade 6: People and Cultures—Representative World Regions			
What unwritten rules shape citizens' behavior?	x		
What rights should minorities have in a democratic society?	x		
What are the expected relationships between the citizens of the United States and the citizens of other nations?	x		
How are the United States and other nations of the world interdependent?		x	
How are the climates in various parts of the world explained?		x	
What contrasts are there between the government of the United States and the governments of selected nondemocratic nations?		x	
What differences are there between the kinds of logic used by individuals in different parts of the world to solve problems?			x
How can cultural perspectives be recognized in a statement of position on a world problem?			x
Why do some problems have neither right nor wrong answers?			x
Grade 7: A Changing World of Many Nations—A Global View			
How are "good citizens" defined in different countries?	x		
Do all countries view "democratic decision making" similarly?	x		
How do countries differ in terms of percentages of citizens who choose to vote in elections?	x		
What geographic advantages and disadvantages characterize selected countries of the world?		x	
How do patterns of historical development of selected countries compare with our own?		x	
What variables are associated with "high status" and "low status" in selected countries of the world?		x	
How is the relative logical strength of an argument determined?			x

Focus Questions	Citizenship	Social Science and History	Reflective Thinking Problem Solving
How can situations arising from conflicts about values that are prized by selected world cultures best be resolved?			x
Do all problems have solutions?			x
Grade 8: Building a Strong and Free Nation—The United States			
What is the definition of a "good citizen"?	x		
What can be done to get people to vote?	x		
What might happen if, over time, people become less and less interested in politics?	x		
Are there revolutionaries today?		x	
What is special about our economic system?		x	
What is the role of interest groups in the American political process?		x	
Why are some problems more difficult to resolve than others?			x
What roles do American values play in how decisions are made in this country?			x
How can problems be solved in ways that protect rights of minorities?			x

number of questions related to each area of emphasis. Think about the issue of focus questions as you do the activity described in Box 1–2.

Deciding on questions to guide our instruction requires thought about the content to be taught and its order of presentation. One fundamental problem is that an enormous volume of information is available about almost any topic we select. For example, universities often have an entire sociology course devoted to "The Family." Obviously, we cannot cram the contents of a sophisticated university course into lessons about the family designed for young elementary school pupils. We have to select a small sample of the total information available. Then, we have to organize it. The "structure of knowledge" can help us do this.

THE STRUCTURE OF KNOWLEDGE

The structure of knowledge approach, built on the work of such important learning theorists and social studies specialists as Jerome Bruner (1960) and Hilda Taba (1962), provides a way to organize kinds of content in terms of their importance.

In the structure of knowledge, a given element of content is viewed as becoming more important as it increases its potential to provide information that applies to

---

BOX 1–2   **Refining your Beliefs and Commitments**

One of the purposes of this chapter is to get you to think about your beliefs and commitments regarding social studies education. Take a minute to reflect on the following questions.

Think About This

1. Choose a grade level that interests you. Review the content normally taught at that level. What ought to be the priorities in teaching social studies at that grade? How would you incorporate citizenship? Reflective thinking? Problem solving? History and social science education?
2. Brainstorm what you know about the learners at that age. What challenges does their age present in teaching social studies to them? Do you think they should be introduced to controversial aspects of society? Do you think they are capable of reflective thinking and decision making? Why or why not?
3. What would be a list of focus questions you might use to guide your planning for teaching social studies at that grade level?
4. What might be some controversial topics at that level? How do you feel about getting into those controversial areas?

---

diverse situations. That is, more all-encompassing kinds of content elements are assigned a higher priority than those with narrower explanatory power.

There are three major content types in the structure of knowledge, shown in Figure 1–4. From the narrowest (and least important) to the broadest (and most important) these are (1) facts, (2) concepts, and (3) generalizations.

Facts

Facts have limited explanatory power. They refer to specific circumstances and have little transfer value. Here are some examples of social studies facts:

- Lincoln was born in 1809.
- Mountains cover between 10 and 15 percent of New Mexico's land surface.
- Wyoming has fewer residents than Colorado.
- Dover is the capital of Delaware.
- Mexico City has a larger population than does New York City.

Facts are important because they form the building blocks for the development of concepts and generalizations. Concepts are not learned in a vacuum. Rather, they are acquired in a process that involves consideration of specific facts.

Because there are so many facts about every subject, it is never possible for us to teach them all. We must choose. The facts we select to teach are those that will help our learners grasp important concepts and generalizations.

Figure 1–4
The structure of knowledge.

The following diagram illustrates the structure of knowledge. At the base is a broad band representing the vast number of facts. There are fewer concepts and even fewer generalizations. Facts have very limited transfer value to other times, places, or events. Concepts and generalizations, however, have wide transfer value that helps an individual who has a grasp of them understand and predict events. Generalizations and concepts, because they have wider transfer value, are less specific than facts. The major point is that facts, concepts, and generalizations are all important. The facts provide specific examples of concepts and generalizations. However, if facts are not tied to important concepts and generalizations, they become mere bits of trivia with little utility. The facts chosen to be taught in social studies classes should be those that illuminate or help pupils learn important concepts and generalizations.

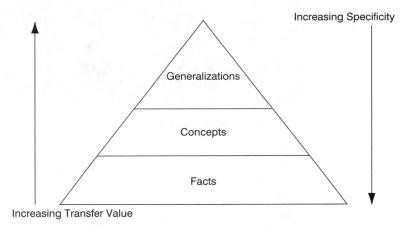

Concepts

Concepts are labels that help people to make sense of large quantities of information. They are wonderful intellectual tools that enable us to simplify our world and to make thinking and problem solving easier. For example, the concept "automobile" helps us organize a vast array of data regarding size, color, shape, and special features. When we see something that has all of these things, we quickly are able to place it in the mental category "automobile." In addition, the concept relates to other concepts, such as "make," "model," "production-line manufacture," "mode of transportation," "highway," and so forth. Unlike facts that are limited to specific situations, concepts have broad applicability. The following are examples of social studies concepts:

- Monsoon wind
- Latitude
- Folkway
- Inflation
- Self-determination

Elementary social studies needs to address "real world" issues such as homelessness.

Concepts have assigned meanings or definitions. The defining characteristics of concepts are called *attributes*. For example, the concept "triangle" is defined by these attributes: (1) it is a two-dimensional figure (2) that is enclosed by no more and no fewer than three straight lines.

In the social studies, few important concepts are as easily defined as "triangle." Concepts such as "democracy," "culture," and "socialization" have many defining attributes. One of our challenges as social studies teachers is developing lesson plans to help pupils master these complex concepts. This is something we must do if we expect our learners to master the even more sophisticated content embedded in generalizations.

Generalizations

Generalizations are statements of relationship among concepts. The "truth" of a generalization is determined by reference to evidence. Some generalizations that we accept today may have to be modified in the future, should new evidence come to light. Generalizations concisely summarize huge volumes of information. This makes them particularly attractive as we plan social studies programs. The following are examples of social studies generalizations:

- Opinions that originate in an earlier period persist to be influential in a later period.

- The more demands a natural environment places on people for physical survival, the less attention people pay to supernatural phenomena.
- As a society becomes increasingly educated and industrialized, its birth rate declines (Berelson & Steiner, 1967).

Generalizations often contain many concepts. Look at the last one in the preceding list. Concepts included are "society," "educated society," "industrialized society," and "birth rate." Pupils need to understand these concepts before we can expect them to grasp the significance of the generalization. There are specialized concepts and generalizations associated with individual academic disciplines. We will identify examples of these in chapters 2 and 3.

THE MOTIVATION PROBLEM

The basic focus of the social studies is people. This ought to make it one of the most fascinating subjects in the school curriculum. However, many surveys have found that social studies ranks close to the bottom of the list of subjects elementary pupils like (McGowan, Sutton, & Smith, 1990). Much of this reputation, we believe, results not from social studies content, but rather from how the subject is taught.

Elementary school learners are concerned about themselves and others. Consider how eager they are to share information about personal experiences. We need to capitalize on this interest and build lessons that use children's personal and family interests as points of departure. The trick is to transfer the interest in the personal and immediate to other peoples and places. Often, this can be accomplished by lessons that provide learners with opportunities to "do something tangible" with the content. Our lessons must have an immediate and personal relevance for learners. Even older elementary pupils will not accept the argument that "you should read this now because it will help you when you get to high school or college."

Our personal interest as teachers in social studies content must be evident. Pupils are quick to spot a teacher who is simply "going through the motions" of teaching social studies, mathematics, science, or any other part of the curriculum. They are also alert to teachers who have a genuine enthusiasm for the subject they are teaching. Teacher enthusiasm is a contagious influence that has high potential for stimulating pupils interest.

As you embark on reading and studying this text, we challenge you to think about your own feelings about the social studies (see Box 1–3). If you now have an indifferent (or even a negative) attitude toward the subject, what can you do to improve it? Perhaps some ideas we introduce in the chapters that follow will help you share some of the enthusiasm for social studies teaching that we have felt during our years as professional educators. We look forward to your joining us in the effort to help learners understand their world and how they can get about the business of making it better.

BOX 1–3   **Motivation and Elementary Social Studies**

Think About This

Take a minute or two and reflect on what you remember about your experiences in elementary school social studies.

1. What are you most vivid memories? Are they pleasant or unpleasant ones?
2. What topics did you study? How did you react to them?
3. Is the current curriculum similar to what you remember?
4. What methods were used to teach social studies? Which ones did you enjoy?
5. How do you feel about social studies now? Do you personally think it is important? If you still find social studies unimportant or boring, how do you think that will influence your teaching? Do you agree that a disinterested teacher will have have disinterested pupils?
6. How might a social studies teacher make the subject interesting to elementary pupils?
7. What do you think you need to learn to become a good social studies teacher? What are your personal goals as you continue to learn about social studies and teaching?

KEY IDEAS IN SUMMARY

1. Social studies lessons provide pupils with tools they can use to make decisions about pressing personal and social problems. There are disagreements about what components should be present in a good social studies program. Some people want a strong emphasis on content from the academic disciplines to assure that all young people leave school with a common core of knowledge. Others want social studies programs to focus on controversial issues and to help pupils to become reflective thinkers and individuals committed to active participation in democratic decision making. Whatever perspective is reflected in a given program, teachers face some risk. Regardless of what they do, some people will challenge their priorities. Social studies teachers must have a clear personal conception of the social studies and be prepared to engage in responsible debate with people holding different views.

2. There is consensus around the idea that preparation for citizenship is one important purpose of the social studies. Other widely acknowledged emphases include focuses on (1) history and social science education and (2) reflective thinking and problem-solving education.

3. There is evidence that levels of citizen participation in the governance process are decreasing. This trend could have dangerous long-term consequences for our country. It is hoped that the emphasis on citizenship education in the social studies will engender more interest in active participation in civic affairs when learners mature.

4. There are three important sub-emphases associated with the major social studies program focuses of citizenship education, history and social science education,

and reflective thinking and problem solving. These are (1) knowledge, (2) skills, and (3) values.

5. The National Council for the Social Studies Task Force on Scope and Sequence made the following recommendations for content in grades K through 8: (1) Kindergarten: Awareness of Self in a Social Stetting; (2) Grade 1: The Individual in Primary Social Groups—Understanding School and Family Life; (3) Grade 2: Meeting Basic Needs in Nearby Social Groups—The Neighborhood; (4) Grade 3: Sharing Earth Space with Others—The Community; (5) Grade 4: Human Life in Varied Environments—The Region; (6) Grade 5: People of the Americas—The United States and Its Close Neighbors; (7) Grade 6: People and Cultures—Representative World Regions; (8) Grade 7: A Changing View of Many Nations—A Global View; (9) Grade 8: Building a Strong and Free Nation—The United States.

6. Well-balanced social studies programs devote at least some attention to each of the emphases of (1) citizenship education, (2) history and social science education, and (3) reflective thinking and problem-solving education. However, because of changing levels of learner maturity and other factors, it is probable that degrees of emphasis on each of these will vary from grade level to grade level and from classroom to classroom.

7. The *structure of knowledge* is a scheme that has been devised to illustrate relationships among facts, concepts, and generalizations. It can be used as a guide to help teachers select content. Key social studies concepts and generalizations help pupils understand the world around them. Teachers select facts carefully with a view to including those that help pupils grasp the focus concepts and generalizations.

8. Surveys often reveal that pupils do not have a high interest in their social studies lessons. The subject matter itself does not appear to be the problem so much as the unimaginative ways social studies lessons are sometimes taught. Some teachers also are not enthusiastic about this part of the elementary school program. Pupils are quick to sense teacher indifference. When they do, they tend to develyouped diminished enthusiasm levels for the subject. To the extent possible, teachers need to develop a personal interest in the social studies topics they teach and to approach teaching social studies lessons with genuine enthusiasm. Where this kind of instruction occurs, pupils' levels of motivation tend to increase.

CHAPTER REFLECTIONS

Directions: Now that you have completed the chapter, reread the case study at the beginning. Then answer these questions:

1. How would you now respond to the student questions posed in the case study?

2. Have your responses to the questions changed? If so, in what ways and why?

3. Can social studies lessons be made to connect to lives of elementary pupils? What would you do to make a topic you might teach relevant to your learners?

4. What do you see as the central purposes of social studies instruction?

5. If your school adopted the central purposes you believe to be important, what kinds of topics would your pupils study?

6. What do you think you still need to learn that will help you to make your social studies more interesting and meaningful to pupils you will teach?

EXTENDING UNDERSTANDING AND SKILL

1. Choose a curriculum guide for a grade level of your choice. Evaluate the guide using the "Social Studies Purposes Matrix" illustrated in Figure 1–2. To what extent are the emphases of (1) citizenship education, (2) history and social science education, and (3) reflecting thinking and problem-solving education represented in the guide? For each of these emphases, what attention is given to (a) knowledge, (b) skills, and (c) values?

2. Choose a topic that you might teach at a grade level of your choice. Write a short paper presenting at least one example of how you might include each major social studies purpose (citizenship education, history and social science education, and reflective thinking and problem-solving education).

3. Interview the person in charge of the social studies program for a local school district. (Depending on the size of the district, the person might hold a title such as "Director of Social Studies," "Coordinator of Social Studies," "Social Studies Curriculum Director," "Director of Elementary Education," or "Curriculum Director.") Your instructor may be able to suggest the name of person for you to contact. Ask this individual to tell you the major social studies content taught at each grade from kindergarten through grade eight. Compare this arrangement with the recommendations of the National Council for the Social Studies Task Force on Scope and Sequence. Prepare an oral report in which you comment on similarities and differences.

4. Prepare a complete list of focus questions to guide social studies instructic n at a grade level of your choosing. Your instructor will critique your list.

5. Interview several children in a grade level you would like to teach. Ask them what they like and dislike about their social studies lessons. Summarize their comments in a short paper. Make particular note of those things they like. Suggest how you might build on their ideas to make your own social studies program more appealing to your pupils.

6. Take time to reflect on your views about the importance of social studies and about your interest in the subject. Are your feelings positive or negative? What is the source of your feelings? How might they interfere with or help you as you teach social studies content to elementary pupils? What might you do to develop more positive attitudes and feelings toward the social studies? Share your views with others in your class.

REFERENCES

BARR, R. D., BARTH, J. L., AND SHERMIS, S. S. (1977). *Defining the Social Studies.* Arlington, VA: National Council for the Social Studies.

BERELSON, B., AND STEINER, G. (1967). *Human Behavior: An Inventory of Scientific Findings.* New York: Harcourt, Brace & World.

BERMAN, S., AND LA FARGE, P. (1993). (eds.). *Promising Practices in Teaching Social Responsibility.* Albany, NY: State University of New York Press.

BRUNER, J. (1960). *The Process of Education.* Cambridge, MA: Harvard University Press.

CHERRYHOLMES, C. (1992). "Knowledge, Power, and Discourse in Social Studies Education." In K. Weiler & C. Mitchell (eds.), *What Schools Can Do: Critical Pedagogy and Practice*, pp. 95–115. Albany, NY: State University of New York Press.

HIRSCH, E. D., JR. (1987). *Cultural Literacy: What Every American Needs to Know.* New York: Houghton Mifflin.

LEMING, J. S. (1989). "The Two Cultures of Social Studies Education." *Social Education, 53* (6), pp. 404–408.

McGOWAN, T. M., SUTTON, A. M., AND SMITH, P. G. (1990). "Instructional Elements Influencing Student Attitudes Toward Social Studies." *Theory and Research in Social Education, 18* (1), pp. 37–52.

"Minutes of the 36th Delegate Assembly." (1993). *Social Education, 57* (4), pp. 193–196.

National Council for the Social Studies Task Force on Curriculum Standards for the Social Studies. (1994). *Curriculum Standards for Social Studies: Expectations of Excellence.* Bulletin 89. Washington, DC: National Council for the Social Studies.

National Council for the Social Studies Task Force on Scope and Sequence. (1989). "In Search of a Scope and Sequence for Social Studies: Report of the National Council for the Social Studies Task Force on Scope and Sequence." *Social Education, 53* (6), pp. 376–385.

PARKER, W. (1991). *Renewing the Social Studies Curriculum.* Alexandria, VA: Association for Supervision and Curriculum Development.

"Poll Finds Nation of Cynics." (1994, 21 September), Riverside, CA: *The Press Enterprise*, p. 1.

TABA, H. (1962). *Curriculum Development: Theory and Practice.* New York: Harcourt, Brace & World.

TAYLOR, P. A. (1990). "A National Morale Problem—Americans Feel Increasingly Estranged from Their Government." *Washington Post National Weekly Edition.* (14 April–20 May), pp. 6–7.

THORNTON, S. J. (1994). "Perspectives on Reflective Practice in Social Studies Education." In W. Ross (ed.), *Reflective Practices in Social Studies.* Bulletin No. 88, Washington, DC: National Council for the Social Studies, pp. 5–11.

2

THE CONTENT SOURCES: HISTORY, GEOGRAPHY, AND ECONOMICS

CHAPTER GOALS

This chapter provides information to help the reader:

- identify the role of history and the social sciences in the social studies curriculum,
- describe the unique perspectives of history, geography, and economics,
- identify selected concepts and generalizations from history, geography, and economics that can be incorporated in the elementary social studies program, and
- develop social studies lessons that focus on content from history, geography, and economics.

CHAPTER STRUCTURE

Introduction
History
    History of the Curriculum
    *Civilization, Cultural Diffusion, and Innovation / Human Interaction with
    the Environment / Values, Beliefs, Political Ideas, and Institutions / Conflict
    and Cooperation / Comparative History of Major Developments / Patterns of
    Social and Political Integration*
    History-Related Classroom Activities
    *Time and Chronology / People as Resources / The Local Community / Investi-
    gating Artifacts / Children's Literature / Holiday Observances*
    How Historians Judge the Truth
    External Validity / Internal Validity
    A Selection of Information Sources
    *The National Council for History Education / The National Council for the
    Social Studies*
Geography
    The Geography Curriculum
    Location / Place / Human–Environment Interactions / Movement / Region
    Geography-Related Classroom Activities
    Thinking Geographically
    Investigating Location
    Noting Spatial Interactions
    Observing Human–Environment Interactions
    A Selection of Information Sources
    *National Council for Geographic Education / Joint Committee on Geo-
    graphic Education / Geographic Alliance Network*
Economics
    Categories of Economic Systems
    Traditional Economies / Command Economies / Market Economies
    Economics-Related Classroom Activities
    *People Choose / People's Choices Involve Costs / People Respond to Incen-
    tives in a Predictable Way / People Create Economic Systems that Influence
    Individual Choices and Incentives / People Gain When They Trade Voluntar-
    ily / People's Choices Have Consequences that Lie in the Future*
    A Selection of Information Sources
    *Joint Council on Economic Education / National Center for Economic Edu-
    cation for Children / Other Sources*
Key Ideas in Summary
Chapter Reflections
Extending Understanding and Skill
References

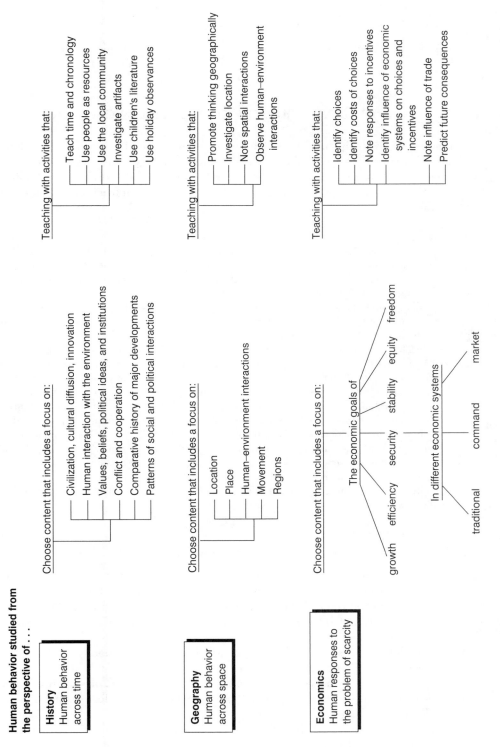

Figure 2–1

Social studies content sources.

35

Chapter 2

Case Study

TOO MANY SUBJECTS, TOO LITTLE KNOWLEDGE

Juan Isaguirre is scheduled to student teach next semester. He is assigned to a fourth-grade classroom. As is typical of university students at this point in their professional development, Juan is both excited and apprehensive as he thinks about his readiness for student teaching. In discussing his feelings about student teaching he made the following comments:

> It's really intimidating to think about all the subjects I'm supposed to teach. I'm more worried about some than others. I mean, in some cases, I can pretty well identify courses I have taken that will help me. The math I have completed at the university is far beyond what I will need to know to teach fourth grade. I'm not really worried about the content I will be expected to teach in arithmetic.
>
> On the other hand, I'm a bit concerned about the social studies. I know social studies is primarily history and geography with some political science. I've had a lot of history at the university. But, there is so much to cover and so many facts to learn. How do I select what to teach? Also, I can't see how the many facts I've learned in those classes transfer to teaching fourth graders. Are they really interested in what happened long ago in some far-off place? I guess I don't see the point. As for geography, I had only one course. That was an intro course that focused primarily on the physical environment. I can see how I can use some of that in science, but is there something else I'm supposed to cover in geography? I guess the focus is on learning the names of state capitals, continents, rivers, and mountain ranges. How do you keep the pupils interested? I feel weak in geography. I've had several political science classes so I guess I'm okay there. I can describe the political system, and how elections work. Again, what is most important for fourth graders to learn about our political system? I know there are many things to cover in a short time. I'm not really sure I know how to go about selecting the content I can teach in the limited amount of time that is available—this is a real worry.

What Is Your Response?

Think about Juan's concerns. Then, briefly respond to these questions:

1. One problem Juan identifies is his own lack of preparation in one of the academic areas (geography) from which content for elementary social studies lessons is often drawn. How do you feel about your own depth of academic preparation in academic subjects related to social studies? If you sense any inadequacies in these subjects, what might you do?
2. Juan defines the social studies as primarily history and geography. How do you react to his definition? Do you agree?
3. Another problem that concerns Juan has to do with the issue of selecting content. What ideas do you have regarding the content you would select for inclusion in the elementary classroom?
4. Juan is also concerned about the interests of fourth-grade pupils and whether the information he learned is really something that will be useful to him. How would

you respond to this concern? How would you relate social studies content to the interests of the pupils? What is the function of university classes in preparing a person for teaching the subject in the elementary school? Is it to present you with content to be translated and then taught in a simplified version to young children?

5. Some critics of elementary social studies programs assert that teachers cannot possibly know all of the content they need in order to teach. They argue that elementary learners would be better served if "social studies" was abandoned and replaced with content focusing on a single subject such as history or geography. If this were done, these critics allege, teachers would have a better chance to develop some academic depth in the subjects they were asked to teach. What do you see as the strengths and weaknesses of this idea?

INTRODUCTION

The focus of social studies is on human behavior—past, present, and sometimes future. It is unrealistic to expect elementary social studies programs to expose pupils to everything that might be taught about this vast subject. Teachers must make content choices. Which choices are "correct"? There is no single answer to this question. What *is* clear is that rapidly changing conditions in our society are making these decisions more difficult (Risinger, 1992). In making choices, social studies teachers consider questions such as these:

- What do pupils need to study to learn how to participate effectively in society?
- What examples of human behavior are most effective for teaching people how to live together and solve difficult social problems?
- What content is most useful for helping individuals understand their cultural heritage and decide what needs to be retained and what needs to be changed?
- Out of the wide array of human cultures, past and present, which ones should be studied in the elementary school?
- What content is important for individuals as they try to make sense of the personal and economic worlds outside the classroom?

These questions have no simple answers. Individuals have responded to them in different ways, depending on their own particular sense of what is important. Answers to these questions have been made even more difficult for teachers who must deal with learners from highly diverse cultural and ethnic groups. Meeting needs of today's pupils requires teachers to draw on content that has potential meaning for people who bring extremely diverse cultural and social perspectives with them to school each day.

Recent events have demonstrated the need for American citizens to develop a comprehensive and connected understanding of human affairs. The memorization of names, dates, and other isolated facts drawn from a single culture is not sufficient for young people who are growing up in an increasingly interdependent world. Citizens of the United States today must understand that their decisions may have implications for people living thousands of miles from our shores and that decisions made abroad often have significant effects on the the United States. This new world reality requires a social studies that is global and inclusive in its outlook. As the National Commission on Social Studies in the Schools (1989) points out, these challenges require people whose thinking is broadly based: "Individuals do not think well if they do not understand their own history, appreciate political and cultural diversity, and understand the economic and sociological realities of a changing world (p. xi).

This statement hints at the importance of information drawn from history and the social sciences. Specialists in these fields have identified concepts and developed generalizations that help us to explain the complexities of our world. In the elementary social studies program, information from these fields helps pupils to better understand the world and themselves. To be useful, information from history and the social sciences needs to be integrated and applied to important practical problems. The information needs of future citizens cannot be met through the study of a single subject. That is, it no longer suffices to study history alone, or geography alone, or economics alone. These and other social science disciplines need to be combined into a systemic and interrelated study of people (National Commission on Social Studies in the Schools, 1989).

This chapter and Chapter 3 provide a brief introduction to history and the social sciences, and suggest how you might use content from these disciplines in planning and implementing sound elementary social studies programs. This is not meant to imply that these are the only content sources elementary social studies teachers use. Teachers often also draw on information from music, art, religion, philosophy, and even the physical and biological sciences. However, it probably is fair to say that more elementary social studies content comes from history and the social sciences of geography, economics, political science, sociology, anthropology, and psychology than from other sources.

The focus on this chapter is on history, geography, and economics. Chapter 3 introduces material related to political science, sociology, anthropology, and psychology.

HISTORY

History has long been one of the key subjects in the social studies curriculum. In fact, some people consider the terms *history* and *social studies* to be synonymous. The importance of history in elementary social studies is reflected in many ways. For example, American history is the featured subject of the grade-five curriculum almost everywhere in the United States. History is mentioned in the third goal of the National Goals for Education (1990). The History–Social Science Framework that governs social studies programming in California draws heavily on history.

History has played and continues to play such a dominant role in the elementary social studies curriculum for several reasons, not least because it has long been viewed as an important element of general citizenship education. Many people have assumed that systematic study of the origins of our nation and key events in our history will socialize young people to accept values critical for the maintenance of our democratic tradition.

Some people believe that history as a subject lends itself well to integrating content from the various social sciences and from the humanities. A focus on history, some say, promotes learning efficiency. The unifying element of time can draw together content from many separate subjects and can help pupils recognize the interrelatedness of many different kinds of content. The Bradley Commission on History in Schools is a national group strongly committed to the importance of history in education. In one of its reports, the commission (1988) suggested that history provides a unique avenue for helping learners to understand themselves and their society. The report went on to maintain that the principal aim of teaching history is to help pupils develop alternative perspectives and modes of thoughtful judgment.

Helping pupils improve their thinking skills through the study of history requires teachers to think carefully about the particular history they are teaching to pupils. Sometimes this point is not widely appreciated. For example, in the History–Social Science Framework for California Public Schools there is emphasis on history as a "story well told" (p. 4). While certainly well-written history often presents a good story, the real issue for teachers and their learners should be on *whose* story is being told, the *accuracy* of the story, and the *intended purposes* of the story.

No historical account is "true" in any absolute sense. Knowledge of past events must be reconstructed from artifacts and surviving accounts. The historian must make judgments about what to include and what to omit. His or her own values come into play when such choices are made. For example, a historical account written by a person who sees the class struggle as the most important theme in human affairs will write an account of settlement of the American West that differs from one written by someone who sees technological change as the dominant theme.

When they encounter history, pupils should be taught to approach it much as they approach a mystery. They need to think about the author's perspectives, and they must be provided with other opportunities to develop critical thinking skills. Good history teaching sensitizes pupils to the idea that all people do not experience the same event in the same way. Helping pupils think about issues of perspective as they study historical content can nurture the development of a worldview that recognizes and appreciates multiple realities.

Lesson Idea 2–1

RESOLVING CONFLICTING ACCOUNTS OF EVENTS

Grade Level:	5–6
Objectives:	Learners can (1) identify bias is historical accounts, and (2) state the importance of identifying bias in the things they read.
Overview:	To help pupils recognize bias and different perspectives on a single event, it is helpful to present them with two or more conflicting accounts of the same event and have them identify and explain discrepancies.

Procedure:

Learning Set   Ask pupils if they have ever had two different people tell them about the same thing, and each one's story was very different. Ask them why they think this happens.

Presentation   Place a chart on the board with two columns, one marked Account 1 the other Account 2. Head the chart "The Burning of Washington in the War of 1812." Give the pupils Account 1 and have them read it.

Account 1: Victorious troops of the crown swarmed into Washington. With huzzahs all around, torches were passed. Officers led their men on a block by block campaign to torch the rebel capital. Officers of the general staff believe that this action will soon break the back of the American resistance. There is talk that before the year is out these rebel colonies will be rightfully returned to the crown. American resistance is said to be crumbling. Loyal subjects of the king are said to be waiting in Canada for the signal to return south and re-establish proper colonial governments (Report filed by a cor-respondent of the *London Gazette*.)

When all have read the account, fill in the chart with student answers to the following questions: Was the burning viewed as a positive event? What was the reason? How were the troops viewed? How were the Americans viewed? What words are used to describe each side? Give the pupils Account 2 and have them read it.

Account 2: The British barbarian showed his true colors today. Consistent with the pattern of 25 years ago when American rights were trampled into the ground, the undisci-plined British troops took Washington today with unprinci-pled savagery. With little regard for the safety of women and children, they went on a rampage that resulted in the burn-ing of most of the buildings in Washington. American troops, shocked by the brutality, are rallying. Determination has never been higher. All look forward to taking a revenge that will forever free this continent from the tyranny of the British. (Report filed by a correspondent of the *New York Review*.)

Use the same questions, reversing the nationality as appropri-ate, and fill in the chart under Account 2. After completing both sides of the chart, lead a discussion using the following questions:

1. How are the accounts similar?
2. How are the accounts different?
3. How do you explain the differences?
4. What do you think the reaction would be to people who would read each account?
5. Can you identify an incident where a similar thing hap-pened recently?

6. What do you think this means you should do when you read or hear an account of an event?

Closure: Ask the class, "What did we learn today? Why is what we have learned important?"

The History Curriculum

The history curriculum is generally organized around the study of topics. For example, United States history is usually the topic of study in the fifth grade. Other topics include state history, for example the history of Texas. The Bradley Commission (1988) defined six themes that could be used as a focus for the history curriculum:

- Civilization, Cultural diffusion, and Innovation
- Human interaction with the environment
- Values, Beliefs, Political ideas, and Institutions
- Conflict and Cooperation
- Comparative history of major developments
- Patterns of social and political interaction

Civilization, Cultural Diffusion, and Innovation
Content associated with this theme is directed at promoting an understanding of how civilizations have developed and changed over time. It includes an emphasis on the creation and spread of new ideas, especially regarding how they have affected people and nature. Content in this theme deals with many issues that are of interest to anthropologists.

Human Interaction with the Environment
This theme is concerned with the relationship between human civilizations and the physical environment. It includes content focusing on how people, by using technology and other innovations, have changed their environments and how environments influence human affairs. The role of agriculture comes in for serious consideration. Much content has close ties to geography.

Values, Beliefs, Political Ideas, and Institutions
This theme pays particular attention to the development and spread of values and beliefs of major world religions and ideologies. The development of political values and ideas and the creation of political institutions are important content issues. Some material related to this theme has close ties to the disciplines of sociology and political science.

Conflict and Cooperation
This theme deals with the causes and consequences of wars and international conflicts as well as with instances of cooperation and peacemaking. Issues associated with isolation and interdependence are a central concern. Study often focuses on different ways particular civilizations have interacted with outsiders.

Learning about the United Nations provides an opportunity for pupils to consider the concepts of conflict and cooperation.

Comparative History of Major Developments

Content associated with this theme centers on key events in history and how they have affected how people live and what they do. It includes the study of great human achievements as well as great human failures. Lessons frequently illuminate the impact of great events as stimulators of revolution and reform.

Patterns of Social and Political Integration

Topics relating to this theme include such issues as immigration and social mobility. Studies often focus on changing patterns of race, class, and gender, particularly as they pertain to shifts in political power. Often this kind of content involves themes from sociology and political science.

As noted in the preceding brief descriptions, content from history often overlaps with topics treated in one or more of the social sciences. In history lessons, the unifying thread is treatment of human behavior over time. Concepts central to the discipline of history are change and continuity. Instruction is guided by such questions as, "How have things changed, and why?" and "How has there been continuity over time, and why?" Lesson planning that draws on content from history attends carefully to questions, concepts, and generalizations that are central to the discipline. Some of these are noted in Figure 2–2.

History-related Classroom Activities

Because history reflects the perspectives of those who write it, study of the subject requires learners to go beyond recalling information that is reported in historical accounts. Pupils need to be taught to rethink arguments of historians, to ask questions about interpretations of facts, and to suggest alternative explanations of events (Gagnon, 1989). This suggests that elementary social studies lessons should actively involve pupils in the processes of historical inquiry. The following are ideas for accomplishing this purpose.

The following are examples of central questions, concepts, and generalizations that are important when studying history. They are useful to the elementary social studies teacher when making decisions about what to include in lessons related to history.

Central Questions (a selection)

What are the values and the biases of the writer?
What parts of the account are fact? What part is fiction?
Are the conclusions warranted by the facts?
What kind of language is used to describe the event or person? How does this language influence the view of the reader?
Where did the writer get this information?
Where else could one get information about this event?
What do other writers say about what happened?

Concepts (a selection)

Change, continuity, innovation, multiple causation, interpretation, movement, primary sources, secondary sources, era, period, epoch, century, A.D., B.C.E., season, year, prehistory, ancient, medieval, middle ages, modern, validity, chronology.

Generalizations (a selection)

Continuous change is universal and inevitable.
The rate of change in a society varies with such factors as the values of the people, the extent of pluralism, and the amount of contact with other cultures.
Events of the past influence events of the present.
The history of a culture provides guidelines for understanding the thought and action in the culture's present-day affairs.
The history of a nation influences the culture, traditions, beliefs, attitudes, and patterns of living of its people.

Figure 2–2
Central questions, concepts, and generalizations associated with history.

Lesson Idea 2–2

YESTERDAY ON THE PLAYGROUND

Grade Level: 3–6

Objectives: Pupils can (1) write an eyewitness account of an event, (2) identify why historical accounts differ, and (3) state different ways history can be written.

Overview: Students can be made aware of how history can be written from different perspectives and in different ways by having them try to reconstruct an event that they all have experienced. This activity can be useful helping them begin to understand the problems that historians face when trying to write an account, how to begin to judge the accuracy of information, and how to organize the information into a good story.

Procedure: *Learning Set*   Begin by telling the class that today they are going to learn about a past event of great importance, lunch time yesterday. Ask them, What happened on the playground yesterday at lunch? Let a few share their experiences. Then state that it is obvious that many things happened.

Presentation: *Day 1*   Tell the class that they are going to write some histories of yesterday on the playground. Ask them how they will need to begin and what they will need to do. You might ask if any others should be interviewed about what happened. For example, they might want to interview the teacher who was on playground duty, the secretary in the office to see if anyone was hurt or sent to the office, pupils from other grades who might have been on different parts of the playground. They might also want to find out if anything happened before lunch that might have influenced later events. Maybe a new game was introduced in a class or perhaps some balls were flat and could not be used. Perhaps someone had an injury that prevented them from participating in some activities.

At this point the class can be grouped into groups of four or five to plan their research and how to write their history. As they gather data, suggest to them that they can write their history in several ways. One way would be chronologically, from 12:00 to 12:10, and so on. Another approach would be geographically: at the ball field, at the primary area, in the office, and so on. A third approach would be to organize their histories by important episodes or events.

Day 2   After the pupils have gathered data, discuss with the class what they might need to consider to make their history interesting. Have each group write their history. Some may want to attach drawings or photographs of the playground or playground events. When completed, the accounts can be bound as a book.

Closure: Ask, "What did you learn about writing history? What does a historian have to think about when deciding what to include? How can you use this information as you read historical accounts in our social studies book or in the library?"

Time and Chronology

History requires familiarity with many time concepts. These include "seconds," "minutes," "hours," "years," "decades," and "centuries." Time is an abstract concept. Many children, particularly those in the primary grades, have distorted ideas about time. For example, some of them believe that conditions long ago were much as they are today. Others think that practically every aspect of modern life has been created within the last four or five years. Teachers typically begin helping pupils to get a more adequate understanding of time by relating the concept to learners' own experiences. Pupils may be asked to mark off passing days on room calendars and to observe changes associated with changes of the seasons. To help pupils gain improved understanding of time and change, a timeline chart is useful. Such a chart might include information about (1) birth dates of members of the class, (2) birth dates of parents and grandparents, and (3) dates when specific items were invented. An example of a timeline chart is provided in Table 2–1.

The timeline chart personalizes human events. They become more interesting to pupils because they are introduced in a context that includes birth dates of relatives who were alive when certain events occurred. Information on the chart often prompts pupils to ask their relatives about some of the events listed.

A diorama, such as this one in a museum, provides a concrete way of learning about the past.

Table 2–1

Sample timeline chart.

Birthdates							
1905	**1915**	**1925**	**1935**	**1945**	**1955**	**1965**	**1980**
Grand-father (father's side)	*Grand-father (father's side)*	*Grand-father (father's side)*		**Fathers**	**Fathers**		**Our Class**
Jones	Adams Barnes Cole Finn	Daly		Adams Cole Daly Finn Howe	Barnes	Adams	Barnes Cole Daly Finn Howe etc.
Grand-father (mother's side)	*Grand-father (mother's side)*	*Grand-father (mother's side)*		*Mothers*	*Mothers*		
Barnes	Adams Barnes Cole	Daly Finn Howe		Adams Daly Howe	Barnes Cole Finn		
	Grand-mother (father's side)	*Grand-mother (father's side)*					
	Cole Finn Howe	Adams Barnes Daly					
	Grand-mother (mother's side)	*Grand-mother (mother's side)*					
	Adams Barnes Cole	Daly Estes Howe					
electric vacuum cleaner (1907)	automatic toaster (1918)	T.V. (1927) electric razor (1931)	parking meter (1935)	long-playing record (1948)	laser (1958)		**Inventions**
							Games children played
							Presidents

Using the Timeline Chart: Each column represents ten years of time (i.e., information in the first column relates to events occurring during the time period of 1905–1914). The types of events recorded in the rows below the birthdates can vary according to type of content being emphasized. The main point is to try to tie events from the past to the birthdates of people with whom pupils can identify. For example, a student whose grandmother was born during the decade 1925–1934 can identify her as someone who was born during the same decade that television was invented.

People as Resources

People are an important resource for teaching historical content to elementary pupils. For example, learners may be asked to interview older people who were alive when certain events occurred and who can describe "what it was like." Parents and grandparents are good human resources. When they interview several people about a common past event, learners sometimes are surprised that everyone does not remember it in the same way. Such conversations are valuable for helping them learn that events can be interpreted in different ways and that historical inquiry requires consideration of information from multiple sources.

Lesson Idea 2–3

FAMILY ORIGINS AND TRADITIONS

Grade Level: K–2

Objectives: Pupils can (1) learn how to interview a family member, (2) identify how change and continuity have taken place, and (3) share information with the class.

Overview: This lesson may take place a few days before some or all students celebrate almost any recognized holiday or commemorative event. During any holiday season it is useful to make sure that all pupils are included. This also provides an opportunity for pupils to begin appreciating the diversity of cultures and to develop some simple understanding of time.

Procedure: *Day 1: Learning Set*   Discuss the upcoming holiday season and ask pupils about some of the different things they do during the holidays. State that different people have different holidays and different ways of celebrating the holidays. Tell them that they are going to talk with their parents and or grandparents about how they celebrated holidays when they were young. On chart paper, record some of the questions they might want to ask. Discuss the questions and select five or six. Write these on a questionnaire along with some directions to the parents to enlist their help in discussing the questions and completing the questionnaire along with the children.

Day 2: Discussion   When the questionnaires have been returned, place pupils into groups of four and have them share their information with each other. Change the groups three or four times so that class members experience a variety of responses.

As a group, construct a chart listing the changes that have taken place in the celebrations. Those who identified traditions and customs brought from other countries can identify the location of that country on a map.

Closure: Ask pupils, "What did you find out about how things have changed? Do you think things will be different when you are grown up?"

Thanks to Gayle Chew and Theresa Squires, Vicentia Elementary School, Corona, CA, for this idea.

The Local Community

The local community is an excellent resource for lessons focusing on history. Communities have important historical residues including buildings, people, cemeteries, museums, and statues that can be used for historical inquiry (Armstrong & Savage, 1976). Pupils are familiar with local communities. As a result, lessons built around local community resources often have more motivational appeal than those focusing on distant places that have few, if any, ties to learners' personal experiences. One of the authors enjoyed great success in getting a group of initially unmotivated fifth and sixth graders interested in social studies by starting with some questions about origins of street names and buildings in the urban community where they lived.

Investigating Artifacts

Artifacts are tangible reminders of times gone by. In the classroom, they function well as prompts for historical inquiry lessons. For example, artifacts such as old photographs, objects of various kinds, letters, documents, artwork, and music can be used to stimulate thought about the ways of life of people in the past. The study of the lyrics of a song sung by immigrants lamenting their permanent separation from their native land often will "connect" to pupils more effectively than any prose narrative describing the immigrant experience. A youngster who hefts a heavy iron used by Chinese laundry workers during the California Gold Rush has tangible evidence that such a life existed and also gains some important insights into the kind of fatigue laundry workers must have experienced after having spent 10 or 12 hours on their feet doing this kind of hard work.

Lesson Idea 2–4

GOD SAVE THE SOUTH

Grade Level: 5

Overview: Art and music often capture the moods, fears, values, and aspirations of many of a culture's people. These forms of expression can be important sources of information in social studies classrooms for developing understanding and insight that might not be possible through standard textbooks.

Procedure: *Learning Set*   Tell the class, "We can learn about history from many different places. One of those places is by the songs people sing. Why do you think that might be a good source of information?"

Presentation   Say to the class, "The following is a song that was popular in the Confederacy at the beginning of the Civil War. Read the verses and see if you can find clues about how the Southerners viewed the war."

GOD SAVE THE SOUTH

Words by George H. Miles

God Save the South!

God Save the South!

Her altars and firesides—

God Save the South

Now that war is nigh

Now that we arm to die—

Chanting our battle-cry,

Freedom or Death!

God make the right

Stronger than might!

Millions will trample us

Down in their pride—

Lay Thou their legions low

Roll back ruthless foe,

Let the proud spoiler know

God's on our side.

Discussion Questions:

1. What do you think it means that they ask God to protect their altars and firesides?
2. Where does that indicate they think the war will take place?
3. What does it mean that they ask God to make right stronger than might?
4. What words indicate what Southerners thought about the Northerners?
5. On the basis of this song, what do you think the attitude of the South was toward the Civil War?
6. What could we do to find out if the view presented in this song was accurate?

(Note: This song can be played to the class. It is on the tape *Civil War Songs*, by Keith and Rusty McNeil, WEM Records, Riverside, CA: 1989.)

Closure:

Ask the class, "What did we learn today about how songs might help us understand history? What did we learn about the attitude of the people in the South toward the Civil War?"

Children's Literature

Children's literature is another fine resource for helping pupils master historical content (Savage & Savage, 1993). Works of children's literature are written in a more engaging style than school texts. They feature stories with a clear beginning and end. There are books that satisfy even very young elementary school pupils.

Biographies represent a particularly useful genre for teaching historical information. For example, Jean Fritz has written a number of well-researched biographies about famous people in American history. Historical fiction also has a place in the instructional program. Two good titles are *Sarah Bishop* by Scott O'Dell (Houghton Mifflin, 1980) and *My Brother Sam is Dead* by James Lincoln Collier and Christopher Collier (Four Winds Press, 1974). Both books provide some unusual perspectives on the American Revolution. Similarly, some interesting views of the Civil War are presented in Irene Hunt's *Across Five Aprils* (Follett, 1964).

Holiday Observances

A common method for helping young children develop a sense of history is through observances of the various holidays that occur during the school year. Lessons built around holidays take advantage of learners' interest in holidays. Some teachers introduce pupils to the origins of each holidays. Studying changes in the ways individual holidays have been celebrated over the years develops an appreciation for the point that human behavior changes over time. Lessons on holidays should take into consideration celebrations of different cultural groups. It is important to provide opportunities for pupils from diverse backgrounds to learn about their own heritage.

Lessons focusing on holidays need to be planned carefully. The learning benefits of proposed holiday-based activities must be weighed against the amount of time required to do them. Such lessons make sense when the holiday theme acts as a motivator for a lesson that deals with important social studies content. If the lesson cannot be defended on the basis of its ability to transmit important content and the lesson represents little more than a cosmetic acknowledgment of the existence of a particular holiday, the holiday focus should be scrapped in favor an approach that ties more clearly to serious content.

How Historians Judge the Truth

Good history is not just a matter of the writer's opinion. It rests on the careful examination of evidence. As appropriate to their age, developmental level, and intellectual sophistication, elementary pupils should be introduced to the ways that historians identify and evaluate evidence. When historians consider the truth or validity of a historical document, they consider (1) external validity and (2) internal validity.

External Validity

External validity has to do with the issue of authenticity. Suppose a historian found a document that was supposed to have been written in England in the year 1610. The historian might arrange for a chemical analysis of the paper and ink to establish whether they represented types available in 1610. The words used in the document might be compared to words used in other documents known to have been written in the early seventeenth century. While doing this, the historian would be trying to find words in the mystery document inconsistent with what logically might be expected in a document of this date. Detective work associated with external validity often unmasks forgeries.

Internal Validity

Internal validity seeks to determine the accuracy of information contained in a historical record. For example, it would be possible for a document that really was produced in 1610 to contain inaccurate statements. Even if the external validity tests indicate that the document was written in 1610, the historian must be careful not to accept without question everything that was written. In the search for internal validity, the historian must consider whether the person who allegedly wrote the material was really capable of doing so. For example, did the writer have an education that would account for the kinds of words and sentences found in the document? Perhaps someone else wrote the material. Why did the person write the material? Did the author have an interest in writing the truth, or was there some reason to distort some, or even all, of the information? For example, public speeches or political documents designed to be read by a wide audience sometimes are designed not so much to illuminate absolute truth as to support the case for a particular point of view. On the other hand, a letter to a personal friend or relative that was not intended for dissemination to others may more accurately reflect what the writer personally believes to be true.

In the search for internal and external validity, the historian looks for explanations that go beyond the obvious. The search is part of the excitement of the historian's craft. History is not just a matter of collecting and writing down information about the past. Rather, historians must make careful judgments about the validity and reliability of evidence. Good history is the product of disciplined thinking.

A Selection of Information Sources

Teachers look constantly for material they can incorporate into lessons that interest and excite their pupils. The following subsections describe information sources that many teachers find useful when planning social studies lessons.

The National Council for History Education

During the latter half of the 1980s, concerns about the quality of history instruction led to the formation of the Bradley Commission on History in the Schools. Bradley Commission members included leading historians, history education specialists, and public school educators with an interest in history. Many symposia, conferences, and curriculum projects were supported by the Bradley Commission.

In 1988, the Bradley Commission issued curriculum guidelines that have been widely discussed by individuals interested in improving the quality of history in both elementary and secondary schools. The commission initiated publication of a monthly newsletter, *History Matters*. This publication often includes information of interest to elementary teachers.

In 1990, the Bradley Commission changed its name to the National Council for History Education. The organization continues to publish *History Matters* and to provide other services to educators who wish to improve history teaching in the schools. For membership information, write to the National Council for History Education, 26915 Westwood Road, Suite A-2, Westlake, OH 44145.

The National Council for the Social Studies

The National Council for the Social Studies (NCSS) is the largest national organization of educators interested in social studies education. For many years, NCSS has published *Social Education*. The "Elementary Education" section of this journal often includes ideas for teaching historical content to young learners. A subscription to *Social Education* is included in the basic NCSS membership fee.

NCSS also publishes *Social Studies and the Young Learner*. This professional journal is dedicated exclusively to issues of interest to elementary school teachers. For subscription information, membership information, and information about other services provided by NCSS, write to the National Council for the Social Studies, 3501 Newark Street, NW, Washington, DC 20016.

GEOGRAPHY

Geography has been traditionally viewed as one of the major pillars of the social studies curriculum. While history views human affairs from the perspective of time, geography places human affairs in a locational context. Risinger (1992) states that "geography is the stage upon which the human drama is played" (p. 4). An idea central to geography is that each place on earth is unique. This means that an understanding of diverse settings is prerequisite to real understanding of the human condition.

Geographers focus on patterns of spatial distribution and on interactions of phenomena as they occur across space. Studies of distribution make sense because resources, people, and other environmental features are not evenly distributed. Some places lack things that other places have. These differences prompt flows of people and resources from place to place. These flows take the forms of human migration and of trade. Because of movements of people and goods from place to place, there are interactions among different places on the earth's surface. Geographers interested in spatial interaction study relationships among different world regions, paying particular attention to factors that enhance or inhibit the volume or intensity of these interactions.

Professional geographers have long been concerned that many public school programs fail to introduce students to much of what geographers do. Some critics of school practices have suggested that, in some schools at least, geography is conceived of as involving little more than teaching students to recognize locations of continents and countries and to name capitals of the states. To develop a more adequate appreciation of what should be included in sound geography-based school programs, several national organizations of geographers have joined forces. As a result of this collaboration, the Association of American Geographers (AAG) and the National Council for Geographic Education (NCGE) published *Guidelines for Geographic Education: Elementary and Secondary Schools* (Natoli et al., 1984). This publication lays out arguments supporting the idea that geographic ignorance can have dire consequences for our nation's future economic and social development and international competitiveness. It includes a framework for teaching geography in elementary and secondary schools that is designed to help learners acquire better self-understanding, appreciation of their relationship to the earth, and recognition of their interdependence with other world peoples (Natoli et al., 1984).

The Geography Curriculum

To combat geographic ignorance, there needs to be a change in how geography has sometimes been viewed in the elementary curriculum. Geography is not primarily concerned with memorization of state capitals, names of mountain ranges, and lists of imports and exports of various world places. Good lessons in geography focus on involving students in critical thinking and problem solving. This means that pupils not only need to know where things are located, but why they are there and what the consequences of these locations might be.

Guidelines for Geographic Education (Natoli et al., 1984) identifies five major themes educators can use in planning geography-based lessons:

- Location
- Place
- Human–environment interactions
- Movement
- Regions

Location

Location refers to where phenomena are located on the face of the earth. There are two aspects of location. One is absolute location, and the other is relative location. *Absolute* location refers to a precise place on the earth's surface. This can be determined with reference to grid lines such as latitude and longitude. *Relative* location refers to where something is located in relationship to other things, for example bodies of water, transportation routes, climate types, population centers, or various kinds of natural resources. Relative location helps individuals understand why places are interdependent.

Place

Each place on the earth's surface has unique characteristics. The nature of the interaction of people with the physical environment varies, both because of cultural differences and because of place-to-place differences in physical environments. Lessons focusing on the theme of place emphasize both environmental characteristics and special cultural characteristics of the people who live in various places across the earth's surface.

Human–Environment Interactions

This theme draws attention to how human beings modify physical landscapes and how landscapes also exercise influence on the range of human activities at particular places. Changes in local environments may result from cultural, economic, social, political, and technological characteristics of individual human populations. Lessons emphasizing this theme are designed to promote an understanding of human–environment interactions and their possible consequences.

Lesson Idea 2–5

ENVIRONMENTAL PERCEPTION

Grade Level:	Primary
Objective:	Students can state the influence of experiences on their ideas and perceptions.
Overview:	Geographers interested in environmental perception believe that human relationships with the environment are not adequately explained by the world "as it is." Rather, these relationships are the result of what people "believe" the world to be. Personal experiences help shape how people view the world. For example, surveys of people in different regions of the United States have revealed great variations in opinion about the location of the "best" place to live. Similarly, experiences often lead to misperceptions of distance. Longtime residents of the Northeast often underestimate the distance separating western cities such as Los Angeles and San Francisco. Westerners have difficulty understanding the proximity of eastern cities such as Boston and New York. Pupils can begin to understand how their personal experiences have influenced their view of the world by focusing on elements of their own neighborhood.
Procedure:	*Learning Set* Discuss with the pupils the kinds of things that they can do in a park. Tell them that they are going to be allowed to design the "perfect" park. Ask the following questions and write the responses on the board:

- What kinds of things should be in the park?
- Where did you get your ideas?

Give cooperative groups an opportunity to draw a park to include the things they have identified and where they think the best place would be for the items they want to include. Then discuss the following questions:

- How do you think your ideas of a perfect park would be different if you lived in the center of a city? In a farming community? In a snowy region? In a desert region?
- Why do you think people in different places would have different ideas about what would be best?

Debrief the class, pointing out that the experiences people have influence the choices they make. What might look like a good place for a park for us might not be the same place and type of a park that someone else would choose. This could be extended by asking pupils why some people prefer to go to the mountains for vacations and others prefer to go to the beach or to the city.

Closure: Ask the class, "What did we learn about the way people view the environment? How is our view influenced by our experiences?"

Movement

Movement focuses on interaction between and among places. Lessons may emphasize the patterns of movement of people, resources, and ideas. Pupils are challenged to think about why things move across the face of the earth as they do, and about what factors might enhance or restrict movement. For example, learners might be asked to think about how physical features such as mountains or human creations such as political boundaries and laws might influence the movement of people and ideas. Lessons also often encourage learners to think about how technological change might affect movement.

Transportation systems facilitate human movement and interactions.

Lesson Idea 2–6

MIGRATION

Grade Level: 5–6

Objectives: Learners can (1) locate places on a map, (2) identify movement patterns, and (3) state reasons for movement from one place to another.

Overview: The movement of people and goods from place to place is an important feature of our world. Understanding the reasons for movement, the impact of the movement, and the patterns of movement can help pupils to understand the linkages between places and the changes that have resulted from such movement, and to predict problems that might arise as a result.

Procedure: As a homework assignment the night before the lesson, have the pupils find out from their parents the birthplaces of their parents and their grandparents.

Learning Set   Ask class members, How many have moved? Discuss reasons why they moved. Tell them that movement from place to place is very common and that understanding those movement patterns can help us understand different places and the advantages and problems they might have.

Give each child a set of six circles with "sticky" backs, and have them put their name or initials on each one. On one sticker write *father*, on another *mother*. On the other four, indicate the grandfather and grandmother on the father's side of the family, and the grandfather and grandmother on the mother's side of the family.

Divide the class into groups of five or six. Give each group a world map and have them locate the places of birth of their grandparents and parents. Have each group share their maps with the rest of the class.

Discuss the maps, using the following questions:

- Did you notice any patterns of movement in our class?
- Why do you think there were patterns?
- Why did your parents or grandparents move?
- What causes people to move?
- What problems might occur when many people from many different places decide to move to the same place?

Closure: Conclude the lesson by asking, "What did we learn about movement? What did we learn about our class? What other types of movement might be interesting to study?"

Region

The concept of "region" is fundamental to geography. A *region* is defined as an area of any shape or size that has a certain common characteristic or set of common characteristics. Regions need not be based only on physical characteristics. For example, some regions are defined by a common language or a common set of religious beliefs. Other regions are defined by density of population or by predominance of a certain kind of economic activity (corn belt, wheat belt, and so forth). There are almost endless possibilities for dividing the surface of the earth into regions.

Regions provide convenient units of analysis for studying the world. Study of the development and characteristics of regions can promote the discovery of important relationships. For example, a number of years ago researchers divided the United States into regions based on rates of occurrence of certain types of cancer. This then allowed researchers to investigate other variables that were present in the high-incidence regions (for example, amount of industrial air pollution, percentage of the population smoking several packs of cigarettes a day, and so forth) to determine whether any of them might be contributing to the unusually high percentage of the population with cancer.

Lesson Idea 2–7

REGIONS

Grade Level:	Primary
Objectives:	Learners can (1) identify criteria for establishing a region, and (2) draw boundaries for a region.
Overview:	A region is an area of any shape or size that has some common characteristic. This does not mean that other activities or things do not occur in the region. For example, the corn belt includes many other things besides farmers growing corn. Regions do not need to be areas of vast size. They can be as small as the painting region of the classroom, or as large as the continent of Asia. Pupils can begin to develop the idea of region by beginning with an area familiar to them. This might include area of the room, the playground, or the neighborhood.
Procedure:	***Learning Set*** Begin by stating to the class, "In our homes and in our school, there are certain places we go for certain types of activities. For example, if we want to eat, where do we go? We could call this the 'eating region.' At home, if we want to sleep, where do we go? We could call this the 'sleeping region.' Today we are going to go out to the playground and see if we can identify different areas or regions on the playground."

Provide groups of pupils with a simple map of the playground. Walk around the playground and discuss with the pupils a few of the different regions and labels they could give to the region. Those might include the following:

- Tether ball region
- Soccer region
- Baseball region
- Swings region
- No running region
- Primary-grade region
- Upper-grade region

Have each group decide where they would draw the boundaries of each region on their maps. Encourage them to think of other regions they might include on their maps. After returning to the room, have groups share their maps. Discuss why they drew the boundaries where they did. Ask them if the only thing that ever happens in their region is the activity they identified. Point out that people called geographers divide the earth into regions. Sometimes they disagree where the boundaries of a region might be. Those regions also include many things other than the one thing identified for the region.

Closure: Ask the class to define a region and state what they have learned about regions. Encourage them to think about regions in the neighborhood.

Geography is an important part of the social studies program. It provides more than just a "stage for the human drama." Techniques geographers use allow for sophisticated thought about important human–environment relationships. Its tools have potential for unlocking solutions to critical political, economic, and social problems. The five major themes of geography from *Guidelines for Geographic Education: Elementary and Secondary Schools* provide important planning anchors for teachers as they plan their lessons. Some central questions, concepts, and generalizations associated with geography are presented in Figure 2–3.

Geography-related Classroom Activities

Thinking Geographically

One purpose of classroom lessons oriented around geography is to teach pupils how to "think geographically." This requires them to develop sophisticated observation and thinking skills. Such lessons prompt them to ask questions as they observe the world around them.

Efforts to prompt geographic thinking can be started in the primary grades. Taking pupils for walks around the school or the neighborhood and asking them to identify

The following are examples of central questions, concepts, and generalizations that are important when studying geography. They are useful to the elementary social studies teacher when making decisions about what to include in lessons related to geography.

Central Questions (a selection)

Where are things located? Why are they there?

What patterns are reflected in the grouping of things?

How are these patterns explained?

How can things be grouped to form a region?

How do people influence the environment? How does the environment influence people?

What causes changes in the patterns of distribution?

What problems does unequal distribution cause?

What are the links and interactions between different parts of the world?

Concepts (a selection)

Environment, environmental perception, landform, climate, weather, latitude, longitude, elevation, spatial distribution, density, diffusion, interaction, accessibility, location, relative location, region, land use, central place, Equator, North Pole, South Pole, natural resource, area differentiation, settlement pattern, migration, rotation, revolution (of the earth)

Generalizations (a selection)

Human use of the environment is influenced by cultural values, economic wants, level of technology, and environmental perception.

Each culture views the physical environment in a unique way, prizing aspects of it that may be different from those prized by others.

More change and conflict occur near the boundaries of regions than in the interior of regions.

The accessibility, relative location, and the political character of a place influence the quantity and type of its interactions with other places.

The character of a place is not constant; it reflects the place's past, present use, and future prospects.

Innovation and change influence the accessibility and desirability of places.

Successive or continuing occupancy by groups of people and natural processes together give places their uniqueness.

Figure 2–3
Central questions, concepts, and generalizations associated with geography.

items in the environment is a good starting point. You might ask the following prompt questions during such a walk:

- Why do you think a school was built here?
- What things are near the school? What things are near your home?
- How is our community changing?
- Where do you think things in the grocery store come from?

As pupils grow older, their curiosity about geography can be stimulated by asking more sophisticated questions:

- How is our community different from other communities?
- Why is it colder in the winter in the interior of the continent than on the west coast?
- Why are there some many vacant buildings in the old downtown area?
- What changes will take place when those new houses that are being built are finished?
- Why are deserts where they are?

The roles of the teacher in helping pupils to think geographically are that of one who asks questions and that of a resource person who can help learners find needed information. The emphasis is on urging the pupils to do the thinking, not the teacher. When young people begin to do so, they become much more confident in their own abilities to deal with situations where interpretation is required.

Investigating Location

Pupils can learn to identify both absolute and relative locations by working with things in their immediate environment. For example, they might consider locations of their classroom, home, school, and community. Many teachers find it useful to use simple grid systems to introduce learners to the idea of absolute location. A simple grid might have letters A, B, C, D, and so forth along one axis and numbers 1, 2, 3, 4, and so on along the other. For example, pupils in a class might be provided with a simple drawing of their classroom featuring locations of individual student desks with letters and numbers along the axes. Then, the teacher might ask individual youngsters to identify the location of their desks by referencing the grid. (My desk is at location B-3, and so forth.) These simple grid lessons can be followed by more sophisticated exercises involving use of grid systems to locate places on community and state maps.

You may begin a relative location lesson by asking pupils to describe locations of several places they know in their own communities. Pupils often will talk about locations of such places schools, markets, shopping malls, and movie theaters. Once identified, you may then ask pupils about where these places are in relation to one another. They might describe locations in terms of direction and distance from well-known locations such as rivers, parks, harbors, and major streets and highways. You may then lead them into a productive discussion of why certain places might be located where they are. Questions such as the following help pupils think about reasons some kinds of places are located either close to or far away from others:

- Why are many residential areas not located close to where factories are located?
- Would you expect lots of doctors' offices to be located close to hospitals? If so, how would you explain this pattern?
- Why are there often many gas stations near entrances and exits of major highways?

- If there were three stories in a school, would you expect to find all the drinking fountains on just one floor, or would you expect to find some on each floor? Why do you think so?

Noting Spatial Interactions

Spatial interaction refers to the interaction that occurs between and among places. Pupils can begin to understand this idea by discussing and mapping relationships between where they live and where their parents or guardians work. Primary pupils often are taught interactions between urban and rural areas. People get their milk from others, who work on farms in rural areas. In turn, people on farms purchase many items from stores in urban areas. A trip to the supermarket affords an excellent opportunity for a lesson focusing on spatial interaction. Many products have labels indicating their origin. Pupils may take note of this information. Back in the classroom, the class can plot some of the locations on a large map and discuss the variety of places supermarket merchandise comes from.

One class conducted an interesting experiment that led to a great deal of information about interactions among people in different parts of the world. The class purchased a stuffed animal. A letter was drafted and attached to the animal asking anyone who encountered it to write a postcard to the class telling where they had seen the animal and how the animal got there. The respondent was asked to pass the animal along to someone else, particularly to someone who might be doing some traveling. A parent in the class started the activity by giving the animal to an airline flight attendant. Soon postcards began coming to the class from people all over the world. The teacher and the pupils plotted locations of the stuffed animal and its movement on a large world map. This activity greatly heightened the students' awareness of spatial interaction and stimulated their interest in learning about some of the places the animal had visited.

Observing Human–Environment Interactions

It is important to identify how humans change their environment as well as how the environment changes human behavior. As a beginning, pupils might look at the local community and seek answers to questions such as these:

- How is the local community changing?
- Are new homes being built?
- Are trees being eliminated or planted?
- What changes in the environment might take place as the result of a new highway?

Such questions afford an opportunity to tie questions tied to geography to historical information about the community. Answers encourages pupils to understand not only what is happening now but also what has existed in the past.

A study of weather and climate is often included as a component of units focusing on human–environment interactions. Lessons help learners discover how people living under different climatic conditions interact with their circumstances to build special kinds of buildings and wear particular types of clothing. Kinds of recreational activities pursued by people in different climatic regions often also interest elementary school children.

The activities that we have briefly described here are samples of what can be done with geography-related content. Most of these activities require active pupil involvement. Further, they demand that learners think. Sound geography-based lessons require learners to do much more than learn locations and memorize names of capitals. That kind of boring, mindless activity has given geography instruction a bad name. The discipline of geography has marvelous explanatory powers. Good geography-based lessons both interest learners and contribute to the development of their mental powers.

A Selection of Information Sources

National Council for Geographic Education

The leading national professional organization for educators interested in geography is the National Council for Geographic Education (NCGE). NCGE publishes the excellent *Journal of Geography*. A subscription is included as part of the annual membership fee. Many issues feature articles describing imaginative approaches to teaching geographic content to elementary school pupils. For information, write to the National Council for Geographic Education, NCGE Central Office, Indiana University of Pennsylvania, Indiana, PA 15705.

Joint Committee on Geographic Education

Members of the Joint Committee on Geographic Education were drawn from two professional groups whose members have long been interested in improving the quality of geographic education, the National Council for Geographic Education and the Association of American Geographers. The Joint Committee's work led to the publication of *Guidelines for Geographic Education: Elementary and Secondary Schools* (Natoli et al., 1984). As noted previously, this document includes important information regarding kinds of geographic content that should be taught at each grade level. Copies of this material are available from the National Council for Geographic Education.

Geographic Alliance Network

The National Geographic Society has become interested in revitalizing the quality of geographic education in the schools. To this end, the Society has sponsored the formation of more than 40 state-based Geographic Alliances. The alliances seek additional support from state government and private sources.

Each alliance draws together professional geographers and classroom teachers. An alliance coordinator helps to organize activities and to disseminate information about each state's activities. Alliances sponsor summer geographic education institutes, put on one- and two-day workshops, and support the development of high-quality instructional materials. Many Geographic Alliance activities are directed toward elementary school teachers.

For information about the Geographic Alliance Network, write to Geographic Education Program, National Geographic Society, Washington, DC 20036.

ECONOMICS

Scarcity is the fundamental concern of economics. People's wants often exceed the resources needed to satisfy them. Hence, decisions must be made regarding how limited resources are to be allocated and which wants are to be satisfied. *Economics* is the study of approaches used in making decisions in response to the universal scarcity problem.

Traditionally, many elementary economics lessons focused on consumer and personal economics. Consumer economics lessons focused on teaching pupils how to be alert, careful buyers. Personal economics focused on skills such as personal budgeting, management of savings accounts, and (for older learners) balancing checkbooks.

Today's more comprehensive economics programs go beyond consumer and personal economics. Increasingly, economics-oriented instruction attempts to provide pupils with a basic understanding of how the entire American economic system operates and how economic decisions affect everyday life.

Some economics content often can be included in lessons that draw most of their information from other subjects. For example, economic motivations of immigrants can be brought into history lessons focusing on movement of people from other lands to the United States. Lessons that describe decisions of particular kinds of businesses to locate in given places draw content from both geography and economics. Problems governments face in making laws that limit choices people can make and that allocate tax revenues in certain ways are issues with relevance for both economics and political science.

Categories of Economic Systems

All economic systems try to accommodate several important social goals:

- Economic growth
- Economic efficiency
- Security
- Stability
- Equity
- Freedom

As economic systems attempt to respond to the central issue of scarcity, they attend to each of these goals. Individual goals never receive equal emphasis in a given economic system. Economics lessons help pupils to understand that different economic systems have established different priorities. For example, some societies place more emphasis on the goal of economic security than on the goal of economic freedom.

When they are taught to think about how different economic systems respond to the six basic economic goals, children in the middle and upper grades are introduced to three basic types of economies:

- Traditional economies
- Command economies
- Market economies

Traditional Economies

Traditional economies respond to the problem of scarcity by following longstanding patterns or customs. These patterns or customs guide decisions about deciding how scarce resources will be divided, who will get them, and how much will be diverted to the use of each individual or group of individuals. Most frequently, traditional economies are found in technologically underdeveloped societies.

Command Economies

Command economies allocate scarce resources by following a master plan. This plan is devised and enforced by a strong central government. Until quite recently, many countries in Eastern Europe had command economies. Some of the recent troubles in Russia have resulted from conflicts between those who want to remain elements of the old command economy that characterized the former Soviet Union and those who want to move away from this approach to a system more closely approaching the market economies of Western Europe and the United States.

Market Economies

Market economies allocate resources in a decentralized way. There is no master plan. Governments play a relatively minor role. Decisions about what is produced, how much is produced, and how goods are allocated are largely driven by demands of consumers. This kind of economic system characterizes the United States, much of Western Europe (and, increasingly, Eastern Europe as well), Japan, and many other countries in the world. Market economies seem to be increasing in popularity. Because of this trend, social studies programs now pay particular attention to how they operate. Lessons often focus on such market characteristics as the following (Allen & Armstrong, 1978):

- Private property
- Economic freedom
- Incentives
- Decentralized decision making
- Special and somewhat limited role for government

When they plan economics-related lessons, teachers refer to central questions, concepts, and generalizations associated with the discipline. Some examples of these are shown in Figure 2–4.

Economics-related Classroom Activities

Some people see economics as an abstract subject of interest only to those who can generate enthusiasm for working with complex graphs and mathematical formulas. This is not true. Perspectives of economics have great practical value. Further, basic content can be taught in ways that interest pupils. Doubters should take a look at Wentworth and Shug's (1994) excellent *Social Education* article titled "How to Use an Economic Mystery in Your History Course." In this article, the two authors introduce a *Handy Dandy Guide* you can use to help pupils think and reason from an economics perspec-

The following are examples of central questions, concepts, and generalizations associated with economics. They provide guidelines for elementary teachers interested in planning economics-related lessons.

Central Questions (a selection)

How have different societies coped with the problem of scarcity?
How do innovation and change influence the wants and needs of people?
How can resources be allocated responsibly and fairly?
What is the proper role of government in limiting the economic choices of people?
Does the economic system provide for an equality of opportunity?
Is the economic system stable or is it characterized by periods of uneven growth?
What are the possible consequences of alternative economic choices?
What is the overall quality of life provided by the economic system?

Concepts (a selection)

Scarcity, resources, costs, benefits, opportunity costs, private property, public property, land, labor, capital, specialization, division of labor, trade, supply, demand, producer, consumer, price, competition, incentives, goods, market, traditional economy, command economy, market economy, money

Generalizations (a selection)

The wants of people are unlimited whereas the resources to meet those wants are scarce; hence, individuals and societies must make decisions as to which wants will be met.
Scarce resources are allocated to meet needs according to the values of those making the decisions.
When individuals choose to allocate scarce resources to meet one need, they give up the opportunity to meet other needs.
Unequal distribution of resources and population makes trade a necessary ingredient of economic well-being.
Specialization and division of labor promote the efficiency of an economic system.
The economic development of a nation is related to the availability of resources, capital, and the quality of the labor force.
The government plays an important role in the economic development of every society, but that role varies from place to place.

Figure 2–4
Central questions, concepts, and generalizations associated with economics.

tive. Content is based on an assumption that guides the work of professional economists, namely, "Human behavior results from choices people make based on expected costs and expected benefits." This assumption led Wentworth and Shug (1994) to develop six important related corollary statements:

- People choose.
- People's choices involve costs.

- People respond to incentives in predictable ways.
- People create economic systems that influence individual choices and incentives.
- People gain when they trade voluntarily.
- People's choices have consequences that lie in the future.

People Choose

This statement is based on the assumption that actions of individuals are rational. People make choices by considering alternatives and deciding how to use their scarce resources. The better people understand the alternatives open to them, the better their choices will be. This idea can easily be incorporated into elementary social studies lessons. For example, you may give pupils some imaginary money to spend, then have them decide how to spend it. They must think about their options. Their choices are likely to be better as they learn more about each option and as the number of options they know about increases. From this, it is a short step to discussing the idea that many things are scarce other than money. For example, recess time is a scarce resource: only a limited amount of time is available. Children must think about how they will spend it. A discussion of this issue with a group of young children can provide them with important insights into the human need to choose and allocate scarce resources wisely. Older learners may apply their understanding of positives and negatives associated with individual decisions to content from other kinds of lessons. For example, you might discuss the choices that were available to people who, in the end, decided to move to a new community, a new country, or a new continent.

People's Choices Involve Costs

Choices involve costs. People choose things that appear likely to provide them with more benefits than would the alternative. This idea can be incorporated into many kinds of elementary social studies lessons. For example, you might ask pupils to reflect on the costs borne by people in the United States during the previous two centuries who decided to move west. In addition to monetary costs, these people paid other prices. They gave up opportunities to visit old friends and relatives. They lost the comfortable familiarity of the terrain they had known for much of their lives. They gave up the relative safety of a well-developed society for the dangers of a rough-and-ready frontier. Why did they accept these costs? A discussion of this issue with learners might lead to several conclusions, including the possibility of riches from new lands, new opportunities for their children, and the ability to participate in setting up new governments in the new western lands.

Lesson Idea 2–8

MAKING CHOICES

Grade Level: Primary

Objectives: Learners can (1) identify choices they have to make, and (2) explain how choosing one thing eliminates another that could have been chosen.

Overview:

Scarcity requires people everywhere to make many choices. The choices that people make in their everyday life reflect expected benefits and costs. One of the costs is that when one makes a choice, the possibility of having something else is eliminated. By focusing on the choices that they make in everyday life, young pupils can begin to appreciate this economic idea.

Procedure:

Learning Set   Ask pupils what they like about events such as Christmas or their birthday. After discussing several things they like, focus on the receiving of gifts. Tell them that deciding what gifts to request involves making choices because people can't buy everything we might want.

Presentation   Tell the class, "I would like you to pretend that I am going to get you a gift for one of those special occasions. I would like you to draw me a picture of five things you want." Collect the pictures when they are finished drawing.

Select one student's picture. Tell the class that the items in the picture are all good things; however, you don't have enough money to buy them all. The price of each item is two dollars and you only have four dollars. Ask the pupil who drew the picture to tell you which two things you should choose. Ask the student why he or she chose those items. Make sure and discuss what the pupil is choosing to give up by not making the other choices. Help the class see that the student is making choices based on expected benefits assumed to be more important than what is being given up.

Repeat the process with a couple of other pupils. Then discuss the following questions:

- Why couldn't we get everything?
- How do you decide what things you really want?
- How do you feel when you have to choose?
- Do you think people are able to get all the things they want? (This can lead to a discussion of how human wants expand more rapidly than the resources needed to satisfy them.)

Closure:

Conclude the lesson by asking, "What did we learn about people's wants? Because people have many desires, what do they have to do? What do you need to think about when making choices?"

People Respond to Incentives in a Predictable Way

Incentives encourage people to make a particular choice when they are confronted with alternatives. For example, in elementary schools the incentive of more recess time may encourage pupils to finish assigned tasks rather than talk to their neighbors.

The study of economics involves the study of choices.

Changes in incentives often cause individuals to change the choices they make. If new incentives are attached to a particular option, this option is more likely to be selected. Similarly, when incentives associated with an alternative diminish, the likelihood decreases that that option will be chosen.

Pupils can be introduced to the idea of incentives through role-playing activities that require them to make choices. For example, youngsters might act out roles in a situation the teacher explains in the following way:

> All right, I want two people to play roles. This is going to be a situation involving two friends. One person wants to play a game that requires the other person as a player. The other person would rather watch a TV program. The student who wants to play the game must try to make the friend want to play the game and give up the idea of watching television. Let's try and make this as real as we can. Do I have two volunteers?

After pupils have finished role playing this situation, the teacher can engage the class in a discussion focusing on the incentives offered to encourage the person who wanted to watch television to play the game. Learners probably will suggest some incentives that didn't occur to the pupil who took the part of the friend who wanted to play. The discussion might focus on *disincentives*, things designed to discourage the person from wanting to watch the television program. For example, the person who wanted to play the game might have suggested that the program was going to be a rerun that the child who wanted to watch TV had already seen. As part of the discussion, the teacher might point out the variety of incentives that are used to get people to do things. Coupons printed in newspapers are designed as incentives to encourage people to shop at certain stores. Advertisements regularly try to encourage a belief that their products will give more satisfaction or pleasure than those of competitors. To the extent individuals believe these claims, advertisements provide incentives for consumers to buy.

Lesson Idea 2–9

ECONOMIC INCENTIVES

Grade Level:	3–4
Objectives:	The learners can (1) identify example of incentives used to influence people's behavior and (2) apply the idea of incentives to understanding the behavior of people in the past.
Overview:	Incentives are those things that are used to influence human behavior. Understanding the role of incentives in making choices helps individuals understand the choices people made in the past. Incentives are commonly used in everyday life. Beginning with examples that pupils meet everyday and then applying this lesson to historical events facilitates student understanding of the past.
Procedure:	*Learning Set* Begin by asking pupils if they would be willing to perform an undesirable task. Then ask them if they would perform the task if they received something they desired. Tell them that this is an example of an incentive, and that incentives are frequently used to get people to make choices they might not otherwise make.
	Procedure Divide the class into small groups and give each group a newspaper. Tell them you want them to go through the paper (especially the advertisements) and see how many examples of incentives they can find. Have them cut out the examples and paste them to on a chart labeled "Incentives." Each group can then share their chart with the class.
	Tell them that incentives can be anything that a person thinks will be beneficial to them. For example, the people who settled our community or our state had some incentives that led them to think that their life would be better if they settled here than at other places. Ask them what the incentives might have been for people to settle in our community or state. List these on the board and then tell them that in the next few days the class will do some research to see if their ideas about incentives are correct.
Closure:	Ask class members to define incentives. See if someone can provide an example of an incentive. Have someone state how they are going to use their knowledge of incentives in their study of the local community or state.

People Create Economic Systems that Influence
Individual Choices and Incentives

This statement speaks to the relationship between the issue of economic freedom and the role of government. To help pupils begin to grasp the complex nature of the relationship between the twin ideas of economic freedom and economic justice, prompt questions such as these might be used to spark a discussion:

- Do you believe people should be completely free to make any choices they want to?
- What if someone exercises his or her freedom and makes a choice that hurts you? Is this right?
- What should be done about the problem of some people making choices that might hurt others?

These questions can lead pupils to an appreciation that even in market economies that place a high priority on giving economic decision-making authority to individuals, there is a need to place limitations on economic freedom in the name of fairness and justice. Much governmental policy is directed toward this end. The idea is that the government allows the maximum possible amount of economic freedom while making sure that individual rights and freedoms are protected. For example, regulations place restrictions on where industries can dump certain waste materials. These rules are designed to prevent pollution and to protect the health of the general population. Even elementary pupils need to begin to understand that there is controversy regarding how much economic freedom is needed and how much government control is required. They will be thinking about and debating this general issue all their lives.

Traditional economies and command economies often place severe restrictions on the economic freedom of individuals. In traditional economies, more attention often is given to making economic decisions that favor certain high-status groups such as older people or important group leaders. In command economies, choices often are made based on what is perceived to be most efficient for the economy as a whole, regardless of the issues of fairness or justice to particular individuals or groups of individuals.

Pupils relate easily to the need for rules to limit choices. When they play games, they learn to follow rules that place restrictions on what they can do. Discussions of simple rules, such as "three strikes and you're out" in baseball, can lead students to consider governmental actions to limit choices for the purpose of promoting fairness. Role-playing exercises often work well to expand pupils' understanding of this issue. For example, to promote a better understanding of decision making in traditional and command economies, you might set up a situation where you make every rule with no reference to learner wishes (command economy illustration) or where certain pupils, such as the oldest or all the boys or all the girls, are allowed to make decisions for the entire class (traditional economy illustration).

Lesson Idea 2–10

ECONOMIC SYSTEMS

Grade Level:	5–6
Objective:	Learners can identify the features of traditional, command, and market economies.
Overview:	The choices people have are influenced by the economic system. Learners can begin to understand this by having them participate in an exercise that simulates the way each of these systems works. Teaching this lesson requires a number of small items that pupils desire. These could be marbles, pencils, pictures, and so on. Three tagboard cards labeled (a) "Traditional Economy," (b) "Command Economy," and (c) "Market Economy" are also needed.
Procedure:	*Learning Set* Ask the pupils if they can define what is meant by choice and what is meant by freedom. Explain, "Today you are going to learn about three different ways groups of people around the world have decided to deal with the freedom people have in making choices."

Presentation   Ask all pupils who are the eldest children in their family to stand. Inform them that they can have all the wealth (the collection of desirable items). Others in the class will receive nothing. Tell pupils that in some places in the world all the wealth of parents is left to the oldest child. Ask them who has the most choices in this type of a system. Get their reactions. Have them state what types of problems they think this system might create. Tell them this is called a traditional economy. Show them the card labeled "Traditional Economy" and place it at the front of the room.

Next, announce that you are the "government" of a country. You have decided that a few of the pupils can have a choice of any item they want. You will decide who gets the rest of them. Go about arbitrarily giving a few pupils a wide choice and distributing items to others. Leave out a few pupils so that they do not receive anything. Ask the pupils what type of freedom and choice they had in this way of distributing the wealth. Ask for their reactions. Have them state what types of problems they think this system might create. Tell them this is an example of a command economy, where one person or a few people decide who gets what things. Place the card labeled "Command Economy" at the front.

Next tell the class that you are going to let them decide which items they would like to have and that they can work to make money to buy whatever item they would like. Ask them to compare this way of distributing the items to the first two ways. Inform them that this is a market economy. Place the card labeled "Market Economy" with the previous two cards. Tell students that individuals in a market economy have the freedom to buy what they want. However, the prices of some items might be higher and some lower. If many people want some things, they would be willing to pay more to get it. Those things they didn't want would be less expensive. Ask them what they see as potential problems with this system.

Closure: Ask pupils to give a definition of each of the three types of systems discussed. Ask them, "What type of a system do you think we have?" Tell them that in coming lessons the class is going to study different countries to identify the type of system they use and to see if they can find the advantages and disadvantages of each system.

People Gain When They Trade Voluntarily

Because people are not self-sufficient, they need to trade. We do not make all of our clothes or grow all of our own food. People who are allowed to trade things they have in surplus for things they lack increase their ability to satisfy their needs. Many pupils have an intuitive grasp of this idea. They frequently trade things such as lunch items and baseball cards.

Simple activities can be used even in the primary grades to reinforce the idea that trade provides benefits to people. For example, two pupils might be asked to come to front of the class. One can be given bread, and one can be given lunchmeat. As everyone in the class will see, without trade, one has only bread to eat and the other has only meat. However, if they trade, both can make sandwiches. Older pupils can investigate how communities, states, and regions trade things they have for things they want and need. All of this leads logically to such ideas as the interdependence of people and regions, the importance of transportation, and the function of money.

People's Choices Have Consequences that Lie in the Future

The choices people make do not have perfectly predictable consequences. People try to make decisions in ways that will provide them with benefits that outweigh the costs. Sometimes they are right; sometimes they are wrong. It is always possible that, even when people choose carefully, unforeseen circumstances may lead to unanticipated consequences. Elementary school children need to learn that they cannot simply "go to a book" to find out how they should make a difficult choice. However, they also need to understand that good thinking about choices can help reduce the probability of making an unwise decision.

To help pupils think about what goes into making smart decisions, you can initiate a discussion focusing on examples in learners' lives when their decisions have not worked out as expected. For example, they may have chosen to play outside only to find that rain cut their games short. Or, they may have purchased a new game and found some pieces were missing when they arrived home and opened the package. These personal examples provide a link to the more general understanding that unanticipated events are a constant of life. Many examples from the social studies illustrate this point. For example, founders of new communities in thousands of locations across the American West were convinced that their towns would blossom into huge metropolises. Despite these high hopes, few of these places became thriving cities; many disappeared entirely after a few years.

You will have many opportunities to introduce content from economics into social studies lessons. Because issues associated with economics are so intimately associated with decisions people must make throughout their lives, it is important to give pupils opportunities to experience economic reasoning in the elementary social studies program.

A Selection of Information Sources

Joint Council on Economic Education

The Joint Council on Economic Education is dedicated to the improvement of economics-related instruction in the nation's schools. It is an independent, nonprofit, nonpartisan organization. The Joint Council produces many materials suitable for use in elementary school social studies classes. For information, write to the Joint Council on Economic Education, 1212 Avenue of the Americas, New York, NY 10036.

National Center for Economic Education for Children

The National Center for Economic Education for Children is particularly concerned about improving economic understanding of elementary school learners. It publishes a quarterly journal, *The Elementary Economist*. Each issue features practical teaching suggestions for the elementary grades. Information about the center's activities can be obtained by writing to the National Center for Economic Education for Children, Lesley College, 35 Mellen Street, Boston, MA 02138.

Other Sources

Many economic education centers exist around the country. Most of them are located on college and university campus. These centers are dedicated to the improvement of the nation's economic literacy. Many have materials designed for use in elementary school classrooms. These centers also frequently sponsor inservice programs designed to help teachers prepare and deliver economics-related instruction.

Chambers of commerce, unions, manufacturers, and many other private and public organizations produce learning materials focusing on economic issues. Some of these reflect narrow points of view. They need to be selected carefully to assure that the total program of instruction presented to learners reflects a good balance of competing perspectives.

KEY IDEAS IN SUMMARY

1. Content selection in the social studies is challenging. This is true because of the tremendous range of information that, logically, might be considered for use in social studies lessons. In general, the idea is to select content that will help pupils develop a complete and connected view of the world. Most content used in social studies teaching comes from history and the social sciences.

2. Content drawn from history can be used to help pupils develop an appreciation for multiple perspectives on events and more sophisticated thinking skills. The Bradley Commission on History in Schools (now the National Council for History Education) is an organization committed to improving the quality of history instruction in the schools. The Bradley Commission has suggested six themes teachers can use to organize effective history-based lessons: (1) civilization, (2) cultural diffusion and innovation, (3) values, beliefs, political ideas, and political institutions, (4) conflict and cooperation, (5) comparative history of major developments, and (6) patterns of social and political interactions.

3. Historians, as they attempt to determine the "truth", are concerned about both internal and external validity of information sources. Procedures used to determine external validity focus on the likelihood a document or other historical artifact could have been produced at the time it was alleged to have been produced. Internal validity procedures seek to verify the accuracy of information in the material.

4. Geography focuses on spatial patterns. Guidelines produced by major organizations concerned about geographic education identify five major themes that should be reflected in a geography education program: (1) location, (2) place, (3) human–environment interactions, (4) movement, and (5) regions.

5. The National Geographic Society has encouraged the development of Geographic Alliances in each state. These are coalitions of professors of geography and classroom teachers who are interested in geography. Alliances sponsor summer programs and workshops, and engage in the development of geography-related classroom materials.

6. Economics lessons focus on scarcity and how people respond to this universal human problem. Three types of systems have evolved to deal with scarcity, (1) traditional economies, (2) command economies, and (3) market economies. Recently, some experts in economic education (Wentworth & Schug, 1994) have

suggested five key ideas that should be introduced to help pupils develop their economic thinking skills: (1) people choose; (2) people's choices involve costs; (3) people respond to incentives in predictable ways; (4) people create economic systems that influence individual choices and incentives; (5) people gain when they trade voluntarily; and, (6) people's choices have consequences that lie in the future.

CHAPTER REFLECTIONS

Directions: Now that you have finished reading the chapter, reread the case study at the beginning. Then, answer these questions.

1. What is your reaction to Juan's view of the social studies as primarily consisting of history and geography?

2. How would you respond to Juan's question about how to select content for inclusion in the elementary school program?

3. How do you react to Juan's question about what should be taught about geography in elementary social studies classes?

4. What do you think you need to learn about different subjects to teach them successfully?

5. Have your ideas about what should be taught changed as a result of reading this chapter? If so, in what ways?

EXTENDING UNDERSTANDING AND SKILL

1. Review several issues of *History Matters*. Share with other members of your class some arguments included in this publication for including history instruction in the elementary school program. For information about receiving *History Matters*, write to the National Council for History Education, 26915 Westwood Road, Suite A-2, Westlake, OH 4414.

2. Compare the themes identified in the chapter for history and geography and the basic ideas introduced in Wentworth and Schug's (1994) *Handy Dandy Guide*. How much overlap is there? Do you think it is possible to create lessons that integrate history, geography, and economics?

3. Prepare a position statement in which you defend history, geography, and economics as important components of the elementary social studies program.

4. Select four or five key concepts each from history, geography, and economics. Begin building resource files you can use in the classroom to teach these concepts

to children. Include such things as photographs, newspaper accounts, journal articles, and cartoons.

REFERENCES

ALLEN, J., AND ARMSTRONG, D. (1978). *Hallmarks of a Free Enterprise System*. College Station, TX: Center for Education and Research in Free Enterprise, Texas A&M University.

ARMSTRONG, D. G., AND SAVAGE, T. V. (1976). "A Framework for Utilizing the Community for Social Learning in Grades 4–6." *Social Education, 40*(3), pp. 164–167.

Bradley Commission on History in Schools. (1988). *Building a History Curriculum: Guidelines for Teaching History*. Westlake, OH: National Council for History Education, Inc.

GAGNON, P. (1989). *Democracy's Half-Told Story: What American History Textbooks Should Add*. Washington, DC: American Federation of Teachers.

History–Social Science Framework for California Public Schools: Kindergarten through Grade Twelve. (1987). Sacramento, CA: California State Department of Education.

National Commission on Social Studies in the Schools. (1989). *Charting a Course: Social Studies in the 21st Century*. Washington, DC: American Historical Association, Carnegie Foundation for the Advancement of Teaching, National Council for the Social Studies, Organization of American Historians.

NATOLI, S. J., BOEHM, R. G., KRACHT, J. B., LANEGRAN, D. A., MONK, J. J., AND MORRILL, R. W. (1984). *Guidelines for Geographic Education: Elementary and Secondary Schools*. Washington, DC: Association of American Geographers and National Council for Geographic Education.

RISINGER, C. F. (1992). *Current Directions in Social Studies*. Boston: Houghton Mifflin.

SAVAGE, M. K., AND SAVAGE, T. V. (1993). "Children's Literature in Middle School Social Studies." *The Social Studies, 84*(1), pp. 32–37.

WENTWORTH, D. R., AND SCHUG, M. C. (1994). "How to Use an Economic Mystery in Your History Course." *Social Education, 58*(1), pp. 10–12.

3

THE CONTENT SOURCES: POLITICAL SCIENCE, SOCIOLOGY, ANTHROPOLOGY, AND PSYCHOLOGY

CHAPTER GOALS

This chapter provides information to help the reader:

- identify the relationships among the social science disciplines of political science, sociology, anthropology, psychology, and the curriculum of elementary social studies,

- describe the special perspectives of each discipline in studying human action and behavior,

- identify central questions, concepts, and generalizations for each discipline, and

- develop social studies lessons that draw content from each social science discipline.

CHAPTER STRUCTURE

Introduction
Political Science
    Political Science in the Curriculum
    Micropolitical Organization / Macropolitical Organization
    Political Science-related Classroom Activities
    Making Rules / Resolving Conflicts / Basic Foundations of Democratic Government
Sociology
    Institutions
    Primary Groups
    Secondary Groups
    Stratified Groups
    Relationships within and Among Groups
    Social Change
    Communication
    Social Problems
    Sociology-related Classroom Activities
    Group Membership / Investigating Communication / Community Studies / Identifying Social Problems
Anthropology
    Archaeology and Prehistory
    Human Evolution
    Culture
    Cultural Change
    Anthropology-related Classroom Activities
    Native Americans / Cultural Conflict / Storytelling
Psychology
    Individual Differences
    Perception
    Fears
    Aggression
    Psychology-related Classroom Activities
    Observing People / Individual Differences / Perception / Emotions
Key Ideas in Summary
Chapter Reflections
Extending Understanding and Skill
References

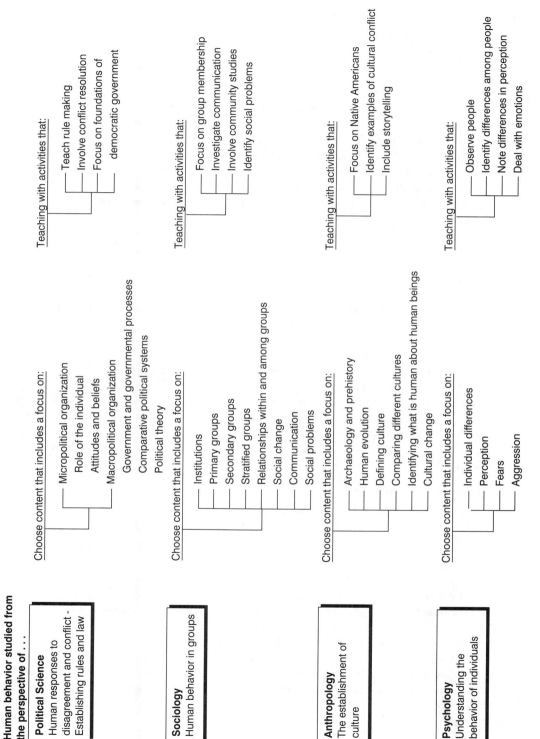

Human behavior studied from the perspective of . . .

Political Science
Human responses to disagreement and conflict - Establishing rules and law

Choose content that includes a focus on:
- Micropolitical organization
  - Role of the individual
  - Attitudes and beliefs
- Macropolitical organization
  - Government and governmental processes
  - Comparative political systems
  - Political theory

Teaching with activities that:
- Teach rule making
- Involve conflict resolution
- Focus on foundations of democratic government

Sociology
Human behavior in groups

Choose content that includes a focus on:
- Institutions
- Primary groups
- Secondary groups
- Stratified groups
- Relationships within and among groups
- Social change
- Communication
- Social problems

Teaching with activities that:
- Focus on group membership
- Investigate communication
- Involve community studies
- Identify social problems

Anthropology
The establishment of culture

Choose content that includes a focus on:
- Archaeology and prehistory
- Human evolution
- Defining culture
- Comparing different cultures
- Identifying what is human about human beings
- Cultural change

Teaching with activities that:
- Focus on Native Americans
- Identify examples of cultural conflict
- Include storytelling

Psychology
Understanding the behavior of individuals

Choose content that includes a focus on:
- Individual differences
- Perception
- Fears
- Aggression

Teaching with activities that:
- Observe people
- Identify differences among people
- Note differences in perception
- Deal with emotions

Figure 3–1
Social studies content sources.

Chapter 3

Case Study

WHAT IS CITIZENSHIP?

The faculty of Glen Eden Elementary School were gathered for their first faculty meeting of the year. After a few welcome back comments and some routine business, the principal launched into the first substantive agenda item, the social studies curriculum.

"As you are all aware," she began, "our student population has been changing in the past few years. We now have many of our pupils who are immigrants or children of immigrants. These individuals often lack an understanding and a commitment to our form of government. If these new members of our community do not develop this understanding and commitment, our form of government and way of life could be in jeopardy.

"I am sure you are also aware that right-wing groups have been active in monitoring school programs and protesting policies and activities that they perceive to be inconsistent with citizenship and patriotism. I'm sure you are familiar with the difficulty and embarrassment caused by these protests. We want to avoid that here. We want a quiet, peaceful school year.

"Putting together these two forces, the need to educate an immigrant population in our democratic tradition, and the protests of these conservative groups, lead us to consider what should be taught in the social studies program. As you teach social studies this year, I want you to avoid controversial topics and discussions. Don't be discussing problems in our government. Teach the positive accomplishments of our government so that pupils will develop a positive image of our nation and will grow to be committed and patriotic citizens. This will also ensure that no group can have any grounds for criticizing what we are doing in school."

What Is Your Response?

Read the information above and imagine that you are a teacher in the Glen Eden School. Then, briefly respond to these questions:

1. Do you agree that recent immigrants need to be inculcated into a commitment to our form of government?
2. Is avoiding discussion of controversial of negative aspects of our political system the best way to develop a commitment and understanding?
3. Should the social studies curriculum be influenced by the actions of protest groups at either end of the political spectrum?
4. What should be the role of the school in responding to the concerns of various groups interested in the school curriculum?
5. Do you think that social problems and some of the failures of our political system should be included in the elementary curriculum, or are such topics best left until later?

6. What would be a proper way to include controversial issues in the classroom?
7. How would you respond to the principal's remarks if you had attended this faculty meeting?

INTRODUCTION

Human behavior is complex. Answering the questions posed at the beginning of Chapter 2 requires more than a knowledge of the past and of place. Developing an understanding of human behavior that is useful in making sense out of the complex social world requires information and perspectives from a variety of subjects. The social science disciplines are among those sources that are most useful for selecting the content and the perspectives needed by future citizens. Scholars in these disciplines have central questions that guide their inquiry. They have developed concepts and generalizations that are useful in understanding human behavior and the possible consequences of choices that people might make.

We must remember, however, that the reason for including content from these disciplines in the social studies is not to create "miniature social scientists" or to teach these subjects in isolation. The purpose is to draw from a variety of content sources those insights and perspectives that are most useful in helping future citizens face enduring social issues and make informed choices. The following sections provide a brief summary of selected social science disciplines and present sample activities based on their content.

POLITICAL SCIENCE

Content drawn from political science has been a key element of elementary social studies programs. In fact, it has been viewed as essential to citizenship education because it involves the study of government. In the past, this content was often labeled *civics* or *government* and in many of these social studies programs was narrowly focused on ways to "Americanize" the children of immigrants, to inculcate them with the political values and perspectives of the United States government. Educators, as well as politicians and many citizens, believed that teaching students about the Constitution, the Bill of Rights, how bills become laws, how our government is organized, and other related facts would result in individuals who would be committed to our democratic form of government and who would be eager to participate in our nation's political life.

The process of learning about the government and acquiring values and perspectives about one's role is called *political socialization*. Some early efforts to include the content of political science in the social studies curriculum were largely attempts at political socialization. The results of these attempts were not always as anticipated. For example, one state legislator once remarked that social studies had obviously failed because so many individuals were involved in mass protests against the government. For this individual, this was an obvious indication that individuals lacked patriotism. A contrary interpretation might be that the political socialization of those individuals protesting was very successful; it was just that they developed political views that were at odds with those of the legislator.

Though political socialization has a place in school programs, today we appreciate that the discipline of political science has much more to offer the elementary social studies curriculum. In particular, political science has perspectives that can help us teach pupils about themselves and their role in a democracy. Lessons with these emphases go beyond a study of basic structures of government. For example, influences in establishing directions and goals for our society come from sources such as the Chamber of Commerce, National Rifle Association, American Medical Association, Parent-Teacher Association, trade unions, and religious groups. These are special interest groups outside what we might label "formal" government. Institutions of government account for only a part of the decisions made in the political systems.

In addition, in some places in the world, the political functions are performed by family or tribal groups rather than by some special institution called "government." Focusing narrowly on government would exclude study and understanding of these alternative ways of performing political functions.

The study of political science involves the study of controversy and disagreement. In every society there are disagreements between individuals and groups over the goals of the society, the best methods for achieving those goals, the values that ought to be made into law, enforcement of laws, and the rights of various groups and individuals in the society. Informed and well-meaning individuals disagree about these issues. As a result, each society must have a set of institutions to settle these conflicts. This set of institutions can be identified as the political "system."

Political science is the study of this system and, where they exist, the institutions of government. Political science is concerned with the conflicts in the society, how these conflicts are resolved, who makes the decisions, and the consequences of the resolution. Figure 3–2 presents some of the central questions, concepts, and generalizations that have been used to organize the study of political science.

Political Science in the Curriculum

There are different ways these central concepts can be organized for study so that pupils begin to understand political systems and how they operate to resolve conflicts. Sorauf (1965) labeled these approaches "micropolitical" and "macropolitical." One approach focuses on the individual within the political system, and the other is concerned with the big picture or overall operation of the political system.

Micropolitical Organization
The *micropolitical* way of organizing content from political science focuses on the role of the individual in the political system. The following two key questions direct the attention of individuals approaching political science from this perspective:

The following are examples of central questions, concepts, and generalizations that are important when studying political science. They are useful to the elementary social studies teacher when making decisions about what to include in lessons related to political science.

Central Questions (a selection)

Who decides the rules or laws?
Are the rules or laws accepted by the people?
What difference does it make who decides the rules?
Who enforces the rules or laws?
What values are reflected in the rules and laws?
How much impact do the citizens have on the decisions made by the government?
How does the system change?
What happens if the system does not change in the direction that people desire?
What is the decision-making process in different political systems?
What alternative ways have people established for making political decisions?
What are the consequences of different ways of making political systems?

Concepts (a selection)

Distribution of power, authority, equality, conflict resolution, decision making, compromise, Constitution, law, law making, rights, responsibilities, freedom, justice, due process, citizenship, state, nation, civil liberty, separation of powers, common law, legal system, democracy, monarchy, totalitarian, theocracy

Generalizations (a selection)

Every society establishes a system of authority that makes decisions and enforces social regulations on members of the society.
A stable political system facilitates the social and economic growth of a nation.
Some consent of the governed is required in all governments, and without it a government will eventually collapse.
The political system acts to help resolve conflicts when individuals and groups have competing goals and values.
In order for a political system to survive, it must have the ability to change as values and circumstances change.
A democratic society depends on the presence of educated and informed citizens who have a willingness to compromise and a respect for the rights of minorities and the loyal opposition.

Figure 3–2
Central questions, concepts, and generalizations associated with political science.

- How do individual citizens influence the political system?
- What is the impact of the political system on individual citizens?

People who study micropolitical organization are concerned with the goals, beliefs, and responsibilities of individuals and how they acquire them. Each person has some understanding about the political system and the power and responsibilities of individual members of society. The attitudes and beliefs of individuals have a great influence

Political science involves the study of controversy and disagreement.

on the political system of which they are a part. For example, people who believe that the individual is powerless and the system is insensitive to their needs may become alienated. When a high percentage of citizens become alienated, often political unrest results that threatens the continued functioning of the political system.

Another important element of the micropolitical arena is attention to how individuals make political decisions. People often encounter issues where different groups to which they belong favor different choices. For example, we might be involved in a situation in which our occupational group favors one solution to a problem and our religious group favors another. Resolving these competing loyalties, sorting through competing claims of truth, and making a personal decision is an important and demanding task for all of us.

In helping our pupils to grasp some of these difficulties, we need to familiarize them with how various groups use persuasion techniques to influence attitudes and opinions to win a majority in support of a particular public policy. Lessons need to include information about the role of media and the use of various propaganda techniques. Citizenship education implies a need for our pupils to have the kinds of knowledge and skills required for them to sort through conflicting claims so that they may base their decisions on sound criteria.

Macropolitical Organization

Macropolitical study looks at the operation of the political system as it tries to accommodate the conflicting demands of various groups. Lessons designed to provide pupils with this perspective can be organized around the following basic themes:

- Government and governmental processes
- Comparative political systems
- Political theory

"Government and governmental processes" instruction emphasizes how decisions are made and how widely held values become formalized as laws. Our lessons in this area focus on how the leaders of the political system are selected and how authority and power are distributed.

"Comparative political systems" emphasize the way people at various times and in various places have organized themselves to make political decisions. Content emphasizes topics such as the allocation of power, conflict resolution, enforcement, and the rights of individual citizens.

"Political theory" deals with the issue of how people ought to be governed to preserve the rights and freedoms of individuals while at the same time ensuring the continuation of the society as a whole. Concepts such as "justice," "freedom," and "equality" are associated with this emphasis.

Political Science-related Classroom Activities

One of our major purposes in selecting content from political science is to help learners understand the function of rules and laws. They need to realize that there are honest differences between people regarding the goals and directions of a society and the role of government. Activities we select should help youngsters view themselves as individuals with the potential to influence political decisions. Clearly, too, we want them to know how our government works. There are many activities we can use to accomplish these purposes. We introduce examples in the subsections that follow.

An important function of government is making rules.

Making Rules

A central focus in the study of political science content is the function of rules and laws. We want pupils to understand the importance of having fair and just rules that are accepted by most people. They need to learn that rules or laws are ineffective if most people do not agree with them. Our lessons can also help learners discover the differences in the rules that come about as a result of special perspectives of those who make and enforce them.

Rulemaking can be a meaningful activity in classrooms beginning with the primary grades. In these early grades, lessons can be tied to the establishment of rules for the classroom or school. The rulemaking activity that usually takes places at the beginning of the year can be expanded by having the pupils discuss who should make the rules. Should it be the principal, the teacher, the pupils, or a combination of all these? We might have our pupils think about how the rules made by the principal or the teacher might be different from rules made by pupils.

Some teachers have found it useful to involve pupils in an activity to develop a set of rules for the classroom that are organized into a classroom constitution that all of the pupils sign. Not only does this help pupils learn important political science concepts, it helps classroom discipline by providing the pupils with some ownership in the regulations.

Lesson Idea 3–1

RULE MAKING

Grade Level:	K–2
Objectives:	Pupils can (1) identify reasons for and advantages/disadvantages of rules, and (2) practice making decisions about issues that have alternative solutions.
Overview:	To help individuals understand the importance of being involved in decisions and how to influence decisions. They can also recognize the specific purpose for a given decision and the values and assumptions that lead to the establishment of a rule.
Procedures:	***Learning Set*** Identify a given area of the playground that the pupils enjoy using. Discuss why they like playing in that area. Then tell them that there have been some problems in that area. Several people have been injured, so the school has decided to make rules about use of the area. Several rules have been suggested. The class is going to discuss these rules and decide what to do.
	Presentation The first possible rule is to only allow the older pupils to play in the area. It is thought that this would reduce problems because the older children would not have to worry about younger children getting in the way. The younger children would have to play in another (less desir-

able) area of the playground. Ask the class what they think about this rule. Use the following questions to prompt discussion:

- What is good about this idea?
- What do you think the people who thought about this idea liked about it?
- Do you think this rule would solve the problem of people getting hurt?
- Why do you think the upper-grade pupils like it?.
- What problems might this rule create?
- Do you think this is a fair rule?

The second proposed rule is that only those people who have demonstrated that they are good citizens will be allowed to play in this area. Buttons will be made and those children who work hard in class and who follow the rules will be given a button by the teacher that they can wear. They can then go and play in the area and all others will have to stay out. If someone misbehaves, they will lose their button. Discuss this idea using the questions posed previously.

At this point have the class suggest other rules for use of the area. Have them think about issues of fairness and equality as they propose new rules. When they have identified a rule they agree with, they can then discuss what they can do to encourage its adoption. They could decide to send a group to the student council or the principal, or discuss the issue with other classes to get their support. The point is for the pupils to begin to understand that group action can influence political decisions.

Closure: At this point, inform the class that this was only a make-believe issue. Asked them what they learned about making rules. Why might different groups propose different rules? What should people consider when making rules? What can people do when they do not like a proposed rule?

Resolving Conflicts

An important function of government is resolving conflicts between individuals and groups. Every society has individuals and groups with different ideas about the goals of the nation and how to achieve these goals. It is important for children to understand that disagreement does not mean that one side must be "good" or "right" and the other "bad" or "wrong." There are honest disagreements between good and intelligent people concerning the best course of action.

We also have to help our learners understand that some people and groups try to resolve conflicts by force or violence. We can develop lessons that involve pupils in exploring the consequences of this type of conflict resolution. These situations can be compared to our system where we try to resolve conflicts through voting and through a court system designed to uphold the ideals of fairness and justice.

Conflict resolution is something that pupils of all ages will confront. They are constantly facing conflicts in the playground and the classroom. They frequently lack knowledge of alternative means for resolving disputes, and they are prone to resort to fighting or other forms of violence. The basic issues of conflict and conflict resolution that confront young children in play parallel those that arise within and between nations.

We need to begin classroom discussions on the issue of conflict resolution with a focus on pupils' personal experiences. In the primary grades, discussion might center on the use and sharing of toys or materials. We can encourage class members to discuss alternative ways of resolving these disagreements. To conclude the lesson, we might involve pupils in voting on a preferred solution.

In the upper grades, the pupils can be presented with conflicts that might be occurring in the local community over policies or actions of the local government. We can help pupils trace the actions of different groups as they try to resolve the conflict. For example, one of the authors is living in an area where the Mediterranean fruit fly has been discovered. Because of a threat to the extensive agricultural industry in California, the state has embarked on an eradication program that involves aerial spraying of the entire city with malathion every few weeks. The spraying covers everything with a sticky spray that residents must then clean up. School children must spend the entire day in the classroom until everything can be washed clean. The city has tried to stop the spraying because of potential health threats. Children in school were very aware of the problem, and having them trace the actions of different interest groups as they tried to resolve the issue provided valuable insights into our political system and into processes associated with conflict resolution.

Older children can look at the issues of the loyal opposition in our political system and the always difficult problem of resolving international conflicts. Unfortunately, numerous examples of international conflict are available for discussion.

Lesson Idea 3–2

CONFLICT RESOLUTION

Grade Level:	4–6
Objectives:	Pupils can (1) identify steps that can be followed in resolving conflict and (2) identify the potential role of governments in conflict resolution.
Overview:	One of the most important functions of government is resolving conflict among citizens. Government acts as a referee that brings conflicting groups together, sets forth rules on how to resolve these conflicts, and specifies how the decisions are to be enforced. Mock government focusing, as appropriate to the issue, on a city council, a state legislature,

the United State Congress, or the United Nations can help pupils become more familiar with the potential conflict resolution role of government.

Procedure:

Learning Set   Present to the class a newspaper report on a current issue in the news. It is best to present one with merit to both sides of the issue. Read the article to the class and have them discuss their thoughts and feelings. Tell them that an important role of government is trying to resolve conflicts like this while preserving stability and order. Tell them that the class is going to establish a mock government to try to find some solutions.

Presentation:

Step 1: Assigning Roles   An important part of the mock government is assigning roles to class members. It is best if the whole class can be involved. One way of accomplishing this would be to divide the class into at least three groups. One group could be assigned to gather information and to make a presentation on one side of the issue. A second group could be assigned the task of finding and presenting information on the other side of the issue. A third group would be assigned the role of the governmental body hearing both sides of the issue and proposing a solution. This group's preparation task would be to meet as a group and try to identify the criteria that should be followed in judging the arguments and in arriving at a decision. For example, they might identify "fairness" as an important criterion. They should also set the rules for the hearing they will conduct.

Step 2: Defining the Issue   At this stage, hold a discussion before the pupils begin to work in their groups. Focus on identifying the specific issue and the goals of the opposing groups.

Step 3: Establishing the Hearing Rules   Before the hearing is to take place, the third group needs to present their rules on how the meeting will be conducted. They need to state how long each side will be allowed to present their position and whether they will be allowed rebuttal time. The role of the members of the government in asking questions should also be presented and a person designated to chair the meeting. The power of that person to stop arguments should also be considered. When the rules are presented to the class, they can be provided with an opportunity to discuss them. The government group can then decide if they want to change them.

Step 4: Presenting the Positions   The hearing begins and the sides present their case.

Step 5: Establishing Decision Criteria and Deciding   At this point, you and the governmental body discuss what the criteria should be in deciding the issue. Try to get the whole class involved in discussing the criteria. They should also decide how they will resolve the issue. Will they take a vote on one side or the other or will they propose a third alternative that might then be voted on?

Step 6: Debriefing   This is an important part of the lesson and should not be overlooked. Lead a discussion of the entire decision-making process, noting how the process works in local, state or federal government.

Closure: Ask the pupils to review what they learned about conflict resolution during this activity. Ask them to compare this approach to other possible approaches, such as one authority (a king or queen) making the decision, or solving it using force.

Basic Foundations of Democratic Government

One purpose of the social studies is providing future citizens with a basic understanding of how government works. This has been an item of considerable concern in recent years. Several studies have revealed that about one-half of high school graduates have only superficial knowledge of the institution, principles, and processes of their government (Patrick & Hoge, 1991). Since many of the attitudes and beliefs about government begin to emerge during the elementary grades, considerable attention must be devoted to teaching about the foundations of our government.

Teaching about the basic foundations of democratic government requires teaching about the Declaration of Independence, the U.S. Constitution, the Bill of Rights, and other great documents of our nation. However, our approach should not emphasize rote memorization, leaving pupils with the impression that these are musty old documents with little relationship to contemporary issues. We need to teach this material in ways that illustrate the drama and the contemporary relevance of these documents. The Constitution, for example, outlines the basic values that serve as criteria for judging the actions and laws of the people of the United States.

One useful approach is to teach the relevance of these documents using case studies, simplified statements of issues relating to questions of individual and societal rights, privileges, and obligations. Learners can discuss whether they believe the constitutional rights of the individuals involved were violated. As they are involved in the discussion, they usually begin to understand how difficult it is to write clear laws that are fair. They also begin to appreciate those values and laws that serve as a foundation for our nation.

Lessons focusing on our government allow pupils many opportunities for discussion of controversial issues, which we want to encourage. Attempting to avoid controversy eliminates much of the excitement and relevance of social studies instruction and can result in a cynical rather than a supportive attitude toward government. In addition, we should orient instruction in this area toward interesting pupils in active participation in governmental affairs. Some lessons should encourage pupils to take some action in support of those topics that are of interest to them. This active participation might begin with letter writing and move on to other forms of involvement in efforts to resolve local or national issues.

Social studies teachers should include lessons deriving content from political science beginning with the primary grades. Understanding the function of laws, how to influence government, and the rights and responsibilities of citizens help youngsters to become informed and to develop a commitment to active involvement in the processes of democratic governance. The activities that we have briefly described here are only a few examples of what we can do to help pupils grasp relevant and useful principles from political science. This aspect of the elementary social studies curriculum has rich potential for producing citizens who are committed to a form of government that truly provides "liberty and justice for all."

SOCIOLOGY

Sociology is a social science that has received scant attention in the elementary social studies curriculum. Part of the reason for this may be the absence of groups actively seeking to improve the teaching of sociology at the precollegiate level. Nelson and Stahl (1991) contend that some policymakers see the main emphasis of sociology, the role and function of groups, as not supportive of their narrow definitions of citizenship focusing on nationalism and patriotism. If this is true, it may suggest why there has rarely been a strong push for sociology as a source of school lessons for young children.

We disagree with this perspective. Adults must confront pressures of all kinds that result from actions taken by formal and informal groups. Content from sociology provides pupils with insights into very important group processes. Citizens today are also confronted with a daunting array of social problems. How should we respond to youth gangs? What is to be done about crime problem? What are the implications of the changing structure of the American family? Individuals familiar with important concepts and generalizations from sociology have special tools that can help them analyze and make rational choices among action alternatives related to these questions.

People everywhere live in groups. Further, each person belongs to several different groups beginning with the family and including social organizations, ethnic groups, political parties, and religious affiliations. Sociologists study groups; why they are formed, how they are organized, how they influence the behavior and the values of their group members, and why they fall apart. They investigate the formation of norms and values, how these are passed on from one generation to the next, and how they change over time. Sociologists have helped us understand that social behavior is complex. Their research has taught us that there are multiple causes and multiple effects of social behavior. Changes in one area, such as the role of women in the workplace, have widespread effects because all institutions in a society are interrelated, and a change in one will result in changes in others.

An important concept in sociology is *socialization*, or how individuals learn what is right and wrong. Closely related to the concept of socialization is that of *role*, or how individuals learn their place in society and what is expected of them. A current issue related to the concept of role is that of gender bias and how males and females are influenced to accept a role based solely on gender.

We have numerous opportunities to incorporate perspectives from sociology into our elementary social studies lessons; some content has long been included. For example, primary-grade youngsters typically spend a great deal of time studying families. They may investigate roles and relationships between family members and examine family structures in other cultures. The study of groups is extended in subsequent elementary grades when pupils begin investigating their local community and how its residents live and work together. In the upper grades, pupils can deal with more sophisticated issues, including how group membership influences public opinion and why it is easier to have influence through groups than through individual action. You may use the following basic concepts to organize content based on sociology:

- Institutions
- Primary groups
- Secondary groups
- Stratified groups
- Relations within and among groups
- Social change
- Communication
- Social problems

Institutions

Sociologists look at the institutions that society creates to influence its members, such as the family, the tribe, the school, the government, religious groups, and the military. These groups have expectations that affect behavior of their members. They represent an important influence that helps explain what individuals do.

Primary Groups

Groups can be differentiated by the kinds of relationships that exist among group members. The *primary group* is that group where members learn the primary skills of interaction and communication. The family is a good example of a primary group. The primary group exerts a powerful influence on the socialization of its members.

It is important for individuals of all ages to be a member of a primary group. This is an important point when addressing the issue of gang membership. When the home or the school fails to meet the needs of the individual to be a part of a primary group, the gang becomes a primary group and socializes the individual by communicating ideas of right and wrong. It may well be that solving the problem of gangs will require the development of primary groups to which individuals can belong that will serve as a positive alternative.

The family is an example of a primary group.

Secondary Groups

Any group not a primary group is called a *secondary group*. Typically, an individual belongs to several secondary groups. One type of secondary group is the voluntary group. The *voluntary group* is one where members have some common interest or a common problem. Examples are the Girl Scouts and Boy Scouts, political parties, taxpayer associations, labor unions, and professional associations such as the NEA or AFT. Voluntary groups help individuals communicate with others that have the same interests and keep members informed about what is going on in their area of interest. This allows them to exert some political power by lobbying for items of interest to the group. These activities give individual group members some sense of control and power. Some individuals develop such close relationships within a voluntary group that it becomes their primary group.

Stratified Groups

Membership in *stratified groups* is open only to those who have command of certain social resources such as wealth, power, and prestige. An example of a stratified group might be membership in an exclusive country club. Political parties often have a subgroup to which an individual can belong by making a contribution of sufficient size. Sociologists are interested in how the members of these groups are identified, how they exercise power, and how these groups influence the rest of society.

Relationships within and among Groups

Because different groups have different goals, teach different norms and values, and have different levels of power, conflict between them is inevitable. Some sociologists consider the study of this conflict to be second only to the study of socialization in importance. Conflict is pervasive in society; children in families fight, students in school compete with each other in numerous ways, religious groups have conflicts with school boards over the content of the curriculum, political parties try to defeat each other, and nations go to war. Of special importance today is the study of conflict based on prejudice. This might be conflict between different ethnic groups, between individuals of different gender, or between individuals with different sexual preferences. A stable society learns how to control and limit conflict. An important thrust of sociology is to discover how these conflicts arise and how they are resolved.

Social Change

Social change results in anxiety. Some people have trouble adjusting to the social changes happening around them. Sometimes they seek relief by attempting to return to "the good old days," when they understood societal norms and expectations. However, "the good old days" are not going to return. We need to help our pupils appreciate that social change is a constant force. It has always been occurring, and older generations have always felt uncomfortable with this situation. Today, changes seem to be occurring more frequently and more rapidly than in times past. Content drawn from sociology can help pupils identify factors that lead to change, learn how to anticipate change, and master positive ways of coping with change.

Communication

Communication is an important theme in sociology. Through various media, common values, expectations, and ideas are transmitted to people. Because communication is so important, we need to help pupils know something about both the content of communication and the identity of those who control communication. Useful lessons here might include those focusing on "messages" communicated through mass media such a television, newspapers, and movies. We might want to include in these lessons a focus on propaganda, a particularly dangerous form of communication that can spread stereotypes and distorted ideas. Our overall purpose is to help learners understand that free and open communication is an important ingredient of our democratic society.

Social Problems

Social problems such as poverty, homelessness, crime, delinquency, alienation, racism, prejudice, and the breakdown of social control are topics of great interest to sociologists. It is hoped that through the study of social problems methods of prevention can be implemented and solutions found. Solutions are required as an antidote to social disintegration. Because our society is faced with so many difficult problems, we have little difficulty in identifying issues for lessons that relate to this important concept from sociology.

Figure 3–3 presents questions, concepts, and generalizations associated with sociology. These are useful when preparing lessons that draw content from sociology.

Sociology-related Classroom Activities

Sociology deals with our society and with many current issues. Hence, content from sociology has high potential as an information source for lessons pupils will find inter-

---

The following are example of central questions, concepts, and generalizations that are important when studying sociology. They are useful to the elementary social studies teacher when making decisions about what to include in lessons related to sociology.

Central Questions (a selection)
What are the influential social institutions in society?
What happens when groups disagree with each other?
How do individuals learn what is appropriate and what is inappropriate in society?
How is disapproval for inappropriate behavior given?
How are family relationships different today than in the past?
How are family relationships similar or different in other cultures?
How does mass media influence public opinion?
What forces facilitate societal change and what forces hinder such change?
What are the various levels of status, class, and power in society?
What are the evidences of prejudice and discrimination in society?

Concepts (a selection)
Socialization, roles, norms, values, sanctions, conflict, prejudice, racism, discrimination, customs, traditions, beliefs, social institutions, social stratification, social class, status, primary group, secondary group, ethnic group, cooperation, assimilation, immigration, competition, collective behavior

Generalizations (a selection)
The family is the basic social unit in most societies and the source of most fundamental learning.
Social classes have existed in every society, although the basis of class distinction has varied.
Every society develops a system of roles, norms, values, and sanctions that guides the behavior of individuals within society.
The roles that a given individual plays often clash, which leads to role conflict.
Societies must develop ways of solving conflict without violence or they may disintegrate.
People behave differently in groups than they do individually.
Primary groups play an important role in socializing individuals by communicating values and expectations.
Status and prestige are related to the values held by primary social groups. Behavior that is rewarded in one group may be discouraged in another.

Figure 3–3
Central questions, concepts, and generalizations associated with sociology.

esting and relevant. The following are ideas for including sociological content in the curriculum.

Group Membership

Pupils are members of a number of different groups. Understanding group membership and the impact of the group on the individual can be the focus of lessons, beginning in the primary grades. Class members can list the various groups to which they belong. This might include the family, religious groups, sports teams, classroom groups, and neighborhood play groups. A discussion of why people belong to different groups can follow.

In later grades pupils can begin to distinguish between primary and secondary groups by classifying the groups to which they belong as either one or the other. They should also begin investigating what they learn from different groups. Of special importance here would be discussing groups such as gangs that might teach unacceptable or antisocial behaviors and attitudes. The problems that arise when groups teach competing values, for example the differences between gang and the school or family, makes an interesting focus for lessons. Pupils can also discuss the consequences of group membership in a group that advocates unacceptable behavior.

The study of religious groups has received increased attention in recent years. Some individuals are calling for more attention in the social studies curriculum to the role of religion. Religion has been an important element in all societies and any study of humans would be incomplete without addressing the religious dimension. Students can investigate the different types of religions in the local community and identify the part they play in influencing attitudes and behaviors of people. In many communities, religious organizations spend considerable time and resources volunteering and addressing social problems. These topics are important additions to the social studies curriculum.

Lesson Idea 3–3

LEARNING ROLES

Grade Level:	1–3
Objectives:	Pupils can (1) list the similarities and differences in the roles of men and women, and (2) state where people learn their roles.
Overview:	All individuals in society learn roles. Youngsters sometimes think that the roles they have learned are the "natural" or "right" roles. When they encounter individuals who have a different understanding of roles, conflict can occur. This is an important understanding in current society as the gender roles are being challenged. In addition, many youngsters from other cultures have different understanding of the roles of men and women in their culture. This activity can provide the teacher with insight as well as serving as a useful lesson for pupils.

Procedure:

Provide the pupils with the following homework assignment the night before you are going to do the activity in class: Tell them you would like to get their parents' permission to look through magazines and cut out pictures of men and women performing different tasks.

Learning Set   Allow a few pupils to share some of the pictures they gathered. Then collect all the pictures. Tell them that the class is going to put the pictures together in groups.

Presentation   Separate the pictures of men and women. Then tell the class that you want to group all the pictures of women and those of men into groups. Ask them what pictures of women could be placed into the same group and why. Allow the class to identify their own criteria for grouping the pictures. On the chalkboard, have a section labeled *women* and one labeled *men*. When all the pictures of women performing tasks have been grouped, ask the class for a label for each group, and write these labels on the chalkboard. Repeat the procedure for men. When the lists are complete, compare the two lists. What are the similarities and differences between the two lists? Why do you think there are differences? Where do people learn about what is appropriate for men and women to do? How are these ideas changing?

Closure:

Use the following questions to review with the class: What did we do today? What did you learn about how to group things? What did you learn about the kinds of tasks men and women do? As a final task, paste the pictures that go together on a large piece of butcher paper and write the label of the group at the top.

Investigating Communication

The impact of communication on the values and beliefs of people is an important dimension of learning. Citizenship education requires that individuals have what might be called "media literacy." Individuals must learn how to identify and analyze the messages sent by television, newspapers, movies, and radio just as they learn how to read and analyze messages in literature. The impact of mass communication on the attitudes and actions of people is especially important.

For example, recent media attention created the impression of an out-of-control American crime wave, whereas statistics revealed that the crime rate actually decreased. The result of the impression caused by the media was to make people suspicious of one another and afraid to leave their homes or to participate in civic functions. These behaviors resulted because of "perceptions" (e.g., the impressions received from the inaccurate media accounts) rather than the reality (the actual statistics on the incidence of reported crime). We need to help pupils understand that communication can influence their behavior and that they need to know how to check the accuracy of what they hear.

The newspaper is an excellent source for lessons dealing with issues associated with accuracy of communication (and for many other sociology-oriented topics, as well). Many newspapers have a program for schools that delivers newspapers to the class-room for a specified time. Pupils can review the paper looking for articles that focus on the behavior of people in groups, what is acceptable and unacceptable behavior, social problems, and conflict between groups on the local as well as the international scene. Pupils enjoy using the newspaper as a text because the material is current, and they recognize the newspaper as something that is a part of the "real" world.

Another interesting unit can be developed focusing on the impact of television or movies. Television viewing guides can be developed to help pupils look for specific items as they watch programs. We might have pupils focus on how conflicts arise, the types of conflicts portrayed, and how they are resolved. Older pupils can identify the messages being sent and how these are likely to affect viewers. Another appropriate focus might be advertisement and the logic used to influence behavior. In preparation for these experiences, we can introduce pupils to different forms of persuasion and pro-paganda. They can look for examples as they view television programs and commer-cials, and report their findings back to the whole class.

A useful technique for studying communication is to teach the pupils how to per-form a *content analysis*. We begin by asking members of the class to identify an idea or an attitude they are interested in researching. We then assign them to count the num-ber of instances that certain words, ideas, or attitudes are used in the media. For exam-ple, if pupils are interested in gender roles, they might count the numbers of time women are portrayed as professionals in television programs. Another example might be to simply count the number of stories included in the local newspaper about various topics such as crime, education, poverty, or politics. Comparing the number of stories on these topics can lead to a discussion of the image one might get of the local commu-nity by reading the newspaper.

Lesson Idea 3–4

IDENTIFYING ISSUES IN THE NEWSPAPER

Grade Level:	3–5
Objectives:	Pupils can identify instances of group conflict and conflict resolution.
Overview:	It is important for pupils to learn that group conflict needs to be resolved without resorting to conflict. They can begin by identifying examples of group conflict and of various forms of conflict resolution in the newspaper. They can then apply it to the resolution of conflicts they experience.
Procedure:	*Learning Set* Ask the pupils to describe examples of con-flict between groups at school. These might be conflicts over

the use of playground equipment or participation in activities in the classroom. State to the class that solving disagreements between groups is something they will have to deal with all of their lives. State that for the next few days the class is going to look for examples of conflict using the newspaper.

Presentation   Divide the class into groups. Provide each group with a large chart divided in the following manner:

Examples of Conflicts	How Conflicts Were Handled	Consequences

Each group is to look through the paper and find articles describing a conflict between groups. These might include disagreements between groups in the community that go to the city council as well as international disagreements between countries or groups. They are to cut out the article and paste it in the first column. They should then briefly identify how the conflict was handled. In some cases it may involve a compromise or a vote; others could involve fighting or even war.

Pupils can then identify or speculate on the consequences of the attempt to resolve the conflict. When all groups have finished, post the charts in front of the room. Each group presents their chart. When this is completed, lead a discussion focusing on the different types of conflict resolution that were discovered and the consequences of each type. Ask each group, "How can we use this information in helping us decide how to solve problems between groups?"

Closure: Ask class members to share at least one thing they learned from the lesson. They can then be asked to watch television that night and identify at least one other example of a conflict and how it was resolved, using either a news broadcast or one of their favorite programs. When reviewing, ask the class, "What does television seem to be saying about how we resolve conflict?"

Community Studies

Community studies have long been an interest of sociologists. Because much of the primary-grade social studies curriculum emphasizes the local community, this forms a natural bridge for including sociological concepts. Young children can begin to study their local community through their own experience by identifying the different groups in the community. These might be ethnic groups, religious groups, business organizations, recreational groups, and social groups. We can ask our pupils, "Why do you think people join groups?" They can discuss how it feels when a person goes to a new place and does not belong to any groups. They can then discuss the need for different groups in the community to learn to work together and accept the differences that exist among them.

In the upper grades, pupils can investigate the groups found in a community and the ways group members try to resolve conflicts between groups. They can investigate this issue as they study the past or as they look at communities in other parts of the world. The newspaper can be useful for identifying different groups in the community. Many papers produce a local "calendar of events" that mention activities of a large number of community groups and organizations.

Identifying Social Problems

Studying social problems has been a typical use of sociological content in the social studies curriculum. Problems that might serve as the focus for study are crime and delinquency, racism and prejudice, poverty, homelessness, war, drug and alcohol abuse, and divorce. These are issues that intrude on the life of a large number of pupils. While some of these issues, such as drug and alcohol abuse, might be discussed in the health curriculum, the social dimensions of these issues are at least as important as the health dimension.

Homelessness is a relatively new concern, and has not been addressed by most schools. Pupils in many communities see homeless individuals daily. They have questions about these people: "Who are they? Why are they homeless? Should I be afraid of them?" Homeless pupils are present in many classrooms. These pupils often feel different, excluded, and embarrassed because they do not have a home. Discussions on the many causes of homelessness, the problems that homeless people face, and possible solutions can lead to interesting lessons because it is a current topic of concern for many pupils.

When including current issues and social problems in the classroom, emphasize social action. Taking action based on personally held beliefs is one of the most important outcomes of social studies programs. Through social action pupils learn that their involvement can make a difference and that social studies is an important and relevant subject. In addition, pupils get highly motivated and get much personal gratification when they see that their efforts make a difference.

Lesson Idea 3–5

THE BENEFITS OF COOPERATION

Grade Level: 4–6

Objective: Pupils can state at least one benefit from working cooperatively on a problem.

Overview: Cooperative learning has become an important approach to learning. Cooperation is essential in working in groups to solve problems. This exercise is designed to get pupils thinking about the benefits of cooperation, and may be used to introduce cooperative learning to the class as well as teach some important sociological content. The basic design is for the teacher to identify two relatively similar problems. The pupils attempt to identify possible solutions to one problem individually and to the second problem in groups. They then compare the outcomes and feelings associated with each approach. There are usually more solutions generated, more comprehensive solutions, and more satisfaction associated with the cooperative approach.

Procedure: ***Learning Set***   Tell the class of a time when you faced a problem all alone and had trouble coming up with a solution. Ask the pupils to share similar incidents. Tell them that today you are going to conduct an experiment on solving problems.

Step One   Pose the following problem to the class: You are a member of an army in the days of knights in armor. You and your fellow knights have ridden far ahead of the other troops. You discover another group of knights preparing to attack, so you must get a message back to your troops. You are selected to deliver the message and you ride off. After hours of riding, you find the headquarters of your army. However, there is a big problem. The army has made their camp on the other side of a river that is too wide and too deep for your horse to swim. It is too noisy for them to hear you if you shout. How are you going to get your message across the river? Tell the class, "I'm going to give you five minutes to write down every idea that you have. Write as quickly as possible until you hear me say 'Stop.'|"

Step 2   After five minutes, share everyone's solutions. Tally the number of different solutions identified by the members of the class. Ask pupils how they felt while trying to solve problem.

Step 3   Pose a second problem to the class: The class is on a field trip together on a school bus. You are on a mountain road where there is no traffic. Coming around a corner, the bus skids into a ditch and is stuck. You need to get a tow truck to come and get you. Someone discovers that through a break in the trees they can see a service station with a tow truck way off at the bottom of the mountain. It is too steep and too far to climb down the mountain to get help. How will you get a message to the people at the station? This time, thinking as a group, have everyone share their ideas. Take five minutes to find solutions. Listen carefully to the ideas of others and then tell us what you think. After five minutes, stop the discussion.

Step 4   Compare the solutions for the first problem and the second problem. Ask, "Which problem generated more solutions? Which had better solutions? How did you feel working alone and working with the whole class? What do you think this experiment shows? Can you think of other, similar experiments we could do that involve the action of people in groups?"

Closure: Review with the class what was done. Ask, "What was one thing we learned today? How might we use what we learned?"

In summary, although there has not been much attention on the sociological dimension of social studies, there are many natural bridges between the elementary social studies curriculum and sociological concepts. Social studies lessons should take advantage of the experiences and interests of pupils. Sociological content, perhaps more than that drawn from other disciplines, is well suited to do this. Lessons focusing on sociology allow us to address current issues that are interesting to pupils and that have potential for contributing to their understanding of the nature of their membership in the total human community.

ANTHROPOLOGY

Anthropology is the study of the history of human culture. It examines the various ways in which people interpret and assign meaning to their social and physical world. Lessons in anthropology help pupils understand that the members of each culture tend to be *ethnocentric*—that is, they tend to believe that their own culture and interpretation of the world around them are the most "natural" and "logical" ones.

Anthropology shares many concepts with sociology, but tends to focus more on the comparison of different cultures. Some anthropological studies focus on exotic and different cultures and therefore lead individuals to erroneously conclude that anthropology is the study of "funny people and strange lands."

As is the case with sociology, there has been little recent emphasis placed on anthropology content in the social studies curriculum. This has not always been the case. A number of years ago an interesting fifth-grade social studies program, titled "Man: A Course of Study," was developed around anthropological concepts. This program focused on three basic questions: "What is human about human beings?"; "How did they get that way?"; and "How can they be made more so?" The program compared a nonurban culture, the Netsilik Eskimo, to our own. In addition, human behavior was compared to that of animals, such as to a baboon troop. Because of the obvious connection to evolution and other somewhat controversial content and because of the program's cost, "Man: A Course of Study" was not widely adopted. Another elementary social studies program was developed at the University of Georgia in the 1960s that included materials for integrating anthropology in the elementary school curriculum. As with "Man: A Course of Study," few schools today use any of the Georgia anthropology project materials (Nelson & Stahl, 1991).

This does not mean, however, that no content related to anthropology is being taught. Some topics associated with this discipline have long been a part of the elementary social studies curriculum. Units with such titles as "Native Americans," "People of Other Lands," and "Early Civilizations" all have roots in anthropology. Current interests in ethnic studies and multicultural education provide opportunities to include even more anthropological content. When taught from an anthropological prospective, these and similar topics provide pupils with significant insight about what it means to be human and help them develop an appreciation for the rich diversity of cultures and people. Several basic themes can be developed through the study of content associated with anthropology: archaeology and prehistory, human evolution, culture, and cultural change. Figure 3–4 presents central questions, concepts, and generalizations around which you may build lessons focusing on these themes.

Archaeology and Prehistory

This area of anthropology tries to reconstruct the nature of human existence before written history. Archaeologists find and study *artifacts* (material remains of human occupation) and try to reconstruct history by analyzing them. This aspect of anthropology is interesting to even the young child because it carries so much mystery. Reconstructing the past from artifacts is much like piecing together the clues to solve a mystery, and pupils are easily motivated to try and study the mystery.

Human Evolution

Anthropology is concerned with the development of the human species, bridging the gap between the biological and social sciences. Anthropologists are interested in the question, "How did humans get to be as they are?" They are concerned with how

The following are examples of central questions, concepts, and generalizations that are important when studying anthropology. They are useful to the elementary social studies teacher when making decisions about what to include in lessons related to anthropology.

Central Questions (a selection)

What is uniquely human about humans that sets them off from other species?
How did humans get those qualities?
What elements do different cultures seem to have in common?
How do changes in one part of a culture influence the other parts?
What are the values and beliefs of this culture and how are they interconnected?
What does the language tell us about the culture?
What part does religion play in the culture?
How do individuals achieve adult status in the culture?
How does the culture adapt to change?
How are wealth, status, and power determined in the culture?
How are values, beliefs, and traditions passed from one generation to the next?

Concepts (a selection)

Culture, cultural change, cultural borrowing, cultural lag, adaptation, diffusion, cultural disintegration, ritual, religion, tradition, race, ethnocentrism, nuclear family, extended family, innate behavior, learned behavior, technology, invention

Generalizations (a selection)

Every society has a set of interconnected beliefs, values, and knowledge, called *culture,* that influences its life.
People around the world have responded to common needs and concerns in unique ways, thus creating different cultural systems.
Each group of people believes that their cultural system is the most natural and logical way to view the world and relationships.
Increased contact between cultures results in cultural conflict and cultural change.
The art, music, architecture, food, clothing, and customs of people produce a cultural identity and reveal the values of the culture.

Figure 3–4
Central questions, concepts, and generalizations associated with anthropology.

humans have developed and changed throughout their existence. The world continues to change and individuals must learn to adapt to that change to survive. An understanding of how individuals and civilizations did and did not meet the challenges of change in the past will provide clues to help students make predictions about future adaptations and change.

Culture

This concept is central to the study of anthropology. *Culture* is defined as the constellation of values, beliefs, and institutions unique to a given group of people. It is important that pupils learn that these elements are interconnected in a culture and that as mentioned previously, a given people believe that their unique culture is the most "logical and natural" one. This ethnocentrism can be a barrier to multicultural understanding because each culture believes others are somewhat "strange." The primary research method of the cultural anthropologist is that of the *participant observer*. The anthropologist tries to become a part of the culture and so view it through the eyes of participant. The anthropologist then attempts to identify the ways the members of the culture view the world and integrate their cultural and physical environments into a meaningful whole. This idea can be applied to many elementary classrooms as teachers use role play to get pupils to dress, act, play, and eat as members of another culture. Comparing another culture with our own provides insights into our own society and behavior and helps us make discoveries we might otherwise overlook.

Cultural Change

This theme is of great contemporary interest. Cultures throughout the world continue their pace of rapid change. Studies of how others coped with such rapid change can provide insights into the process in our own culture and may suggest ways to respond to preserve valued cultural elements. Studying people who lived long ago or far away becomes more interesting and meaningful when such study is used to learn ways to handle current problems of rapid change, social upheaval, and cultural conflict.

Traditions, such as this Mexican Quinceañera, help pupils develop a sense of identification with their culture.

Anthropology-related Classroom Activities

When developing activities for use in the classroom, it is important that we foster respect for other cultures. We should not exaggerate unfamiliar customs; pupils should not feel that they are studying about "funny people." When possible, the interrelationship between cultural elements should be presented so that the pupils do not get a distorted view of a culture. Care needs to be taken to make sure that lessons get beyond stereotypes of groups or people. A goal should be to begin to break down destructive ethnocentrism. This does not mean that pupils are encouraged to give up their own culture. Rather, it means that individuals develop a respect for other cultures and realize that we may learn something from each other. The following are ideas for accomplishing these purposes.

Native Americans

Studies of Native Americans are common throughout the elementary social studies program. Studies may be included in the third grade as pupils study about the local area, in the fourth grade as they study about the state, and in the fifth grade as they study about the history and geography of the United States. The current problem is that what is taught about Native Americans is often based on stereotypes and myth rather than fact. It is not uncommon to visit classroom where the tipi is used to illustrate the type of housing used by "Indians." The fact is that Native American dwellings have varied significantly, and the tipi is an artifact of only one cultural region, the Great Plains.

We need to remember that there was and is a rich diversity of Native American cultures. For example, some Native American groups had permanent homes and engaged in farming. It is estimated that true farming existed among the southeastern tribes about 6,000 years ago (Gallant, 1989). Great cultural variation exists from region to region and what is taught to pupils needs to be based on accurate information. It is important that teachers challenge television and movie stereotypes and not teach about Native Americans as if they belonged only to the past (Harvey, Harjo, & Jackson, 1990).

There is an abundance of material available that can be used to teach about Native Americans, including numerous books and other instructional resources. Excellent selections of children's literature that can be used to teach the anthropology concepts of culture and cultural change include Paul Goble's retelling of myths and legends of the Great Plains, such as *The Gift of the Sacred Dog* (Bradbury, 1980), Tomie De Paola's *The Legend of the Bluebonnet: An Old Tale of Texas* (Putnam, 1983), Shonto Begay's Navajo story, *Ma'ii and Cousin Horned Toad* (Scholastic, 1992), Michael Lacapa's Apache folktale, *Antelope Woman* (Northland, 1992), and Ekkehart Malotki's Hopi folktale, *The Mouse Couple* (Northland, 1988). Share these stories with pupils, comparing their themes and settings. They can provide pupils with insight into cultural beliefs as well as an understanding of how different Native American groups related to their environment in different ways.

Some excellent nonfiction books are also available. These include *Cherokee Summer*, by Diane Hoyt-Goldsmith (Holiday House, 1993), *Sequoyah's Gift*, by Janet Klausner (HarperCollins, 1993), *The Gift of Changing Woman*, by Tryntje Van Ness Seymour (Henry Holt, 1993), and *Proudly Red and Black*, by William Loren Katz and Paula Franklin (Atheneum-Macmillan, 1993). (This latter book is about individuals of mixed

Native American and African American heritage.) Roy Gallant's *Ancient Indians: The First Americans* (Enslow, 1989) is a useful book for helping older students understand the stories of prehistoric Native American cultures. In a similar vein, Byrd Baylor's *One Small Blue Bead* (Charles Scribner's Sons, 1992) captures the excitement and significance of finding artifacts.

One approach that can help pupils to understand similarities and differences and to form generalizations is to construct *data retrieval charts*. These charts organize information according to the concepts you wish to teach to the class. For example, you may construct a chart showing how characters in different stories face the issue of change. The following sample chart is based on the book, *Annie and the Old One*, by Miska Miles (Little, Brown, 1971), a story about Navajo culture and beliefs.

Book	Character	Feelings	Result
Annie and the Old One	Annie	Tried to stop change	Felt guilty
	Grandmother	Accepted change	Taught Annie an important lesson

Other examples from other books could be added as you read them. Once the data retrieval chart has been completed, you may ask: "Why did Annie dislike change? What did Annie try to do to stop change? Was she successful? What was the lesson that grandmother tried to teach her? Can we stop change? What is the lesson we should learn about facing change?"

From the story and discussion, pupils can learn about another culture as well as about how to cope with change in their lives. While they discover that change is inevitable, you may help them realize that there is also continuity. They can begin to look for elements of change and continuity in their environment.

Lesson Idea 3–6

LEARNING FROM AN ARTIFACT

Grade Level: 4–6

Objectives: Pupils can (1) make at least one statement about a culture based on an investigation of an artifact and (2) explain how wrong conclusions can be drawn.

Overview: Learning how an anthropologist might work in trying to get an object to tell a story need not require exotic materials of costly preparation. Pupils can have fun learning how to extract the story from an artifact by beginning with common objects in their environment. This activity can be enjoyable as well as educationally useful.

Procedure:

Learning Set   Begin by asking the class how they think textbook authors know what conditions were like long ago. Inform them that written records or descriptions of historical life and times are often destroyed or lost. The things people have left behind, like tools, pictures, and houses are what we call "artifacts." Scientists named anthropologists and archaeologists find these things and analyze them to see if they can put together the story of the people who made them. Tell pupils that today they are going to pretend to be these scientists and see if they can discover what life was like for a civilization that lived long ago.

Presentation   Tell students the following: "I want you to imagine that you live 3,000 years from now, in about the year 5,000 A.D. You now live on another planet and you have made a trip with a group of scientists to a planet called Earth. On this planet are many ruins. You begin digging in these ruins. After much hard work someone finds a jar full of coins. You don't find anything else. It is your job to see what you can tell about the people who lived here by looking at these coins and seeing if they can tell their story. (Provide each pupil with a nickel.) What can well tell about these people by only looking at this coin?" You may need to provide some hints and a model to get the class going. The following ideas are among those that typically emerge:

- The people must have been fairly advanced. They knew how to refine ore into metal to make the coins.
- They might have been bilingual because the coins seem to have two languages printed on them.
- The people were religious and believed in a god.
- They might have been skillful architects. There is a building on the back that shows some good building design.
- The term "United States of America" might mean that a group of governments banded together.
- The figure has a pigtail. Perhaps all the people who lived in the 1970s and the 1980s had pigtails and long hair.
- The male figure might be a king, a hero, or maybe even a god.
- They may have had a calendar because there is a large number that might represent the year the coin was made.
- The term *five cents* seems to indicate some sort of unit designation. What might that indicate?

It is sometimes useful to introduce some other coins. You might state that someone in another location found these coins. Provide a few pennies, dimes, and quarters for them to compare. Other statements might emerge as they note that most of the figures seem to be men and that the coins picture different buildings and symbols.

Have pupils discuss how statements drawn from artifacts can sometimes lead to wrong conclusions about the life of people. We do not all dress as the people pictured or live in buildings like those on the coins. Anthropologists and archaeologists need to find other ways of making sure their conclusions are correct. What could students do to check conclusions to make sure they are correct? The class might mention that they could look for other evidence such as pictures, the ruins of buildings, or perhaps written records to validate the conclusions.

Closure: Review with the class. Ask, "What did we do today? Why did we do this? What did you learn from this activity that might help you as you read about ancient times? How might you use this when you look at items in a museum?"

Cultural Conflict

Cultural conflict is present in all of our lives. As times change, accepted customs and beliefs are challenged. Some cultures are able to adapt to challenges and others are not. Studies of cultural change and adaptation can begin by focusing on those aspects of your pupils' environment that are facing the prospect of change. For example, many school districts have changed the school calendar to year round from the traditional calendar with a summer break. There are many who oppose this change simply because it changes a long-held custom. Pupils can discuss the possibility of changing to a year-round calendar and what that might mean. They can predict other changes that might result from this one change. Other examples of customs that have changed or that are being challenged can be discussed.

Related to the concept of change are the problems that occur when two cultures come into contact. The results can be very disturbing for members of both cultures. Books such as the *Lotus Seed*, by Sherry Garland (Harcourt Brace Jovanovich, 1993), *The Double Life of Pocahontas*, by Jean Fritz (Puffin, 1983), and *The Talking Earth*, by Jean Craighead George (Harper & Row Junior Books, 1983) all deal with the conflict that occurs when two cultures come into contact.

Many communities have individuals who have immigrated from other countries. They can be invited to the class to share their customs and talk about the difficulties they experienced trying to change and adapt to a new culture. Most classrooms will have pupils who have moved from one school or one community to another. There is a need to adapt to new customs and new ways of living even in this type of change. Pupils can be asked to share the problems they experienced when adapting and trying to fit in to a new place.

Lesson Idea 3–7

INVENTIONS AND TOOLMAKING

Grade Level: 4–6

Objectives: Pupils will (1) create a tool from limited resources, (2) identify the difficulties in inventing something new, (3) identify the importance of new inventions and, (4) predict the changes that might occur in a culture as the result of an invention.

Overview: The making of new tools or new inventions can have a profound effect on a culture. Throughout the ages, inventions, such as moving from the creation of stone tools to using metals such as bronze, have characterized dramatic changes in civilization. Creating new tools or inventions from items existing in the environment demands a high level of creativity. In this lesson, pupils will have fun trying to create something as well as develop a deep appreciation for inventors.

Procedure: *Learning Set*   Ask the pupils to define the word *invention*. Ask them to identify some inventions that they think are important. Ask them how they think life was different before the invention (include positive as well as negative influences). Tell the class that today they are going to invent a new tool.

Presentation   Provide teams of three or four pupils with the following items, an ice cream stick, a piece of string, and a 3- × 5-inch card. Tell the class that they need to invent a new tool using only these three objects. They do not need to use all the objects. Allow ample time for them to discuss and experiment with different types of things they can create. They can get additional supplies of these three items as they experiment.

Have each of the groups share their inventions. Choose one of the inventions and predict what changes might occur if people were to use the new invention. As an alternative activity, provide them with a hypothetical invention and have them predict the consequences. For example, what would happen if a car was invented that never needed to stop for gas?

For an extension activity, have the class map an invention. They might begin with a common object, such as a clock, and begin to map the prerequisites that led to the invention of a clock. To do this, place the word *clock* in the center of a large piece of paper. On the top, write a statement describing the need that led to the invention. Drawing lines outward from the clock, list the prerequisites as the class thinks of them. These might include things such as electricity, gears,

Closure: wheels, numbers, wires, etc. At the bottom of the page, iden-
                        tify some of the consequences of the invention.

                        Debrief by asking the class, "What have you learned from the
                        lesson?" Emphasize the point that an invention, although
                        small, might have some long-term consequences and can
                        even change our way of life.

Storytelling

Storytelling has been a common method for passing on the customs and beliefs from
one generation to another. Gathering the stories of a people is of interest to anthropologists. Books such as *Why Mosquitoes Buzz in People's Ears*, by Verna Aardema (Dial
Books, 1975) can be used to illustrate how the stories people tell communicate the values and beliefs of people. All children like to hear and tell stories. A beginning point for
including storytelling would be to have them share stories they have been told, discussing what they think the stories mean and what they tell us about the culture that
told them. Class members can have fun collaborating as they then try to develop new
stories that they could tell to younger brothers and sisters to teach them something
important. An interesting extension would be to have the pupils think about the stories
that are told in popular music. Ask, "What do these songs tell us about ourselves?"

   In summary, anthropology is a fascinating subject that can help us learn about and
develop a respect for our own and other cultures. The subject offers an opportunity to
deal with significant issues such as ethnocentrism, racism, cultural change, and ethnic
and cultural pride. There are numerous opportunities to include anthropology content
in the elementary curriculum.

PSYCHOLOGY

Few topics spark more interest than the idea of *self*. We are interested in many aspects
of the self, such as why we think and feel the way we do, how we are alike or different
from others, why some people seem to be smarter than we are, how we can learn to be
smarter, how we can be happier, and how we can understand the forces that influence
our behavior. Evidence of this interest is easily found in the popularity of radio talk
shows, newspaper columns dealing with self-help, and the many current books with
psychological topics. In the school arena, psychology courses at the high school level
are among the elective courses most often taken for social studies credit (Nelson &
Stahl, 1991). Unfortunately, many elementary social studies teachers have not considered psychological topics as a legitimate component of the social studies curriculum.

   Psychology focuses on understanding ourselves and the behavior of those around us.
This kind of content makes perfect sense for an elementary social studies program dedicated to helping pupils understand themselves and their social world.

As a discipline, psychology has far-ranging concerns. Most lessons that include content from psychology focus on pupils' self-concept and sense of self-acceptance. Many lessons with psychological orientation are now found in programs that focus on drug and alcohol abuse. It has been recognized that these types of programs must help individuals develop a positive self-image to help them cope with life's pressures and stress.

Although including psychological content in programs aimed at preventing drug abuse is necessary, opportunities for including content drawn from psychology in other parts of the social studies program are often overlooked. We need to understand human behavior if we are to understand history and the social sciences. If we know our own hopes, fears, aspirations, and motivations we then have a foundation for thinking about these elements in other people at other times and places. Understanding what motivates people to do different things can, for example, help pupils understand the risks explorers were willing to take by venturing into unknown lands or the willingness of soldiers to enter into a battle in which they could lose their life.

Another advantage of including psychological perspectives in the social studies curriculum is that pupils already have experienced many feelings and have observed others in their social world. As a consequence, they have formed some hypotheses about why people behave the way they do. Teachers can use these understandings as springboards to study others. Figure 3–5 presents questions, concepts, and generalizations central to psychology that are useful for organizing lesson content. We discuss several of these in the subsections that follow.

Individual Differences

Many of the questions young children have about people relate to individual differences. Pupils frequently ask, "Why are some people smart and others are not? Why are some people bigger than others? Why are some people nice and others mean?" Children learn at a very young age that people are different. In fact, this awareness of differences seems to develop to such an extent during adolescence that individuals believe they are totally different from everyone else.

An understanding of individual differences develops a foundation for much school learning. It helps pupils develop the foundation for a healthy self-concept and an appreciation for individuals who are different from them. This understanding becomes even more crucial as the elementary years unfold and acceptance by the group becomes more important. Boys who mature late and girls who mature early often feel "different" and believe they are abnormal. That some individuals tend to learn some things quickly or be more talented in certain highly respected areas may diminish pupils' self-concepts and lead to frustration and failure.

Understanding individual differences is also central to understanding the behavior of others, both past and present. The actions of individuals when confronted with challenges may be explained, in part, by their unique skills and abilities.

Perception

"Seeing is believing" is a common quotation. However, it is not entirely accurate. Perception is selective, and what we see in a given situation is colored by many factors

The following are examples of central questions, concepts, and generalizations associated with psychology. They provide guidelines to elementary teachers interested in planning psychology-related lessons.

Central Questions (a selection)

In what ways are people alike and how are they different?

What accounts for differences among people?

Why do people who observe the same event have different explanations of the event?

Why do people act as they do?

How do we use different senses to learn?

Why do people grow and develop at different rates?

What are the consequences of different developmental rates on personality?

What makes people afraid?

How do people react differently when they are fearful?

What makes some people more aggressive than others?

What are the basic needs of people?

How do different people go about meeting those basic needs?

Concepts (a selection)

Learning, self-concept, individual differences, personality, acceptance, security, normal, abnormal, achievement, aggression, fear, perception, habit, motivation, uniqueness, innate behavior, heredity

Generalizations (a selection)

All individuals have common needs, yet each individual is different in significant ways.

Heredity and environment both play an important part in shaping the personality of individuals.

Human behavior is influenced by learned patterns much more than is the behavior of other species.

Fear is a natural emotion that can be helpful in certain situations, but that can be harmful if it is irrational or left unrecognized.

Humans are social beings who seek to establish positive relationships with others.

All individuals have the needs to achieve, belong, be accepted, and achieve freedom from fear.

Aggression is a natural reaction. It can be used in productive and unproductive ways.

Individuals who use aggression in socially unacceptable ways often feel guilty.

Figure 3–5
Central questions, concepts, and generalizations associated with psychology.

including our mood, attitude, previous knowledge, and self-concept. Many arguments between elementary-aged pupils are based on different perceptions of the same event. Youngsters will argue at considerable length, with parents as well as peers, that they have accurate or correct perception. Perception also accounts for much of the variety of individual behavior. In geography, different people have different perceptions regarding the potential uses of a given environment. Wars have been fought because individuals perceived something differently from others. An important part of studying history is learning that events can be viewed from different *viewpoints*, an aspect of perception.

Fears

Everyone has fears. Fear has been a crucial element in many historical events. Individuals under the influence of fear may behave in ways that appear inconsistent with their normal behavior. Understanding fear and distinguishing between rational and irrational fear is an important educational outcome.

Young children have fears, and these fears may interfere with their ability to relate to others or to function in a productive manner. On the other hand, pupils may sometimes be unable to distinguish those situations where fear is appropriate. Learning how to recognize and cope with fear is a topic of great interest to pupils throughout the elementary grades.

Aggression

Aggression is another psychological theme with significant social studies applications. Many student questions are directed toward understanding aggressive behavior, such as, "Why do individuals fight? What do I do when I get mad? Why do some people seem to hate each other?"

One application of the study of aggression is to view world events that involve it. The news media are usually filled with examples of aggression. These might involve aggression between nations that result in war or the aggression between neighbors or ethnic groups. Answering the question, "Can't we all get along?" requires an understanding of aggression. This study needs to begin with individuals and what causes them to feel and react aggressively.

However, aggressive behavior is not always viewed as inappropriate. Employers often praise individuals who "aggressively" attack problems or go after business. Coaches of athletic teams praise athletes who play the game "aggressively." Knowing when to be aggressive and how to use aggression in an acceptable manner can be confusing to pupils.

Psychology-related Classroom Activities

Psychology deals with the uniqueness of each individual and how personality is developed. Because of this focus, it is of great interest to pupils. Lessons focusing on psychology should begin with the experiences of the pupil and then move to the study of the behavior of others. An important goal of lessons should be to help individuals develop an understanding and an acceptance of self. A word of caution is in order: we need to take care that our lessons in this area are not overly intrusive and that they do not invade the privacy of our pupils.

Observing People

Observation of human behavior is a major research technique used by psychologists. This tool can be very profitably used in the classroom. Pupils enjoy assignments that actively involve them, and they enjoy watching other people. To use observation in the classrooms, we need to begin by showing members of the class how to record their observations. They need to learn only to describe what they see rather than to make interpretations about the behavior. They can describe both the circumstances and the reactions of those they observe.

Once they have learned the technique of observing, we may then teach them how to interpret what they have witnessed. We can assign them to observe people in different situations. For example, they may begin by observing the reactions of young children to certain stimuli or situations. They can watch them as they play, interact with others, or handle frustration. Older pupils might observe individuals at different ages to begin to understand some basic principles of growth and development. Other observations might take place using common situations around the neighborhood. For example, what happens when people are crowded together on an elevator or a bus? How do they react when something unexpected happens? Why might these reactions have occurred?

The school, playground, and cafeteria are good places for observing behavior. Pupils might observe to see what individuals do when they do not want to participate in a game with others. Do some individuals go off by themselves rather than play? What do they do? Why might they behave that way? Pupils can observe what happens when different people win or lose a game or what they do when there is a disagreement. Lively discussions of these episodes can take place back in the classroom as pupils share their observations and try to explain why people behave the way they do.

Lesson Idea 3–8

OBSERVING HUMAN BEHAVIOR

Grade Level:	4–6
Objectives:	Pupils will (1) collect data through systematic observation and (2) identify patterns and form conclusions from data.
Overview:	Psychologists observe individuals and study their reactions to different situations. Elementary social studies lessons can help sharpen pupils' observational behaviors and help them begin to develop insight into why people behave the way they do.
Procedure:	***Learning Set*** Ask the class if they know what a psychologist does. Tell them that a *psychologist* is a scientist who studies and tries to understand human behavior. One of the ways the psychologist does this is by observing how people react to different situations. Tell the class that they are going to get to practice observing as psychologists.

Presentation   Introduce the Observation Record Form shown here. Tell them that it is important to record only what they see, and not interpretations of what they think is happening. Present them with an example of how to make a systematic recording.

Observation Record Form

Place of observation:
Time of observation:
Situation:
People who are observed:
Observation sequence:
Time   Behavior observed

_____   _____

_____   _____

_____   _____

Divide the class into teams to collect data by observing people in different settings. For example, assign one team the task of observing younger children on the playground and another team the task of observing older children. Those who do not play games could be observed by a third group. Make other group assignments as appropriate for the situation.

After the observations have been completed, have the members of each team see if they can identify patterns in the data. They might try to answer questions such as the following:

- How was the behavior of people in groups different from those who were alone?
- How did they respond to disagreements and problems?
- Were there differences in the way younger children play and older children play?
- What special features of the place might have contributed to what the people did there?

Have each of the groups share their findings and any patterns they noticed. Conduct a whole-class discussion of what the class thinks might account for the different behaviors of patterns that they observed.

Closure: Ask the class to review what they did. Ask, "Why is it important to record only what we see, not what we think? What did we learn about making observations? What did we learn about human behavior?"

Individual Differences

There are a great number of things that we can do to help pupils begin to understand that although all people have some things in common, they are also different from each other. Lessons focusing on individual differences can begin with young children by getting them to observe the physical differences between pupils in the classroom. This can easily be integrated with mathematics by making charts showing the different colors of eyes and hair, and different heights of pupils in the room. Other opportunities for identifying individual differences can focus on different interests and hobbies that pupils might have. Discussion should emphasize that differences are natural and that it is important for people be different to meet the diverse needs of society. We might ask members of our class to think about what it would be like if everyone was good in reading and no one liked or had skill in math or music.

Pupils in upper grades can begin to focus on trying to understand what causes individual differences. They can begin to understand that some differences are the result of heredity and others the result of environment.

Perception

Pupils are often surprised to discover that not everyone perceives things in exactly the same way. Helping them understand that perception is selective and is influenced by age, gender, values, prior experience, and motivation can result in interesting lessons. These lessons can be organized around a series of experiments that focus on (1) comparing "eyewitness" accounts of pupils who all witness the same event, (2) comparing reactions and interpretations to art prints, (3) discussing something that all students have read, or (4) comparing individual interpretations of athletic events.

For example, heated debates can take place when the fans of two different teams are brought together to discuss a game. Fans of one team will see some incidents and tend to overlook or not notice other incidents that are noticed and interpreted differently by other fans. Discussing what happened and why it happened can lead to an understanding of some of the basic principles of selective perception. A number of simple experiments in perception, described in most basic psychology books, can be adapted for use in the classroom.

Lesson Idea 3–9

UNDERSTANDING PERCEPTION

Grade Level:	K–3
Objectives:	Pupils will state one reason why people might see a thing differently than others do.
Overview:	Individuals' values and previous experience influence how they perceive reality. The following exercise combines art and social studies into a lesson to help pupils appreciate individual perception.

Procedure:

Learning Set   Tell the class that today they are going to see if people always see the same thing when they look at a picture.

Presentation   Give pupils pieces of construction paper folded down the middle. Ask them to unfold the paper. Place a drop of paint right on or near the fold line. The paper is then refolded and pressed together. This produces a symmetrical image as the paint spreads on both sides of the fold line.

Allow the paint to dry for a few minutes and choose several of the prints to post in front of the room. Ask individuals to describe what they see in each of the paintings (encourage them to express different answers). Ask why they think that different people see different things in the paintings.

- How might things that are of interest to them have influenced what they saw?
- Did something you are familiar with help you "see" things in the painting?
- How do you think the descriptions might be different for people who live in other places?

Closure:

Review with the class. Ask, "What did we find out today? How might this information be helpful when we listen to people tell us about something they saw?"

Emotions

Emotions are everpresent in our lives, ranging from happy to sad, loving to hating, peaceful to angry, confident to fearful and insecure. All of us experience the whole range of emotions. Young children often have questions about them and may not understand what influences their emotions. They want to know, "Why do people fight? Should you ever be afraid? What causes people to like each other? Why do parents sometimes yell at you? Why do parents sometimes get mad at each other?" The important learning that can come out of a study of emotions is that all people have them and that it is okay to sometimes feel sad or angry.

Perhaps the best approach to studying emotions is to help pupils learn to be sensitive to their own emotions and to those around them. Emotions as a topic should be openly discussed in the classroom rather than be ignored. We can set the tone by acknowledging when pupils are experiencing emotions through a simple response such as, "You are feeling sad." A nonthreatening way to introduce and include this topic is through role playing. Pupils can be placed in a role that has the potential for evoking an emotional response. They can then discuss how they felt and what caused that feeling. Different individuals might have different reactions to the same situation, and the reasons for this may be profitably explored.

Classroom meetings where pupils are gathered in a circle and encouraged to participate in a discussion of a topic, such as, "What makes you feel happy?" or "Why do people fight?" can result in valuable lessons. Hearing about the feelings of others is often eye opening to pupils as they begin to see that individuals have different reactions to common events.

A topic that has generated interest in recent years has been death education. Teachers and parents are realizing that death is a common occurrence in the life of many pupils. Pupils experience the loss of grandparents, parents, friends, and pets. The traditional reaction of ignoring the loss can lead to unhealthy reactions. Although the immediate grief reactions of young children tend to be shorter and milder than those of adolescents, the long-term consequences in terms of psychiatric disturbance are greater (Grismer, 1994). Omission of discussion about death sends the message to pupils that this subject is not to be discussed and therefore blocks communication that would help youngsters learn to cope with loss (Wass, 1982). Several studies indicate that death education components in the curriculum do reduce pupil anxiety and help children develop better coping abilities (Grismer, 1994). A basic theme in effective programs is that death is a natural part of life and that grief is a natural and healthy response.

Although there is a shortage of material on death education, one place to begin is with children's literature. *The Fall of Freddie the Leaf*, by Leo Buscaglia (Charles B. Slack, 1982) and *Lifetimes*, by Bryan Mellonie and Robert Ingpen (Bantam, 1983) deal with the life cycle and can be used with primary level pupils. *Goodbye Max*, by Holly Keller (Greenwillow, 1987), *The Tenth Good Thing About Barney*, by Judith Viorst (Alladin, 1984), and *When a Pet Dies*, by Fred Rogers (Putnam's, 1988) discuss the loss of pets. The loss of relatives is dealt with in *The Two of Them*, by Aliki (Greenwillow, 1979) and *Everett Anderson's Goodbye*, by Lucille Clifton (Henry Holt, 1983). The Clifton book is also useful as it takes the reader in poetic form through the five stages of the grief process. *Bridge to Terabithia*, by Katherine Paterson (Harper & Row, 1977) and *Annie and the Old One*, by Miska Miles (Little, Brown, 1971) are well-written books that deal with different responses to loss and grief. They are appropriate for older children and are likely to elicit good discussions of life, death, fear, grief, and guilt.

KEY IDEAS IN SUMMARY

1. Political science topics have long been a part of the social studies curriculum. Such content was often labeled "civics" and its intent was to "Americanize" individuals by convincing them of the virtues of the American political system. Current emphases go beyond this narrow focus to help pupils learn key concepts as power, authority, freedom, and justice, and to learn about alternative political systems.

2. Sociology is concerned with the behavior of individuals in groups. Lessons dealing with sociological content should help pupils learn about the influence of groups on their behavior, about group processes, and about why some groups change and adapt and others disappear.

3. Anthropology focuses on the central concept of culture and on how different cultural groups view the world. Lessons drawn on anthropological content can help pupils learn about different cultures and how these cultures respond to basic human concerns.

4. Psychology is often overlooked as a source of content for the elementary grades. However, it is a topic that has the potential for high pupil interest. Many pupils come to school already having observed human behavior and with ideas and theories about that behavior. Lessons focused on the content from psychology have great potential for helping pupils learn how to understand self and to cope with situations they may face.

5. Lessons drawn from the social science disciplines are not intended to turn pupils into miniature "social scientists." Rather, the intent is to include content that will help pupils develop complete understanding of their social environment.

CHAPTER REFLECTIONS

Directions: Now that you have completed the chapter, reread the case study at the beginning. Then, answer these questions.

1. How would you now respond to the comments of the school administrator?

2. What is the role of political science in the development of citizenship?

3. Do you agree that subjects such as sociology and anthropology are generally not supportive of citizenship education?

4. How do you feel about bringing controversial topics into the social studies curriculum?

5. What do you think can be done to prevent problems from groups who may not want certain topics discussed?

6. Do you agree that pupils in the elementary grades are too immature to understand and deal with controversial topics?

EXTENDING UNDERSTANDING AND SKILL

1. Write a short (three to five pages) paper on good citizenship. How do you define *good citizenship*? How do individuals learn citizenship? What does this imply for what you will teach and how you will teach it?

2. Review several social studies textbooks written for a grade level that interests you. Identify topics in the book where you could include political science, anthropological, sociological, and psychological content. Briefly state your ideas about what you might include.

3. Select four or five key concepts from the disciplines covered in the chapter. Begin to build a resource file of pictures, cartoons, newspaper articles, case studies, artifacts, and charts that would be useful in teaching these concepts to elementary pupils.

4. The chapter identified a number of children's books that could be used to teach the social studies. Identify other books that could be used. Briefly give a summary of each book, and identify the social science concepts that could be taught using the book.

5. Interview several teachers of a grade level of interest to you. Ask them about how social problems such as gangs, drug abuse, homelessness, and prejudice influence their classrooms. Identify example lessons that might help address these problems.

REFERENCES

GALLANT, R. (1989). *Ancient Indians: The First Americans*. Hillside, NJ: Enslow.

GRISMER, L. M. (1994). *Death Education in the Primary Elementary Classroom*. Unpublished master's project, California State University, Fullerton, Fullerton, CA.

HARVEY, K., HARJO, L., AND JACKSON, J. (1990). *Teaching About Native Americans*. Washington, DC: National Council for the Social Studies, Bulletin no. 84.

NELSON, M. R., AND STAHL, R. J. (1991). "Teaching Anthropology, Sociology, and Psychology." In J. Shaver (ed.), *Handbook of Research on Social Studies Teaching and Learning*. Englewood Cliffs, NJ: Merrill/Prentice Hall, pp. 420–426.

PATRICK, J., AND HOGE, J. (1991). "Teaching Government, Civics, and Law." In J. Shaver (ed.), *Handbook of Research on Social Studies Teaching and Learning*. Englewood Cliffs, NJ: Merrill/Prentice Hall, pp. 427–436.

SORAUF, F. (1965). *Political Science: An Informal Review*. Englewood Cliffs, NJ: Merrill/Prentice Hall.

WASS, H. (1982). *Resources for Helping Young Children Deal with Death*. (Report No. CG0116831) Gainesville, FL: University of Florida, (ERIC Document Reproduction Services No. ED 233254).

PLANNING FOR INSTRUCTION

CHAPTER GOALS

This chapter provides information to help the reader:

- define aims, goals, intended learning outcomes, and instructional objectives,
- describe relationships among aims, goals, intended learning outcomes, and instructional objectives,
- write instructional objectives of different types at different levels of complexity,
- describe basic characteristics of taxonomies in the cognitive, affective, and psychomotor domains,
- list levels of each of the three major domains of learning,
- develop instructional units, and
- write lesson plans.

CHAPTER STRUCTURE

Introduction
Aims, Goals, Intended Learning Outcomes, and Instructional Objectives
    Aims
    Goals
    Intended Learning Outcomes
    Instructional Objectives
    The ABCD Format / Instructional Objectives and Domains of Learning
Information Needed in Making Instructional Planning Decisions
    Information About Learners
    Pupil Expectations and Prior Experience
    Knowledge About Content
    Knowledge of Teaching Methods
    Knowledge About Available Resources
Organizing Planning Information
    Unit Plans
    Identifying the Grade Level / Identifying a Topic or Theme / Identifying Features Associated with High-quality Social Studies Programs / Opportunities to Integrate Content / Identification of Prerequisite Knowledge / Intended Learning Outcomes / The Organizational Scheme / Suggested Teaching Approaches / Identifying Assessment Ideas / Criteria for Reviewing the Unit
    Lesson Plans
    Instructional Objectives / Teaching Approaches / Organizing and Managing Learners
Key Ideas in Summary
Chapter Reflections
Extending Understanding and Skill
References

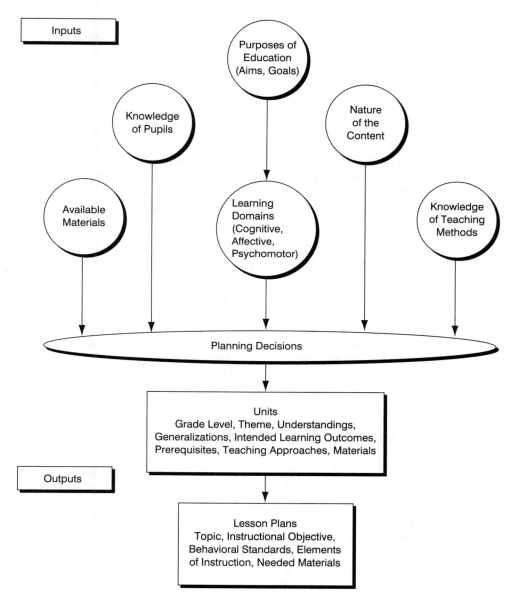

Figure 4–1
Planning for instruction.

Chapter 4

Case Study

IT SEEMED LIKE A GOOD IDEA

Carlos Cortez is in his first year of teaching fifth graders. He has been trying to develop some imaginative social studies lessons. Several days ago, he decided that a simulation would be just the thing to get his pupils interested and involved.

At the beginning of the social studies period, he said, "Today we're going to do something different. I'm going to divide you into groups. I want people in each group to identify the name of an explorer and plan this person's trip to the New World. I want everyone to make a presentation to the class at the end of the week."

Carlos had barely gotten these words out when members of the class began shouting out questions:

"What happens if everybody wants to be the same explorer?"

"Do we have to do what the 'real' explorer did, or can we just make stuff up?"

"What if we don't want to be an explorer?"

"Exactly what are we supposed to present to the class?"

"We don't have enough information. When can we go to the library?"

"How come we're doing this, anyway?"

Carlos tried to answer the questions. Then he moved quickly to get members of the class organized into groups. That's when the real "fun" began. Problems started popping up all over the place. Carlos found himself racing from group to settle conflicts and answer questions. Some members of the class did nothing at all. They just sat and talked. It was unclear whether they were unwilling to get to work or were unaware of what they were supposed to be doing. The noise level rose higher and higher. What had seemed a splendid idea a day or two earlier was turning into a disaster.

What Is Your Response?

Take a few minutes to respond to these questions.

1. Why do you think Carlos's plans went awry?
2. What would you have done if you had been in his place?
3. How do you think members of the class felt about the new activity? Why?
4. Was the activity itself a poor choice, or might it potentially have merit?
5. How might better planning have helped Carlos? Specifically, what might he have done before initiating this lesson to increase its likelihood of success?

INTRODUCTION

Skilled professionals perform in ways that make their tasks seem effortless. An artist sitting at an easel creating a beautiful painting gives the appearance of doing something so easy that we may be tempted to pick up a brush and try. Most of us soon become frustrated when we attempt tasks that pose few challenges for experts. Our mistake is one of judgment. We see only the public performance of someone who may have spent years perfecting a special ability. The halting, tentative, and not always successful early attempts of today's proficient performer usually were never put on public display.

People who observe skilled teachers often suppose that "teaching is easy" and that it is something that "anybody can do successfully." This is not true. Good teachers' performances have been honed by practice, and they are daily sharpened further by careful planning. The preparation that goes into a successful lesson is largely invisible to a casual observer. Because it cannot be seen, novices often fail to grasp the importance of instructional planning.

At its heart, teaching is a decision-making process. The success individual teachers enjoy relates directly to the quality of their decisions. During a typical day, researchers have found, teachers make decisions about once every two minutes (Clark & Peterson, 1986). In addition to decisions they make about learning experiences, teachers also decide how to organize and pace their content, how to respond to questions, how to react to pupils' behavior, and how to manage paperwork of all kinds.

Further adding to the complexity of the teacher's role is the complexity of the classroom setting. It is a public, multidimensional environment where many things are happening at the same time (Doyle, 1986). This complexity adds pressure to teachers that can cloud their judgment and interfere with their abilities to make good decisions.

To cope with these challenges, teachers need to take actions to reduce the unpredictability of the classroom. This can be achieved through good planning. Planning includes careful attention to the following:

- Characteristics of learners
- Nature of content to be taught
- Alternative teaching approaches available
- Availability of resources and materials
- Alternative ways to sequence presentation of material
- Ways to apply basic principles of teaching and learning

AIMS, GOALS, INTENDED LEARNING OUTCOMES, AND INSTRUCTIONAL OBJECTIVES

Planning begins with consideration of purposes. Purposes focus on student learning. These vary in terms of their specificity. Many teachers use the following four levels of specificity and generality as they plan learning experiences for pupils in their classes:

- Aims
- Goals
- Intended learning outcomes
- Instructional objectives

Aims

Aims are broad statements that establish a general sense of direction for school programs. They include those general purposes that the public has established for the schools. For example, the public generally expects students who graduate from high school to be informed individuals who are familiar with responsibilities of adult citizenship.

Sometimes aims developed by educators are controversial. This is true because not everyone has the same views regarding what education's purposes should be. Debates often reflect a clash of philosophies. For example, some people think the primary mission of schools should be to prepare young people to assume vocational roles. They favor "practical" courses that tie clearly to the world of work. Others feel the school's major mission is to transmit academic knowledge that may not necessarily have "practical" value in the workplace. Public discourse about the purpose of schools helps educators determine what society in general and the local community in particular expects of the schools.

Though there are variations from place to place, the following social studies aims are among those supported in large numbers of American communities (adapted from *History–Social Science Framework for California Public Schools*, 1987):

- Understand the basic principles of democracy.
- Understand what is required of citizens in a democracy.
- Develop social and political participation skills.
- Solve problems and draw conclusions.
- Recognize the sanctity of life and the dignity of the individual.
- Recognize history as common memory.
- Understand world regions and their historical, cultural, economic, and political characteristics.
- Understand the basic economic problems facing all societies.

Goals

Goals are narrower statements of purpose than aims. They indicate specific directions for a given subject or grade level. For example, goals for third-grade social studies help identify the specific material that should be taught at that grade to contribute to the general aim of "producing good citizens."

Goals frequently are established at the school district level. They may be identified by school boards, curriculum committees, or even textbook selection committees. Goals often are printed in official school district curriculum guides. The following are examples of goals that might be adopted for the purposes of narrowing a broader aim and identifying more specific instructional responsibilities for teachers:

- Learn basic geographic features of the state.
- Know responsibilities of a citizen.
- Understand that history is an interpretation of past events.

- Grasp basic economic concepts including scarcity, specialization, trade, and economic interdependence.
- Explore relationships of people in homes and schools.
- Gather information from maps.
- Compare lifestyles of people living in different regions.
- Analyze contemporary events.

Goal statements help teachers to define general responsibilities they have in working with lessons directed at a particular group of learners (first graders, second graders, and so forth). Goal statements, though, still are rather broad in scope. They must be further refined and made more specific as teacher planning goes forward. Goals represent a distant achievement. The stops along the way must also be considered. These "stops" include intended learning outcomes.

Intended Learning Outcomes

Intended learning outcomes boil down goal statements into a set of specific items a teacher expects a class to learn in a given unit of study. The focus is on what pupils are to learn, not on the activities they may experience or on what the teacher will do. For example, the statement, "Read the chapter on the Westward Movement," is an activity, not an intended learning outcome. An intended learning outcome related to this activity would be, "State some causes of the Westward Movement." Wording of intended learning outcomes clearly identifies how pupils will demonstrate what they have learned (Gronlund, 1991). In this case, the intended learning outcome calls on them to "state some causes . . . "

Intended learning outcomes provide teachers with guidance regarding what to teach and how to teach it. They also add specificity to teachers' attempts to communicate with parents and others about their instructional intents. For example, much more is communicated about teachers' expectations when parents are told, "Pupils will be expected to state economic differences between the North and South that contributed to the outbreak of the conflict," than when they are simply told, "The class will be reading about the Civil War."

Instructional learning outcomes are especially useful to teachers when they plan a unit of instruction for a particular group of learners. Examples of intended learning outcomes for elementary social studies follow:

- Define the roles of different people in the community.
- Point out the regions in the state and describe them.
- State the basic ideas in the Declaration of Independence.
- Demonstrate respect for the opinions of others.
- Describe steps in a procedure that will lead to solution of a problem.
- Define some concepts associated with scarcity.
- Apply generalizations to new problems.
- State questions pertinent to solution of a problem.
- Distinguish between fact and opinion.

Instructional Objectives

Instructional objectives are an extension of intended learning outcomes. Similar to outcomes, they state in specific terms what pupils will be able to do as a result of their exposure to instruction. Additionally, they include criteria teachers can use to determine how well learners have mastered the content. They also specify the conditions under which pupils will be expected to demonstrate what they have learned.

Sometimes different instructional objectives specify different things learners can do to demonstrate what they have learned. For example, an intended learning outcome that calls on pupils to define "scarcity" might be demonstrated in a number of ways and at several levels of sophistication. A teacher might assign some of these alternatives to pupils to demonstrate how well they grasp the concept:

- Match a definition of scarcity to the term.
- Draw an illustration of the concept scarcity.
- State a definition of scarcity orally.
- Identify an example of scarcity.
- Distinguish between examples and nonexamples of scarcity.
- Role play an example of scarcity.
- Apply the concept of scarcity to a present-day issue.
- Write an essay about how scarcity influences the pupil's own life.

In a classroom enrolling a diverse group of learners including many who are limited English proficient (LEP) pupils, the teacher might allow some to draw an illustration or orally state the concept and require others to write definitions or match the concept with an appropriate definition. Specific indicators a teacher chooses should vary depending on characteristics of learners in the class.

Teachers use instructional objectives to guide preparation of lesson plans. Several formats have been developed for writing them. One that is widely used is the ABCD format.

The ABCD Format

Instructional objectives that follow the ABCD format have four components—audience, behavior, conditions, and degree.

Audience: The "A" component of the objective identifies the person or persons to whom the instruction is directed. This might be the entire class, a small group, or an individual. When they plan lessons, teachers consider whether pupils have the necessary prerequisites to accomplish the proposed objective. Sometimes teachers find it useful to develop different objectives for individual members of their classes. Examples of the "A" component follow:

- All fifth grade pupils will . . .
- Zelda Zike will . . .
- Ben's cooperative group will . . .

Behavior: The "B" component defines the behavior that pupils will be expected to demonstrate. Note the emphasis is on the pupil behavior that *results* from the lesson, not on what pupils or the teacher do while the lesson is being taught.

It is important to describe behaviors with verbs that indicate clearly observable pupil actions. Verbs such as *know, appreciate,* and *understand* are not precise enough to serve as behavior components of instructional objectives. The behavior component requires precise language that will allow the teacher to observe clearly whether pupils can demonstrate what they have learned. Examples of the "B" component follow:

- . . . trace the route of the Lewis and Clark expedition . . .
- . . . describe the sequence of events leading to the adoption of the Bill of Rights . . .
- . . . draw a graph showing the exports of Japan . . .
- . . . identify an example of interdependence . . .

Conditions: The "C" component describes the conditions under which pupils will be allowed to demonstrate the behavior. The conditions component of an objective may specify whether pupils will be able to use other resources such as books and notes, whether they will be expected to demonstrate the behavior individually or in a group, and whether there will be a time limit for the task. They also may specify whether the demonstration will take the form of a test, require the creation of a "learning product" of some kind, or require some other demonstration of learning. The specific conditions a teacher chooses to incorporate in an instructional objective vary depending on the type of learning task and specific characteristics of pupils. Examples of the "C" component follow:

- . . . working in a team of two . . .
- . . . working alone with a map . . .
- . . . on a multiple-choice test . . .
- . . . constructing a model of a theater . . .

Degree: The "D" component focuses on the issue of proficiency. It establishes a standard that tells teachers how well pupils must perform for them to conclude that the new behavior has been mastered. Teachers often apply the criterion of successful repeated performance of new learning. A single correct response could result from chance factors, and may not be a valid indicator that learning has occurred.

As they develop the "D" component of their objectives, teachers may consider such things as the number of correct responses on a test, the kinds of things that must be included in a project, the categories of information to include in an essay, or the number of inferences pupils can make when confronted with a novel situation. The specific degree selected is determined by the type of learning that is the focus of the individual objective. For example, a major league baseball player who gets at least 3 hits for every 10 times at bat is considered to be proficient; a clerk in a store who gives correct change to only 3 customers out of every 10 served is not.

In addition to thinking about the nature of the learning task, teachers must also consider pupils' skill levels when establishing the "D" component. Lower proficiency levels logically are expected of pupils who are less advanced in their grasp of given content or their abilities on a skill task than pupils who are more proficient at the time instruction begins. Examples of the "D" component follow:

- . . . will locate 8 out of 10 cities on a map.
- . . . will respond correctly to 8 of 10 test items that relate to the journey of Lewis and Clark.
- . . . will make three inferences about a place from a climatic map.
- . . . will state two differences between families now and long ago.

Putting It All Together: The "A," "B," "C," and "D" components are always present in a complete instructional objective, but they do not always appear in the same order. The following are examples of two complete instructional objectives. Note the "A," "B," "C," and "D" components in each.

"A"   "B"
Each pupil in the first grade will cite the names of the days of the week and the
                          "C"   "D"
months of the year orally from memory with no mistakes.

"C"   "A"   "B"
On a true/false test, pupils in the orange group will label examples of
                                        "D"
counties, countries, and continents with 90 percent accuracy.

Instructional Objectives And Domains Of Learning

Instruction in the elementary school involves several types of learning. Some instructional objectives need to be written to address each major learning category. Traditionally, learning has been divided into three major categories or domains:

- Cognitive domain
- Affective domain
- Psychomotor domain

Cognitive Domain: The cognitive domain refers to what might be termed intellectual learning. The sample learning objectives in the section about implementing the ABCD format are examples of cognitive domain objectives. They focus on the learning and processing of information. In the 1950s, Benjamin Bloom and several colleagues set out to define categories of cognitive learning. The result of their work was a book that has become an educational classic, *Taxonomy of Educational Objectives: Handbook 1: The Cognitive Domain* (Bloom, Englehart, Furst, Hill, & Krathwohl, 1956). This book, usually

---

BOX 4–1   **Does Planning Stifle Creativity?**

A beginning teacher commented as follows to some colleagues in an elementary school faculty lounge:

> I think we plan too much. It can get in the way of good teaching. I mean, sometimes my youngsters get off on an exciting topic or issue I haven't planned for at all. I think this is the real "teachable moment," and I think it's my responsibility to take advantage of these opportunities to help kids learn. Lessons plans can turn us into robots who mechanically plod through what we have written, regardless of how the kids are reacting. We would all do a better job if we simply "went with the flow" of the class and made the most of opportunities as they spontaneously develop.

Think About This

1. What evidence does this teacher use to defend the position taken in these comments?
2. What counterarguments to this position can you identify?
3. How comfortable would you be to stand in front of a group of learners with no plan?
4. What do you see as potential consequences of teaching delivered according to this teacher's position?

---

referred to simply as "Bloom's Taxonomy," describes six types or levels of cognitive thinking. These levels, introduced in Figure 4–2, range from low-level intellectual tasks such as memorizing to highly sophisticated thinking requiring analysis, synthesis, and evaluation.

Intellectual objectives calling on pupils to demonstrate more sophisticated thinking patterns demand more preparation and teaching time than those that ask them to perform at less challenging levels of thinking. Teachers must take into account time requirement differences when they consider the cognitive difficulty of individual instructional objectives.

Affective Domain: The affective domain embraces learning that involves attitudes and values. Some of the purposes of the social studies program clearly tie to a desire to help students commit to such core American values as respect for the individual and toleration for diversity. Lessons directed to these kinds of ends often are guided by affective instructional objectives.

Over the years, a number of specialists have made important contributions to our understanding of the affective domain. Krathwohl, Bloom, and Masia (1956) developed an affective taxonomy that identified different levels of affective learning. Raths, Harmin, and Simon (1966) made important contributions to our knowledge of how people acquire values. These specialists determined that value formation becomes possible when people open themselves to receive and interpret new ideas and points of view. A willingness of a person to publicly affirm and act upon her convictions evidences deeply-rooted personal values.

Knowledge

This lowest level of the taxonomy refers to the recall of specific elements of previously learned information. A pupil at this level is asked to do little beyond naming or describing something.

Objective: Each pupil will orally name the seven days of the week without error when asked to do so by the teacher.

Comprehension

This level implies an ability to simultaneously recall several bits of information. The individual should be able to change the form of the original information, translate the information, or extrapolate from the information.

Objective: Each fifth grader will identify with 90% accuracy the steps that a bill goes through to become a law by developing a flow chart outlining the steps when given the text description of the process.

Application

Application-level thinking requires that information learned in one context be used in a different or new setting. Pupils are called upon to "do something" with their learning.

Objective: The student will calculate the approximate distance between four out of five pairs of cities to within 50 miles using the scales provided in the classroom atlas and classroom maps.

Analysis

Analysis calls on pupils to describe the characteristics of something by identifying the relationship between various parts. Analysis requires pupils to break something into smaller components and note the relationship among the components.

Objective: Each sixth-grade pupil will write a short description of life in ancient Egypt. The description will include: (1) indications of the relationships between religion and everyday life, (2) roles of various classes in Egyptian society, and (3) dependence on the Nile.

Synthesis

Synthesis-level thinking calls on pupils to put together elements of something in a new way (at least in a way that is new to them). This usually involves an element of creativity or imagination.

Objective: Each cooperative learning group will predict the probable consequences for California and neighboring states if there were no Sierra Nevada Mountain range. Pupils will include at least three of the following: climactic consequences, economic implications, types of agriculture, probable changes in the history of the region, population distribution, and location of major cities.

Evaluation

Thinking at the evaluation level requires pupils to make judgments about something considering specific criteria. The "specific criteria" provision is important. Without these criteria, attempts at evaluation-level thinking may result in little more than unsupported personal opinions or preferences.

Objective: Each second-grade pupil will decide which of two rules would be most fair for all pupils and would be most likely to promote good feelings and cooperative work.

Figure 4–2
Levels of the cognitive domain and examples of objectives.

Several schemes have been developed that describe different levels of the affective domain. One of them is displayed in Figure 4–3.

The affective area poses a problem for social studies educators. Teachers do not want to intrude on pupils' personal and family values. Yet, they sense an obligation to transmit certain widely held perspectives. Our society does have norms regarding what is "right" and "wrong." Pupils must learn that important limits on individual behavior are necessary to our social survival. Murderers are never excused on the ground that "they were just doing their own thing."

In addition to teaching values associated with certain social imperatives, it is important that pupils understand areas of life where there is less consensus regarding which

---

Receiving

Behavior at the level of receiving is characterized by a pupil's willingness to be exposed to new ideas or values with an open mind. The intent is to remove any "blockages" that might exist because of misconceptions, prejudice, or general hostility to the content.

Objective: Each pupil will allow opposing viewpoints to be presented without interruption or ridicule.

Approaching

The level of receiving is concerned with a pupil's general willingness to take in new content. Approaching goes a step farther. It refers to a predisposition to investigate and gather more data, and involves a willingness to suspend judgment and to seek additional information before making a commitment. An individual at this level actively seeks additional information or evidence.

Objective: Each pupil will gather and orally present information on both sides of an issue presented to the class.

Deciding

Decision-level thinking is characterized by pupils' arriving at personal decisions after consideration of the individual merits of issues. This involves a willingness to commit and take a stand.

Objective: Each pupil will personally choose an opinion from among conflicting viewpoints expressed in readings presented in class. Pupils will write their choice and their reason and present them to the teacher.

Sharing

At the sharing level, pupils demonstrate a willingness to share their personal decisions about issues with others. Sharing is characterized by commitments that run so deeply that pupils are not hesitant to state them publicly.

Objective: Each pupil will freely and without coercion make a public statement of one position taken on at least one values-related issue presented during the unit.

Figure 4–3
Affective categories and objective examples.

values are appropriate. Many decisions people make are not the inevitable result of dispassionate consideration of evidence; personal values often come into play. Pupils need to be helped to understand value positions that underlie specific political and personal decisions. Lessons guided by affective instructional objectives help them gain this important understanding.

Psychomotor Domain: The psychomotor domain includes kinds of learning that depend on fine-muscle coordination, for example jumping a rope or hitting a baseball. Pupils' levels of psychomotor development also influence their abilities to accomplish tasks associated with academic learning. For example, social studies lessons requiring learners to measure distances on a map with a ruler require the use of motor skills as well as cognitive knowledge.

Several schemes have been developed to describe levels of the psychomotor domain. One of these (Armstrong & Savage, 1994) is illustrated in Figure 4–4.

Higher levels of psychomotor learning require more instructional time than lower levels. For example, "free practice" assumes a level of proficiency at which pupils are

---

BOX 4–2   **Social Studies and the Affective Domain**

Selection of affective domain content is a problem for many social studies teachers. Surveys reveal that many people in our country believe that the teaching of values should be a high priority. However, attempts to include the teaching of values-laden issues often result in attacks from other citizens, who accuse the schools of inappropriately "indoctrinating" children.

Complaints sometimes are made about surprising topics. In a school district close to the home of one of the authors, a group of parents protested lessons focusing on cleanliness and washing hands. They took the position that cleanliness was an individual matter and that schools had no business intruding in an area that, in their view, should remain the responsibility of parents.

Because the potential for public protest is very real, many school districts are reluctant to promote the teaching of content that reflects a specific values orientation. Administrative pressures to maintain positive relations with the entire community often discourage teachers from emphasizing affective domain content.

Think About This

1. Does the school have a responsibility to teach certain attitudes and values?
2. What kinds of social studies content might lend itself well to lessons with an affective emphasis? Why do you think so?
3. What are some affective objectives you believe should be emphasized in the social studies program?
4. What considerations should guide a teacher's decision when selecting affective objectives at the levels of "deciding" and "sharing"?

Awareness

At this level, pupils must be able to correctly describe what they must do to perform a given psychomotor task properly. This psychomotor level is closely related to the knowledge and comprehension levels of the cognitive domain.

Objective: Each pupil can correctly state how to hold and manipulate the tape measure and mark units of scale when determining point-to-point distances on a map.

Individual Components

Psychomotor learning at this level requires the pupils demonstrate the individual parts of a complex activity. The student should be able to do each step called for with no errors.

Objective: Each pupil will demonstrate, with no errors, each of the following: (1) align the tape on the map properly, (2) point to the lines indicating centimeters and millimeters, (3) mark the number of centimeters and millimeters representing 100 kilometers on the map, and (4) count the number of 100-kilometer intervals between two locations.

Free Practice

At this level the pupils are expected to demonstrate a mastered sequence of psychomotor behavior in diverse settings, with no direct teacher assistance or supervision.

Objective: Each pupil, on request, will measure point-to-point distances on a work map, using a tape measure with a millimeter and centimeter scale. The estimated distances will be within 100 kilometers of the actual distance.

Figure 4–4
Psychomotor domain and objective examples.

able to perform the task with no teacher supervision. It takes much longer for pupils to reach this proficiency level than to develop an "awareness" level of familiarity with a new learning task.

Interrelationships Among The Three Learning Domains: Though we often separate the cognitive, affective, and psychomotor domains when planning for instruction, they are in reality interconnected. Think about the connections among these three domains as you read the following:

> At 9:45 Joey, a second grader, was building a snow fort on the playground. Jamie, unseen by Joey, crept up silently behind him. She scooped up a handful of snow and, in a flash, pushed it down Joey's back. Joey jumped up, whirled around, and howled. He zipped open his jacket and worked furiously to shake out the snow.

What did Joey learn? First, he probably already knew that snow is cold. He also was aware that cold things feel uncomfortable against warm skin. These two cognitive understandings helped him react.

Second, this experience triggered an emotional, or affective, response. The depths of his anger and any followup action (revenge?) he might take may well be based on a personal view of "right" and "wrong." If he and Jamie are good friends, he may laugh off the incident and look for an opportunity to play a similar prank on her. If Joey has never liked Jamie, he may think about a more serious response.

Third, Joey had a psychomotor reaction. When the snow touched his skin, the nerve endings in his body flashed a message to his brain that something was amiss. He reacted quickly to this messages and began unzipping his jacket and shaking out the snow. All of these reactions involved the use of his psychomotor abilities.

As with this playground incident, classroom learning also involves interplay among cognitive, affective, and psychomotor responses. What teachers mean when they talk about "cognitive," "affective," or "psychomotor" objectives is that one or another of these domains tends to be more heavily emphasized in a given objective. But the others are usually present, to some extent, as well.

For example, suppose a group of pupils were asked to read about Thomas Jefferson. On the surface, this activity seems to be almost exclusively cognitive. However, depending on how the assignment is designed and introduced by the teacher, pupils may have affective reaction of acceptance or rejection. If the assignment requires them to write, draw, or engage in other manipulative activities, psychomotor abilities will also be required.

INFORMATION NEEDED IN MAKING INSTRUCTIONAL PLANNING DECISIONS

Researchers who have studied instructional planning find that the activity gives teachers a mental picture of what to teach (Clark & Peterson, 1986). This picture often includes routines to be used in setting up and managing the classroom environment, key points to emphasize, the sequence of activities, and probable pupil responses to various parts of the instructional experience. The more detailed and accurate the image that results from planning, the higher the likelihood instruction will yield learning.

Good planning takes into account information from several distinct categories. These include information about the following:

- Learners to be taught
- Specific content to be introduced
- Alternative instructional approaches
- Available resource materials

Knowledge about Learners

Pupils in the schools today are diverse, representing a surprising range of interests, motivations, and abilities even in a single classroom. These differences are appreciated by knowledgeable teachers. They plan in ways that will promote the likelihood that as many pupils in the class as possible will learn the new content. Success on one learning task engenders self-confidence. It has few peers as a motivator. Hence, experienced teachers devote considerable time thinking about how their instruction can help each child learn the material.

Pupil Expectations and Prior Experience

Pupils' personal expectations and prior experiences influence their academic performance. Young people who are confident in their abilities and who believe that learning the material is important react differently to instruction than pupils who lack these characteristics. This issue is particularly of concern in the social studies component of the elementary program. Many pupils, initially at least, do not think social studies content is either important or personally relevant. Because of past experience, some of them expect social studies learning to be boring.

Pupils' attitudes toward the social studies are influenced by the kinds of social studies instruction they have received. Some learners may have experienced problems because of their exposure to instruction that failed to take into account their entry level of knowledge. It is imperative that planners not make unwarranted assumptions about what pupils already know. One of the authors once taught a group of pupils who had never seen an ocean. During a lesson, it became apparent that many in the class had the mistaken idea that a person could stand on a Pacific beach, look west, and clearly see the shores of Asia on the other side. Learners who start with misinformation of this magnitude are almost certain to experience difficulties grasping more sophisticated content—a situation with a high likelihood of producing failure, diminished levels of self-esteem, and low opinions of the social studies.

For a variety of reasons, some students have developed a negative view of the social studies. This problem is sufficiently widespread that we need to plan all social studies instruction with care. In time, the cumulative effect of well-designed, interesting, learner-involving instruction that takes into account pupils' backgrounds can promote more positive attitudes.

Knowledge about Content

Instructional planning requires teachers to identify specific elements of content that pupils should learn. Listing general topics to be covered will not suffice. Careful plans deal with much more detailed information about key ideas and concepts that will be emphasized.

Knowledge of content to be taught requires more than identifying particular items of information. Lessons develop material in a sequential fashion. Therefore, teachers must think about how new material can best be sequenced to promote learning. Sequencing decisions require careful consideration of the characteristics of the pupils you will be teaching. The sequence of material provided in a textbook may not be appropriate. As a professional, you have an obligation to develop a plan that best responds to the needs of the young people who will be doing the learning.

BOX 4–3   **Mandated Content and Preplanning Questions**

Identify a grade level that interests you. Gather information from individuals such as a teacher who works at that grade level, a social studies supervisor, and your course instructor. You may also want to consult library resources in preparation for your responses to these questions.

Think About This

1. Is there content that your state requires to be taught at this grade level? If so, what are the state content requirements?
2. Are there local content requirements for this grade level? If so, what are they?
3. What topics seem to be typically treated in social studies lessons at this grade level?
4. How are the topics typically sequenced throughout the year?
5. What are some ways in which these topics are often subdivided?
6. What important social studies goals can be addressed at this grade level?
7. What key social studies concepts can be taught at this grade level?

Knowledge of Teaching Methods

Identifying the instructional approaches you will use is an important part of the planning process. Usually, you will incorporate several techniques within a given instructional sequence. This introduces a variety that can motivate learner interest. Also, certain objectives may be better served by some instructional techniques than by others.

In identifying specific techniques, consider the characteristics of the pupils, the potential of individual techniques to prompt pupil interest, the kinds of behaviors called for in the instructional objectives, and the specific nature of the content to be covered. A teacher thinking about preparing an instructional experience focusing on "how a bill becomes law" might engage in the following kind of thinking:

> "Well, I could have them just read about it in the text, but I don't think so. That's pretty dull. Besides, some of these kids aren't good readers. Also, the stuff in the text doesn't give them much feel for the drama of argument and debate that's part of the legislative process. So, that's three strikes against that idea: (1) boring; (2) some of them can't do it; and (3) it will give them an incomplete idea of the process.
>
> Okay, then, how about a simulation? They'll probably like it. More opportunities for them to talk. They *always* like to talk. It will also give the slower ones a chance to pick up on ideas of some of the more able kids. Finally, it will get them actively involved in debates . . . a pretty good stand-in for the kind of thing legislators do. I think we'll do the simulation."

Knowledge about Available Resources

The kinds of resources available to support their instruction strongly influences what teachers can do. As they plan, teachers must know what resources will be available. They need specific information about the availability of equipment (projectors, televi-

Planning requires the identification and organization of a variety of instructional materials.

sions, videocassette players, computers, and so forth), appropriate instructional space (rooms with appropriate work spaces, rooms where specific equipment is located, and so forth), learning support resources for pupils (maps, globes, supplementary texts, library books, simulations games, and so forth), and, as needed, human resources (special outside speakers, school librarians, and so forth).

Planning resources teachers often use while designing instructional experiences include district-level social studies curriculum guides or state social studies program frameworks. These documents often provide guidance regarding what content should be taught at each grade level and how it might be sequenced. Sometimes these guides also provide lists of useful instructional support materials and suggestions regarding teaching techniques.

ORGANIZING PLANNING INFORMATION

Once you have gathered information about learners, content, alternative instructional techniques, and available resources, you must organize it into a plan of action. Whether this plan is prepared in a careful, formal written form or drafted as a sketchy outline is largely a function of experience. In general, less experienced teachers benefit from committing more time to the process of organizing planning decisions in a formal way. This helps them to identify areas where more planning specificity is needed.

Instructional planning goes forward at several levels of specificity. More general, long-term planning often results in the preparation of unit plans. Planning focusing on shorter instructional periods takes the form of lesson plans.

Unit Plans

Teachers engage in both long-term and short-term planning. They may develop broad outlines of what they intend to do over an entire instructional year. Such extremely long-term plans need to be broken down into smaller segments that feature more specific information. A term often applied to plans that cover between approximately two to four weeks of instruction is *instructional unit*. An instructional unit describes an organizational scheme for the content to be taught and identifies teaching approaches to be used in introducing material to pupils.

Unit planning typically begins with a consideration of content that state or local authorities require at a given grade level. Once this high-priority, "must-be-included" information is identified, teachers go on to select additional content. In doing so, they weigh alternatives and consider questions such as the following:

- What social science concepts and generalizations relate to this topic?
- How can this topic be tied to pupils' personal goals and interests?
- What skills can be included?
- What values might be emphasized?

Instructional units function as building blocks of the elementary social studies program. It is from units that individual lessons are directed. Completed units also prompt thinking about how content in the social studies can be integrated with information in other subject areas. For example, social studies unit topics can suggest kinds of books pupils might be asked to read as part of their reading lessons. Often it is possible to tie experience from mathematics, science, music, and many other learning areas to content organized in social studies instructional units.

Instructional units must be planned in advance. Often, materials will need to be gathered and special arrangements made. For example, there may be a need to order videotape titles, to get approval for proposed field trips, and to obtain commitments from speakers. As a rough guideline, it is a good idea to plan an instructional unit at least a month before teaching lessons related to it.

Units may be formatted in many ways. Good formats make clear relationships among intended learning outcomes, objectives, teaching approaches, and needed materials. Figure 4–5 displays a format that many teachers have found useful.

In planning a unit, teachers must develop specific information about each of the following:

- The grade level for which the unit is intended
- The topic or theme of the unit
- Elements associated with a high-quality social studies program
- Descriptions of opportunities to integrate content
- Identification of prerequisite knowledge

Unit Title:
Grade Level:
Social Science Understandings Emphasized:
Citizenship Understandings Emphasized:
Problem-solving Opportunities:
Content Integration Possibilities:
Prerequisite Knowledge and Skill:
Focus Generalization(s):

Intended Learning Outcomes	Teaching Approach	Materials
Unit Initiation		
Unit Development *1.* *2.* *3.* *4.* *5.* *etc.*		
Unit Culmination		

Evaluation Procedures:

Figure 4–5
Sample unit planning format.

- Specification of intended learning outcomes
- The unit organizational scheme
- Suggested teaching approaches
- Ideas for assessing learners
- Criteria for reviewing the unit

Identifying the Grade Level

Specification of the grade level gives potential unit users important information about the target audience for the described instructional program. Identification of the intended grade level early in unit development serves to remind the developer to keep the proposed instructional program appropriate for learners in the specified grade.

Identifying a Topic or Theme

The topic or theme helps delimit content to be introduced. Good topic titles describe the unit's contents clearly. For example, a title such as, "Family Life in Revolutionary America," provides a better picture of the kind of content to be emphasized in a unit than a less precise alternative, such as, "Interesting Happenings in Revolutionary Days."

Including Features Associated with High-Quality Social Studies Programs

Units should include elements that build pupils' understandings in the areas of social science and history, citizenship, and problem solving. To ensure attention is given to each of these three critical areas, developers consider questions such as the following:

- What will be the citizenship outcomes? What knowledge, skills, values, and decision-making opportunities associated with citizenship will be included?
- What will be the history and/or social science outcomes? What generalizations, concepts, values, skills, and decision-making opportunities associated with history and/or the social sciences will be emphasized?
- What problem-solving opportunities will be provided?

Opportunities to Integrate Content

Social studies instruction can provide an excellent focus for integrating learning from many school subjects. To take advantage of these possibilities, experienced unit developers think about how content from reading, mathematics, science, language arts, music, art, and physical education can be woven into new units.

Identification of Prerequisite Knowledge

Individuals who develop instructional units begin with certain assumptions about pupils who will be taught unit content. Since instructional units often are used by people other than those who develop them, it is important that assumptions about these pupils be made explicit. This information can help a potential teacher decide whether unit content might be appropriate for the particular class.

Intended Learning Outcomes

As noted earlier in the chapter, intended learning outcomes are succinct statements that specify what pupils will be able to do as evidence that they have mastered unit content. Including intended learning outcomes in unit plans helps teachers keep a clear focus on key instructional priorities. They also provide teachers with guidelines to follow when planning individual lessons and converting intended learning outcomes into instructional objectives used in planning lessons for specific groups of pupils.

Intended learning outcomes need to be arranged in an appropriate sequence. Those listed first should identify content introduced at the beginning of the unit. They may tie closely to initial learning activities that are designed to prompt pupils' interest in the general content of the unit. Subsequent intended learning outcomes will focus on the main body of content. The final intended learning outcomes will be broad in scope and will refer to pupil behaviors that call on them to synthesize, apply, and extend content introduced throughout the entire unit.

The Organizational Scheme

Units need to be organized so that relationships among their parts are clear. The organizational plan illustrated in Figure 4–5 is one that functions well. An outline or other general unit organizational plan need not be long. Often, three or four pages will suffice. You can keep in a file specific information you will need when teaching unit content (e.g. assignments, pictures, artifacts, outline maps, and so forth) and bring it out for use at appropriate times.

Suggested Teaching Approaches

Developers do not need to specify ideas for teaching unit content in instructional units. Teachers will do this when planning individual lessons. What is needed in units are brief ideas that will help teachers as they begin thinking about alternative teaching approaches. The following example is appropriate for use in an instructional unit:

> Role play the decision to move west by assigning pupils to different roles such as a father, a mother, a sick child, and an elderly grandfather. Discuss perspectives of each of these people. As a class, discuss how each might feel if the family makes a final decision to move west.

This overview indicates the general kind of teaching activity the unit developer has in mind. It leaves specific details regarding introducing the activity, assigning roles, specifying appropriate behavior standards, debriefing questions, and other details to the teacher who will be planning lessons based on the unit.

Sometimes, suggestions for teaching approaches included in unit plans mention needed instructional materials. These might include such things as titles of specific books, names of films, descriptions of maps, and other support resources.

Identifying Assessment Ideas

In this part of the unit plan, developers provide ideas about how to gather and evaluate information related to pupil learning. There may be suggestions recommending the use of approaches including checklists, project critiques, portfolios containing a broad sampling of pupils' work, and formal testing techniques. These ideas are provided as suggestions. Teachers should consider these and other alternatives when unit instruction begins and they prepare specific lesson plans.

Criteria for Reviewing the Unit

When preparing units, it is useful to develop important quality criteria. These can be used as a quality check before teaching the unit for the first time, and can be applied more or less continuously throughout the unit. This kind of systematic and ongoing review is consistent with the idea that units "are never done." They are always being reviewed and revised for the purpose of making them better. Typical quality check questions include the following:

- Is the whole range of social studies outcomes included?
- Is the material in the unit sequenced logically?
- Is content appropriate for the pupils who will be asked to learn it?
- Are suggested teaching approaches the best that can be devised? Are these approaches consistent with behaviors referred to in the intended learning outcomes?
- Are assessment procedures as good as they can be?

Figure 4–6 presents an entire sample unit plan embodying the characteristics discussed in this chapter.

GRADE LEVEL: SECOND
UNIT THEME: KNOWING MYSELF AND MY FAMILY

Social Science Understandings
Students should begin to acquire several social science and history understandings. They can begin to develop an understanding of change and continuity through the investigation of how their family has changed and how some aspects have remained the same throughout generations. They can begin to develop a simple understanding of the historical approach by gathering data through interviewing others.
Plotting the movement of families can help them begin to understand geographic concepts such as movement, location, and differences between places. An emphasis on sociological concepts such as role, norms, values, and interdependence should be included as the roles of different family members are compared. Economic concepts such as wants, needs, division of labor, money, and employment can be developed as pupils discuss reasons why families might move.

Citizenship Understandings
Citizenship understandings can be developed as each pupil understands that each person in the family has responsibilities to the family. The place of rules and authority in families can also help them begin to realize the importance of rules in an orderly society. An appreciation of diversity can be enhanced by making public the wide variety of families in the classroom and the diverse backgrounds of pupils. Pupils can develop a sense of pride and identity as they explore their cultural and ethnic heritage.

Problem-Solving Understandings
Pupils can begin to learn problem-solving and conflict-resolution approaches as they identify problems and conflicts that individuals have in families. They need to learn the importance of compromise and of taking others into account as they resolve conflicts.

Content Integration
There are numerous opportunities for content integration in the unit. Reading can be integrated by reading selections of literature that deal with families in different contexts. Numerous opportunities for writing are available as pupils write about their families, favorite events that they remember in their family, and letters to family members such as grandmothers or aunts. Math can be integrated through the counting and adding of extended family members. Each family unit can be characterized as a "set." Music can be integrated by bringing in music that is representative of different eras. Pupils can make some crafts or toys that might have been made or used by grandparents as one way of integrating art. The whole class can put together a quilt or mosaic by having each pupil draw a picture of their family and then constructing a class quilt or mosaic.

Figure 4–6
Sample unit.

Prerequisite Knowledge and Skill
For maximum success in this unit pupils should have the following:
The ability to write simple sentences.
A basic understanding of a map of the world.
A beginning understanding of time and chronology.
Knowledge of terms such as family, parents, grandparents, etc.

UNIT OUTLINE

Focus Generalizations
Similarities and differences are to be found among all families.
Family members are some of the most important people on whom we depend.
While families change over time, many practices and traditions continue.

Intended Learning Outcomes	Teaching Approach	Resources
Unit Initiation Identify similarities and differences.	Read selections from the book, *Family Pictures*. Ask pupils how these situations are similar and different from their family. Ask the pupils to identify questions they would like to know about different families. List and keep the questions as a reference for the unit development. Inform the pupils that the class is going to be studying families, both their own and others from around the world.	Garza, Carmen Lomas, *Family Pictures* (San Francisco, Children's Book Press, 1990). Large piece of chart paper or overhead transparency.
Unit Development Define terms.	Introduce the term *ancestors*. Ask if anyone knows what it means. Define the term, provide examples, and share personal examples.	Pictures of families now and long ago. Pictures of individuals from years past.

Locate places on map.	Send letter home to parents at beginning of unit. Have them identify their ethnic heritage and countries of origin for both mother's and father's side of family. Return this on a 3- by 5-inch card. Introduce a map of the world and point out main features. Choose a few pupils and mark the country of origin of their ancestors. During the day the others can identify country of origin on map.	World map, stickers, cards from parents on family origins.
Identify problems. Estimate distances. Construct a grid to help find places on a map.	Review map of world. Show pupils how to use a simple grid system to locate places on a map. Have a few people identify location of countries when given grid coordinates. Have pupils estimate which families had to move the greatest dis-tance to get to the local community. Break into small groups and have each group identify problems they think their ancestors might have experienced in moving.	World map, paper for each group to write problems.

Figure 4–6
continued

Construct a graph. Interpret relationships on a graph.	Present own family tree. Discuss various branches of the family tree. Have pupils construct their own family tree. Pose the questions, "What does a family tree tell us about families? Why is this type of a chart useful?"	Construction paper, markers, student photographs.
Identify cause-and-effect relationships.	Discuss some of the reasons immigrants came to America and the problems they faced. List causes for moving under one column and the problems and benefits under another.	Immigrant stories, chart paper with columns labeled "Cause" and "Effects."
Gather data through listening.	Invite a parent or grandparent who has immigrated to America to talk to the class about their experience. Have class identify how the story is like those they have already learned about.	Guest speaker.

Identify change and continuity in family customs.	Have pupils interview family members about customs and practices when they were young. In a group session, identify a selection of practices. Have them identify which customs and practices are the same today and which are different. Ask the class, "Why do you think some things stay the same and some things change?" View filmstrips.	Interview sheets for pupils to take to interview family members. Filmstrips, "Seasons and Holidays Around the World."
Identify roles and responsibilities of various family members.	Ask pupils to identify the different "jobs" people in their family have. List parents, children, etc. Ask, "How are these responsibilities different in different families? Why do you think they are different? What happens if someone doesn't do his or her job?"	
Compare roles and responsibilities of families in different parts of the world.	Show a videotape or a film of a family from another part of the world. Have the class identify the roles and responsibilities of various family members and compare them to those of class members.	Film or videotape of families around the world.

Figure 4–6
continued

Apply problem solving and conflict resolution.	Have the class share problems that often occur in families. In groups, have class members state how they think these problems might be solved. Discuss how rules might be developed to prevent some problems.	
Culminating Activity Integrate what they have learned from the unit.	Have each class member, in conjunction with their family, develop a picture of the family doing something together (the book *Family Pictures* could be used as an example).	Instruction sheets to go home, construction paper to go home, book: *Family Pictures.*
Working together in groups.	Divide the class into work groups to share and discuss the pictures they have developed and begin gluing or taping them onto a classroom mosaic or quilt.	Large piece of paper for each group, glue or tape.
Review of important ideas. Formulations of generalizations about families.	After all of the sections of the mosaic have been joined together, review some of the illustrations. Ask the class members, "What have we learned in our study of families? What kinds of things could we say about families?" Review the questions that were identified at the beginning of the unit to see how many of the questions were answered.	Completed classroom mosaic.

Evaluation Procedures

1. Keep a checklist of the participation of individuals and groups on all assignments.
2. Have each pupil keep a portfolio that includes the interviews they conduct, the stories they write, the pictures they draw, and the assignments they complete.

Figure 4–6
continued

Lesson Plans

Short-term planning results in the creation of lesson plans, which outline what the teacher and pupils will do during specific lessons. Sometimes these plans cover more than one day. Usually, though, teachers tend to develop plans for what they wish to accomplish during a single day.

The level of detail in individual lessons plans varies. Inexperienced teachers often need to do more detailed planning than teachers who have had many years of successful classroom experience. A rule of thumb is that a lesson plan should include enough detail that a substitute teacher could implement the intended lesson without much difficulty.

Lesson plans often feature the following categories of information:

- Instructional objectives
- Teaching approaches
- Organizing and managing learners

Instructional Objectives

All lessons should focus on a specific instructional objective. Some lessons may have more than one. In addition to establishing a focus on what pupils should do as a result of the lesson, the objective also provides guidance regarding what kinds of learning materials should be used and what kinds of teaching approaches might be appropriate.

Teaching Approaches

Decisions about instructional approaches reflect the following considerations:

- The entry point for instruction
- Motivating learners
- Procedures to inform pupils about objectives and to establish a learning set
- Alternative ways to present lesson content

Determining the Entry Point for Instruction: Identification of an appropriate beginning point for teaching a lesson requires thought about the pupils who will be taught. If

Effective teachers spend many hours alone planning lessons and units.

they are to succeed, pupils must have certain prerequisite skills and knowledge. The entry point should be selected to help them see connections between what they already know and the new information.

Motivating Learners: Successful lessons prompt and maintain pupils' interest. Planning for motivation requires more than attention to an interesting lesson beginning. It needs to take into consideration specific things you might do to periodically reinforce pupils' motivation throughout the entire time a given lesson is taught. Teachers respond to the following basic questions in planning for motivation:

- How can I gain pupils' attention so they will see a need to learn the content of this lesson?
- What can be done at various places in the lesson to maintain their interest?
- What can I do at the end of the lesson to make sure pupils feel successful and to help them maintain their interest in the subject?

Informing Pupils about the Objective and Establishing a Learning Set: Pupils need to know what is expected of them. For this reason, it is important for the teacher to explain lesson objectives to them in language they can understand. They also need a frame of reference, or *learning set*, to orient them to the new content. This provides a context that will help them to fit new information into what they already know. Often a simple sentence or two can be used to communicate information both about learning set and an objective. Consider this example: "Remember how we have been learning about people in the community who can help us. After today's lesson you'll be able to tell me how a letter carrier, the person who delivers the mail, knows where to deliver letters."

Presenting Content: Presentation of new information is the heart of a lesson. Procedures selected for doing this bear directly on what pupils will learn, retain, and transfer to new situations. Decisions about which teaching approaches to use depend on the objective of the lesson, the nature of the content, the characteristics of learners in the class, the availability of instructional support materials, and the teacher's experience and skill.

Basic instructional principles guide teachers as they decide how to best transmit content to a specific group of pupils. For example, new content is more likely to be learned when pupils recognize its relationship to what they already know.

Teachers must also consider the time required for a given approach. Attention spans of pupils, particularly those in the primary grades, are short. Successful lessons respond to this reality by including a variety of activities within a single lesson. Learners also retain content better when they process it actively. They need opportunities to see, hear, discuss, and, most importantly, to apply what they have learned. The needs for variety and active involvement can be accommodated when teachers vary teaching approaches to include such alternatives as reading, demonstration, questioning, modeling, role-playing, simulations, and work in cooperative learning groups.

Many teaching approaches require the teacher to make verbal presentations to the class. When this is done, it is important for the teachers' comments to be concise, logically organized, and free from vague and ambiguous terms. Point-to-point transitions must be clear and logical.

Few people remember detailed information the first time they hear it. Therefore, good lessons feature some planned redundancy. This means that teaching methods incorporate opportunities at different points in the lesson for pupils to encounter important content in various examples and activities.

Pacing of the lesson should be fairly brisk, but slow enough to allow most of the pupils to achieve success. It is particularly important to allow enough time for practice and application activities. These help pupils to solidify their grasp of new content. Figure 4–7 presents a sample lesson plan designed as discussed in this section.

Organizing and Managing Learners

Some teaching approaches require a change in seating arrangements or in space available for teachers and pupils to walk. When planning lessons, teachers must consider problems in spatial arrangements that might be caused by requirements of specific lessons (e.g., learning centers taking up space ordinarily used for other purposes). This is particularly true when pupils will be required to move from one area to another at some point during the lesson. Unless the room is organized to facilitate quick and easy movement and specific directions developed that will communicate clearly to pupils what they are to do, important instructional time will be lost.

Lesson Topic _____ Unit Theme_____ Lesson Plan Number _____
Instructional Objective:
_____
_____

New Vocabulary or Concepts_____
Behavioral Standards _____

Time Allocation	Lesson Sequence	Materials
	Lesson Introduction: Gain attention Stimulate pupil interest Establish learning set Inform learners of objective	
	Presentation of Material: Logical organization Questions Examples/Models Checks for understanding Elicit samples of desired behavior/Provide feedback	
	Application/Practice Guided practice/Monitor pupil work Provide corrective feedback Give independent practice	
	Lesson Conclusion Review key ideas Reinforce success Build bridge to next lesson	

Teacher Evaluation of Lesson Effectiveness _____
_____
_____

Figure 4–7
Sample lesson plan format.

KEY IDEAS IN SUMMARY

1. Competent instructional planning is a hallmark of a professional teacher. During the planning process, the teacher establishes priorities for instruction, identifies needed learning materials, considers organizational issues, and makes decisions related to pupil and program evaluation.

2. Instructional planning begins with a consideration of aims and goals. Aims are broad statements of purpose that describe what society expects of the schools. Goals are related to aims, but are much more specific statements. They point out specific directions for people planning instruction for particular subjects and grade levels.

3. Intended learning outcomes focus teacher attention on what pupils should be able to do as a consequence of their exposure to instruction. They are particularly useful to planners of instructional units. They convey to other interested parties the purpose or intent of the instruction described in the unit.

4. Instructional objectives are related to intended learning outcomes, but convey additional information. Complete objectives include a specification of the intended audience, the specific behavior pupils will be expected to demonstrate and the conditions under which they will demonstrate it, and the degree or proficiency level students will be expected to achieve for the teacher to assume content has been mastered.

5. Intended learning outcomes and instructional objectives may be developed for each of the three major domains of learning: cognitive, affective, and psychomotor. The cognitive domain refers to the intellectual or academic aspects of learning. The affective domain is concerned with feelings, attitudes, and values. The psychomotor domain is concerned with physical movement and muscle control.

6. As they prepare to make instructional decisions, teachers need information related to (1) the pupils to be taught, (2) the content to be presented, (3) alternative instructional methods, and (4) available resources.

7. Long-term planning often results in the development of instructional units. A typical unit organizes instruction for a three- to four-week period of time. Short-term planning often culminates in the development of lesson plans. Lesson plans describe how teachers will meet broader purposes outlined in instructional units as each day's teaching unfolds.

CHAPTER REFLECTIONS

Directions: Now that you have completed reading the chapter, return to the case study at the beginning. Reread it, then answer the following questions.

1. How would you now diagnose the problems Carlos had with his lesson?

2. What planning elements might have helped him avoid the problems?

3. Do you think advance planning would have interfered with his creativity, or would this kind of planning have enhanced it?

4. Describe learning outcomes that might have been included in the unit to which the lesson was related.

5. Suppose you were hired to teach social studies in a district with no social studies curriculum guides. How would you begin to plan your social studies program?

6. Pupils in elementary classrooms have diverse needs. Which need do you feel least capable of accommodating? What might you do to prepare yourself to respond to them more confidently?

7. Educators frequently discuss the issue of motivation. Some people argue that today's pupils are less motivated to do school work than pupils were in the past. Do you agree or disagree? Why, or why not?

EXTENDING UNDERSTANDING AND SKILL

1. For a grade level you would like to teach, identify a theme and plan a unit around this theme. Include intended learning outcomes and a selection of different teaching approaches.

2. Write at least two lesson plans for the unit you developed. Use the ABCD format for your instructional objectives. Describe how parts of your proposed lessons respond to specific pupil and content needs.

3. Motivation should occur not only at the beginning of a lesson, but at intermediate points and at the end as well. Describe places in each of your lessons where you will take specific actions to motivate learners.

4. Teach a group of peers a social studies lesson lasting 5 to 10 minutes. Ask them to critique your introduction, your sequencing of activities, and your actions to check for understanding.

5. Describe how you would adapt one of the two lessons you developed in question 2 to respond to needs of pupils with each of these characteristics:
    • Hearing challenged
    • Visually challenged
    • Attention deficit
    • Physically challenged
    • Gifted and talented

REFERENCES

ARMSTRONG, D., AND SAVAGE, T. (1994). *Secondary Education: An Introduction*, 3d ed. Englewood Cliffs, NJ: Merrill/Prentice Hall.

BLOOM, B., ENGLEHART, M., FURST, E., HILL, W., AND KRATHWOHL, D. (1956). *Taxonomy of Educational Objectives: Handbook I: The Cognitive Domain*. New York: David McKay.

CLARK, C., AND PETERSON, P. (1986). "Teachers' Thought Processes." In M. Wittrock (ed.), *Handbook of Research on Teaching*, 3d ed. Englewood Cliffs, NJ: Merrill/Prentice Hall, pp. 255–296.

DOYLE, W. (1986). "Classroom Organization and Management." In M. Wittrock (ed.), *Handbook of Research on Teaching*, 3d ed. Englewood Cliffs, NJ: Merrill/Prentice Hall, pp. 392–431.

GRONLUND, N. E. (1991). *How to Write and Use Instructional Objectives*, 4th ed. Englewood Cliffs, NJ: Merrill/Prentice Hall.

History–Social Science Framework for California Public Schools: Kindergarten through Grade Twelve. (1987). Sacramento, CA: California State Department of Education.

KRATHWOHL, D., BLOOM, B., AND MASIA, B. (1956). *Taxonomy of Educational Objectives: Handbook II: Affective Domain*. New York: David McKay.

RATHS, L., HARMIN, H., AND SIMON, S. (1966). *Values and Teaching*. Englewood Cliffs, NJ: Merrill/Prentice Hall.

II

FUNDAMENTAL APPROACHES TO INSTRUCTION

CONCEPTS, GENERALIZATIONS, AND INDIVIDUALIZED LEARNING

CHAPTER GOALS

This chapter provides information to help the reader:

- distinguish between concepts and generalizations,
- describe procedures used in concept-attainment and concept-formation/diagnosis lessons,
- identify steps in an inducing-a-generalization lesson,
- point out variables that can be altered to individualize instruction, and,
- explain features of learning centers, learning activity packages, activity cards, and learning contracts.

CHAPTER STRUCTURE

Introduction
Concepts
    Types of Concepts
    Conjunctive Concepts / Disjunctive Concepts / Relational Concepts
    Teaching Concepts
    Concept Attainment / Concept Formation / Diagnosis
Inducing Generalizations
Individualized Learning: Basic Features
    Altering the Rate of Learning
    Altering the Content of Learning
    Altering the Method of Learning
    Altering the Goal of Learning
Examples of Formal Approaches for Individualizing Learning
    Learning Centers
    Learning Activity Packages
    Activity Cards
    Learning Contracts
    Open Learning Contracts / Closed Learning Contracts
Key Ideas in Summary
Chapter Reflections
Extending Understanding and Skills
References

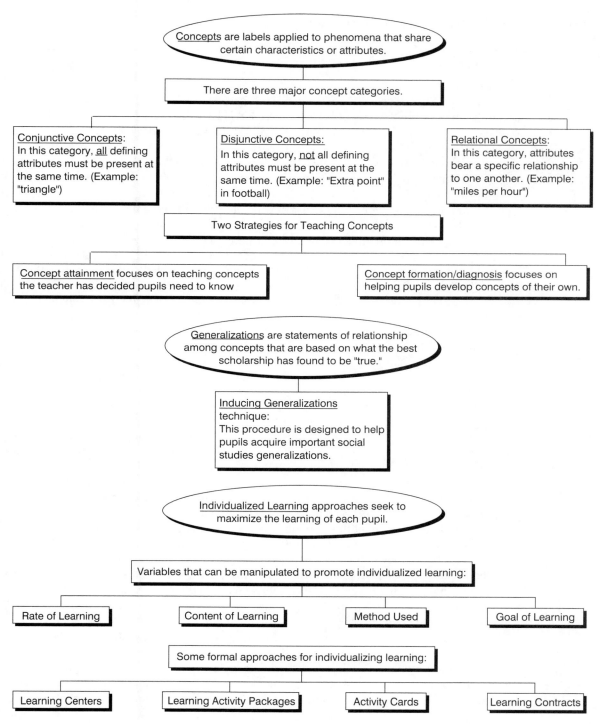

Figure 5–1
Concepts, generalizations, and individualized learning.

Chapter 5

Case Study

DO GENERALIZATIONS REALLY HELP US SELECT SPECIFIC INFORMATION TO TEACH TO LEARNERS?

The school district where Naomi Schwartz works as a fourth-grade teacher sponsored a workshop on teaching social studies. At the end of the session, Naomi raised this issue for the group to consider:

"I'm not sure I agree with the use of generalizations to guide the selection of content. For one thing, the state has a curriculum mandate specifying the content that needs to be taught in the fourth grade. Our pupils are tested every year to see how well they learned this content. If I start teaching generalizations, how will I make sure that I cover the content that will be tested? If our pupils don't do well, we all know that this will result in a headline in the local paper.

"I also think there is a value concern that has not been discussed. For example, because of our state's location on the Great Plains and because the fourth-grade social studies program emphasizes state history, I might develop a focus generalization something like this:

> Development of patterns of living on the plains resulted from technological developments that allowed people to adapt to this new environment and from successful efforts to deal with challenges posed by the original Native American population of this region.

"The problem I am having is that this generalization contains some subtle value preferences and bias. It implies that technology is a beneficial force that was properly applied to 'tame' nature and that the land was not productive. Was this always true? What about the ecological damage technology has brought to some parts of the plains? Shouldn't we teach content that points out that environmental costs have sometimes been high when new technologies have been applied?

"Similarly, what about the cultural clash between the European American residents and the original Native American residents? Just because someone has a technological superiority, are they entitled to displace others, take their land, and cause the deaths of thousands of people and their cultures? Are we to present the settlement of the plains as a triumph of 'good' over 'evil,' or is there a place to discuss how this settlement was viewed by the Native Americans? Shouldn't we be discussing the value implications of the application of technology?

"I realize this is only one of many generalizations that could be chosen. However, I'm concerned that we are going to blindly accept this way of organizing content without considering these issues. Just how should we deal with the value assumptions that inevitably are embedded within any generalization we might choose? How do we make sure that we avoid presenting a single perspective as the only one that is 'right' or 'correct'?"

What Is Your Response?

Think about Naomi's comments. Then, respond briefly to these questions:

1. How do you respond to her argument that pupils must be prepared for taking the standardized test? Do you think that teaching toward a generalization means that pupils will not learn specific information? Why, or why not?
2. Naomi argues that generalizations often assign higher priorities to some values than others. Do you agree? Can you identify generalizations that are value free?
3. Suppose you were asked to prepare lessons designed to help pupils understand the generalization Naomi used in her example. How would you deal with some of the values issues she identified?
4. Try to take some different perspectives as you consider these issues. If you were a pupil, do you think you would prefer units organized around the learning of generalizations, or units presenting information designed to help you do well on a test? What do you think is best for pupils in the long run? That is, which approach will help them most as high school students, college students, and adult citizens? Why do you think so?
5. If you were a parent, how would you react to an announcement from teachers at your child's school that they proposed to organize social studies units around focus generalizations? What advantages might you see to this approach, and what might be some of your concerns?

INTRODUCTION

Chapter 1 introduced the "structure of knowledge." Two content types included in the structure of knowledge, concepts and generalizations, are important organizers of information. Both concepts and generalizations have great explanatory power and potential for transfer of learning to new situations. Special instructional procedures have been designed for teaching these important content organizers and for helping pupils understand how concepts and generalizations can be introduced. This chapter introduces several examples of these techniques.

When teaching concepts, generalizations, and other kinds of content, you must consider pupils' individual differences. Individualized instruction seeks to capitalize on pupils' differences by providing instructional experiences that have a high probability of succeeding with individual students. In the social studies, individualized instruction does not necessarily mean that pupils will work in isolation. Much social studies learning requires interaction with others. Therefore, lessons that attend to individual differences often involve groups but build in provisions that will allow individual pupils to pursue needed content in different ways. In this chapter, we suggest several alternative approaches to responding to pupils' personal differences.

CONCEPTS

Concepts are labels applied to phenomena that share certain characteristics or attributes. For example, the concept "automobile" refers to something that has these attributes (among others):

- Functions as personal vehicle, almost always with four wheels
- Powered by a gasoline or diesel engine (also, but rarely, by an electric motor)
- Direction of movement controlled by a circular steering wheel

Teaching pupils concepts such as "automobile" helps simplify their understanding of the world around them. Concepts provide a scheme that allows them to classify under a single label hundreds, even thousands, of individual examples that fit into the classification category. Once a young child grasps the basic requirements of what something must have to be called an automobile, he can quickly recognize examples that are associated with this concept or class regardless of differences in size, color, make, model, or age.

Recognition of a given concept also helps pupils distinguish between examples and nonexamples. For instance, mastery of the concept "automobile" makes it possible for learners to distinguish examples of this concept from trucks, buses, and motorcycles—examples of related, but somewhat different classes of objects. In short, concepts function as a kind of shorthand that allows people to group and recall information about a large number of things that share certain important characteristics.

Concept learning helps pupils learn how to organize information into categories that are useful for storing and retrieving.

Types of Concepts

There are three basic types of concepts:

- Conjunctive concepts
- Disjunctive concepts
- Relational concepts

Conjunctive Concepts

All defining attributes of a *conjunctive concept* must be present for something to be considered a proper example of this type. For example, the conjunctive concept "triangle" has these three attributes: (1) three sides, (2) a closed, two-dimensional figure, and (3) three interior angles. If any of these attributes is missing, the "thing" is not a triangle.

Disjunctive Concepts

In the case of *disjunctive concepts*, it is not necessary for *all* possible defining attributes to be present for something to be considered a proper example of the concept. The "extra point" in football is an example of a disjunctive concept (Fraenkel, 1980). There are three possible defining attributes (e.g., ways in which an extra point can be scored), but not all of them need to be present for an extra point to be awarded. The three defining attributes of the concept "extra point" are: (1) the ball can be run into the end zone following a touchdown; (2) the ball can be passed into the end zone and caught by an offensive player following a touchdown; or, (3) the ball can be kicked (not punted) through the uprights and over the crossbar following a touchdown. If any one of these three conditions (attributes) is present, an extra point is scored. Multiple attributes and the point that not all of them need to be present make disjunctive concepts somewhat more difficult for pupils to learn than conjunctive concepts.

Relational Concepts

Attributes of *relational concepts* bear a specific relationship to one another. Consider the concept "miles per hour." There is a relationship between an attribute related to distance covered (miles) and an attribute concerned with time (hours). Mastery of relational concepts require pupils to understand not only each attribute but also the nature of the relationship among attributes. As a result, relational concepts sometimes are difficult for pupils to learn.

In addition to problems associated with concept types, the number of defining attributes associated with a given concept affects the probable difficulty learners will have in mastering it. Concepts that have large numbers of associated attributes are particularly difficult. Abstract concepts that often are featured in social studies lessons, such as "democracy," "citizenship," "power," and "socialization" are examples of these kinds of complex, difficult-to-learn concepts. Because these concepts are important building blocks in many social studies lessons and are included in powerful explanatory generalizations, special attention needs to be devoted to teaching them to pupils in ways that are likely to promote real understanding.

Teaching Concepts

Concepts can be taught in various ways. Two formal approaches that are widely used are concept attainment and concept formation/diagnosis.

Concept Attainment

Concept attainment focuses on teaching concepts that the teacher has determined are important for pupils to know. The approach follows six basic steps:

- The teacher introduces the concept by name.
- The teacher presents examples of the new concept.
- The teacher presents nonexamples of the new concept.
- The teacher introduces a mixture of examples and nonexamples of the new concept; pupils attempt to distinguish between the examples and nonexamples.
- Pupils are asked to develop a definition of the concept of their own (e.g. explain what they see as its defining attributes).
- Pupils demonstrate their understanding of the concept by finding additional examples on their own.

The concept-attainment technique can be used to teach a variety of concepts. For example, a teacher who wishes to teach a relatively simple concept such as "desert" might begin by showing pupils pictures of a variety of desert regions. Next, he would introduce pictures of nondesert regions, and pupils would be told that the depicted places were not deserts. During the next step, the teacher would show pupils a mixture of desert region and nondesert region pictures. Pupils would be asked to identify those that were of desert regions. Next, the class would be asked to come up with a definition of "desert region." If pupils experienced difficulty, the teacher would provide some cues by asking them to look both at the pictures of desert regions and those of nondesert regions and ask them to describe characteristics in the desert region pictures that were not present in the nondesert region pictures. (It is important that pictures of desert regions clearly reflect characteristics common to deserts.) Finally, pupils would be asked to identify other examples of deserts, possibly by looking through photographs in back issues of publications such as *National Geographic*.

More complex concepts, such as "justice" or "democracy," can also be taught using this general approach. They will require more time because they have more defining attributes than a simple concept such as "desert." Several class periods might be required. If the focus were on "justice," a case study approach might be taken. After introducing the concept, presenting brief examples, and describing brief nonexamples, the teacher may present pupils with short "cases," some of which illustrate examples of "justice" and some of which provide examples inconsistent with "justice." Pupils could be asked to identify cases in which the described situation was consistent with their understanding of "justice." Next, the teacher could ask them to define the concept in their own words. Finally, pupils might find and present to the class examples of justice they have witnessed in their own lives.

Concept Formation/Diagnosis

The concept-attainment technique focuses on teaching pupils concepts the teacher feels pupils must know in order to understand important social studies content. It also is important for young people to learn how to develop concepts of their own. By learning how to categorize fragmented information into general categories, the world's complexity is reduced. Concepts basically are category labels that provide convenient "containers" for vast quantities of related information. One procedure for helping pupils develop their own category labels is called *concept formation/diagnosis* (Taba, 1967).

Concept formation/diagnosis helps pupils to group and label isolated pieces of information. The teacher functions as a guide as pupils go through the process. Specifically, the teacher attempts to elicit a range of information from class members, encourages them to organize this information into groups sharing common characteristics, and concludes by asking them to generate labels descriptive of items in each group. These are the basic steps:

- The teacher asks an open-ended question designed to elicit as much data as possible from the class. As members of the class supply information, it is listed on the chalkboard, a chart, or an overhead projector transparency.
- When step one is complete and there is a great deal of unorganized information written where all class members can see it, the teacher asks pupils to organize information into groups. The teacher devises a symbol to place by items that "go together." (Sometimes letters of the alphabet or numbers are used; sometimes the teacher develops other kinds of symbols.) Pupils need to be told that some items might go into more than one group.
- After items have been placed into groups, pupils are asked to develop concept labels. They are encouraged to come up with labels that define the general characteristics of items in each labeled group.

A key to the success of this technique is selection of a good open-ended question. This question should be one that prompts large numbers of pupil responses. It also is best if it is a question to which many members of the class will be able to contribute possible answers. (If larger numbers of pupils are involved in this early phase, the whole group will have a larger sense of "ownership" as the lesson unfolds.) Specific questions will vary depending on pupils' grade levels and interests, content being studied, and priorities of the teacher. Examples of opening questions appear in Figure 5–2.

After asking the open-ended question, the teacher should list *all* pupil responses. One of the purposes of this exercise is diagnostic. By listing all pupil responses without comment, the teacher is able to identify incorrect information that some members of the class believe to be true. This enables the teacher to correct misimpressions later when there are opportunities to share new information with the class. One of the authors, when using the concept-formation/diagnosis technique with a group of sixth graders, asked, "What would you expect if you were to visit Brazil?" Among responses were: "dark-skinned Africans," "Spanish-speaking people," and "primitive living conditions." Obviously, some class members did not know Brazil's location, were unaware that Portuguese rather than Spanish is spoken there, and had little idea that such cosmopolitan places as São Paulo, Rio de Janeiro, or Brazilia existed.

The second step in a concept-formation/diagnosis activity requires pupils to group the listed items. A prompting question often works well, such as this: "As you look at

Questions used in the concept formation/diagnosis approach should relate to the content of the unit being studied. These are examples of the kinds of questions that might be developed:

> What jobs do people have?
> What kinds of things can you buy at the supermarket?
> Can we draw a picture of something we do at school?
> What do you think about when you hear the word *democracy*?
> If you were to tell another person about our state, what would you say?
> What would you expect to see on a visit to _____?
> What are the buildings like in our town?
> If you were a pioneer moving west, what would you take with you?
> Can we draw pictures of some things families buy with their money?
> What are some ways people can earn money?
> What did you see on our field trip?
> What do you think of when someone says the word *summer*?

Figure 5–2
Opening questions for concept formation/diagnosis.

the items on our list, which ones go together, and why do they go together?" This question helps pupils to think about criteria or attributes they are using as a basis for grouping. Sometimes pupils do not agree on where a given item should go. It is important to tell them that there is no one "correct" way to group information and that a single item can be assigned to more than one group.

The final phase of the lesson also begins with teacher questions. For example, the teacher might say, "What can we call each of the groups? We have used letters of the alphabet to designate them, but now let's give each group a real name. What names can we come up with that will tell us something about the kinds of things in each group?" Disagreements among pupils may arise. When pupils suggest several possibilities for labeling a given group, they should be asked to consider which one best describes items in the group.

In summary, the concept-formation/diagnosis approach gives pupils practice in forming concepts. It gives them a process they can use to organize complex information into categories—a useful thinking skill for many areas of living. Teachers sometimes use the technique at the beginning of a new unit of study. The focus question and pupil responses center on the unit topic. The exercise promotes high levels of pupil involvement and establishes an initial context for what pupils will be studying. Sometimes, teachers keep information from the pre-unit concept-formation/diagnosis exercise and involve learners in a similar lesson using the same focus question at the conclusion of the unit. Differences in pupil responses serve as an indicator of changes in learners' understanding as a result of their exposure to unit content.

INDUCING GENERALIZATIONS

Generalizations are statements of relationship among concepts. They are idea-dense condensations of what the best available scholarship has been found to be "true." They are useful for pupils learning social studies content because they provide efficient summaries of vast quantities of information.

The *inducing-a-generalization* technique is commonly used to help pupils acquire important social studies generalizations. It helps pupils learn how to form generalizations through gathering evidence and applying their own thought processes. Before a teacher initiates an inducing-a-generalization lesson, it is important that he know that pupils understand the basic concepts associated with the focus generalization. Suppose a teacher wanted learners to master this generalization: "The global location of a nation or region contributes to its importance in international affairs." Pupils with no grasp of concepts such as "global location," "nation," "region," and "international affairs" would have great difficulty in learning the generalization.

These steps are followed in an inducing-a-generalization activity (see Figure 5–3 for an example):

- Pupils look at evidence that the teacher has made available. They organize this information into appropriate categories.
- Pupils compare and contrast data in the categories and note relationships.
- Pupils develop statements (generalizations) that can explain the relationships and that they can apply to other similar situations.

In step one, the teacher introduces information related to the generalization. (Remember that pupils are not given the focus generalization. They receive only *information related to* the generalization. The purpose of this exercise is to encourage pupils to organize data, look for relationships, and develop explanatory generalizations of their own.) The next step involves organizing the information. Sometimes teachers may provide the class with information already organized into categories More mature and sophisticated learners may themselves be required to do this.

During step two, pupils look at the information that has been gathered and organized. The teacher asks pupils questions related to the information. Examples of teacher questions are, "What do you notice about information in category A? In category B? What are the similarities? What are the differences?"

Step three requires pupils to develop generalizations of their own. This step may frustrate pupils who are not accustomed to "going beyond what they are given." The teacher needs to encourage pupils to take chances and make educated guesses based on their analyses of the data. Often teachers ask prompt questions, such as: "How do you account for these differences? What statements could we make that might apply to similar situations or places?"

As learners attempt to formulate generalizations, the teacher encourages them to justify their responses with reference to appropriate evidence. All pupil-developed

The following chart is a visual illustration of how the data for an inducing-a-generalization lesson might be organized and displayed to facilitate the discovery of relationships among categories and the development of statements explaining the relationships. This generalization was selected by the teacher as the focus generalization of this activity: *The types and varieties of services change as the size of the community changes*. One axis of the chart identifies communities of different sizes. The other axis indicates the types of services and businesses. In this manner, the relationships between the two major concepts of *community size* and *services* can be easily displayed. Each cell of the chart is filled in as data are gathered. The teacher usually makes the chart to help the pupils organize the data. As they become older and more sophisticated thinkers, they may develop their own chart.

Types of Services

Community Size	Government Services	Types of Stores and Businesses	Types of Industries
Small Rural Community			
Moderate-sized City or Community			
Large City			

After information has been added to each cell, following the steps and questions listed here will assist pupils in arriving at generalizations about the relationship between community size and types of services.

Step 1: What do you notice about the types of governmental services, stores and businesses, and industries in small communities? Moderate communities? Large cities?

Step 2: What are the similarities and differences you notice among these different communities?

Step 3: Why do you think there are differences among these communities? What statements can we make that might help us predict or explain what we might find in other communities we study?

Figure 5–3
Organizing an inducing-a-generalization lesson.

generalizations are accepted. The adequacy of individual generalizations will be tested later when they are applied in unfamiliar contexts. As pupils apply their own generalizations to new situations, they will discover that some of them have a great deal of predictive power. Others will need to be revised as new evidence comes to light. A few may have to be abandoned altogether because there is simply too much contradictory evidence available. Lesson Idea 5–1 illustrates how an inducing-a-generalization activity might proceed.

Lesson Idea 5–1

COMPARING TWO COLONIES

Grade Level:	5–6
Objective:	After reviewing the information presented on the chart, the pupils will make at least two generalizations that explain the differences between the two colonies.
Introduction:	Say the following to the class: "How many of you have traveled to cities in other parts of the country? How are those places like where we live? How are they different from where we live? Every place in the world is different in some way from all other places. There are some things that explain why places grow to be very different. Once we understand these reasons, we can begin to understand places all over the world. Today I have some information on two colonies that were settled and established about the same time. Let's look at the information on the chart."
Procedure:	Ask the following questions:
Step One	"What do you notice about the nationality of settlers in Amstead and Martinville? What do you notice about the location of these two colonies? How would you describe Amstead 50 years after settlement? How would you describe Martinville 50 years after settlement?"
Step Two	"Why do you think these two colonies grew so differently in those 50 years?"
Step Three	"What statements could we make that would explain the growth of these communities that might be useful in understanding the growth and change of other places?"
	Write the statements that the pupils give on a chart or transparency to save for future reference.
Closure:	"Ask the class: "What did we do today? What did you learn? How might we use what we have learned?"

Name of Colony	Nationality of Settlers	Location of Colony	50 Years After Settlement
Amstead	Swedish	Inland, away from the ocean	One political party in power.
		Rich farm land	Most people go to the same church
		Lots of water	Not very much industry.
		Five-month growing season	
		Surrounded by high mountains	Most people live by farming.
		Lots of forests	Change is very slow and most people continue to do things the same way for years.
			There are few new people moving into the community.
Martinville	English French Germany Italian Spanish	Located on ocean	Several different political parties.
		Good harbor	Most people work in factories or businesses.
		Very rocky, poor soil	
		Short growing season	People go to several different churches
		Coal found in nearby hills	There is lots of disagreement between people in the community on how to run things.
		Lots of water for power	
			There is constant change in the community.
			Lots of new people are coming into the community.

INDIVIDUALIZED LEARNING: BASIC FEATURES

Successful teachers are able to respond to pupils' diverse needs and interests. One way they do this is through the use of individualized instruction. We introduce in this section several approaches to individualizing instruction.

The term *individualized instruction* means different things to different people. Some think of individualization as implying an independent study environment in which each pupil works alone. In our view, individualized instruction is not synonymous with isolated study and by no means requires that pupils always work by themselves. Indeed, working alone may be totally inappropriate for some pupils and for meeting certain kinds of needs. Many needs are best met through interaction with others in group settings.

Several variables are manipulated when teachers plan for individualized instruction:

- The rate of learning
- The content of learning
- The method used in learning
- The goal of learning

Altering the Rate of Learning

The rate of learning refers to the pace of instruction and learning. In a classroom where the entire class is taught as a single group, it is often assumed that all pupils learn at the same rate. In reality, some pupils grasp information rapidly; others require much more time. When there is no planning for these differences, pupils who finish quickly may become behavior problems, and those who do not master the material in the allotted time may come to see themselves as failures. Neither of these outcomes is desirable. Individualized instruction that alters the rate of learning makes provision for pupils who learn at different speeds. When this variable is manipulated, the goals, content, and methods of learning remain the same for all pupils. What is changed is the time allowed for individual pupils to complete the learning task.

Altering the rate of learning requires the teacher to break a learning task into several parts, and develop a *criterion task* for each part. Pupils must successfully complete the criterion task for each part before moving on to the next one. Pupils who do not master the criterion task continue to work on instructional material related to the part of the lesson that has proved difficult for them. They are *recycled* back to more learning material related to this lesson part. After doing additional work, they are allowed to attempt the criterion task again. This general approach allows pupils to proceed as quickly or slowly as they need to master individual lessons. Self-paced materials in a programmed learning text or self-paced computer programs are approaches to individualization that alter the rate of learning.

Learning how to develop and use a computer database is a method that is useful in helping pupils learn concepts.

Altering the Content of Learning

In individualized programs that alter the content of learning, different pupils in a class are allowed to study different content to reach a common objective. For example, when the program objective focuses on helping pupils master research and writing skills, individual pupils may be given wide latitude in selecting their personal research topics.

When individualization is attempted by altering the content of learning, pupils may choose the content they will study from among several provided alternatives. This allows them to choose options holding more interest for them than some of the choices they do not commit to. As a result, pupil motivational levels tend to go up. A learning activity package is one format that can alter content of learning. (A complete description of a learning activity package appears later in this chapter.) A typical learning activity package describes the learning goals and suggests several options learners might follow to achieve them.

In individualized programs that vary the content to be learned, some pupils may elect to work alone. Others may choose to work in groups. To succeed, individualized learning that depends on varying content must be supported by many different kinds of learning resources. Such lessons typically demand a considerable amount of teacher planning time.

Altering the Method of Learning

Individualized instruction that focuses on varying the method of learning seeks to respond to pupils' different learning styles. Some people prefer to learn new things by reading about them. Others must see them or touch them. Approaches to individualizing that alter learning method often require all learners to master the same content and objectives, but allow individual members of the class to learn the material in different ways. Often pupils have permission to select from among several alternatives. For example, pupils learning about the role of law in our society may choose to read about this topic, view films or filmstrips, listen to audiotapes, see a videocassette, or participate in a simulation exercise. Pupils may also be allowed to provide evidence of their learning in different ways. Some may choose to participate in a role-play exercise. Others might paint pictures. Still others might compose rap music or write a formal report.

There are general instructional formats that assume that it is desirable to alter the method of learning for individual pupils. Among these are learning activity packages and learning centers.

Altering the Goals of Learning

Instructional programs that respond to the need to individualize by altering the goals of learning are uncommon. This approach allows pupils to make major decisions about what they study and learn. In these days when teachers feel the public is holding them accountable for teaching certain prescribed skills and knowledge to learners, the political environment does not favor widespread adoption of instructional programs that appear to give young learners "too much" control over what they study. Where such programs exist, the teacher functions primarily as a facilitator who tries to sort out and respond to pupils' personal interests. It is an approach that presumes each learner to be the best judge of his instructional needs.

Instructional programs that allow learners to control what is taught and learned are much more common in community education programs than in public schools. Community education course offerings are largely driven by student demand. If enough people want to learn how to play the banjo, usually someone will be found to teach the course. If no one expresses this interest, the course will not be offered.

Table 5–1 summarizes ways in which the four variables discussed can be manipulated to individualize instruction.

EXAMPLES OF FORMAL APPROACHES FOR INDIVIDUALIZING LEARNING

Decisions about which variables to manipulate to individualize instruction reflect teachers' values and school and community expectations. The specific subject matter to be studied also plays a role. For example, it is reasonable to expect all pupils to learn

Table 5–1
Altering variables to individualize instruction.

Variable	Pupil Role	Teacher Role
Learning rate	Works at own pace; seeks assistance when needed.	Makes assignments; monitors work; provides assistance; checks for mastery.
Content	Chooses topics to be studied in achieving goal; finds resources; works alone or with others interested in the same topic; works at own pace.	Sets learning goals; provides alternative topics for study; helps find resources; monitors work; evaluates final product.
Methods	Decides how to study a topic; arranges the environment for study; works at own pace; may work with others interested in doing the same activity.	Establishes goals; identifies content to be learned; provides alternative approaches to learning; monitors work; evaluates final product.
Goals	Chooses own goals to achieve; helps establish criteria for evaluation; submits final product for evaluation when satisfied.	Challenges pupils to consider what is important for them to learn; negotiates goals, evaluation, and timeline with pupils; provides assistance when needed; monitors progress; evaluates final product using criteria established with pupil.

basic arithmetic processes such as adding and subtracting. It is unlikely that teachers would consider allowing pupils to "alter the goals of learning" to avoid dealing with this kind of content. On the other hand, altering methods and pace might make perfectly good sense.

Several formal instructional approaches have been developed as ways of "packaging" individualized instruction, including the following:

- Learning centers
- Learning activity packages
- Activity cards
- Learning contracts

The use of learning centers is an effective method for individualizing instruction.

Learning Centers

Learning centers frequently are used to individualize instruction in elementary social studies programs. They are designated areas of the classroom that contain materials for learning and directions telling pupils what they are to do. Often an attractive visual display at the center is provided to motivate interest in the focus topic. Centers often include a variety of learning resources such as books, pictures, audiotape recorders, computers and software, videocassette players and videotapes, assignment sheets, and study guides.

Fold-down learning centers with cardboard sides, which include general instructions and some needed information, are popular. These can be set up on tables, and are easy to store once lessons requiring their use are over. Figure 5–4 illustrates a learning center that focuses on map and globe skills.

In the learning center illustrated in Figure 5–4, a projector with a filmstrip and an accompanying audiotape recorder with a cassette containing important information have been set up. The earphones allow individual pupils to listen to this information without disturbing others. Pupils may be instructed to use this center one or two at a time. Each pupil is free to go to the center when others are not using it. Often several centers are available for pupils to use. This makes it possible for several pupils to be working in centers at the same time.

Learning centers typically include study guides. A learning center's study guide includes questions pupils must answer and descriptions of activities they are to complete. Figure 5–5 displays a study guide designed for use in the center featured in Figure 5–4.

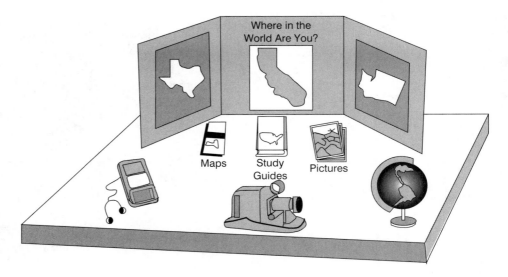

Figure 5–4
A learning center: Map and globe skills.

Learning centers allow teachers to manipulate several of the variables associated with individualized instruction. They can accommodate different rates of learning by allowing pupils to take as much time as they need to respond to questions and complete activities. Methods can be altered by providing pupils with alternative learning options. For example, directions at a learning center may allow pupils to choose ways of getting information from among the alternatives of listening to an audiocassette, reading a prose selection, or looking at a videotape.

When several learning centers are set up at the same time, the teacher may have to establish general time limits. For example, pupils may be told, "All learning center work must be finished by Friday." It is important that pupils be monitored when they are working at centers to assure they are spending their time in a productive way. Pupils who complete their work before slower-working classmates need to be provided with enrichment activities. These will occupy them while others complete their learning center work. Sometimes teachers find it useful to allow talented early finishers to serve as tutors to help other learners.

Learning centers are a good option for teachers who have not had much prior experience in individualizing instruction. Their use does not represent a revolutionary break with familiar classroom routine. As a beginning, a teacher may wish to have only a single learning center. Others can be added as both teacher and pupils become more familiar with the approach.

Good learning centers require careful planning. Care must be taken to establish an appropriate content focus, to decide on appropriate learning activities for pupils, to

Topic: Where in the World Are You?
Grade Level: 4–5
Objective: Pupils can identify the type of map needed to solve a given problem.

Where in the World Are You?

Objective:
When you complete this learning center you should be able to identify different types of maps that are used to solve different problems.

Sequence of Activities:
1.   Take a minute to look at all of the material in the learning center. What do you think is the possible use of each of the things in the center? What do you already know about maps and globes? Write down any questions that you might want to get answered as you work through the center.
2.   Pick up the worksheet that goes with the filmstrip. Look at the filmstrip and listen to the tape. When you have completed the worksheet, turn it in to the teacher. If you do not understand a part of the filmstrip, look at it again until you do or ask the teacher for some help.
3.   Use the maps in the middle of the center to help you answer the following questions.
　 (a)   Which maps are best when trying to compare the population of cities?
　 (b)   Which maps help you compare the elevation of different places?
　 (c)   Which maps help you identify the types things grown in different regions?
　 (d)   Which maps help you compare the size of different places?
　 (e)   Which maps tell you which people have the same government?
4.   *Application Activity:* Construct a map of our community. In your map, decide on something you want to show that is not usually included on a street map. (Examples: the types of stores, the location of apartment houses, the location of traffic lights and stop signs, etc.) Make up symbols for this item and place it on your map. Make sure to include a map legend and an appropriate title for your map. Completed maps will be placed on the bulletin board.

Figure 5–5
Example of learning center study guide.

gather needed learning materials, and to develop directions for center users that are clear enough that pupils will not need to ask for much clarification.

Learning Activity Packages

The *learning activity package* (LAP) provides a way for organizing individualized instruction. LAPS typically include these features:

- Pretest
- List of learning objectives
- Explanation of resources to be used
- Posttest or some other kind of evaluation procedure

To succeed when using LAPs, pupils must have the prerequisite skills and knowledge needed to accomplish the assigned tasks. Otherwise, they will become frustrated when doing work assigned with LAPs and will require a great deal of teacher help.

All of the material and information pupils need to complete work associated with a LAP do not have to be included within the LAP itself. For example, the package may provide instructions directing pupils to information sources such as specific books, newspapers, and evening newscasts.

LAPs are basically instructional management tools. They allow teachers to organize instruction for pupils in convenient packages. They also allow teachers to create individualized packages for learners with specialized needs. For example, materials might be included in a LAP for hearing-impaired pupils allowing them to get information in print form that others might be asked to obtain by listening to audiotapes. A sample LAP is provided in Figure 5–6.

LAPs are useful vehicles for guiding pupils' work on research projects. They provide specific directions to learners regarding what they are to do. Pupils need to be monitored closely while they are doing work associated with LAPs. The teacher needs to help pupils keep busy at their assigned tasks and to counter a tendency many of them have to procrastinate. Careful monitoring also allows teachers to identify and respond to problems individual learners are experiencing.

LAPs allow teachers to alter the rate of learning, the method of learning, and even the content of learning. Pupils complete LAPs at their own pace. They may have opportunities to select from among several alternative learning activities. Sometimes LAPs give pupils choices in kinds of content they may use to fulfill LAP assignment requirements.

Activity Cards

Activity cards describe choices pupils have as they decide how to go about learning assigned tasks. Each card focuses on one learning objective and suggests kinds of tasks students might complete to master the material. Typically a set of activity cards focuses on the same general topic. Each card deals with a part of the topic.

Activity cards can be used in several ways. One approach is to assign certain cards to individual pupils based on their special needs and interests. Another is to allow pupils to select cards focusing on a particular part of the general topic being studied. Teachers often begin work with activity cards by using them as extra credit assignments for pupils who complete other work.

Activity cards are easy to organize and store; a large number can fit in a card file or shoebox. New cards can be added as they are developed. Cards can be kept from year to year and easily modified to accommodate changes in the overall grade-level social

Topic: Primary Sources
Grade Level: 5
Objective: Pupils can identify primary sources
and their importance when studying history.

I. *Pretest*

This learning activity package is about primary sources. If you know what a *primary source* is, answer the following questions and take your answers to the teacher. If you do not know, skip the questions and begin with the introduction.

  1. What is a primary source?
  2. Is our social studies textbook a primary source?
  3. Why are primary sources important when learning about history?

II. *Introduction*

When you read our social studies textbook, do you ever wonder how the writers found out about the events they describe? They were not alive and were not participants in most of these events. How do they know what really happened, and how do we know they are giving us an accurate description?

When you read an account of an event, it is important to know about the accuracy of the description. Most people have to rely on the descriptions provided by others. The descriptions of those who were present are probably the most accurate. Information tends to get confused when it is passed from person to person. People also forget things that happened to them a long time ago. You may recall how stories have changed when you have heard them from different people and some time after they have happened. The same thing is true in history and sometimes the stories we read about historical events are quite different from what actually happened. By completing this LAP you will learn some ways of checking to see if the descriptions of events are accurate.

III. *Objectives*

When you have completed this LAP you will be able to:

  1. Define a primary source.
  2. Define a secondary source.
  3. Identify an example of a primary source.
  4. State how primary sources are used to check the accuracy of a description of an event.

Figure 5–6
A learning activity package.

studies program. Particularly with older elementary pupils, teachers have found it useful to have learners develop activity cards of their own on topics of interest to them. Pupil-developed activity cards sometimes include marvelously imaginative activity suggestions. The process of participating in the development of their own learning tasks can give pupils a motivating sense of ownership in the instructional program.

IV. *Activities*
Definition. A *primary source* is a person or a record written by a person who was a participant or an actual observer of an event. For example, individuals who attended a baseball game or who played in the game would be considered primary sources. Someone who only read about it in the newspaper would not be. Other records, such as pictures, films, or notes written by the coaches or other observers, would also be considered primary sources. Newspaper accounts, stories told by people who did not attend the game but only heard about it would not be primary sources–they would be secondary sources. If your friend attended the game and told you about it, he or she would be a primary source. If you told someone else what they said, you would be a secondary source.

1.   Which of the following are most likely to be primary sources in learning about the American War for Independence?
       (a) A diary of a soldier who was in the war.
       (b) A movie about the war.
       (c) Our social studies textbook.
       (d) The letters of one general to another.

2.   Read the story "The Shot Heard Around the World" in our social studies textbook. Next read the diary account of the British soldier. Identify how the two stories are different. Why do you think they are different?
3.   Why do you think it would be important to use primary sources when trying to determine what happened? Do you think just one primary source would be enough?
4.   If you were to write an account of how our school has changed in the past 10 years, what would be some primary sources that you could use?

V. *Evaluation*
Choose an event from the recent history of our nation or community. Identify some people or some records that could be considered primary sources. If you identify people, ask them to describe the event to you on a cassette tape. You may need to think of some questions to ask those people. Then write your own account of the event. The teacher can help you with this. When you finish, turn in your account and the material you used, such as the tape, to the teacher.

Figure 5–6
continued

Activity cards are useful vehicles for integrating content from many subject areas. For example, an activity card on the westward movement could well include activities drawing on mathematics, the arts, science, music, and other subjects. Figure 5–7 illustrates examples of three activity cards that were developed for use in an elementary social studies class.

Activity Card I

Topic: The Division of Labor
Grade Level: Primary
Purpose: The pupil will state examples of the division of labor.

Activities
1. Look through the magazines in the learning center.
2. Cut out five pictures of jobs that people are doing.
3. For each job, write one sentence describing how this job helps other people.
4. Draw a picture of a job that you have at home.
5. Write a sentence telling how your job helps your family.

Activity Card 2

Topic: Goods and Services
Grade Level: Upper Elementary
Purpose: The pupil will identify businesses that provide goods and those that provide services.

Activities
1. Look through the Yellow Pages. Make a chart like the one below. In the "Goods" column, place at least ten businesses that provide goods. In the "Services" column, place at least ten businesses that provide services. Identify at least three businesses that provide both goods and services.

Goods	Services	Both

2. Interview a relative or friend. Find out whether his or her job provides a good or service. Identify what she or he must know to provide this good or service.

Activity Card 3

Topic: Local History
Grade Level: Middle Elementary
Purpose: The pupil will research an event in local history.

Activities
1. Are there any historical markers or important historical sites in our community? If there is a marker, visit this site. Write down what the marker says. Talk with other people in the community to find out what they might know about the event described on the historical marker.
2. Once you have gathered information about the event, do one of the following:
(a) Prepare an oral report about the event.
(b) Draw a picture of the event.
(c) Write a play about the event, and act it out for the class.

Figure 5–7
Activity card examples.

Learning Contracts

A *learning contract* is an agreement between a teacher and an individual pupil. It states what the pupil agrees to do to satisfy certain learning requirements. The contract is signed by both the teacher and the pupil to indicate that both understand and agree to its terms. Learning contracts are of two types, open and closed.

Open Learning Contracts

Open learning contracts give the pupil a great deal of choice over such issues as the topic to be studied, the objectives, the learning activities, the assignments, and the criteria and procedures to be used for evaluation. They are most suitable for use with motivated, independent, mature learners. However, one of the authors had considerable success in using open learning contracts with some rebellious pupils who had refused to do any schoolwork. When they found they had some voice in what they would do and how they would do it, they could no longer fall back on many of the excuses they had used to justify doing nothing. Many of these students got busy and proved to themselves that they really could be successful learners.

Closed Learning Contracts

Closed learning contracts are more common than open learning contracts. In contracts of this type, the teacher plays a more dominant role. The teacher on the basis of his best professional judgment identifies the objectives, describes learning activities and assignments, and lays out criteria and procedures for evaluating the learner's work.

A basic difference between a learning contract and many other schemes for packaging individualized instruction is that a given contract is designed specifically for a particular pupil. It is designed with a clear focus on this person's unique interests and aptitudes. Specific formatting of learning contracts varies, but large numbers of them include the following descriptions:

- What the pupil is to do.
- What resources are to be used.
- What kind of learning "product" the pupil is to produce.
- What procedures will be used for evaluation.
- When all work is to be completed.

If you want to use learning contracts with learners who have never experienced this approach before, the best advice is to "think easy and think simple." It is important for pupils to understand exactly what they are to do to experience success. Success enhances self-esteem and increases motivation. A learner who succeeds on an initial learning contract will be much more interested in trying another one than a learner who fails. A sample learning contract is presented in Figure 5–8.

Learning Contract

Date _____

Topic:

Objective:

I, _____ agree to do the following social studies activities:

1.
2.
3.
4.

My work will be evaluated/graded using the following criteria:

1.
2.
3.

I agree to have all work completed by _____.

_____   _____
Student Signature   Teacher Signature

Figure 5–8
Sample learning contract.

KEY IDEAS IN SUMMARY

1. Concepts are labels that describe phenomena that share certain characteristics. Generalizations are statements of relationship among concepts. They are succinct statements that summarize what the best available evidence tells us is "true." Because of the explanatory power of concepts and generalizations, specific techniques have been developed for teaching them to elementary pupils.

2. All of the defining attributes must be present for something to be considered a proper example of a conjunctive concept. A disjunctive concept may have several defining attributes, but it is not necessary for all of them to be present at the same time for something to be considered a proper example of this concept category. Relational concepts have attributes that bear a specific kind of relationship to one another. Generally, disjunctive and relational concepts are more difficult for pupils to learn than conjunctive concepts. Concepts that have large numbers of defining attributes are also difficult.

3. The concept-attainment technique focuses on teaching certain concepts that the teacher has selected for pupils to learn. The following steps are typically followed in a concept-attainment lesson: The teacher (1) introduces the concept by name, (2) presents examples of the concept, (3) presents nonexamples of the concept, (4) provides a mixture of examples and nonexamples of the concept, (5) asks pupils to define the concept, (6) provides opportunities for pupils to apply their understanding by finding additional examples of the concept.

4. The concept-formation/diagnosis approach can be used to provide pupils with experience in forming concepts of their own. Lessons with this focus familiarize pupils with the process of forming concepts and, at the same time, provide the teacher with useful diagnostic information regarding misconceptions some pupils may have. The following steps are typical of concept-formation/diagnosis lessons: (1) pupils respond to a stimulus, usually an open-ended question posed by the teacher, that is designed to elicit a large volume of pupil-generated information; (2) pupils are asked to organize the information they have generated into categories and to describe the basis for their grouping decisions; (3) pupils develop labels for each category that clearly define characteristics of the items grouped together under each label.

5. The inducing-a-generalization technique helps pupils arrive at an explanatory generalization by applying their own logical thinking skills. The teacher begins by selecting a well-validated generalization and finding specific examples that support its truth. The learners are presented only with this evidence. They are challenged to develop an explanatory generalization that is consistent with the evidence. These steps typically are followed: (1) pupils look at the evidence the teacher has gathered and organize it into categories; (2) pupils compare and contrast information and note relationships; and (3) pupils develop an explanatory generalization that explains noted relationships and that can be applied to other situations.

6. Individualized instruction seeks to meet the diverse needs of pupils in the classroom. It does not imply that each pupil should work independently of others. Some individual needs are best met when pupils work together.

7. Approaches to individualizing instruction manipulate one or more of four variables: (1) rate of learning, (2) content to be learned, (3) method of learning, and (4) goals of learning. The rate of learning variable is probably the one that is altered most frequently. Lessons that permit pupils to alter the goals of learning are rare.

8. Learning centers are frequently used to individualize instruction in elementary social studies classes. Learning centers are designated classroom areas where specific information is provided for pupils regarding what they are to do to accomplish certain learning task, and which resources they are to use as they work. Sometimes several learning centers are set up at the same time in a single classroom. Learning centers may be used to supplement or replace whole-class instruction. Learning centers provide a means for individualizing instruction by allowing for different learning rates and different methods of learning.

9. Learning activity packages (LAPs) represent another way of packaging individualized instruction. LAPs typically include (1) a pretest, (2) a list of activities to be completed, (3) an explanation of resources that can be used, (4) a posttest or some other means of evaluation. LAPs can be used with learners who have varying interests and instructional needs. They allow for manipulation of a number of the variables associated with individualized instruction.

10. Activity cards are easy to prepare. They provide a useful means of responding to individual learner differences. Sets of cards often provide activities related to a general focus topic. Individual cards often concentrate on parts of this broad topic. Cards offer teachers opportunities to create a variety of activities from which learners can choose to accomplish assigned tasks. Information on cards can be varied to accomplish a variety of special pupil needs. Activity cards are easy to store, and may be deleted or modified easily to accommodate programmatic changes and changes in pupil needs.

11. Learning contracts are agreements between the teacher and an individual pupil. They describe (1) what academic work the pupil will do, (2) what resources may be used, (3) the kind of learning "product" that will be created, (4) how the product will be evaluated, and (5) when the work will be completed. Open contracts allow for the individual pupil to play a role as an equal partner to the teacher in negotiating the contract components. Closed contracts, which are much more common, include terms that are largely made by the teacher and then provided to the pupil in contract form.

CHAPTER REFLECTIONS

Directions: Now that you have read the chapter, reread the case study at the beginning, then answer these questions:

1. How might you respond to issues of bias and perspective when preparing social studies lessons designed to help pupils learn a selected focus generalization?

2. How does the identification of a focus generalization provide guidance for content selection?

3. Are there so many values issues involved that selection of generalizations to guide content selection for elementary social studies programs doesn't make much sense? Why, or why not?

4. How would you defend the use of focus generalizations to others?

5. The "truth" of a generalization can be tested by referring to supporting evidence. Is this also true of concepts? Why, or why not?

6. What is meant by the phrase "inducing generalizations?"

7. What kinds of things can be altered when planning for individualized instruction? What are some advantages and disadvantages of altering each of these variables?

8. Which of the teaching approaches discussed in the chapter would you feel most comfortable with? Why?

EXTENDING UNDERSTANDING AND SKILL

1. Much has been written about concept learning and concept teaching. Review several articles in journals such as *Social Education* and *The Social Studies* that deal with these topics. Take notes on a specific technique for teaching a concept. Share your information with others.

2. Individualized instruction demands careful planning. Planning takes time. Interview several teachers at a grade level that interests you. Ask them how they feel about individualizing, particularly in terms of how any attempts to individualize have affected their planning time.

3. Select a social studies topic and learning objective. Prepare a set of activity cards. Include opportunities for pupils to make choices. Share your materials with others.

4. Prepare a rough sketch of a proposed learning center. List the learning resources you would include were you to set your learning center up in a classroom. Check with your instructor about where to get ideas of the kinds of resources schools might be expected to have available to support this kind of instruction.

5. Work together with two or three others in your class to develop a learning activity package. Choose your own focus topic and a grade level of potential users of your material.

REFERENCES

FRAENKEL, J. R. (1980). *Helping Students Think and Value*, 2nd ed. Englewood Cliffs, NJ: Prentice-Hall.

TABA, H. (1967). *Handbook for Elementary Social Studies*. Reading, MA: Addison-Wesley.

6

GROUP LEARNING

CHAPTER GOALS

This chapter provides information to help the reader:

- recognize the importance of group learning experiences in the social studies program,
- differentiate among basic group types,
- describe the procedures that can be used to prepare learners for group learning experiences,
- state what a teacher must do to plan and implement classroom debates, role-playing lessons, and simulations, and
- list the characteristics of several different cooperative learning techniques.

CHAPTER STRUCTURE

Introduction
Basic Group Types
    The Tutoring Group
    The Equal Roles Group
    The Assigned Roles Group
Preparing Pupils to Work in Groups
    Two-by-Two
    Think-Pair-Share
    Inside-Outside
    Numbered Heads Together
    Buzz Session
Three Popular Group Techniques: Classroom Debate, Role Playing, and Simulation
    Classroom Debate
    Role Playing
    Simulations
    Overview / Training / Activity / Debriefing
Cooperative Learning Techniques
Jigsaw
Learning Together
    Teams Achievement Divisions
Key Ideas in Summary
Chapter Reflections
Extending Understanding and Skill
References

Figure 6–1
Group learning.

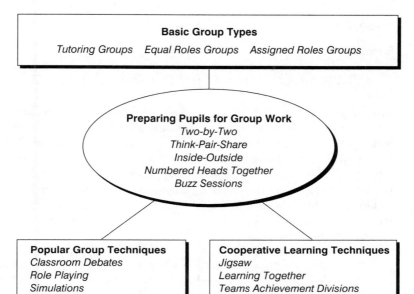

Basic Group Types

Tutoring Groups   Equal Roles Groups   Assigned Roles Groups

Preparing Pupils for Group Work
Two-by-Two
Think-Pair-Share
Inside-Outside
Numbered Heads Together
Buzz Sessions

Popular Group Techniques
Classroom Debates
Role Playing
Simulations

Cooperative Learning Techniques
Jigsaw
Learning Together
Teams Achievement Divisions

Chapter 6

Case Study

DOES GROUP WORK INHIBIT INDIVIDUAL DEVELOPMENT?

Third-grade teacher Ping Yee attended a workshop this summer focusing on small-group work in elementary social studies. She came back to her school eager to implement some of the procedures she had learned. Ms. Yee's principal, Gretchen Stein, thought third graders might benefit from some of the techniques introduced in the workshop. To familiarize parents with these approaches, she asked Ping to address the parents at a meeting of the school's parent-teachers organization. Ping agreed to do so.

On the night of the meeting, most parents seemed supportive. A few were noncommittal. But two or three argued against using more small-group techniques. Their arguments included these points:

- Small-group activities allow individuals to "hide." It is easy for a child to become lazy and let other group members do the real work.
- Small groups put bright pupils at a disadvantage. They end up doing the work for less able learners. This isn't fair. It inhibits the development of less able pupils because, in small groups, they are not held individually accountable for their own work.
- History shows that groups can put severe psychological pressures on individuals who do not see things the way most in the group see them. This can be dangerous. Group pressures can force sensitive young people to publicly express views they don't hold. At best, this promotes lying. It may even do psychological damage to youngsters who do not understand why their views are always seen as "wrong."
- In the "real world," people are held accountable for their actions as individuals and not for the actions of the groups of which they may be a part.

What Is Your Response?

Think about these parents' concerns. Then, respond briefly to these questions:

1. Does small-group learning allow some pupils to escape responsibility for their own actions? If there is a possibility this might happen, what action might a teacher take to remedy it?
2. How do you feel about the claim that bright pupils are required to carry an unfairly heavy load when small-group instruction is used? What evidence from your own experience both supports and argues against this point of view?
3. Do members of small instructional groups in school have the power to exert too much pressure on individual group members? Why, or why not?
4. In the "real world," are individuals treated as they are treated because of what they do as individuals, or because of their membership in certain groups? What evidence could be presented in support of each position? How do you personally feel about this issue?

Successful small-group activities are preceded by a careful examination of what is to be accomplished and what are each group member's responsibilities.

5. Most opposition to increasing the amount of small-group work in third-grade social studies classes is directed against small-group instruction in general. Are some kinds of small-group instruction more likely to cause difficulties than others, or do these concerns apply equally to all small-group techniques? Explain your answer.

INTRODUCTION

Nearly all school instruction is a form of group instruction. Most teaching involves a teacher working with a number of pupils in a classroom. This familiar scene is an example of what might be termed *large-group instruction*. We will use the term *group learning* in a more restricted sense in this chapter to refer to instructional groups ranging in size from about 2 to 15 learners.

In recent years there has been a trend toward more use of group learning. One reason this has happened is that we now know more about the learning process than we used to. A number of learning theorists now believe that learning is more likely to occur when pupils are actively engaged in organizing new information and connecting it previous knowledge (Winitzky, 1991). Ways of organizing learners that maximize their opportunities to engage new material and identify connections with prior knowledge are desirable. Small-group work, properly used, allows for this kind of active pupil exploration.

Another advantage of group work is that it allows individuals to work closely with others who may have different learning styles (Jarolimek & Foster, 1993). Exposure to alternative learning styles broadens pupils' receptivity to information delivered in different ways and helps them to develop more comprehensive and sophisticated problem-solving approaches.

The popularity of group learning has also been abetted by the development of a number of specific instructional approaches that emphasize it, and that include well-defined roles for both teachers and learners. The sophistication of these techniques gives direction to us as we plan to use group approaches and helps us deal with the complaint of some skeptics that group work is merely "sharing ignorance."

Group learning is especially important in social studies. Studies indicate that group learning is used more frequently in this part of the school curriculum than in other subjects. There are several reasons for this. The term *social studies* implies human interaction. Further, some of the intended outcomes of group learning are congruent with the goals of social studies (Winitzky, 1991). These include acquiring the skills necessary for participation in a democratic society, developing an appreciation for racial and ethnic differences, working productively with others, respecting the opinions of others, understanding individual differences, contributing to the welfare of the group, developing positive self-concepts, and accepting a variety of viewpoints.

Group learning approaches vary in the number of pupils assigned to a group. The numbers assigned vary in terms of the purposes of the group activity and the prior experiences of the pupils. Some group activities can accommodate fairly large groups of learners. Others work best when only two or three pupils are working together. Pupils who have little or no previous experience working with groups may need to start by first working with only one or two other pupils and then moving into larger groupings as they acquire the necessary skills. Many classroom groups function well with four to six pupil members. This number seems to work well when the expectation is that group members will discuss content (Cohen, 1986).

Group learning has several advantages for the elementary social studies classroom. Instruction that organizes learners to facilitate idea exchange and high participation levels helps to refine learners' abilities to work well with others. Group learning makes sense for the teacher in other ways. New teachers are often amazed at the range of individual differences within a given classroom. Lessons directed at an entire class often fail to meet needs of some class members. Organizing pupils into smaller groups allows you to respond more directly to particular needs of individual learners and use the range of skills and abilities in a positive manner.

There is evidence that group learning helps to develop warmer relationships between teachers and learners (Olmstead, 1974). This occurs for several reasons, First of all, breaking the class into small groups allows teachers and pupils an opportunity to work together on a more personal basis. This allows pupils to hear better and to feel they are more important as individuals. Additionally, the teacher is better able to appreciate how pupils are reacting to lesson content, and can respond more quickly when

Working in groups facilitates idea exchange and leads to higher levels of pupil involvement.

learners signal confusion or disinterest. The ability of the teacher to adjust instruction as needed often results in enhanced levels of learner success and motivation.

Levels of active pupil involvement increase in small-group work. In part, this occurs because it is difficult to avoid participating when relatively few people are involved. Second, participation is less intimidating. Many learners who hesitate to speak before the entire class willingly participate as members of a small group. Thus small-group learning is especially appropriate for pupils who need to learn oral language skills. This is especially the case for those pupils who may have limited English proficiency.

An important side effect of enhanced levels of learner participation is an increase in individual learners' commitment to decisions made by their group. This occurs because the group experience fosters a sense of "ownership" in decisions. In large-group instructional settings, pupils are less likely to develop such allegiances to conclusions emerging from discussions of issues.

Certainly there are difficulties associated with group learning approaches. For example, we have to engage in careful planning for these approaches to be successful. Pupils need to understand exactly what they are to do and what the expected learning outcome is. They may not know how to work productively with others and how to develop and share ideas in the context of a group. What all this means is we need to provide students with specific instruction on how to work in groups. We also have to be careful how we assign specific individuals to groups. For example, little is gained by organizing a group to "discuss" a controversial issue if, at the outset, each group member holds the same opinion.

In addition, there are always some pupils who are not enthusiastic about working in groups. This may be true of individuals who have been successful in a competitive classroom environment. They tend to think they can do the task better by themselves. They may be reluctant to share their success with others or to compromise their ideas. Sometimes they will simply take over the work and do it by themselves. We have to convince them of the value of working and sharing with others.

This chapter introduces some basic group types; suggests procedures for introducing learners to group work; discusses ways to implement classroom debates, role-playing exercises, and simulations; and points out several cooperative learning approaches.

BASIC GROUP TYPES

Successful group learning lessons do not just happen. They are preceded by careful planning. An important consideration during this planning phase is the purpose to be served by the group activity. Once we are sure of the purposes we want served by group instruction, we can move along confidently to select a particular group activity or set of activities.

Many group organizational schemes represent modifications of three basic group types:

Important responsibilities of for teachers during group work activities are monitoring of group progress and arbitrating disagreements.

- The tutoring group
- The equal roles group
- The assigned roles group

The Tutoring Group

This basic type may be used for two distinct purposes. First, it may be organized to help learners who may be having trouble mastering content introduced in a large-group setting. Second, it may be organized to provide enrichment experiences for pupils who are capable of doing more sophisticated work than that introduced to the class as a whole.

In the tutoring group, our role does not vary greatly from the role we play when working with the whole class. In general, it is a role of directive leadership. We provide general instructions, explain content, and lead discussions.

Pupils are encouraged to participate actively during tutoring group sessions. Often, because of the relatively small number of pupils involved, learners are more inclined to speak up in small-group situations than when a discussion includes all members of class. In the tutoring group, pupils are usually seated close to the teacher. This physical proximity also tends to increase their willingness to participate actively in lessons.

Preparing learners for a tutoring group experience is not difficult. In a large mea-sure, they will be doing work similar to what they have always done in larger, whole-class settings. A few learners may experience initial discomfort as they realize there is "no place to hide" and that they will be expected to participate. If we provide them with a few supportive comments, these anxieties ordinarily can be overcome.

Instructing a tutoring group demands our undivided attention. We have to make arrangements for members of the class who are not in the group. These people must have meaningful tasks to work on while the tutoring group is in session, and they must be supervised. (See Box 6–1.). Sometimes it is possible for some learners to work with aides or other paraprofessional personnel. Parent volunteers occasionally are available to work with some learners. Others might be involved in work with the school librarian or at a media center.

The Equal Roles Group

The equal roles group is used most frequently in elementary social studies classes to involve learners in solving a problem. In implementing this approach, we provide members of the class with experiences designed to make them more familiar with sys-tematic approaches to resolving issues. One widely used problem-solving scheme involves these steps (for more information on problem solving, see Chapter 7, "Devel-oping Thinking Skills"):

- Identify the problem.
- Consider possible approaches.
- Select and apply approaches.
- Reach a defensible conclusion.

BOX 6–1   **Planning Meaningful Work for Other Learners While Working with a Tutoring Group**

Working with a tutoring group is an intensive activity for both teacher and learners. The teacher must devote undivided attention to the group members. This means that plans must be made to occupy other learners in a meaningful way.

Suppose you had 25 pupils in your class, and you are thinking about working with a tutoring group that includes 5 of them. If the tutoring group activity is to succeed, you must have special plans for the other 20 students. Perhaps you will have all of them do a common activity, or perhaps you will involve them in several small-group activities.

Think About This

1. Develop two separate plans for dealing with these 20 learners. What features will each plan have?
2. How will the pupils be supervised?

In the equal roles group, all pupils are required to participate in each step of the process. Often, we assign a group leader to take general charge of the investigation. Other than this role, there are no specialized roles that pupils will assume, although sometimes a group recorder is assigned to take notes on decisions that are reached.

We begin by explaining the problem to be solved. The following problem might be given to a group of sixth graders who are beginning a unit of study on Eastern Europe: "Why are the various groups in the region known as Bosnia fighting with each other?" We have to give group members specific guidelines regarding what we expect to result from their group investigation. They need to know whether they will be required to develop an oral presentation, write a group paper, conduct a role play, participate in a debate, construct a model, or create a mural.

Once the issue is identified, we go on to explain steps to be followed. We must present clear directions as to the activities that the group can engage in. If pupils are going to be allowed to leave the room, we must give them guidelines for doing so. They also need to know what materials are available for their use. Time limits or guidelines should also be presented so that they can gauge their progress. It is often useful for us to present a model or an example so that the group members will have some knowledge of what they are to do. We also have to ensure that sufficient learning materials are available for pupils to use. As the activity develops, we need to circulate among groups to make sure that all members are participating and to respond to questions.

We also play an important role at the conclusion of the exercise. At this time, we challenge conclusions, call on pupils to defend ideas by referring to evidence they have gathered, and ask why other solutions or explanations to the "problem" might not be equally good. This phase of the lesson needs to be handled sensitively. For many pupils, the experience of developing conclusions of their own will be unfamiliar. We need to support their ideas while at the same time asking them to think about alternative answers.

As was true with the tutoring group, we need to make arrangements for learners who will not be involved when we plan lessons that feature equal roles group instruction. Sometimes, it is possible for the entire class to be organized into four or five separate equal roles groups. When this happens, we move quickly from group to group to monitor activities. In situations where multiple groups are at work, it is probable that some groups will complete the assigned task more quickly than others. We need to have a plan regarding what these "early finishers" should do.

The Assigned Roles Group

In the assigned roles group, each member has a particular task assignment (Cohen, 1986). This means that each pupil must do her work if the group as a whole is to have complete information at the conclusion of the activity. Assigned roles groups may work in several ways. In one type, each pupil becomes a specialist or an expert on some part of the assigned task. The scheme is often used when we want learners to be exposed to complex content that can be conveniently divided into parts. For example, fifth graders usually study American history. Often, information about the English colonies is introduced under the headings "New England Colonies," "Middle Colonies," and "Southern Colonies."

If we were teaching a fifth-grade class, we might organize members of the class into assigned roles groups of six or so pupils each. Individual members would be assigned to answer certain questions about (1) family life and religion and (2) locations of major towns and settlements in each of the three colonial regions (a total of six topics).

In another arrangement, we might assign each individual a specific role to play in the group. The roles that might be assigned include facilitator, recorder, timekeeper, materials organizer, and illustrator (the specific roles will vary according to the task and the final product). This assigned role format allows for the incorporation of a wide range of skills. Therefore, heterogeneous grouping becomes a strength for a group. Individuals who are good readers can contribute, as can those who are creative or who might have artistic abilities. All pupils can feel like they are important members of the group and that their particular skills are respected. Overall, the group project can be better than a collection of individual projects.

Sometimes assigned roles groups are organized to familiarize learners with perspectives of groups who see a common problem in different ways. Often controversial current events lend themselves well to lessons of this kind. For example, we might organize learners into groups of four, with each group focusing on a specific perspective regarding the involvement of the United States in Bosnia. One group could represent the Serbs, another the Bosnians, and a third citizens of the United States. Following study within these groups, we could reorganize the class into new groups that would include one pupil from each of the former groups. Each new group would have an expert on the perspectives of each of the parties with interests in Bosnia. In the new groups, individual "experts" can share their perspectives with others.

The teacher plays an important role during the debriefing phase of the lesson. We have to assure that all pupils have an opportunity to share their information and that all members of the group understand it. We also have to be prepared to respond to ques-

Identify a grade you would like to teach. Research the topics normally taught at this grade level. Next, identify a topic that might be suitable for presentation via an assigned roles group activity. Define five different roles that pupils might fulfill in the group activity. State how the activity would be introduced and how the pupils would be taught the role they would fulfill. Pay careful attention to the management aspect of assigning pupils to the groups and breaking the class into small groups. Define any roles or procedures you would use. Finally, define what the teacher would do during the group activity.

Figure 6–2
Designing an assigned roles group activity.

tions and clarify confusing points. Sometimes it works well to encourage learners to write major points of information they have discovered on the chalkboard or on a large piece of butcher paper. (For the above example, the labels "United States," "Serbs," and "Bosnians," would be written. Pupils would write major points at the appropriate places under these labels.) This procedure allows us to help learners make comparisons and contrasts using the information written under the various categories.

As is true for all small-group learning lessons, we have to make plans for pupils who will not be participating in the small-group activity. Procedures followed when using assigned roles group techniques parallel those used with tutoring group and equal roles group lessons (Figure 6–2).

PREPARING PUPILS TO WORK IN GROUPS

Experiences of learners in different classrooms vary. Some may not have had much experience in working in groups. When this is the case, attempts to use group work may be unsuccessful. To enhance the likelihood that small-group assignments will be successful, we have found it useful to put learners through experiences designed to orient them to group work and help them achieve success and satisfaction from the experience.

When first introducing group work, we need to give members of our class a good reason for doing it. They need to understand why they are engaged in this activity. We might point out that this kind of activity will help them learn skills of working together that will be valuable to them in life. We need to help them appreciate the importance of sharing information and participating in democratic decision making. It is important that the initial group activities have very clear, concrete outcomes. Pupils need to have success so that they can gain satisfaction from the experience and begin to see the value of group activity. Group work that produces a clear, tangible result provides a "product" that gives pupils evidence something worthwhile has occurred.

The first tasks that are chosen should be those that rather naturally incorporate a variety of skills and abilities. They should invite collaboration and make it desirable.

This provides them with an incentive to work together. Early on, it is best to have short group activities that are worked regularly into the lessons rather than a long-term group project. These short-term activities allow pupils the opportunity to begin building group process skills and to experiment with different approaches.

It is extremely important that consistent routines and procedures for group work be established and taught to the class. Pupils need to know how to move to groups, how to get materials, what their particular role involves, what to do if there is a question or a problem, and what to do when the activity is completed. Teaching these routines and constantly reinforcing them will help ensure that the group work is efficient and productive. In addition, it helps prevent teacher stress!

Small-group approaches that can be used to acquaint pupils with group activities and allow them to learn how to work productively together include two-by-two, think-pair-share, inside-outside, numbered heads together, and buzz sessions.

Two-By-Two

This approach is especially useful in helping break the ice when forming a new classroom group. To initiate the activity, ask each pupil to find out a specific bit of information about one other person. Once this has been done, pairs of pupils are joined to form groups of 4. Members of the groups share and try to remember the information about all 4 individuals. The groups of 4 are then joined to form groups of 8, the groups of 8 joined to form groups of 16, and the groups of 16 to form one large group. At each stage, pupils are to try and remember information about each person. The multiplication of group size can be conducted up to the size we feel appropriate, given the age and maturity levels of people in our class, and the class size.

Teachers who have never used two-by-two's before are often astonished at the large number of learners who will be able to provide information about everybody in the class at the end of the activity. The exercise makes learners more comfortable with one another, and builds a sense of cohesiveness. Learners who know something about one another tend to settle into academically oriented group work better than those who are assigned to work with comparative strangers.

Lesson Idea 6–1

WORKING IN GROUPS: TWO-BY-TWO

Grade Level:	3–6 (earlier grades with clear instructions and careful monitoring)
Objectives:	Pupils will (1) gain information about their classmates, (2) learn how to work together, and (3) develop a sense of cohesion and friendship in the classroom.
Overview:	This exercise is particularly useful as an "ice breaker" at the beginning of the school year when learners in a class may not know each other well. The example is designed for a

class of 32; group size must be adjusted for smaller or larger classes.

Procedure:

Learning Set   Relate to the class the importance of making friends. Remind them that this class of individuals will be spending a lot of time together over the new year and in order for it to be a fun classroom, making friends is important. Inform them that the beginning of making friends is learning about other people. Today, they are going to learn something about others in the class.

Presentation

Give the following instructions for the seven steps of the exercise.

Step 1   Listen carefully. Do not do anything until I say "Ready . . . go." I want each of you to stand up. Then, walk over and find somebody you don't know well. You will have half a minute to do this. Any questions? (Respond to questions, if any.) Ready . . . go! (Each pupil finds a partner.)

Step 2   I want you to find out three things about your partner. First, find out your partner's name. Second, find out your partner's birthday. Third, ask what your partner would do if someone gave him or her $300 that had to be spent this Saturday. You will have two minutes to do this. (Pupils follow instructions in this and each subsequent step. Monitor activities and call "time" when the limit is reached for each step.)

Step 3   You have done very well. Now let's make things more interesting. I want you and your partner to get together with another pair of partners. This will make a group of four. When you have formed your groups of four, I want each of you to tell the three other members of the group the things you learned about your partner. Remember these are (1) your partner's name, (2) your partner's birthday, and (3) what your partner would do with $300 that they must spend this Saturday. I want everybody in the group to try to remember the answers for each group member. You will have four minutes to do this. Are there questions? Ready . . . go!

Step 4   Now you are really going to be challenged. I want each group of four to get together with another group of four. This will create a group of eight. Do the same thing in the group of eight as you did in your groups of four. That is, take turns providing information about your partner. I want all of you to try and remember information about everybody in your group. Are there questions? You will have six minutes to do this. Ready . . . go!

Step 5   Now let's find out who our memory champions are. I want each group of eight to get together with another group of eight to make a group of sixteen. Follow the same procedure as before. You'll have eight minutes this time. Ready . . . go!

Step 6   Now it's time to really stretch our memories. Let's all get together in a giant circle. Then, I want you to use the same process as before. Let's do this for about eight minutes. Are there any questions? Ready . . . go!

Step 7   Now, is there anybody who can provide all three items of information about everybody in the group? Who wants to start? (if there are learners willing to try, call on them. Provide supporting comments. If no one wants to try this, ask if anyone can provide one or two items about each person in the class.) Are there others who would like to try? (Process continues until as many pupils as wish to volunteer have had a chance to participate.)

Closure: Ask the class, "What did we learn today? What did you learn about listening to other people? What did you learn about remembering information? How might we use what we have learned in other situations?"

Think-Pair-Share

This introduces the idea of small-group learning by getting the pupils together in groups of two. In this technique we begin by giving the class a question or a problem. In the first phase, each student is to think individually about the question or problem. After a short time, we give a signal, and pupils then begin to work in pairs to share their responses. When the pairs have had ample opportunity to discuss, each pair shares its responses with the rest of the class (McTighe & Lyman, 1988).

An advantage of the "think-pair-share" approach is that it helps pupils learn how to discuss and share their ideas with others. It can help them learn that "two heads are often better than one." The technique also helps pupils to understand the importance of integrating ideas and of compromising.

Inside-Outside

This approach is useful in helping pupils begin to learn effective group work skills. In this method, one group, the "outsides," observe the working of another group, the "insides." Each member of the outside group is assigned to watch one person and is told to look for some specific things. It is sometimes best for them to take notes on their observations. The inside group is given a task to complete or a problem to discuss. When the inside group has completed the task or had ample time to discuss the issue, the groups change places. Members of the new outside group are reminded of their assignments. When the new inside group has completed its task or has had ample time for discussion, the whole class then is pulled together, and individuals share the types of things that contributed to the success of the group.

Pupils who have had an opportunity to participate in this type of an activity tend to work more productively when they are assigned to participate in group learning than those who have not. Sometimes the authors use inside-outside with our classes several times during the year to reinforce good group work skills.

Lesson Idea 6–2

WORKING TOGETHER: INSIDE-OUTSIDE

Grade Level:	4–6
Objectives:	Pupils will participate in a class discussion and identify behaviors that contribute to a productive discussion.
Overview:	Small-group learning requires learning group work skills. Many pupils are unaware of the behaviors that contribute to successful group work. This procedure helps them begin to learn group work skills by having them observe others and identify those behaviors that contribute to productive work. Learners who go through an exercise of this type tend to work more productively when they are assigned to participate in group learning activities than are those who have not. Sometimes teachers use inside-outside several times during the school year to reinforce good group participation skills. Pupils tend to like the activity.
Procedures:	***Learning Set*** Ask the class, "How many have watched team sports such as basketball or football? What happens if one person on the team tries to do everything and doesn't work with the other players on the team? The team usually doesn't succeed unless everyone on the team does his or her part. That is the same way it is when we work together in the class. It is important for everyone to work with the others so that the whole group can be successful. Today we are going to see if we can identify those things in group work that helps a group be successful."
	Presentation To begin, divide the class into two large, even groups. For example, if there are 24 pupils in the class, have 12 learners in each group. Arrange enough chairs in a circle to seat all the members of one of the groups, who are asked to sit in the chairs. The seated group is called the "inside group." Members of the other group arrange themselves behind the circle of chairs. This is the "outside group." Each member of the outside group is assigned to observe what one member of the inside group does during a discussion and to take notes on this person's behavior. After giving these instructions, provide the inside group with a controversial topic (this should be a matter of genuine interest to learners). For example, a group of fourth graders might be asked to discuss this idea:

It should be the law that every fourth grader is in bed no later than 9:00 P.M. on school nights.

Before the discussion begins, provide additional information to members of the outside group regarding kinds of information to note. Ask pupils to observe the extent to which their assigned person does each of the following:

- Takes an active part in the discussion.
- Makes comments that logically follow what the previous speaker says.
- Summarizes something said earlier in the discussion.
- Makes comments that keep the group from arriving at a premature conclusion.
- Supports comments made by someone else in the group.
- Refers to evidence to support a point.

At this point, begin the discussion. Allow it to go on for 8 to 10 minutes. At this point, members of the inside group and the outside group change places. Remind members of the new outside group what they are to do. The new inside group begins discussing the topic. This second discussion also continues for 8 to 10 minutes.

To conclude the activity, lead a debriefing discussion with the whole class. Introduce information gathered by the note-takers. Point out the kinds of verbal behavior that help keep discussions going in a productive way (supportive comments, willingness to listen, careful attention to points made by previous speakers, and so forth).

Closure: Ask the class, "Why did we do this activity today? What did you learn that will help you when you work with others?"

Numbered Heads Together

This approach introduces pupils to the idea of group scoring and individual accountability. We begin by organizing pupils into groups of four or five, and we give each pupil a number. We then present a question or problem to the entire class. Each group must discuss the question or problem. We tell pupils that they must make sure that every member of the group knows the answer. After an allocated period of time, we call a number, and the pupils in each group with that number raise their hands. If they are able to give the correct response, their team gets a point (Kagan, 1989).

The advantage of this approach is that all the group members must share and must listen if they want their group to do well. This is really a form of a tutorial group and helps a large number of pupils review and discuss important questions in a minimum amount of time.

Buzz Session

The buzz session is a very simple procedure that we can use to introduce pupils to doing group work in social studies. Often the buzz session is tied directly to academic content when a new unit of study is about to begin. It does not need to take a great deal of time; 10 minutes is usually sufficient. We begin by organizing the class into groups of four or five pupils each. If possible, members of each group should arrange chairs in a circle so everyone faces one another. Each group is asked to select a recorder, who will write down group responses.

We then provide a topic. Group members are to quickly identify a question or an item of information about the topic. All responses are recorded by the recorder. One effective technique when using this at the beginning of a unit is to have each group make two columns. In one column, members state what they think they already know about the topic. In the second column, they write questions about what they want to learn about the topic. At the end of the activity, we collect these lists. We can then record this information on chart paper or on an overhead transparency and share it with the class.

This technique provides useful diagnostic information about what pupils already know and about possible misconceptions they may have. This information is valuable as we ponder content to be included in our lessons. For our pupils, the approach provides an initial focus on a topic we will be studying and also contributes to the development of productive group behaviors.

BOX 6–2   **Do Buzz Sessions "Steal" Valuable Instruction Time?**

A critic of buzz sessions recently made these comments:

> Buzz sessions should be banned from elementary social studies programs. They promise more than they deliver. It is claimed they motivate pupils. I'm not totally convinced on that point. But, even if they do, they simply allow teachers to waste too much time.
>
> Some people claim that a buzz session can be completed in 10 minutes. I'm somewhat dubious about teachers' abilities to restrict them to so short a time. But, even if they do so, 10 minutes can add up to a lot of time over a year. Suppose a teacher uses buzz sessions twice a week. That is 80 minutes a month when learners aren't working hard to master new academic content. The result can be a reduction of overall pupil learning. We simply cannot afford to let this happen.

Think About This

1. Do you think this person has a reasonable concern? Why, or why not?
2. Other might argue that buzz sessions, by helping learners establish a focus for later learning, in the end will increase pupils' levels of achievement. Do you agree?
3. Specifically, how would you respond to this critic?

Lesson Idea 6–3

BUZZ SESSION: MOVING TO AMERICA

Grade Level: 5

Objective: Learners can list questions they have about the settlement of America.

Overview: This activity is especially useful for beginning a unit of study. In addition, it helps pupils learn the group work skills needed to make group learning successful.

Procedures: *Learning Set*   Ask how many members of the class have moved from one community to another. Ask what kinds of things they had to think about as they prepared for the move. Explain that today the class is going to pretend that they are settlers moving from England to America. However, they are going to work together in groups.

Presentation   Say to the class, "We are going to be learning about the lives of some of the early permanent settlers to come to North America from England (point out location of England on a large globe or world map). They landed and established settlements here (point out location of New England).

"I want you to suppose that you were living in England in the early 1600s. You are thinking about coming to America, but you know very little about what America might be like. Knowing which questions to ask could be very important in deciding whether to go and what you might need to take in order to survive. Why do you think knowing the right kinds of questions to ask is so important? (Get a few responses from the class.) Today you are going to work together in groups. Each group is to try and identify as many questions as you can that you think these people might have had about moving to North America. Make sure that one member of your group records the questions on a piece of paper. Do not spend time today trying to answer the questions, just try to identify as many as possible.

"Don't start until I give you the signal. This is going to go fast. I will give you 10 minutes. I would like every member of each group to think of at least one question. Now, before we start, do you have any questions? (Respond to questions, as necessary). All right, let's begin." (Learners begin to talk or "buzz" in their respective groups. Call "time" after 10 minutes.)

After the buzz period has concluded, pick up the question lists from each group, and share these with all learners. You may wish to write some of these on the board or on an overhead transparency. The class in the example above might develop questions such as these:

- How will I get to America?
- How long will the trip take?
- What kinds of animals will I find?
- What will I eat?
- Where will I get my clothes if there are no stores?
- What will happen if I get sick?
- What will the weather be like?

These and other questions can provide a focus for the study of the new unit. Since pupils have developed the questions themselves, they frequently are eager to find some answers. The buzz session often motivates students to learn new material. The interest it generates helps them master content and, at the same time, may increase their interest in doing additional work in groups.

Closure: Ask the class, "What did we do today? What are the advantages of working in a group for this type of an activity? What do we need to do next?"

THREE POPULAR GROUP TECHNIQUES: CLASSROOM DEBATE, ROLE PLAYING, AND SIMULATION

The following are three popular approaches to group learning. Each of the techniques is a well-defined, systematic approach to instruction. Each of the approaches can be used at varying levels of sophistication depending on the abilities of the pupils in the classroom.

Classroom Debate

People whose only exposure to debates has been formal debate tournaments in high schools and universities might wonder how debate might be regarded as a useful group activity. The classroom debate is organized differently from the format used in tournament debates. It features teams of pupils who prepare positions on each side of an issue and who each participate actively during the debate itself.

There are many ways to organize classroom debates. One version features teams of seven pupils each. Assignments are made as follows:

- Three learners take the "pro" position.
- Three learners take the "con" position.
- One learner plays the role of "critic."

The teacher explains that members of the pro team will gather as much information as they can that supports a controversial proposal. Each member will be expected to play an active role in arguing the pro team's case. Similarly, members of the con team will gather information that can be used to attack the same controversial proposal. Each member will play an active role in arguing the con team's case. The critic will learn as much as she can about positions of both the pro team and the con team. This critic's function will be to ask probing questions toward the end of the debate that will highlight weaknesses of the positions of both the pro and the con teams.

To get the activity started, select a controversial issue that will serve as a focus. Make sure that adequate background materials are available for team members. Time must be provided for team members to prepare their case. (Monitor pupils during this time to render assistance and to assure they are staying on task.)

The controversial issue is usually described in terms of a proposal that implies a change. The following are examples:

"Resolved that all people in this school should be required to wear uniforms to school."

"Resolved that the environment of Antarctica should be protected by forbidding tourists to visit that continent."

"Resolved that schools should be in session at least eleven months of the year."

"Resolved that families should be required to pay children for taking out the garbage."

"Resolved that classroom rules should be made by teachers, not members of the class."

The classroom debate follows a general sequence. The following example reflects what might be done in an upper-grades class during a 50-minute period:

1. All pro and con team members speak for two minutes each. Individual pro and con speakers alternate. Approximate time: twelve minutes.
2. Members of the pro team cross-examine members of the con team for a team total of six minutes. Then, members of the con team cross-examine members of the pro team for a team total of six minutes. Approximate time: twelve minutes.
3. Members of each team make final statements. All team members are encouraged to speak. Total time allotted to each team is three minutes. Approximate time: six minutes.
4. The critic is invited to ask probing questions of both pro team and con team members. The critic, at her discretion, may choose to direct a question at either some or all members of each team. The function of the critic is to point out weak spots in arguments made by members of both teams. Approximate time: eight minutes.
5. At this time, the class as a whole votes to determine a winner. Approximate time: two minutes.

6. The teacher debriefs the class. It is important that comments be as supportive as possible. Learners need to understand that speaking up is not going to elicit negative teacher reactions. During the debriefing phase, the teacher might use focus questions such as these:
   • What were the best arguments you heard?
   • What impressed you about those arguments?
   • What other points would you have brought up if you had been on the pro team? The con team?
   • Should the critic have asked some other questions? If so, what should the critic have asked?

Classroom debate is a technique that can generate high levels of interest. It provides an opportunity for large numbers of pupils to get actively involved in the learning process.

Role Playing

Role playing serves several purposes that are consistent with objectives of the elementary social studies program. The technique can help learners do the following:

• Develop their interpersonal relations skills
• Appreciate perspectives of others
• Recognize perspectives of others
• Recognize the impact of one person's decision on others
• Master academic content by replicating roles of people who participated in "real" events

Role playing is adaptable for use with learners at all elementary grade levels. It begins with a problem. We often find it useful to introduce pupils to the technique by presenting them with a situation they or members of their family might have faced.

Lesson Idea 6–4

ROLE PLAYING: HOW CAN NEEDS BE MET?

Grade Level:	4–6
Objectives:	Pupils will identify perspectives of different characters and state the impact of one person's actions on others.
Overview:	Role-playing activities can help accomplish several purposes. They can help pupils develop an understanding of different perspectives by assuming different roles. In addition, they help pupils learn to discuss and share with others in a group setting. This activity is designed to provide the pupils with a realistic setting, one they may experience in their own

homes. Thus, the outcome may help them understand every-day problems. It is best if the entire class is involved in the role playing. Those who are not assigned roles should be observing during the enactment. It is also useful to have two or three enactments so that a variety of perspectives can be presented and the actions of the characters compared.

Procedures:

Learning Set   Begin with the following question: "Do you ever have times in your family when everyone seems to want to do something different and people get upset?" Tell the class that today they are going to talk about those types of situations.

Presentation   Say to the class: "Today we are going to act out a situation similar to what might happen in our families. Here is the situation:

"Mr. Jones is a single parent. He has four children. These are Jill, a 14-year-old high school freshman, the twins, Tom and Sid, 8-year-old third graders, and 7-year-old Jessica, a second grader.

"It is five o'clock on a Thursday evening. Mr. Jones has had a difficult day at work. He had many interruptions, and he wants to get back to the office no later than six-thirty to catch up on some paperwork.

"Jill is panicked about an algebra test she must take on Friday morning. She wants Mr. Jones to go over the material with her. She needs help right after dinner. At seven o'clock she will have to stop studying algebra and watch a special public television production of *The Merchant of Venice* for her English class.

"The twins, Tom and Sid, have a Cub Scout meeting that begins at six-thirty, where they are both receiving awards. They are hopeful that their father be there to see them receive the awards.

"Jessica's church group will be having a short meeting from six-thirty to seven-thirty. The meeting is at the church, about four miles from the house. She will need to be taken to the meeting and picked up after it is over.

"The problem is, how can needs of each person be met? I am going to choose a few people to play the roles of Mr. Jones, Jill, Tom, Sid, and Jessica. I want you to pretend you are that person and see if your team can act out a way of solving this problem. For those of you not acting, I want you to see if you can identify things that contribute to the solution and things that get in the way. Also, try to identify why you think each character acts the way they do, and see if you have some better solutions."

When the enactment is complete, take a couple of min-utes to ask the participants how they felt when certain things

	happened. Then choose another group to see if they can act out the situation in different way.
Closure:	Ask the class, "What do you think are the important things you learned as a result of our lesson today? How do you feel about doing lessons like this? What do we all need to do to make lessons like this successful?"

Once a situation has been developed and presented to learners, participants need to be selected. Sometimes we ask for volunteers; sometimes we appoint pupils to play each part. Learners should have the option to refuse to play a role. The role-playing exercise does not work well when they feel they are being required to do something they would prefer not to do. Most often, we find that more pupils want to participate than there are roles available.

Once players are selected, provide them with background information about their parts, and give them time to think about how the individuals they are playing would react to the basic problem.

A good role-playing lesson involves the entire class, not just the pupils playing parts. Pupils who are not playing roles should be assigned to look for specific things as the enactment proceeds. ("How realistic were Mr. Jones's responses to Jill?" "What other arguments could the twins have made to make a stronger case?") Pupils should be told to be ready to comment during the discussion following the role-playing enactment.

Sometimes, we find it useful to have two or three enactments of the same basic situation. When this is done, numerous learners can be actively involved as role players. Knowing they may be called upon to play roles in a subsequent reenactment, pupils pay closer attention during the initial enactment.

The following steps have been found useful in implementing role playing (adapted from Joyce & Weil, 1986):

1. *Enactment.* Role players act out responses. They are encouraged to be as realistic as possible. The teacher may intervene occasionally to remind learners of their roles, of the basic problem, and of issues relevant to the situation.
2. *Discussion and evaluation.* The teacher leads a discussion. Pupils who were to look for specific things are asked to speak. The teacher highlights motives and priorities of individual characters. Courses of action different from those that came out during the enactment are sometimes discussed.
3. *Reenactment.* When feasible, reenact the situation to give additional pupils opportunities to play roles. Such reenactments also allow for more responses to the problem to be considered.
4. *Final discussion and debriefing.* If there have been reenactments, this phase begins with a discussion and evaluation similar to the one that followed the initial enactment. This phase concludes with the teacher summarizing major points players made during the enactments. Learners' ideas are actively solicited at this time. Some teachers use this final phase to ask learners about other issues they would like to study using the role-playing technique (Figure 6–3).

Identify an issue you might teach as part of your elementary social studies program that could be taught via a role-playing exercise. Describe the problem as clearly as possible. Then, indicate specific roles to be played by the participants. Be sure to indicate participants' unique perspectives on the problem. If circumstances permit, you might ask students in your social studies methods class to assume roles and go through the exercise as part of a class activity. You might play the teacher and take the remainder of the class through the entire role-playing sequence (enactment, discussion and evaluation, reenactment, final discussion, and debriefing).

Figure 6–3
Preparing a role-playing exercise.

Simulations

The terms *games* and *simulations* are often used interchangeably. However, they have somewhat different meanings. Games usually involve a situation where an individual or a group compete with one another within a set of rules where there is a means of determining winners and losers. Simulations are designed to place participants in situations that closely parallel those found in the real world. Simulations simplify reality to highlight certain key ideas. For example, a simulation designed to focus on the legislative process may emphasize negotiation and deemphasize other features of legislative decision making. Simulations may not have winners and losers. The participants in the simulation may all achieve their goals. The object is for each participant in the simulation to make decisions and to experience the consequences of the decision. Simulations are basically more elaborate role-playing activities. Activities that incorporate both the elements of reality as well as game qualities of winning and losing are usually called *simulation games.*

Learners are intensely involved during simulations. Often they have opportunities to talk and to move to different parts of the room. Many pupils find simulations to be highly motivating. They have the potential to add an important real-world dimension to elementary social studies instruction.

Simulations vary enormously in their complexity. Some are simple board activities derived from popular commercial simulation games such as Monopoly®. Others are elaborate schemes that may require computers to manage and take many days to play. An example of a computer simulation appropriate for elementary pupils is the popular "Oregon Trail," available in most computer software stores. The popularity of personal computers and the potential for use of computer simulations as a means of instruction for decision making has increased interest in simulations.

Often simulations divide participants into several groups. For example, there might be a simulation of an international conference on the control of terrorism. Individual groups may be assigned to play the roles of diplomats from individual countries or groups of countries.

Most simulations that are suitable for use in elementary social studies classrooms are not excessively complex. They typically can be played in one or two class sessions, though a few require more time. Many are available from commercial sources. Simulations suitable for use in elementary schools are included in the annual *Grades K–6 Social Studies Catalog*, available on request and free of charge from Social Studies School Service, 10200 Jefferson Boulevard, P. O. Box 802, Culver City, CA 90232-0802.

Simulations require learners to assume roles, make decisions, and face the consequences of their actions. They tend to be more complex in their organization than role playing. Hence, more time typically is required to prepare pupils to participate in them and more support material may be required. A complete simulation activity moves through four phases—overview, training, activity, debriefing.

Overview

During this phase, we introduce pupils to the simulation. Parts to be played by individual learners are described, and assignments to these parts are made. General rules of the simulation are introduced at this time.

Training

This amounts to a "walk through" of processes to be followed once the simulation begins. We select several learners, assign them parts, and use them to illustrate how class members will be involved once the simulation begins. Learners are invited to ask questions as we explain how the simulation will operate.

Following this introductory information, pupils should be allowed to review their roles. If the simulation features several groups, group members should be allowed to meet to discuss their roles and to plot preliminary strategy.

Activity

This is when the actual simulation activity takes place. During this time, we play the roles of discussant, coach, and referee. At times, pupils may not grasp the point of the simulation. We may find it necessary to stop the action for a moment to help pupils think about their decisions and to explain the purpose of the activity.

Some pupils may not know how to respond to certain developments. We can coach them as they consider their options. Our ideas can help inexperienced simulation participants gain in confidence. As pupils' expertise grows, we gradually disengage from the coaching role.

It is common for disputes to arise during simulation activities. Often there are situations for which the rules fail to provide a specific action guideline. When this happens, we need to intervene and make a ruling that will allow the simulation to continue.

Debriefing

This is a critically important part of any simulation activity. During debriefing, we lead a discussion highlighting various events that occurred during the activity. The discussion helps pupils recall things that might have escaped their notice during the fast pace of the activity itself.

Debriefing discussions sometimes focus on specific decisions made and their desirability relative to alternatives. Sometimes debriefing concerns the design of the simulation. What issues were forced to the front because of the rules of the simulation? What did the designers of the simulation omit? Often, individuals will want to critique their own performances and suggest ways they might act differently were they to do the exercise another time.

Teachers with no prior experience with simulations tend to allow insufficient time for debriefing. This severely limits the effectiveness of the simulation as a productive learning activity. It is during the debriefing that the important concepts and procedures are discussed and the learning is reinforced.

COOPERATIVE LEARNING TECHNIQUES

Cooperative learning is an approach that emphasizes working together. This approach to teaching is particularly appropriate for use in social studies lessons, as it replicates the kind of cooperative activity that characterizes much of adult social, economic, and political life. Those advocating cooperative learning point out that it is especially suited for coping with individual differences within the classroom. Individuals with a variety of skills and ability levels learn to work together in heterogeneous groups.

Cooperative learning approaches feature positive interdependence, face-to-face interaction among learners, individual accountability, and instructing students in appropriate interpersonal and small-group skills (Good & Brophy, 1994). *Positive interdependence* refers to situations where pupils realize that they are interdependent and everyone in the group must contribute to achieve success. Positive interdependence can be fostered through a division of labor, giving each group member a specific task, or through the use of group incentives or a group grade. For example, some approaches use total group scores or the improvement scores of group members to determine group rewards. Positive interdependence appears to be a key characteristic of cooperative learning approaches that result in increased achievement.

Face-to-face interaction refers to group tasks that require pupils to interact with each other as opposed to those tasks where each pupil works independently and the material is then just compiled into a final product.

Individual accountability is another key area where many attempts at cooperative learning flounder. Most people are familiar with the situation where one or more group members fail to do their job and depend on others in the group to do all the work. Individual accountability makes each pupil accountable for making a contribution to the group. This can be accomplished by giving individual grades or reinforcements in addition to group grades. However, in cooperative learning approaches these grades are based on the effort and the contributions of the individual in achieving the group goal, not just on individual achievement.

There are several ways this can be done. Individuals within the group can rate the contribution of team members, individuals can perform a self-evaluation, or the teacher can review the contributions of each member by reviewing a portfolio from each pupil that contains material they gathered and used during the group project.

As already indicated, small-group work will not be successful unless pupils are taught the necessary skills. Just being told to cooperate is not enough. Individuals will need to be taught not only the interpersonal skills necessary, but the specific roles they will need to fill in the particular cooperative learning approach being used.

Researchers have found that cooperative learning approaches result in higher levels of mastery and better retention of concepts than situations in which pupils compete against one another as individuals. In addition, peer acceptance and encouragement is improved. This is possible because of the powerful influence of the peer group and the increased opportunity for becoming involved in discussions involving higher levels of reasoning (Good & Brophy, 1994).

A number of cooperative learning approaches have been developed. Three popular approaches are introduced here:

- Jigsaw
- Learning together
- Teams achievement divisions

Jigsaw

The *jigsaw* method is a group learning technique that requires each person in a group to accomplish part of a larger assignment. The entire assignment cannot be finished until all parts of the "jigsaw" are fitted together. There are many possible applications of the jigsaw method in elementary social studies classrooms. One adaptation to the approach is what might be termed "Jigsaw Twins." In this approach, two pupils are teamed together to become the experts on a topic. This is especially useful when pupils may have limited English proficiency or may have learning difficulties that might hinder their ability to learn and communicate the material back to the home team.

Teachers sometimes provide a blank data chart that learners can use to record information. Such a chart for the example presented in Lesson Idea 6–5 would have the names of the five countries listed across the top. The terms *religions, languages, major income sources, major terrain features*, and *educational system* would be written down the left side. Pupils are invited to write notes in the appropriate cells of this matrix.

When pupils in a given group have completed their work, they let the teacher know they are ready for their evaluation. The teacher then assesses their work and provides reactions to members of the group.

In an adaptation of this approach, often called "Jigsaw II," points are given to each group based on the scores of the pupils during an evaluation (Borich, 1996). This addition heightens interest by making it important for each person in the group to learn their expert role and for all members to listen and learn from each other.

Lesson Idea 6–5

JIGSAW: SOUTH AMERICA

Grade Level:

6

Objectives:

Each pupil will (1) learn and chart information about one South American country, (2) become an "expert" about one aspect of a country and will teach it to others in the group, and (3) will work cooperatively in a group.

Overview:

The jigsaw approach is useful in social studies, especially when a topic has several parts to develop and research. If some of the pupils have limited English proficiency or a learning difficulty, team them with another to become an "expert pair" on that particular aspect of the country. In this example, the class is learning about South America. For each of the countries, you want the class to learn something about the history of the relationships with other countries, the ethnic and language backgrounds of the people, the major resources and industries in the country, the terrain and the major regions, the religious beliefs, and the form of government. Rather than try to cover all countries, choose several because they offer some interesting contrasts, such as Brazil, Argentina, Columbia, Paraguay, and Peru.

Procedure

Learning Set   Say to the class, "Today we are going to begin learning about South America. But we are going to do it a little differently. When you work in a company, you usually have different people who are 'experts' on different things. For example, a manufacturer might have an expert on running the machines, an expert on designing the products, an expert on advertising, and an expert on selling. For the company to be successful, each expert must learn as much as possible about the job and must help others in the company understand what needs to be done. For the next several days, each of you is going to become an expert on some aspect of a South American country and will teach others in your group about that part of the country."

Presentation   Divide the class into "home" groups. Present to them the aspect of the country they will study. You can then assign each member of each home group the task of becoming an expert on one aspect. Tell them that they will be responsible for learning as much as possible about that aspect and when they return to their home group, they will have to teach the others what they have learned.

Divide the class into expert groups by having the experts from each group gather together in different parts of the room. For example, all of the experts on government will gather together, all of the experts on culture and language, and so on. Tell the class that the first country they will be studying will be Brazil. Present each group with a packet of material on the aspect of Brazil where they are to become experts. Each group then begins working together, organizing the material and discussing it.

Each expert group may need to work together for more than one day. Part of their assignment will be to develop an outline, maps, diagrams, or pictures that they will use to present their information to their home group.

Closure: This activity will probably take several days. At the end of each day, bring the day to a close by reviewing how the groups are working together, and make suggestions on what they need to do to next.

In summary, the jigsaw method promotes the development of productive group behavior. Pupils learn to listen attentively to others. This is encouraged because contributions of all group members are needed to complete the assigned task. The procedure also helps develop cooperative, mutually supportive attitudes among class members.

Learning Together

The learning together method features a less formal organizational structure than the jigsaw method (Johnson & Johnson 1987; Johnson, Johnson, Holubec, & Roy, 1984). In learning together, we organize pupils into groups whose members reflect a variety of interests and abilities.

Once the groups are formed, we give every group an assignment that requires the attention and involvement of each person. The technique works best when many talents and enthusiasms are represented in each group. This allows individual pupils to work on parts of the overall project that are compatible with their own interests. The assignment usually requires pupils to develop a "product" of some kind. This might be a set of written responses to questions, a research report, a play to be presented to the class, or a group oral report. Members of a group receive grades based on the quality of this final product.

Roles of individual pupils within each group can be quite varied. Typical roles that might be found in a group would be those of group manager, recorder, researcher, illustrator, editor, and materials organizer. However, the roles vary according to the task. For example, if we wanted a group of fifth graders to write a short play about life in colonial New England, we could assign our pupils roles as head writer, general manuscript editor, set designer, and sound effects chairperson. All could assist in preparing the actual content of the play.

In learning together lessons, each pupil receives the same grade. This feature of the technique encourages individuals to pool their talents. There is incentive for each pupil to do her best to ensure that all members of the group receive a good final evaluation.

Johnson and Johnson (1985) report that learners who have had experience in working together tend to support the idea that it is fair to award the same grade to each group member.

During a learning together lesson, we monitor each group carefully. Pupils may have problems that have to be resolved. We try to be available to clear up misunderstandings and to help group members complete the required learning product.

Teams Achievement Divisions

We begin teams achievement divisions by dividing the class into four- or five-member teams (Slavin, 1978). Each team includes some high achievers, some low achievers, some boys, and some girls, ideally from different cultural and ethnic backgrounds. After we introduce new content through traditional large-group instruction, each team is given a set of study worksheets. These worksheets describe tasks to be accomplished and problems to be solved. These tasks and problems relate to the content that has been introduced to the class as a whole.

At this point, each team begins to work. Team members may quiz each other, tutor each other, or take other action they feel is necessary to accomplish the assigned work. Once a group has finished its work, team members take a test over the material. They may not help one another on the test. Group members are scored separately.

There are several approaches to computing team scores. Teachers who have worked with their pupils for some time have a good idea of each pupil's expected test score. The teacher makes a list of these expected or "base" scores. When tests are scored, one point is awarded toward the team's score for every point a member of the team exceeds her base score. Usually there is a maximum number of points that any one pupil can contribute to the team total (often this is set at 10 points.) This would mean, for example, that a learner with a base score of 32 who scored 80 still would contribute only the 10-point maximum to the total team score. An example of a group score for an achievement team is given in Table 6–1.

Note in the table that Calvin, although he had the lowest actual test score, still contributed 10 points to the team total. This happened because his test score of 35 was much higher than his base score of 20.

Table 6–1
Group score for an achievement team.

Student	Base Score	Quiz Score	Team Points
Alan	49	56	7
Bertha	50	48	0
Calvin	20	35	10
Dinah	85	90	5
Carlos	75	100	10
Total			32

Student teams achievement divisions encourage academically challenged pupils. They have an incentive to do as well as they can. Even though their individual scores may not be high, they have opportunities to make important contributions to the total scores of the teams to which they are assigned. This technique also encourages more able pupils to assist less able members of their group to master the content. This is true because all members of the group will profit when these youngsters' performances exceed the expectations reflected in their base scores. Indeed, each member of a teams achievement divisions group has a stake in the learning of each member of the group. Hence, there is an incentive for all group members to help each other.

In summary, cooperative learning techniques require the following teacher decisions:

- Selecting a topic that lends itself to group work.
- Making decisions about group size and composition.
- Providing appropriate materials.
- Identifying the parts of the lesson and sequencing the lesson.
- Monitoring the work of pupils in groups.
- Intervening when necessary to solve problems.
- Evaluating outcomes.

Because of the social nature of many aspects of the subject, cooperative learning approaches are particularly suitable for use in elementary social studies programs. Many teachers find these techniques enhance pupils' interest and improve general levels of achievement.

KEY IDEAS IN SUMMARY

1. Group instruction refers to instruction that is directed at classroom groups ranging in size from about half of the total class to as few as two pupils. Many group instruction techniques feature high levels of interaction. They have the potential to improve learners' abilities to work with others at the same time they promote learning of new content.

2. Successful group learning requires that teachers plan carefully. Pupils must understand exactly what they are to do, and they must know what they are expected to learn from the activity. Teachers must exercise care in assigning individuals to groups. Many group procedures work well when each group includes pupils with diverse academic abilities, interests, and points of view. Materials used in group activities must be prepared in advance, and must be easily accessible to group members. Finally, teachers need to monitor groups carefully when they are working on assigned tasks.

3. Tutoring groups tend to be used (1) to help pupils who have difficulty mastering material when it is introduced in a large-group setting, and (2) to provide enrich-

ment experiences for gifted learners. This arrangement features a teacher who plays a strong leadership role as a provider of instruction, disseminator of information, and leader of discussions.

4. In equal roles groups, learners are grouped together for the purpose of working on a common problem. All members of a given group participate in these general problem-solving steps: (1) identifying the problem; (2) considering possible approaches; (3) selecting and applying approaches; and (4) reaching a defensible conclusion.

5. In assigned roles groups, individual members work on a unique task that represents part of a larger problem assigned to their group. This scheme works well when teachers want pupils to work on complex issues having many parts.

6. Teachers who want to use group learning techniques with their learners sometimes find that their students have had little prior experience working together in small groups. To facilitate learner functioning in groups smaller than the class as a whole, teachers sometimes use several introductory techniques. Among these are Two-by-Two Think-Pair-Share, Numbered Heads Together, Inside-Outside, and Buzz Sessions. Some of the techniques focus exclusively on developing learners' techniques for working productively in groups. Others help them learn how to focus on academic content in a group setting.

7. Many group learning techniques are suitable for use in elementary social studies classrooms. Three popular techniques are (1) classroom debate, (2) role playing, and (3) simulation. Classroom debate features teams of pupils who are assigned to prepare positions to either support or oppose a controversial proposition. Role playing allows learners to appreciate perspectives of others by responding to situations in a manner consistent with the views of a character they are assigned to play. Simulations help pupils learn by involving them in structured simplifications of reality that help them to grasp the complexities of important processes and issues.

8. Cooperative learning techniques seek to replicate in the classroom many of the kinds of cooperative activities that characterize adult social, economic, and political life. Numerous cooperative learning approaches have been developed. Three that are widely used in elementary social studies classes are (1) jigsaw, (2) learning together, and (3) teams achievement divisions. Many cooperative learning methods seek to give each learner a personal stake in the learning of all members of her group.

CHAPTER REFLECTIONS

Directions: Now that you have finished reading this chapter, reread the case study at the beginning. Then, answer these questions.

1. How would you respond to concerns about some of the pupils "doing all the work" for others when small-group instruction is used?

2. Some of the criticisms of small-group learning raised in the case study seem to assume that the concerns apply to all small-group learning approaches. Are there important differences among individual small-group approaches that might make individual concerns more applicable to some techniques than others? Cite examples to support your answer.

3. What is your personal experience with small-group learning? Do you like or dislike small-group learning? Why?

4. Some teachers are uncomfortable with the group grading techniques used for some cooperative learning approaches. What is your personal reaction to group grades?

5. Two-by-Twos and Inside-Outside are used primarily to improve learners' skills at working in groups. Is it defensible to take time away from content-oriented teaching to focus on the development of such skills?

6. Many cooperative learning approaches emphasize cooperation and mutual support. At the same time, they downplay competition. Some people argue that much of life features competitive activity. If this is true, does it make sense for teachers to involve pupils in procedures that are not designed to encourage competitive behavior?

EXTENDING UNDERSTANDING AND SKILL

1. Prepare a list of the group learning techniques introduced in this chapter. Interview an elementary teacher. Ask whether he or she uses any of these procedures to teach social studies lessons. Also, ask whether the teacher uses other group approaches. Summarize what you learn in your interview in an oral report to your social studies methods class.

2. In recent years, there has been an explosion of interest in cooperative learning techniques. (You might want to begin by looking up *cooperative learning* in the *Education Index*, available in your library. Your instructor also may be able to direct you to specific sources of information.) Identify one or two cooperative learning techniques that were not introduced in this chapter. Be prepared to explain to your instructor how these techniques work. If time permits, you might involve other class members in a lesson featuring one or more of these approaches.

3. Identify content from this chapter that might be taught to social studies methods students using the jigsaw method. Plan a lesson involving class members in your suggested approach.

4. To familiarize yourself with Two-by-Twos, use the technique as a means to break the ice when a large group of people get together. You might try it at a party, at a

church function, at an orientation session for new university students, or in some other setting. Share your experiences in using the procedure with members of your social studies methods class.

5. Following procedures for a classroom debate, organize members of your methods class into teams to debate this issue: "Resolved, that exposing learners to cooperative learning techniques in school will diminish their abilities to succeed in a competitive society." Ask other members of the class to observe the debate and to critique the technique.

REFERENCES

BORICH, G. (1996). *Effective Teaching Methods*, 3d ed. Englewood Cliffs, NJ: Merrill/Prentice Hall.

COHEN, E. G. (1986). *Designing Group Work: Strategies for the Heterogeneous Classroom*. New York: Teachers College Press.

GOOD, T., AND BROPHY, J. (1994). *Looking in Classrooms*, 6th ed. New York: HarperCollins.

JAROLIMEK, J., AND FOSTER, C. (1993). *Teaching and Learning in the Elementary School*, 5th ed. Englewood Cliffs, NJ: Merrill/Prentice Hall.

JOHNSON, D. W., AND JOHNSON R. T. (1987). *Learning Together and Alone*, 2nd ed. Englewood Cliffs, NJ: Prentice Hall.

JOHNSON, D. W., JOHNSON, R. T., HOLUBEC, E., AND ROY, P. (1984). *Circles of Learning: Cooperation in the Classroom*. Alexandria, VA: Association for Supervision and Curriculum Development.

JOHNSON, R. T., AND JOHNSON, D. W. (1985). "Structuring Conflict in Science Classrooms." Paper presented at the annual meeting of the National Association of Research in Science Teaching." French Lick, IN, April.

JOYCE, B., AND WEIL, M. (1986). *Models of Teaching*, 3d ed. Englewood Cliffs, NJ: Prentice Hall.

KAGAN, S. (1989). "The Structural Approach to Cooperative Learning." *Educational Leadership, 47* (4), p. 13.

McTIGHE, J., AND LYMAN, F. T., JR. (1988). "Cueing Thinking in the Classroom: The Promise of Theory-Embedded Tools." *Educational Leadership, 45* (7), pp. 18–24.

OLMSTEAD, J. A. (1974). *Small-Group Instruction: Theory and Practice*. Alexandria, VA: Human Resources Research Organization (HumRRO).

SLAVIN, R. E. (1978). "Student Teams and Achievement Divisions." *Journal of Research and Development in Education* (Fall), pp. 39–49.

WINITZKY, N. (1991). "Classroom Organization for Social Studies." In J. Shaver, ed., *Handbook of Research on Social Studies Teaching and Learning*. Englewood Cliffs, NJ: Merrill/Prentice Hall, pp. 530–539.

DEVELOPING THINKING SKILLS

CHAPTER GOALS

This chapter provides information to help the reader:

- describe reasons for teaching thinking skills,
- point out approaches to developing pupils' metacognitive abilities,
- cite general features of inquiry teaching,
- identify steps in a critical-thinking lesson,
- describe a sequence for a problem-solving activity,
- point out features of creative-thinking lessons, and
- suggest how teachers can help pupils become better decision makers.

CHAPTER STRUCTURE

Introduction
Teaching Pupils to Monitor Their Thinking
    Thinking Aloud
    Visualizing Thinking
Inquiry Approaches
    Inquiry Teaching: Basic Steps
    Using Data Charts to Compare, Contrast, and Generalize
    Delimiting and Focusing Pupils' Thinking
Creative Thinking
Critical Thinking
Problem Solving
Decision Making
Finding More Information
Key Ideas in Summary
Chapter Reflections
Extending Understanding and Skill
References

Developing thinking by

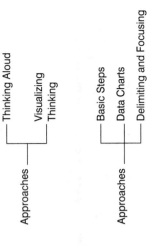

Purposes

Metacognition seeks to help pupils become personally aware of their own thinking processes. The long-range intent is for them to develop an ability to analyze a task and select thinking processes appropriate to complete it successfully.

Inquiry approaches encourage pupils to examine individual pieces of information for the purpose of developing explanatory principles and generalizations. They encourage development of the kinds of rational decision-making skills that pupils will need through their adult lives.

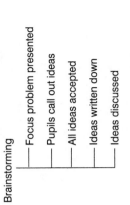

Approaches — Thinking Aloud / Visualizing Thinking

Approaches — Basic Steps / Data Charts / Delimiting and Focusing

Varieties of Thinking

Creative Thinking

Basic Characteristics

Creative thinking seeks novel solutions to perplexing problems. The "product of creative thinking must be both new and useful."

Critical thinking seeks to evaluate ideas. It always involves judgments based on evidence or highly informed opinion.

Critical Thinking

Implementing Procedures

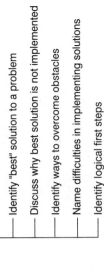

Brainstorming
- Focus problem presented
- Pupils call out ideas
- All ideas accepted
- Ideas written down
- Ideas discussed

Analytic Brainstorming
- Identify "best" solution to a problem
- Discuss why best solution is not implemented
- Identify ways to overcome obstacles
- Name difficulties in implementing solutions
- Identify logical first steps

Figure 7-1
Developing thinking skills.

229

Varieties of Thinking

| Problem Solving |

Basic Characteristics

Problem-solving thinking approaches are used when it appears likely that a given problem or situation has a "best," "correct," "right," or "most appropriate" solution.

Implementing Procedures

Basic Steps
- Identify the problem
- Consider possible approaches to its solution
- Select and apply approaches
- Reach a defensible solution

| Decision Making |

Basic Characteristics

Many questions people must face have no clearly "right" or "wrong" answers. People must make their responses by considering available options, weighing evidence, and considering personal values. This kind of thinking is called decision making.

Implementing Procedures

Basic Steps
- Identify the basic issue or problem
- Point out alternative responses
- Describe evidence behind each alternative
- Identify values implied in each alternative
- Describe consequences that might follow implementation of each alternative
- Make a choice from among alternatives
- Describe evidence and value considerations considered in making this choice

Figure 7–1
Continued

Chapter 7

Case Study

THINKING SKILLS, STUDENT LEARNING, AND EVALUATING THE TEACHER

For many years, elementary social studies specialist Felicia Littlebird has encouraged teachers to develop specific lessons for pupils designed to teach them how to engage in higher-level thinking. At the end of one of her recent presentations, a fifth-grade teacher made the following observations.

"Personally, I think these ideas are great. The research evidence about the importance of helping our young people engage in higher-level thinking is impressive. The findings also support what some critics of our schools have been telling us about how much better thinkers some foreign students are compared to our kids. To save time here, let me assure you that your recommendations make good sense to me. *But . . .* I do have a major concern.

"I'm a new teacher. I feel that everything I do is being watched by the principal and by parents. I don't have a track record yet. I have to watch my step to avoid getting a bad evaluation. Whether right or wrong, my sense is that I'm going to be evaluated mostly on how well my kids perform on tests.

"While I'm convinced that spending time teaching my people how to use higher-level thinking techniques can have a wonderful long-term payoff for them, I'm not at all sure that there will be anything in the short run that will show up in the form of improved test scores. In fact, test scores could go down. The time I take teaching them how to engage in higher-level thinking may come at the expense of lessons I could be teaching on content likely to appear on tests."

What Is Your Response?

Think about this teacher's concerns. Then, respond briefly to these questions:

1. Some critics of elementary school instruction claim that taking time to teach processes such as higher-level thinking skills steals instructional time that could be devoted to teaching more important content. Do you agree or disagree?
2. This teacher suggests that people who support teaching pupils higher-level thinking skills have failed to convince administrators and parents of the worth of this activity. Is this a reasonable concern? Why, or why not?
3. What ideas do you have regarding how a teacher's success in teaching pupils to use higher-level thinking skills might be measured and reported?
4. What kinds of conditions do you think would have to be present for this teacher to feel completely at ease with a decision to implement ideas introduced in Felicia Littlebird's workshop?
5. How would you advise this teacher if you were Felicia Littlebird?

INTRODUCTION

In the early years of our country, few people held out high educational expectations for the general population. As learning strategy specialist Karen Scheid (1993) points out, schools were considered to have succeeded when large numbers of people left able to write their own names. Today we want school graduates who read fluently and who can go beyond the literal meaning of texts to make judgments and inferences. This suggests that schools need to help pupils become sophisticated thinkers.

Social studies specialist Walter Parker (1988) found that few teachers in elementary social studies lessons spend much time helping students develop their thinking skills. Many people believe thinking-skills instruction deserves more emphasis in elementary schools (Nickerson, Perkins, & Smith, 1985; French & Rhoder, 1992; Perkins, 1993–1994). However, not everyone agrees.

Cheney, in *American Memory: A Report on the Humanities in the Nation's Public Schools* (1987) contends that teachers spend too much time teaching children learning processes and too little time teaching them important content. The argument Cheney and others (Ravitch, 1985; Hirsch, 1987) have made is that time devoted to teaching children skills, including thinking skills, steals time that could be better devoted to teaching important academic information. Perkins (1993–1994, p. 84) counters this position by noting, "You can often answer fact-based questions that you don't have answers for by extrapolating from what you know. If we can learn more facts by thinking about what we know, we can also know more facts by thinking about them as we learn them." In other words, good thinking-skills instruction helps rather than hinders pupils as they seek to master academic content.

The view that teachers should devote attention to teaching pupils how to think represents a majority opinion today. There is evidence that when pupils know how to use a thinking-skills strategy and are aware of how it can help them master new content, they will use the strategy in new contexts (French & Rhoder, 1992). Pupils who leave school with highly developed thinking skills have powerful intellectual tools they can apply to problems they will confront throughout their lives.

Many approaches have been developed for helping elementary pupils improve their thinking skills. Among them are ideas for improving learners' abilities to do the following:

- Monitor their own thinking patterns
- Use inquiry approaches
- Engage in creative thinking
- Think critically
- Solve problems

TEACHING PUPILS TO MONITOR THEIR THINKING

Learning psychologists use the term *metacognition* to refer to conscious thought about how we think about a problem or dilemma. Pupils need to learn how to monitor their

Organizing material in a logical manner is an important thinking skill that can be applied to many situations.

own thinking. This will help them select thinking approaches appropriate for various tasks they are trying to accomplish. Two approaches to helping pupils better monitor their thinking patterns are thinking aloud and visual thinking.

Thinking Aloud

The thinking-aloud approach is based on modeling, which research has shown to be a powerful instructional tool. As applied to thinking aloud, modeling requires the teacher to verbalize thought processes followed as he approaches a task. For example, suppose a teacher plans to have some fourth graders use maps to find distances (in miles) between selected pairs of United States cities. In preparation for this activity, the teacher might use a think-aloud approach along the lines of the example introduced in Lesson Idea 7–1.

Lesson Idea 7–1

FINDING DISTANCES

Grade Level:	4–6
Objectives:	Pupils will be able to (1) locate selected cities on a map, and (2) use scale to calculate the distance between two points.
Suggested Procedure:	Give pupils the following directions: "Today, your assignment will be to find the distances in miles between pairs of cities in

the United States. To help you begin, let's pretend that someone gave me the same assignment I've given you. This is how I would go about it.

"I have to find distances between several pairs of cities. The first pair is Chicago and San Francisco. I begin by thinking about where these two cities are. If I don't know, I'll need to look in the back of the atlas, in the index. I need to find Chicago and San Francisco. For Chicago, I find a reference to B9. This tells me to go back to the map of the United States and find the letter B. (Do this.) There is on the left side. Then I need to find the number 9 at the top. (Do this). Now, I'll simply move my finger even with the B until it is under the 9 at the top. Chicago should be near this spot. (Do this.) There it is! Now I know where Chicago is. I'll follow the same procedure to find San Francisco. The index tells me it is at C1. (Find San Francisco.)

"Now what I have to do is figure out the distance between Chicago and San Francisco. The first thing I am going to do is look at the scale at the bottom of the map. Remember we learned that the scale tells how many miles are represented by a given distance on the map. When I look at the scale, I learn that one inch on the map is equal to about 300 miles.

"The next thing I need to do is to measure the distance on the map between San Francisco and Chicago. This is about six inches. Now, I know that one inch equals 300 miles. Six inches, then, has to be six times as far. So, I multiply six times 300 to find out about how far it is from San Francisco to Chicago. This turns out to be about 1,800 miles. (Briefly explain that this is a point-to-point air distance. Because of curves in highways, mountains, and other variables, the highway distance between San Francisco and Chicago is longer.)

"Now that I know how to compute the distance between one pair of cities, I can use the same procedure to compute distances between other city pairs."

Thinking aloud provides children with a model they can follow as they attempt a new task. Further, it points out to them the importance of thinking about how they are going to approach a learning activity before they actually begin working on it.

Visualizing Thinking

Visualizing thinking is another technique used to help pupils monitor their thinking processes. It helps them focus on the essential features of an assigned task. Teachers encourage pupils to prepare diagrams that indicate their understanding of the task and

---

BOX 7–1　　　　**Preparing a Thinking-Aloud Lesson**

Think About This

There are many places where a thinking-aloud approach may be appropriately used in teaching elementary social studies content. The procedure is particularly important when a learning task will require pupils to follow a predictable series of steps. For example, a thinking-aloud approach might be a useful way to introduce pupils to a task requiring identification of elevations at various places using a map showing physical relief. The teacher could begin by pointing out one place on the map and by talking through the thinking processes involved in arriving at an answer. "Let's suppose I wanted to know the elevation of the central part of the Tibetan Plateau. The first thing I would do would be to. . . . ")

When planning a thinking-aloud lesson of your own, first select a topic. Then, indicate what you would say to your class to explain each step that pupils should follow as they work toward your learning goal.

---

the kinds of information they will need. Pupils then use these diagrams to record notes about what they have read and earned. An example of this approach is illustrated in Lesson Idea 7–2.

Lesson Idea 7–2

THE UNHAPPY TALE OF THE MONGOOSE

Grade Level: 　　　　6

Objectives: 　　　　Pupils will (1) recall specific information from a reading selection, and (2) identify cause and effect relationships using a visual diagram.

Suggested Procedure: 　Have all class members read this selection:

> *Pests have always bothered farmers. Crop damage from pests can be costly. At various times and places, landowners have tried to get rid of pests by introducing other animals that will eat them.*
>
> *For example, in the 1800s, farmers in Argentina imported sparrows from England. These birds were brought in to eat moths. This did not work out as expected. The moths were eaten, all right, but the sparrows grew so numerous that they became a serious problem.*
>
> *In the 1700s and 1800s, farmers in the West Indies tried several ideas to get rid of rats living in sugar cane*

fields. Some farmers imported weasels. Unfortunately, the weasels were attacked by a certain kind of fly, and they did not survive. Some farmers even brought in a species of ant that was famous as a "biter." They hoped that the ants would make life miserable for the rats. But, the rats didn't suffer as much as the farmers had hoped, and they continued to be a problem in the fields. One desperate group of farmers went so far as to import a number of giant toads that were reputed to be aggressive rat eaters. The toads, too, failed to get the job done.

In the early 1870s, West Indian farmers finally hit upon a solution that seemed to work. A small meat-eating animal called a mongoose was brought to these islands and released. The mongooses multiplied. Soon farmers noticed that numbers of rats in their fields were decreasing. This good news was not to last.

After about 10 years, rats were becoming a problem again. The mongooses had discovered chickens. They preferred to eat chickens, and many flocks were lost. By 1900, the mongoose itself had come to be viewed as a dangerous pest. Governments in the West Indies paid hunters to kill them. The "solution" to the pest problem had turned into an even bigger problem for authorities.

To help pupils focus on key information as they read this selection, help them develop visual thinking diagrams to guide their reading and as a vehicle for taking notes. Abilities and interests of individual pupils in any class vary. Consequently, you may ask some learners to look for different things than others. One group might be given this assignment:

Learning task: Say to pupils, "Name some examples of animals that were released to control pests. What pests were they supposed to control?"

In preparation for this learning task, students might develop a visual diagram such as the following:

Animals and Pests They Were to Control

Animals   *Pests to be Controlled*

_____   _____

_____   _____

_____   _____

_____   _____

Learning Task: You might ask other pupils in the class to accomplish a task such as this: "What happened when the mongoose was first introduced? What happened that was expected? What happened that was not expected? How do you explain what people thought about the mongoose by 1900?"

A visual diagram such as this might help pupils accomplish this task:

Changing Attitudes Toward the Mongoose

What happened when the mongoose was first introduced?

_____

_____

_____

What happened that was Expected?   **Unexpected**

_____   _____

_____   _____

_____   _____

How did people feel about the mongoose by 1900?

_____

_____

_____

Why did they feel this way?

_____

_____

As pupils read the selection, they fill in the diagram. Teachers typically prepare visual-thinking diagrams for pupils who have not worked with them before. Once they gain experience with the technique, pupils make their own. The process of preparing visual-thinking diagrams helps pupils to pay close attention to the specific requirements of the required learning task. This helps them to monitor and adjust their own thinking processes as they work on assignments. Improved understanding and enhanced self-confidence often result.

INQUIRY APPROACHES

Inquiry teaching introduces concepts to learners inductively. *Inductive learning,* which involves reasoning from the particular to the general, begins with the teacher introduc-

These pupils are engaged in a simple inquiry activity using maps.

ing a number of specific examples. Pupils study the examples and try to pick out general patterns. They conclude by identifying a broad general principle drawn from the characteristics of the examples.

Suppose a teacher working with kindergartners wanted to teach the concept "bird." The teacher might begin by showing these pupils pictures of different birds. A series of questions would prompt class members to identify common features in the pictures. To conclude the lesson, the teacher would help pupils develop their own definition of the concept "bird," perhaps showing additional pictures of birds to help pupils determine the adequacy of their definition.

Inquiry learning might be thought of as an exercise in knowledge production. Learners are asked to develop conclusions based on their own consideration of evidence. The kinds of reasoning involved in inquiry learning parallels the rational thinking learners will be called upon to exercise throughout their lives.

Inquiry Teaching: Basic Steps

Inquiry teaching applies the scientific method to a variety of learning problems, and is widely used in elementary social studies programs. The eminent American educational philosopher John Dewey suggested basic steps for sequencing inquiry instruction in his classic *How We Think*, originally published in 1910. The following steps used in implementing an inquiry lesson closely follow Dewey's recommendations:

- Describe the essential features of a problem or situation.
- Suggest possible solutions or explanations.

BOX 7–2 **"Inquiry Lessons Slow My Class Down."**

Two elementary teachers were discussing their social studies lessons in the school's faculty lounge. One of them made these comments:

"I like the *idea* of inquiry teaching. I mean, I think it really can help my people develop better thinking skills. But, I just can't cover much content when I do inquiry teaching. It takes a long, long time for the kids to see patterns and come up with generalizations. If I do much more of this, we're going to fall way behind. At this rate, we'll never finish the book."

Think About This

1. Do you think this teacher has a legitimate concern?
2. Are the benefits associated with pupils' learning higher-level thinking skills worth the "cost" of giving up some content coverage? Why, or why not?
3. How would you respond to this teacher's comments?

- Gather evidence that can be used to test the accuracy of these solutions or explanations.
- Evaluate the solutions or explanations in light of this evidence.
- Develop a conclusion that is supported by the best evidence.

Inquiry lessons can be used at all grade levels. A simple lesson might be used with pupils in the early primary grades who are beginning to learn how to work with maps and globes. An example of such a lesson is provided in Lesson Idea 7–3.

Lesson Idea 7–3

INQUIRY LESSON: MAPS AND GLOBES

Grade Level: K–2

Objectives: Pupils will (1) identify what selected map symbols represent, and (2) state reasons for using different symbols on a map.

Suggested Procedure Guide pupils through the following steps:

Step 1.

TEACHER: How many of you have ever been to a lake? To a river? Have any of you seen an ocean? How are all of these alike? (Pupils respond to each question. Probe until learners mention that all have water.) Did you know that there is more water in our world than land? People who make maps and globes have a problem. They have to have a way to help people recognize what areas are land and what areas are water.

Step 2.

TEACHER: How do you think people who make globes have solved this problem? How do you think they might indicate where areas of water are located?

Sample pupil responses:

- Maybe they neatly print the word "water" at places where there is water.
- They may draw pictures of waves in areas where there is water.
- They may use a special color to show where the water is.

Step 3.

TEACHER: Now we're going to act like scientists as we see which of our ideas are best. Let's look at this globe. (Hold up globe.) Can anyone give me the name of an ocean? (If nobody can, help the class.) All right, let's look at the Atlantic Ocean. Here it is on the map. How is it shown? (Pupils respond, "It's blue.") Let's look at the Pacific Ocean. Here it is on the map. How is it shown? (Pupils respond, "It's the same color—blue.")

(Put down the globe and point to a large U.S. wall map at the front of the room.) Here is the Atlantic Ocean and over here we have the Pacific. What do they look like? (Pupils respond, "They're blue.") These are what we call the Great Lakes. What do they look like? (Pupils respond, "They're blue.") This long thin part of the map represents our longest river. How is it shown? (Pupils respond, "It's blue, too.")

Step 4.   Ask learners to reflect on evidence they have seen. Encourage them to consider the possible explanations they have suggested in light of this evidence.

TEACHER: Based on what we have seen, what do you think most map and globe makers do when they want to show water? (Pupils respond, "They color it blue.")

Do you have any ideas about why they have chosen this solution to the problem? I mean, why wouldn't they write "water" at various places or draw waves? (Pupils respond. Possible answers might include: "If they had to write 'water,' they would have to write the word over and over again." "Because some areas of water are small, it might be hard to squeeze the word 'water' in the space." "It would be hard to have enough room to write the word 'water' on rivers." "Drawing little waves might be all right for an ocean, but it would be hard to see on rivers." "Drawings of little waves might make it hard to print other information.")

Step 5.   This step concludes the lesson. It is designed to result in a general explanation or principle that can be applied in different situations.

TEACHER: From what we have learned, what can you say about how areas of water are indicated on maps and globes? (Pupils respond: "They are shown in blue.")

Let's work with this idea a little more. We'll spend a few minutes looking at some other maps and globes to see if this idea works. (Look with pupils at other maps and globes.) Conclude by praising learners' work and telling them that they have discovered a principle they can remember: "On most maps and globes, the color blue is used to show water."

Using Data Charts to Compare, Contrast, and Generalize

An important purpose of inquiry is helping pupils to learn how to compare, contrast, and generalize. *Data charts* are useful organizers of information that pupils can use as they engage in these thinking processes. A sample lesson featuring use of a data chart is provided in Lesson Idea 7–4.

Lesson Idea 7–4

NATIONS OF LATIN AMERICA

Grade Level: 6

Objective: Pupils will develop a generalization that explains the relationship among literacy, income level, and life expectancy by comparing data presented on a chart.

Suggested Procedure: Suppose you were about to introduce a unit focusing on nations of Latin America. A data chart constructed for this lesson would include information pupils would use to develop some generalizations. Later in the unit, pupils would spend time testing the accuracy of their generalizations. The data chart might look something like the one that follows:

Selected Characteristics of Four Countries in Latin America and of the United States				
Country	Languages	Percentage of People Who Can Read and Write	Average Annual Income (Dollars)	Life Expectancy (Years)
Bolivia	Spanish and various Indian languages	63	470	53
Costa Rica	Spanish	93	1,290	74
Ecuador	Spanish and various Indian languages	85	1,160	65
Honduras	Spanish	56	730	63
United States of America	English and other languages including Spanish	99	16,400	75

Distribute copies of this chart to each pupil. Alternatively, a large version can be drawn on the chalkboard or projected from an overhead transparency. Begin by asking pupils to look carefully at the chart and to respond to the following sequence of questions:

1. What are some similarities you notice among these countries? Possible student responses:
   • The label at the top refers to all of them as Latin American countries and the United States. So they're all in the same part of the world.
   • Spanish seems to be spoken by some people in each of these countries.
2. What differences do you note? Possible student responses:
   • More people are able to read and write in some of these countries than others. Honduras has the highest percentage of people who cannot read and write.
   • Life expectancies are different. In Bolivia, the age is only 53.
   • The average incomes are very different. In Bolivia, it's only $470. In the United States, it's over $16,000 a year.
3. You have identified several important differences. Can you suggest some causes of these differences? Possible student responses:

- It seems people tend to live longer where income levels are higher.
- People also seem to live longer in places where higher percentages of the people can read and write.
- It seems to me that incomes go up when more people in a country can read and write.

(These are only examples. Members of a real class may develop different generalizations from the chart.)

TEACHER: These are all good ideas. Let me write them on the board. We are going to be studying Latin America for the next several weeks. As we do, let's try to find evidence to test the accuracy of our statements. I want each of you to take notes on these ideas. When you find new information, think about whether it supports or does not support these generalizations. When we finish the unit, we'll look again at these ideas to see whether we need to revise any of them.

The data chart helps pupils develop insights of their own. They become directly involved in the creation of new information. This information, in turn, provides a point of departure for further study. The opportunity to test their own generalizations often results in pupils becoming more enthusiastic as they pursue additional study of a topic.

Delimiting and Focusing Pupils' Thinking

Pupils sometimes are overwhelmed by the volume of information presented to them in social studies lessons. This is a particular problem when they first encounter inquiry lessons. These lessons typically begin with an introduction of a large quantity of information that, at least in the minds of pupils, may seem fragmented and disjointed.

Suchman (1962) developed an approach designed to help pupils focus on relevant information and to dismiss irrelevant details as they begin to solve a problem. Suchman's idea builds on learners' natural curiosity. It begins by presenting learners with a puzzling or perplexing situation that Suchman calls a *discrepant event*. This is something that does not quite fit pupils' understanding of reality. After they are introduced to the puzzling situation, pupils ask the teacher questions about it. The major rule is that all questions must be capable of being answered "yes" or "no." A Suchman lesson has a gamelike feel that pupils enjoy. The basic steps follow.

- Pupils are presented with a discrepant event.
- They are encouraged to explain it by asking the teacher questions that can be answered either "yes" or "no."

BOX 7–3   **Preparing Suchman Inquiry Lessons**

Many elementary pupils enjoy participating in Suchman inquiry lessons. There is a game-like quality to this approach that they find appealing. Additionally, every pupil has a chance to be an active participant. Good Suchman inquiry lessons begin with a *discrepant event*, something that pupils find does not quite "fit" with their previous knowledge.

Think about some social studies lessons you would like to teach. Choose at least five topics you could introduce using Suchman inquiry lessons. Identify the discrepant event you will use to capture pupils' attention and interest.

- The exercise ends with a general discussion of explanations that pupils have suggested and of the processes they used to arrive at them.

To illustrate how you might use Suchman's approach, suppose you were interested in helping pupils understand that many of the foods we consume change form before we eat or drink them. You might build a lesson around cocoa. Cocoa, as a drink, probably will be familiar to most pupils; however, few may know that it comes from seeds or beans that grow in a pod on a tropical tree. Fewer still will understand that a roasting process must intervene before cocoa can be consumed.

An interesting thing about cocoa beans is that they are white. This makes an ideal discrepant event for the exercise. Few children will associate the color white with cocoa. If you wanted to use this lesson, you would have to locate a color photograph of a cacao pod that had been cut open to reveal the seeds. The lesson would begin by a reminder of the rules. You would then show the children the photograph and ask a simple focus question, such as, "What are these things, and what do we use them for?"

After they have experienced several Suchman lessons, pupils become adept at asking good questions. Good questions are ones whose answers eliminate great quantities of irrelevant information. This helps members of the class to focus quickly on issues that are central to the solution of the focus problem.

CREATIVE THINKING

Creative thinking features novel approaches to perplexing problems. Many inventors are creative thinkers. The inventor of the forklift truck was inspired to build it after watching mechanical fingers remove donuts from a hot oven. (Ruggiero, 1988). The usefulness of the forklift makes an important point about the object of creative thinking. It is not thinking devoted to the creation of something bizarre for which there is no immediate or potential use. To be a legitimate "creative product" something must be both *new* and *useful* (Slabbert, 1994).

Creative thinking helps us adapt to change. Experts believe that the pace of change is accelerating. Hence, helping pupils develop creative-thinking strategies that will allow them to accommodate to conditions we cannot imagine today will be useful to them throughout their lives. Slabbert (1994) and others argue that it is just as important to teach young people creative-thinking skills, which will have lifelong relevance, as to teach them traditional subject matter content, which may soon become outdated. There is disagreement about what lasting effects lessons focusing on developing pupils' creative-thinking skills can be expected to have. Some recent studies have suggested that the "cognitive abilities underlying creative performance differ from task to task" (Baer, 1993–1994, p. 80). This seems to suggest that no single creative-thinking lesson can be expected to generate abilities in pupils that will help them to develop creative solutions to all kinds of problems. The lesson for teachers seems to be that they must prepare creative-thinking lessons that focus on many different kinds of problems and tasks. By exposing pupils to a variety of creative-thinking experiences, we increase the probability that they will have developed thinking responses with practical value for different kinds of problems they will encounter as adults.

There is evidence that relatively little attention is being paid in elementary classrooms to development of pupils' creative-thinking abilities (or, indeed, to the systematic development of any other thinking skills) (French & Rhoder, 1992). A number of creative-thinking techniques have been developed. One that is widely used is called *brainstorming*.

Brainstorming developed first in the world of business. It is designed to help people develop original solutions to problems. It places an initial premium on generating a huge volume of possible answers. When it is used in the classroom, pupils are encouraged to develop as many responses as possible to a focus problem. The rules for brainstorming are as follows:

- Pupils are given a focus problem. ("Suppose, because trees release huge amounts of oxygen into the air, all nations in the world decided to ban all further cutting of trees for lumber. What might result from this decision?")
- Pupils are asked to call out ideas as rapidly as possible. A person is free to speak whenever someone else stops speaking. The idea is to generate a rapid outpouring of ideas. Pupils are encouraged to say whatever comes to their minds so long as it is relevant.
- Participants are cautioned not to comment positively or negatively on ideas suggested by others. All ideas are accepted. This rule helps break down pupils' fears about "saying something stupid."
- The teacher or a designated recordkeeper writes down every idea, often on the chalkboard. Whoever is chosen to do this should be a person who can write quickly. Responses from pupils often come fast and furiously.
- The teacher stops the idea-generation phase when the rate of presentation of new ideas noticeably slows.
- A general discussion of the ideas concludes the exercise. This discussion may prompt ideas for additional study. (For example, given the focus question used to illustrate these procedures, there might be followup research on topics such as alternative fuels, substitute materials for furniture, new construction materials for houses, and so forth.)

CRITICAL THINKING

The purpose of critical thinking is to *evaluate* ideas. It always involves judgments based on informed opinion. Properly, these judgments should be supported by defensible criteria (Lipman, 1988).

Critical thinking encourages generation of new ideas. Critical-thinking instruction sometimes is linked to creative thinking. When this is done, the creative thinking part of the lesson occurs first. During this phase, pupils generate new ideas. During the second part of the lesson, they use critical-thinking skills to make judgments about these ideas.

Dunn and Dunn (1972) developed an adaptation of the basic brainstorming technique that encourages learners to think critically. An analytic brainstorming activity that requires use of critical-thinking skills includes the following steps. Pupils brainstorm responses to questions posed at each step. The teacher writes pupil responses so that everyone can see them.

- As an initial focus, the teacher encourages pupils to consider what the "best" solution to a problem might be. A fifth-grade teacher might use this question to begin the activity: "What would be the best thing we could do to make sure first graders don't get hurt on the playground?"
- Next, the teacher asks why these ideas have not already been implemented. ("What things are preventing us from doing any of these things to help solve this problem?")
- After pupils have responded to this question, the teacher asks another, designed to help pupils begin thinking about what might be done to overcome any obstacles. ("How could we overcome some of these difficulties?")
- At this point, the teacher asks pupils to consider problems they might encounter in implementing responses to the previous question. ("What might keep us from overcoming any difficulties we may face in trying to keep first graders from getting hurt on the playground?)
- Finally, pupils are asked to decide what should be the first step toward a realistic solution of the problem. ("Let's think about everything we have considered. What action should we take first to solve this problem? Be prepared to explain your choices.") Class members respond and defend their choices by referring to appropriate criteria.

PROBLEM SOLVING

Some problems have a "best," "correct," "right," or "appropriate" solution given the evidence that is available. In working with these situations, teachers encourage pupils to follow a problem-solving approach. A typical problem-solving lesson includes the following steps:

BOX 7–4   **Are Problem-Solving Lessons Appropriate**
for Younger Elementary School Pupils?

A mother made these comments to her son's first-grade teacher after learning about some simple problem-solving activities that pupils had been working on in class.

"I appreciate what you are trying to do. I want my son to know how to think. But are these formal problem-solving skills really appropriate for first graders? It seems to me that very young children will take an awfully long time to figure out the 'right' answer. This could be dangerous. For example, I don't want my son to take a long time deliberating about whether a red light means 'stop' or 'go.' I want him just to be told that 'red means stop.' If we don't give young children the idea that there are some things they should just listen to and accept as true, we're asking for trouble."

Think About This

1. Specifically, what concerns this parent?
2. How would you respond to points the parent raises?
3. How do you personally feel about the issue of introducing younger elementary pupils to problem-solving skills? Why do you feel this way?

- Identify the problem.
- Consider possible approaches to its solution.
- Select and apply approaches.
- Reach a defensible solution.

An example of a how problem solving can be used in a social studies lesson is illustrated in Lesson Idea 7–5.

Lesson Idea 7–5

WEATHER PATTERNS

Grade Level: 5

Objective: Pupils will identify procedures that explain differences and climate in two different places.

Suggested Procedure: If you are interested in having learners understand weather patterns in different parts of the United States, you might engage pupils in the following dialogue:

> You: I am going to write some information about temperatures in Boston and Seattle on the board. (Write the following information on the board.):

City	Average January low
Boston	23°
Seattle	34°

Does everybody remember where Boston and Seattle are? (Point out locations of the two cities on a large wall map of the United States.) Now let's be detectives. I want you to explain these differences. Why is Seattle warmer than Boston in the winter?

Let's start by reviewing what we already know about what influences a place's climate. Who'll tell me one that that is important?

JOSÉ: Well, places farther north sometimes are colder than places farther south.

YOU: Yes, that's true. What term did we learn to describe how far a place is north or south of the equator?

LASHANDRA: Latitude.

YOU: Latitude. Good. So one thing we might want to look at is latitude. That is, how far north of the equator Boston and Seattle are. All right, what else might we want to know?

SAMUEL: It makes a difference how high these places are. I mean, a place way up on a mountain is going to be colder than a place lower down.

YOU: That's a good idea. Remember, we use the term "altitude" to talk about how high a place is. Remember, too, we always compare its elevation to sea level. So, we may want to find out how high both Seattle and Boston are above sea level. Good. Now, what other things might we want to know?

RHEA: We might want to know if there is a lot of water close by and the direction the winds blow. That could make a difference.

YOU: That's a good idea, Rhea. For your information, class, winds that blow over a place mostly from the same direction are called "prevailing winds." Now let's think about our ideas. There are three of them. First of all, we will want to know how far each city is north of the equator. Second, we will need to find out how far each city is above sea level. Finally, we'll need to look for information about nearby bodies of water and prevailing winds.

I want people at each table to find out information to answer these three questions:

1. How far north of the equator are Seattle and Boston? You can use the back part of the atlas to find out.
2. How far above sea level is each city? Look at page 345 in the almanac on your table to find out.
3. Are there large bodies of water near each city, and what are the prevailing wind patterns? Use your atlas, and see pages 78 to 81 in your text to find this information. (Monitor pupils as they work.)

All right, let's see what we learned. Who will tell me how far north each city is?

ANDREA: Boston is 42°21' north of the equator, and Seattle is 47°36' north of the equator.

YOU: Thank you, Andrea. Now, does this information explain differences in minimum January temperatures?

SUSAN: No, it doesn't make sense. I mean, Seattle's farther north. It should be colder, but it's not.

YOU: Yes, it's a bit puzzling, isn't it? Let's go on to another possible explanation. How about altitude? What did you find?

GRACIELLA: Seattle's about ten feet above sea level, and Boston's about twenty-one feet.

YOU: Does this explain differences in winter temperature?

ROLAND: I don't think so. There isn't all that much difference. I mean, eleven feet doesn't seem like much to me.

YOU: I think you're right, Roland. The ceiling of this room is about twelve feet higher than the floor. If we keep the air circulating in the room, there probably is not going to be much difference in air temperature anywhere in our room. What else might explain differences between winter temperatures in Seattle and Boston?

DEJUAN: Well, both cities are on water. The winds generally blow over both cities from the same direction—out of the west. I'm not sure that this means anything. I mean, why should this make winter temperatures different?

YOU: That's a good question, DeJuan. Let's think about it for a minute. Let me give you a hint. In the winter time, areas of water are warmer than areas of land. Now, where is the wind coming from in the winter that blows over Seattle and Boston?

RENEE: Out of the west.

YOU: Keep working with that idea, Renee. What is west of Seattle? What is west of Boston?

RENEE: Well, it's mostly Pacific Ocean west of Seattle. It's just land, other states and stuff, west of Boston.

YOU: And why might that be important? What effect might the location of these two cities have on their winter weather?

STEWART: Well, you said that water stays warmer than land in the winter. In Seattle, the wind blows over water. Maybe the wind warms up a little before it gets to Seattle.

YOU: Stewart, you're on the right track. Now what about Boston's situation?

STEWART: Well, in the winter time, the winds out of the west blow over cold land before they get to Boston. Maybe that's why its colder in the winter in Boston than in Seattle.

YOU: I think we've solved our problem.

DECISION MAKING

Many questions we face have no "right" answers. Various responses might be appropriate. Issues of this kind force us to choose from among alternatives. We do this by thinking about available options, weighing evidence, and considering personal values. Thinking of this kind is known as *decision making* (Beyer, 1988).

The following steps are included in many decision-making lessons:

- Identify the basic issue or problem.
- Point out alternative responses.
- Describe evidence supporting each alternative.
- Identify values implied in each alternative.
- Describe possible consequences that might follow selection of each alternative.
- Make a choice from among various alternatives.
- Describe evidence and values considered in making this choice.

There are many possibilities for using decision-making lessons. For example, as part of their effort to help develop pupils' citizenship skills, many schools have a student council. Suppose a group of fifth and sixth graders decided that upper-grade members (from grades five and six) ought to be pupils who have been attending the school for at least three years. Their idea is that newcomers are unfamiliar with the school's traditions and won't be able to represent its true interests well. Present school policy allows any student in grade five or six to run for membership on the student council.

A teacher who was presented with this idea might capitalize on the situation and engage pupils in a decision-making lesson. An example of how such a lesson might develop is given in Lesson Idea 7–6.

Lesson Idea 7–6

DECISION MAKING: ELECTING SCHOOL OFFICERS

Grade Level: 5–6

Objective: Pupils will apply steps of the decision-making process to a problem.

Suggested Procedure: Guide pupils through these steps:

Step 1.   Frame the issue as a proposition worded in this (or a similar) way: "No fifth grader should be allowed to run for membership on the student council unless he or she has been in this school for at least three years."

Step 2.   In this case, there are only two basic alternatives. Alternative one is to support this policy. Alternative two is to maintain the present policy, which allows any fifth or sixth grader to seek election to the student council.

Step 3.   Some of the following evidence might be used to *support* the idea that only fifth and sixth graders who have been in the school three years should be allowed to run for the student council.

- This is a special school that is different from all others. Pupils who have been here for at least three years appreciate its special qualities.
- Learners who have been in the school for at least three years tend to know more people than those who are relative newcomers. They will be better able to represent the interests of all people in the school.
- Some issues such as deciding how to keep first graders from getting hurt on the playground have been considered before. Fifth and sixth graders who have been in the school for at least three years will know what has been tried before and what has and has not worked.

Some of the following evidence might be used to *oppose* the idea that fifth and sixth graders on the student council should have been in the school at least three years.

- Bright people who are new to the school quickly learn about its special qualities. It makes more sense to have a fifth- or sixth-grade student council member who really wants to work on the council than another person who may have been in school longer but who isn't especially interested in being a member.

- New people may bring new ideas that can be used to solve problems that others have been unable to resolve.

Step 4.   The following values might be among those expressed by people who *support* the new proposal.

- Traditions are important; they are likely to be better appreciated by people who have years of familiarity with them.
- People with more experience make more responsible decisions than people with less experience.

The following might be values cited by people who *oppose* the new proposal.

- Maintaining broad interest in student government is more important than ensuring individual members meet strict qualifications for office.
- Years in the school do not necessarily translate to a commitment to the school and its traditions.

Step 5.   The following consequences might be noted by a *supporter* of the three-year requirement.

- Pupils who have been in the school at least three years are likely to help the student council adopt decisions that will please more people in the school than council members who have spent less time enrolled in the school.
- If pupils have been in the school three or more years, they will help the council make better and more efficient decisions. This will happen because they will be very familiar with procedures and ideas that have been tried before.

The following consequences might be cited by an *opponent* of the three-year rule.

- Many in the school will become apathetic about the student council. They will not have any sense of "ownership" in the organization and will be little inclined to support its decisions.
- A decision to require people to have been in the school at least three years before allowing them to run for student council will create two classes of pupils. One category, the politically powerful "upper class" will include fifth and sixth graders who have been in the school three or more years. The second, or "lower class," will include all other fifth and sixth graders.

Step 6. At this point, pupils make a decision to either support or oppose the idea of requiring fifth and sixth graders to have been members of the school for at least three years before allowing them to run for student council membership.

Step 7. A person *supporting* this decision might describe evidence and values related to this issue in this way:

> *"I like the idea that people who have been in school here for at least three years know what the school is really like. I think the school is pretty good just as it is. I think people who have been here for a few years feel more like I do than someone new would. These people are also likely to know a lot of people in other grades. I think that's important, too."*

A person *opposing* the idea might describe values she or he thought relevant to the issue in this way:

> *"I think we need to have the smartest people in the fifth and sixth grades on the student council. Some of them may not have been in our school all that long. I want to be sure we don't have a rule that keeps them from running. Also, if I ever had to go to another school, I wouldn't like being shut out of things because I hadn't gone there as long as somebody else."*

In summary, the decision-making sequence allows pupils to think through alternative solutions to problems. Teachers, as they encourage class members to think about these alternatives as well as evidence and values related to each, involve children in kinds of thinking challenges that daily face adults. As a link to the adult world, decision-making lessons have a definite place in the elementary social studies program.

BOX 7–5   **Decision-Making Issues for Different Grade Levels**

Think About This

Decision-making lessons are used widely in elementary school social studies programs. Because of developmental differences and interest differences of pupils, kinds of problems used as subjects for these lessons vary across grade levels.

- Based on what you know about developmental levels of children and about kinds of issues addressed in social studies classes, identify three or more issues that might be appropriate for decision-making lessons.
- Point out three issues that might be appropriate for pupils in grades K through three and three issues that might be suitable for pupils in grades four through six.

FINDING MORE INFORMATION

Interest in helping pupils develop their thinking capacities has spawned an enormous amount of writing on this topic. You may wish to look over some information sources that we have found to be particularly useful:

- Beyer, B. K., *Developing a Thinking Skills Program* (Boston: Allyn & Bacon, 1988).
- Costa, A. L. (ed.), *Developing Minds: A Resource Book for Teaching Thinking*, Vol. 1 (Alexandria, VA: Association for Supervision and Curriculum Development, 1991).
- Costa, A. L. (ed.), *Developing Minds: Programs for Teaching Thinking*, Vol. 2 (Alexandria, VA: Association for Supervision and Curriculum Development, 1991).
- Garner, R. and Alexander, P. A., "Metacognition: Answered and Unanswered Questions," *Educational Psychologist*, 24 (2, Spring 1989), pp. 143–158.
- Scheid, K., *Helping Students Become Strategic Learners* (Cambridge, MA: Brookline Books, 1993).

KEY IDEAS IN SUMMARY

1. Should teachers spend time teaching thinking skills directly? Today, many people think so. Some critics, however, argue that time spent teaching thinking skills diverts time from instruction that could better be spent on more purely academic subject matter. In response, some authorities claim that pupils learn academic subject content better when they also receive instruction focusing specifically on thinking-skills development.

2. *Metacognition* refers to the process people use to monitor their own thinking as they confront problems or dilemmas. Several instructional approaches seek to help pupils more carefully monitor their thinking processes. The "thinking ₂loud" technique, based on the principle of modeling, requires the teacher to verbalize the steps followed in approaching a task similar to the one pupils will be assigned to do. The "visualizing thinking" technique encourages pupils to develop diagrams they can use to take notes that are clearly relevant to an assigned learning task.

3. Inquiry approaches utilize inductive learning processes. They begin by introducing pupils to isolated pieces of information. Pupils proceed through a series of steps that culminate in their development of an explanatory generalization. General steps in an inquiry lesson are (1) describing essential features of a problem or situation, (2) suggesting possible solutions or explanations, (3) gathering evidence to test these solutions or explanations, (4) evaluating solutions or explanations in light of this evidence, and (5) developing a conclusion based on the best evidence.

4. Data charts can be used to develop pupils' abilities to compare, contrast, and generalize. They typically feature information displayed in a matrix. Pupils use individual cells as they look for patterns, identify similarities and differences, and draw general conclusions.

5. Suchman (1962) developed an inquiry approach that can help pupils reduce the volume of information they must consider when confronted with a problem. It features a focus issue introduced by the teacher and pupil interrogation of the teacher with questions that can be answered either "yes" or "no." Through this procedure, pupils learn to reject broad categories of irrelevant information and to focus on information that will help them solve the problem.

6. Creative thinking requires learners to consider perplexing problems in novel ways. The "product" of good creative thinking must be both new and useful. Brainstorming is one technique teachers use to develop pupils' creative-thinking skills. This procedure encourages them to generate responses in a lively, uninhibited way.

7. Critical thinking requires that judgments be made in light of defensible criteria. Dunn and Dunn (1972) developed an analytic adaptation of brainstorming that is useful for developing pupils' critical-thinking abilities.

8. Problem-solving techniques are used when issues have "correct," "right," or "most appropriate" answers. A typical problem-solving lesson includes four steps: (1) identify the problem, (2) consider possible approaches to its solution, (3) select and apply approaches, and (4) reach a defensible solution.

9. Some problems have several possible solutions. The specific decision a person reaches results from considering evidence and weighing personal values. Decision-making lessons can be used in a variety of circumstances in elementary social studies programs.

CHAPTER REFLECTIONS

Directions: Now that you have finished reading the chapter, reread the case study at the beginning. Then, answer these questions:

1. Should tests be designed that focus on pupils' abilities to use specific higher-level thinking techniques, or should the success of these techniques be measured indirectly by looking at pupil scores on more traditional content tests?

2. Are there really differences among what we call "inquiry approaches," "critical thinking," "problem solving," and "creative thinking," or are these just fancy labels used to describe processes that are more alike than different?

3. Monitoring one's own thinking takes time. Can a logical case be made for teaching pupils to monitor their own thinking when time spent doing so substitutes for lessons focusing on more traditional academic content? Why, or why not?

4. Interest in developing higher-level thinking skills has been a priority of many educational leaders for decades. If this is true, why do you suppose social studies specialist Walter Parker (1988) found so little classroom instructional time dedicated to this kind of teaching?

EXTENDING UNDERSTANDING AND SKILL

1. Think about a social studies topic you might teach at a particular grade level. Find a passage in an elementary text that deals with this issue. Identify at least two learning tasks you might develop for pupils of different ability levels. For each, prepare a visual-thinking diagram.

2. Articles on inquiry teaching frequently are featured in journals such as *The Social Studies* and *Social Education*. Copy two or three articles that describe the use of inquiry techniques at the elementary level. Share them with others in your class. Use material from one of the articles to develop a lesson plan that features inquiry learning.

3. Review chapter material on Dunn and Dunn's analytic brainstorming technique. Identify a social studies topic suitable for presentation using this procedure. Develop a plan outlining what you would do at each phase of the lesson.

4. Review material in this chapter on data charts. Prepare a data chart for making comparisons and contrasts among creative thinking, critical thinking, and problem solving. Share the chart with others in your class. Class members may wish to keep copies as review material for a quiz.

5. Suppose you are asked to address your school's parent-teacher organization on this topic: "Approaches to Improving Thinking Skills." Prepare a draft of your remarks. Ask your instructor to critique your work.

REFERENCES

BAER, J. (1993–1994). "Why You Shouldn't Trust Creativity Tests." *Educational Leadership, 51*(4), pp. 80–83.

BEYER, B. K. (1988). *Developing a Thinking Skills Program*. Boston: Allyn & Bacon.

CHENEY, L. V. (1987) *American Memory: A Report on the Humanities in the Nation's Public Schools*. Washington, DC: National Endowment for the Humanities.

DEWEY, J. (1910). *How We Think*. Boston: D. C. Heath.

DUNN, R., AND DUNN, K. (1972). *Practical Approaches to Individualizing Instruction*. New York: Parker.

FRENCH, J. N. AND RHODER, C. (1992). *Teaching Thinking Skills*. New York: Garland.

HIRSCH, E. D., JR. (1987). *Cultural Literacy: What Every American Needs to Know*. Boston: Houghton Mifflin.

LIPMAN, M. (1988). "Critical Thinking—What Can It Be?" *Educational Leadership, 46*(1), pp. 38–39.

NICKERSON, R. S., PERKINS, D. N., AND SMITH, E. E. (1985). *The Teaching of Thinking.* Hillsdale, NJ: Lawrence Erlbaum Associates.

PARKER, W. C. (1988). "Restoring History to Social Studies—Had It Ever Left?" *Educational Leadership, 45*(7), p. 86.

PERKINS, D. (1981). *The Mind's Best Work.* Cambridge, MA: Harvard University Press.

PERKINS, D. (1993–1994). "Thinking Centered Learning." *Educational Leadership, 51*(4), pp. 84–85.

RAVITCH, D. (1985). *The Schools We Deserve.* New York: Basic Books.

RUGGIERO, V. R. (1988). *Thinking Across the Curriculum.* New York: Harper & Row.

SCHEID, K. (1993). *Helping Students Become Strategic Learners.* Cambridge, MA: Brookline Books.

SLABBERT, J. A. (1994). "Creativity Revisited in Education: Reflection in Aid of Progression." *Journal of Creative Behavior, 28*(1), pp. 60–69.

SUCHMAN, J. R. (1962). *The Elementary School Training Program in Scientific Inquiry.* Report to the U.S. Office of Education, Title VII, Project 216. Urbana, IL: University of Illinois Press.

DEVELOPING PROSOCIAL BEHAVIOR

CHAPTER GOALS

This chapter provides information to help the reader:

- describe the importance of prosocial behavior as an outcome of the social studies program,
- identify the relationship between (1) values and attitudes and (2) prosocial behavior,
- describe sensitive issues related to teaching values and morality,
- point out components of a four-level framework for organizing learning associated with values and morality,
- explain how a moral-dilemma approach can be used in helping develop pupils' moral reasoning abilities, and
- prepare role-playing experiences for use in the elementary classroom.

CHAPTER STRUCTURE

Introduction
Values, Morality, and Prosocial Behavior
    Aesthetic Values
    Moral Values
    James Rest's Framework
    Moral Sensitivity
    Moral Judgment
    Moral Decision Making
    Moral Action
Dealing with Values, Morality, and Prosocial Behavior in the Classroom
    Clarifying Personal and Aesthetic Values
    Values-Situation Role Playing
    Kohlberg's Approach to Developing Moral Judgment
    1.   *Punishment and Obedience Orientation Stage*
    2.   *Instrumental Relativism Stage*
    3.   *Interpersonal Concordance Stage*
    4.   *Law and Order Orientation Stage*
    5.   *Social Contract–Legalistic Orientation Stage*
    6.   *Universal Ethical Principle Orientation Stage*
        Moving From Stage to Stage
    Moral Dilemma Discussions
    Introducing the Moral Dilemma
    Asking Pupils to Suggest Tentative Responses
    Dividing Pupils Into Groups to Discuss Their Reasoning
    Discussing the Reasoning and Formulating a Conclusion
    Teaching Formal Decision Making: Issues, Values, and Consequences
        Analysis
Key Ideas in Summary
Chapter Reflections
Extending Understanding and Skill
References

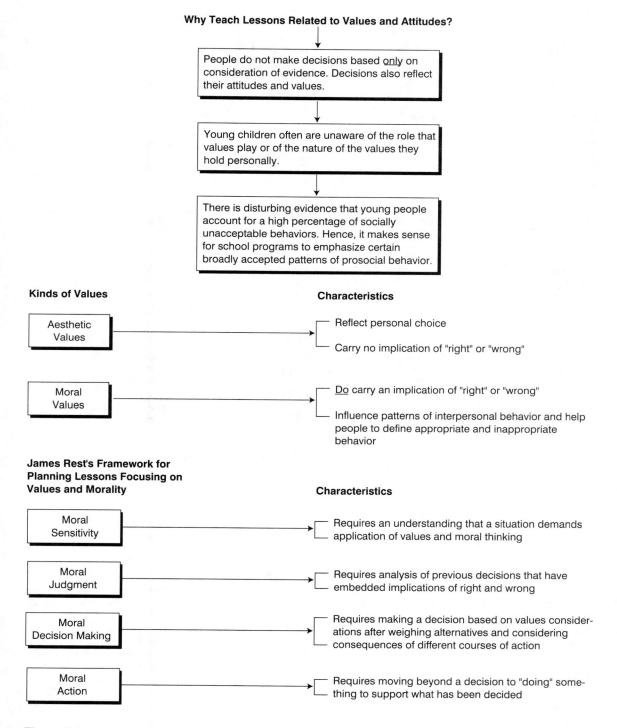

Why Teach Lessons Related to Values and Attitudes?

People do not make decisions based <u>only</u> on consideration of evidence. Decisions also reflect their attitudes and values.

Young children often are unaware of the role that values play or of the nature of the values they hold personally.

There is disturbing evidence that young people account for a high percentage of socially unacceptable behaviors. Hence, it makes sense for school programs to emphasize certain broadly accepted patterns of prosocial behavior.

Kinds of Values

Characteristics

Aesthetic Values
— Reflect personal choice
— Carry no implication of "right" or "wrong"

Moral Values
— <u>Do</u> carry an implication of "right" or "wrong"
— Influence patterns of interpersonal behavior and help people to define appropriate and inappropriate behavior

James Rest's Framework for Planning Lessons Focusing on Values and Morality

Characteristics

Moral Sensitivity
— Requires an understanding that a situation demands application of values and moral thinking

Moral Judgment
— Requires analysis of previous decisions that have embedded implications of right and wrong

Moral Decision Making
— Requires making a decision based on values considerations after weighing alternatives and considering consequences of different courses of action

Moral Action
— Requires moving beyond a decision to "doing" something to support what has been decided

Figure 8–1
Developing prosocial behavior.

Classroom Applications

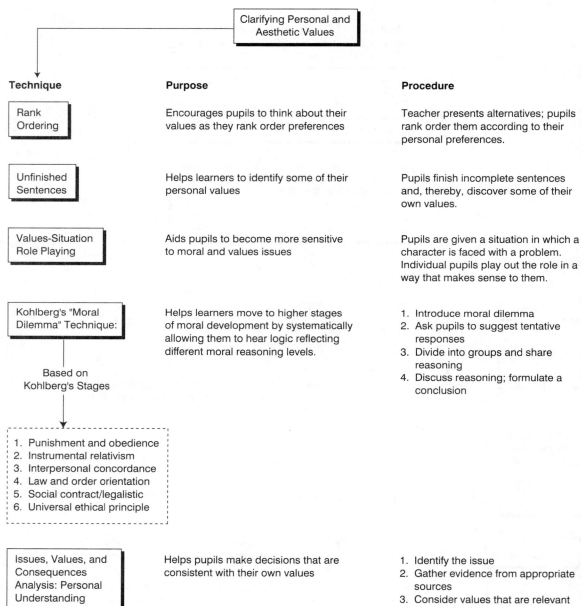

Clarifying Personal and
Aesthetic Values

Technique	Purpose	Procedure
Rank Ordering	Encourages pupils to think about their values as they rank order preferences	Teacher presents alternatives; pupils rank order them according to their personal preferences.
Unfinished Sentences	Helps learners to identify some of their personal values	Pupils finish incomplete sentences and, thereby, discover some of their own values.
Values-Situation Role Playing	Aids pupils to become more sensitive to moral and values issues	Pupils are given a situation in which a character is faced with a problem. Individual pupils play out the role in a way that makes sense to them.
Kohlberg's "Moral Dilemma" Technique:	Helps learners move to higher stages of moral development by systematically allowing them to hear logic reflecting different moral reasoning levels.	1. Introduce moral dilemma 2. Ask pupils to suggest tentative responses 3. Divide into groups and share reasoning 4. Discuss reasoning; formulate a conclusion

Based on
Kohlberg's Stages

1. Punishment and obedience
2. Instrumental relativism
3. Interpersonal concordance
4. Law and order orientation
5. Social contract/legalistic
6. Universal ethical principle

Issues, Values, and Consequences Analysis: Personal Understanding	Helps pupils make decisions that are consistent with their own values	1. Identify the issue 2. Gather evidence from appropriate sources 3. Consider values that are relevant to the issue 4. Identify possible solutions 5. Point out consequences of possible solutions 6. Make a decision and provide a rationale

Figure 8–1
continued

Technique	Purpose	Procedure
Issues, Values, and Consequences Analysis: Appreciating Personal Decisions Made by Others	Helps pupils grasp values dilemmas others faced when they have had to make difficult choices.	1. Identify the issue 2. Describe Faction A 3. Identify information seen as relevant by Faction A 4. Describe relevant alternatives open to Faction A 5. Point out possible consequences of each Faction A alternative 6. Describe Faction B 7. Identify information seen as relevant by Faction B 8. Describe the relevant alternatives open to Faction B 9. Point out possible consequences of each Faction B alternative 10. Relate and compare alternatives open to each Faction, relate and compare probable consequences of each alternative, make decisions 11. Apply to another setting

Figure 8–1
continued

Chapter 8

Case Study

DOES IT MAKE SENSE TO TEACH COMMON VALUES TO PROMOTE PROSOCIAL BEHAVIOR?

Joe Simpson and Marie Bellaby, both fifth-grade teachers, recently were designated by Manisha Ramy, the principal of Culver Elementary School, as members of a team charged with identifying certain values that all teachers in the school should be teaching to their pupils. Both have found this to be an extremely frustrating assignment. Joe recently shared his concerns with Ms. Ramy. This is what he said:

"I want you to know that Marie is a great colleague. I respect her. But we just don't see things in the same way. I am 'pro choice' all the way; Marie is just as committed to the 'pro life' position. I am totally opposed to capital punishment; Marie supports it and thinks it's a real deterrent to crime. I think the government should provide some tax support to all schools, including those run by churches and private organizations; Marie is opposed to this idea, especially to using tax money to support parochial schools. I think there are important strength differences between men and women that make it legitimate for some occupations such as firefighting to be restricted to males; Marie thinks every occupation ought to be equally open to both sexes. I think spanking children, assuming parental permission has been obtained, is a perfectly legitimate way for teachers to discipline members of their class; Marie is totally opposed to corporal punishment in the schools. I think the government has gone too far and has caused our country to lose jobs to overseas competitors by placing an excessive number of environmental regulations on industry; Marie thinks the health of future generations is seriously at risk from pollution and that more government regulation is needed.

"As you can see, our values simply differ. We just don't see a lot of issues in the same way. If the two of us can't agree on these things, how can we propose a set of values that should be taught to every pupil in school?"

What Is Your Response?

Read the information above. Think about Joe's concerns. Then, respond briefly to these questions:

1. Are the differences Joe describes so serious that any attempt to identify a set of values to be taught to all learners will fail? Why, or why not?
2. Joe claims to have identified quite a few important differences in how he and Marie see key issues. Are these differences common, or is this a rather unusual situation? Why do you think so?
3. If the principal insists that Joe and Marie continue to try to identify common values to be taught to all pupils in the school, what do you think will happen?
4. If you were the principal, how would you respond to Joe's comments?
5. Does the school have a legitimate interest in passing on certain values to all pupils? Support your answer.

INTRODUCTION

Fans of the *Star Trek* series know that people from Vulcan make decisions in ways that strike Earthlings as strange. They look *only* at evidence and then apply their logical reasoning powers. We do more than that. Any time we make a choice, values and attitudes come into play. Since these predispositions influence adults as they go about the business of daily living, schools have an obligation to help young people understand issues associated with values and attitudes.

Researchers have found some interesting variables that influence how people feel about certain kinds of things. For example, we now know that individuals empathize more with people they believe to be similar to themselves and with people they are likely to personally meet than with people living in distant places (Hoffman, 1993). The "familiarity-similarity" bias and the "here and now" bias have important implications for us as social studies teachers. They suggest a need for lessons that emphasize similarities among people and that attempt to "make real" people who are unlikely ever to be in the physical presence of our learners. Instruction must strive to inculcate a truly global perspective that helps pupils to break down feelings that there is a "they" out there who are fundamentally different than "we" are (Perry & McIntire, 1994).

Though instruction tied to issues associated with values can be controversial, increasingly there is a recognition that "we share a basic morality, essential for our survival; that adults must promote this morality by teaching the young, directly and indirectly, such values as respect, responsibility, trustworthiness, fairness, caring, and civic virtue" (Lickona, 1993, p. 9).

There is nothing new about the expectation that public schools should be concerned about these issues. As an institution, "the school has always been seen as one of the means by which the culture transmits its values from one generation to the next" (Rogers & Freiberg, 1994, p. 277). There is disturbing evidence that we have not been succeeding as well as we would like in encouraging young people to embrace behaviors widely held to be "moral." Some frightening statistics support this point. In one recent year, almost half of the hate crimes in this country were committed by young people under 21 years of age. On another topic, a survey of middle school and high school students found that nearly one-third of the students claimed they would willingly participate in a hostile act against a member of another cultural group (Heller & Hawkins, 1994). Given the increasing ethnic diversity of our country, these views hint at significant social problems to come. Will there be warring factions in the United States similar to those that strain social fabrics in Northern Ireland, parts of Africa, and Bosnia? We like to think not; *but*, present trends suggest a need for countervailing measures in the schools.

Social studies teachers have a delicate balancing act to play. One the one hand, they foster the development of pupils as individuals. On the other, they seek to nurture a commitment to certain core moral perspectives that represent a kind of "social glue" that binds together everybody in the country. Collectively, the behaviors that are thought to contribute to the stability and betterment of our society are called *prosocial behavior*.

Developing prosocial behavior requires more than providing information to pupils. It involves consideration of values and personal ethics. People take action only when "evidence" is supported by a strong sense of personal commitment and belief. Since this is true, the social studies program, as it seeks to promote the development of pupils' prosocial behavior, must permit them to consider individual values and morality and allow them opportunities to act on their beliefs.

There is broad support for the general idea of teaching moral behavior patterns in school. However, some schools are criticized for what they are trying to do. This criticism often comes from people who approve of the general idea of teaching moral behavior but do not like the specific types of prosocial behavior that the schools seem to be encouraging. Some parents, for example, may feel that values and patterns of morality espoused in some lessons conflict with those being stressed at home.

Lessons that deal with values and morality must be prepared and presented carefully. They should encourage learners to act in informed and intelligent ways as they seek to bring about change. This chapter offers suggestions about how the social studies program can contribute to the development of these behaviors.

VALUES, MORALITY, AND PROSOCIAL BEHAVIOR

Prosocial behaviors include those individual actions that contribute to the general well-being of humankind. They are directed toward the good of others as opposed to an exclusive concern for self.

Prosocial behavior rests on the values and sense of morality of the individual. *Values* are those bedrock beliefs that give direction to a person's life. They are convictions that are so deeply rooted that they guide people as they make decisions about how they spend their time, talents, and money. Types of values range from aesthetic values, concerned with issues relating to beauty and style, to moral values, concerned with broad questions of right and wrong.

Aesthetic Values

Aesthetic values reflect personal choice. They carry no connotations of "right" and "wrong" or of "good" and "bad." For example, one person may prefer classical music, another may prefer country-western music. Neither preference is "right" or "wrong." Each is a simple aesthetic preference of an individual. Aesthetic values add a stimulating variety to life.

Aesthetic values deserve attention in the social studies program. First of all, it is important for pupils to learn that others may have aesthetic preferences that differ from their own. Tolerance for diversity of aesthetic perspectives is an important outcome of social studies instruction.

Second, pupils need opportunities to clarify their own aesthetic values. Individuals who are clear about those things they prize and value need to be encouraged to develop commitments and to take actions in support of these values. For example, a person who strongly values the beauty of nature might choose to spend time on community beautification projects.

Third, though individuals have different sets of aesthetic values, there tend to be groups of people who share compatible sets. Comparative study of aesthetic values of different cultures and societies adds an important dimension to lessons in elementary social studies programs.

Moral Values

Moral values *do* carry connotations of right and wrong. Moral values influence patterns of interpersonal relationship, and they help people define appropriate and inappropriate behavior. Among moral values that are of particular interest to the social studies teacher are those focusing on justice, equality, fairness, basic rights such as life and liberty, freedoms such as religion and speech, respect for human worth and dignity, and the rule of law. Some moral values are deeply held throughout the world. For example, all world cultures hold human life to be sacred. Murder is everywhere considered to be an immoral act. Such basic moral values ought to be emphasized in every social studies program. The actions and lives of others and the study of other cultures has little meaning unless it is related to these concepts of morality.

James Rest's Framework

James Rest (1983) developed a four-level framework to identify the elements included in lessons focusing on values and morality:

- Moral sensitivity
- Moral judgment
- Moral decision making
- Moral action

Moral Sensitivity
At the moral sensitivity level, people must understand that they face a situation that calls on them to apply values and moral thinking. In the elementary social studies program, this stage requires pupils to appreciate that making a decision demands more than a simple consideration of evidence. They must appreciate that a value or moral judgment precedes the final act of deciding.

Moral Judgment
At the moral judgment level, there is analysis of previous decisions that have implications of right and wrong embedded within them. In the social studies classroom, lessons focusing on this level engage pupils in considering decisions they or others have made. They proceed to analyze the principles or values that led to these decisions. Pupils learn that people who have different basic values have different conceptions about what constitutes moral behavior. As a result, they learn that it is possible for people to defend, on moral grounds, very different decisions about a common issue.

Moral Decision Making

The moral decision-making level requires people to move beyond the analysis of decisions based on the values of the decision maker. Individuals are confronted with an unsolved problem. They are introduced to evidence related to the problem, and are challenged to consider different value positions related to associated issues. They are asked to describe decisions that would be consistent with different value positions. Typically, they are also required to comment on the possible consequences of these decision alternatives. Finally, they are asked to make personal decisions about the problem and to defend their positions.

Moral Action

At the moral action level, a person is asked to move beyond a statement about what she would do about a given problem. The individual is required to go beyond "talking" to "doing." This requires action in support of the decision that has been made. For example, in an elementary classroom, if a pupil (or several pupils) decided that the best way to "improve school" was to eliminate the trash on the playground, the moral action level would require them to remove it. Merely "saying" that trash removal would be the preferred action would not suffice. The level of moral action reflects a much stronger value commitment than the moral decision-making level.

DEALING WITH VALUES, MORALITY, AND PROSOCIAL BEHAVIOR IN THE CLASSROOM

Several instructional approaches have been developed for addressing values issues and morality issues in the classroom. The best of these call for active pupil participation and

---

BOX 8–1   **Should Young Children Learn about Values?**

A State Board of Education recently held public hearings on a proposed new elementary social studies program. Members of the public were invited to testify. The following comments were made by one person who spoke at the hearing:

"The proposed new social studies program asks children to inquire into the personal values of some of the historical people they're studying. These children will even be asked to comment about whether they personally approve of the values of these people.

"It seems to me that this is going to lead boys and girls to ask their parents about their attitudes and values. I don't think this appropriate for children who are this young. It may be fine when they're older. The job of younger children is to accept their parents as they are. I think the social studies program should just stick to teaching youngsters the facts."

Think About This

1. Why do you think designers of the program included lessons focusing on values?
2. The person giving this testimony felt that such instruction might cause problems for parents. Do you agree?
3. What is your personal reaction to this testimony?
4. How does your reaction reveal some of your own values?

demand high levels of personal involvement. Certain techniques are useful for developing moral sensitivity and moral judgment. Others are appropriate for encouraging decision making and moral action. In this section, we discuss aspects of clarifying personal and aesthetic values, and introduce the technique of values-situation role playing. We then discuss Kohlberg's (1975, 1980) approach to developing moral judgment, and conclude with suggestions for teaching for moral decision-making, with special attention given to teaching relating to issues, values, and consequences analysis.

Clarifying Personal and Aesthetic Values

Clarifying those things that are important in one's life is an essential step toward developing commitments and taking action. People often are confused about the values that influence their choices. Instructional techniques designed to heighten pupils' sensitivity to their own values do not focus on issues that have right or wrong answers. Neither do they force them to select any one position. Their purpose is to help learners think about what values are important to them and whether their behaviors are consistent with these values. Simon, Howe, and Kirschenbaum (1978) outline several procedures that are useful for this purpose, including rank ordering and unfinished sentences. Lesson ideas 8–1 and 8–2 illustrate how you might choose to implement these approaches.

Lesson Idea 8–1

WHAT WOULD YOU DO WITH YOUR TIME?

Grade Level: 3–6

Objective: Pupils will identify the influence of values on the choices people make.

Overview: This is a "rank ordering" lesson. It begins with the teacher giving pupils several alternative actions, and asking learners to rank them in terms of their individual preferences. Pupils are given a minute or two to think. Then they are invited to share their rankings and their reasons for making their choices.

Suggested Procedures: *1. Focus Component*   Introduce this component by saying the following: "All of us have made decisions about what we do with our free time. Today, I would like you to pretend that it is Saturday morning. You have three things you can do. I would like you to think about these three things. Then, decide which one would be your first choice, which one would be your second choice, and which one would be your third choice. When we finish, if you want to share your choices with others in the class, you may. But, you may also keep your ideas to yourself if you want to. Here are the three choices:

• You can watch your favorite program on television.

- You can play with your best friend as his or her house.
- You can spend the day with your family at the park.

Think for a minute about your choices. Would anyone like to share his or her ideas with us?"

2. Discussion Component   Initiate a whole class discussion of the alternatives (sample beginning follows):

JOSÉ: I would want to go and play with my friend.

YOU: Why did you choose that first?

JOSÉ: Well, I don't get to see my friend much anymore, and I thinking playing with friends is more fun than the other things.

SHARON: I would want to go with my family because we always have fun when we do things together. I think a person's family is more important than friends or TV.

(Discussion continues until all who want to respond have had an opportunity to do so.)

3. Debriefing   Bring closure to the discussion by making generalizations, such as the following: "Today we have discussed how people might make different choices about what do with their time. Some think that spending time with their families is important. Others think that spending time with friends is a good idea. Others feel it is a good idea sometimes to do something just by yourself. All three of these are reasonable ideas. When we make choices we have to think about what is most important to us. We also need to think about the possible results of our choices. For example, will spending time with a friend hurt the feelings of a member of our own family? If so, we might need to rethink our choice."

Lesson Idea 8–2

UNFINISHED SENTENCES

Grade Level: 5–6

Objective: Pupils will state things they value by completing sentences.

Suggested Procedures: Unfinished sentences help pupils think about what they value. Begin by preparing some partial sentences, called *sentence stems*. They deal with ideas that interest pupils. Next, tell learners to complete the sentences. Younger pupils usually are asked to do this orally. Older pupils may write complete sentences that incorporate the given sentence stems.

1. Focus   Begin by saying the following: "Today I am going to read you the first part of a sentence. I would like you to complete the sentence using your own words. Write your new sentences on your own paper. We will do several sentences. When we finish, I will ask any of you who want to share your sentences to read aloud what you have written. Here are the unfinished sentences I would like you to complete" (read stems one at a time, giving pupils time to add their own words to build complete sentences):

- "If I could describe myself to someone else, I would say that I am . . . "
- "The person we have read about who I would most like to be like is . . . "
- "The thing I am best at is . . . "
- "I am happiest when . . . "

2. Discussion   Initiate discussion, as in the sample beginning that follows:

YOU: Who would like to share some sentences with us? Chou.

CHOU: I am happiest when I draw pictures.

YOU: Why does that make you happy?

CHOU: Well, people tell me I draw good pictures, and I like to hear them say that.

YOU: Are there other reasons why some people might like to draw?

BILLY: Some people can tell about what they feel better by drawing pictures than by talking. It makes them feel good to draw about their feelings.

YOU: Does anyone else wish to share a sentence? (Discussion continues as long as pupils are willing to share their sentences.)

3. Debriefing   Provide closure by making generalizations, such as the following: "Today we have all had an opportunity to respond to some sentence stems that allowed us to think about ourselves. If we think about the kinds of people we want to be and the things we enjoy, then we need to think about what we can do to become those kinds of people. Some of you might want to spend more time thinking about and writing these sentences. You may do so during the rest of the day when you have finished other work. If some of you want to talk to me individually about your sentences, I will be glad to talk with you."

Values-Situation Role Playing

As pupils begin to develop a personal sense of morality, they become more sensitive to situations where moral principles need to be applied. Role-playing activities help them recognize these situations. They call on learners to make value judgments as they make decisions consistent with their understanding of the worldview of the person whose part they are playing.

Learners' moral sensitivity levels can also be enhanced by lessons calling on them to look for values and moral issues as they occur in history and in present political and economic conflicts. Values-situation role playing is a technique that helps learners become more sensitive to moral and values issues. It confronts them with a values and moral dilemma that calls on them to test alternatives and to explore possible consequences of various responses. In a short debriefing session, the teacher and members of the class discuss each response. These are the typical steps:

- Introduce pupils to a situation.
- Select individuals to role play their responses.
- Discuss each response with the class as a whole.
- Debrief at the end of the exercise. Draw attention to the pros and cons of each response, and call attention to other possible responses that pupils may not have considered.

There are several ways to introduce pupils to a focus problem for a values-situation role-playing activity. You might propose a simple situation, or pupils might respond to a question such as, "Can you think of a time when you had a hard time deciding the right thing to do?" Another approach is to provide class members with an unfinished short story. Typically, a character in the story is faced with making a difficult choice. Pupils role play this character and make a choice that seems sensible to them. The short-story approach works well because, when the stories are well written, they capture pupils' interest and generate enthusiasm for the role-playing activity. Values-situation role playing can focus on many kinds of issues. In the lower grades, teachers often focus on self-understanding and on understanding of others. In the middle and upper grades, pupils are exposed to more content from history and the social sciences. At these grade levels, values-situation role-playing lessons often are used to help learners better understand value dilemmas that people have faced in other times and places. Lesson Ideas 8–3 and 8–4 present samples of this approach.

Lesson Idea 8–3

VALUES-SITUATION ROLE PLAYING: SELF-UNDERSTANDING

Grade Level: K–2

Objective: Pupils will identify difficulties associated with solving personal problems and state alternative choices to a given problem situation.

Overview:

The purpose of values-situation role playing lessons that focus on self-understanding is to help pupils think through some of their personal problems. Lessons might relate to such issues as self-doubt, worries about the future, concerns about grades, and fear of the dark. They are designed to help pupils realize that many personal problems are complex. They do not have absolutely right or wrong answers. Solutions depend on many factors, including personal values.

Suggested Procedure:

Focus Story   Begin by telling the class the following story:

> *Joel hates the dark. When his mother tucks him in at night and turns out the light, he waits quietly until she leaves the room. Then he leaps out of bed and silently runs to the light switch. When he hops back into bed, he feels good and goes right to sleep.*
>
> *Joel's mother has told him there is nothing scary about the dark. His uncle has offered to take Joel fishing this weekend if he can go a whole week without turning on the light in his room after his mother tucks him in and leaves. Joel really wants to go fishing. But he knows something terrible will happen to him and that he'll never get to sleep if he's alone all night in a dark room.*
>
> *On Monday night, Joel's mother puts him to bed, reminds him about the possible fishing trip, turns off the light, and leaves the room. Joel is nervous. What should he do?*

2. Role Playing and Discussion   Initiate role playing and encourage students as in the following sample:

> You: John, you go first. Pretend that you're Joel. You're in the bedroom trying to decide what to do. Tell us your idea.
>
> John: I really want to go fishing, but there's no way I can go to sleep in the dark. I'm going to stuff a pillowcase along the bottom of the door and turn the light on. That way, my mom won't know I've turned it back on.
>
> You: All right, class, we've heard John's idea. How do we feel about it?
>
> Rosa: I don't think Joel will be able to sleep. He'll worry about whether his mother will look in to see whether the light's out.
>
> James: Maybe Joel won't feel good inside. I mean, he may fool his mom, but he'll know he's done something wrong.

(Other comments from pupils follow.)

> You: Sarah, why don't you play Joel this time?

SARAH: I really want to go fishing, but I'm so scared of the dark that I just can't stand it. I'd tell my mom that I just can't go to sleep with the light off.

YOU: How about some ideas about Sarah's approach to the problem?

RODNEY: That idea is going to make Joel unhappy. He's not going to go fishing. It's also going to make his mother unhappy. Joel still won't be sleeping with the light off. I don't think it's much of an answer.

JILL: Maybe Joel's mom should come up with a new plan. If Joel is this afraid of the dark, a whole week is going to be too hard. Maybe she should expect only one or two nights of sleeping in the dark at first.

(Other pupil comments follow.)

3. Debriefing   Bring closure by making generalizations, encouraging further discussion as appropriate.

YOU: Let me list some of the ideas we've identified:

- Joel should give up the fishing trip because he's too afraid of the dark.
- Joel should pretend he's sleeping in the dark by putting a pillowcase at the bottom of the door so his mother won't know he's turned the light back on.
- Joel's mother should be asked to set a more reasonable number of nights with no light. This will give Joel a better chance to succeed.

PAULA: Maybe Joel's mother should talk to him about why he's so afraid of the dark.

JOYCE: It might help if his mom said she used to be afraid of the dark, too. Maybe she could explain how she got over this problem.

LUIS: I think Joel's mom should buy him one of those small night lights. You know, the kind that uses a Christmas tree light bulb. Maybe she'd let him keep this small light on when the big light was turned off.

YOU: These are interesting ideas. Any others?

(Discussion continues.)

YOU: Have any of you faced a situation similar to Joel's? What did you do? Why did you act in this way?

(Discussion continues.)

BOX 8–2   **Should Pupils Be Taught That Some Things Are Absolutely Right or Wrong?**

The following editorial appeared in a local newspaper:

> We applaud efforts of local school authorities to put important new substance into the elementary social studies program. The new curriculum provides young people with much-needed training in making complex decisions.
>
> The program works like this. Pupils are given unfinished stories. At the end of each, a major character faces a difficult choice. There is no clear-cut "right" answer. Pupils are asked what they would do in this situation. They role play their responses. The teacher follows with a discussion focusing on the values implicit in the decisions they have made.
>
> This kind of activity is outstanding. It helps young people understand that life's issues are complex. They need to understand that there are no easy and simple answers to many of the dilemmas we face.
>
> On the other hand, our society has determined that answers to some questions are *not* open to debate. For example, we do not countenance a discussion that murder might be "right." That it is wrong is nearly universally acknowledged.
>
> We at *The Journal* would be pleased if the proposed new social studies program would add a few lessons pointing to youngsters that there are some positions we do not debate. All truths are not relative.

Think About This

1. What danger does the editorial writer see associated with the present proposal for a new elementary social studies program?
2. What kinds of things might be among those that are "not open to debate"?
3. What would you say in a letter to the editor commenting on this editorial?

Lesson Idea 8–4

VALUES-SITUATION ROLE PLAYING: USING CONTENT FROM HISTORY

Grade Level:	5
Objectives:	Pupils will (1) identify conflicting values when confronted with choices and (2) state possible consequences associated with alternative choices.
Overview:	Values-situation role-playing lessons with a historical focus seek to help pupils appreciate value dilemmas people have faced in the past. They help them understand that value conflicts have always been a part of the human experience.
Suggested Procedures:	***1. Focus Story*** Begin by telling the following story to the class: In 1862, Joseph Fender was 17 years old. He lived with his mother and father in central Kentucky. For months, talk had been of little other than the Civil War. Joseph looked

forward to June when he would become a soldier. But which side should he choose?

Joseph's mother's family, the Gibsons, came from central Ohio. All of his Gibson cousins were fighting in the Union army. His father's family came from Tennessee. His uncles and cousins on his father's side were fighting in the gray uniforms of the South.

"Joseph," his mother called, "here's a letter for you from Grandfather Fender." Grandfather Fender lived in Memphis, in western Tennessee. Joseph's grandfather wrote, "Your father writes that you will be going off to join the war in June. In my heart, I know you will remember your southern roots. All of the Fenders are fighting for the South. Your father's Kentucky tobacco lands are really part of the South. Your speech is like that of the rest of the family here in Tennessee. You belong in a gray uniform. May God give you the insight to make the right decision."

Grandfather Fender's letter certainly didn't make matters easier. Just yesterday, Joseph had received a letter from Cousin Norman, his mother's nephew, who lived in Cincinnati. Joseph recalled the words of Cousin Norman's letter: "I am home on leave from the Union forces. Believe me, I'm proud to be in a blue uniform. With all of our factories here in the North, we have excellent equipment and supplies. There is little doubt we'll win. But even more important, we have 'right' on our side. All of the Gibson people have joined up. We expect to see you in a Union uniform soon. The Ohio River joins Ohio and Kentucky. Kentucky has more shared interests with Ohio and the North than with the South. Remember, even our brave President, Abe Lincoln, was born in Kentucky."

2. Role Playing and Discussion   Initiate role playing and encourage students, as in the following example:

YOU: I am going to ask several of you to pretend that you are Joseph. I want you to tell us what you would have done and why. Who wants to be first? (Several pupils play the role of Joseph. After each portrayal, lead a followup discussion.)

3. Debriefing   Bring closure by making generalizations, discussing all of the positions mentioned by the several role players. Steer the discussion to assure that pupils emerge with a thorough understanding of the value conflicts inherent in the focus situation.

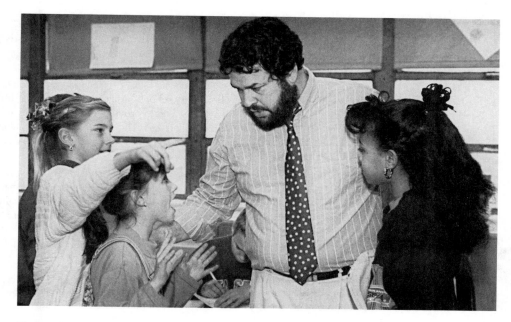

Understanding alternative solutions and possible consequences is an important part of learning value and prosocial behavior.

These role-playing exercises actively involve pupils in making choices involving conflicts of values. They help them to recognize that choices have consequences. Often, even the "best" choice has accompanying results that are not completely desirable. Lessons such as those illustrated in Lesson Ideas 8–3 and 8–4 help pupils think seriously about consequences tied to alternative courses of action. They help them realize, too, that difficult problems rarely have easy solutions.

One key to success in values-situation role playing is using good focus stories. Many teachers write these themselves. Several other sources are available. One that we particularly like is *Role Playing in the Curriculum*, by Fannie R. Shaftel and George Shaftel (1982).

Kohlberg's Approach to Developing Moral Judgment

When people make moral judgments, they make subjective decisions about right and wrong. In doing so, they apply certain criteria. Kohlberg (1975) identified six stages of moral development. People at each stage apply certain criteria and logic when they make moral judgments.

1. Punishment and Obedience Orientation Stage

People at this stage make decisions based on their respect for raw power. They may feel that if they make a decision that runs counter to the views of "authorities" something

---

BOX 8–3   **Do Lessons Focusing on Values Help or Hinder Elementary Pupils?**

Two teachers recently exchanged these views:

TEACHER A: Children in our elementary schools are going to be making difficult decisions all of their lives. We need to provide them with plenty of opportunities to think about complex issues. They need practice in making these
kinds of decisions. It is not too early even in the elementary grades to learn
that not all questions have easy answers.

TEACHER B: We push our elementary school children too fast. Are they really capable
about thinking about sophisticated values conflicts? I think many of them
become confused by lessons that require them to consider values. Perhaps
we should leave the job of dealing with values to teachers of older children
and to parents.

Think About This

1. Are elementary pupils too young for lessons focusing on values?
2. What personal experiences can you draw on to support your position?
3. Suppose you were to join these teachers in this discussion. What would you say?

---

terrible may happen. An elementary child at this stage might say something like, "I
made my bed this morning because my father would have spanked me if I hadn't made
it."

2. Instrumental Relativism Stage

People who are at this stage make their decisions based on feelings that they might
receive a certain advantage if they make a particular choice. It is the logic of the reciprocal back-scratching variety: "If you help me with my arithmetic, I'll help you write
your theme."

2. Interpersonal Concordance Stage

At this stage, individuals make decisions consistent with the feelings of a group with
which they identify: "If I give to the charity drive, then our class will have 100 percent
participation, and we can display the special door banner."

4. Law and Order Orientation Stage

People at this stage decide issues based on their respect for established rules, regulations, and traditional social practices. They prize duty and formal authority: "I may not
like the speed limit, but if that's the law, I'll drive no faster."

5. Social Contract–Legalistic Orientation Stage

Decisions at this stage are not based exclusively on laws. Rather, they involve consideration of the formal rules and guidelines of the entire society, and of personal values and

opinions. When no guidelines for a particular situation are available, people at this stage rely on personal insights. Their reasoning is characterized by a willingness to take action to change formal rules: "I'm going to challenge the way the school district has drawn these attendance boundaries. They are unfair to some people."

6. Universal Ethical Principle Orientation Stage

At this stage, people make decisions based on individual conscience, taking into account such universal principles as respect for human life, love, and dignity. There is no necessary reliance on formal rules, traditions, or other guidelines. The universal principles guiding decisions are chosen by people who make the decisions; they need not be suggested by others: "I know what I say will not be popular, but my words are not my real message. I want to take a stand in support of the idea of freedom of speech. In the long run, respect for this principle will make people happy, even though, in the short run, my words may anger them."

Moving from Stage to Stage

People progress through these stages sequentially. No one can be a third-stage decision maker who has not previously passed through the first and second stages. Moral development stops at different stages for different people. Some never go beyond stage one. Only a very small number of people reach the highest stages of moral development (Kohlberg, 1980).

According to Kohlberg's theory, a person at a given stage is capable of making decisions based on the logic of this and all lower stages. A high percentage of decisions will display reasoning patterns associated with the uppermost stage attained. People are not thought capable of making decisions based on the logic of stages they have not attained.

Movement upward from one moral stage to another is believed to be facilitated by exposure to higher-stage moral reasoning. People are thought capable of understanding the logic associated with one stage above their own highest-attained stage, but not likely to understand moral reasoning involving logic more than one stage above that level.

Moral Dilemma Discussions

Because as people at higher stages of moral development tend to have more concern for others than people at lower stages, followers of Kohlberg are interested in helping people move from lower to higher moral-development levels. One approach that has been used in social studies classes is the "Moral Dilemma Discussion." This technique features these steps:

- Introduce the moral dilemma.
- Ask pupils to suggest tentative responses.
- Divide pupils into groups to discuss their reasoning.
- Discuss the reasoning and formulate a conclusion.

BOX 8–4   Moral Reasoning and Individual Pupil Counseling

Moral reasoning can be used to counsel individual pupils as well as to consider moral dilemmas in class. In listening to a pupil's explanation for misbehavior, the teacher can note the logic and try to identify the moral reasoning stage it represents. Then, the teacher tries to respond with logic that is a single stage higher than that represented by the pupil's explanation. Consider these examples:

Episode 1

TERESA: Yes, I did look at Anne's paper. I mean, I did it just a little.

TEACHER: Tell me exactly what happened.

TERESA: Anne's terrible in math, and I'm pretty good. I said I'd let her peek at a few of my math answers if I could see a few of her social studies quiz answers.

TEACHER: Teresa, I'm concerned about your reputation. Do you want all of your friends thinking you're a cheater?

Episode 2

TERESA: Yes, I did look at Anne's paper. I mean, I did it just a little.

TEACHER: Tell me exactly what happened.

TERESA: Anne's terrible in math, and I'm pretty good. I said I'd let her peek at a few of my math answers if I could see a few of her social studies quiz answers.

TEACHER: Teresa, I want to read you a section from our school handbook. It says that "any pupil who cheats may be subject to appropriate punishment as designated by the principal or by district policy." We simply must follow the rules.

Think About This

1. What moral stage is suggested by Teresa's response?
2. What moral stages are reflected in the teacher's response in each episode?
3. Which teacher response is the more appropriate? Why do you think so?
4. What other, different, responses would you make if you were this teacher?

Introducing the Moral Dilemma

The dilemma selected should be an issue that has meaning for pupils. It should also have some of the complexity of the issues they will face as adults. The material introducing the dilemma should be short and tightly focused on the situation. A dilemma can be introduced in prose form, on film, on cassette tapes, or in some other suitable manner. The following is an example of a moral dilemma that might serve as a focus of a moral reasoning discussion:

Kim Kamatsu is in the sixth grade. She has an older brother in junior high school. Her twin sisters are in the third grade.

Kim's father, Henry, used to make a good living as a steelworker. The plant where he was employed closed six months ago. He has taken odd jobs here and there, but has not found anything permanent. The family has had a difficult time financially. Savings are gone. Kim's mother, Katherine, works at a low-paying job. She worries about how she will feed and clothe her family.

Today, Kim is shopping with her mother in a large grocery store. As she walks down the aisle, she notices seventy-five dollars worth of food stamps that have fallen from a shopper's purse. She stoops to pick them up. Kim looks at the stamps and thinks about what they will buy. Should she keep them, or should she return them to the person who lost them?

Asking Pupils to Suggest Tentative Responses

After the class has been introduced to the dilemma, each pupil is asked to write down what she or he would do, along with a brief explanation of the decision. Next, the teacher asks (for the above example) for a show of hands of those pupils who think Kim should keep the food stamps and of those who think she should return them.

Dividing Pupils into Groups to Discuss Their Reasoning

The teacher then divides the class into five or six groups, taking care to assure that each group includes pupils who want Kim to keep the food stamps and others who want her to return them. The teacher instructs pupils to take turns in their groups explaining their choices, emphasizing that the discussion is to focus on *why* pupils made their decisions, not on what they chose. The teacher circulates from group to group to keep pupils on task.

There is a good chance that most groups will contain pupils at different moral reasoning levels. As a result, many pupils in a group may have an opportunity to be exposed to logic characteristics of a moral-development level that is one stage higher

Group discussion of a moral dilemma facilitates pupil movement to the next higher stage.

than their own. This can help them move to higher moral reasoning stage. These discussions should be kept brief. With fifth and sixth graders, for example, five or ten minutes is plenty. The idea is to maintain intense interaction. When the teacher senses the discussions have gone on long enough, she asks each group to select a spokesperson.

Discussing the Reasoning and Formulating a Conclusion

During the concluding phase of the exercise, the teacher provides either a large chalkboard area or strips of butcher paper and marking pens. The spokespersons write their group's reasons supporting each viewpoint. The reasons are displayed so the whole class can see them.

The teacher leads a discussion covering all noted reasons, being careful to remain nonjudgmental and accepting of each pupil's idea. The teacher tries to elicit comments reflecting a mixture of moral reasoning states.

After this discussion, the teacher asks each learner to take a piece of paper and write down the three or four best reasons that support the position he or she does *not* support personally. This requires pupils to think carefully about logic other than their own. Learners then write down the three or four most compelling reasons supporting their own position. The teacher does not collect these papers, but may choose to elicit this information from learners during individual conferences.

In summary, moral reasoning discussions help learners think about their own logic as well as that of others. During the exercise, opportunities arise for them to be exposed to levels of reasoning different from their own. This exposure may help some pupils advance to higher moral reasoning levels.

When we use moral reasoning discussions in the classroom, we should not set our expectations too high. There are many variables over which we have little personal control influencing what goes on during a discussion. For example, in a given group, there may be little disagreement among members about the course of action to be taken in response to the provided problem. It is possible, too, that only a few moral reasoning levels will be represented among group members. Finally, some pupils may not be able to articulate their reasons for selecting a particular response.

Despite these limitations, moral reasoning discussions are a useful tool. They have the potential to sensitize some pupils to the perspectives of others. For these individuals, the technique may well promote growth toward higher stages of moral development.

Teaching for Moral Decision Making: Issues, Values, and Consequences Analysis

Teaching for moral decision making is an approach designed to encourage pupils to make decisions that are consistent with their own values and understandings of morality. Lessons typically require learners to analyze several value positions related to a single issue. They are asked to suggest possible decisions consistent with each value position and to identify probable long-term consequences that might result from each

Figure 8–2
Promoting pupils' self-under-standing or social understanding: A framework for issues, values, and consequences analysis.

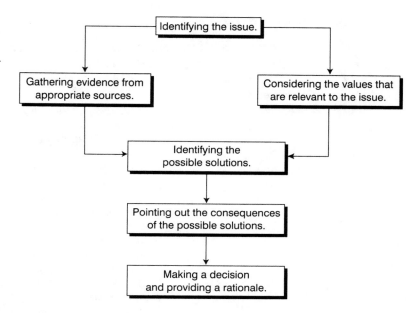

choice. At the conclusion of these lessons, the teacher asks pupils to make and defend a personal decision about the focus issue.

Issues, values, and consequences analysis helps pupils understand that the decisions individuals make reflect their values. The technique is applicable in a variety of situations. It can be used in lessons designed to promote learners' self-understanding, and in those designed to foster an appreciation of decisions made by others. For this latter purpose, we often use subject matter content from history or the social sciences.

When the purpose is to work with content focusing on self-understanding, these steps are followed:

- Identifying the issue
- Gathering evidence from appropriate sources
- Considering the values that are relevant to the issue
- Identifying possible solutions
- Pointing out consequences of the possible solutions
- Making a decision and providing a rationale

Figure 8–2 illustrates these steps and indicates the general flow of this activity.

An example of how issues, values, and consequences analysis might be used to promote self-understanding is provided in Lesson Idea 8–5.

Lesson 8–5

ISSUES, VALUES, AND CONSEQUENCES: SELF-UNDERSTANDING— WORRY ABOUT THE FUTURE

Grade Level: 5–6

Objectives: Pupils can (1) state values relevant to a given issue, (2) identify possible actions and probable consequences tied to each, and (3) apply their values to a task requiring them to choose a course of action.

Procedure: *1. Identifying the Issue*   Evidence suggests that many young people in the upper elementary grades worry about the future. For example, they may wonder whether they will be able to "make it" when they get to high school. Older brothers, sisters, and friends often tell them how difficult high school work is.

Some fifth and sixth graders even worry about their future social lives. Will they develop good personalities? Will they be popular? Will they find a job? Many other concerns bother young people in this age group.

Some authorities suggest that these anxieties will resolve themselves as these people mature. They contend that worries will naturally disappear as these fifth and sixth graders grow older and become more confident in their ability to meet challenges of all kinds. Other experts believe that these worries do not always "just go away" as people grow older. Some young people may continue to be plagued by serious anxieties about the future well into their late senior high school years. These authorities believe that fifth- and sixth-grade pupils should receive systematic help to relieve them of anxiety brought on by excessive worry.

The issue is simply this: Should there be specific programs for fifth- and sixth-grade pupils to help them deal with their worries?

2. Gathering Evidence from Appropriate Sources   Introduce information directed to helping pupils understand both sides of the issue. In looking for information to present, we have found it useful to develop guiding questions that suggest kinds of information that might be needed, such as the following examples:

- What is worry? Is all worry bad?
- Do adults worry, too?
- What conditions bring on worry?
- What ways are there to deal with worry?

3. Considering the Values that are Relevant to the Issue   Your questions at this point help pupils identify some values relevant to the discussion. Here are examples:

- If a person says people should not have worries, what does this tell us about what this person considers to be important in life?
- Some people say worries will go away in time. Others say they won't and that we need to help people with worries right now. What priorities would people in each of these groups assign to an effort to "do something" about the worries of young people in school?

4. Identifying Possible Solutions   A number of possibilities might arise in a discussion. You might receive the following suggestions from pupils after asking, "What should be done about the worries of fifth and sixth graders?"

- The school should have special "worry" counselors.
- Parents should take these problems seriously and make time to listen to their children as they talk about their worries.
- The school should introduce a course on dealing with worries about the future.
- Nothing should be done. Worrying will go away in time.

5. Pointing Out the Consequences of Possible Solutions   At this point, ask pupils to think about the consequences of the possible solutions to the problem they have suggested. Possible questions and potential pupil responses follow:

"What might happen if we established special "worry counselors" in each school?"

- More people might have worries because now there is somebody to talk to about them.
- Worries would not bother people so much because the "worry counselors" could help.
- Counselors maybe couldn't do some of the things they do now because they would be so busy dealing with worry problems.
- People might worry just as much but not be so concerned about their worries. This would be true because they would know that the counselors could help.

"What might happen if we did nothing at all about this problem?"

- Some would continue to worry so much that it would interfere with their ability to do well in school. That's what happens now.
- When they get to high school, most people will have outgrown the worries they had in the fifth and sixth grade.
- Some people will always worry no matter what. So if we do nothing, it won't make much difference.

6. Making a Decision and Providing a Rationale   At this point, ask questions that encourage pupils to make a personal decision about the problem. Also, ask pupils to suggest their reasons for making this decision. During this phase of the lesson, you might ask questions such as the following:

- What should we do about the "worrying" issue?
- Why did you make this choice?
- What convinced you this choice was better than any other?
- What would your choice tell others about the things in life you consider to be really important?

Closure   To conclude the lesson, refocus on its central points, asking questions such as the following:

- What have we learned about what people think about when they make decisions?
- How can decisions tell us about what the decision makers think is important?
- What has this lesson taught you about your own priorities?

Often, the issues, values, and consequences analysis technique is used to help pupils appreciate that decisions made by others reflect certain values' priorities. For example, decisions that leaders in the past made to shape historical events often required agonizing choices among competing values. An issue suitable for a lesson of this type is one for which at least two competing viewpoints can be identified. The steps followed are slightly more complex than for lessons focusing on personal or social understanding.

- Identify the general issue.
- Describe Faction A.
- Identify the information seen as relevant by Faction A.
- Describe the relevant alternatives open to Faction A.
- Point out possible consequences of each Faction A alternative.
- Describe Faction B.
- Identify the information seen as relevant by Faction B.
- Describe the relevant alternatives open to Faction B.
- Point out possible consequences of each Faction B alternative.
- Relate and compare the alternatives open to each Faction; relate and compare the probable consequences of each alternative; make decisions.
- Apply to another setting.

Figure 8–3 provides a graphic of the flow of events in a lesson of this kind.

Lesson Idea 8–6 features an issues, values, and consequences analysis lesson designed to help pupils appreciate values dimensions of issues faced by people in the past.

Figure 8–3
Developing pupils' sensitivity to decisions others have had to make: A framework for issues, values, and consequences analysis.

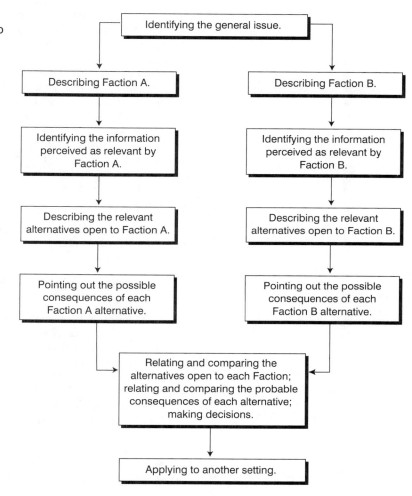

Lesson Idea 8–6

ISSUES, VALUES, AND CONSEQUENCES: APPRECIATING DECISIONS MADE BY OTHERS

Grade Level: 5

Objectives: Pupils will (1) state views, possible actions, and conflicts associated with two competing positions and (2) apply the steps of this analysis to a new problem.

Procedures: Provide the class with the following information, initiating discussion and asking questions as indicated.

1. Identifying the General Issue   In 1710, when today's United States was still a colony of Great Britain, John Peter Zenger came to New York from Germany. He started a newspaper called *The New York Weekly Journal*. All went well until 1732. In that year, a new governor, William Cosby, came to New York colony from England. When he arrived, he found that the man who had been acting as temporary leader in New York had been drawing his salary. Cosby wanted the man to pay him the money, even though, in truth, the man had been doing Cosby's job. By using some shady tricks, Cosby succeeded in having a court decide in his favor, and there was a decision that Cosby should get the money.

After this happened, John Peter Zenger reported in his newspaper all of the questionable things Cosby had done. Cosby was furious. He accused Zenger of libel. *Libel* means damaging a person's reputation by publishing false, defamatory information about that person in a public forum such as a newspaper. Zenger denied that he was guilty of libel because the things he printed were true.

The issue is: Should John Peter Zenger have been found guilty of libel?

2. Describing Faction A: Cosby and His Judges   Cosby was the Governor of New York, the king's own representative. He had responsibility for the overall administration of the colony. He was concerned about letting the colonists develop the idea that they had any real powers of their own. He felt that any attack on him was also an attack on the king.

3. Identifying the Information Perceived as Relevant by Faction A   The judges selected by Cosby felt Zenger had committed libel. English law at this time did not allow a jury to make this decision. The judges, alone, decided whether a given act was libelous. The only job of the jury was to decide whether a person accused of writing a libelous article had actually written it.

4. Describing the Relevant Alternatives Open to Faction A   In response to your questions about these alternatives, pupils might generate answers such as the following:

- They could have done nothing. This might just be something that would have "blown over" in time.
- They could have brought Zenger to trial.
- They could have banished Zenger from the colony.

5. Pointing Out the Possible Consequences of Each Faction A Alternative   In response to prompting questions, the pupils might suggest the following:

- If they decided to do nothing, attacks on the governor might have gotten worse. This could have led to real problems.

- If they took Zenger to trial, some unexpected outcome might have resulted. However, in the past Cosby had had good luck in getting judges to see things his way.
- If they sent Zenger out of the colony, he might have made trouble elsewhere in America. If he went to England, he might have made trouble for Cosby by planting vicious rumors among his enemies there.

6. Describing Faction B John Peter Zenger was a journalist. He was eager to increase the circulation of his paper over that of the rival *New York Gazette*. He was interested in appealing to readers who were interested in extending the rights of the colonists.

7. Identifying the Information Perceived as Relevant by Faction B Zenger and his attorneys believed that the old English idea that judges should decide whether something was libelous should be changed. Judges were too easy for the English to control. Juries, on the other hand, were something else. They tended to be made up of colonists. Zenger and his lawyers felt that juries, not judges, should decide whether the crime of libel had been committed.

Zenger's people also felt that someone should not be able to claim he had been libeled if the information printed in a newspaper could be shown to be true. Thus, they were interested in demonstrating the truth of what Zenger had written.

8. Describing the Relevant Alternatives Open to Faction B In response to your questions, pupils might identify the following alternatives:

- Zenger could have retracted what he had originally printed, and he could have published an apology to the Governor in the hope that the libel suit would be dropped.
- Zenger could have agreed to stand trial in the hope that he would win his case.
- Zenger could have fled the colony.

9. Pointing Out the Possible Consequences of Each Faction B Alternative Pupils might generate answers such as the following in response to prompting questions:

- If Zenger had retracted what he had said, he would have weakened the case the colonists were trying to make for extending their authority.
- If Zenger agreed to stand trial, the took a chance of being found guilty. On the other hand, a trial would provide an opportunity for him to share his views with a larger audience. Also, he might win his case.
- If Zenger fled, he would lose any immediate influence he might have in New York in support of increasing the

authority of the colonists. On the other hand, he might be able to make life uncomfortable for Cosby if he could get to England and talk to some of Cosby's enemies.

10. Relating and Comparing the Alternatives Open to Each Faction; Relating and Comparing the Probable Consequences of Each Alternative; Making Decisions Ask questions to help pupils contrast the positions of the two factions. The following are some questions you might ask, and possible pupil responses:

"What similarities and differences do you see between the alternatives open to each side?"

- Both sides thought about the possibility that Zenger might choose to leave.
- Both sides considered pluses and minuses of taking the case to trial.

"What differences in viewpoint are represented by the two sides?"

- Cosby and his people felt that a libel had already been committed. The trial would be simply to see whether Zenger was responsible for writing the libelous article. Zenger and his people denied that libel had been committed. They claimed that there was no libel since the material printed in the newspaper was true.
- Cosby and his people were afraid of extending the power of the colonists. Zenger and his supporters were eager to extend the power of the colonists.

"What was most important to each side?"

- Cosby saw preserving his authority as most important. He viewed Zenger as a threat to his authority and to that of the king.
- Zenger wanted to extend the rights of the colonies. He wanted to do this by establishing the idea that anything can be printed about a person so long as its truth could be proved. This would give great freedom of expression to the colonists.

"Did Zenger have a right to print articles critical of the Governor?"

- I don't think so. The Governor was the king's representative. Zenger was a threat to law and order.
- Yes. If he couldn't be critical, then very bad governors could have done all kinds of terrible things, and few people would ever have known about them.
- He might have had this right some place, but not in New York. If he wanted to print critical articles, he should have gone to England.

"What do you think really happened in this case?"

Lead a discussion focusing on this question. To conclude the discussion, tell the class what actually happened to Zenger and Governor Cosby.

The outcome of the Zenger case shocked Governor Cosby. First, the jury was convinced by the arguments of Zenger's attorney that judges should not decide whether something is libelous. This should be left to juries. Second, the jury decided that there was no libel in a case where the person writing the article could prove the truth of what he or she had written. John Peter Zenger, as a result, was found innocent.

The Zenger case established the principle that juries, not judges, decide when a libel has occurred. Further, it established the important freedom-of-the-press principle that there is no libel when material printed can be shown to be true.

11. Applying to Another Setting The final phase of the lesson attempts to tie such an episode from another time or place to something more familiar to pupils' own experiences. At this point, you might ask questions such as the following:

- The Zenger case changed some rules that courts had followed for a long time. Can you think of any new rules that have changed how we live and do things? (If pupils have trouble, provide examples—55 MPH speed limit, racial integration, changes in local school rules, and so forth.)
- How do people react to change? Do all people like change? Why do you think some people may support a given change and other people oppose it?
- Are newspapers today free to criticize public officials? Is this right a result of the famous Zenger case?
- How do you feel personally about what can be printed in a newspaper? What does your answer tell us about some things in life you believe to be really important?

KEY IDEAS IN SUMMARY

1. Prosocial behavior contributes to the betterment of society. It rests on the morality of individuals. One purpose of the social studies is to help young people develop a sense of concern that will lead them to take positive action to improve the community, state, and nation. It is particularly important that schools attend to this matter. A high percentage of the total number of antisocial acts are committed by young people.

2. There is general agreement that schools have some obligation to promote the development of moral patterns of behavior among learners. However, some school programs that have attempted to do so have been criticized for allegedly encouraging patterns of behavior inconsistent with those espoused in some pupils' homes.

3. Aesthetic values reflect personal choices. They do not carry connotations of right or wrong. Moral values, on the other hand, do carry implications of right and wrong. They help people define what kinds of behavior are appropriate and what kinds of behavior are inappropriate.

4. James Rest (1983) developed a four-level framework for identifying components that can be included in lessons emphasizing values and morality. These levels are (1) moral sensitivity, (2) moral judgment, (3) moral decision making, and (4) moral action.

5. Many instructional techniques are available for helping learners clarify their personal and aesthetic beliefs. Simon, Howe, and Kirschenbaum (1978), for example, recommend procedures involving rank ordering and unfinished sentences.

6. A widely used approach to increasing pupils' levels of moral sensitivity is values-situation role playing. This technique allows learners to become more sensitive to moral and values issues. It is applicable to issues ranging from those focusing on present personal problems of pupils to those drawn from historical contexts that center on moral dilemmas people have faced in the past.

7. Lawrence Kohlberg (1975, 1980) developed a six-stage framework for analyzing individuals' stages of moral development. People at each stage are thought to apply certain criteria to problems and to use certain logical patterns as they seek solutions. These stages are (1) punishment and obedience orientation, (2) instrumental relativism, (3) interpersonal concordance, (4) law and order orientation, (5) social contract–legalistic orientation, and (6) universal ethical principal orientation.

8. According to Kohlberg, people progress through the stages sequentially. Because those at higher levels are thought to have more concern for others than people at lower levels, followers of Kohlberg are interested in having individuals move to higher stages. One instructional approach that has been developed for this purpose is the moral dilemma discussion. Moral dilemma discussions expose learners to moral reasoning at stages of moral development higher than their own. This exposure is thought to facilitate their movement toward higher moral development stages.

9. Moral decision-making activities help pupils make decisions that are consistent with their own values and personal understandings of morality. Lessons with this focus involve learners in analyses of issues that feature a problem with a number of potential solutions. Each possible solution tends to reflect a somewhat different set of values priorities. Pupils are taught to recognize values underlying each alternative, make choices among the alternatives, and defend their choices. Issues, values, and consequences analysis is a technique that can be applied to many kinds of issues.

CHAPTER REFLECTIONS

Directions: Now that you have finished reading the chapter, reread the case study at the beginning. Think about other chapter content. Then, answer these questions:

1. What are the obligations of the schools regarding transmitting certain key values to all pupils?

2. What are some uses you might be able to make in your own classroom of James Rest's values and morality framework?

3. How do you feel about using moral dilemma discussions in elementary school classrooms? What problems might you have to overcome to use this technique successfully?

4. Why might a teacher wish to use issues, values, and consequences analysis when teaching elementary social studies?

EXTENDING UNDERSTANDING AND SKILL

1. Interview a district-level social studies curriculum director (if that cannot be arranged, find an elementary teacher involved in social studies program planning). Ask about the amount of emphasis given to lessons focusing on attitudes and values. Seek details about the nature of instruction provided, any problems with parents and other school patrons, and teachers' reactions to working with this kind of content. Prepare a report and share it with your class.

2. Survey two or more elementary social studies textbooks. How many of the suggested activities focus on attitudes or values? Prepare a chart to display your findings.

3. Read 10 articles in professional journals that provide practical ideas for dealing with attitudes and values in the elementary social studies classroom. (You may wish to consult the *Education Index* to locate your articles.) Write a brief description of each suggested approach. Share what you have found with others in your class.

4. Prepare three role-playing situations, two moral reasoning dilemmas, and one situation to be used as a focus for an issues, values, and consequences analysis lesson. Develop these for a grade level you would like to teach. Write a description of each approach. Ask your instructor to review your descriptions.

5. Start a newspaper clipping file featuring conflicts among people having different value priorities. Try to include at least 12 items. Discuss some of these items with others in your class. Point out how they might provide beginnings of elementary social studies lessons.

REFERENCES

HELLER, C., AND HAWKINS, J. (1994). "Teaching Tolerance: Notes from the Front Line." *Teachers College Record, 95* (3), pp. 337–368.

HOFFMAN, M. L. (1993). "Empathy, Social Cognition, and Moral Education." In. A. Garrod (Ed.), *Approaches to Moral Development*. New York: Teachers College Press, pp. 157–179.

KOHLBERG, L. (1975). "The Cognitive-Developmental Approach to Moral Education." *Phi Delta Kappan, 56* (10), pp. 670–675.

KOLHLBERG, L. (1980). "Education for a Just Society: An Updated and Revised Statement." In B. Munsey (Ed.), *Moral Development, Moral Education, and Kohlberg*. Birmingham, AL: Religious Education Press, pp. 455–470.

LICKONA, T. (1993). "The Return of Character Education." *Educational Leadership, 51* (3), pp. 6–11.

PERRY, C. M., AND McINTIRE, W. G. (1994). "High School Seniors' Concern for Others: Predictors and Implications." *High School Journal, 77* (3), pp. 199–205.

REST, J. (1983). "Morality." In P. Husen (Ed.), *Handbook of Child Psychology*, vol. 4. New York: Wiley.

ROGERS, C., AND FREIBERG, H. G. (1994). *Freedom to Learn*. 3rd ed. Englewood Cliffs, NJ: Merrill/Prentice Hall.

SHAFTEL, F. R., AND SHAFTEL, G. (1982). *Role Playing in the Curriculum*. Englewood Cliffs, NJ: Prentice-Hall.

SIMON, S. B., HOWE, L. W., AND KIRSCHENBAUM, H. (1978). *Values Clarification*. New York: A&W Visual Library.

WILLIAMS, M. W. (1993). "Actions Speak Louder Than Words. What Students Think." *Educational Leadership, 51* (3), pp. 22–23.

A SELECTION OF THEMES

LAW-RELATED EDUCATION

CHAPTER GOALS

This chapter provides information to help the reader:

- explain why law-related education is in the social studies curriculum,
- define law-related education,
- list goals of law-related education,
- define curriculum topics for law-related education,
- find information and material useful for teaching law-related topics,
- explain how the case study method can be applied in the elementary classroom,
- list the steps for using mock trials in the classroom, and
- state how local community resources can be used for teaching law-related topics.

CHAPTER STRUCTURE

Introduction
What is Law-Related Education?
Goals of Law-Related Education
Law-Related Education Topics
  Basic Legal Concepts
  The Constitution and Bill of Rights
  The Legal System
  Criminal Law
  Consumer Law
  Family Law
Sources of Information
  Special Committee on Youth Education for Citizenship
  Constitutional Rights Foundation
  Law in a Free Society
  Center for Civic Education
  Consumer Law Resource Kit
  Opposing Viewpoints Series
  National Institute for Citizen Education and the Law
  Public Affairs Pamphlet Series
  Law in Action Units
  Cases: A Resource Guide for Teaching about the Law
Classroom Approaches to Law-Related Education
  Using Case Studies
  Selecting Cases for Classroom Use
  Preparing a Case
  Presenting Case Studies
  Debriefing
  Storyline
  Children's Literature
  Mock Trials
  Developing Mock Trials
Community Resources
Key Ideas in Summary
Chapter Reflections
Extending Understanding and Skill
References

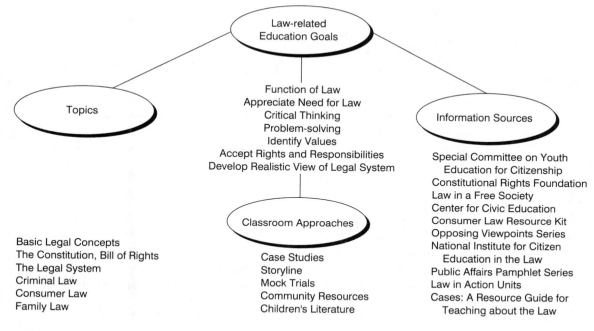

Figure 9–1
Law-related education.

Chapter 9

Case Study

GOING BACK ON THE TEACHER'S WORD: A DILEMMA

Lloyd Fitzjohn teaches at Jim Thorpe Elementary. He is in his first year of teaching third grade. Recently, he made these comments to Jamella Littlehorn, who has been teaching third graders at Thorpe for many years.

"In my social studies lessons, I've been trying to ease them into the idea that in our country citizens make the rules we live by. My third graders are so used to having parents or even older brothers and sisters tell them what to do that they just aren't catching on quickly to the idea that people who are governed should have some say in making rules and laws.

"Falling back on my old principle that 'hands-on experience is the best teacher,' I decided to get my class directly involved in making some simple rules we would agree to follow. To make this credible, I agreed to enforce the rules that they came up with.

"It took the kids a little while to get my drift, but once they caught on to the idea they took it and ran. They got so excited about having some real 'power' for the first time in their lives, that they generated quite a list of rules.

"Their interest really pleased me. Unfortunately, I am less than thrilled with some of their rules. A couple that bother me are (1) a rule that anyone who doesn't pass a test will have to stay in from recess for three weeks and (2) a rule that someone who gets out of his or her seat without permission will have to see the principal.

"I think in both these cases the proposed punishment is much too severe for the 'crime.' I would really like to suggest some alternatives. But, I've boxed myself in. I told the members of the class before we started that it was their responsibility to develop the rules and the list of consequences for infractions. I'm afraid if I jump in and assert my authority and tell them that the proposed punishments are too severe, I will undercut the whole purpose of the exercise. My credibility is on the line. At the same time, I don't think I can stand by and in good conscience enforce these proposed punishments."

What Is Your Response?

Read the information above. Think about these concerns. Then, respond briefly to these questions:

1. Lloyd suggests that his third graders seem to be only vaguely familiar with the idea that American citizens are expected to assume some personal responsibility for establishing rules and regulations governing their lives. Do you think this is likely to be true of most third graders? Why, or why not?
2. In his comments, Lloyd indicates that he has great faith in the learning power of personal experience. Are there any pitfalls to relying on "learning by doing"? If so, what might some of them be?
3. If it is true that these third graders are used to having most decisions regarding their behavior being made by others, how adequate a transition to the idea that

individuals should have some responsibility for "making the rules" was Lloyd's approach?

4. Would the problems that seem to have developed been less likely to occur had the children been asked only to establish the rules, leaving consideration of appropriate punishment to the teacher?

5. If you were Jamella Littlehorn, what specific comments would you make to Lloyd?

INTRODUCTION

Have you ever had a defective product that the maker refused to fix? Have you ever been frustrated while trying to read the small print on a contract or warranty? Did you ever receive a class grade that you believed was an unfair measure of your performance? Have you ever felt that you were wronged by someone to the extent that you wanted to file a lawsuit?

Nearly all of us have had these or similar experiences. When such situations occur, we often do not know what to do and end up feeling powerless, frustrated, and angry. At such times, an understanding of the law is helpful. The law has an enormous influence on our lives. Laws govern television advertising, products we purchase, the way we drive our cars, and the social relationships we have. The law provides processes to resolve disputes and to respond to perceived injustices. It helps individuals to live secure and peaceful lives.

Unfortunately, many individuals do not understand how the law can help them in these situations. Most young people have inadequate concepts of the law, distorted by television and movie dramas. One result is that individuals begin to believe that rights are available only to others (Wasson, 1994). This perception can lead them to a sense of powerlessness and frustration where violence and lawlessness are considered acceptable. This alarming condition is at the root of many contemporary problems. A growing concern about the alienation of individuals from the law has led to a number of academic programs labeled *law-related education.*

The basic premise of law-related education is that individuals who understand the laws and legal system that underpin a democratic society are less likely to feel powerless and to resort to destructive, antisocial behavior. Dissemination of information about law, the legal system, and those who are involved in it is a basic requirement of effective citizenship. The issue, then, is not whether elementary school children should learn about the law, but rather what they need to know and how they should learn it.

WHAT IS LAW-RELATED EDUCATION?

Some forms of law-related education have been found in social studies classrooms for many years. Instruction in "civics," for example, has been a common feature of many school programs. Traditional civics instruction has placed a heavy emphasis on the study of the United States Constitution and its first ten amendments, the Bill of Rights. Even when this traditional content has been well taught, the relatively narrow focus of the instruction has made it difficult for some learners to appreciate its relevance for their daily lives. Another type of law-related education often included primary-grades lessons, such as, "Our Friendly Police." Although well intended, these lessons seldom helped pupils develop an understanding of the role of law enforcement in our society or created positive attitudes that endured the test of time.

Modern law-related education programs are different from these earlier attempts in several ways. Although law-related education overlaps political science content, it is much more specifically focused on an understanding of the function of law in our everyday life. The intent is to help pupils understand how laws can help us. In addition, these programs attempt to help pupils think rationally and critically about important social problems and conflicts. This does not mean that emphases on the Constitution and the Bill of Rights have been abandoned. It does suggest that these documents are studied in different ways. Today, the focus is on them as living documents that embody many of our basic values and that very much influence how we live. It also suggests that the curriculum be expanded to include topics such as family law and consumer law.

Law-related education, by helping learners to appreciate more fully how our legal system works, seeks to produce future citizens who will view the law and the legal system as something positive rather than negative. It is hoped that pupils who are exposed to such instruction will develop a personal commitment to working within the structure of the American system of governance. It is hoped, too, that they will more fully appreciate the roles of those who make, administer, and enforce the law.

Law-related education programs emphasize both common values of our society that draw us together and values conflicts that divide us. Pupils are invited to examine social problems and controversial issues. Lessons are designed to help children understand that difficult problems seldom have absolutely right or wrong answers and that decisions result as much from a consideration of values priorities as from a consideration of evidence. Teaching children processes associated with legal conflict resolution is an important feature of law-related education programs.

GOALS OF LAW-RELATED EDUCATION

A series of definite goals guide law-related education programs in the elementary school classroom. Law-related programs should help pupils do the following:

- Identify the basic functions of law in society.
- Develop an appreciation of the need for a society governed by law.
- Develop an ability to think critically about issues related to laws and the legal system.

- Apply problem-solving skills in proposing solutions to legal issues and problems.
- Identify societal values that guide the development of laws and legal processes.
- Accept the rights and responsibilities of a citizen.
- Develop realistic and honest views of our legal system, its strengths, and its weaknesses.

Law-related education is not intended to turn students into miniature lawyers. Its purposes are consistent with the overall goals of the social studies. They include emphases on learning substantive content, identifying and clarifying values, and applying critical-thinking and problem-solving skills. Some basic questions related to the goals of law-related education are the following:

- What are rules and laws?
- Why do we need rules and laws?
- Who makes the laws?
- What do I do if I think a rule or a law is unfair?
- What happens if a person breaks the law?
- What are my obligations as a citizen to follow the laws?
- How does the law protect me and my rights?
- What do I do if I feel I have been wronged?
- Why does the legal system seem so complicated?

BOX 9–1   **What is the Purpose of Law-Related Education?**

A parent was informed that the teacher was integrating law-focused content into the social studies program of a fifth-grade classroom. The parent wrote these comments to the school board.

> I am very concerned about this so-called emphasis on law-related education. I have been told that one of its purposes is to teach children critical thinking. There is already too much criticism of the laws of this nation. It is time we stopped being critical and simply told the children that it is their patriotic duty to abide by the laws that have been established. I do not want my youngster to grow into some irrational fanatic who protests every law and rule. The schools have enough to do without encouraging this sort of disruptive behavior.

Think About This

1. Do you see any validity in the arguments of this parent?
2. What points would you make in response to this person?
3. How would you approach issues that might prove to be controversial?

LAW-RELATED EDUCATION TOPICS

Historically, a limited number of curriculum topics could be considered law-related education. In recent years, however, the list of topics has expanded dramatically, and now ranges from basic legal concepts, the Constitution and the Bill of Rights, and the legal system to criminal, consumer, and family law.

Basic Legal Concepts

The intent of this topic is to help pupils understand the function of law in society. Lessons often focus on where laws come from, limitations of laws, relationships between values and laws, and a free society's need for laws. The basic concepts of fairness, justice, liberty, equality, property, due process, and power are highlighted.

The Constitution and Bill of Rights

The Constitution and the Bill of Rights are the basic documents around which our legal system is built. Pupils need to understand how these two important documents embody key legal concepts that influence our lives every day. Lessons often emphasize the relationship of these documents to situations familiar to learners. For example, they may focus on issues related to education, discrimination, and privacy.

Lesson Idea 9–1

APPLYING THE BILL OF RIGHTS

Grade Level:	5–6
Objectives:	Pupils can (1) define in their own words the meaning of articles in the Bill of Rights, (2) identify contemporary applications of the articles, and (3) work together in cooperative groups.
Overview:	The Constitution and Bill of Rights are often taught in ways that lead pupils to the conclusions that they are dusty historical documents with little relevance to current issues. This lesson applies the cooperative learning approach to help them identify contemporary applications of the articles of the Bill of Rights.
Procedure:	***Learning Set*** Ask the class how many have heard of something called the Bill of Rights. Ask several if they know what it is, when it was written, and if it is important to know. Inform them that they are going to be involved in a project to learn about the Bill of Rights and how it applies to us.
	Presentation Divide the class into groups of four pupils. Assign each group the responsibility for becoming an expert on one of the first ten amendments to the Constitution. Each group should be provided with a handout that includes the

amendment along with some questions to guide their thinking about the amendment's meaning. The outcome of this phase of the group work is for pupils to state in their own words what the amendment means. Each of the definitions can then be placed on the top of a large sheet of paper.

The second assignment for each group is to search through newspapers and magazines to find headlines, articles, cartoons, letters to the editor, or advertisements related to the issues raised in the amendment. They are to make a collage or a poster on the large sheet of paper that contains their definition of the amendment. When these have been completed, each small group shares its findings with the larger group. They may choose to do this with a role playing of one of the items on their collage or through other creative methods.

Closure: This procedure will take several days. At the end of each day, review the group work skills demonstrated and what was learned during that day. At the conclusion of the lessons, pupils should state what they learned about the Bill of Rights and how it applies to the present.

The Legal System

This topic focuses on how our legal system operates. Lessons with this emphasis may consider law enforcement agencies, courts, lawyers, judges, and juries. Learning experiences that emphasize the duties of police officers and the nature of and limitations on their power help pupils develop an honest and realistic understanding of the roles these individuals play in our society. Lessons focusing on what attorneys do are often

Pupils need to learn that attorneys operate within limits prescribed by law. This involves a considerable amount of research.

A good beginning point for teaching law-related material is to identify pupils' misconceptions. Interview several learners at different grade levels to identify their understandings of the roles of police officers, attorneys, and judges. You may wish to use
the following questions. When the interviews are complete, compare them with those
conducted by other class members. Try to identify common misconceptions and any
pattern that might be related to the developmental levels of the children.

1. What types of things do _____ do when they are working?
2. How does a person get to be a _____ ?
3. Where did you get your information about _____ ?
4. When might you need a_____ ?

Figure 9–2
Identifying misconceptions.

featured. Children who do not understand how the system works often view lawyers as
extremely powerful individuals who "have all the answers." This perception, no doubt,
is influenced by television programs that glamorize the roles attorneys play. Young people need to understand that attorneys are not magicians who can "get you off," but
rather that they are professionals who must operate within limits prescribed by law.

Young people often also have mistaken understandings of the roles of judges and
juries. (See Figure 9–2 for a suggested method for identifying these misconceptions.) It
is common for them to believe that judges and juries make laws. They need to understand that judges act to interpret laws made by others, and that their decisions must
conform to these laws. Similarly, it is important for children to recognize that there are
important limitations on what juries can do.

Criminal Law

The crime rate in the United States has become a much-discussed national problem.
Serious students of this situation point out that law enforcement alone can never
reduce the crime rate. A low crime rate depends on a population committed to lawful
behavior. Lessons focusing on criminal law help pupils understand what constitutes a
crime, why society has defined certain acts as crimes, and what can happen to individuals who choose to violate the law. Of special importance here are topics related to the
typical problems youth have and to how the juvenile justice system works. Other topics
of interest include trial and courtroom procedures, punishment, probation rehabilita-
tion, and the rights of the accused.

Consumer Law

Young people in our society have disposable income and have considerable influence in
the national marketplace. As consumers, they need to know their rights and responsi-

---

BOX 9–2   **Demonstrating Sensitivity When Dealing with Family Law**

Many family law issues, such as divorce, death, child abuse, and spousal abuse, are highly personal. Teachers need to treat them sensitively.

Think About This

1. Suppose you have several children in your classroom whose parents have divorced. How might you handle the legal aspects of divorce without upsetting the children or the parents?
2. When dealing with wills and death, how could you demonstrate sensitivity to the feelings of a child who has recently experienced a death in the family?
3. Suppose you were dealing with the issue of child abuse or spousal abuse and a youngster volunteered that it was common in her or his home. What would you do?
4. Legal issues surrounding abortion are hotly debated. Would you teach the legal issues related to abortion in your classroom? Why or why not?

---

bilities. There are laws that protect them from fraud as well as laws that protect producers from irresponsible consumers. Some areas often covered under the heading of consumer law are advertising, contracts, guarantees, labeling, and consumer fraud. Lessons also often inform learners about options that are open to them when they find they have purchased a defective product or when they feel they have been pressured into buying something they really do not need or want.

Family Law

The family is a basic unit in society, and there is a body of law that governs family relationships. Pupils tend to be very interested in issues associated with family law. Lessons related to this topic often emphasize laws governing marriage, parental responsibility, adoption, child abuse, spouse abuse, divorce, wills, and death. The personal nature of many of these issues requires us to be sensitive in our instructional approaches. We must know our pupils well and deal with the content in an honest, nonjudgmental way.

Abundant resources are available to help teachers teach these topics. Organizations, including bar associations, have developed programs that sometimes include speakers as well as resource materials.

SOURCES OF INFORMATION

One key to the success of any social studies program is the availability of quality learning materials. Several organizations have been actively developing materials for teachers to use in law-related education programs. These materials cover many subjects and are written for a variety of grade levels. Individual organizations will be happy to provide information about the specific materials they have available. We identify several excellent information sources in this section.

Special Committee on Youth Education for Citizenship

For several decades, the American Bar Association has actively promoted law-related education in the schools. It has sponsored several publications for teachers. One of these, *Update on Law-Related Education*, includes articles introducing new topics and provides examples of classroom techniques for teachers at all grade levels. The American Bar Association also publishes other classroom materials and a special catalog of law-related audiovisual material. For information, write to Special Committee on Youth Education for Citizenship, American Bar Association Administration Center, 1155 East 60th Street, Chicago, IL 60637.

Constitutional Rights Foundation

This organization has developed material on the Bill of Rights and other law-related topics. Published material includes simulations, filmstrips, resources for learners, and lesson plans. In addition, the foundation publishes the *Bill of Rights Newsletter*, available to teachers and students. Although much of the material is written for learners in grade seven and above, some of it can be useful to teachers in the upper elementary grades. The foundation also sponsors conferences and workshops for teachers. For information, write to Constitutional Rights Foundation, 6310 San Vincente Blvd., Los Angeles, CA 90048.

Law in a Free Society

This organization has been very active in developing high-quality materials for use in K–12 classrooms. These include case studies and lesson plans that promote the sequential development of the concepts of authority, justice, freedom, participation, diversity, privacy, property, and responsibility. The group also provides materials and assistance for people charged with planning and administering inservice training workshops for teachers. For information, write to Law in a Free Society, 606 Wilshire Blvd., Santa Monica, CA 90101.

Center for Civic Education

This group has developed some excellent material for use in the schools. Most of their material is designed for upper elementary grades or higher. In conjunction with the Commission on the Bicentennial of the United States Constitution, the center developed excellent pupil books as well as teacher guides and resource materials. Two of the more useful titles are *We the People* and *With Liberty and Justice for All*. For information write to Center for Civic Education, 5146 Douglas Fir Road, Calabasas, CA 91302.

Consumer Law Resource Kit

This resource kit contains units on topics of interest to consumers. Titles include, "Avoiding Gyps and Frauds," "How to Use Advertising," "Spending," "Borrowing,"

"Saving," "Budgeting," and "Safeguards for Shoppers." Although much of the material was published several years ago, it is still useful as a resource for teachers planning lessons focusing on consumer issues and consumer law. For information, write to Consumer Law Resource Kit, Changing Times Educational Service, 1729 H Street, N.W., Washington, DC 20006.

Opposing Viewpoints Series

Over the past 20 years this series has addressed a variety of topics that are useful in teaching law-focused studies. These materials are especially valuable because they give opposing viewpoints on each of the issues. They can be used to stimulate classroom debates and sharpen critical-thinking skills. For information, write to Opposing Viewpoints Series, Greenhaven Press, Box 831, Anoka, MN 55303.

National Institute for Citizen Education in the Law

This organization was created to promote the teaching of law in the schools. Its programs focus on teacher training and on the development of curriculum materials and courses. The institute also assists individuals interested in starting law-related education programs. One noteworthy publication is a set of materials on family law. For information, write to National Institute for Citizen Education in the Law, 605 G Street, N.W., Suite 401, Washington, DC 20001.

Public Affairs Pamphlet Series

Although these pamphlets are not specifically designed for teaching law-related content to elementary school learners, they provide a wealth of background for the teacher on a range of topics such as job discrimination, delinquency and the law, abortion, justice for the poor, and consumer issues. For information, write to Public Affairs Pamphlet Series, Public Affairs Pamphlets, 381 Park Ave. South, New York, NY 10016.

Law in Action Units

This series of units includes materials and lesson plans on the topics, "Lawmaking," "Juvenile Problems and the Law," "Courts and Trials," "Youth Attitudes," and "Police and Young Consumers." The units are planned for learners in grades five to nine. For information, write to Law in Action Units, West Publishing Company, Inc., 50 West Kellogg Blvd., St. Paul, MN 55165.

Cases: A Resource Guide for Teaching about the Law

This book includes juvenile crime cases covering a variety of topics. The cases are designed for learners between the ages of 8 and 16. In addition to the cases, questions are posed for learners. The book also contains presentation ideas and a discussion guide, and includes sample test items. For information, write to Cases: A Resource

Guide for Teaching about the Law, Good Year Books, Scott, Foresman and Company, 1900 East Lake Avenue, Glenview, Illinois 60025.

CLASSROOM APPROACHES TO LAW-RELATED EDUCATION

Law-related education can be integrated into the social studies classroom in several ways. As with other approaches, it is important for us to consider pupils' background, interests, and developmental levels in deciding how to introduce the content. Case studies and simulations have been found to be particularly effective in law-focused education programs. Many commercially prepared materials encourage the use of these techniques.

Using Case Studies

Case studies have long been used to introduce people to the law. Most law schools use this approach in teaching prospective attorneys. This method was extended to the elementary and secondary schools when law-focused programs began to appear in public school curricula. Cases prepared for use in elementary schools tend to be short, often only two to three paragraphs in length, with reading difficulty reduced to make them accessible to elementary school readers.

Sometimes cases used in elementary schools are derived from famous and important cases that have been decided by the Supreme Court. Others focus on cases heard by lower courts that feature situations particularly interesting to younger learners. The case study approach helps children to identify key issues and to make decisions about where they stand.

Selecting Cases for Classroom Use

You should follow several guidelines when selecting or creating cases to present to learners. First, the cases selected should be ones that focus on significant issues of enduring value. For example, the issue of the right to privacy was included in the Bill of Rights over two hundred years ago. Although the original writers had specific events of the time in mind, the larger issue continues to be relevant, such as with cases concerning eavesdropping. Cases focusing on freedom of speech, religion, the press, and other Bill of Rights concerns continue to be litigated in our courts. These issues remain very important.

In addition to having the potential to focus on significant and enduring legal issues, cases selected for study should also be of interest to the learners, and should allow for a variety of viewpoints. Legal cases centering on trivial matters that have little interest for people other than the litigants will not generate much pupil interest.

Preparing a Case

Cases prepared for classroom use are available from several commercial sources. Individual teachers often find it necessary to modify these materials to make them suitable for their own learners. There are useful guidelines you can follow when modifying a case that has already been prepared for classroom use or when developing a case from original sources.

First, basic facts need to be introduced. Language used in doing this needs to be uncluttered, jargon free, and appropriate for the learners who will be studying the case. New terms need to be identified and explained. Often it is worthwhile to apply a readability formula to any prose material to be sure that reading levels are consistent with pupils' abilities. Next, important legal issues raised in the case need to be identified. Often this is accomplished by developing a sequence of questions to which learners must respond. For example, a case focusing on the issues of privacy rights and powers of the police might feature questions such as these: Do the police have the right to stop anyone walking down the street? Do individuals stopped by the police have the right to refuse to be searched? Can the police protect citizens if they lack the freedom to go about their work as they see fit?

Some case studies begin with a narrative of events. An alternative beginning is to present a situation's events from the viewpoints of involved individuals. Lesson Idea 9–2 illustrates how this might be done.

When preparing a case for classroom use it is helpful to identify the factors that the courts take into account when deciding similar issues. Most legal issues involve a clash between two or more rights. We need to help learners understand how the courts go about balancing these two rights and reaching a decision. Many commercially prepared classroom cases provide information for teachers about lines of legal reasoning that the courts have used in past cases. Although you need not present this material formally to the class, it is helpful for answering pupils' questions. If the classroom case is based on an actual court case, information about the final decision is useful. However, the decision should not be shared with class members until they have had ample time to discuss the case and to reach their own decisions. At this time, you may share the decision and use it to begin a discussion of the strengths and weaknesses of the reasoning learners used in arriving at their conclusions.

Presenting Case Studies

The case study approach seeks to get learners actively involved in discussing a case, identifying important issues, and making decisions. These purposes are best met when you exercise indirect rather than direct leadership in the classroom. You need to motivate pupils by pointing out the importance of the case, presenting the facts of the case, making sure they understand the facts, prompting discussion and exploration of legal issues, and getting learners to think about their own reasoning and to make a decision.

Debriefing

Debriefing is an important part of lessons featuring case studies. During debriefing, learners evaluate their own reasoning. They may compare their thinking to the thinking of others, including the judge who may have decided the case in a real court of law. You make sure that the basic legal principles and issues are summarized and understood by the class members. During this time, it is important for you to keep your personal views to yourself until pupils have had ample opportunities to share their own points of view.

Lesson Idea 9–2

A CASE STUDY: POLICE SEARCH

Grade Level: 5–6

Objective: Learners can (1) apply the principles of the Bill of Rights to a hypothetical situation and, (2) state the difficulties faced by law enforcement officials in performing their role.

Overview: Pupils are usually unaware that the police must also follow rules. Their job can be a difficult one where they must make decisions that sometimes that may lead to legal troubles for them. The intent of using a case study like this is to show that there is no obvious right and wrong. This can prompt intense discussion by pupils.

Procedure: ***Learning Set***   Ask the class, "Can anyone tell me if the police have rules they must follow? Where do they get those rules?" Inform them that one place where they get the rules is from the U.S. Constitution. One of the rules in the constitution is the following:

> *Amendment IV: Security from Unreasonable Searches and Seizures*
>
> *The right of the people to be secure in their persons, houses, papers, and effects, against unreasonable searches and seizures, shall not be violated, and no Warrants shall issue, but upon probable cause, supported by Oath or affirmation, and particularly describing the place to searched, and the persons or things to be seized.*

After reading this to the class, ask pupils what they think it means. Clarify any difficult terms or words.

Presentation   Tell the class, "What I want us to do is to apply this amendment to the following incident to see if you think the police acted correctly." Read the following event description aloud.

> *The Event*
>
> *At 1.30 A.M. on the morning of November 7, two men were seen walking down the street. Both wore dark clothing. As they walked, they made frequent stops. They seemed to be looking into houses each time they stopped. A police officer sitting in an unmarked car watched them for about five minutes. He was in the neighborhood because there had been reports of house burglaries. The officer approached the two men, stopped them, and asked them why they were in the neighborhood. Then, he proceeded to search them.*

Use the following questions to prompt discussion.

Legal Issues

- Did the officer have a right to search the two men?
- Under what conditions do you think the police should have the right to search someone?
- What right or rights do you think would be involved in a case such as this?
- If you were to write a law that would protect the rights of people and yet allow for the police to do their job, what would it say?

After some discussion, ask the class what they might do to find out whether the police followed the correct procedure. They might propose asking a police officer or an attorney how this case might be judged by inviting them to class or by writing a letter to them.

Closure

Conclude the lesson by asking, "What did we learn today about the rules police must follow? What did we learn about how difficult or easy it is to know exactly what to do? How does this apply to all of us?"

Teachers who use case studies frequently report that pupils find them to be motivating. Case studies do not require learners to come up with answers that are right or wrong in any absolute sense. Further, activities require them to deal with challenging and puzzling situations. Many children find these learning activities to be a welcome change from the more traditional read-and-recite fare they have come to associate with social studies lessons. A good followup to the use of case studies in the classroom is a classroom visit by an attorney, perhaps asking the attorney to discuss basic legal principles used in deciding cases similar to the ones discussed in class. In summary, the case study approach is an especially good vehicle for introducing law-related issues to children in elementary school classrooms. It motivates pupils. More importantly, the approach has excellent potential for introducing them to principles related to the function of law in society and to their rights and responsibilities as citizens.

Lesson Idea 9–3

A CASE STUDY: HURT ON THE JOB

Grade Level: 4–5

Objective: Pupils can (1) interpret conflicting viewpoints and (2) apply legal considerations to a hypothetical case.

Overview: Case studies of real situations can be very motivating to pupils. The following case study, although fictional, is based on a real incident. Discussing the case helps pupils better understand their rights and responsibilities and how the law functions to protect the rights of people.

Procedure:

Learning Set   Ask class members to share the types of jobs they would like. Ask them if they know what the "boss" does. Pose the following situation, "What would you do if you were working and your boss asked you to do something that you thought was dangerous?" After they have shared their ideas tell them that today you are going to study what happened in a situation like that.

Presentation   Read the following case study to them. Stop after the facts as seen by Mr. Chiu have been presented and ask them what they think about this situation. Then inform them that there are usually two sides to a situation. Read them the facts as seen by the boss. Use the questions on legal issues to conduct a discussion.

The Facts as Seen by Mr. Chiu

I arrived in the United States just a couple of years ago. I came looking for a better life. I didn't have lunch money when I arrived. Finally, I found a job working in a warehouse. It was hard work. But, I was willing to do what I had to do to make money.

One day my boss told me to get some boxes from the back of the warehouse and take them to the loading dock. I don't know how to drive the mechanical loader most of the people use to move boxes. I usually use a hand cart. This day the boss was in a big hurry. He insisted that I use the mechanical loader. I told him I didn't want to, but he insisted. He told me he'd fire me if I didn't do it. So, I got on the loader and tried to use it. Because I didn't know what I was doing, a large crate fell. It hit me and broke my arm. Now the boss says it was my fault. He fired me. I can't pay my medical bills, and I can't get a job right away because my arm is broken.

The Facts as Seen by the Boss

Mr. Chiu worked hard for me from the minute he was hired. But, he was afraid of machinery. He always wanted to do everything by hand. I suppose this is how it is done in his native country. We tried to teach him to use our machinery, including the mechanical loader. But he wasn't eager to learn, and he always went back to doing everything by hand. On the day of his accident, we had to get out an important order in a hurry. The truck was at the loading dock and was about ready to leave. I told Mr. Chiu to use the mechanical loader to save time. When he started to operate it, he got very nervous. A box fell. It hit him and narrowly missed another employee. I have a business to run. I have to operate efficiently. Also, I can't put up with an employee who does things that might endanger the safety of others. For this reason, I had no choice but to fire Mr. Chiu.

Legal Issues

1. Who do you think was responsible for the accident?
2. Should the boss pay for Mr. Chiu's medical treatment since he was hurt on the job?
3. Did Mr. Chiu have a right to refuse to operate the mechanical loader?
4. Did the boss have a right to fire Mr. Chiu because he could not operate the machinery properly?
5. Did Mr. Chiu have obligation to learn how to operate the mechanical loader?
6. In general, can an employer require an employee to do something that might be dangerous?
7. To what extent must employers justify their reasons for firing someone?

In using a case formatted in this way, teachers often find it useful to summarize information on both sides of the issue. This helps class members recognize that each side has reasonable arguments favoring its position.

Closure

Bring the lesson to a conclusion by reviewing the main points made by the class. Ask them what might be done to find out what laws may apply to situations like this. You may wish to assign additional research or invite a guest speaker to help the pupils understand the legal issues involved.

Storyline

Storyline is an interesting approach to teaching social studies that fits nicely with law-related studies, and may be adapted to younger children. The storyline method has been developed in Scotland over the past couple of decades (Barr & McGuire, 1993). Advantages of storyline are that it helps integrate the curriculum, and capitalizes on pupils' enthusiasm for storytelling. It is an active approach that utilizes students' prior learning and experience and engages them in active dialog as they construct meaning (Barr & McGuire, 1993).

The first step in storyline is informing the class that they are going to be creating a story together. You then may establish the time and the setting for the story based on your curriculum objectives. For example, to meet objectives related to learning about contemporary applications of law, you may choose the present as the time frame and a setting that would be of interest to the pupils. This is then communicated through a description of the time and place that helps the pupils develop an image in their minds. The following is an example of a description you might present to the class:

Sunshine reflects off the waves as they roll toward the sandy beach. Houses are built running down the hillsides almost to the edge of the water. Many of the houses have views of the ocean and the beach. The houses are generally small, of one story. Most of the houses have small yards containing many colorful flowers. Palm trees line the narrow streets that crisscross the community. On weekends the streets tend to become crowded with cars as people come to the beach.

Scattered throughout the community are several businesses, stores, a couple of schools, and a few churches. There are no large factories or buildings in the community. This is a place where people live who work in the large city nearby.

Once given this description, the class discusses the community. They can discuss what they think the climate might be like and what they think might be important to the residents, and ask any questions they might have. Pupils who may live lived or visited in a place similar to this can share their experiences. The class can then create a mural of a map depicting their visual image of this place.

The next step is for the class to create some characters for their story. They can discuss who some of the people might be who live in this community. You might go on to break the class into small groups, with each group creating families who live here. They need to think about the names, ages, personalities, and special interests of the people in their families. Each group then introduces the characters to the rest of the class. They could do this through by drawing pictures of their characters or even by role playing a family situation.

Once the time, setting, and characters are in place, present the class with a series of episodes based on the main points and objectives of the unit. Pupil response to these episodes leads them into the storymaking. For example, you might present an episode where the people coming to visit the beach leave lots of litter. The class can then create a story of what they would do. As they begin to construct their story, they can research litter laws and the rights of people. For example, would be it possible for them to decide that they were not going to let anyone who did not live in the community visit the beach? In this way their stories become something more than just an exercise in imagination. They are learning about the function of law as they are trying to solve the problems they face.

Other episodes you might present could include disputes between people within the community or land-use issues such as what they would do if a developer bought all of the land along the beach and proposed to build highrise buildings that would block the view of many of the residents. During the unit, you also can include other activities such as writing persuasive letters, role playing conflict resolutions, making speeches, drawing pictures and maps, and passing laws. The class writes or records their stories so that they have narrative of the life of the community. There are numerous ways to use the storyline technique. Another setting might be a family situation, where different episodes could introduce aspects of family law. The essential ingredient is that the setting and the characters are constructed in such a way that the pupils can relate to them and care about what happens. This personal involvement is what makes the approach a powerful and motivating one.

Children's Literature

As with many topics in social studies, children's literature can be a useful stimulus for dealing with law-related topics. For example, *A Family Apart*, by Joan Lowery Nixon (Bantam, 1988) deals with a family that is divided because of the death of the father and the inability of the mother to provide for the six children. Chapter four includes a court scene that could be used to discuss some of the issues of family law.

Books such as *A Picture Book of Frederick Douglass, A Picture Book of Rosa Parks*, by David Adler (both Holiday House, 1993), and *Free at Last*, by Sara Bullard (Oxford University Press, 1993) provide examples of individuals who sought to secure rights for all people and were even willing to violate unjust laws. Other books, too, often have themes or episodes you can adapt for law-related lessons in our elementary classrooms.

Mock Trials

The mock trial is widely used in school law-related education programs. Mock trials are simulation activities that feature enactments of trials. Because they include an element of competition between the contending parties, mock trials frequently stimulate high levels of pupil enthusiasm. Although mock trials have been used more widely at the secondary level, they have been applied successfully at the elementary level (Hickey, 1990). Mock trials can be developed either from actual trials that have taken place or around controversial issues that, at some point, might result in litigation.

If you are interested in engaging learners in experiences based on actual trials, you can draw on an enormous volume of materials developed by firms that produce learning materials for schools. These include complete sets of directions for mock trials based on real court cases, videocassettes, and classroom simulations. Increasing numbers of these materials are directed toward elementary school learners. An excellent general source for such materials is Social Studies School Services. For their elementary school social studies catalog, write to Social Studies School Services, 10200 Jefferson Boulevard, Room 1, P.O. Box 802, Culver City, CA 90232-0802.

Many options are available if you wish to develop mock trial lessons based on controversial issues that may not have resulted in court cases. Such lively public controversy can serve well as a focus for a teacher-developed mock trial. Because the media give heavy exposure to an issue of this type, pupils (and certainly their parents) may well be familiar with the basic situation. This gives credibility to the mock trial experience in that it focuses on something that is of clear concern to the world beyond the school classroom. In addition, by assisting learners to focus carefully on arguments on both sides of a divisive issue, mock trial experiences help pupils learn basic information about how our legal system operates, such as about the operation of courts and trials and the roles of participants. They also afford excellent opportunities for guest speakers from the community to come in to broaden learners' understandings. You may have good opportunities, for example, for attorneys and judges to share information with learners about how trials operate and about more general aspects of our justice system.

Developing Mock Trials

Using mock trials in a classroom involves the three stages of preparation, enactment, and debriefing. The success of a mock trial depends on careful teacher attention to each of these stages.

Preparation   One of the first steps is to introduce the learners to the purpose of a mock trial. They need to know something about the focus of the trial and what they will do to prepare for it. The basic purpose of this step is to motivate students and to teach them any rules or procedures that they will need to know. You then provide basic information concerning the facts of the case, preparing and distributing facts related to both sides of the disputed issue, often in the form of a simple fact sheet. Once it is distributed, take time to check for pupil understanding and to respond to questions.

Next, identify the roles needed and assign them to individual members of the class. Typically, these roles include a judge (or panel of judges), attorneys for both the prosecution and defense, jurors, and court assistants such as court reporters and bailiffs. Some trials require witnesses and people to play the accused person or persons.

Once you have assigned roles, give each pupil specific information about his role and responsibilities. Often this is done by providing each person with a sheet that summarizes the role to be played and provides some specific suggestions. You may also ask learners to do additional research in preparation for the trial. This preparation may require one or two class days. If pupils have never been involved in a mock trial before, often it is helpful to stage a short rehearsal trial. To do this, select a focus issue that will not require pupils to do much by way of background preparation. Assign learners roles. Guide students through the process, answer questions, and generally help them understand the flow of the event.

Enactment   The enactment stage involves the actual running of the trial in the classroom. This general sequence is followed:

- The opening of the court
- Opening statements by attorneys, with the prosecuting attorney going first and the defense attorney second
- Witnesses for the prosecution, with cross-examination by the defense attorneys
- Witnesses for the defense, with cross-examination by the prosecuting attorneys
- Closing arguments, with the defense going first and the prosecution second
- Jury deliberations
- The verdict and adjournment of the court

Certain specific statements are made by the clerk and the judge at each step of the process. You may provide these to the pupils playing these roles so the enactment more closely resembles a real court session. During the enactment, serve as an adviser and a monitor. Your basic task is to keep the enactment on track.

Debriefing   You need to monitor time carefully so ample opportunity remains for this important component of the learning process. During debriefing, focus pupils' attention on issues that have been raised, logic that has been used, and processes that have been implemented. Typically, you would lead a discussion in which you solicit observations and feelings of the different participants. Ask learners about what they have learned. Often, pupils are tempted to dwell only on the verdict. Although this is an important component of the experience, discussion of the verdict should not be allowed to overshadow significant learning about the general trial process.

Mock trials require a considerable amount of class time, often a full week. The need to commit such a substantial block of time is an important drawback to their use. Realistically, most teachers find that they can conduct a mock trial only once or twice during a school year. Those who use them find the commitment of time is more than repaid in terms of pupil learning and excitement.

In addition to formal mock trials, there are numerous simulations that can be used to teach law-focused content. Simulation is a very useful approach for teaching processes and decision-making skills. A number of simulations have been developed that focus on topics such as juvenile hearings, constitutional conventions, mediating conflicts, and even serving as a police officer on patrol. Chapter 6, "Group Learning," provides guidelines for using simulations in the classroom.

COMMUNITY RESOURCES

In nearly every community there are people who can be invited to school to share their insights with learners involved in law-related activities. Such resource people include those working for governmental agencies involved in law enforcement and corrections—police departments; highway patrols; corrections institutions; city, county, and district attorneys' offices; and all levels of courts. Representatives from these agencies

---

BOX 9–3   Are Mock Trials Worth the Time?

Two teachers were discussing approaches to social studies lessons. One mentioned a plan to use a mock trial. The other made these comments:

"I tried mock trials once. I just don't think they are worth the effort. It took me two weeks to get the material together and another two weeks of class time to implement. I just don't think my people learned much from it. Let's face it, the classroom is nothing like a courtroom, so they don't really learn what a trial is like. In addition, the class was difficult to control. There is so much content to cover that I just can't put up with the time and hassle of another mock trial."

Think About This

1. What strengths do you find in this argument?
2. What weaknesses?
3. How would you try to avoid some of the problems mentioned by this teacher?
4. How would you respond to this teacher?

Local law enforcement agencies can be excellent resources for law-related lessons.

are often willing to come to a classroom to talk. Their visits add an important dimension of reality to the content of law-focused lessons.

For example, the problems of law enforcement and the decisions a police officer must make take on added significance when they are explained by an actual officer who comes to the classroom. Bar associations and law schools are possible sources of attorneys who may be willing to come to the school. (There also may be an attorney who is a parent of a child in the class and who would like to talk to a group of elementary school learners.) Attorneys are in a position to share information related to a range of legal topics, and often are willing to assist teachers interested in creating mock trials or simulations. Some may even be willing to help debrief learners after they have experienced a simulation on a law-related topic.

Judges are also frequently willing to serve as guest speakers. Their comments can help learners understand difficulties judges face as they grapple with complex issues. They can also help pupils understand that judges face certain constraints as they do their work.

A field trip to view a court in session is often an enlightening experience for learners. In planning for a court visit, it is important that the teacher understand that not all courtrooms are open at all times to the public and that there are some cases that are not appropriate for young learners. Usually, court visits should be arranged through the court clerk. This person is able to help the teacher work out details for a visit.

Observing a court prepares pupils for a mock trial.

There may be branches of the Better Business Bureau and the American Civil Liberties Union in the local community. The Better Business Bureau has information that may help you develop lessons focusing on consumer law and consumer fraud. The American Civil Liberties Union is particularly interested in civil rights cases.

Lesson Idea 9–4

WHAT ARE YOUR RIGHTS?

Grade Level: 5–6

Objectives: Pupils can (1) define the term *warranty*, (2) state how a warranty protects a consumer, (3) and state what to do if they believe a right has been violated.

Overview: Social studies lessons that pupils perceive to be related to their everyday concerns are more interesting to them. This lesson acquaints pupils with some consumer law by using a situation likely to be of interest to them.

Procedure: *Learning Set* Bring a few examples of warranties to class. Ask the pupils if they know what they are. Read the following situation to the class:

> *Maria's favorite activity was riding a bicycle. She often looked at the new bikes in the store and wished that she had one. She really liked the 10-speed mountain bikes. There were several children in her family and she*

knew that her parents could not afford to buy her one. One day, after looking at a new bike, she decided that the only way she was going to get one was for her to try and save enough money.

Maria started by asking neighbors if she could help them with work around their houses. She collected aluminum cans and took them to the recycling center.

It took a long time, but, finally, Maria had enough money to buy a new mountain bike. She talked to her father about it and he agreed that since she had worked and saved the money, she could buy a bike. They went to the store, where they had lots of new bicycles. Maria found a red, 24-inch, 10-speed bike that she could afford.

Maria was so excited about her bike that she rode it all over the neighborhood. One day, after she had the bike for one week, she was riding it down the street when she hit a bump. When she hit the bump, the right pedal broke completely off! Maria was so upset! She didn't know what to do. He brother told her that she should take the bike back and make them give her a new one.

Discuss the situation with the class. What do you think? Would her bike be covered by a warranty? How could she find out? Under what conditions might a warranty not take care of her bike? What could she do if they told her at the store that they would not fix or replace her bike because she had mistreated the bike?

Some of the conditions of the warranties brought to class could be reviewed to help the class decide whether the bike was still covered by a warranty.

Closure

Ask, "What did we learn today about warranties? What does this tell us about our rights as consumers? What do we need to do when we buy a new product?" Give the class a homework assignment to find some warranties on things their family might have at home and to bring them in so that they can be analyzed and used in other lessons.

Finally, the local newspaper should not be overlooked as a source. Newspapers provide material that can be used in constructing episodes, using storyline, or in creating case studies and mock trials.

KEY IDEAS IN SUMMARY

1. Law-related education programs, particularly those labeled "civics," have been in public schools for many years. These traditional programs have placed a great deal

of emphasis on the study of the Constitution and the Bill of Rights. Contemporary law-focused programs, available both in secondary and elementary schools, are broader in their focus. They emphasize topics that try to explain to learners how various aspects of the legal system influence their daily lives.

2. Law-related programs seek to help pupils (1) identify the basic functions of law, (2) think critically about issues related to laws and our legal system, (3) develop problem-solving skills related to solving legal issues, (4) identify values that guide the development of laws and legal processes, (5) accept the rights and responsibility of citizenship, and (6) develop realistic and honest views of our legal system, including both its strengths and weaknesses.

3. Law-related lessons often focus on basic legal concepts; the Constitution and the Bill of Rights; our legal system; and criminal, consumer, and family law.

4. Teachers with interest in law-related education are able to choose from many materials that have been developed by organizations and commercial publishers. Organizations with materials and information of interest to public school teachers include (1) the Special Committee on Youth Education for Citizenship, (2) the Constitutional Rights Foundation, (3) Law in a Free Society, (4) Changing Times Educational Service, (5) the Opposing Viewpoints Series, (6) the National Institute for Citizen Education and the Law, (7) the Public Affairs Pamphlet Series, (8) Law in Action Units, and (9) Cases: A Resource Guide for Teaching about the Law.

5. Case studies are excellent instructional vehicles for teaching law-related content. Many cases are available from commercial sources. Teachers also write cases of their own. Case studies sometimes are devised from important cases that have already been heard and decided by the courts. At other times, case studies are built around controversial issues about which formal court decisions have yet to be rendered. Cases selected for classroom study should focus on issues of enduring value. For elementary school learners, cases should not be excessively long. Sometimes a few paragraphs of information will suffice. Case studies typically introduce learners to important facts related to the case and to relevant legal issues. Following the enactment of the case, the teacher leads a debriefing discussion to clear up misunderstandings and to reinforce learning.

6. The mock trial is another instructional approach that teachers often find useful. Mock trials are simulations that feature enactments of trials. Mock trials involve preparation, enactment, and debriefing phases. A sequence is followed that to some degree parallels the flow of activity in an actual trial. Mock trials are time-intensive activities. Often a full week of instructional time is required. For this reason, many teachers find it practical to use mock trials only once or twice during a given school year.

7. There are resources in local communities that can supplement law-related programs in the schools. Human resources appropriate for this purpose include law enforcement officials, attorneys, and judges. Organizations such as the Better Business Bureau and the American Civil Liberties Union produce materials that may prove useful to teachers planning law-related lessons. The local newspaper is

an excellent source of information about current controversies that might serve as bases for preparing case studies or mock trials.

CHAPTER REFLECTIONS

Directions: Now that you have completed reading this chapter, reread the case study at the beginning. Then answer these questions.

1. Should the elementary school social studies program place some emphasis on law-related education? Why or why not?

2. If law-related education is incorporated into the elementary social studies program, what should pupils be expected to learn from their exposure to this kind of content?

3. How can case studies and mock trials be incorporated into law-focused education lessons?

4. Describe some community resources that can be used to support law-focused lessons.

5. Do you think law-related studies might help prevent alienation, apathy, and hostility? Why or why not?

6. How would you respond to the argument that using case studies in the classroom when students have little legal knowledge amounts to little more than a sharing of ignorance?

7. Some people feel that case studies focusing on unresolved community controversies can stir up trouble for the schools. They argue that only issues that have already been decided should be used as the focus for case studies. What is your reaction?

EXTENDING UNDERSTANDING AND SKILL

1. Interview two or three elementary teachers who teach at a grade level that interests you. Ask them to comment on the extent of their use of law-related lessons. Also, ask them about their views regarding the relative importance of such studies in the classroom.

2. Write to one or more of the information sources identified in the chapter. Ask for a list of the materials and services available for assisting teachers in implementing law-related content in the classroom. Share information you receive with others in your class, and begin developing a materials file for teaching law-focused content.

3. Develop a case study related to criminal, consumer, or family law that could be used for teaching law-related content to a group of pupils. Prepare a lesson plan that outlines how the case study will be taught.

4. Develop a plan for using a mock trial in the classroom. Identify the case to be discussed, the role profiles that will be needed, and the format that will be used in presenting and debriefing the mock trial. Share your mock trial ideas with others in the class. Keep ideas provided by others in a "mock trial teaching ideas" notebook.

5. Collect newspaper articles on law-related study topics. Suggest how these articles might be used to motivate discussion of law-focused topics, or how they might be developed into case studies.

REFERENCES

BARR, I., AND McGUIRE, M. (1993). "Social Studies and Effective Stories." *Social Studies and the Young Learner, 5* (3) pp. 6–8.

HICKEY, M. (1990). "Mock Trials for Children." *Social Education, 54* (1), pp. 43–44.

WASSON, D.R. (1994). "Real-life Scenarios for Teaching the Bill of Rights." *Social Education, 54* (3), pp. 169–170.

10

GLOBAL EDUCATION

CHAPTER GOALS

This chapter provides information to help the reader:

- recognize the interdependence of people living in different world places and cultures,
- understand arguments made in favor of increasing global education experiences in the elementary social studies program,
- describe the relationship between citizenship education and international understanding,
- develop alternative schemes for infusing global education experiences into the elementary social studies program,
- identify sources of information that can be used to support global instruction, and
- describe classroom activities for helping learners increase their sensitivity to perspectives of people in other places and cultures.

CHAPTER STRUCTURE

Chapter Goals
Introduction
What is Global Education?
Global Education: Issues
Organizing Global Education Learning Experiences
      Monocultural Emphasis
      Experience Emphasis
      Oral History
      Case Studies
      Contributions Emphasis
      Intercultural Emphasis
      Personal Emphasis
Key Ideas in Summary
Chapter Reflections
Extending Understanding and Skill
References

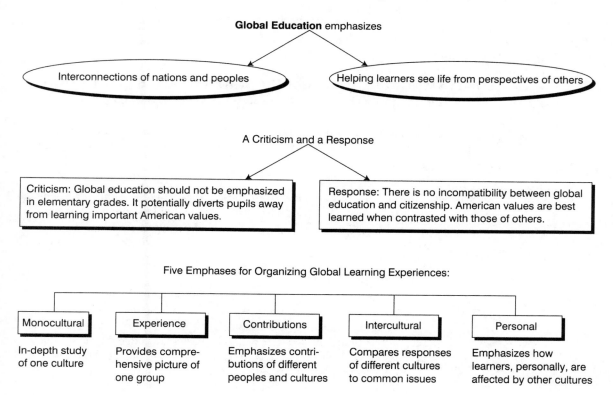

Figure 10–1
Global education.

Chapter 10

Case Study

IS IT DANGEROUS TO TEACH FOURTH GRADERS TOO MUCH ABOUT OTHER COUNTRIES AND CULTURES?

Nolan Karpanen and Ruth Ciopoloto, both of whom have children in the fourth grade at Millard Fillmore Elementary School, recently had this conversation during a coffee hour for parents at the school.

NOLAN: You know, I'm always amazed by these interviews television correspondents in foreign countries have with people whom they seem to encounter in almost any crowd. They have no trouble in finding people who can speak English, and these people seem to have amazingly detailed information about the United States.

RUTH: Yes, I've noticed that too.

NOLAN: These people must learn a great deal about the United States and other countries when they are in school. I doubt seriously if correspondents from France, China, or Nigeria could come to this country and pick people out of a typical crowd who would be very knowledgeable about the peoples and cultures of those countries. It seems to me we should be doing more in our elementary social studies program to help our young people become more knowledgeable about other places. If we are going to do the job right, we should start when kids are young. Maybe some serious international study should begin about the fourth grade.

RUTH: I know what your objective is, but I have a real problem with teaching elementary students too much about foreign countries and about cultures other than our own. I would really not like to see us start doing this with kids as young as fourth graders.

NOLAN: Why not?

RUTH: These kids are still pretty young. They still don't have a good grasp of what our country is all about. I think teaching international issues to children who are too young will just confuse them. Besides, they might fail to appreciate the importance of some of the values we treasure as Americans.

What Is Your Response?

Read the comments above. Think about points made by each speaker. Then, respond briefly to these questions:

1. Nolan indicates that many people in foreign countries seem to know more about the United States than citizens of the United States know about those countries. Do you agree or disagree?

2. Nolan suggests that Americans might know more about other countries and other peoples if more systematic instruction focusing on international topics was featured in the elementary social studies program. What do you see as strengths and weaknesses of this argument?

3. Ruth agrees that many people in foreign countries seem to have an impressive store of information about the United States, but she has doubts about the wisdom of introducing elementary pupils to information about other countries and peoples. What argument does she make in support of this position? How do you react to it?

4. How do you personally feel about committing time in elementary social studies classes to instruction designed to familiarize pupils with perspectives of people in other countries? How would you go about defending your position to someone who might question your stand?

INTRODUCTION

One hundred years ago, people living in the United States had only the haziest notion of what was happening in far-off countries. Today, television allows us to see and hear events happening tens of thousands of miles away. Other communication marvels also have drawn us closer together. Millions of computers worldwide are now linked electronically. Events occurring almost anywhere can be known almost instantaneously throughout the world. Indeed, within minutes, people separated by thousands of miles may be sharing views about what has happened by sending electronic messages on the Internet.

This revolution in communication has been accompanied by a growing international economic association (Tye & Tye, 1992). Today, fully one-third of American corporate profits are generated by global trade. An ever-increasing number of jobs are being created by firms engaged in international commerce. In short, what goes on in other countries has a profound impact on our lives. One implication of this growing interdependency among nations is that American prosperity increasingly is tied to our ability to compete effectively in the world arena. Many people believe that knowledge about other world peoples and cultures is vital to our future economic well-being. As President Bill Clinton stated, "By promoting global education, we are strengthening our ability to compete economically with the rest of the world" (Clinton, 1992, p. xi).

To cope with our growing involvement in the international community, we must become sensitive to other people and cultures. Tye and Tye (1992) suggest that, to prepare young people for this new reality, schools need to develop programs having these characteristics:

- A focus on situations that are international in scope and that emphasize the interconnectedness of nations and peoples

Current events provide an excellent opprtunity for pupils to engage in global studies.

- An emphasis on helping learners see life from the perspective of people in other cultures

In this regard, writers of *The United States Prepares for Its Future: Global Perspectives in Education* (Study Commission on Global Education, 1987) point out that "effective citizens must have knowledge and understanding of the world beyond our borders . . . its peoples, nations, cultures, systems, and problems; knowledge of how the world affects us, and knowledge of how we affect the world" (p. 12). In schools, this concern has been reflected in instruction often organized under the general heading *global education*.

WHAT IS GLOBAL EDUCATION?

Global education seeks to sensitize learners to perspectives of people in other lands and cultures. A leader of the American Forum has suggested that this be accomplished through school programs that emphasize (1) values that are unique to individual cultures as values that are common to all, (2) differing world political, economic, technological, and ecological systems, (3) broad international problems such as peace, international security, and human rights, and (4) aspects of world history emphasizing that contacts between peoples of different cultures have occurred for centuries (Colman, 1989). The following characteristics have been recommended as features of high-quality global education programs (American Forum for Global Education, 1992):

- Instructional materials are factually accurate and devoid of stereotypes.
- Human commonalities receive as much emphasis as human diversity.
- There is an emphasis on human interconnections.
- Future citizenship responsibilities are emphasized, but there are no attempts to propagandize for particular points of view.
- Global challenges are presented as an exciting arena that is worthy of learner interest.

Subsequent sections of this chapter will illustrate applications of these general characteristics of global education programs.

GLOBAL EDUCATION: ISSUES

Not everyone believes that global education is a good idea. Some people question whether such an emphasis is appropriate for elementary school learners. They argue that a longstanding priority of the elementary school program has been developing pupil commitment to American ideals. They wonder whether this commitment can be developed in a program that systematically exposes pupils to non-American values and perspectives. O'Neil (1989) frames the issue in this way: "Is it possible to teach students to appreciate the diversity and pluralism of other cultures while still maintaining their commitment and loyalty to democratic ideals?" (pp. 39, 90).

We believe there is nothing incompatible between global education and citizenship education. Indeed, American values may be more adequately appreciated when seen in contrast with values of people in other lands and cultures. Because of the widespread commitment here to such values as toleration for diverse opinion, learners sometimes find it difficult to suppose such values are not universally accepted. Exposure to situations where this is not the case may highlight unique features of our own worldview.

The technology that draws peoples of the world closer together also provides exciting new ways for young people to learn about other peoples and cultures. The Internet electronically ties together millions of computers around the world. Some teachers now have established programs that allow pupils to "talk" (by typing messages on the computer) to pupils in countries thousands of miles away. This kind of person-to-person dialogue can help learners understand that people everywhere share some common interests and concerns but that there are interesting differences as well.

In addition to linking pupils with learners and classrooms in different countries, computers today also are being used to establish electronic ties with other U.S. classrooms where class members are interested in global education issues. The World

School for Adventure Learning, administered through the University of St. Thomas in St. Paul, Minnesota, facilitates electronic contacts among U.S. classrooms pursuing global education activities (Kadrmas, 1994). These contacts allow pupils and teachers to share questions and ideas about common topics of interest. (See Chapter 13 for additional information about technology and the social studies program.)

Today, global education programs are increasing in number. Professional journals in education reflect great interest in this approach. Many organizations, including private foundations and universities, actively promote global education. Following is a partial listing of these organizations:

- Center for Public Education in International Affairs at the University of Southern California
- Global Education Center at the University of Minnesota
- Center for Teaching International Relations at the University of Denver
- Social Studies Development Center at Indiana University
- Stanford Program on International and Cross-Cultural Education at Stanford University
- Global Awareness Program at Florida International University
- Bay Area Global Education Project (San Francisco area)
- Mershon Center at Ohio State University
- Stanley Foundation (Muscatine, IA)
- World School for Adventure Learning (University of St. Thomas, St. Paul, MN)

Two excellent sources of information about global education activities for schools are The American Forum for Global Education, 45 John Street, New York, NY 10038 (phone 212-732-8606), and the Stanford Program on International and Cross-Cultural Education (SPICE), Littlefield Center, Room 14, 300 Lassen Street, Stanford University, Stanford, CA 94305-5013 (phone 415-723-1114).

ORGANIZING GLOBAL EDUCATION LEARNING EXPERIENCES

Global education learning can be integrated into the elementary social studies program in several ways. The following five emphases represent organizational patterns teachers have found useful:

- Monocultural
- Experience
- Contributions
- Intercultural
- Personal

It is possible to use any one of these emphases to develop global experiences at every grade level that respond to learners' needs and to teachers' personal and professional backgrounds. Further, they allow for the development of global education lessons that are consistent with a variety of grade-level social studies programs. For example, in a traditional expanding horizon program featuring a grade-two emphasis on "the Family," lessons can be prepared that study families in different world settings.

Monocultural Emphasis

The monocultural emphasis features an in-depth study of a single culture. The purpose is not so much to teach another culture's unique characteristics as to suggest how people from different cultures share characteristics. The idea is to help students develop a sensitivity to the broad global human community. Though there are interesting local differences, people in all cultures have developed mechanisms for nurturing the young to maturity, for providing shelter for their members, and for administering justice.

Depending on the grade level of learners and the nature of the local community, global education lessons with a monocultural emphasis might focus on issues such as these:

- A brief history of a particular group of people in their native land and a brief history of the group since members began arriving in the United States.
- Values and traditions that are particularly important to members of the culture.
- How members of the group living in the United States retain their cultural identity.
- Influences members of the group may have had on American life.
- Influences the United States and its people may have had on the place from which members of the group originally came.

Lessons built around a monocultural emphasis can be easily fitted into the traditional elementary school social studies curriculum. The following are examples of questions you might have learners consider at selected elementary grade levels:

Grade 1: Do both mothers and fathers sometimes have jobs outside the home in this country? How is this similar to or different from what we have here?

Grade 4: What is the geography like of these people's native country? In what ways is it similar or different from our geography? What ideas do you get from this country's geography about what people there might do?

Grade 6: How is this country similar or different from other countries you have studied? How might you explain similarities and differences?

Some monocultural lessons build on the experience immigrants have had in coming to terms with their new country. Teachers often find it helpful to invite to class members of the group under study to talk about problems of adjustment they faced. Many recent immigrants to this country have come from Southeast Asia. If, for example, the Vietnamese are chosen as the focus for a monocultural study, members of the local Vietnamese community might be invited to come to school to share their experiences with the children. These visitors could be asked to point out similarities and differences between their lives in Vietnam and their lives as residents of the United States.

Experience Emphasis

The monocultural approach, ideally, tries to provide learners with a comprehensive picture of one cultural or ethnic group. The experience approach tends not to look at members of a single group but rather at how events experienced by people throughout the world influence their attitudes and priorities. The power of events to mold individual perspectives is presented as a characteristic shared by human beings everywhere.

Global education lessons with an experience emphasis often focus on a number of different cultural or ethnic groups. Many teachers have found it useful to organize these lessons around oral history and case studies.

Oral History

Oral histories are particularly popular with fifth- and sixth-grade learners. They can prepare these oral histories as a class project, possibly basing them on student interviews with people from different groups who have immigrated to this country. They might ask questions such as the following in the interviews:

- What was it like to leave your old country? What were your feelings when you left?
- What things in this country were pretty much as you had imagined them?
- What things were different? What surprised you the most when you came here?
- How did your experience as an immigrant change you as a person? Do you think your reaction to this experience was typical? Why, or why not?

Case Studies

Case studies involve learners in the study of a limited number of aspects of one or more cultures. For example, a second-grade class might focus on neighborhood life in several

---

BOX 10–1   Surveying Community Cultures

If you are going to plan good lessons with a monocultural emphasis, you need to know something of the cultural and ethnic makeup of your local community. The following questions will serve as useful guides as you gather this information.

Think About This

1. What are the major cultural and ethnic groups in this community?
2. Approximately how large is each?
3. Are there any individuals who are widely regarded as leaders or spokespersons for these groups?
4. Are there clubs or other organizations that draw their membership from members of individual cultural and ethnic groups?
5. Are there ethnic neighborhoods in the community?
6. Have you identified and contacted representatives from one or more groups who have expressed a willingness to talk to pupils in your class?

Learning about other parts of the world can begin in primary grades.

countries. The lesson might introduce learners to housing patterns in neighborhoods, how letters are mailed (does a mailperson come to the door, must mail be taken to a central deposit, or is there some other arrangement?), and typical patterns of interaction among residents.

A grade-five class might examine how governments operate in one or more foreign lands. Such a lesson could be included as part of their regular study of the government of the United States. The contrasts between the practices of selected foreign governments and more familiar U.S. practices may help learners appreciate some special features of their own government.

Regardless of the focus of the case study, general questions such as the following function well to guide learners' thinking:

- What similarities to what we have in this country do you see? What differences do you see?
- What are some of your ideas about why these differences might exist?

Contributions Emphasis

As the title suggests, this emphasis focuses on contributions to our world by people in different lands and cultures. For example, if you chose this approach, you would develop lessons designed to highlight contributions of people who came to this country from original homelands elsewhere, selecting such topics as, "Distinguished African Americans," "Famous Italian-Americans," "Contributions of German Immigrants,"

"French Influences in America," "Hispanic Americans: A Proud Legacy for America," and so forth. The following focus questions might be useful:

- In what ways have people from other lands and cultures helped our country?
- In what ways have people from our country influenced other lands?
- Are people from other lands and cultures continuing to influence us today?
- Are we continuing to influence them? Can you think of some specific examples?

It is important that learners not be left with the impression that the only important contributions were made by people who chose to move to the United States. Global education seeks to help young people appreciate contributions that have been made in the past and that continue to be made by people living in many parts of the world. Possible topics for lessons with this broad focus include the following:

- African origins of iron smelting
- The work of Louis Pasteur
- Tea: An agricultural gift from Asia
- South America's wonderful potato
- Brave navigators of Portugal and Spain
- Japan's haunting "Noh" plays
- Speaking different languages and working together: Switzerland's special story

Intercultural Emphasis

The intercultural emphasis involves learners in lessons that help them compare and contrast how different cultures respond to common issues. Lessons are designed to help learners appreciate that people in many parts of the world face common challenges and have developed different ways of responding to them.

Some teachers find it convenient to use *retrieval charts* in organizing lessons featuring an intercultural emphasis. A retrieval chart is simply a grid, with one axis listing several countries whose people and cultures are being studied, and the other axis listing common challenges faced by people in each country. For example, all people have a need for food, shelter, clothing, and recreational outlets. Hence, this axis might include these concepts as labels.

You may, of course, select other focus issues. For example, if you wanted to use an intercultural focus, you might want members of your class to compare and contrast several countries in terms of their attitudes toward women, their views on capital punishment, and the nature of their school systems. In such a case one axis of the retrieval chart would include these headings. Figure 10–2 illustrates a simple retrieval chart.

The retrieval chart has several advantages. Pupils may use large printed versions to take notes, writing information in each of the cells as they learn it. You might also consider using retrieval charts to differentiate assignments, having learners find information related to specific cells. A poster-sized version of the chart can be displayed on one wall. Learners can take turns writing information they have gathered in the appropriate

Figure 10–2
Sample retrieval chart.

	Food	Shelter	Clothing	Recreation
Country **A**				
Country **B**				
Country **C**				

places. The completed chart then becomes your basis for debriefing. Using the chart in Figure 10–2 as an example, you might ask questions such as these:

- What are some similarities among countries A, B, and C? What are some differences?
- Do these differences necessarily mean people are "better" in some of these countries than in others? (You must be prepared to deal with an occasional "yes" response to this issue. Learners need to be helped to understand that responses to life's challenges in one country may be different than in another, but that this difference does not imply inferiority. It speaks rather to the rich diversity that is one of our world's real treasures.)
- How might you explain any differences?

This general sequence helps students to move beyond given information to make inferences. Such a lesson has the advantages of deepening their sensitivity to differences among peoples and cultures and developing their higher-level thinking skills.

Another intercultural approach that some teachers use teaches children games that are played by young people in other cultures. Sunal (1988) points out that "learning about a facet of childhood in another culture is likely to be the most concrete means by which children can come to form an initial understanding of that culture" (p. 232).

Lesson Idea 10–1

INTERCULTURAL EMPHASIS: HIDE AND SEEK

Grade Level:	3–6
Objective:	Pupils will identify selected features of a culture by playing a game popular in the culture.
Suggested Procedure:	In one of many examples from Nigeria, Sunal (1988) describes a game similar to our familiar hide and seek. This version is often played by children who are members of a small Nigerian group, the Unemeosu. In this game, the blindfolded person who is "it" counts silently while other children hide. After a reasonable period of time, the person who is "it"

starts looking for the children who have hidden. While trying to keep from being spotted by the child who is "it," those who are hiding try to run quietly and touch a small mound of stones that they have built in the middle of the area of play. If they succeed in touching the stones (and if they are undetected by the person who is "it"), then they must say a phrase meaning, "I have touched the earth." When the person who is "it" finds someone, that person becomes "it" for the next round.

This version of hide and seek is "supposed to remind children of Unemeosu history. The hiders are like heroes of the past who were believed to be smart enough to seem to disappear from an attacking enemy, hide, and reappear quickly in a position to defeat the enemy" (p. 234). Since this game is so similar to our hide and seek, pupils take to it quickly. You may organize a game, perhaps during recess, and have a followup discussion to pinpoint differences between the Nigerian and American versions. As Sunal suggests, you might remind children that many Nigerians are farmers and for this reason the phrase, "I have touched the earth," might be especially important to them. A discussion of this phrase might lead children to consider whether there are special phrases American children sometimes say at certain times during their games.

If you are interested in specific directions for playing other games from foreign lands, read Sunal's article, cited in full in the "References" section at the end of this chapter. In addition to directions for playing the games, the author provides excellent ideas for followup discussions.

Personal Emphasis

Some elementary pupils have regular contact with people from other countries. They may have relatives with whom family members correspond, or may be fortunate enough to travel regularly outside the United States. They may live in a community where large numbers of people have come relatively recently from other lands.

On the other hand, children in many other families and communities have had very little direct personal contact with people from other lands and cultures. Though their lives are very much influenced by people outside the United States, they may not be aware of the extent to which they are members of an interactive international community. Some direct instruction can help underscore this point. You may use several instructional approaches to help pupils appreciate how much they personally are affected by other cultures. Lesson Ideas 10–2, 10–3, and 10–4 illustrate three of these approaches.

BOX 10–2   **Is There Time for Global Education Lessons?**

Recently, a critic of elementary school global education lessons made these comments.

> The elementary program is choked with too much content. Some say we can still give our children a good basic grounding in Americanism and, at the same time, teach them about other cultures. I disagree. There simply is not time to do both. What we are going to end up with is a group of young people who are ignorant both of their own traditions and of those of other cultures. It makes good sense to defer the study of other cultures until junior or senior high school. By this time, most young people will be well informed about the proud heritage of our own country.

Think About This

1. What strengths do you find in this argument?
2. What weaknesses?
3. How would you respond to this critic?

Lesson Idea 10–2

THE PARKING LOT SURVEY

Grade Level: 5–6

Objectives: Pupils will (1) locate nations on a map and (2) state the interdependence and influences of various nations on each other.

Suggested Procedure: This activity works particularly well with older elementary school youngsters. Ask each pupil to look at 25 to 50 cars parked in a row at a shopping center. (For safety's sake, suggest that a parent accompany them.) Have the pupils write down the name of the make, not the model, of each car (not Thunderbird, but Ford, for example). Ask pupils to bring the results of their survey to class.

Prepare a master list of all the car makes the children saw. Write these on the board. Next to each make, indicate the number of cars of this kind that pupils saw. Continue by asking them to name the country of origin of each make. Be prepared to help if learners are unsure.

Next, use a large world map to indicate the locations of these countries. It is probable that the learners' lists will include cars from Japan and Germany. Often, there will also be some that came from Sweden, England, France, Italy, and Korea. Perhaps there will be a few from Yugoslavia and other countries. Conclude with a discussion that helps make these points:

- Many countries now manufacture automobiles, and many foreign car companies currently manufacture automobiles in the United States.
- Usually countries that manufacture automobiles have many highly skilled workers and access to needed raw materials.
- Because large ships can easily transport cars throughout the world, consumers enjoy a wider choice than they would if they had access only to cars made in their country.

Lesson Idea 10–3

WHERE CLOTHING IS MANUFACTURED

Grade Level: 4–6

Objectives: Pupils will (1) locate places on a map, (2) give reasons why different countries manufacture different items, and (3) state the impact of importation on a nation's economy.

Suggested Procedure: This activity can be combined with a family trip to a local discount department store, such as K-Mart. In preparation, provide learners with a short list of clothing items, such as shirts, socks, and jackets, to look for during their trip to the store. At the store, pupils (assisted by their parents) should attempt to determine the countries that manufactured these items. They will find that many of these familiar pieces of clothing are manufactured in other countries.

Have pupils take notes on their observations. Notes should include the category of each item observed and the name(s) of the countries where it was manufactured. When these notes are shared with the class, write the items and countries of manufacture on the chalkboard or on an overhead transparency. Then, using a large wall map of the world, point out the locations of these countries. Additional activities may highlight certain aspects of these countries and their people.

A followup discussion can help learners develop insights such as these (specific information emphasized will vary with grade level, academic ability, and interests of learners):

- Common items of clothing are manufactured in many countries outside of the United States.
- Much clothing comes to this country from countries in Asia.
- Foreign clothing manufacturers know about likes and dislikes of American buyers. Hence, it often is not possi-

ble to distinguish on the basis of styles, fabrics, and colors between clothing made in this country and clothing made in other countries.

• It costs something to ship clothing from another country to the United States. Often this means that clothing comes from areas where wages paid to workers in clothing factories are less than they are in the United States (If they weren't, transportation charges would require sellers to sell these clothes at prices higher than American buyers are willing to pay. Lacking buyers, foreign manufacturers soon would stop shipping clothing here.)

Lesson Idea 10–4

WHERE DO DIFFERENT DOG BREEDS COME FROM?

Grade Level:	3–6
Objectives:	Pupils will (1) gather data from available resources, (2) identify patterns in data, and (3) state possible explanations for observed patterns.
Overview:	Children like dogs. Some teachers have used this interest to stimulate interest in learning about other world places and peoples. Several approaches can be taken to this activity; the one suggested here is representative.
Suggested Procedure:	Planning requires access to a source of information about dog breeds that includes specific details about where each breed originated. One excellent source is Gino Pugnetti's *Simon & Schuster's Guide to Dogs* (New York: Simon & Schuster, 1980). Select 5 to 10 breeds. While these need not necessarily be breeds that each child has seen, it is not a good idea to select rare breeds that children may never see. The idea is to emphasize that the local and the familiar, represented here by the humble dog, has important international ties. Dogs should be selected whose roots trace to a number of different countries. Note that authorities do not agree about where some breeds of dogs began. Thus, it is possible that two pupils may research origins of the same dog and find different information. As a teacher, you need to be prepared for this possibility. It affords an opportunity to point out that there are some matters about which even qualified experts disagree.

After acquiring a reference book, select several breeds as a focus for the lesson. The following list shows a sample selection.

Breed	Presumed Country of Origin
Boxer	Germany (originated in Munich)
Poodle	France
Chihuahua	Mexico
Shih-Tzu	China
Basenji	Egypt
Cocker Spaniel	England

Place photographs of these dogs around the borders of a large wall map of the world. Then help the class to locate the countries from which these dogs came. Finally, invite individual pupils to place brightly colored yarn between the photographs of the dogs and their countries of origin.

A number of followup activities and lessons can be pursued. For example, help the class to notice that large number of breeds originated in European countries. This does not mean that there have not always been large numbers of dogs elsewhere. What it suggests is that Europeans were among the first to keep breeding records and become concerned about the purity of breeds. Attitudes of people in other lands toward dogs might be a productive avenue of inquiry. Do people everywhere like dogs? This is an interesting question to pursue.

Learners can do some research of their own to determine where other breeds originated; they may bring in photographs of these dogs. When they find this information, add the new photographs to those around the map, and string additional colored yarn between these dogs and their probable countries of origin.

KEY IDEAS IN SUMMARY

1. Technological developments are drawing peoples of the world closer together. The increasing internationalization of life makes a strong case for school programs that increase learners' sensitivity to other countries and cultures. Some people also feel that our young people must become sensitive to peoples and perspectives everywhere if our country is to participate successfully in international commerce.

2. Global education seeks to familiarize learners with perspectives of others. Programs emphasize, among other things, values of individual cultures; differing world political, social, and economic systems; challenging international problems such as the search for peace, international security, and human rights; and aspects of world history that stress the long history of contact among peoples of different places and cultures.

3. Some critics have charged that global education programs undermine the effort of elementary programs to develop learners' appreciation for the unique qualities of their own country. Supporters of global education argue that American values can be better understood when seen in contrast with values of other peoples and cultures. Today, supporters of global education seem to be prevailing. Global education experiences are increasingly included within elementary social studies programs.

4. Some global education lessons reflect a monocultural emphasis, designed to provide pupils with an appreciation of characteristics of a single culture. Such lessons may focus on the history of the studied group, its values and traditions, and its past and present interactions with the United States.

5. Lessons featuring an experience emphasis are designed to help learners appreciate that attitudes and perspectives of people everywhere are influenced by what they have experienced in life. Often teachers who plan lessons with this emphasis use oral history and case studies as vehicles for delivering instruction.

6. The contributions emphasis in global education focuses on contributions that have been made to our world by people from different cultures. Lessons are designed to help learners understand that the quality of our lives today has been greatly enhanced by the contributions of people living in other countries and cultures.

7. The intercultural emphasis helps learners grasp how people in different cultures may respond to common issues in different ways. These lessons help young people understand that problems may have several effective solutions.

8. The personal emphasis attempts to take advantage of experiences learners may have had personally with influences from other countries and cultures. People living even in isolated inland areas of the United States have more contact with other lands and peoples than they may realize. Personal emphasis lessons help students to appreciate that exchanges of ideas and goods among the world's peoples have become commonplace.

CHAPTER REFLECTIONS

Directions: Now that you have finished reading the chapter, reread the case study at the beginning. Then answer these questions:

1. How would you respond to critics who suggest that global education lessons interfere with the effort to develop elementary school pupils' sense of patriotism?

2. Describe different approaches to global education learning experiences that are organized around a monocultural emphasis, an experience emphasis, a contributions emphasis, an intercultural emphasis, and a personal emphasis.

3. In addition to the ideas presented in the chapter, what might you do to provide learners with global education learning experiences having a personal emphasis?

4. If you were asked to develop a publicity campaign to build public support for more emphasis on global education in the elementary social studies program, what would you do? Think about people you would involve and about specific arguments you might make. Also, consider points people who oppose global education might want to make and possible responses to their arguments.

5. How would you go about the task of identifying people in your local community who came to this country from other lands and cultures?

EXTENDING UNDERSTANDING AND SKILL

1. Invite a social studies director or coordinator from a local school district to your class. Ask this person to comment on the extent to which the local elementary program emphasizes global education. Inquire about any special difficulties teachers may have had in implementing such lessons.

2. Survey the professional journals in education for articles focusing on global education. (You may wish to begin by referring to the *Education Index* in your library. Your course instructor may have other ideas about article sources.) Make copies of three articles that you feel contain good ideas. Share these ideas with others in your class.

3. Review a social studies curriculum guide for an elementary grade level you would like to teach. (Such guides may be available in the library, or at local school district offices. Your instructor may also know where to find them.) Prepare a brief oral report for your class on the extent to which this document reflects a global education emphasis.

4. Prepare a lesson with one of the following global education emphases: (1) monocultural; (2) experience; (3) contributions; (4) intercultural; and (5) personal. Present your lesson to your course instructor for review.

5. Organize a debate on this question: "Resolved that an increased emphasis on global education will irresponsibly take away from other important social studies content." Select teams of individuals to prepare a case in support of both the pro and the con positions. Conduct the debate as a class, and conclude with a general discussion of the merits of including global education experiences in the elementary social studies program.

REFERENCES

American Forum for Global Education. (1992). *The New Global Resource Book*. New York: American Forum for Global Education.

CLINTON, W. J. (1992). "Foreword." In B. B. Tye and K. A. Tye, *Global Education: A Study of School Change*. Albany, New York: State University of New York Press. pp. xi–xii.

COLMAN, P. (1989). "Global Education: Teaching for an Interdependent World." *Media & Methods, 25* (3), pp. 21–23, 59–61.

KADRMAS, S. R. (1994). "Teaching Global Studies with Technology." *Media & Methods, 30* (4), pp. 24–25.

O'NEIL, J. (1989). "Confronting Controversy in Global Education." *Media & Methods, 25* (4) pp. 39, 90.

PUGNETTI, G. (1980). *Simon & Schuster's Guide to Dogs*. E. M. Schuler, ed. New York: Simon & Schuster.

Study Commission on Global Education. *The United States Prepares for Its Future: Global Perspectives in Education*. (1987). Report of the Study Commission on Global Education. New York: Global Perspectives in Education.

SUNAL, C. S. (1988). "Studying Another Culture through Children's Games: Examples from Nigeria." *The Social Studies, 79* (5), pp. 232–238.

TYE, B. B., AND TYE, K. A. (1992). *Global Education: A Study of School Change*. Albany, NY: State University of New York Press.

11

MULTICULTURAL AND GENDER-EQUITY EDUCATION

CHAPTER GOALS

This chapter provides information to help the reader:

- recognize the diverse character of American society,
- describe issues teachers often consider when they plan multicultural and gender-equity lessons,
- point out basic goals of multicultural and gender-equity education,
- explain differences between single-group studies and multiple-perspective studies,
- cite examples of classroom activities that can help sensitize pupils to multicultural and gender-equity issues, and
- identify sources of information available to use in multicultural and gender-equity lessons.

CHAPTER STRUCTURE

Introduction
Multicultural Education's Many Faces
Gender-Equity Education: Purposes
Basic Goals of Multicultural and Gender-Equity Education
Monitoring Teaching Procedures
Classroom Approaches to Multicultural and Gender-Equity Studies
  Single-Group Studies: General Characteristics
  Single-Group Studies: Examples of Classroom Approaches
  Multiple-Perspectives Approach: General Characteristics
  Multiple-Perspectives Approach: A Classroom Example
Sources of Information
  Multicultural Lessons
  Gender-Equity Lessons
Key Ideas in Summary
Chapter Reflections
References

Lessons focusing on **multicultural** and **gender-equity** issues help pupils to:

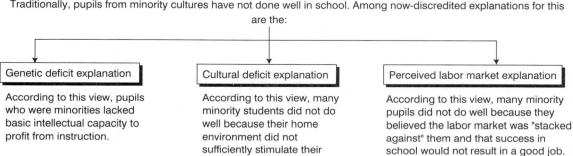

| Understand our increasingly diverse society and appreciate the contributions people from many cultures make to our national life. | Recognize that gender should not be an automatic barrier to any occupational role for which a person is otherwise qualified |

1. **Multicultural Issue**

Traditionally, pupils from minority cultures have not done well in school. Among now-discredited explanations for this are the:

Genetic deficit explanation	Cultural deficit explanation	Perceived labor market explanation
According to this view, pupils who were minorities lacked basic intellectual capacity to profit from instruction.	According to this view, many minority students did not do well because their home environment did not sufficiently stimulate their intellectual development.	According to this view, many minority pupils did not do well because they believed the labor market was "stacked against" them and that success in school would not result in a good job.

> **Today there is an emerging consensus around the idea that failure of minorities to achieve has been a failure of educators to prize cultural differences and to plan for the success of <u>all</u> learners.**

2. **Gender Discrimination Issue**

| Gender discrimination has often been guided by such myths as "boys are poorer writers than girls" and "girls have more trouble with math than boys." | As a consequence of gender bias and discrimination, for many years certain occupations were reserved for males and certain other ones for females. |

> **Gender discrimination has tended to restrict choices more for females than for males. Social studies programs have an obligation to help girls recognize that responsible roles of all kinds are now open to females as well as males.**

Figure 11–1
Multicultural and gender-equity education.

Chapter 11

Case Study

IS A FOCUS ON MULTICULTURALISM AND GENDER EQUITY INCONSISTENT WITH CORE AMERICAN VALUES?

The following comments were prepared by writers of two different newspaper opinion columns:

Writer "A's" Comments

The population of America's schools is more diverse than it has ever been. Providing learning programs that connect to the psychological worlds of young people from many different cultural traditions is a national imperative. Lessons that reflect a multicultural perspective signal to learners that we prize diversity.

Our nation cannot afford school programs that fail to ignite sparks of intellectual interest in *all* pupils. We must signal to young people of all cultural and ethnic backgrounds that they are individuals of consequence for whom our society imposes no artificial upper limits. Sound school programs that respond to multicultural and gender-equity concerns are vital to our nation's future. They deserve our support.

Writer "B's" Comments

Fragmentation that pits group against group is one of the most vexing problems we face today. Cosseting of interest groups, especially those cultural and ethnic minorities whose self-appointed, politically ambitious leaders use inflammatory language to win special treatment, denies the common "Americaness" we share as citizens of this country.

School programs that emphasize multiculturalism and gender equity deny the importance of the social glue that binds us together as a people. Emphases on the importance of the "common good" and our "shared American perspective" are shunted aside in an irresponsible attempt to highlight those things that divide us. Lessons focusing on widely accepted American values are desperately needed in the schools today. We urge a renewed commitment to the idea of the "melting pot"—an image around which all of our citizens should be able to rally.

What Is Your Response?

Read the comments of each columnist. Think about the points each makes. Then, respond briefly to these questions.

1. Writer "A" comments on the changing ethnic and cultural makeup of schools and suggests that today's diverse group of pupils require different kinds of programs than have traditionally been provided. Do you agree? If so, what changes would you recommend?
2. Writer "A" implies that many present school programs fail to encourage some learners, particularly those from ethnic and cultural minorities and those who are female, to develop their capacities to the fullest. Is this a real problem? Why, or why not? Can you cite examples to support your position?

3. Writer "B" argues that school programs that seek to respond to special perspectives of individuals from different ethnic and gender groups are divisive. It this true? Can you cite examples to support your view?

4. Writer "B" suggests that school programs ought to emphasize a common set of core American values rather than perspectives of diverse groups. What strengths and weaknesses do you see in this argument?

5. If you were asked to take a position on the issues raised by writer "A" and writer "B," what would you say?

INTRODUCTION

Olivia Escobar, a first-year teacher, works in a largely white, affluent community. Her interactions with learners have convinced her that most of her pupils have little understanding of cultural groups other than their own. Many of their comments suggest that they believe people who are different from themselves, especially minorities, are less deserving and less intelligent. These young people have little appreciation for the diversity that characterizes American society today.

Steve Stepanovic, also a beginning teacher, is employed in a community very different from Olivia's. Most pupils in his class come from a cultural background not at all like his own. Many seem not to understand the importance of arriving at school on time and are often not prompt in turning in assigned work. Others in his class appear to have little respect for his own personal property. These attitudes contrast sharply with those shared by people in the small town where he grew up. The attitudes of his fifth graders make Steve uncomfortable, and he is not sure what he should do.

Challenges such as those facing Olivia Escobar and Steve Stepanovic confront many teachers in today's schools. The diversity of American society assures that many learners come from cultural backgrounds different from those of their teachers. Responding to this difference requires more than simply learning something about perspectives of individual ethnic groups. Behavior patterns of individuals are shaped by many influences other than ethnicity. For example, a given child may at the same time be a member of a black culture, an urban culture, a youth culture, and a poverty culture. Many influences contribute to the diversity of today's elementary school population.

Schools must serve *all* children who attend. An important obligation of the social studies is to help pupils understand the diversity of our society. One way we can do this is by preparing lessons that focus on multicultural and gender-equity issues. The future stability of our country depends on citizens committed to the idea that perspectives of others are important and that the specific cultural groups to which they belong are parts of a larger, more diverse whole.

The issue of equity is a central theme in school social studies instruction. The concept extends beyond the perspectives of individual ethnic groups to embrace gender as

---

BOX 11–1   **Are New Roles for Women Undermining Families?**

A speaker at a recent parent-teacher organization meeting made these comments:

> We hear much these days about the importance of encouraging girls to think about many kinds of employment options. I'm not sure this makes good sense. Too many women today are working hard to build careers as professionals. Their work takes them out of the home and away from their children. The result is that thousands of children are being left to "raise themselves." It would be better for everybody if more bright women stayed home and gave their children the kind of nurturing needed for them to grow into responsible adults.

Think About This

1. What are the strengths of this argument?
2. What are the weaknesses?
3. How would you respond to this person?

---

well. Historically, women have not had as many personal and career options as men. Though there have been great changes in this situation in recent years, much work still remains.

Multicultural and gender-equity education form a natural partnership, linked by the social goals of equality and fairness. The elementary social studies program seeks to produce young people who, as they begin assuming their responsibilities as citizens, will work to overcome injustice and inequality wherever they find them.

MULTICULTURAL EDUCATION'S MANY FACES

Educators have long recognized a trend toward increasing diversity among the nation's learners. In the early 1990s, more than 40 percent of the nation's children were members of cultural and ethnic minority groups and were from economically impoverished families (*Beyond Rhetoric*, 1991).

We also have known that, traditionally, many children from minority cultures have not done well in school. This situation has resulted in under representation of minorities in professional roles demanding college and university preparation. For example, African Americans comprise slightly over 12 percent of the total U.S. population; yet, they represent only 2 percent of all employed scientists and engineers (Strutchens, 1994).

Earlier in this century, some argued that minority learners failed to do well in school because they suffered from a "genetic deficit." According to this view, learners from minority ethnic groups and cultures lacked the basic intellectual equipment to profit from instruction. Not surprisingly, individuals who subscribed to this position were reluctant to commit resources to serve the needs of ethnic and cultural minorities.

By the 1960s, scholarship had polished off the genetic deficit view as a serious explanation for academic problems experienced by minority group learners (although individuals occasionally still try to make a case for the theory). In its place, some people emphasized a "cultural deficit" explanation. Proponents of this view suggested that many learners from minority groups did not do well because they did not have a "cognitively stimulating environment" at home (Erickson, 1987, p. 335). Erickson, who studied changing attitudes toward minority learners in school, pointed out that the cultural deficit view allowed educators to avoid responsibility for minority learners' failure to profit from instruction. Their failure to achieve was the fault of the home, not the school.

Over time, many educators came to see the cultural deficit view as a prescription for inaction and as a convenient escape from responsibility. Among more recent explanatory theories for academic difficulties of cultural and ethnic minorities have been the "communication process" and the "perceived labor market" views. According to the former, language patterns of minority students differ so dramatically from those of their teachers that they fail to understand much of what occurs in the classroom. The communication process explanation has been criticized because it fails to suggest why some students from ethnic and cultural minorities do extremely well in school.

The perceived labor market explanation suggests that minority learners believe the employment market is rigged against them. Hence, they see no point in taking schooling seriously because they do not think that academic success will result in a good job once they have finished. This view has been attacked by critics who point out that some minority students who do not do well in school are strongly committed to the idea that there is an important connection between academic success and a good job.

In general, present-day critics have little use for explanations for minorities' poor academic performance that have attempted to place blame somewhere other than on schools and school programs. They argue that the real culprit has been our failure as educators to plan seriously for the success of *all* pupils in our classes, not just pupils from "traditional" white families. Instructional practices are needed that will develop levels of self-confidence among all young people in our classes.

Diversity is one of our strengths. As social studies teachers, we have an obligation to assure that our learners appreciate the many cultural and ethnic threads that go together to make up our national tapestry. This most certainly has not always been the prevailing view. Multicultural education specialists Reece L. Peterson and Sharon Ishii-Jordan (1994) point out that "prior to the movement toward multicultural education, cultural differences were characterized as detrimental and seen as barriers in obtaining status and value in the American mainstream" (p. 3).

In recent years, many excellent models have evolved for creating lessons that illuminate perspectives of individual ethnic groups and cultures. One approach suggests developing instructional experiences with the following kinds of emphases:

- Lessons and programs directed specifically at culturally different children for the purpose of equalizing educational opportunities for them
- Lessons and programs designed to promote an appreciation for cultural differences among all learners

- Lessons and programs designed to preserve and maintain perspectives of individual cultures and ethnic groups
- Lessons and programs that seek to help children function in multicultural contexts

These approaches place important obligations on us as teachers. We must plan experiences that support an acceptance of multiple perspectives. This requires us to be on the lookout for examples of contributions made to our society by people who are members of many different cultural and ethnic groups.

The diversity of cultures represented in today's classrooms underscores the importance of teachers' need to learn about the background of their learners. Teachers who seriously consider cultural diversity are much more likely to succeed with youngsters from minority cultures than teachers who fail to take important cultural differences into account. To illustrate how children's cultural backgrounds can influence their expectations about what education and schooling are about, let's think about pupils recently arrived from Southeast Asia.

Many cultures in this part of the world expect young people to acquire new information through rote learning, and their schools emphasize this kind of instruction. If newcomers from Southeast Asia come into a classroom of a teacher who uses different instructional approaches, they may well be confused. As teachers, we need to be alert to these kinds of situations. With young new pupils from Southeast Asia, we might take time to teach them about how other teaching techniques work and, especially, about

Role models help break down gender stereotypes.

how we expect them to participate. These young people need assistance as they come to understand that rote memorization, while a worthy way of learning some content, is not the only reasonable approach.

GENDER-EQUITY EDUCATION: PURPOSES

For many years, certain occupations were widely believed to be the "property" of one sex. Many more roles were open to males than to females. Today, employers have begun to remove gender-based employment barriers, and now are more inclined than before to focus solely on each applicant's qualifications.

Despite considerable progress toward gender equity in all areas of our national life, residual attitudes persist. Such myths as, "females are not good in mathematics," and "males tend to be poor writers," still have their adherents. Some people also continue to feel that males should not do such work as teaching kindergarten, nursing, and so forth, and that females, in turn, should not attempt firefighting, carpentry, surgery, and so forth. An important purpose of the social studies is to confront these gender-based biases openly. Pupils need to understand that many occupational roles will be open to them as adults. This kind of perspective has not always been reflected in the schools (Schmuck and Schmuck, 1994). Even today there is evidence that many "teachers continue to have different expectations for boys and girls. For example, boys are expected to excel in math and science, and teachers often encourage and challenge them more in those subjects" (Flynn & Chambers, 1994, p. 59).

Gender discrimination has tended to restrict choices more for females than for males. Social studies programs, therefore, have an obligation to provide pupils with examples of females who occupy a variety of responsible roles. Girls must recognize that increasing numbers of females play leadership roles in government, engineering, the physical sciences, and medicine.

The standard of living of citizens of the United States is being challenged by economic successes of other nations. There is a pressing need for us to develop *all* of our nation's intellectual resources. To this end, young people must be unconstrained by gender-related barriers as they pursue their personal and vocational objectives.

BASIC GOALS OF MULTICULTURAL AND GENDER-EQUITY EDUCATION

The following are among the most important social studies goals addressed by multicultural and gender-equity lessons.

- *The social studies program should help pupils develop a respect for cultures other than their own.* To accomplish this, we need to take action before instruction begins to find out how our learners feel about other groups and cultures. This kind of diagnostic information provides insights regarding pupils' initial levels of sensitivity toward others. We can use this baseline information to prepare lessons to challenge stereotypes and extend pupils' appreciation of diversity.

- *Pupils should be provided opportunities to work directly with members of different ethnic and racial groups.* Direct contact with members of other groups helps young people to value new friends. These relationships help pupils to appreciate the ethnic and cultural groups to which their new friends belong.
- *Pupils need to recognize the validity of different cultural perspectives.* This goal seeks to expand pupils' conception of what it means to be human. Lessons directed toward this end celebrate the rich diversity of the human experience. If successful, these lessons help pupils understand that different people have developed many acceptable responses to common human problems. Our goal here is

---

BOX 11–2   Diagnosing Stereotypes

This procedure can be used with all but the very youngest pupils. Children in the primary grades should be asked to respond orally. Middle and upper grades pupils can write their responses.

To prepare for the exercise, gather together 8 to 12 photographs of members of different racial and ethnic groups. Ask pupils to look at each photograph and to assign one of the following descriptive words that they believe might "go with" the person who is depicted:

a. helpful	k. energetic
b. troublesome	l. hard-working
c. doctor	m. poor
d. teacher	n. wealthy
e. janitor	o. dirty
f. delivery person	p. kind
g. friendly	q. ignorant
h. hot-tempered	r. wise
i. lazy	s. sad
j. generous	t. helpless

Terms *a, c, d, g, j, k, l, n, p,* and *r* are associated with people who are viewed positively or who are perceived as having higher status. Terms *b, e, f, h, i, m, o, q, s,* and *t* are associated with people viewed negatively or as having lower status.

Think About This

If large numbers of pupils assign negative/low-status terms to photographs of nonwhite American men and women, this suggests that a negative stereotyping problem exists. Lessons can then be planned to break down these narrow, unrealistic views.

Perform this exercise before and after a series of lessons designed to eradicate stereotyping. Compare the results to indicate whether pupils have developed more appreciation for members of groups that they initially negatively stereotyped.

to attack the ethnocentric view that the experiences of any single cultural group represent the "right" or "natural" way to live.

- *The social studies program should help pupils develop pride in their cultural heritage.* This goal seeks to help pupils recognize that there is no one "American way." Though as a nation we commit to such core values as toleration of minority opinion, the right to choose one's occupation, and so forth, the fabric of our society is enriched by many cultural threads. Hence, it is quite proper for pupils to take pride in their own cultural roots. Lessons associated with this goal seek to help pupils develop a positive self-image. When this occurs, pupils grow in their sense of self-worth, feel less threatened by people who "are different," commit more strongly to the school program, and often get better grades.

- *The social studies needs to emphasize that values conflicts are often at the root of conflicts between and among groups.* Many issues that are in dispute in our society are not the result of disagreements about facts. People argue about them because their different values cause them to interpret the facts in different ways. Values orientations often are at the root of conflicts among members of different cultural groups. As social studies teachers, we have an obligation to help pupils recognize that not all groups share the same values and priorities. (For an example of a general instructional approach to highlight values' differences, refer to the discussion of decision making in Chapter 7, "Developing Thinking Skills.")

MONITORING TEACHING PROCEDURES

Multicultural and gender-equity purposes of the social studies program require us to think carefully about procedures we use in implementing instruction. What we do as we teach can greatly affect how individual pupils feel about themselves. Attention to the following guidelines can contribute to the development of a classroom atmosphere that supports successful multicultural and gender-equity lessons.

- *We should include learners of different ethnic, cultural, and social backgrounds when we organize pupils into groups.* There is evidence that this kind of mixing is not as common as one might hope. Sometimes race, socioeconomic status, and sex have been considered when teachers have made decisions about which pupils should be included in a given group. Grouping based on such variables can inhibit academic development and can lead to low self-images.

- *As teachers, we need to be aware of our own cultural perspectives and to recognize how these may vary from those of some of our pupils.* Researchers have found that individuals differ in their learning styles and that cultural background contributes to a person's preference for a given style (Grant & Sleeter, 1989). In a classroom that includes learners from different ethnic and cultural groups, several style preferences will be represented. Some pupils will need to manipulate objects, others will learn better by reading about new content, still others may respond well to graphic representations of information. Lessons that accommodate different learning styles are more likely to help pupils learn than are those in which content presentation assumes all youngsters learn in the same way.

- *Our evaluation procedures should be as free from cultural and social bias as possible.* Improper testing and evaluation procedures present serious obstacles even to highly motivated pupils from minority cultures. Standardized tests pose particularly difficult problems. The vocabulary used and assumptions made about prior life experiences of those who take standardized tests often are unrelated to the backgrounds of pupils from certain ethnic and cultural groups. Some tests even reflect a regional bias. For example, a test developed in Texas that asked pupils to identify an armadillo might well bewilder a pupil in New England where armadillos are not a common roadside sight, as they are in parts of Texas.

One way we can avoid bias in standardized tests is to develop assessments of our own. When we do this, we can take into account particular characteristics of members of our own class when preparing evaluation procedures. These kinds of assessments often do a much better job of providing accurate evaluation information than procedures developed by others who lack our insights about the special characteristics of the young people we teach.

- *We need to monitor what we do in the classroom to assure that we are not favoring any single group of learners.* Researchers have found that teachers' attitudes toward and expectations of individual learners influence their achievement (Good & Brophy, 1994). These expectations often are communicated to learners through teachers' actions. For example, we may ask certain pupils more challenging questions, provide them more feedback, and spend more time with them. It does not take others in the class long to figure this out. When pupils see what is going on, those who see that they are not in the "favored" group often develop less positive

---

BOX 11–3   The Problem of "Pigeonholing"

Some people tend to assign certain allegedly fixed characteristics to whole groups of individuals. Often these characteristics are negative stereotypes. The term *pigeonholing* refers to evaluating people based on characteristics thought to be associated with their ethnic group or gender.

Think back on your own experiences in school. Did you ever feel certain people had prior conceptions about what you could or could not do even before they had an opportunity to assess your real abilities? Did you ever see pigeonholing happening to others?

Think About This

1. If you ever felt yourself to be pigeonholed, describe your feelings. If you saw it happening to others, how did they feel and react?
2. In your opinion, what might cause a teacher to pigeonhole a pupil?
3. As a beginning teacher, what are some things you might do to minimize the possibility of assigning certain expectations to a given pupil based on nothing more than ethnic group membership or gender?

attitudes toward the teacher and the class, and their level of academic performance often declines.

If we truly want all of the people in our class to learn, we must behave in ways that signal that we truly believe that each person has the potential to succeed. If we somehow signal to pupils that "it is natural for girls to have trouble doing math" or that "pupils from low-income homes can't be expected to read well," we are asking for trouble. These kinds of assumptions quickly reveal themselves to pupils. Further, these biases affect what the teacher does. For example, if a teacher believes that certain pupils are not going to read as well as some others, there is a tendency for less effort to go into instruction directed toward those individuals for whom the teacher has low expectations. This becomes a vicious circle in which the teacher's unfortunate *a priori* assumptions lead to half-hearted instruction which, not surprisingly, ends up with poor performance on the part of those pupils for whom the teacher had low initial expectations.

CLASSROOM APPROACHES TO MULTICULTURAL AND GENDER-EQUITY STUDIES

Approaches used in developing these lessons feature either a single-group or a multiple-perspectives focus. The single-group approach, as its name implies, looks at a single group or culture in depth. For example, one instructional sequence might center on women's roles during a specific historical period. Another might focus on experiences of immigrants from Southeast Asia.

Typically, the multiple-perspectives approach takes a given problem and explains how it is seen by two or more groups. These lessons help pupils "step into the shoes" of others and become more sensitive to their views. For example, to accomplish this purpose, we might select settlement of the United States as a theme and introduce the topic by emphasizing how this phenomenon was viewed by men and women who were English, French, Spanish, or Native American.

Single-Group Studies: General Characteristics

Single-group studies must be free from damaging stereotypes and distortions. In preparing lessons of this kind, we have to become well informed about the group to be studied. Single-group studies are designed to help pupils learn more about special perspectives of the group they are studying. Optimally, they will complete their study with a good idea of how group members interpret reality. To accomplish this, lessons have to go beyond superficial introduction of the group's clothing, food, and religious preference. There has to be careful attention to the group's values, ethics, and special cultural traditions.

Single-group studies should provide information about the group's history. This content helps pupils identify with struggles and experiences that, over time, have helped to shape members' attitudes. Additionally, historical content highlights relationships

Face-to-face interaction with people from another culture is a powerful means of learning about other culture.

between the group and the larger society of which it is a part. Changes in this relationship over time often reveal much about present perspectives of group members. For examples, individuals who are suspicious of the motives of others may be members of groups that have been systematically and officially repressed in the past by representatives of a larger, majority culture.

Contributions of the focus group in such areas as art, music, literature, science, mathematics, and government often are included in these lessons. The study of cultural adaptation provides opportunities for pupils to understand that some groups have made innovative responses to trying conditions. For example, studies of certain Inuit groups (native peoples living in the far north, from Alaska across Canada to Greenland) often emphasize their adjustment to extremely cold climatic conditions. Many of their practices were adopted by early European explorers of the far north. Without the contributions of the Inuit, successful exploration of the world's polar regions by people of European descent would have been impossible.

Single-group studies also focus on issues that reveal values of the group. Positions taken on key issues help define the group's priorities and help pupils recognize that individual groups have their own agendas. This insight contributes to pupils' grasp of the idea that healthy conflict is a hallmark of our democratic society.

Single-Group Studies: Examples of Classroom Approaches

A group's music reveals much about how its members view the world. In the example provided in Lesson Idea 11–1, the national anthem of Mexico serves as beginning point for learning about Mexican values and culture.

Lesson Idea 11–1

WHAT DOES A NATIONAL ANTHEM TELL US ABOUT PEOPLE?

Grade Level: 4–6

Objectives: Pupils will (1) develop one or more hypotheses about the history of Mexico, (2) identify two or more values or basic beliefs of the Mexican people, and (3) identify two or more sources that they can consult to validate and clarify their hypotheses.

Suggested Procedure: Ask class members if they know what is meant by the term *national anthem*. Discuss the "Star Spangled Banner" with the class. Ask pupils why the song is important. Go over the words. Ask members of the class to try to identify what the song tells us about the history and values of people of the United States.

Provide learners with copies of the English translation of the words of "Himno National," the national anthem of Mexico. (If available, play a recording of the anthem to familiarize pupils with the music as well as the words.) Review some of the unfamiliar words and symbols. Answer any questions. Ask pupils to state several hypotheses about what the

Single-group studies are designed to help pupils learn the perspectives of the group they are studying.

anthem reveals about the history of Mexico. Write their ideas on an overhead transparency and project for all to see or, alternatively, write them on the chalkboard.

Himno National

Mexicans when the trumpet is calling,

Grasp your sword and your harness assemble.

Let the guns with their thunder appalling

Make the Earth's deep foundations to tremble.

May the angel divine, O Dear Homeland,

Crown thy brow with the olive branch of peace;

For thy destiny, traced by God's own hand

In the heavens, shall ever increase.

But shall ever the proud foe assail thee,

And with insolent foot profane thy ground,

Know, dear country, thy sons shall not fail thee,

Ev'ry one thy soldier shall be found, thy soldier ev'ry one shall be found

Blessed Homeland, thy children have vowed them

If the bugle to battle should call,

They will fight with the last breath allowed them

Till on thy loved altars they fall.

Let the garland of life thine be;

Unto them be deathless fame;

Let the laurel of victory be assigned thee,

Enough for the tomb's honored name.

Lyrics by Francisco Gonzales Bocanegra

Music by Jaime Nuño

Ask members of the class what they think the anthem suggests is important to the Mexican people. Write their ideas on another transparency or on the chalkboard.

Ask pupils where they think they might get information about Mexico that they could use to test the accuracy of their ideas. Encourage them to think about such resources as books, films, interviews with people who have traveled to Mexico, and guest speakers of Mexican descent.

Divide the class into cooperative learning groups. Ask each group to work with one or more of the hypotheses generated by the class. Have each group find information relating to their hypotheses and make a report of their findings to the whole class.

Challenge group members to present their information in interesting and creative ways. Encourage pupils to use pictures, murals, or charts. Some groups may wish to use role playing as a way of making their reports to the class. After each group reports, ask the class to decide whether the focus hypotheses should be retained, modified, or rejected. This portion of the activity may generate new hypotheses, which you may then also discuss.

As a followup, some pupils might enjoy learning the Spanish words of the anthem.

Another rich source of material for lessons focusing on single groups is children's literature. Good literature for young people has a great deal of appeal for many of our pupils. The growing trend of using children's literature to teach reading ought to have a counterpart in the social studies. Outstanding children's literature provides a useful vehicle for teaching the perspectives of particular cultural groups. The example introduced in Lesson Idea 11–2 focuses on Native Americans. It draws on two well-known, popular books for young people, *The Legend of the Bluebonnet* by Tomie DePaola and *The Girl Who Loved Wild Horses* by Paul Goble.

Lesson Idea 11–2

HOW DO LEGENDS HELP US UNDERSTAND PEOPLE?

Grade Level:	1–3
Objectives:	Pupils will (1) identify two or three specific aspects of Native American culture as reflected in their legends, (2) cite one or more examples that illustrate how Native Americans view their relationship with nature, and (3) point out one or more aspects of Native American culture that might conflict with aspects of the dominant Western culture
Materials Needed:	*The Legend of the Bluebonnet* by Tomie DePaola (New York: G. P. Putnam's Sons, 1983) and *The Girl Who Loved Wild Horses* by Paul Goble (New York: Bradbury Press, 1978).
Suggested Procedures:	1. Begin by asking the class whether anyone has had experience riding or taking care of horses. Encourage pupils to share their experiences. Ask them to tell how they feel about horses. Introduce them to *The Girl Who Loved Wild Horses* by Paul Goble. Tell the class that you are going to read them a Native American legend about a girl who loved horses.
	2. Read the story. Stop as needed to clarify meanings of words, respond to questions, and share illustrations with the class.
	3. Ask questions such as, "What do you think this story means?" "What does it tell us about how Native Americans feel about their world?" "What things are

important to them?" Read aloud the two songs at the end of the book. Then, ask questions such as, "What do these songs tell us?" "Do they reveal feelings that are different from those most of us have?" "What are the differences?"

4. Read aloud *The Legend of the Bluebonnet* by Tomie DePaola. Ask questions similar to those you asked about *The Girl Who Loved Wild Horses*. Ask pupils what they think these people might have felt if others arrived and began hunting the wild horses and plowing under the bluebonnets to make room for houses and factories.

5. Conclude the study by helping pupils find other books dealing with lives of Native Americans. Ask them to think about traditional Native American customs as they read these materials. Particularly, urge pupils to consider how these customs might conflict with dominant Western cultural practices.

Using language appropriate for learners, explain that when two different cultures come together, changes occur. Sometimes these changes bring harm to members of certain cultural groups. Often this happens because people in the larger or dominant cultural group fail to understand aspects of the other culture. As a class, consider what might be done to minimize this kind of damage to members of minority cultural groups.

To help pupils understand that females have many occupational roles open to them, we might develop a single-group lesson focusing on stereotyped views of what jobs are "proper" for women. Pupils need to understand that today's situation differs from past times when relatively few employment roles were thought "suitable" for females. Lesson Idea 11–3 illustrates an instructional approach designed to help pupils grasp this point.

Lesson Idea 11–3

WHAT JOBS CAN A WOMAN HAVE?

Grade Level: 4–6

Objectives: Pupils will (1) recognize that all jobs are open to women who qualify for them and that their gender is no longer a critical factor, (2) describe differences in kinds of jobs open to women today and those open to them 30 or more years ago, and (3) suggest two or more reasons why women enjoy more employment choices today than they did earlier in the century.

Suggested Procedures:

1. Ask class members to think about kinds of jobs women can have today. Write ideas on the chalkboard under the heading, "Jobs Women Can Hold." Then, ask if there are any jobs women cannot hold. Write any pupil responses on the chalkboard under the heading, "Jobs Women Cannot Hold." Save this information.

2. Divide class members into groups of about five pupils each. Provide each group with one or two copies of magazines that are at least 30 years old. (These can frequently be found at rummage or garage sales. Often they are available at modest cost from used book stores and from resale shops such as Goodwill Industries.) Ask learners in each group to look for pictures of women at work. For each woman pictured, ask pupils to write down the nature of the occupation shown (teacher, nurse, steelworker, and so forth).

3. Ask a spokesperson from each group to report the group's findings. Write this information on the chalkboard next to the information generated in step one. Lead a discussion that requires pupils to examine both the original lists and the list developed after their work with the magazines. Ask them to point out differences and similarities between the lists.

4. Have students re-form into groups. Give each group several copies of current magazines. Again, ask them to look for illustrations of women at work and to note the occupational roles.

5. Ask a representative from each group to share the group's findings. Write the information on the chalkboard. Repeat the discussion outlined in step three. Pupils should find more job roles represented in the current magazines than in either the step one or the step three lists.

6. Next, ask pupils to compare the kinds of jobs for women found in magazines 30 or more years old with those found in current magazines. Ask them if they can explain any differences. Ask each pupil to write a short paragraph beginning: "As I think about jobs available to women 30 years ago and today, I conclude that . . . "

7. As a followup activity, some pupils may enjoy preparing a bulletin board featuring women in a wide variety of occupational roles. (You may also wish to display some of the excellent posters available from the Organization for Equal Education of the Sexes, Inc. The address of this group is given later in this chapter.)

BOX 11–4   Ideas for Multiple-Perspectives Lessons

Think About This

Events in history frequently were viewed in surprisingly different ways by various groups that experienced them. Such events work well as focal points for multiple-perspectives lessons. Think about at least two events from American history. Identify perspectives on these events of at least two different groups.

As one example, during World War II, many women found employment as industrial workers. When the war ended, many lost their jobs when male soldiers were released from military service. The men and women involved undoubtedly had very different reactions to this situation. Show your class a videotape of a film made on this subject, such as *The Life and Times of Rosie the Riveter* (directed by Connie Field, 1980). Afterwards, discuss with the class issues raised in the film, and compare peoples' attitudes and feelings then and now.

Multiple-Perspectives Approach: General Characteristics

The multiple-perspectives approach focuses on a single issue, presented from the perspective of several groups. The approach is easily integrated into the elementary social studies program. For example, as we introduce a given event, such as the early European settlement of the Atlantic coast of what is now the United States, we might examine this event from the perspectives of both the settlers and the indigenous Native Americans.

Multiple-perspectives lessons help pupils realize that common events often are interpreted in varied ways by different people. Their interpretations often are tied to the values of the groups to which they belong. Solutions that make sense to people in one group, because they are consistent with this group's values, may not seem good at all to members of other groups whose values are different.

Multiple-Perspectives Approach: A Classroom Example

Many films and books romanticize the westward movement of settlers across lands that today comprise the continental United States. Accounts of this settlement often fail to give serious attention to the impact of the arrival of new people on individuals who were already occupying these lands. Lesson Idea 11–4 illustrates an instructional experience designed to help pupils understand that a common event often affects some people differently than others.

Lesson Idea 11–4

MOVING WESTWARD

Grade Level: 3–6

Objectives: Pupils will (1) identify two or more groups of people who were living in the western United States prior to the arrival of pioneers from the eastern United States, (2) identify several customs and ways of living of these people, and (3) state at least two influences on the ways of life of these people that were a direct result of the pioneers' arrival.

Suggested Procedures:

1. Have the class view a film or read a romanticized account of the Westward Movement or of the Old West. Ask pupils to think about what they saw or read. Ask them whether they would have liked to have lived at this time. Follow up with a question about the extent to which their opinions are based on what they have just seen or read. Introduce pupils to the idea that there were people already living in the western United States before the arrival of the pioneers.

2. Divide the class into several groups. Ask each group to find locations of people inhabiting the Old West in the early 1800s. One group might be assigned to identify places where different groups of Native Americans were living. Another might focus on locations occupied by settlers who originally entered the area from Mexico. Others might focus on European groups such as the British, French, and Russians. Each group should be given a small outline map of North America. A spokesperson from each group should plot the location of the assigned population on the group's map.

3. After the small-group work has been completed, reconvene the class as a single large group. Ask spokespersons from each group to plot the location of the group's assigned population on a large map. If possible, make copies of this map and distribute them to everyone in the class.

4. Next, reconstitute the small groups. Ask each group to find additional information about its assigned population. In particular, have pupils find out the following:
   • When members of the assigned population first began to occupy the area they settled
   • What their motives for coming were
   • How they made a living
   • Interesting customs and lifestyles of these people

5. Bring the pupils back together as a single large group. Pose the possibility that pioneers from the eastern United States are about to move into the lands occupied by the people each group has studied. Challenge pupils to think about the probable reactions to this situation of the people who were already occupying these lands.

6. Ask pupils to go back into their small groups. Tell people in each group to develop a response to the

movement of the pioneers into the area their assigned population occupies. Ask them to prepare this response from the perspective of members of the assigned population. Give pupils options. For example, some groups may wish to write a simulated editorial as a way of sharing their views. Other groups may elect to have one or two pupils deliver reactions orally.

7. To follow up on the presentations of the individual groups, add the perspective of yet another group of people who were involved in the Westward Movement: the women. Read the following account to the class. It comes from the diary of a young woman who moved west with her husband:

Only women who went west in 1859 understand what a woman had to endure. There was no road, no stores, and, many times, no wood for a fire. I had a new baby, and it was teething and suffering from fever. The child took nearly all my strength. I became weak. My weight fell and fell. In the end, I was all the way down to ninety pounds.

After reaching Denver, we heard that gold had been discovered in the mountains. On the nineteenth of February, 1860, I was taken from my sick bed and placed in a wagon, and we started for the new mines. No woman had yet been there. After several days' travel we came late at night to Salt Creek. We tried the water and found it was no good. We tied the oxen to the wagon so they couldn't drink. Then we went to bed with nothing to eat. That night it got very cold.

The next day we moved to Trout Creek and found the water good. Several men had left Denver a few days ahead of us. We wanted to join up with them but had seen no sign of them. Our men decided to mount a search. They shouldered rifles and headed out looking for footprints. Each went in a different direction. The men had not returned by dark, and I felt very alone. I allowed the small donkey to come into the tent with me. I put my head on him and cried in the loneliness of the soul. (Adapted from W. M. Thayer, Marvels of the New West, Norwich, CT: Henry Bill Publishing, 1888, pp. 246–253.)

8. After pupils have finished making their group reports and have read and thought about the diary excerpt, ask them to make general statements about the impact of the Westward Movement on different groups of people. As a culminating activity, involve learners in developing a play, drawing a wall mural, or writing a personal history of the Westward Movement.

Other multiple-perspectives lessons can introduce pupils to conflicting accounts of historical events by using letters to the editor or editorials from different newspapers that present conflicting views of contemporary issues, and by exposing learners to opposing viewpoints by scheduling class speakers from groups with different views on controversial issues.

SOURCES OF INFORMATION

Multicultural Lessons

There are many idea sources for both single-group and multiple-perspectives approaches to multicultural learning. The *Education Index* includes many listings of articles in professional education journals that provide guidelines for such lessons. Specific examples frequently appear in journals such as *Social Education, Social Studies and the Young Learner*, the *Journal of Geography*, and *The Social Studies*. Books are also available that include ideas for multicultural lessons. One that is particularly good is Carl A. Grant's and Christine E. Sleeter's *Making Choices for Multicultural Education: Five Approaches to Race, Class, and Gender* (Prentice Hall, 1994). This volume contains detailed directions for implementing a variety of multicultural lessons.

A particularly useful classroom supplement for multicultural lessons is the Ethnic Cultures of America Calendar. This calendar is published annually and is available from Educational Extension Systems, P. O. Box 259, Clarks Summit, PA 18411. The calendar features information for each day of the year about celebrations and events that are meaningful to different ethnic groups residing in the United States. In addition, it contains several pages of information about the ethnic cultures of America, about various calendars in use throughout the world, and about holidays of many world religious groups.

The following information sources also may be useful in planning multicultural lessons:

- The Balch Institute for Ethnic Studies, 18 South 7th Street, Philadelphia, PA 19106
- Center for Migration Studies, 209 Flagg Place, Staten Island, NY 10304
- Center for the Study of Ethnic Publications, Kent State University, Kent, OH 44242
- Immigration History Research Center, University of Minnesota, Minneapolis, MN 55455
- Institute of Texan Cultures, University of Texas, San Antonio, TX 78294

Gender-Equity Lessons

Many sources of information are available to help you plan gender-equity lessons. The Upper Midwest Women's History Center for Teachers makes available a long list. Write for details to the address given here.

A good source of visual materials is the Organization for Equal Education of the Sexes, Inc. This group makes available more than one hundred 11- by 17-inch posters. Many feature women from history and contemporary women in nontraditional occupations. The collection is multicultural and includes women with disabilities. Each poster features a brief biography of the woman or women depicted. The materials are inexpensive. Write for details.

The Population Reference Bureau publishes "The World's Women: A Profile." This large wall chart contains information about women throughout the world. Write for ordering information.

Following are addresses of those groups previously mentioned, and others, producing materials of interest to teachers who wish to plan lessons with a gender-equity focus:

- ISIS—Women's International Information and Communication Services, P.O. Box 25711, Philadelphia, PA 19144
- National Women's History Project, P.O. Box 3716, Santa Rosa, CA 95402
- Organization for Equal Education of the Sexes, Inc., P.O. Box 438, Blue Hill, ME 04614
- Population Reference Bureau, Inc., 2213 M Street, N.W., Washington, DC 20037
- Upper Midwest Women's History Center for Teachers, Central Community Center, 6300 Walker Street, St. Louis Park, MN 55416

KEY IDEAS IN SUMMARY

1. Schools should serve *all* enrolled pupils. In our increasingly diverse society, this means that instruction must take into consideration learners who bring with them many different cultural and ethnic perspectives.

2. At various times, the academic performance of minority-group children has been viewed in different ways. The "genetic deficit" explanation, the "cultural deficit" explanation, the "communication process" explanation, and the "perceived labor market" explanation have all been offered as reasons many children from minority cultures have not done well at school. Today, these explanations have been dismissed as weak excuses for the system's failure to serve the needs of minorities.

3. Multicultural and gender-equity lessons are designed to (1) help pupils develop a respect for cultures different from their own, (2) provide learners with opportunities to work with people from different groups, (3) help pupils recognize the validity of different cultural perspectives, (4) assist learners as they develop pride in their own cultural heritage, and (5) help pupils appreciate that values differences often lead to conflicts between and among groups.

4. Teachers can use the following guidelines to help pupils become sensitive to diversity: (1) Learners of different backgrounds should be included in each group when the class is divided into smaller units for special projects. (2) As teachers, we

need to be aware of how our own cultural perspectives may differ from those of some of our pupils. (3) Teaching methods need to be modified to accommodate a variety of learning styles. (4) Evaluation procedures must be free from cultural and social biases. (5) We need to monitor our teaching behavior to make sure that we are not unconsciously favoring any one group of pupils.

5. Classroom approaches to multicultural and gender-equity learning include the single-group approach and the multiple-perspectives approach. The single-group approach seeks to help pupils become so familiar with one group that they can appreciate how its members interpret reality. The multiple-perspectives approach focuses on a single issue, introduced in a way that highlights views of several different groups.

6. Many sources of information are available for teachers who wish to develop multicultural and gender-equity lessons. These include examples of lessons, background materials for pupils, instructional support items, and background information for teachers.

CHAPTER REFLECTIONS

Directions: Now that you have finished reading the chapter, reread the case study at the beginning. Then answer these questions:

1. What do you see as major purposes of multicultural and gender-equity lessons? What are some strengths and weaknesses of arguments supporting and opposing increased emphases on these topics?

2. What are the implications of explaining low academic achievement of some minority learners as being caused by one of the following factors?

   - a genetic deficit
   - a cultural deficit
   - a communications problem
   - a perceived labor market problem

3. What are the arguments of and social remedies proposed by individuals who identify with each of the perspectives listed in question 2?

4. Have you personally experienced any problems as a result of either too little or too much emphasis in schools on lessons dealing with multicultural or gender-equity issues?

5. In what ways might your personal cultural heritage inhibit your ability to develop good multicultural lessons?

6. What are characteristics of multicultural programs that feature single-group studies? That feature multiple-perspectives approaches?

7. Is it possible for social studies programs to develop pupils' sensitivity to cultures other than their own and still develop an appreciation for their own culture? What problems might you face as a teacher in dealing with this potential difficulty, and what ideas do you have for responding to it?

8. When you were in school, were you or any of your friends directed to take certain courses because they were "better for boys" or "better for girls"? If your answer is "yes," how did you or your friends feel, and what are your thoughts about the long-term consequences of this kind of gender-based advice?

9. How would you defend gender-equity lessons in a community where many parents continue to believe that certain social roles and jobs should be reserved for males and others for females?

EXTENDING UNDERSTANDING AND SKILL

1. Observe an elementary social studies class. Note how the teacher interacts with male pupils, female pupils, and pupils from different cultural groups. Can you identify patterns that may cause difficulties for some learners?

2. Reflect on your own cultural background and your personal life experiences. What values are most important to you? What are your images and expectations of members of different cultural groups? How might your perspectives affect your ability to teach people with different world views?

3. Prepare a report on images of minority cultural groups and females in photographs in an elementary social studies text. Choose a text used at a grade level you would like to teach. Look for kinds of jobs being performed by minority group members and females. If time permits, do this with two books, one published recently and one published 20 or more years ago.

4. Prepare a plan for a single-group lesson for a cultural group different from your own. Include at least two suggested instructional approaches. Ask your instructor to critique your plan.

5. Organize a group of five or six people from your class. Identify two or three key episodes from American history (settlement of the west, initial legalization of slavery in some states, the Homestead Act and its provision of free lands, the annexation of Texas, the Gadsden Purchase, the Boston Tea Party, and so forth). For each selected episode, brainstorm to identify as many approaches as you can to teach pupils how these events were viewed by members of different cultural groups. Prepare a copy of all ideas generated, and distribute this information to others in your class.

REFERENCES

Beyond Rhetoric: A New American Agenda for Children and Families. (1991). Final report of the National Commission on Children. Washington, DC: United States Government Printing Office.

ERICKSON, F. (1987). "Transformation and School Success: The Politics and Culture of Educational Achievement." *Anthropology and Education Quarterly, 18* (4), pp. 335–356.

FLYNN, V., AND CHAMBERS, R. D. (1994). "Promoting Gender Equity: What Can You Do?" *Learning 94, 22* (5), pp. 58–59.

GOOD, T. L., AND BROPHY, J. E. (1994). *Looking in Classrooms*, 6th ed. New York: HarperCollins.

GRANT, C. A., AND SLEETER, C. E. (1994). *Making Choices for Multicultural Education: Five Approaches to Race, Class, and Gender.* Englewood Cliffs, NJ: Prentice Hall.

PETERSON, R. L., AND ISHII-JORDAN, S. (1994). "Multicultural Education and the Education of Students with Behavioral Disorders." In R. L. Peterson & S. Ishii-Jordan (eds.), *Multicultural Issues in the Education of Students with Behavioral Disorders.* Cambridge: MA: Brookline Books, pp. 3–14.

SCHMUCK, P. A., AND SCHMUCK, R. A. (1994). "Gender Equity: A Critical Democratic Component of America's High Schools." *NASSP Bulletin, 78* (558), pp. 22–31.

STRUTCHENS, M. (1994). "Culture Inclusive Mathematics: Breaking Down Barriers." *Minority Teacher Recruitment, 3* (1), pp. 1, 8–9.

ENVIRONMENTAL AND ENERGY EDUCATION

CHAPTER GOALS

This chapter provides information to help the reader:

- point out examples of events that have focused attention on the environment,
- describe specific environmental problems including global warming, deforestation, toxic waste pollution, and ozone depletion,
- suggest potential long-term results of failure to respond to threats to the environment,
- develop instructional activities designed to sensitize pupils to environmental concerns,
- describe progress that has been made in developing alternative, renewable energy resources, and
- point out classroom procedures that might help pupils more fully grasp issues associated with electrical energy conservation.

CHAPTER STRUCTURE

Introduction
Pressing Environmental Challenges
    Global Warming
    Deforestation
    Toxic Waste
    Ozone Depletion
    Issues Associated with Energy
Classroom Approaches to Building Environmental and Energy Awareness
    Sensitizing Learners to the Problem of Unnecessary Waste
    Developing Environmental Sensitivity Through Children's Literature
    Learning What is Biodegradable
Key Ideas in Summary
Chapter Reflections
Extending Understanding and Skill
References

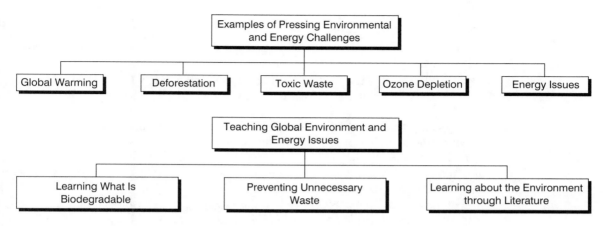

Figure 12–1
Environmental and energy education.

Chapter 12

Case Study

ARE LESSONS FOCUSING ON THE ENVIRONMENT APPROPRIATE FOR ELEMENTARY SCHOOL PUPILS?

A group of teachers recently discussed kinds of content that ought to be included in the elementary social studies program. One of them made these comments:

"You know, we're dealing with young kids. They have a whole lifetime ahead of them. And, in a few years, they're going to be a lot more secure about themselves and a lot more sophisticated than they are now.

"All of this brings me to a concern about this environmental business. I don't for a minute deny that we should all be worried about leaving the world in decent shape for future generations. The problem I'm having is that so much of what we hear and read is so incredibly negative and discouraging. The basic message seems to be that the world is going to be just a terrible place in the future.

"What kind of impression does this give our elementary youngsters? I'm really wondering about the wisdom of focusing on lessons that seem to be presenting such a sad vision of the future. These young folks need to be encouraged. We need to help them believe in themselves and to be convinced that there will be some wonderful years ahead for them. I'm afraid that lessons focusing on environmental issues just don't do that."

What Is Your Response?

1. Is it true that much information related to the environment is inherently "discouraging"? If this is generally true, would teachers do a disservice to their pupils by selecting environmentally related content that tended to paint a more positive view? Why, or why not?
2. Should teachers be concerned about protecting elementary pupils from information that may be difficult for them to deal with, given their ages and levels of maturity? If this is a concern to you, how would you react to the suggestion that lessons dealing with these issues should be offered only to pupils in the later elementary grades?
3. How real is the concern that introducing pupils to content that does not always paint a positive view of the future may undermine students' self-confidence and sense of personal optimism? What evidence supports your view?

INTRODUCTION

Today, environmental issues command much public attention. In part this has resulted from extensive media coverage of threats to the environment. This kind of coverage notably increased after the Russian nuclear disaster at Chernobyl in 1986. Radiation from this explosion crossed national frontiers, and underscored the multinational nature of environmental issues. What affects the environment in one nation also affects the broader, global environment. Recognizing that irresponsible action in one location may undermine the planet's ability to sustain life, citizen concerns worldwide now range across a broad spectrum of issues.

These concerns will be even more important in the future. It is important for young people in the schools to be introduced to them. Resolving pressing environmental problems may require social, political, economic, and personal adjustments. Hence, environmental and energy questions have a legitimate place in the elementary school social studies program.

PRESSING ENVIRONMENTAL AND ENERGY CHALLENGES

Global Warming

Large numbers of scientists believe that the world is experiencing a global warming trend (Jacobson, 1989). This trend has resulted from widespread use of carbon-based fuels such as coal and petroleum products and from excessive cutting of trees in the world's tropical forests (Durning, 1994). When carbon-based fuels burn, they give off carbon dioxide and other gases. Trees and other kinds of vegetation absorb gases such as carbon dioxide. When there are fewer trees, more of these gases are released, causing a *greenhouse effect* as these gases retain heat in the lower atmosphere.

Warming poses a number of serious challenges. If the trend continues, large volumes of water that are now locked in the polar ice caps may be released. Brown, Flavin, and Postel (1989) note that "a temperature rise of three degrees Celsius by the year 2050 would raise sea level by 50–100 centimeters. By the end of the next century, sea level may be up as much as two meters" (p. 10). This will pose a tremendous threat to low-lying, densely populated lands where much of the world's rice and other crops are grown. It is estimated that as many as 17 million people in Bangladesh and as many as 8.5 million in Egypt could be forced from their homes (Brown et al., 1989).

Certain kinds of sea life are also greatly threatened by the possibility of continued increases in ocean temperatures. In some parts of the world, "reefs have suffered extensive die offs of corals associated with higher temperatures" (Weber, 1994, p. 50). In addition, global warming may influence kinds of crops that can be grown. Tree crops are particularly likely to be affected. Trees take years to develop, and cannot adapt to rapid climatic change. Some of the world's great orchard areas may be destroyed. Replacement of tree crops by planting new areas will take decades.

Deforestation

Deforestation, destruction of the world's supply of trees, has been occurring at an astonishing rate. In one recent year, people cleared Amazon rainforest acreage equal in area to the entire country of Austria (Brown et al., 1989). Over the past decade, tropical forests occupying an area nearly the size of France have been cut down (World

---

BOX 12–1   **Teaching the Concept "Deforestation" at Different Grade Levels**

Think About This

Think about what you have learned in your teacher preparation program about learning characteristics of pupils of different ages. Develop a list of ideas for introducing the concept "deforestation" to learners in the following grades:

- K, one, and two
- three and four
- five and six

Share your ideas with your instructor and the class, and solicit their comments.

Resources Institute, 1994). The rate of cutting of the world's forests has increased tremendously since about 1950. Today, of the timber cover that existed one hundred years ago, only about three-eighths remains (Durning, 1994).

Deforestation has been accompanied by many serious problems. For example, thousands of species dependent on forest environments have become extinct. As noted previously, a reduction in the world's forest cover seems to be contributing to a damaged ozone layer and global warming. Denuded hills cannot hold topsoil, and excessive cutting of trees has contributed to loss of soil and excessive sedimentation of rivers. In some places, resultant water pollution has damaged productive fisheries (Durning, 1994).

Industrial abuse and resource mismanagement are responsible for much of the world's timber loss. Deforestation has also resulted from high rates of population growth. For example, destruction of Amazon forest lands has been attributed to a population increase that has led people to move away from high-priced lands to create new affordable farms elsewhere in the Amazon Basin. In other world areas, population pressure has resulted in desperate searches for inexpensive fuels, often leading people to cut down available timber.

Toxic Waste

The problem of toxic waste is one of chemical contamination. As Jacobson (1989) points out, this can result suddenly from a specific event, for example a wreck involving a truck carrying dangerous chemicals, or it can develop slowly over time. This latter condition has been found in many places throughout the world where dangerous chemicals have been dumped over a period of years. In time, water supplies, food products, and even the surrounding air may become contaminated.

Certain species of trees have proved particularly vulnerable to the effects of toxic waste. A recent United Nations report found that 43 percent of the world's cork oak trees have been damaged. Problems are particularly bad in heavily industrialized areas where environmental controls have been relatively lax. For example, one recent survey found that 77 percent of fir trees over 60 years old were damaged. Even in the much more heavily regulated United States, toxic wastes are suspected of damaging trees in the Great Smoky Mountains, in the Ohio River Basin, and in some areas around the Great Lakes (Denniston, 1993).

Toxic waste contamination has brought disaster to people in many parts of the world. In this country, 900 people were forced to move from their homes built along the Love Canal, a filled-in chemical dump site in New York State. The government of Poland offered to resettle villagers from one area of the country where chemical pollution had become a severe problem (Jacobson, 1989).

In recent years, the world's major industrial countries have tightened regulations governing dumping of dangerous chemicals. One unpleasant result has been a tendency for industries to ship these dangerous wastes to less developed countries for disposal. Increasingly, these countries are becoming more sophisticated about the dangers of these chemicals. More and more governments throughout the world are acting to place severe restrictions on the kinds of wastes they will accept for disposal.

Ozone Depletion

Ozone is a form of oxygen with an altered atomic structure. A large ozone layer exists in the upper atmosphere. This layer helps to keep dangerous ultraviolet radiation from reaching the earth's surface. In recent years, evidence has been accumulating that points to a gradual destruction of this atmospheric ozone. Scientists first noted that a hole in the ozone layer was occurring periodically over Antarctica. More recent evidence has suggested that the ozone layer around the entire globe is eroding.

A primary cause of this erosion is release into the atmosphere of chlorofluoro-carbons, or CFCs. CFCs are used predominantly as refrigerants in air conditioning units and as aerosol propellants. They also are used in some forms of insulation, and in certain important commercial solvents.

Destruction of the ozone layer can have serious consequences for animal and plant life. A diminished ozone layer poses the probability of increased levels of ultraviolet rays striking the body, which can lead to skin cancer and to eye cataracts. Cynthia Pollock Shea, an authority on the threat to the ozone layer, states that "reduced crop yields, depleted marine fisheries, materials damage, and increased smog are also attributable to higher levels of radiation. The phenomenon is global and will affect the well-being of every person in the world" (1989, p. 78).

Nations of the world have recognized the seriousness of this problem. More than thirty countries have signed the Montreal Protocol on Substances that Deplete the Ozone Layer. This agreement calls for nations of the world to work to cut CFC emissions in half by 1998. Some experts hope that replacement chemicals can be developed that will allow for a total ban on CFCs by the year 2000.

Among actions taken to deal with the CFC problem are efforts to prevent their release directly into the atmosphere. It has been a common practice for CFCs in car air conditioners to be released into the atmosphere when units are taken for repair. New equipment has now been developed that allows service personnel to recapture CFC coolant, store it, and recharge it back into units once they are repaired.

Serious efforts are under way to find replacement chemicals for CFCs that retain their useful properties without posing threats to the environment. Much progress in this area has been reported. For example, hydrocarbons have largely replaced CFCs as aerosol propellants. In many countries of the world, special equipment has been installed to recover CFCs that remain in old refrigerators and air conditioning units. As a result of these efforts, world output of CFCs by the early 1990s had fallen fully 50 percent below record levels established in 1988 (Brown, 1993). Environmental expert Lester Brown (1993) suggests that, if present trends continue, diminished CFC levels will cease to affect the ozone layer and that, by the middle of the twenty-first century, much present damage to the ozone layer will be repaired.

Issues Associated with Energy

Concerns about energy have come in for special attention in recent years. Many energy sources that are used today produce side effects that can damage plants, soils, and even human health. Common fuels such as coal, oil, natural gas, and wood produce huge quantities of carbon dioxide as a byproduct of combustion. As has been noted previously, this buildup is associated with a dangerous global warming trend.

Additionally, many widely used fuels are nonrenewable. The supply of coal and oil, for example, is finite. Quantities of these nonrenewable fuels are not likely to be sufficient to meet future energy needs (Flavin, 1988). Nuclear energy is not an attractive alternative because of serious safety concerns. Today, the search is on for safe, renewable energy sources.

Hydropower, power generated through water, is a safe energy source whose capacity does not diminish over time. One difficulty with hydropower is that sites suitable for development of hydroelectric plants are limited. Most of the best ones have already been utilized.

Efforts appear particularly promising for increasing the use of renewable plants and animal wastes as fuel. Shea (1988) points out that energy from these sources already contributes 15 percent of the energy used worldwide. In some tropical areas, measures are being taken to increase acreage devoted to fast-growing varieties of sugar cane. Alcohol fuels derived from the sugar provide a reliable renewable energy source as well as a dependable market for farmers. Brazil has worked particularly hard at increasing use of alcohol-based fuels. In 1986, half of that nation's automobile fuel came from this source (Shea, 1988).

Rice is one of the world's most abundant agricultural products. Preparing rice for market requires removing the husks. Every five tons of finished rice yields about one ton of rice husks. These husks have an energy content about equal to wood, and have great promise as a fuel source. Other crop byproducts that are potential fuels include coconut shells, cotton stalks, fruit pits, and seed hulls of all kinds (Shea, 1988).

In addition to energy from plants, work is being done to tap more directly into the sun's energy. Solar collection devices are being promoted as a means of transferring this energy to air and water. Research is underway that may result in large-scale production of electricity produced by the *photovoltaic effect*, electricity generated when the sun's rays strike certain substances.

In some parts of the world, wind power is being harnessed to drive electricity-generating turbines, though this is possible only in areas where winds blow relatively consistently. Today, groups of windmills are providing substantial quantities of electricity to parts of California and to other world areas as well.

Scientists are seeking still other alternatives to traditional energy sources. Exploratory work is underway to determine if it is feasible to exploit temperature differences between shallow and deep ocean water to produce energy. A priority for those interested in practical use of renewable energy is the development of systems to store energy from windmills and solar devices for later use. Pollution problems and dwindling supplies of coal, oil, natural gas, and wood demand that research into dependable renewable energy sources increase in the years ahead.

These environmental and energy concerns are but a few of those that are attracting attention of people throughout the world. Others include such issues as acid rain, general air pollution, general water pollution, desertification of productive agricultural lands, and maintaining environments to sustain the continued existence of endangered species.

Learning about endangered animals is especially useful in helping young children develop environmental awareness.

BOX 12–2   **Should Elementary School Pupils Deal with Difficult Environmental Issues?**

A parent who was informed about a school district's interest in requiring an instructional unit on "environmental challenges" in the elementary social studies program made these comments:

> I am very sensitive to the need to preserve our environment for future generations. But, I also recognize that many environmental issues are extremely complex. Often, proposed "solutions" seem to produce more problems than they are solving. In fact, even experts are discouraged by the magnitude of the problems we will be facing in the next 10 to 20 years. Are young elementary children ready to confront these discouraging problems? I don't think so. I am afraid that this instructional unit might leave them with terribly negative feelings about the future. Let's reserve this kind of content for the high school years when they will have a more mature perspective on these issues.

Think About This

1. What are the major concerns of this parent?
2. Do you believe they are valid?
3. How would you respond to this person?

Good information sources are available for teachers interested in general environmental education and energy education. Publications of the World Watch Institute are particularly recommended. This respected organization publishes the annual *State of The World* report, which contains well-researched articles and up-to-date reports on environmental issues of all kinds. World Watch Institute also publishes *World Watch*, a bimonthly journal. Each issue features articles centering on important environmental topics. For information write to The World Watch Institute, 1776 Massachusetts Avenue, N.W., Washington, DC 20036.

Another excellent source is World Resources Institute. Every two years, this group publishes a new edition of *World Resources*. This book is an excellent compendium of short articles and detailed statistical information related to the global environment. For information, write to World Resources Institute, 1709 New York Avenue, N.W., Washington, DC 20006.

Many other organizations and government agencies publish materials related to the environmental and energy education. A particularly fine program has been produced by the Missouri Department of Conservation. The materials, entitled "Conservation Seeds," include environmentally related activities for kindergarten and early primary-grades pupils and are outstanding. For information about available materials, write to Missouri Department of Conservation, Education Section, P.O. Box 180, Jefferson City, MO 65102.

CLASSROOM APPROACHES TO BUILDING ENVIRONMENTAL AND ENERGY AWARENESS

Elementary social studies lessons focusing on the environment and on energy seek to develop youngsters' sensitivity to these issues. O'Connor (1983, pp. 2–3) has developed a useful list of purposes for such lessons, which we have adapted here. Environmental lessons seek to help learners do the following:

- Develop an appreciation for the immediate environment
- Note the existence of interrelationships that tie together all living things
- Point out what individuals can do to maintain healthy local, regional, national, and global environments
- Appreciate the necessity of protecting certain natural areas
- Point out threats to environmental quality and how they might be met

Suggestions introduced in this section are not meant to be exhaustive in scope. They simply illustrate kinds of approaches some teachers have found to be successful. Specific lessons need to be tailored to age levels, interests, and levels of sophistication of children in individual classes.

Sensitizing Learners to the Problem of Unnecessary Waste

Most elementary school children (and many adults, too) have not thought much about how much garbage we generate. More specifically, few have considered whether too much is being thrown away and whether some items that end up in the trash might have additional uses.

Elementary teachers have developed several approaches to helping their pupils become more aware of problems associated with excessive litter and waste. Two widely used lessons are "Contents of the Wastebasket" and "The Dreaded Litter Creature."

Lesson Idea 12–1

CONTENTS OF THE WASTEBASKET

Grade Level:	6
Objective:	Pupils will develop a plan for conserving resources.
Suggested Procedure:	This activity can be organized in many ways. One alternative involves a careful examination of all trash contained in the wastebasket at the end of the school day. In preparation for this activity, bring a large plastic garbage bag to school. At the end of the day, contents of the class wastebasket are emptied into the garbage bag and kept in a safe place until

needed (usually the next day). The following steps are involved in the activity:

1. Organizing learners and displaying the contents of the wastebasket.
2. Sorting contents of the wastebasket into categories.
3. Describing sources of litter in each category.
4. Discussing what items might have been more effectively used or might be capable of reuse.
5. Establishing an action plan.

Organizing Learners and Displaying Wastebasket Contents   At the appropriate time, gather members of the class around and carefully empty the garbage bag containing the wastebasket contents onto newspapers or sheets of butcher paper spread on the floor (or on the surface of a large table).

Sorting into Categories   Invite members of the class to suggest categories into which items might be sorted. You may wish to ask one or more learners to move individual items into piles, and then organize the piles. Categories may be of many kinds. Some learners may decide to put all paper items in one pile, wooden ones in another, and items made of plastics and other materials in still another pile. Some children may decide to sort objects by color. You may decide to write category names on the board or on an overhead transparency and to list all items from the wastebasket belonging to each category. Ask children to speculate on why some categories have more items than others.

Describing Sources of Litter   Ask children to suggest where litter in each category may have come from. Additional questions include, "Do you think the amount of litter we found in this category today is more, less, or about the same that we would find on any day? Why do you think so? If we wanted to reduce the amount of litter in any one of these categories, what could we do?"

Discussing Reuse or Better Use of Items   This step flows logically from the previous one. Ask questions designed to focus learners' attention on conservation-related issues, such as, "Are there some things we found that were thrown away too soon? Could people have used them more before throwing them away? For example, there is only writing on one side of this paper. How might this paper have been used longer before being thrown away? Could some of these things that have been thrown away been used for other things? What other things might they have been used for? If too many people throw away things that still might be used for something, what do you think might happen?"

Establishing an Action Plan   Ask learners to make some decisions that will result in behavioral changes that reflect the need to conserve resources. The class might decide to try to reduce the amount of paper being thrown away. Pupils may then recheck the wastebasket contents periodically to see if less paper was going out each day. Another possibility might be to retrieve all paper not written on both sides. The blank sides could be placed in a "scratch paper" bin. Class members could be encouraged to use paper from this source for practice drawings, informal note taking, and so forth.

Followup: A variety of followup activities can conclude the wastebasket activity. Some teachers involve learners in schoolwide or neighborhood cleanup projects. Sometimes these feature similar analyses of the sources of litter and what might be done to decrease the volume of litter produced. Teachers also often have pupils prepare posters with a litter-reduction theme.

Lesson Idea 12–2

THE DREADED LITTER CREATURE

Grade Level: 2–4

Objectives: Pupils will (1) identify ways of preventing litter, and (2) demonstrate that they understand the importance of cleaning up litter.

Suggested Procedure: This activity sometimes is designed to be used in conjunction with the wastebasket lesson or with a campaign to clean up the school and its immediate neighborhood. Provide children with large plastic garbage bags in which to collect litter. After they have followed your directions and have filled the bags with litter, pupils bring them back to the classroom. Organize class members into teams, each with three or four pupils.

Challenge each team to create a "dreaded litter creature" using items in their bags. Provide paste, staples, poster board, pipe cleaners, and other art supplies that might be used by team members as they make their creature. Often teachers find it useful to show class members a previously completed "litter creature." The example may suggest to pupils ways in which the project might be approached.

As a final assignment, ask each group to make a sign to accompany their creature. The sign should focus attention on the issue of litter elimination. Signs might include such phrases as, "Zap the Litter Creature!" "Make the Litter Creature an Endangered Species!" "No Litter Creatures Allowed Here!" "Let's Starve the Litter Creature!" To conclude the lesson, the class can display their "dreaded litter creatures" and accompanying signs in the classroom or in a hallway where others in the school can see them.

Developing Environmental Sensitivity through Children's Literature

Many books directed at elementary school pupils deal with environmental education issues. O'Brien and Stoner (1987) identify several of these books. One title they recommend is Brian Wildsmith's *Professor Noah's Spaceship* (Oxford University Press, 1980), which features content relevant to the topic of pollution.

O'Brien and Stoner point out that this book can provide an excellent starting point for classroom discussion focusing on effects of pollution on human beings and on specific animal species. They suggest followup activities centering around efforts to make records of evidence of pollution in and around pupils' homes, in the school, and in local neighborhoods, and suggest that class members might also make collages or engage in other art projects illustrating problems associated with pollution. Reading and discussing the book might also prompt interest in a class-sponsored environmental cleanup project.

Active involvement is critical in helping students learn about environmental issues.

O'Brien and Stoner list many other books and include suggestions for developing related environmental education activities. Their article is well worth reading. (See the complete citation in the "References" section at the end of this chapter.)

Learning What Is Biodegradable

The adjective *biodegradable* means, "capable of being broken down by natural processes such as the action of bacteria." The biodegradable characteristic of grass clippings, for example, make them suitable for use in compost piles. In time, they break down and become part of enriched new soil. Litter and waste products that are biodegradable produce fewer threats to the environment than those, such as many plastics, that are not biodegradable.

To help pupils determine whether some common items are biodegradable, Sisson (1982) suggests a classroom exercise based on burying different items in small containers of soil. Lesson Idea 12–3 is a modified version of that exercise.

Lesson Idea 12–3

BIODEGRADABLE LITTER

Grade Level: 5–6

Objectives: Pupils will (1) define the term *biodegradable* (2) state the importance of using biodegradable products, and (3) develop a course of action to reduce nonbiodegradable litter.

Suggested Procedure:
1. Select six containers, and fill each with garden soil.
2. Bury selected items.
3. Dig up and examine each item once a week for two months and make notes on conditions of the items.
4. Discuss differences in conditions of items as observed over time.
5. Consider further action.

Select Containers Half-gallon ice cream containers work well. Fill each container with moist garden soil. Assign individual pupils to keep soil watered to maintain moisture levels. This must be done throughout the entire two months of the activity.

Bury Selected Items Select items to be buried in each container. Take care to select some items that are biodegradable and some that are not. The following items work well:

- leaf
- piece of a paper bag
- foil wrapper from inside a pack of cigarettes or gum
- piece of orange peel
- pull-top from an aluminum can

• small plastic spoon

Bury one item in each half-gallon carton. Label the container with the name of the item it contains. Bury items approximately in the center of each container.

Dig Up and Examine   Once a week, involve the class in digging up and examining the buried items. To do this, gather the class around a large table. Place a plastic sheet over the table top. Select a pupil to dig up each item. Do one container at a time. Caution the pupils to dig carefully to minimize the amount of dirt spilled and to prevent unnecessary damage to the item.

Provide each learner with a note-taking chart. A sample chart is provided in Figure 12–2. Prompt pupils to observe changes in the condition of each item and to take notes on their charts.

Discuss Observed Differences   At the conclusion of the eight-week period, lead a discussion. Encourage learners to refer to their note-taking charts. Ask questions such as these to guide the discussion:

Figure 12–2
Sample note-taking chart for an exercise on biodegradable litter.

	Condition and Comments			
Object	**Week One**	**Week Two**	**Week Three**	**Week Four**
Leaf				
Paper bag				
Foil wrapper				
Orange peel				
Can pull-top				
Plastic spoon				

Duplicate chart with appropriate changes for weeks five through eight.

- What things changed the most?
- What things changed the least?
- How might we explain why some things changed a lot and others didn't change much at all?
- What do our observations tell us about differences in how some kinds of litter might harm the soil?
- Why do you think we should be concerned about harming the soil?

Learners should be helped to appreciate that environmentalists generally believe biodegradable litter poses fewer threats to soil quality than nonbiodegradable litter. The teacher should point out that the breakdown of biodegradable material sometimes even provides additional nutrients to the soil.

Consider Further Action   To conclude the activity, ask members of the class to think about things to do to reduce the amount of nonbiodegradable litter. Have them consider actions they might take personally as well as what they might do to encourage others to do. For example, the group might decide to urge their parents to ask for paper bags at the grocery store rather than nonbiodegradable plastic ones. Or they may encourage their parents to take their own reusable fabric or plastic shopping bags to the store. They might suggest ways of reusing aluminum can pull-tops that would make people less likely to throw them away. They might wonder whether items such as chewing gum that are often wrapped in foil might be wrapped in a more biodegradable substance. They might make a personal inventory of the trash basket in their own bedrooms to determine which items are more biodegradable than others. As a result, they might decide to try to reduce the amount of nonbiodegradable trash they throw away each week.

The purpose of this final phase is to help learners understand that biodegradable alternatives are often available for many commonly used nonbiodegradable items. If more biodegradable materials were used, the threat to the world's soils could be reduced.

Much of the effort of environmentalists concerned with the negative impact of nonbiodegradable litter focuses on recycling material. Recycling reduces the volume of material that is thrown away and also reduces the demand for new raw materials. Sisson (1982) has developed a number of practical classroom lessons focusing on littering and recycling. These lessons appear in her book, *Nature with Children of All Ages,* cited in full in the "References" section at the end of this chapter.

Lesson Idea 12–4

POLLUTION

Grade Level:	K–2
Objective:	Pupils will describe how automobiles contribute to air pollution.
Suggested Procedure:	Griffin (1988) suggests a lesson designed to introduce pupils in kindergarten or the earliest primary grades to the concept of pollution. Begin by taking the class outside to the school parking lot. (It is a good idea to have some parent volunteers or another teacher along to monitor learners during this exercise.) Children gather around the car of a parent who has volunteered to help.

Take a piece of clean white cloth and attach it with a strong rubber band to the car's tailpipe. Ask learners to share ideas about what the cloth might look like if the car were driven with the cloth attached to the tailpipe. Accept all ideas.

Next, tell pupils that they are going to be scientists and conduct an experiment. The parent volunteer is going to drive the car around the block. The class will then remove the white cloth and look at it. When the white cloth is removed, ask learners to report what they observe. Compare the condition of the cloth with what they said would happen before the experiment began.

Point to the dark smudges on the cloth and explain that it is pollution. Ask class members their thoughts on what happens to the air when there are lots of cars. Conclude the lesson by discussing some ideas, such as car pooling, that can reduce the amount of air pollution.

Lesson Idea 12–5

ELECTRIC APPLIANCE SURVEY

Grade Level:	4–6
Objective:	Learners can develop an action plan for conserving energy. At the elementary school level, an important objective of energy education lessons is to help pupils understand that, ultimately, many energy resources are used for the production of electricity. Demand is especially high in societies such as ours that are heavily dependent on electricity sources to

run sophisticated equipment, light homes and businesses, and operate heating and cooling systems. Our reliance on electricity can be highlighted during an appliance survey activity.

Suggested Procedures: This activity can be organized in several ways. Sowards (1985) suggests that the teacher ask pupils to draw a rough floor plan of their house or apartment. When they have done so, ask them to draw in locations of household appliances, such as washing machines, dryers, electric stoves, refrigerators, lamps, radios, televisions, vacuum cleaners, ceiling lights, and hair dryers. Alternatively, pupils may simply develop a list indicating numbers of such items in their homes. This procedure should produce a list such as the following:

Appliance	Quantity
Stove	1
Refrigerator	1
Vacuum cleaner	1
Ceiling lights	7
Lamps	9
Radios	4
Televisions	2
Washing machine	1
Clothes dryer	1
Hair dryers	2
Room air conditioners	3

From individual pupil lists, compile a master list. Use this information as the basis for a discussion focusing on such questions as these:

- Which of these items do you regard as essential?
- Which items would you give up?
- If you didn't have to give up an item, but did have to use it less often, which item or items might you select?
- Which items seem to be turned on for the longest period each day?
- How do you account for differences in amounts of time individual items are used?
- Do you think that because an item is "on" longer during a given day than another item that it necessarily uses more electricity? (Point out here that some appliances use less electricity than others.)
- If you wanted to save electricity in your home, what might you do?
- What could we do here at school to save electricity and to encourage others to do so as well?

Lesson Idea 12–6

MAKING ENERGY-COLLAGE POSTERS

Grade Level: 2–4

Objectives: Pupils will (1) identify different sources of energy, and (2) classify items according to the type of energy they use.

Suggested Procedure: An energy-collage poster activity serves well to help younger learners appreciate that there are different kinds of energy resources. To begin, point out that energy is provided to us in many forms, including electricity, natural gas, oil, coal, solar, and wind. Divide learners into teams of about four pupils each. Provide each group with the following materials:

- Several old magazines or catalogs
- Paste or glue
- Scissors
- Light poster board
- Marking pens or pencils

Ask pupils to draw a line across the bottom of the poster board about five inches from the bottom. Tell them not to paste anything on this part of the poster. (They will write information here later.)

Next, instruct pupils to go through the magazines and catalogs and find pictures of items that use energy, such as small appliances, furnaces, automobiles, windmills, and so forth. Have them cut these items out and paste them on the poster board. Carefully monitor pupils while they are engaged in this activity. Urge pupils to fill in all areas of the poster board except for the five-inch "reserved" strip at the bottom.

When students have completed this phase, each team should have a poster collage. At this time, pause to lead a discussion centering on the question of what energy sources are used for each of the items depicted on the posters. After this discussion, instruct team members to write labels indicating the various power sources (e.g., electricity, oil, natural gas, solar, wind) across the top of the "reserved" section at the bottom of the posters.

Next, ask members of each group to write the names of items appearing on their posters that use each of these energy sources under the appropriate label. For example, under the heading "natural gas," they may list items such as "stove," "clothes dryer," and "furnace." When all students have completed this phase of the activity, display the posters in the classroom or elsewhere in the school building.

KEY IDEAS IN SUMMARY

1. Environmental and energy concerns attract much public attention today. In part, this interest is due to extensive media coverage of events, such as the explosion at the nuclear facility in Chernobyl, that have had a dramatic impact on the environment. Environmental issues are worldwide in scope. Their resolution will require social, political, and personal adjustments. Hence, environmental education plays an important role in the elementary social studies program.

2. Many scientists today are concerned about global warming, which appears to be associated with a carbon dioxide buildup in the lower atmosphere. This buildup results from widespread burning of carbon-based fuels. Global warming may produce many problems. The world's low-lying areas may flood as the polar ice caps melt and sea level rises. There also may be negative effects on kinds of crops that can be grown, threatening the total supply of available food.

3. There is evidence that global acreage occupied by trees is diminishing rapidly. If this trend continues, supplies of oxygen could be threatened. Green leafy surfaces take in carbon dioxide and give off oxygen, and a diminished supply of trees may result in a buildup of carbon dioxide, thus contributing to global warming.

4. Toxic waste pollution is chemical contamination of the environment. Toxic waste problems have already forced populations out of some areas of the world. More and more governments are placing severe restrictions on places authorized for disposal of dangerous chemical wastes.

5. The ozone layer in the upper atmosphere acts as a filter to keep dangerous ultraviolet radiation from reaching the earth's surface. In recent years, scientists have discovered that the ozone layer is gradually eroding. This destruction is thought to be from release into the atmosphere of chlorofluorocarbons (CFCs). A diminished ozone layer can have serious consequences for animal and plant life. Exposure to ultraviolet radiation may increase the incidence of skin cancer.

6. Use of energy sources such as coal, oil, wood, and natural gas produces carbon dioxide. In addition to their association with the problem of global warming, these energy fuels exist in limited supplies, and in time will be exhausted. Efforts are underway today to expand use of hydroelectric power, solar power, and other renewable energy sources. There is particular interest in using plant derivatives for fuel, such as alcohol made from sugar cane.

7. Classroom lessons focusing on the environment and energy seek to develop learners' sensitivities to these issues. Among other things, these lessons seek to help them (1) develop an appreciation for their immediate environment, (2) note the interrelationships among all living things, (3) suggest what people can do as individuals to maintain healthy environments, (4) appreciate the need to protect certain natural areas, and (5) point out threats to environmental quality and how they might be met.

CHAPTER REFLECTIONS

Directions: Now that you have finished reading the chapter, reread the case study at the beginning. Then answer these questions:

1. Is it appropriate to introduce content related to the environment to elementary school pupils? Why, or why not?

2. What do scientists believe to be the major causes of global warming, and why might this trend pose a threat?

3. What are some environmental consequences of deforestation?

4. What evidence is there that problems associated with toxic waste have become serious?

5. What is one of the primary causes of deterioration of ozone in the upper atmosphere?

6. What are some examples of renewable fuels, and why do many experts favor expanding their use?

7. What are some classroom activities that can be used to introduce students to issues associated with the environment and with energy?

8. Suppose the global warming trend were to continue. Consider the impact on plants, especially on food crops. What might some consequences of this trend be for your own local area?

9. Some environmentalists are proposing that broader use be made of renewable fuel sources, such as alcohol. Alcohol can be produced from many plant sources, including corn. Describe what might happen were a regulation imposed requiring people to use only fuel from renewable fuels. (This would mean an immediate end to the use of such traditional fuels as gasoline, diesel oil, other petroleum-based fuels, and coal.)

10. Not everyone agrees with positions espoused by environmentalists. Some people argue that environmentalists take too pessimistic a view of the future. These critics suggest that human beings have always successfully met whatever challenges that confronted them and that there is no reason to fear the future. How receptive are you to these arguments? Why do you take this position?

11. Much has been written about threats to the environment. In your own view, which threat is the most serious? Why do you think so? What might be done to respond to it?

EXTENDING UNDERSTANDING AND SKILL

1. Identify four or five major environmental issues. Prepare a clipping file of news articles related to each. Try to include at least 10 articles for each issue you select. Information about environmental issues changes rapidly in the light of new scien-

tific developments, so include only materials published within the past three years. Prepare a table of contents for your file that will enable you to locate individual items quickly.

2. Prepare an environmental/energy education "how-to" idea collection. Include specific suggestions for introducing content related to environmental and energy concerns to learners. Examine such information sources as *Social Education, The Social Studies, Learning,* and *The Instructor.* Your course instructor may know of additional source materials. Include at least 10 different ideas in your collection.

3. Select a major environmental issue that you might use as a focus for a lesson at a grade level you wish to teach. Develop a complete lesson. After your lesson has been reviewed and approved by your instructor, make copies to share with others in your class.

4. Interview two or three elementary teachers who teach at a grade level that interests you. Ask them how much attention they give to environmental and energy issues in their classrooms. Specifically, what kinds of lessons do these teachers teach in these areas? Find out whether there are any state or local requirements to include content of this kind. Write up results of your interviews in the form of a report. Submit it to your instructor for review.

5. Organize a brainstorming session in your class. For each elementary grade, solicit responses to this question: "What kinds of environmental and energy issues might be appropriate for learners at this grade?" Select someone to write responses on the chalkboard. Your instructor will lead a followup discussion focusing on the appropriateness of the suggestions.

REFERENCES

BROWN, L. R. (1993). "A New Era Unfolds." In L. Starke (ed.), *State of the World 1993.* New York: W. W. Norton, pp. 1–21.

BROWN, L. R., FLAVIN, C., AND POSTEL, S. (1989). "A World at Risk." In L. Starke (ed.), *State of the World 1989.* New York: W. W. Norton, pp. 3–20.

DENISTON, D. (1993). "Air Pollution Damaging Forests." In L. Starke (ed.), *Vital Signs 1993.* New York: W. W. Norton, pp. 108–109.

DURNING, A. T. (1994). "Redesigning the Forest Economy." In L. Starke (ed.), *State of the World 1994.* New York: W. W. Norton, pp. 22–40.

FLAVIN, C. (1988). "Creating a Sustainable Energy Future." In L. Starke (ed.), *State of the World 1988.* New York: W. W. Norton, pp. 22–90.

GRIFFIN, S. (1988). "Conservation Seeds: Pollution Awareness." *Day Care and Early Education, 15* (4), pp. 28–29.

JACOBSON, J. L. (1989). "Abandoning Homelands." In L. Starke (ed.), *State of the World 1989.* New York: W. W. Norton, pp. 59–76.

O'BRIEN, K., AND STONER, D. K. (1987). "Increasing Environmental Awareness through Children's Literature." *Reading Teacher, 41* (1), pp. 14–19.

O'CONNOR, M. (1983). *Living Lightly in the City: An Environmental Education Curriculum for Grades K–3*. Milwaukee, WI: Schlitz Audubon Center.

SHEA, C. P. (1988). "Shifting to Renewable Energy." In L. Starke (ed.), *State of the World 1988*. New York: W. W. Norton, pp. 62–82.

SHEA, C. P. (1989). "Protecting the Ozone Layer." In L. Starke (ed.), *State of the World 1989*. New York: W. W. Norton, pp. 77–96.

SISSON, E. A. (1982). *Nature with Children of All Ages: Activities and Adventures for Exploring, Learning, and Enjoying the World around Us*. Englewood Cliffs, NJ: Prentice Hall.

SOWARDS, A. (1985). *"Energy Curriculum Guide for Science, Grades K–6."* Austin, TX: Texas Mid-Continent Oil and Gas Association.

WEBER, P. (1994). "Safeguarding Oceans." In L. Starke (ed.), *State of the World 1994*. New York: W. W. Norton, pp. 41–60.

World Resources Institute. (1994). *World Resources 1994–1995: A Guide to the Global Environment*. New York: Oxford University Press.

SUPPORTING AND ASSESSING SOCIAL STUDIES LEARNING

13

TECHNOLOGY AND THE SOCIAL STUDIES

CHAPTER GOALS

This chapter provides information to help the reader:

- describe several technologies that can be integrated within elementary social studies lessons,
- suggest specific ways of using computers and computer programs in the social studies program,
- point out characteristics of CD-ROM and how this technology can enrich social studies instruction,
- explain potential classroom uses of the Internet, and
- speculate about how emerging technologies, for example programmable personal digital assistants (PDAs), may influence elementary social studies instruction.

CHAPTER STRUCTURE

Introduction
Computers in the Schools
    Traditional Computer Programs
    Processing Information / Locating Social Studies Software
    CD-ROM
    Internet
    Integrating Computer-Based Instruction
    Some "PROs" and "CONs" Related to Computers and Schools
    Some Arguments for More Extensive School Use of Computers / Some Cautionary Arguments About School Use of Computers
Videocassettes
Videodiscs
Personal Digital Assistants (PDAs)
Key Ideas in Summary
Chapter Reflections
Extending Understanding and Skill
References

Figure 13–1
Technology and the social
studies.

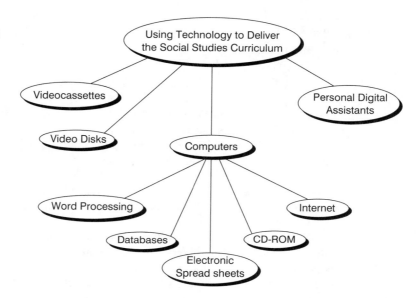

Chapter 13

Case Study

CD-ROM AND TRADITIONAL LIBRARY RESEARCH

This exchange took place between Henry Duforge and his friend, Francelle Dupuis, during a party at the home of a mutual friend.

"So how's the wonderful world of grade four education?" asked Francelle. "Let's see, you're about halfway through your second year now. Right?"

"That's right," Henry replied. "Basically, things are fine. The kids are super. The other teachers have been great, and my principal has been really supportive. I'm having trouble getting some of the parents up to speed, though."

"What do you mean?"

"Well, Francelle," Henry replied, "these parents got out of school years before anyone dreamed there would be personal computers in classrooms. Many use them at work, but hardly any of these parents have an idea about what we can do with computers in the schools. As a result, some of them don't quite understand what I'm trying to teach."

"Give me an example," said Francelle.

"Well, when you and I were in school, we did a lot of work in the library, right? When we had to find some specialized information, we didn't really have a choice. It was go to the library and look at the card catalog or ask the librarian for help. A lot of my kids' parents remember library work, and they don't understand that, for the most part, library assignments just aren't necessary anymore."

"Why not?" inquired Francelle.

"Because we now have these great computers equipped with high-speed CD-ROM drives. We've got CD-ROM disks containing huge volumes of information. They are easy to store in the classroom. They allow kids to find specific information quickly. And they represent an up-to-date technology that young people today need to know about."

"Have you tried to explain this to your parents?"

"Well, Francelle, I have," replied Henry. "A few of them nod their heads, but many of them think their kids are 'just playing' when they are working with computers. They don't see the computer as a tool for doing serious work. I know lots of them would be happier if their kids came home and announced that they had been doing work in the library.

"To tell you the truth," Henry went on, "I'm a bit worried. I'm afraid some parents may think that I am not seriously trying to teach important content and to improve the thinking skills of their children."

What Is Your Response?

After reading the conversation between Henry and Francelle, respond briefly to these questions:

1. Do parents' personal experiences during their school years influence their expectations of their children's teachers?

2. Is there a bias in this country in favor of educational innovation or is there a bias in favor of traditional ways of doing things? Explain your answer.
3. Do teachers have an obligation to familiarize pupils with the latest technology, or is this simply "faddism" that may result in an emphasis on something that may be forgotten in a few short years?
4. Some critics have charged that schools are extremely slow to adapt to change. Is this accurate? What leads you to your conclusion?
5. If you were Francelle, what specific advice would you pass on to Henry?

INTRODUCTION

Jodie McCracken told her mother she was going up to her room to work on her social studies speech. Her assignment was to compare and contrast typical daily experiences of 10-year-olds in two quite different parts of the United Kingdom, London and the Shetland Islands (north of Scotland). From her backpack, she extracted the portable CD-ROM unit provided by the school. She inserted the tiny CD-ROM disk, connected the unit to a color monitor, and began scanning for appropriate information.

Quickly she located information she needed. On the monitor, digitized images depicting a typical day of a young resident of the Shetland Islands played out, accompanied by a sound commentary. Jodie looked, listened, and took notes. At the end, she was invited to ask specific questions. Answers to many of them were built into the memory of the CD-ROM program. Where answers were not immediately available, the monitor suggested Internet addresses Jodie might query. This same general sequence reoccurred as Jodie sought information about a typical day of a young resident of London.

After working with the portable CD-ROM, Jodie briefly used a computer to log on to the Internet. She directed queries to several of the Internet addresses that had been recommended as she watched and listened to the CD-ROM, and gathered additional information.

Now she was ready to put the elements of her presentation together. She sat down at her computer and developed a basic speech outline. She went back to the CD-ROM and identified some of the graphics she would like to include to support her talk. During her presentation, she would have access to a large monitor and a CD-ROM unit. She would "call up" appropriate visual clips to support her points. As an experienced user of technology, Jodie felt her presentation would be a good one.

Does this all seem a bit farfetched? Will technology really change how young people go about the business of gathering, organizing, learning, and presenting information? Though some places will embrace these changes more rapidly than others, evidence mounts that technology is playing an ever-larger role in education. Let's consider some examples.

In a recent textbook adoption in California, of the eight programs that were considered, only two included a traditional pupil text. *Seven* of the eight packaged learning experiences in formats depending on one or more of these technologies: videodiscs,

*Advances in technology con-
tinue to create exciting new ways
for pupils to explore the world.*

computer software, videotapes, and audiotapes ("Technology Products Adopted in California," 1992).

Large numbers of public libraries are beginning to purchase CD-ROM titles. These are available for checkout in the same way books are ("Public Libraries will Lend CD-ROM Titles," 1993).

The Internet, a nonprofit collection of computer networks that links millions of computer users in 100 countries, enables users to communicate with one another and exchange information. Recently, the United States Library of Congress established an Internet address that allows computer users to inquire about Library of Congress holdings on topics that interest them ("Internet Access to the Library of Congress," 1993). Information from the Library of Congress, and from many other government agencies, can be accessed through the Internet by using Gopher (the Internet information search system) to open the general category, "Government Information." Information can also be accessed with any of several World Wide Web browsers.

Technology has spawned the development of a number of parent–school communication systems. Educational Telephone, a Tennessee-based company, allows teachers to leave messages with parents about absences, homework, or other topics. Parents can also call in for recorded messages about school events. A typical system holds as many as 500 30-second messages. Homework Hotline is another parent–school communication system. It features recorded messages in multiple languages and is proving particularly useful in schools enrolling large numbers of pupils who speak languages other than English at home (Stearns, 1993).

Technology is now available that allows individual school districts to create their own CD-ROM disks. This is making possible a tailoring of the curriculum to meet special needs. For years, teachers working with pupils in schools on the White Earth Reservation in northern Minnesota wanted materials focusing on the culture of the Ojibway Native American culture. With money from a grant, a Native American researcher who was an expert both on the Ojibway and in technology teamed up to produce a CD-ROM disk. It includes complete lesson plans for teachers and self-guided lessons for pupils that focus on the Ojibway language, history, and culture ("CD-ROM Spins into Schools," 1993).

These developments hint at the kinds of changes that implementation of new technologies may bring to our classrooms. Change is so rapid that it is hazardous to guess which technologies will have the most impact on the schools. Present trends, however, suggest that the late 1990s may witness an explosion of CD-ROM use in the schools much as personal computers and accompanying floppy disk software became common features of many schools in the 1980s and early 1990s. Slightly farther into the future, it seems a good bet that school use of multifunction technology devices such as personal digital assistants (PDAs) will increase. These small, hand-held units combine multiple technologies. Pupils may soon use sophisticated PDAs to gather, process, and produce information.

COMPUTERS IN THE SCHOOLS

The number of computers in schools has soared over the past 15 years. Early on, teachers had problems integrating computer-based instruction into their programs because insufficient machines were available. Today, some elementary schools have large numbers of computers in each classroom. Many other schools have large, well-equipped computer rooms that are staffed by teachers trained to help pupils master computer-based lessons.

The availability of computers in the schools has increased for several reasons. Perhaps the most important has been the public demand that they be made available for learner use. Many people believe that the future growth of our economy depends on innovative applications of technology. Employers in the future may be even more insistent than they are today that employees be fluent computer users. Large numbers of parents want to be sure their children leave school with these skills.

The huge demand for computers in this country and throughout the world has resulted in economies of scale in their manufacture. Prices have come down dramatically. A computer that might have sold for thousands of dollars in the early 1980s can be had today for a few hundred dollars. As a result, schools have been able to buy more of them for classroom use.

In recent years, there have been great improvements in the quality of educational software. This has been true in elementary social studies as well as in other areas of the

BOX 13–1   Are Computers Better than Textbooks?

A teacher recently made these comments:

> I am tired about hearing technology enthusiasts talk nonstop about much more pupils can learn from computers than textbooks. I'm not against computers, but I think some claims for what they can do are exaggerated.
>
> What we get from people pushing for more computers are examples of the finest computer programs used in responsible ways by talented teachers. These are invariably contrasted to the worst possible use of textbooks by teachers whose instructional skills could only charitably be rated as "mediocre."
>
> This is the reality as I see it: There are outstanding computer programs, and there are terrible computer programs. We should stop this nonsense about computer technology being superior to textbook technology in any kind of absolute sense. Neither is inherently "good" or "bad." We need the best examples of both technologies in our schools, and we need outstanding teachers who can take advantage of what each has to offer our young people.

Think About This

1. What are your reactions to this teacher's position?
2. If you agree that computers should be "sold" to educators in ways that avoid irresponsibly negative comparisons to other technologies, how might you make a case supporting their use?
3. Do you believe any instructional technology can be good enough to overcome a lack of proficiency in the teacher?

school curriculum. Consequently, teachers today are more inclined than previously to incorporate computer-based lessons into their programs.

Finally, computers today are much more compact than they used to be. Early word processors were about the size of an upright piano. Today, much more powerful computers take up only a modest amount of space on a tabletop or desktop. Notebook and subnotebook computers including hard disks with enormous storage capacities are small enough to fit easily into a briefcase. The physical space required for computer-based instruction is much less today than it was when the first units came on the market.

Traditional Computer Programs

Most computers in schools today utilize programs that are stored either on internal hard disk or floppy disk drives. Social studies teachers and their pupils use programs to process information and to engage new content.

Processing Information

Word processing capabilities of microcomputers are well known. Computers enable learners to develop drafts quickly and to revise easily. Rewriting with a computer using a word processing program takes much of the tedium out of the process. In elementary social studies classes, this means that teachers whose pupils have access to computers and good word processing programs may be able to demand more written work and to expect better final versions of learners' papers.

A number of excellent word processing programs are available today. Some pupils may have learned sophisticated programs such as *WordPerfect, Word*, or *WordStar* that their parents use on their own computers at home. Other programs have been designed specifically for school use. Several of these are appropriate for learners in the middle and upper elementary grades.

Databases are enormous collections of data that users can draw on in response to their specific information needs. Information for some databases is kept at a central location. Users who subscribe to these services access this information using a telephone line, a modem (a device that allows a computer to "talk" over a telephone line), and a personal computer. Prodigy, CompuServe, and America Online are examples of databases of this basic type. They have information on a variety of subjects that subscribers to their services use.

Other databases are self-contained. That is, the information is contained on one or more disks that the user inserts into the computer when needing to access the data. Sometimes it is possible for users to add information to that initially provided.

Electronic spreadsheets store information in rows and columns displayed on a computer monitor. Typically, individual rows and columns have their own labels. A teacher might use an electronic spreadsheet instead of a traditional gradebook. The rows at the left would contain names of pupils in the class. The individual columns would have labels indicating particular assignments, tests, and other evidence to be used as a basis for grading. Electronic spreadsheets allow users to do more than simply record existing information. They can engage in speculative thinking by engaging in "what if" sorts of activities. For example, the impact on a given pupils' grade of a 10 percent improvement on every assignment could be quickly reflected on a spreadsheet. The procedures for adding new information and making calculations are quite simple.

There are many possible applications for using spreadsheet programs in social studies programs. These programs are particularly valuable for engaging learners in lessons designed to develop their skills in making inferences. Rooze and Northup (1989) cite an example of using spreadsheets to calculate the impacts of different rates of population growth in different places. Columns at the top are labeled, "Place A and its rate of population increase" and "Place B and its rate of population increase." Rows are labeled with individual years. Cells that result from this matrix contain population information for each place at each year. Learners can review the displayed data and draw conclusions about the impact of the different growth rates (see Table 13–1).

Locating Social Studies Software

Numerous firms are now selling software suitable for use in elementary social studies classrooms. A list of 10 firms selling software of interest to elementary social studies teachers is given here.

Table 13–1
A completed spreadsheet showing the impact on populations of
two countries of differing rates of
population increase.

| Year | Population Projections | |
	New Zealand (annual rate of natural increase = 0.08%)	Jordan (annual rate of natural increase = 3.60%)
1989	3,397,000	3,031,000
1990	3,424,000	3,140,116
1991	3,451,392	3,253,160
1992	3,479,003	3,370,273
1993	3,506,835	3,491,603
1994	3,536,890	3,617,301
1995	3,565,185	3,747,524
1996	3,593,706	3,882,435
1997	3,622,456	4,022,203
1998	3,651,436	4,167,002
1999	3,680,647	4,317,014

Note: Data assume that rate of natural increase for
each country stays the same for every year cited.

1. Aquarius, P.O. Box 128, Indian Rocks, FL 33535
2. Broderbund Software, 345 Fourth Street, San Francisco, CA 94107
3. Educational Activities, 1937 Grand Avenue, Baldwin, NY 11510
4. Grolier Electronic Publishing, Sherman Turnpike, Danbury, CT 06816
5. Learning Arts, P.O. Box 179, Wichita, KS 67201
6. MicroEd, P.O. Box 24750, Edina, MN 55424
7. Milliken, 1100 Research Boulevard, St. Louis, MO 63132
8. SVE, 1345 Diversey Parkway, Chicago, IL 60614
9. Tom Snyder Productions, 90 Sherman Street, Cambridge, MA 02140
10. Unicorn Software, 2950 E. Flamingo Road, Las Vegas, NV 89121

The annual elementary school social studies catalog produced each year by Social Studies School Services is available free to educators. It includes large numbers of excellent programs for supporting social studies instruction. For a copy, write to Social Studies School Service, 10200 Jefferson Boulevard, Room 1, P.O. Box 802, Culver City, CA 90232-0802.

Another useful source of information about current software titles is *Only the Best*. This is an annual guide to the highest rated software directed at learners in grades pre-K through 12. It is available from ASCD, Technology Resource Center, 1250 N. Pitt Street, Alexandria, VA 22314.

CD-ROM

CD-ROM stands for "compact disc—read only memory." This powerful technology allows for integration and management of tremendous quantities of digital, audio, and visual information. A CD-ROM disk holds as much information as 1,500 floppy disks. Pupils and teachers using CD-ROM have access to sound, text, and visuals of all kinds. Full motion video can even be encoded and played back in interactively. The technology has the potential to provide social studies teachers with extraordinary flexibility in planning and delivering instruction.

CD-ROM is among the most rapidly expanding technologies in the schools. Several reasons account for this trend. First, many computers now being purchased by schools feature a built-in CD-ROM drive. This means the capability to use the technology "comes with the machine" and is not something that must be purchased as an expensive "add on."

Second, increasing numbers of CD-ROM titles have been developed specifically to support school instruction. Many of these go beyond the supplementary materials (electronic encyclopedias and so forth) that were featured on many early CD-ROMs. More and more CD-ROM titles are are curriculum based. That is, they treat the actual subjects that are being taught in school.

Third, CD-ROM equipment that allows individual schools to produce CD-ROM disks of their own to meet unique local needs are coming down in price. (Recall the earlier mention of a successful effort to produce a CD-ROM curriculum program for learners who are members of the Ojibway Native American group.) Many districts have special populations for whom few relevant learning materials are available. CD-ROM technology provides a mechanism to create and distribute learning experiences that respond to special local needs.

How is CD-ROM technology helping teachers today? Here are two examples. Because of today's emphasis on inclusion of pupils with special needs in regular classrooms, elementary teachers must be prepared to respond instructionally to pupils with varying personal conditions. For example, many elementary classrooms include learners with severe hearing impairments. Educators have long recognized that deaf and severely hearing impaired learners need many visual representations of new concepts to help them learn. The tremendous storage capacity of a CD-ROM disk makes thousands of images available. One interesting project in New York City, called *StreetSigns*, is working on the preparation of a CD-ROM program that will be an American Sign Language Dictionary. Visual image will facilitate translation between sign language and English equivalents.

In today's elementary classrooms, individual pupils may have family ties to the Dominican Republic, the Philippines, Haiti, Mexico, Vietnam, and many other countries around the world. CD-ROM disks are available that allow pupils to easily retrieve information about these lands. This permits individuals to learn about and take pride in their roots and the entire class to develop a greater appreciation for the multicultural characteristics of our country.

An interesting program with a multicultural perspective called *Ethnic Newswatch*, is in use in the Miami, Florida, area. This application of CD-ROM technology features the full text of 100 ethnic newspapers published in the United States. Learners who use it have an opportunity to see how current events are perceived by different cultural groups and can promote sensitivity to the diversity that is a special American strength.

Several compilations of good current CD-ROM titles are available. Two useful ones are the *CD-ROM Buyer's Guide and Handbook*, from Eight Bit Books, Online, Inc.,

462 Danbury Road, Wilton, CT; and *Only the Best*, from ASCD, Technology Resource Center, 1250 N. Pitt Street, Alexandria, VA 22314.

The following is a sample of available titles and sources of CD-ROM programs suitable for use in elementary social studies classrooms:

Countries of the World on CD-ROM
Bureau of Electronic Publishing
141 New Road
Parsippany, NJ 07054

Time Table of History: Science and Innovation
Compton's NewMedia
2320 Camino Vido Robo
Carlsbad, CA 92009

U.S. History on CD-ROM
Bureau of Electronic Publishing
141 New Road
Parsippany, NJ 07054

Who Built America?
The Voyager Company
1351 Pacific Coast Highway
Santa Monica, CA 90401

World Factbook
Wayzata Technologies
2515 East Highway 2
Grand Rapids, MN 55744

Compton's Interactive Encyclopedia
Compton's NewMedia
2320 Camino Vido Robo
Carlsbad, CA 92009

Internet

The Internet is a connection of over 5,000 electronic networks that embraces every continent on the planet (Dyrli, 1993). Telecommunications technology allows individual computer users to tap into an incredible array of information sources. Data can be easily sent and received along this "electronic highway." Special browsers, such as Netscape Navigator or Quarterdeck Mosaic, make it easy to locate specific information.

Only in recent years has access to the Internet become easily, and relatively inexpensively, available to individuals and schools. Such commercial services as Applelink, American Online, Compuserve, and Prodigy have made Internet access widely available. Many schools subscribe to services that allow learners and teachers to become Internet users. This allows them to access information such as instructional programs maintained on distant computers, lists of library holdings, and databases. It also allows for almost instantaneous person-to-person communication between individuals at separate geographic locations.

Every computer linked to the Internet has its own special electronic address. These addresses are typed in by distant Internet users when they wish to contact a specific individual or group. For example, if you, as a user of this book, wanted to ask David Armstrong, one of the authors, a question using Internet, you would type in this Internet address: DGA@Tamu.edu.

For elementary social studies teachers, the Internet opens up an array of potentially useful information sources. Several states have developed special Internet services to serve K–12 educators, among which are the following:

CORE
California Technology Project
P.O. Box 3842
Seal Beach, CA 90740-7842

Florida Information Resource Network
Florida Educational Center
B1–14 325 W. Gaines Street
Tallahassee, FL 32399

Merit MichNet
2901 Hubbard, Pod G.
Ann Arbor, MI 48109-2016

TENET
Texas Education Network
Texas Education Agency
1701 North Congress Avenue, Room 4159
Austin, TX 78701

Public Education Network (PEN)
Information Systems
Virginia Department of Education
P.O. Box 6-Q
Richmond, VA 23216

Integrating Computer-Based Instruction

Computer-based instruction works best when it is not a stand-alone procedure. Computer learning should be integrated both with learning in other subject areas and with other instructional techniques used to introduce social studies content. Such integration promotes the development of cumulative learning experiences that have more total impact on learners' development.

Ties with other subjects make especially good sense because computer software in these other areas often is designed to develop competencies with relevance for the social studies. For example, many mathematics programs help learners to become more proficient in working with graphically depicted information. It is clear that an ability to learn from graphical displays of information is also critically important in the social studies.

Integration of computer-based instruction with other methods used to introduce social studies content is also important. If there is no real link between what pupils do when they work with computers and what they do when other instructional techniques are used, they may well view their computer time as a recreational diversion with little real connection to the academic social studies program. Many teachers find it useful to select software that ties closely to academic content also being treated in other ways. For example, when studying a social studies unit on the American Revolution, learning experiences requiring the use of the textbook, learning centers, special library resources, and other materials provide an excellent context for a computer simulation of some aspect of the revolutionary experience.

Some "Pros" and "Cons" Related to Computers and Schools

It has been widely recognized that our economy is becoming more and more dependent on high technology. Consequently, many parents have come to believe that their children must have a thorough grounding in using computers, and these parents—often supported by members of the business community—have successfully lobbied school boards for more computers in the schools.

As more schools place computers in their classrooms, and as prices have dropped dramatically, more hardware and software developers have entered the educational marketplace. The quality of educational software has gotten better in elementary social studies as well as in other areas of the school curriculum. Consequently, teachers have become more enthusiastic about incorporating computer-based learning experiences into their lessons.

Despite the increasing number of computers in schools, there is no universal agreement that computers should be extensively used in educational programs. There continue to be arguments on both sides of this issue.

Some Arguments for More Extensive School Use of Computers

Exposure to computer use provides learners with numerous personal benefits. These skills have high transfer value. For example, expertise in computer use gained in a social studies lesson may enable the learner to use skills such as word processing to

Well-done software programs are exciting and motivating to students.

increase performance levels in language arts or in other areas where writing is required. Basic computer competence acquired in the elementary grades may facilitate learning in a number of areas when pupils go on to secondary school. Finally, the computer provides a direct link to the "real world" of the employment marketplace.

Computer programs can be developed that respond well to special needs of individual pupils. The possibility exists of delivering instruction in ways that can help larger numbers of learners succeed. For example, programs may include features that provide pupils with immediate feedback when they respond to questions related to an assignment. Because immediate feedback helps learners identify their mistakes quickly, it contributes to overall learning efficiency. Research has revealed that "computer-assisted instruction can reduce the instructional time necessary for students" (Schug, 1988, p. 112). As Schug points out, the prospect of increasing instructional efficiency is especially attractive in a content-crowded subject such as the social studies.

Some Cautionary Arguments about School Use of Computers

Enthusiasm for school use of computers has grown so widespread that some school officials may have installed them quickly into their buildings to avert a public relations disaster. The tendency of some school districts' public relations materials to emphasize the numbers of computers available for school use suggests the political capital to be gained by schools with high-profile computer-based learning programs.

In some cases, computers have been purchased before teachers have been trained adequately in their use. Further, though instructional programs have improved tremendously in recent years, some of the available software is not good. For example, some simple (if not simplistic) programs are nothing more than electronic versions of pupil workbooks. Little learning difference should be expected when the only change made is that pupils type answers into a blank on a computer screen rather than write them on a blank in a printed workbook. This kind of computer use raises serious costs-benefit questions. Dollar-conscious critics of school programs might well ask why a five hundred dollar computer is needed to replace a five dollar workbook.

Certain characteristics of computers impose limitations. For example, many computers in schools are not portable. Notebook and subnotebook computers represent a tiny fraction of the computers purchased for use in schools. The typical school computer does not begin to approach the portability of the typical textbook. Further, computers, particularly when subjected to heavy use, break down. Specially trained technicians must be hired by the schools to keep them up and running.

Although arguments continue between those who support and oppose computers in schools, there are so many computers now being used in schools that supporters' views have carried the day. Evidence is overwhelming that computer use in schools is increasing. All signs point to a continuation of this trend in the years ahead.

VIDEOCASSETTES

Videocassette technology is widely used in elementary schools. Nearly all schools have the necessary playback equipment. Social studies materials catalogs feature large numbers of titles appropriate for use with elementary school pupils.

Videocassettes have largely displaced 16 mm films. This has happened because of cost. Sixteen millimeter films are expensive. A half-hour color film may cost more than $500.00; many videocassettes are available for a less than a tenth as much. Tight instructional budgets stretch further with videocassettes than with 16 mm films.

Videocassettes are easy to store; a single shelf may hold several dozen. The playback equipment is simple to use. Most units require the operator to do little more than turn on a switch and insert the cassette. The cassette containers are durable. The playback system, itself, places little stress on the film. These features make it possible for videocassettes to last many years, given reasonable care.

In addition to playing prerecorded videocassettes, many teachers use videocassette equipment to record information of their own choosing. For example, in social studies classes, some teachers make video recordings of pupils working in groups, engaging in role-playing activities, and participating in simulations. Portable equipment can be taken into the field to make permanent audio and video records of field trip experiences.

VIDEODISCS

On videodiscs, a laser beam is used to store and retrieve information. As the disks turn, the beam senses information that has been stored and converts it to audio and visual signals. Since only a beam strikes the disk surface, no physical wear occurs when the disk plays. Hence, videodiscs do not wear out as do traditional phonograph records as a result of abrasion from the playback needle.

The sound reproduction quality of digital audio- and videodiscs can be superb when signals are played back through a good speaker system. This feature makes them much prized in music programs, where faithful reproduction of sound is important. Today, relatively few audiodiscs have been developed specifically for use in elementary social studies classes.

GTV, an extremely high-quality social studies program that relies heavily on videodisc technology, has been developed with the support of the National Geographic Society. This interactive American history program is designed for use in grades 5 through 12. There are two full hours of available video divided into 40 segments that last from three to five minutes each. Users can identify which segments they want, and can sequence them. Learners can be involved in sequencing decisions. The program allows them to pursue a common theme across a number of selected segments, to develop short programs to support content in the text, and to otherwise get directly involved in decisions involving selection and organization of information. A word processing feature allows either teacher or pupils to write scripts to accompany the visual stories. For information about GTV, write to National Geographic Society, Department GTV, Washington, DC 20077-9966.

PERSONAL DIGITAL ASSISTANTS (PDAS)

Personal digital assistants (PDAs) bring together multiple technologies in a device small enough to be held in the hand. Some units now on the market contain functions that not too long ago would have had to be accommodated by as many as seven different technologies—clipboards, memo pads, telephones, file cabinets, fax machines, e-mail transmission and reception systems, and typewriters (D'Ignazio, 1994).

The potential for PDAs to establish wireless ties to the Internet and other points of access to the fast-emerging "information superhighway" may make it possible for pupils to gather and exchange information from almost any location. The "wireless" feature involves an arrangement whereby PDAs will be able to access cellular telephone networks. Cellular telephones, which have made it possible for people to use phones from automobiles or planes or to dial up a friend or business associate while walking down the street, allow for wireless, over-the-air transmission of information. Availability of cellular phone facilities is expanding rapidly, as is the number of users. By the year 2005, it is estimated that there will be 60 million subscribers to cellular services in the United States alone (Santelesa, 1994).

PDAs offer the possibility that children in the future will have a hand-held device they can take back and forth to school that will provide them instant access to a whole world of information. This has enormous potential implications for educators. For example, today's teachers often are constrained to provide instruction that can be supported by resources materials available at their own schools, or at least by resources available in their school district. PDA technology can make information available to pupils everywhere that today is either not available at all or available only to learners in affluent school districts. Further, these devices offer the possibility for establishing frequent and personal links between pupils in different parts of the country and, indeed, in different parts of the world. Obviously, this portends a future in which learners will be able to have many more direct contacts with people from cultures different from their own than is possible today.

PDAs, so far as schools are concerned, are devices of the future. They are only now coming to market in large numbers. Prices remain high. However, if observed market patterns hold true, prices will fall rapidly as production levels increase and additional vendors begin bringing competitive models to the market. It is estimated that when PDA prices fall below $300.00 that the market for these devices will explode. Specialists who follow electronic innovations anticipate this will happen before the year 2000. PDAs may then begin to appear in the schools in large numbers.

KEY IDEAS IN SUMMARY

1. New technologies are playing increasingly important roles in elementary social studies and in other parts of the elementary curriculum. New technologies are beginning to increase options of teachers as they plan to help students gather, organize, manipulate, and think about new information.

2. Computers are now well established in schools. Increasingly, computers are featuring CD-ROM drives. Development of the Internet gateway to the "information superhighway" makes it possible for computers in schools to link to thousands of information sources worldwide. Technology is also facilitating improved parent–school communication links. A number of systems are now in place that provide parents with information about homework assignments, upcoming school events, and other matters. In the future, personal digital assistants (PDAs), handheld devices that blend together many sophisticated technologies, may allow pupils literally to carry around a world's worth of information.

3. Personal computers are now available in most schools. In social studies programs, word processing capabilities allow pupils to write and edit reports easily. Databases allow them to make sophisticated comparisons and contrasts. Electronic spreadsheets have many applications in social studies lessons, including the potential to allow teachers and pupils to engage in sophisticated "what if" speculations.

4. CD-ROM technology is perhaps the fastest-growing electronic technology in schools today. Several reasons account for this. Many new computers being sold to schools include CD-ROM drives. Also, there has been a tremendous expansion in the number of CD-ROM disks developed specifically to support instruction in the social studies and other traditional subjects. CD-ROM allows students to access and manipulate enormous quantities of information. Also, equipment is now avail-

able that allows local school districts and schools to develop CD-ROM disks of their own. This capability has the potential to allow instructional programs to be developed that are uniquely suited to special characteristics of learners at a particular place.

5. The Internet is a connection of over 5,000 electronic networks. It allows individual computers to be tied electronically to a vast array of information sources. School use of the Internet is increasing. Some states have developed special Internet services specifically designed to assist elementary and secondary school educators.

6. Computer-based instruction has been found to be most effective when it is not introduced as a stand-alone procedure. It works best when integrated as a regular part of the instructional program, much as textbooks today.

7. Though computers seem destined to be permanent features of public schools, "pros" and "cons" of their use continue to be debated. Economic arguments often are made by people who enthusiastically support early introduction of computers in schools. They argue that technological proficiency of the workforce is essential if we are to be economically competitive with other nations in the future. Supporters also point to the great improvements that have been made in the quality of software designed for classroom use. On the other hand, some argue that certain school leaders have been more interested in buying computers as a public relations gimmick than as a sincere effort to help learners. They point out that some teachers have had little training in their use and that, at least in some instances, expensive computers are used as little more than expensive equivalents of old-fashioned pupil workbooks.

8. Videocassettes have tended to displace 16 mm films in school programs. They are less expensive than 16 mm films, and numerous titles are available to support lessons in the social studies and other curricular areas. The technology is very "user friendly." Individual cassettes last a long time, given reasonable care. Videocassette equipment is also available that allows teachers to record activities of their own pupils in the classroom or on field trips.

9. Videodiscs use laser beams to store and retrieve information. Because there is no direct contact with the surface of the disk, videodiscs do not easily wear out. They have the potential to store thousands of units of visual and graphic information that can, depending on the design of the system, be modified to meet specific pupil learning needs.

10. Personal digital assistants (PDAs) are just now coming to the consumer market in large numbers. They still are expensive and, experts believe, probably won't represent a mass-purchase item for schools, and for individuals who must watch expenditures carefully, until prices drop considerably from present levels. This price drop is anticipated some time before the end of the century. PDAs integrate into small hand-held units a large number of other technologies. They offer the possibility that someday teachers and learners may have constant access to quantities of information barely imaginable today.

CHAPTER REFLECTIONS

Directions: Now that you have read the chapter, reread the case study. Think about other topics and issues raised in the chapter. Then answer these questions.

1. What are some reasons that new technologies have not always been eagerly embraced by professionals working in schools?

2. What can the newer electronic technologies help teachers to do?

3. Today there is much talk about an electronic "information highway" that will enable people everywhere to connect to almost limitless numbers of information sources. What changes might the "information highway" produce in how elementary social studies programs are delivered in the future?

4. You learned in the chapter that some school districts are using CD-ROM technology to produce instructional programs to serve needs of pupils for whom relevant instructional materials are not available. Can you think of some pupils you might teach for whom this situation continues to exist and for whom special instructional programs might be developed for district-produced CD-ROM disks?

5. Suppose you had access to equipment for making videocassette recordings of your pupils. What kinds of things might you record? What would you do with this information? How would it help your pupils, and how would it help you to improve your instructional program?

6. Traditionally, schools have lagged behind many private sector enterprises in utilizing new technologies. What might be done to encourage schools to be leaders rather than followers in the adoption of innovations?

7. Suppose PDAs were available to each pupil in your class. What kinds of social studies lessons might you develop to take advantage of this technology?

EXTENDING UNDERSTANDING AND SKILL

1. Reports of how technology is being used to support instruction in social studies classes often are published in *Social Education* and in *The Social Studies*. Review the last three years of each publication for articles focusing on classroom applications of technology. Prepare a report for members of your class.

2. CD-ROM technology is rapidly becoming available in the nation's elementary schools. At the same time, many more CD-ROM titles are being produced that may be useful for teaching elementary social studies. Review such sources as the annual catalog of Social Studies School Services (10200 Jefferson Boulevard, Room 1, P.O. Box 802, Culver City, CA 90232-0802). Prepare a list of CD-ROM titles suitable for use in elementary social studies programs and where they can be ordered. Share the list with members of your class.

3. With a group of three or four others, do some reading about the Internet. Make a panel presentation to your class on possible ways that linking school computers to the Internet might enhance the elementary social studies program.

4. Assume you are in a school with computers and that this school has software titles you wish to use with pupils. Develop a lesson plan that incorporates use of computer technology as one of your approaches to involving pupils in mastering the new material. Ask your instructor to critique your plan.

5. Start a clipping file focusing on educational applications of technology. Look for articles in newspapers, general circulation periodicals, and journals directed at educators. In particular, look for examples with possible relevance for elementary social studies teaching.

REFERENCES

D'IGNAZIO, F. (1994). "Beyond Multimedia: The Student as Sherlock Holmes." *The Computing Teacher, 21* (5), pp. 38–40.

DYRLI, O. E. (1993). "The Internet: Bringing Global Resources to the Classroom." *Technology & Learning, 14* (2), pp. 50–58.

"Internet Access to the Library of Congress." (1993). *Electronic Learning, 13* (special edition, October), p. 6.

McCARTHY, R. (1993). "CD-ROM Spins into Schools: How These Shiny Little Discs Will Revolutionize Education." *Electronic Learning, 13* (special edition, October), pp. 11–17.

"Public Libraries Will Lend CD-ROM Titles." (1993). *Electronic Learning, 13* (special edition, October), p. 5.

ROOZE, G. E., AND NORTHUP, T. (1989). *Computers, Thinking, and Social Studies.* Englewood, CO: Teachers Ideas Press.

SANTELESA, R. (1994). "PDAS Here, There, and Everywhere." *Computer Shopper, 14* (3), pp. 201–208.

SCHUG, M. C. (1988). "What Do Social Studies Teachers Say About Using Computers?" *The Social Studies, 79* (3), pp. 112–115.

STEARNS, P. H. (1993). "History Comes Alive." *Electronic Learning, 13* (special edition, October), pp. 8–9.

"Technology Products Adopted in California." (1992). *Electronic Learning, 12* (10), pp. 6, 8.

UNDERSTANDING MAP
AND GLOBE SKILLS

CHAPTER GOALS

This chapter provides information to help the reader:

- recognize problems often experienced by elementary pupils when they work with maps and globes,
- identify key map and globe skills,
- describe map and globe skills appropriate for pupils in different grades,
- point out basic characteristics of maps and globes,
- suggest teaching approaches useful for helping pupils master certain map and globe skills, and
- identify basic concepts pupils must know to before they can cope successfully with map and globe activities.

CHAPTER STRUCTURE

Introduction
Globes
     Kinds of Globes
     Readiness Globes / Elementary Globes / Intermediate Globes
     Parts of the Globe That Need to Be Emphasized
Maps
     Conformal Maps
     Equal Area Maps
Basic Map and Globe Skills
     Recognizing Shapes
     Utilizing Scale
     Recognizing Symbols
     Utilizing Direction
     Determining Absolute Location
     Pointing Out Relative Location
     Describing Earth–Sun Relationships
     Interpreting Information on Maps and Globes
Teaching All of the Skills at Each Grade Level
Key Ideas in Summary
Questions
Extending Understanding and Skill

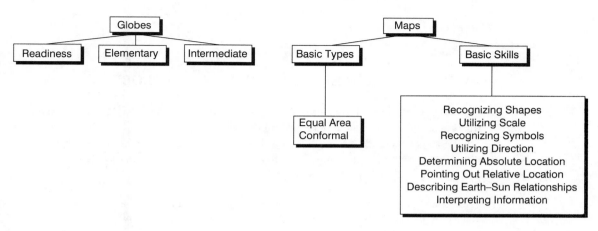

Figure 14–1
Understanding map and globe skills.

Chapter 14

Case Study

WHY SO MUCH EMPHASIS ON MAP AND GLOBE SKILLS?

Recently, the Director of Social Studies in the State Department of Education asked for written reactions from teachers regarding the adequacy of the social studies program in grades three to six. Ingrid Stein, who has been teaching sixth graders for many years, included these comments in the letter she wrote in response to the director's invitation.

> I am concerned about why there is so much emphasis on map and globe skills, particularly on manipulation of latitude and longitude, in the present program. Pupils encounter this kind of content over and over and over again. Why?
>
> Is this really a "critical life skill"? I doubt it. Certainly adults *do* need to know how to identify places on simple grid maps such as the highway maps available at service stations. However, I doubt if one person in a hundred, as part of his or her job responsibilities, is ever called on to use latitude and longitude. Mind you, I have no problem with teaching this content. My concerns relates to what I believe to be a heavy overemphasis on content that is only marginally important to the lives of most adult citizens.
>
> I have been doing a lot of thinking about why we ever began this business of redundant teaching of latitude and longitude in the elementary social studies program. I've concluded that it got started for reasons having nothing to do with the importance of the content. I think we teach this material because pupils' proficiency in manipulating latitude and longitude is easy to assess on standardized tests.
>
> Should "ease of test question construction" be a rationale for establishing instructional priorities in the elementary social studies program? I don't think so. For this reason, I recommend a reduction of emphasis on teaching about latitude and longitude and increased emphasis on more "meaty" academic content. This may pose problems for the test preparers. If that is so, it's a price we should pay. We need to teach content that is important, not content that is in the program because it is easy to test.

What Is Your Response?

Read this teacher's comments. Then, respond briefly to these questions:

1. This teacher suggests that some content is in the elementary program primarily because it is easy to test. From your own experience, were certain topics covered in schools you attended because it was easy for test developers to prepare relevant examination questions?
2. The writer of this letter implies that relatively few adults need to use latitude and longitude as they go about the business of living. Should social studies content be selected in terms of its relevance for the lives of adult citizens? Why, or why not?
3. One argument made in the letter is that latitude and longitude are "overtaught" in the elementary program. Is this sort of redundant teaching a general problem in elementary social studies programs or in other parts of the elementary curriculum? Can you cite examples to support your views?

4. Are there other arguments supporting Ms. Stein's views that too much time in elementary social studies classes is devoted to teaching about latitude and longitude? Would any of these arguments be stronger than the ones she presents in her letter?
5. If you were asked to react to the position taken in this letter, what would you say?

INTRODUCTION

Are the following statements "true" or "false"?

1. Reno, Nevada is west of Los Angeles, California.
2. The west coast of South America is in the same time zone as New York City (Eastern time zone).
3. If a person flew first from New York to San Francisco and then flew an equivalent distance west from San Francisco, he or she would be more than one-third of the way across the Pacific Ocean.
4. Because Juneau, Alaska, is much farther north, it has colder average January weather than Philadelphia, Pennsylvania.

Here are the answers: Numbers 1 and 2 are true, and numbers 3 and 4 are false. Do not feel bad if you missed a couple. Many adults find such questions difficult. They would be even more perplexing to elementary pupils who have little experience in working with map and globe skills. On the other hand, children and adults who are solidly grounded in these skills should be able to respond confidently to questions such as these. Before going on, let us pause a moment to explain the answers.

The question about Los Angeles and Reno is confusing because most people look at flat maps of the United States rather than at globes. Many of these maps distort the shape of the west coast. They make it look like a relatively straight north-south line. Since Los Angeles is on the coast and Reno is inland, it is only natural for people to conclude that Los Angeles must be farther west. In reality, the southern part of the west coast lies in a generally southeasterly direction from the northern part. This is why it is possible for Los Angeles to be east of Reno. The relationship is quite apparent on a globe. Perhaps because of the names of the two continents—North America and South America—many people *assume* that South America lies directly south of North America. It does lie south, but it is also considerably east of most of North America. This is why it is true that the west coast of South America lies in the same time zone as the eastern United States.

Children and adults, too, often greatly underestimate the size of the Pacific Ocean. The Pacific Ocean covers about one-third of the earth's surface. In very rough terms, it is about 10,000 miles (16,090 kilometers) from the west coast of the United States to the western boundaries of the Pacific. This is more than three times the distance from New York to San Francisco.

Many middle-grade children have some understanding of the parts of the globe, such as the equator and the poles. They also recognize that, on the average, the winter temperatures in the northern areas of the northern hemisphere are colder than in the southern areas. Many of these pupils, though, have not grasped that other local conditions, such as elevation, proximity to warm water, and wind patterns also influence temperature. They need this kind of understanding to correctly answer the question about the January temperatures in Juneau and Philadelphia.

Though it is much closer to the equator than Juneau, Philadelphia sits at the eastern edge of a large continental land mass, Because the prevailing winds here blow off the cold continental interior in the winter, the January weather can be very cold. Juneau, by way of contrast, sits on the coast and enjoys moderate winter temperatures because the prevailing west winds blow in off the warm Alaska current.

Map and globe skills taught in elementary social studies classes help pupils to understand the many important physical dimensions of the world. Technological advances draw the peoples of the earth closer together. Map and globe skills provide learners with analytical tools they can use to make sense of the world beyond their local communities. These skills have long received heavy emphasis in social studies programs, and this emphasis will certainly continue.

GLOBES

Globes deserve more attention than they receive in many social studies classrooms. Some of the misunderstandings learners have about the world might be eliminated if they were provided more experience in working with globes and relatively less in working with maps. Globes provide the best representation of our spherical planet. Maps, dealing in only two dimensions, distort shapes and areas; this distortion can lead to serious misconceptions.

For example, many flat world maps use a projection that makes Africa look smaller in area than North America. Surprisingly large numbers of middle grade pupils believe that this is true. Such maps also make Greenland look as large as South America. In fact, South America is nine times larger. Globes avoid these distortions. The relative sizes of the world land masses appear on the globe as they actually exist.

Though the increased use of globes can help pupils gain a better appreciation of size relationships, their use poses problems as well. Globes are bulky. Ideally, there should be enough globes so that no more than three or four pupils at a time need to work with one. In a class of twenty-five, this would mean six or more globes. Often, there is simply not sufficient space to accommodate such a large number.

There are serious problems associated with using globes to teach certain kinds of content. Globes include the entire earth's surface. Consequently, the individual areas of the earth appear to be quite small. If there is an interest in studying only a small part of the earth's surface, a globe might not be as good a choice as a map.

Suppose that a teacher wanted to teach something about Romania. Romania is about 425 miles (684 kilometers) across from east to west. On a standard 16-inch globe, Romania occupies less than one inch of space from east to west. Very little detail can be included in such a small space. A larger globe would involve other difficulties. A globe

---

BOX 14–1   **Children's Misinformation about World Geography**

Not long ago, a group of middle-grade pupils was surveyed about selected geographic top-ics. The following are some of the "facts" about the world many of these young people believed to be true.

1. On any map, the Atlantic always lies to the right.
2. It is impossible for a river ever to flow in a northerly direction.
3. In the northern hemisphere, every place north of location A has colder winters than does location A.
4. Africa is a country.
5. More Spanish-speaking people in the world live in Spain than in any other Span-ish-speaking country.
6. The most northern part of the 48 connected states is the northern tip of the state of Maine.
7. It is about the same distance from New York to London as from Seattle to Tokyo.

Think About This

1. Which of the above misinformation do you believe to be most widespread? Why do you think so?
2. In general, what are the sources of this misinformation?
3. As a teacher, what might you do to help learners correct such mistaken impressions?

---

large enough for Romania to be 36 inches across would be 48 feet in diameter. Such a globe would need to be installed in a special building.

Though they do have limitations when the purpose is to study small parts of the earth's surface, globes are ideally suited to helping learners grasp other kinds of con-tent. As noted previously, they are excellent vehicles for displaying the proper area and location arrangements. They can be used to help develop the locational skills that involve the use of latitude and longitude. The concept of the great circle route is much better taught by using a globe rather than a map. Earth–sun relationships—as they relate to issues such as day and night, the seasons of the year, the 24-hour day, and time zones—are best taught using globes.

Kinds of Globes

Three common globe types are found in elementary schools: (1) readiness globes, (2) elementary globes, and (3) intermediate globes.

Readiness Globes
Readiness globes are designed to introduce basic information about globes. They are used mostly in the primary grades. Bright colors are often used to depict the individual countries. The detail does not go much beyond labels for the major countries, the

names of capital cities and other large population centers, the names of major oceans and seas, and the labels for the equator and, sometimes, for the Tropic of Cancer and the Tropic of Capricorn. Occasionally, a few additional details are found.

Even readiness globes sometimes contain a bewildering array of information for very young children. Some pupils in the early primary grades experience great difficulty in distinguishing between the areas of land and water. One teacher reported having a readiness globe that used the color blue to depict certain political areas as well as water areas. One child in the class described Wyoming as a major lake!

Elementary Globes

Elementary globes are good for use in fourth, fifth, and sixth grades. They include *much* more detail than readiness globes. This detail may overwhelm children in the primary grades. The additional information often includes the lines of latitude and longitude, the details regarding the scale of the globe, the indications of major world wind

Figure 14–2
An **analemma** is used to indicate the latitudes at which the noonday sun is directly overhead on each day of the year. The northern limit of the analemma is the Tropic of Cancer, where the sun is directly overhead on June 21–22. The southern limit is the Tropic of Capricorn, where the sun is directly overhead on December 21–22. The sun is directly overhead at noon at the equator twice each year: once on March 21–22 and again on September 21–22. The apparent movement of the sun is a result of the earth's annual movement around the sun. Because the earth's axis always points to the North Star, at some times of the year the sun's rays strike most directly at points south of the equator, at the equator, or north of the equator. To receive a clearer picture of why this happens, see Figure 14–9. Some teachers find that pupils enjoy pointing out where the sun will be overhead at noon on their birthdays.

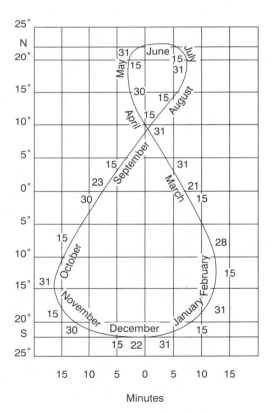

patterns, and the depictions of the directions of the major ocean currents. They often will include the locations of many more cities and towns than will readiness globes.

Intermediate Globes

Intermediate globes are best suited for use with older, intermediate-grades learners. They include even more detail than elementary globes. Many of them, for example, will include the notations of world time zones. Many, too, will include an analemma. An *analemma* is the figure-eight-shaped figure that cuts through the equator (Figure 14–2). It indicates the locations where the sun is directly overhead at noon on each day of the year.

Some intermediate globes also have a horizon ring. A *horizon ring* is a circular band that surrounds the globe. It has the degrees marked off on its inner surface. The globe can be rotated at will within the ring. By using the degree markers, pupils can engage in relatively sophisticated calculations of degree differences and time differences between pairs of locations on the globe.

Parts of the Globe That Need to Be Emphasized

The information presented on globes is of no use until youngsters understand what it means. There are substantial differences in the types and amounts of information introduced on various kinds of globes. By the end of their elementary social studies experience, youngsters should recognize the functions of features of the globe such as the equator, the Tropic of Cancer, the Tropic of Capricorn, the North Pole, the South Pole, the International Date Line, the Prime Meridian, the horizon ring, the distance scale, the world time zones, and the analemma.

They should be able to apply basic globe skills to solve problems such as finding locations using latitude and longitude, explaining the seasonal changes in terms of earth–sun relationships, pointing out the function of the international dateline, and explaining the time difference between selected pairs of world locations. Examples of how proficiency in these skills might be developed are introduced later in the chapter.

MAPS

Maps are used more frequently than globes in most elementary social studies classrooms. Properly used, maps can be very effective instructional resources. They can be designed to accomplish many purposes, they cost less than globes, and they do not consume much storage space.

The strengths of the map as a teaching devise need to be counterbalanced by an understanding that maps are an imperfect representation of the earth. A three-dimensional surface cannot be transformed into a two-dimensional surface without distortion. To illustrate how this might happen when explaining maps to children, some teachers carefully remove half of the peel from an orange. By placing the peel on a flat surface and pushing down on the peel, it can be illustrated that something must "give" before the spherical surface can be converted to a flat plane.

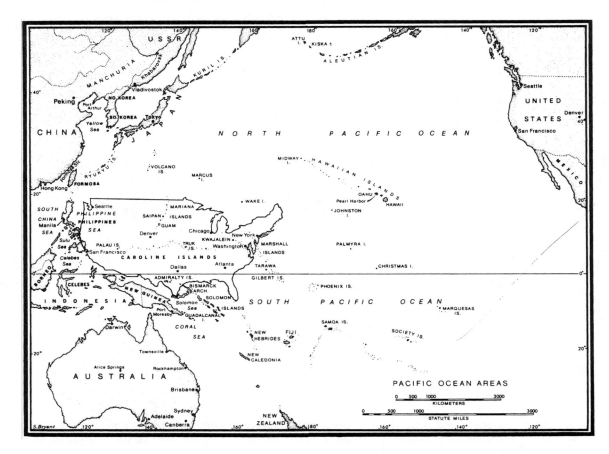

Figure 14–3
General Douglas MacArthur's wall map. General MacArthur had this map in his headquarters during World War II, and he used it to illustrate the vast size of the Pacific Region to his incoming officers.
Source: William Manchester, *American Caesar: Douglas MacArthur: 1880–1964*. New York: Dell Publishing Co., copyright © 1978 by William Manchester. Illustration section between pp. 320 and 321. Reprinted with permission.

Many maps illustrate only a portion of the earth's surface. A survey of the wall maps permanently on display in elementary classrooms in this country would probably reveal more United States maps than maps of other parts of the world. Pupils' continuous exposure to such maps has the potential to lead to false conclusions. The widespread notion among middle-grade pupils that "the Atlantic is always found on the right-hand side of a map" may be the result of years of seeing it so positioned on U.S. maps attached to classroom walls.

Constant exposure to a large wall map of the United States also has the potential to confuse pupils about the proper size relationships among world places. Elementary school children often tend to overestimate the physical size of the United States (this is also a problem with some adults). This results in their failure to appreciate the magnitude and importance of other places in the world. For example, one of the authors was once amused on a flight to Hawaii by a fellow passenger. After crossing the Pacific coast, the passenger observed that the stewardess had better serve the meals so that there would be time to eat before landing. Upon the approach to Honolulu, he mused that perhaps he would hop on out to Japan since he was so close!

During World War II, General Douglas MacArthur recognized this problem. He was concerned that many incoming officers to the Pacific Theater of the war did not recognize the huge size of the Pacific area. To help the officers grasp this point, he had a special map prepared to illustrate the size of the United States relative to the area of the Western Pacific Ocean. This map is reproduced in Figure 14–3.

World maps are a common wall feature in elementary school classrooms. To some degree, individual maps reflect characteristics of one of these two basic types: conformal maps and equal area maps.

Conformal Maps

Conformal maps are prepared in such a way that the shapes of the land areas, for example Australia, are the same on the map as on a globe. An important example of a conformal map is the *Mercator projection* map, named for a famous map maker who lived in the sixteenth century (Figure 14–4).

To understand how a Mercator projection map is made, imagine a clear glass globe with land areas outlined in dark ink and a tiny light in the center. The globe is placed on a table so a line passing through the North Pole, the light in the center, and the South Pole is perpendicular to the tabletop. A cylinder of paper is slipped over the globe. The light source causes shadows to be cast on the paper cylinder from the boundaries of the land areas. These shadows are carefully traced by the map maker. When the cylinder is unwrapped, the result is a Mercator projection map of the world. (In reality, the process is done mathematically. But the principles are as described here.)

The Mercator projection produces a world map that maintains accurate shapes of land masses. However, relative sizes of places are not accurately portrayed; areas of places more distant from the equator are less accurately displayed than are areas closer to the equator. Places in extreme northern and southern locations are depicted as much larger than they appear on a globe.

The distortion in land areas on Mercator projection maps can lead to unfortunate misunderstandings. As noted, pupils who do not often work with globes and who see a Mercator map every day often mistakenly conclude that Greenland is as large as or even larger than South America. Greenland's apparent size on a Mercator projection map is a result of its great distance from the equator. South America, on the other hand, lies across the equator and hence is relatively undistorted.

When conformal maps are the only world maps available, it is particularly important to give pupils opportunities to work with globes, and to explain to them why the sizes of land masses in extreme northern and southern regions are distorted on Mercator

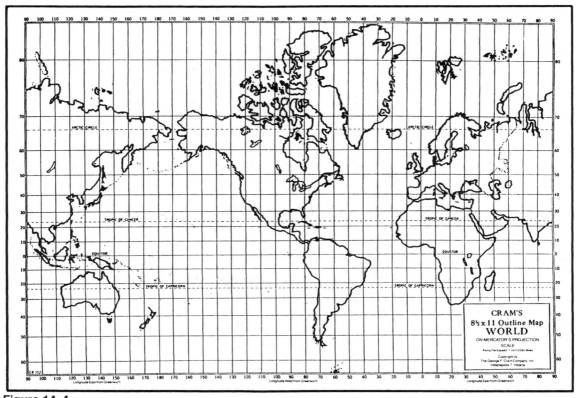

Figure 14–4

An example of a conformal world map: Mercator's projection.

Source: Copyright George F. Cram Co., Inc., Indianapolis, IN. Reprinted by permission.

maps. Pupils should be given opportunities to compare and contrast globes and world maps so they can appreciate that conformal maps distort sizes of some land masses.

Modifications of the Mercator projection reduce some of these extreme area distortions. In general, though, these modifications give up the Mercator projection's total consistency with the shape of land masses as depicted on the globe as a tradeoff for less distortion in area. Such maps are not truly conformal.

Equal Area Maps

Equal area maps of the world are drawn in such a way that the relative size of land masses, as reflected on the globe, are preserved. As noted previously, Greenland is approximately one-ninth the size of South America. On an equal area map of the world, Greenland and South America are drawn to reflect this true size relationship. Compare areas of Greenland and South America as they appear in the Mercator projection map in Figure 14–4 and in the Robinson's (equal area projection) map in Figure 14–5.

Figure 14–5

An example of an equal area world map: Robinson's projection.

Source: Reprinted with permission from Edward B. Espenshade, Jr., ed., *Goode's World Atlas*. 18th ed., p. xi. Chicago: Rand McNally, 1990.

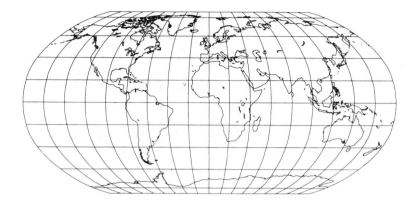

Preserving proper size relationships among land areas requires that some distortion occur in their shapes. It is not possible for an equal area map to be drawn so that all shapes are as they appear on the globe.

There are relatively few equal area world maps hanging in classrooms as compared to conformal world maps. Traditionally, educators (many with little formal training in issues associated with maps and globes) have opted for maps featuring land masses shaped as they appear on globes.

Because of the enormous distortions of areas of some important world land masses on conformal maps, equal area maps should be available in every elementary classroom. Ideally, each classroom should have one world map of each type. Exposure to both conformal and equal area maps and to globes provides children with a solid grounding in relative sizes and areas of land masses. Such lessons, too, reinforce the idea that all renderings of a sphere onto a flat surface result in important distortions.

BASIC MAP AND GLOBE SKILLS

Eight basic map and globe skills are of interest to the elementary social studies teacher:

- Recognizing shapes
- Utilizing scale
- Recognizing symbols
- Utilizing direction
- Determining absolute location
- Pointing out relative location
- Describing earth–sun relationships
- Interpreting the information on maps and globes

In the subsections that follow, we introduce basic information about each basic skill. In addition, we provide ideas about sequencing instruction from the early grades, through the middle grades, and into the upper grades.

Recognizing Shapes

Recognizing shapes is one of the most fundamental map and globe skills. Though the skill may appear to be simple or even simplistic, many sophisticated analyses in geography require a grasp of the importance of physical shapes, particularly those of land masses. For example, to appreciate that a narrow peninsula may have a climate that varies dramatically from that of a central location at the heart of a continent, a person must know what a peninsula is. The kinds of learning associated with recognizing shapes increase in complexity as children move through the elementary program.

Utilizing Scale

Scale is an abstract and very difficult concept. Teachers often find that teaching students to understand and use this concept is one of their most challenging assignments (see Box 14–2). Scale is difficult because it requires the concurrent understanding of two subordinate understandings. Each of these can frustrate pupils, especially those in the early elementary grades.

First, to appreciate scale, a person needs to know that geographical features (mountains, rivers, oceans, and so forth) can be visually depicted in a convenient way. For example, it is possible to represent a mountain by taking a photograph of the mountain. Learners need to grasp that the mountain is real; they need to know the photograph is real; and, most importantly, they need to understand that there is a connection between the mountain as depicted in the photograph and the actual mountain itself.

BOX 14–2   **Helping Young Children Learn about Scale**

Scale is a challenging concept for children in the early grades. Some teachers have found it useful to take pictures of familiar objects in the classroom using a camera that produces instant prints. They ask students to measure the object as it exists in "real life" and the object as depicted in the photograph, then ask how many heights of the object in the photograph would be required to reach the same height as the real object.

This exercise can help learners grasp the idea that multiples of units on a scale can be used to determine how large something is in reality. It is often useful to take pictures of similar objects at different distances. This helps develop the idea that scales can change.

Think About This

1. What major misconceptions do you think children in the early grades might have at the beginning of this exercise? Why do you think so?
2. What kinds of objects in the classroom might be best suited as subjects for a photograph used to introduce the idea of scale?
3. What difficulties might you expect learners to have in understanding the scale differences revealed by photographs of the same object taken at different distances? How might these difficulties be overcome?

Second, a child looking at a photograph of a mountain needs to recognize that there is a knowable physical size relationship between the size of the mountain as it exists on the earth's surface and the size as it is depicted in the photograph. A sound understanding of the principle of using small, convenient representations as reliable indicators of the size of large phenomena is fundamental to an appreciation of scale. Pupils who lack this basic knowledge have a difficult time grasping the idea that the scales on maps and globes can be used to make accurate statements about the actual sizes of the physical features of the earth.

Recognizing Symbols

Both maps and globes feature many symbols. These symbols are a convenient shorthand representation for the kinds of phenomena that exist in the world. For people who understand them, they efficiently communicate a tremendous amount of information. But for individuals who do not know what they mean, they are confusing marks that can lead to serious misunderstandings. Because symbols are so basic to an understanding of maps and globes, recognizing symbols has long been recognized as one of the most important map and globe skills.

Pupils must recognize that symbols represent real objects. Maps and globes in their entireties are symbols. They are representations of part or all of the earth's surface. It is important that pupils understand that even the colors on maps and globes function as symbols. Younger pupils are sometimes confused about this. When they see Kansas depicted in orange, they may receive the impression that everything in Kansas literally is orange. We need to be careful to explain the symbolic nature of maps as a whole as well as the meaning of the more specific symbols indicating things such as airports, highways, boundary lines, and large cities.

Lesson Idea 14–1

LEARNING ABOUT MAP SYMBOLS

Grade Level: 1–3

Objectives: Pupils will create symbols to represent real objects.

Suggested Procedure: Six ideas for helping beginning learners understand map symbols follow.

1. Cut out well-known symbols for businesses and other organizations from newspapers and magazines. For example, you might select symbols representing the Olympics, the United Nations, Volkswagen, Texaco, and many other organizations, firms, and groups. Ask how many youngsters recognize each symbol. Explain why symbols are used (to save time, to provide for ready recognition, and so forth). Does the school have a mascot? Is there a symbol that repre-

Creating their own map legend is a useful strategy for helping pupils learn map symbols.

sents a favorite sports team? Lead into the idea that map makers and globe makers use many symbols.

2. Let pupils decide on five new clubs that should be started in the school. Once they have identified these groups, set them to work developing a symbol for each club. Sometimes it works well to organize learners into teams for this activity. Follow up with a discussion about what goes into a good symbol. (It is easy to remember, and quickly communicates a great deal of information about the group or thing for which it stands.)

3. To prepare children to work comfortably with the symbols that will appear on the maps or globe they will use, develop sets of flashcards. On one side will be the symbol. On the other side will be the thing for which the symbol stands. These cards can help youngsters grasp the meaning of symbols.

4. Another technique to help pupils learn the meanings of symbols used on maps involves the use of simple two-part puzzles. These can be made from construction paper. From sources such as *National Geographic*, find pictures of things that are depicted by symbols on maps. Paste a picture on the top half of a sheet of construction paper. On the bottom half, draw the symbol used for the thing depicted. Then cut the

Figure 14–6
Example of a simple symbol for a church. Pupils put the two parts of this simple puzzle together in an exercise designed to help them see the connection between the symbol and the object for which it stands.

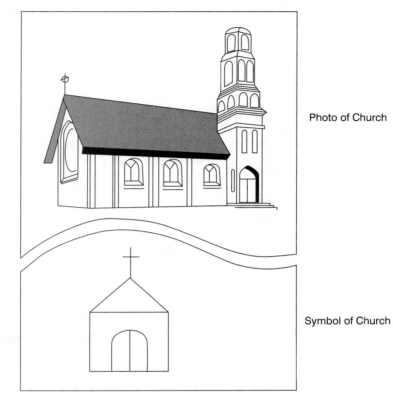

Photo of Church

Symbol of Church

sheet into two parts. Give pupils a mixed group of top and bottom sheets, and have them try to fit the sheets together by using their knowledge of symbols. When the sheets fit properly, they know they have matched the symbol to the thing it depicts. See Figure 14–6.

5. Ask pupils to develop symbols for the school desks or tables, for the teacher's desk, for the doors, and for the chalkboards. Then give them a blank outline map of the classroom. Ask them to use their symbols to indicate the locations of these objects. Display the finished products, and ask several volunteers to explain their maps.

6. Have pupils create a simple map featuring a key that explains the symbols they choose to include. Ask them to explain what they might see if they took a trip along a specified route depicted on the map. Remind them to refer to the meanings of the symbols provided in the key. An example of such a map appears in Figure 14–7.

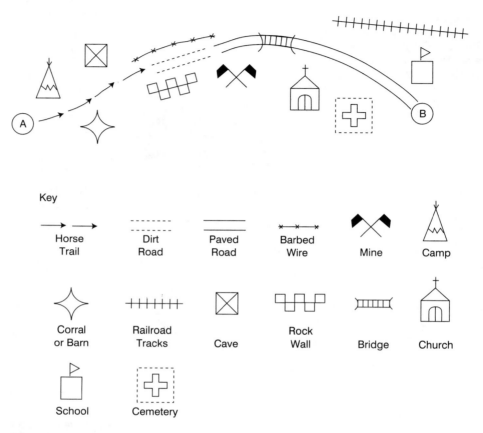

Figure 14–7
Example of a pupil-produced map using simple symbols.

Directions: Describe a trip a person might make along this route, starting at point A and finishing at point B. Use the key below to interpret the symbols on the map.

Recognizing shapes, utilizing scale, and recognizing symbols all have different educational emphases at different grade levels. These emphases are summarized in Table 14–1.

Utilizing Direction

The proper use of globes and maps depends on an ability to become properly oriented to direction. A sound understanding of the major and intermediate compass directions is basic to pinpointing locations. It is particularly important that learners master and use the concept of direction before working with wall maps. Otherwise, students will tend to

Table 14–1
The grade-level emphases for (1) recognizing shapes, (2) utilizing scale, and (3) recognizing symbols.

	Kindergarten to Second Grade Emphases	Third to Fourth Grade Emphases	Fifth to Sixth Grade Emphases
Recognizing Shapes	Introduction to basic information about shape. Recognition that the earth is basically round. Recognition of the basic shapes of the continents and oceans (near end of second grade).	Recognition of the shapes of smaller land masses, such as islands, peninsulas, and isthmuses. Recognition of the shapes of smaller bodies of water, such as lakes, bays, and sounds.	Recognition of certain kinds of map distortion. Identification of the patterns of flow of the major rivers. Identification of the shapes of the major physical regions.
Utilizing Scale	Introduction of the basic concepts such as "larger" and "smaller." Recognition of the simple increments of measure (city blocks, for example). Identification of the objects of different sizes in pictures.	Utilization of the scale on simple maps. Solution of simple distance problems using scale. Recognition that scale may vary from map to map and globe to globe.	Utilization of the many kinds of scales. Recognition that the amount of detail on a map varies with its scale.
Recognizing Symbols	Recognition of the meanings of common signs (stop signs, for example). Recognition that some colors on maps are regularly used to represent land and water. Recognition that symbols stand for things in the real world.	Utilization of symbols for the major landscape features on maps and globes. Recognition of the traditional symbols for cities, railroads, rivers, and highways.	Utilization of the symbols on special purpose maps. Recognition that the same symbol may mean different things on different maps and globes.

Figure 14–8
An example of a grid activity to help pupils learn how to find places when given the coordinates of latitude and longitude. Directions: Find the secret word by placing an *X* in each of these squares: C2, C5, C8; D2, D5, D8; E2, E3, E4, E5, E8; F2, F5, F8; G2, G5, G8.

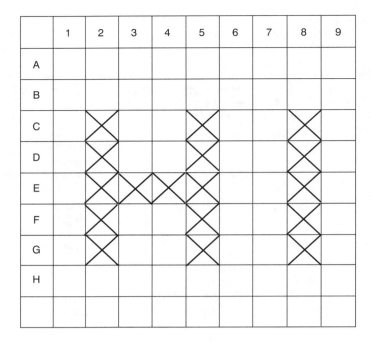

use such terms as "up" and "down" when referring to "north" and "south," and "right" and "left" when referring to "east" and "west." These inappropriate terms can contribute to the development of inaccurate information (the Pacific Ocean always lies to the left).

Determining Absolute Location

Determining absolute location requires pupils to locate any point on the earth's surface. To adequately perform the skill, learners must be familiar with the lines of latitude and longitude. Specifically, they must understand how a longitude–latitude grid system can be used to identify the "address" of every location on earth. Generally, teachers have pupils work with very simple grids before they introduce the global system of latitude and longitude (Figure 14–8; see also Lesson Idea 14–2).

Pointing Out Relative Location

Relative location refers to the location of one place in terms of one or more other places. When Chicago is described as being north of Houston, east of Omaha, and west of New York, we are referring to Chicago's relative location.

Many elementary social studies programs begin building the skill of pointing out relative location by helping pupils to first recognize their relative location with regard to familiar places. For example, we might help them understand the relative location of the school by pointing out its position in terms of nearby parks and homes. Often the local community is pinpointed by referring to its location relative to other places in the state. Later, we might go on to reference its location to places in the nation and the world.

Lesson Idea 14–2

LEARNING ABOUT ABSOLUTE LOCATION

Grade Level: 2–4

Objectives: Pupils will apply knowledge of the grid system to locate places on maps.

Suggested Procedure: Five ideas for helping beginners learn about relative location follow.

1. Prepare a simple grid with squares along the top identified by numbers and squares along the side identified by letters. Determine in advance which squares, when colored in, will spell a word. Give learners the directions to shade in squares that are identified by coordinates. (Shade in these squares: A-1, A-3, B-2, B-3, B-4, C-1, C-5, C-6, and so forth.) When pupils have completed the exercise, they should be able to see the secret word. See the sample provided in Figure 14–8.

2. Provide children with a simple outline map of the world. The map should include the lines of latitude and longitude, and a simple compass rose. Play a Find the Continent game with the members of the class. Give map coordinates. Then ask pupils to name the nearest continent. (What is the nearest continent to 30° south latitude and 150° east longitude? [Australia])

3. In a learning center, provide several short books about various countries of the world. Inside each book, neatly print a coordinate of latitude and longitude that would fall within the boundaries of the country about which the book is written. Provide pupils with an outline map of the world featuring the political boundaries of the nations. Ask them to use the latitude and longitude coordinate to identify the location of the country the book describes, then shade in or color this country on the outline map.

4. In a learning center, place several newspaper articles with datelines from a number of cities around the world. Attach each article to a sturdy piece of paper. Above the article, write the latitude and longitude of the dateline city. Then have pupils use a globe or an atlas to locate the city.

Table 14–2
The grade-level emphases for (1) utilizing direction, (2) determining absolute location, and (3) pointing out relative location.

	Kindergarten to Second Grade Emphases	Third to Fourth Grade Emphases	Fifth to Sixth Grade Emphases
Utilizing direction	Introduction to the four cardinal compass directions. Introduction, very basic, to latitude and longitude (referred to at this level as north-to-south lines and east-to-west lines).	Description of the locations of continents in terms of their directional locations from one another. Location of the Prime Meridian. Utilization of a compass to orient a map, and of the compass rose on a map. Introduction to the intermediate directions.	Recognition of the difference between true and magnetic North. Utilization of intermediate direction to provide precise information about locations and paths of travel.
Determining absolute location	Utilization of relative terms such as "right," "left," "near," "far," "up," "down," "back," "front." Location of the places on a globe as being north or south of the equator.	Introduction to the use of grid systems. Location of the places on maps and globes using simple grid systems.	Location of places using the coordinates of latitude and longitude. Identification of the degree position of important lines of latitude including the equator, the Arctic and Antarctic circles, and the Tropics of Cancer and Capricorn.
Pointing out relative location	Description of one place in a room in terms of the other places in the room. Identification of the location of the school in terms of the other parts of the community.	Description of the location of the state within the nation. Identification of the local community in terms of its location in the state and nation.	Location of the local community relative to any other place on the globe. Description of the relative location of any two points on the globe.

   5. Write an itinerary about a journey to various cities in the world. Instead of naming the cities, identify them only by coordinates of latitude and longitude. Give these to pupils. Ask them to name the cities and plot the route the traveler took on a world outline map. Here are some possibilities:
   - Latitude 22° 53' 43" S, Longitude 43° 13' 22" W (Rio de Janeiro, Brazil)
   - Latitude 62° 28' 15" N, Longitude 114° 22' 00" W (Yellowknife, Northwest Territories, Canada)
   - Latitude 48° 50' 14" N, Longitude 2° 20' 14" E (Paris, France)

Different aspects of utilizing direction and of determining absolute and relative location are emphasized when these concepts are taught at different grade levels. These emphases are summarized in Table 14–2.

Describing Earth–Sun Relationships

Proper understanding of earth–sun relationships is an essential ingredient of knowledge regarding diverse topics such as global time, the seasons, and the changing annual wind patterns. Many elementary youngsters find content related to earth–sun relationships to be difficult.

Part of the problem is our language. We speak of the sun "rising" and "setting." This terminology is based on an illusion that makes sense. As residents of the earth's surface, we are not physically aware that the globe is spinning on its axis. Hence, the "rising" and "setting" terminology does accurately describe what we see, but this language does not properly describe what is going on. Adults (most of them, at least) know that the sun does not move, but rather that the earth's spinning only makes it appear to do so. Younger elementary children lack this understanding. Many of them really believe that it is the sun that does the moving.

As they progress through the elementary program, learners are exposed to the concepts of the "seasons." They are taught that the seasons change because the angle of the sun's rays strikes some parts of the earth's surface more directly at certain times of the year than at others (Figure 14–9). Many children who grasp this basic idea have trouble understanding exactly how this happens. Some conclude erroneously that the earth wobbles back and forth on its axis, thus causing a change in where the sun's rays strike most directly. Teachers find they must work very hard if pupils are to grasp exactly how the seasonal change can occur without "global wobble."

Interpreting Information on Maps and Globes

The skill of interpreting information on maps and globes is the broadest of them all. It is perhaps the most important for elementary social studies programs because it establishes a purpose for many of the other map and globe skills. Unless programs involve

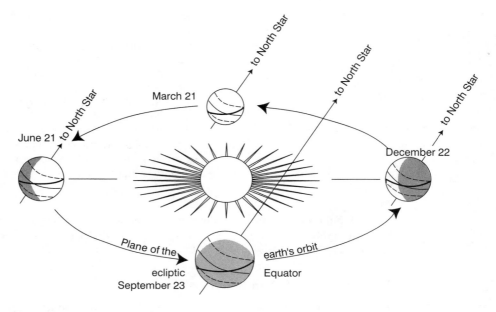

Figure 14–9
The location of the earth in relation to the sun on key dates. Many elementary pupils have difficulty accepting the idea that the earth does not swing back and forth or wobble on its axis. A figure such as this can help to explain what actually happens. The earth's axis always points toward the North Star. Note that the sun directly strikes its surface at different points at different times of the year.

pupils in using the other skills, they may see the instruction that focuses on these skills as boring and directed toward no useful end. But when these skills are used to produce new information, pupils tend to appreciate their importance. Table 14–3 summarizes the different grade-level emphases used when teaching pupils how to describe earth–sun relationships and when teaching them how to interpret map and globe information.

TEACHING ALL OF THE SKILLS AT EACH GRADE LEVEL

Sometimes, new teachers assume that the more basic skills (such as, perhaps, symbol recognition) should be taught to younger children and that these learners should not be exposed to the more advanced skills. There are two difficulties with this approach. First, there is nothing inherently either easy or difficult about any of these skills. Each can be taught at varying levels of complexity. A teacher would not expect kindergarten children and sixth graders to engage in similar learning activities or to develop similar depths of understanding about a given skill. Yet each group should be exposed to appropriate learning experiences for each skill.

Table 14–3
The grade-level emphases for (1) describing earth–sun relationships and (2) interpreting
the information on maps and globes

	Kindergarten to Second Grade Emphases	Third to Fourth Grade Emphases	Fifth to Sixth Grade Emphases
Describing earth–sun relationships	Recognition of the terms "summer," "fall,""winter," "spring," "day," and "night." Identification of the direction of sunrise and sunset. Description of how the turning of the earth causes night and day.	Description of how the earth moves around the sun. Description of the inclination of the earth on its axis.	Description of the relationship of the sun to the equator, Tropic of Cancer, Tropic of Capricorn, Arctic Circle, and Antarctic Circle. Recognition that the globe is divided into 360 degrees. Recognition that the earth has twenty-four time zones that are each fifteen degrees wide. Utilization of the analemma to determine where the sun's rays strike the earth most directly on each day of the year.
Interpreting the information on maps and globes	Interpretation of the information from pictures and simple maps. Recognition that no one, not even an astronaut in space, can see the whole earth at one time. Construction and interpretation of simple local neighborhood and community maps.	Preparation of more complex local community maps and the interpretation of information contained on these maps. Description of the population distributions and terrain features on maps. Explanation of the basic causes of climate by referring to the information on maps.	Prediction about the probable climate of a place by viewing maps to determine its elevation, proximity to ocean currents, latitude, and continental or coastal position. Explanation of the geographical constraints on historical or current events through reference to maps. Prediction of elevation change by examining river flow direction on maps.

There is a variety of globes. The kind of globe used in the classroom should be appropriate for the developmental level of the pupils.

Second, when teachers of younger children decide to omit the teaching of a "difficult" skill, they often eliminate that of interpreting information. This is a serious mistake. This skills allows pupils to put to work the other skills they have learned as they try to solve problems.

Interpreting exercises help pupils see a purpose for lessons that require them to master map and globe skills. These activities extend their abilities to make sense out of their world. If such activities are eliminated in the early grades, many pupils will see little use in learning the other basic map and globe skills. As a result, teachers may face serious motivational problems, which can inhibit learning.

KEY IDEAS IN SUMMARY

1. Many adults have confused ideas about locations of places on the globe. Elementary pupils are even more likely to insufficiently grasp the map and globe skills needed for the proper understanding of geographical location. Some misunderstandings result from a complete lack of information, others from inadequate information. For example, large wall maps sometimes distort shapes and sizes of land masses.

2. Globes should receive more attention in elementary social studies classrooms. Only the globe shows places on earth with a minimum of shape and size distortion and with accurate relative placement of water and land areas. To be useful as teaching tools, there should be at least one globe available for every three or four pupils.

3. Globes have disadvantages. They are bulky. They are rather expensive. They do not lend themselves well to teaching certain kinds of content. For example, if a teacher wanted to teach about a relatively small area, perhaps the state of South Carolina, the area of interest would be too small on a globe to be of any practical value. A globe large enough to display South Carolina at a size sufficient for learners to see easily might be too large to fit in the classroom.

4. Three common types of globes are found in elementary schools. These are (1) readiness globes (2) elementary globes, and (3) intermediate globes. Readiness globes include only basic information. Elementary globes include latitude, longitude, and other details not included on readiness globes. Intermediate globes include even more information.

5. Maps are useful for teaching certain kinds of content, such as the study of relatively small areas. Typically they are less expensive than globes, and are much easier to store.

6. Because they attempt to represent a sphere on a flat surface, all maps include distortions. On conformal world maps, shapes of land areas are as they are on the globe, but the areas of land masses distant from the equator are greatly distorted. On equal area world maps, areas of land masses are consistent with areas as they appear on the globe, but shapes may be distorted. Teachers need to instruct students about the problem of distortion. Ideally, students should have opportunities to compare and contrast depictions of places in the world as they appear on the globe, on a conformal world map, and on an equal area world map.

7. There are eight basic map and globe skills. They are (1) recognizing shapes, (2) utilizing scale, (3) recognizing symbols, (4) utilizing direction, (5) determining absolute location, (6) pointing out relative location, (7) describing earth-sun relationships, and (8) interpreting information on maps and globes.

8. It is desirable to introduce all eight map and globe skills at each level of the elementary school program. The skills remain common throughout the program, but the activities used to introduce and reinforce them change with grade levels.

9. It is especially important that pupils have opportunities to use map and globe skills to solve problems. Such experiences help establish the importance of these skills. Additionally, they can extend learners' sense of understanding of the world and, by so doing, build interest in other aspects of the social studies program.

CHAPTER REFLECTIONS

Directions: Now that you have finished reading the chapter, reread the case study at the beginning. Then answer these questions.

1. What factors contribute to misunderstandings many pupils have about the relative locations of places on the earth's surface?

2. What are some advantages of using globes when providing learners with basic understandings about shapes and sizes of different lands?

3. What are the characteristics of readiness globes, elementary globes, and intermediate globes?

4. What are general characteristics of conformal world maps and equal area world maps?

5. What are the eight basic map skills?

6. Suppose you were challenged to defend the inclusion of map and globe skills instruction in the elementary social studies program. How would you respond?

7. In the past, some people have said that the skill of interpreting information on maps and globes is too sophisticated for pupils in kindergarten to second grade. How do you feel about the suggestion that this skill be reserved for older learners? Why do you take this position?

8. Many pupils have a difficult time understanding that the earth does not wobble back and forth on its axis. The axis always points to the North Star, regardless of the time of year. What might you do to help learners grasp this point?

9. Suppose you were assigned to teach map and globe skills to a group of third graders. What would you use maps for? What would you use globes for?

10. Children in the elementary grades often greatly underestimate the size of the continent of Africa. What might you do to help them understand the size of this continent relative to the size of North America? Relative to the size of the United States?

EXTENDING UNDERSTANDING AND SKILL

1. For each of the eight basic map and globe skills, prepare a lesson directed at the age group you would like to teach. Discuss your suggestions with others in your class and with your instructor.

2. Interview four or five pupils who are at a grade level you would like to teach. Ask questions to determine the accuracy of their information about subjects such as (1) the relative locations of major U.S. cities, (2) the directions of flow of major U.S. rivers, and (3) the relative sizes of the continents. Share your findings with others in your class.

3. Look at at least two elementary social studies textbooks. Do a content analysis of each to determine how much attention is paid to developing pupils' understandings of the eight basic map and globe skills. Prepare a short paper in which you describe the relative attention paid to each skill.

4. Earth–sun relationships are difficult for many pupils to understand. With one or two other students, gather needed materials and prepare a lesson that you would use to teach earth–sun relationships to a grade level of your choice. Deliver the lesson to your class and solicit suggestions for its improvement.

5. Prepare a complete plan for a field trip designed to strengthen learners' basic map and globe skills. Identify the preplanning procedures, learning objectives, teacher activities, pupil activities, and evaluation procedures. Turn your plan into your instructor for review.

15

SOCIAL STUDIES AND THE INTEGRATED CURRICULUM

CHAPTER GOALS

This chapter provides information to help the reader:

- state the rationale for an integrated curriculum,
- define the steps in preparing an integrated curriculum,
- identify how different subjects can be integrated with social studies,
- state how children's literature can be used as an integrating focus,
- define *readers' theater*,
- plan how to teach study skills appropriate for helping pupils during the pre-reading, reading, and postreading phases, and
- explain how each of the seven language functions can be integrated into social studies lessons.

CHAPTER STRUCTURE

Introduction
Choosing Appropriate Themes
> Feasible
> Worthwhile
> Contextualized
> Meaningful

Mapping the Integration
Integrating Units Around Selections of Children's Literature
The Arts
Music
Mathematics
Science and Technology
Language Arts
> Readers' Theater
> Reading Study Skills
> Prereading Techniques
> *The Structured Overview / ReQuest*
> During-Reading Techniques
> *Visual Frameworks / Multipass Reading*
> Postreading Techniques
> *Graphic Post-Organizers / Interaction Frames*
> Writing and the Social Studies
> *Instrumental Function / Regulatory Function / Interactional Function / Personal Function / Heuristic Function / Representational Function / Imaginative Function*

Key Ideas in Summary
Chapter Reflections
Extending Understanding and Skill
References

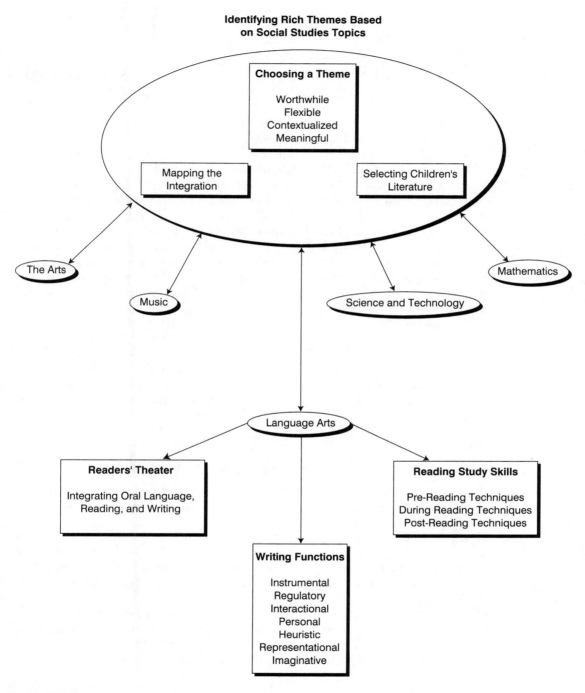

Figure 15–1
Social studies and the integrated curriculum.

Chapter 15

Case Study

SHOULD TIME BE DEVOTED IN SOCIAL STUDIES LESSONS TO IMPROVING PUPILS' WRITING SKILLS?

Two fourth-grade teachers recently had this discussion as they sat at a table waiting for a meeting of the district's Central Curriculum Council to start.

"The guidelines we adopted last year calling on us to emphasize development of writing skills are really helpful." The speaker was Loren McPhee, a teacher at Persimmon Creek Elementary School. "Writing ties in particularly well with my social studies lessons. I've found it easy to get students to write about interesting social studies content. They like writing paragraphs about what life was like in the Old West. They're getting much more experience in developing their writing skills than they used to get. I think these people will turn out to be much better writers given this kind of additional writing practice."

Loren's remarks were directed to Moira O'Roark, a third-grade teacher at Bluff Point Elementary School. After listening politely to Loren, Moira shook her head and said, "I'm sorry, I just don't go along with you on this. This 'writing across the curriculum' business sounds good in theory, but in practice it doesn't make much sense. Every time we ask students to write during a social studies lesson we are using valuable time. This time could better be used to present new social studies content. It seems to me that writing instruction is something we should do when we teaching reading and language arts. When we're teaching science, we should concentrate on science. When we're teaching social studies, content that is clearly related to the social studies content should be our focus. Too much time spent on writing skills robs pupils of other valuable learning experiences."

What Is Your Response?

Read over these teachers' positions. Then, respond briefly to these questions:

1. "Writing across the curriculum" (the idea that some writing instruction should occur in all subject areas) has many supporters. How do you feel about this idea? On what do you base your opinion?
2. Loren McPhee suggests that writing instruction complements instruction focusing on more traditional social studies content. How can this be? Do you agree with this view?
3. Do you think a directive to include some writing instruction in all elementary subject areas could be implemented more easily in some subjects than others? Explain your answer.
4. Moira O'Roark argues that imposition of a requirement to teach writing when also teaching subjects other than reading and language arts is irresponsible. What is the basis for her position? Do you agree or disagree with it? Why?
5. Suppose you had been present when Loren and Moira were having this discussion. What would you have said if they had asked your opinion?

INTRODUCTION

Traditional school organizational patterns allocate specific time slots to each subject. Reading is taught during the reading period, social studies during the social studies period, and mathematics during the mathematics period. Today this pattern is being questioned. Should pupils be concerned with correct spelling only during the typical Friday spelling test? Should they be concerned with good writing only during the language arts period? Most teachers would answer with a resounding "No!" We agree. This kind of artificial separation of learning into separate subject matter "boxes" runs counter to how we really experience the world. Many school programs today are working to break down barriers that too often have stood in the way of helping pupils understand interconnections among different kinds of information.

Too much subject-by-subject separation interferes with learning efficiency. This has been recognized by specialists in the teaching of many school subjects (Eisner, 1991). For example, large numbers of mathematics educators have concluded that pupils master basic mathematical facts and operations when they are taught in a context that "connects" them to problems learners sees as practical and real. Similarly, reading and language arts educators point out that reading and writing are best taught in the context of "real language," topics that are interesting and significant to pupils. We in the social studies also support the idea that many school experiences should be integrated so that learners see the practical utility of information drawn from many different subject areas.

A recent trend has been to focus on the integration of the curriculum around important and interesting themes or topics. Knowledge is drawn from a variety of subject areas and organized into thematic units (Beane, 1992). To implement this approach, we might choose these themes ourselves or organize them around significant questions

The integrating of writing and social studies enhances the accomplishment of objectives in both subjects.

asked by our pupils. We believe the concern of the social studies for the experiences and problems of people makes it an ideal subject around which to organize the curriculum. Eisner (1991) points out that the very term *social studies* suggests an integrative approach. Subject areas—for example art, music, reading, language arts, science, and math—offer alternative ways of learning information, different perspectives, and significant insights into the actions and motivations of people. When we plan lessons that bring these subjects together, we extend learners' critical- and creative-thinking powers and also increase the likelihood that they will see the content as interesting and important.

Developing an integrated curriculum is not easy. Such an approach must have a strong structure. If anything, successful curriculum integration takes a good deal more planning and thought than the typical pattern of teaching separate subjects. These kinds of lessons place obligations on us to teach important content from several subjects. We do not quit teaching reading skills, mathematical operations, or forms of artistic expression in an integrated curriculum. We do teach them in the context of rich themes or topics. This chapter introduces approaches to integrated teaching using the social studies as a source of themes and topics.

CHOOSING APPROPRIATE THEMES

A key task in planning an integrated curriculum is identifying the basic organizational themes. We need to select themes or topics that are of high potential interest to learners. If they are not, much of the advantage of the integrated curriculum will be lost.

We begin the planning process by reviewing the curriculum normally taught at the grade level we are teaching. Suppose we are teaching a fifth-grade class. In grade five, the social studies curriculum focus is usually United States history. We might begin by looking at topics into which the grade-five program frequently is divided, which include of the following:

- Native American tribes
- Colonization
- Forming a new government
- Growth of a new nation
- Westward expansion
- Sectional conflicts

Next, we might work with pupils to ask questions about each of these topics. For example, we might develop questions about how different kinds of people reacted to proposals for a new government. What kinds of people supported these proposals? What kinds of people did not? How might we explain differences in their feelings?

As an approach to developing questions related to these major content themes, sometimes we find it useful to ask pupils to generate questions about present-day issues that are of interest to them. For example, one of the authors recently conducted a discussion with a group of fifth graders, who had significant concerns and questions. They wanted to know why people can't get along, why some people act like bullies, why people join gangs, why people pollute the environment, why companies close and people lose jobs, why earthquakes happen, and were concerned about what the future will be like. These questions raise issues about human behavior and human feelings that often can be tied back to the major content themes.

Such questions sometimes function well as focuses for integrated units that are not tied specifically to the academic content of the traditional grade-level program. Since the social studies has an obligation to promote citizenship education and an appreciation of varying values perspectives, such lessons have a legitimate role to play in the social studies program.

Successful planning of integrated lessons requires us to know our pupils and their concerns well. This is particularly true because of our interest in selecting a learning focus that our students will find interesting. There are a few topics that almost all pupils seem to find fascinating. For example, many primary-grades pupils get really excited about dinosaurs. Other topics may have a less general appeal. Some of these will be functions of local conditions. For example, a group of third graders living in western Nebraska may well have different questions and concerns than those living in Chicago.

Blumenfeld, Krajick, Marx, and Soloway (1994) suggest useful guidelines that can help you identify good themes or questions that can become the focus of thematic units. They suggest that questions or topics need to be feasible, worthwhile, contextualized, and meaningful.

Feasible

Feasible means that the question or theme can potentially lead to successful pupil learning. We need to consider whether pupils have access to the resources they will need in their investigation. Do they have the sufficient prerequisite skills and knowledge to successfully complete the task? Themes that are not feasible will result in frustration. Frustrated pupils often lose interest quickly, and may resist active involvement in future thematic instruction activities. In planning for integrated instruction, we have to do a good job in diagnosing entry-level and performance-level abilities of our learners. We also have to make sure that the materials they will need to complete tasks successfully are available.

Worthwhile

Worthwhile refers to the issue of the importance of what we intend to teach, particularly in terms of helping pupils understand complex content and situations that have practical relevance to the lives they and their families live in the world beyond the school. If we are creative, we can find ways of integrating content around almost any theme. The objective is not to draw on multiple content sources to address trivial issues. We want to select themes that offer a real possibility of integrating a variety of subjects in ways that truly extend pupils' intellectual, social, and personal development.

BOX 15–1   **Does Thematic Instruction Mean a "Watered Down" Curriculum?**

During a "back-to-school" night, a teacher described the thematic instruction approach to a group of parents. After the meeting, one of them approached the teacher and made these comments:

> I'm not sure that your classroom is the right place for my child. I don't agree with this emphasis on thematic teaching. It seems to me that all you are doing is letting the children do what they want to do. It doesn't seem rigorous, and I'm afraid my child won't learn the basics. It will be a tragedy of these young people don't learn reading, math, writing, science, and history. I don't want these basics watered down and ignored in favor of learning about some "theme" that might be of only passing interest to these children. I want my youngster in a room where the teacher teaches and where the pupils are expected to learn.

Think About This

1. Which points made by this parent are valid? Which are not?
2. How can a teacher made sure that important content from all areas of the curriculum is included in a program featuring thematic teaching?
3. What are your own views about thematic teaching?
4. How would you respond to this parent?

Contextualized

Contextualized content relates to real and practical concerns of pupils. If our learners regard the topics we have selected as "phony" or "unimportant," their motivational levels will plummet. Contextualized learning helps pupils to transfer school learning to outside-of-school tasks. When pupils begin to see the connection between what they are doing in school and in their own lives, their attitudes toward their social studies lessons are likely to improve.

Meaningful

Questions or themes need to be *meaningful*, that is, they must be relevant, interesting, and exciting to our pupils. This requires us to have some knowledge about learners' interests and concerns. It also means that we need to make sure that the interesting and exciting components of the subject are brought into the classroom. An initial interest may soon wane unless effort is directed toward keeping that interest high during the investigation.

Once themes or questions are identified, the subjects of the curriculum need to be integrated. Most of the activity of the school day will revolve around the theme. Spelling words will be ones pupils will be using during lessons related to theme. Similarly, math problems, science investigations, and reading and writing assignments will all be tied to this common focus. This general model is basically an extension of what often goes on in kindergarten classrooms (Eisner, 1991). These young learners often experience stories, create and act out plays, and draw pictures related to a single idea. What we and other proponents of integrated instruction are suggesting is that this general approach be extended to instructional planning for older elementary school pupils.

MAPPING THE INTEGRATION

One useful technique for planning an integrated unit is to develop a graphic organizer illustrating the connections among the various subjects. The organizer assists in identifying specific lessons to develop. Figure 15–2 is an example of a graphic organizer used in preparation for developing a complete integrated unit for a fifth-grade classroom.

The ideas mentioned in Figure 15–2 are only a beginning. For example, some reading skills might need to be taught to help the pupils comprehend the text. Other books,

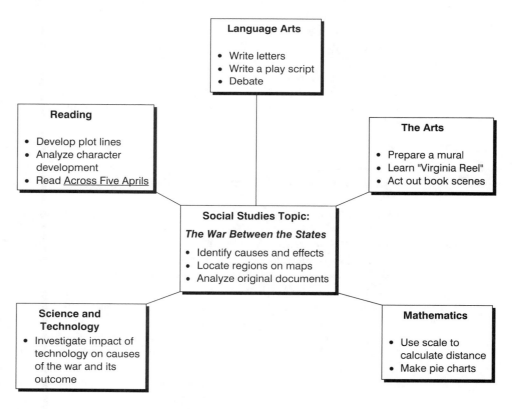

Figure 15–2
Sample graphic organizer for a fifth-grade unit.

such as *Harriet Tubman*, by Judith Bentley (Franklin Watts, 1990) could also be added. In language arts, the pupils might need to be taught the correct form for writing letters and the oral language skills needed to participate effectively in a debate. In the arts, it would be useful for the pupils to begin to understand how art is used as a communication medium. Art prints and pictures help convey the tragedy of the war in ways not captured in print. Many songs are available that could be used to teach music concepts as well as provide insight into the feelings of people. Advances in technology helped create some of the strains between the two sections of the country, and technological developments such as the railroads played a large role in determining the outcome. Technological advancements and their impact could be studied, and then extended to a study of the impact of technology on our lives. Finally, the typical math curriculum of the fifth grade could be taught be applying the skills to problems that might have arisen while studying the theme.

A final dimension needs to be added to this pre-unit plan: identification of the ways the content contributes to a theme, such as learning how to get along together.

When the possible connections and a culminating project have been identified, then formal unit planning can begin. It should be noted that there are numerous opportunities for cooperative activities, whole-group activities, inquiry exercises, individualized learning, and the use of technology and media. The unit and lesson planning suggestions presented in Chapter 4 will help you put all of these possibilities together into a coherent plan.

Developing integrated units requires basic understanding of different subject areas and how they relate to the social studies. The following sections suggest how content from different subject areas can be incorporated into social studies–based integrated lessons.

INTEGRATING UNITS AROUND SELECTIONS OF CHILDREN'S LITERATURE

Many good children's books are useful for teaching social studies material. These books can also become the central focus in an integrated unit (Savage & Savage, 1993). For example, *Carlota*, a story of early California by Scott O'Dell (Dell, 1977), can support integrated instruction focusing on such social studies topics as war, prejudice, and roles of women; on such language arts topics as the use of figurative language and character development; on Spanish-language instruction (the book features approximately 125 Spanish words); on mathematics-based word problems created from the events in the book; and on science experiments relating to weather prediction and adaptations to cold.

In preparing for a literature-based unit, we begin by identifying the themes or the questions for the integrated unit. Next, we begin our search for selections of children's literature that relate to the theme. Texts such as *Through the Eyes of a Child* (Norton, 1995) or *Children's Literature: An Issues Approach* (Rudman, 1993) identify good selections of literature related to a variety of themes and issues. Lessons built around children's literature provide a degree of realism and vividness not ordinarily found in other sorts of educational material (Savage & Savage, 1993).

THE ARTS

The objectives of the arts and the social studies are complementary in many ways. Eisner (1991) points out that what pupils learn about a culture is constrained by the forms of representation, or the ways they learn about it. If the chief means of learning about a culture is through the written word, this places some limits on what children will learn. Therefore, attention to art, music, and literature helps enlarge understanding as well as making social studies instruction more vivid and interesting to learners.

Works of art can be treated as artifacts that provide revealing glimpses into a culture (Collins & Chandler, 1993). Artwork can capture the mood, the color, the fears, the joy of a group of people much better than can many written representations. In addition, we can use art in lessons designed to teach children to make inferences. A teacher known to one of the authors begins many of his social studies units with a collection of art prints. The pupils investigate the prints in depth and try to make as many inferences and develop as many questions as they can. These provide a focus for subsequent instruction. Pupils find this to be an exciting activity, and this teacher has experienced great success over the years in using this approach to increase pupils' interest in social studies units.

To gain information from a work of art, a person needs to be artistically literate (Eisner, 1991). This means that we have to provide basic information to our learners about art and art processes. Those of us who have had some formal instruction in art have advantages when we work to develop integrated lessons that include material from the arts. Such lessons do not make contributions only to learners' understanding of social studies content; they also enrich their appreciation for the arts by placing works of art in a particular social, cultural, or historical context (Eisner, 1991). Learners who know this contextual information can derive much more from their art lessons than those who do not.

MUSIC

Much of what has been said about art can be repeated for music. Music is another source of information about people. Music created by members of a given group gives insight into their values, beliefs, hopes, and fears. It evokes the emotions and communicates aspects of a culture that cannot be communicated in any other way. For example, listening to the song, "God Save the South," tells us something about the attitudes of the people living in the South during the Civil War. This kind of a perspective is one we simply cannot expect our learners to get by reading a textbook. Folk songs are particularly good sources about views of the common people. Textbooks rarely devote much attention to this kind of information.

As with art, the goals of music and social studies are complementary. An understanding of the culture and the social conditions are important in developing a full appreciation of music. Music is created within specific contexts. When learners understand these, they develop more sophisticated understanding of content introduced during music lessons.

Music is an excellent vehicle for learning about other cultures.

An abundance of tapes, records, and pieces of music that reach far back in history and cross many cultures are available to classroom teachers. In many parts of the nation, groups have preserved a part of their cultural identity through music and dance groups. Some of us are fortunate enough to have musical talents of our own. This is a great advantage in planning integrated social studies lessons that include some emphases on music. One of the authors once worked with a teacher who was an accomplished cellist. He captivated his middle school class by beginning many class periods with a short selection of music related to the day's social studies objectives.

MATHEMATICS

More and more, mathematical literacy is becoming an imperative of effective citizenship. We are bombarded daily with massive amounts of data and figures. Much public policy is decided based on such figures. One example is the establishment of monetary policy based on such things as inflation indexes, interest rates, and unemployment rates. Many political campaigns include figures and claims that need to be verified by mathematical analysis. Similarly, consumers need to be prepared to protect themselves in a marketplace that requires a least some mathematical diligence. Advertising daily tries to take advantage of the limited mathematical sophistication of many potential buyers.

A society with a large percentage of mathematically illiterate individuals is in danger of making poor choices that can influence their lives in profound ways. Mathematical knowledge is relevant to our everyday lives. Mathematics educators are aware of this and have been seeking ways of teaching mathematical operations in applied and meaningful contexts. The social studies is seen as a key area for incorporating these context-based learning experiences.

Teachers have numerous opportunities for teaching mathematical concepts in the social studies. One of the more obvious examples is in the teaching of map scale (see Chapter 14). Understanding the ratio of a map scale is important in order for pupils to compute distances between points on a map.

Another important area is in the teaching of economics. Many economics and mathematics concepts are best taught together. Even in the primary grades, we can use the classroom store to teach concepts such as scarcity, addition, and subtraction. An interesting application in the middle grades is that of using the consumer price index to help pupils understand that the value of a dollar has fluctuated over the years (Savage & Armstrong, 1992). Table 15–1 displays the consumer index for the years 1860 through 1994 and instructions for using the index to convert historic prices to current dollar values. Applying this procedure to convert the price of such items as automobiles in the 1920s to their equivalent cost today is very enlightening and helps destroy the myth that things were much cheaper in times past. See Lesson Idea 15–1 for an example.

Lesson Idea 15–1

SEWARD'S FOLLY

Grade Level:	5–8
Objective:	Pupils will use the formula to convert the purchase price of Alaska to present-day dollars. They will state whether the purchase was a good deal for the United States.
Overview:	Individuals often draw erroneous conclusions based on flawed information. This is especially true when it comes to comparing the cost of particular items over time. The value of the dollar does not stay constant. It changes over time because of inflation and deflation. Most of us appreciate that what the dollar buys today is different than what it would buy only a few years ago. For pupils to understand the real meaning of prices and wages mentioned in texts and other sources dealing with historical information, they need to know how to compute the present-day values of those dollar amounts.
Procedure:	*Learning Set* Ask the class, "How many of you have heard your parents talk about how cheap things were in the past? Can anyone give us an example?"
	Presentation Tell the class the following:

Table 15–1
Consumer price index numbers: 1860–1994.

YEAR	PRICE INDEX	YEAR	PRICE INDEX	YEAR	PRICE INDEX	YEAR	PRICE INDEX
1860	9.0	1887	9.0	1914	10.0	1941	14.7
1861	9.0	1888	9.0	1915	10.1	1942	16.3
1862	10.0	1889	9.0	1916	10.9	1943	17.3
1863	12.4	1890	9.0	1917	12.8	1944	17.6
1864	15.7	1891	9.0	1918	15.1	1945	18.0
1865	15.4	1892	9.0	1919	17.35	1946	19.5
1866	14.7	1893	9.0	1920	20.3	1947	22.5
1867	14.0	1894	8.7	1921	17.9	1948	24.1
1868	13.4	1895	8.3	1922	16.8	1949	23.8
1869	13.4	1896	8.3	1923	17.1	1950	24.1
1870	12.7	1897	8.3	1924	17.1	1951	26.0
1871	12.0	1898	8.3	1925	17.5	1952	26.0
1872	12.0	1899	8.3	1926	17.7	1953	26.7
1873	12.0	1900	8.3	1927	17.4	1954	26.9
1874	11.4	1901	8.3	1928	17.1	1955	26.8
1875	11.0	1902	8.7	1929	17.1	1956	27.2
1876	10.7	1903	9.0	1930	16.7	1957	28.1
1877	10.7	1904	9.0	1931	15.2	1958	28.9
1878	9.7	1905	9.0	1932	13.7	1959	29.1
1879	9.3	1906	9.0	1933	13.0	1960	29.6
1880	9.7	1907	9.3	1934	13.4	1961	30.2
1881	9.7	1908	9.0	1935	13.7	1962	30.6
1882	9.7	1909	9.0	1936	13.9	1963	30.6
1883	9.3	1910	9.3	1937	14.4	1964	31.0
1884	9.0	1911	9.3	1938	14.1	1965	31.5
1885	9.0	1912	9.7	1939	13.9	1966	32.4
1886	9.0	1913	9.9	1940	14.0	1967	33.4

While it is true that prices of things in the past were different than they are today, we need to remember that there are other things to consider. For example, although prices may have been lower, people also did not make as much money on their jobs. How can we find out what something really cost in the past? By this I mean, how can we figure out what the item would cost today? To help us do this, the government produces something called the "Consumer Price Index." This is a table we can use to find out differences in what a dollar would buy in different years. (Pass out copies of the CPI [see Table 15–1].)

Let me explain this chart to you. When it was first put together, someone had to identify a beginning point we could use in determining how the value of the dollar has

YEAR	PRICE INDEX	YEAR	PRICE INDEX	YEAR	PRICE INDEX	YEAR	PRICE INDEX
1968	34.8	1975	43.8	1982	96.5	1989	126.0
1969	36.7	1976	56.9	1983	99.6	1990	133.8
1970	38.8	1977	60.6	1984	103.9	1991	136.2
1971	40.5	1978	65.2	1985	107.2	1992	141.9
1972	41.8	1979	72.6	1986	110.4	1993	145.8
1973	44.4	1980	82.4	1987	115.4	1994	150.1
1974	49.3	1981	90.9	1988	121.2	1995 (Feb.)	150.9

CONVERTING OLD PRICES TO NEW USING INDEX NUMBERS

1. Divide the index number of the most recent year by the index number for the historic year. For example, suppose we wanted to find out how much a 1911 price would be in terms of February 1995 dollars. In this case, we would divide the index number for February 1995, 150.9, by the index number for 1911, 9.3: 150.9 ÷ 9.3 = 16.2.

2. We take this figure (16.2) and multiply it by the 1911 price. For example, suppose a small table in a catalog cost $16.00 in 1911. To convert this to a February 1994 equivalent price, we simply multiply $16.00 by 16.2. This is what we get: $16.00 x 16.2 = $259.20. This latter price is what the table would cost in February 1995 dollars.

GETTING UPDATED CPI INFORMATION

Updated CPI information is available from a number of sources, including the following:

1. *CPI Detailed Report* (monthly). Washington, DC: U.S. Department of Labor, Bureau of Labor Statistics.

2. *Statistical Abstract of the United States* (annual). Washington, DC: U.S. Department of Commerce, Bureau of the Census.

3. Also, nearly all almanacs have up-to-date CPI information.

changed. The rest of the table tells us whether the dollar was worth more or less at times other than this beginning point. At the present time, the chart is based on what the dollar was worth in the years 1982–1984. The index number assigned for those years is 100. You'll notice that for some other years, the index number is less than 100. This means that something that costs one dollar in 1982–1984 could be purchased for less money in this year. In other years, the index number is more than 100. In these years, it cost more than one dollar to buy what could be had for one dollar in 1982–1984. Notice that no year has an index number of *exactly* 100.

Let's look at an example. Remember the index for 1982–1984 is 100. When we look at the latest index number for February 1995, we find the number 150.9. This tells us that it cost about $1.50 in early 1995 to buy what could be had for $1.00 in the period 1982–1984. Now, let's look at a famous price from our own history.

In the year 1867, the American Secretary of State, William Seward, negotiated a deal to buy what is now the state of Alaska. The purchase price was $7,200,000. Many people at the time claimed that this was a terrible waste of money, and they called the purchase "Seward's Folly." Today, we look at that price and think was incredibly cheap. Today seven million dollars is not enough money to build even one medium-to-large-sized high school. (If possible, cite a local example.) However, we have to remember that a dollar could buy more in 1867 than it can today. Look again at the index. We find that the index for 1867 is 14. This means that it took only 14 cents in 1867 to buy what cost a dollar in 1982–1984. How much did Alaska cost us in terms of what the dollar was worth in early 1995? Here are the steps we need to follow to get the answer:

1. Note that the index number for 1867 is 14.0. The latest index number for February 1995 is 150.9. We begin by dividing 150.9 by 14.0. What do we get? (10.8)
2. Now, we multiply the original price (the price that Seward paid in 1867) by 10.8. Remember that the original price was $7,200,000. What do we get when we multiply? ($77,760,000). This tells us that the February 1995 dollar equivalent of $7,200,000 1867 dollars is $77,760,000.

Did Seward get a good deal? Most of us would say, "Yes." Although 78 million dollars is a lot of money, it is still a ridiculously low figure to have paid for the wealth and resources of our largest state. Today, people looking back on what Seward negotiated probably would be more inclined to describe the deal as "Russia's Folly," not "Seward's Folly."

(For practice, give pupils some other historic prices to convert to present-day equivalents using the index numbers in Table 15–1)

Closure: Ask, "What did we learn today? Why is it important? How can we apply this information?"

SCIENCE AND TECHNOLOGY

Science and technology are significant social forces. Any understanding of people and their actions in the past or present requires an understanding of prevailing levels of technology. Today's rapid scientific and technological changes have important, and often unforeseen, consequences for our society (Marker, 1992). This can be disconcerting and can result in a perception that technology is out of control and that individuals are powerless. These feelings often play a role in debates about important public policy, which frequently feature discussions heavily weighted with ethical and values issues, and strengthen a case in support of social studies programs developing future citizens who have a solid understanding of science and technology (Giese, Parisi, & Bybee, 1991).

Marker (1992) suggests several big ideas or generalizations related to science and technology that need to be taught to elementary youngsters. Among the ideas he suggests are the following:

- Technological changes seldom have an equal impact on all groups in society.
- Technology often changes more rapidly than the social institutions.
- In a democratic society, citizens have a right and a responsibility to participate in the development of laws that control the uses of technology.

As a beginning point for teaching our elementary school pupils about technology, we might have them identify ways that technology changes our lives. How has the automobile changed the way people live? How has it made living easier? What problems has it created?

Many science concepts and lessons are easily integrated with social studies lessons. For example, understanding climate patterns requires application of some basic concepts of physics. In addition, science and social studies both advocate the use of inquiry processes. This makes the two subjects natural partners.

LANGUAGE ARTS

The ability to communicate effectively is an essential skill for any individual. The literacy rate for a democratic society is an important contributor to its stability. Effective communication is often referred to as "communicative competence" (Tompkins & Hoskisson, 1991). Communicative competence involves two major components: (1) transmitting meaning through speaking and writing and (2) comprehending meaning through listening and reading (Tompkins & Hoskisson, 1991). Because of the importance of communicative competence, school subjects such as reading, spelling, writing, and oral language have been included in the elementary curriculum specifically for the purpose of transmitting these important skills to learners. In recent years, educators have realized that language and communications skills are best learned in genuine, functional, and meaningful communication contexts rather than through contrived skill lessons and practice experiences (Tompkins & Hoskisson, 1991).

Social studies teachers typically use a variety of print resources. These include textbooks, encyclopedias, almanacs, magazines, and newspapers. Because of the heavy reliance we place on printed materials and because our pupils' success may be strongly influenced by their reading abilities, social studies has become a prime candidate for lessons that integrate both reading and writing.

At one time *literacy* was defined as the ability to read. However, in recent years the definition of literacy has been expanded to include both reading and writing. As with reading, social studies lessons provide numerous opportunities for teachers to support the development of learners' writing abilities. The following subsections provide some general suggestions for integrating reading and writing in our social studies lessons.

Readers' Theater

Readers' theater is an exciting language arts approach that can easily be integrated with social studies. Reader's theater involves two or more pupils reading from a script and using voice and body action to portray a scene. Readers' theater presentations are not plays; hence, little practice is required. Readers' theater promotes the development of oral language abilities as pupils learn how to communicate effectively in front of an audience, to read critically to identify the emotion and the dynamics of a scene, to master effective writing skills as a script is prepared, and to develop good listening skills (Laughlin, Black, & Loberg, 1991). Effective readers' theater experiences require pupils to understand the setting of the passage they are presenting. This understanding of context provides a logical tie to the social studies.

One way we implement readers' theater is to assign pupils to select an episode from a book they are reading and to write a script and present it to the class. Historical fiction that has a great deal of dialogue is especially well suited to readers' theater adaptations.

A good way of beginning is to have pupils work in cooperative learning groups. They can select an episode from a book they enjoy. The whole group should read the episode together and discuss what is happening. They might want to discuss the feeling of the characters and how they think the words would sound if spoken. Then they may begin preparing a script by identifying the speaking parts of the different characters. They then can decide who will play each character and practice reading through the script. They can go on to discuss what they can do to make the presentation interesting to the audience. When they are ready, they present their scene to the class.

Laughlin, Black, and Loberg (1991) have developed a number of scripts from a variety of children's books. These scripts can provide models for pupils to use until they feel comfortable enough to develop their own scripts.

In summary, readers' theater includes many of the skills that need to be developed in a total language arts program. In addition, it is an exciting way for young people to learn social studies content. Pupils enjoy good readers' theater both as active participants and as listeners to others' presentations.

Reading Study Skills

A key need in helping pupils learn how to read and comprehend social studies material is mastering basic reading and study strategies. These strategies provide pupils with a set of "tools" they can apply across subject areas. In developing study and reading strategies, we need to know something about how the human brain functions.

Our brain does not act as a camera that passively records its exposure to reality. Instead, the brain actively looks for patterns that it can organize and transform into

Social studies tends to be a print-heavy subject. Teaching reading study skills is an important part of social studies instruction.

storable information. The way a person's brain does this has an important bearing on how well the person retrieves information and uses it later. Pupils can be taught to monitor the way they organize and store information and, thus, improve their learning from printed material. They need special help during three important reading stages:

- Prereading
- Reading
- Postreading

Instruction during the prereading stage is designed to help pupils discover a personal purpose for reading and establish a scheme to organize information they will be learning as they read. We assist in this process by relating new information from the reading assignment to previously mastered material. We also tell our pupils what they will be expected to do after completing reading to demonstrate that they understand what they have read.

During the reading stage, learners read the assigned material. We monitor them to spot individuals who may have difficulty understanding what they are reading. This monitoring involves questioning pupils about what they are reading and encouraging them to think about the content. We sometimes ask pupils to develop questions of their own that can be answered using the content from the reading assignment, and encourage pupils to take notes focusing on major points.

During the postreading stage we encourage pupils to reflect on and evaluate what they have read. Often we do this by discussing one or more of the major ideas introduced in the reading assignment. Our effort here is to involve the entire class in the postreading discussion. This allows us to identify and help individuals who may still be experiencing difficulty.

Prereading Techniques

Prior experiences help readers fit what they read into meaningful patterns. When people are lacking any experiential base related to what they read, they may find the information difficult to understand, and they may fail to grasp certain important ideas.

In elementary social studies classes, pupils often become frustrated when asked to read about people and places that are totally unfamiliar to them. Prereading techniques are designed to provide a frame of reference for pupils that will help them better grasp information introduced in prose materials. We want to help pupils establish a link between what they already know and what they will be reading as part of a learning assignment. Two techniques that teachers have found useful are the structured overview and ReQuest.

The Structured Overview

A structured overview provides pupils with a graphic or pictorial display that illustrates relationships among concepts that will be featured in a reading assignment. Pupils should be involved in developing the overview. We may ask them to brainstorm what they know or think they know about the topic to be read. We also may inquire about experiences they have had that might help them understand the subject to be studied.

Suppose a group of fifth graders were assigned to read material on "the Westward Movement." We might begin by asking them to think about the general issue of moving. What are things people have to think about when deciding whether to move or to stay where they are? What must they think about after the decision to move has been made? Responses to such questions can be graphically organized into a structured overview. An example is provided in Figure 15–3.

Figure 15–3
Structured overview for westward movement.

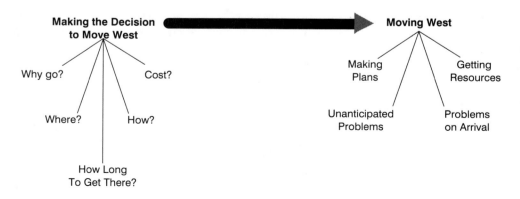

The structured overview diagram is used by pupils as they begin their reading. They are invited to add components to it as needed. The overview suggests things for them to think about as they read. It gives purpose to the activity. It helps them to fit new information into an orderly pattern and to make sense out of what they read. The structured overview can also play a role during postreading. Its categories provide a framework we can use to discuss and debrief content with our pupils.

ReQuest

"ReQuest" is an acronym for "reciprocal questioning" (Manzo, 1969). It involves both teacher and pupils in asking and answering questions related to a prose selection. Learners' active participation in framing questions helps them draw on prior knowledge related to new content to be introduced in the reading assignment. It also helps them to see relationships between their own interests and topics to be covered in the reading. Questions guide pupils toward appropriate content once they begin working on the assignment.

These steps are followed in the ReQuest technique:

- The teacher and pupils read together the first sentence of a reading assignment.
- The teacher closes his book while pupils keep theirs open. Pupils are invited to ask the teacher any question they wish that relates to the first sentence. The teacher answers the questions as accurately as possible. If one sentence is not enough to stimulate questions, another sentence or two may be read. During this phase the teacher may guide the general direction of learners' questions.
- The pupils close their books. The teacher asks questions. These questions are designed to help pupils recall information from their own experience that may help them understand content introduced in the reading material.
- Procedures outlined in steps one, two, and three may be repeated several times. When the teacher senses pupils are ready, he asks, "What do you think you will be reading about in the rest of this material?" This question helps learners develop expectations that can help them better understand what they will be reading.

During-Reading Techniques

As they read, pupils need to know how to recognize important information and to make connections among the ideas presented. Many elementary school learners have difficulty distinguishing between important and unimportant content. Many also have problems identifying relationships among important content elements. Two techniques that can be used to help learners are visual frameworks and multipass reading.

Visual Frameworks

Visual frameworks help pupils to organize content from material they read. Many teachers have traditionally responded to the need to help learners organize material by teaching them to outline what they have read. Some pupils find outlining to be very tedious. Often they fail to appreciate its value in helping them grasp new content.

Younger elementary pupils often lack outlining skills. The visual frameworks approach overcomes some of the difficulties with content outlining.

The number of reading purposes that might be established for a prose selection of only two or three paragraphs is enormous. Assignments might require learners to focus on a specific category of fact. Others might require them to identify certain cause-and-effect relationships. Still others might ask pupils to make predictions of future trends based on information introduced in the reading assignment. See Lesson Idea 15–2 for a sample comparing two teachers' use of the same text material for different purposes.

It is clear that an assignment asking learners to focus on certain kinds of facts requires them to look differently at the reading content than when they are asked to identify cause-and-effect relationships. To assist pupils in developing an appropriate approach to their reading assignments, it makes sense for us to explain the nature of the task clearly. Then additional assistance can be provided through visual frameworks. These are devices that will help learners "see" which elements of content they should focus on. They also provide a means for taking good notes on the reading.

Visual frameworks can take many shapes. Some teachers help their pupils to work out their own frameworks. Whether developed by the teacher alone or with some active pupil participation, visual frameworks help learners master content assigned in required reading.

Lesson Idea 15–2

SPANISH COLONIZERS AND THE CARIBBEAN

Grade Level:	5
Objective:	Pupils will identify the relationship between specific items of information using a visual framework.
Overview:	This lesson plan is somewhat different in that it displays how visual frameworks will vary according to the purposes of the teacher. This illustration supposes that two teachers had very different purposes in mind when they assigned their pupils to read exactly the same material. Teacher "1" wants the pupils to identify which islands were discovered by vhich explorers. Teacher "2" wants pupils to identify how the settlers tried to meet their need for workers and what happened as a result.
Procedure:	*Learning Set* Display a picture or a brochure of a cruise ship visiting one of the Caribbean islands. Ask the students what they know about cruise ships and why people like to visit the Caribbean islands. Tell them that today they are going to read about some of the first people who took a "cruise" to the islands, the Spanish explorers.
	Presentation Give each pupil a copy of the visual framework. Tell members of the class that they should fill in the blank spaces as they read. When they have completed their reading, have the class discuss what they read.

Visual Framework for Teacher One

Teacher One's focus:

The Islands and Spanish Explorers

N

Islands

_____

Puerto Rico _____

_____

_____

Spanish Explorers

Columbus

_____

_____

_____

Visual Framework for Teacher Two

Teacher Two's focus:

Finding Workers

Why were workers needed

_____

_____

_____

This was tried first

_____

_____

_____

Results

_____

_____

This was tried second

_____

_____

_____

Results

_____

_____

Final Outcome

_____

_____

_____

The Reading Passage   Christopher Columbus first landed on San Salvador Island. This happened in 1492. San Salvador is one of the islands that today we call the Bahamas. Later, Columbus went on to discover many Caribbean islands. He set up a fort on one of the biggest islands, Hispañola.

Another famous Spanish explorer was Nicolas de Ovando. In 1502, he was sent to become governor of Hispañola. He brought many colonists with him. The colonists tried to make money in two ways. Some of them tried farming. Some of them tried mining. One of their biggest problems was finding people to do the hard work.

One thing the early Spanish colonists tried was to make slaves of the Indians. This did not work. The Indians died when they were forced into slavery. At first, the Spanish tried to solve the problem by capturing Indians from other islands. But many of these Indians died, too. Later, slaves were brought from Africa.

After all of these things were tried, there were still not enough people to do the work. Many of the original colonists from Spain gave up on Hispañola. They moved to other islands of the Caribbean. Some of these colonists were led to the island of Puerto Rico. This happened in 1509. The Spanish leader who led them there was Juan Ponce de Leon. This happened in 1508. Another leader, Juan de Esquival, took another group to Jamaica in 1509. The largest Caribbean island, Cuba, was reached by Spanish settlers in 1514.

When the class has had a chance to complete the visual framework, review the findings with learners by completing a copy of the framework on an overhead projector. Add details and additional questions as they are brought up in class.

Closure: Review the visual framework constructed by the class. Ask what was learned and how such a framework can be used to help them remember information.

Multipass Reading

"Multipass reading" encourages readers to go over the same material several times, approaching the reading with a different purpose each time. The purpose of the first pass is to help learners develop a framework for the content and to relate it to what they already know. This is accomplished quickly. During this phase, we encourage learners to skim the content, note major chapter divisions, and glance at the illustrations.

Once pupils have completed the first pass, we ask general questions, such as the following:

- What is this chapter or section about?
- What do we already know about these events?
- How is the chapter organized? What comes first, second, and so forth?
- What kinds of photos or illustrations did you see? Why do you think they might have been included?

The second pass through the material helps pupils to identify major ideas. During this pass, learners read major headings, subsection headings, and the first sentences of paragraphs. Most writers include the major ideas of their paragraphs in the first one or two sentences. When pupils read only the first sentence of each paragraph, they are able to pick up a surprising amount of key information. Even slow readers find they can learn a good deal about the content when they follow this procedure.

After learners have completed the second pass, we ask questions such as these:

- What are the main ideas you found?
- Are these ideas similar or different from those you already knew?
- What additional information do you need to find out whether the ideas you read about are true or false?

During the third pass, learners look for specific details. At this point they typically have a good idea about how the content is organized. This allows them to find needed details relatively quickly. Often this phase concludes with specific questions, such as the following:

- What do people in Ethiopia eat?
- How are their houses different from ours?
- Is the climate there in summer different from ours?
- What different things are taught in school to boys and girls?

The final pass is for review. Pupils quickly read the entire assignment from beginning to end. This last pass helps individuals who may have missed important information to fill in the gaps.

Teachers who have not used multipass reading sometimes wonder about how much time it takes. The technique is not so time consuming as one might suppose. Some of the passes are completed very quickly. Once pupils have developed a general feel for how content is organized, even reading for details does not require a great deal of time. The higher rates of comprehension that often result with this technique save time later. Less time is needed for reteaching and review.

Postreading Techniques

What teachers do after learners have completed reading assigned material has an important influence on pupils' comprehension of the information. We need to help them relate new information to what they have learned previously.

Small-group activities are particularly useful during the postreading stage. Sharing information with other learners stimulates pupils to reflect on and react to what they have read. Also, the setting allows group members to benefit from the thinking processes of pupils who have successfully grasped the new content. This experience often helps pupils who are not well informed about what they have read to recognize and use approaches employed by more successful pupils. Approaches we often use during postreading include graphic post-organizers and interaction frames.

Graphic Post-Organizers

Graphic post-organizers represent an extension of the structured overview approach introduced previously. The basic differences center on timing and on who is responsible for preparing the material. Structured overviews are prepared before reading takes place, and are prepared jointly by pupils and their teacher. Graphic post-organizers are developed by pupils after they have completed reading the assigned material. The outcome is the development of a graph of the main ideas and supporting information.

In preparing learners to develop graphic organizers, we divide the class into groups of four to six members each. Each group is provided with two packs of index cards, each pack a different color.

To begin the activity, we tell class members that they are first to use the note cards in only one of the packs. ("When we start, use only the pink cards. We will use the green ones later.") Pupils are instructed to individually identify as many different major ideas or concepts from the reading as they can. ("Let's think about what we have read. First of all, take several pink cards. Quietly, write on the cards as many major ideas from the reading as you can recall. Write only one idea on each card.")

After pupils have completed writing on their cards, we move on to the next phase of the activity. This requires members of each group to share their main ideas with the rest of the group. Each group then develops a master set of cards containing the group's major ideas. As this phase unfolds, we sometimes need to establish a ground rule about the maximum number of major ideas each group will be allowed to have. The purpose of the exercise is for learners to identify the truly important ideas. Pupils sometimes indiscriminately identify both important and unimportant ideas. If we sense that this is happening, we might require each group to agree on no more than five or six major ideas. ("Some ideas you have identified probably are more important than others. As a group, I want you to identify no more than six major ideas. If you have more than six, discuss the ideas in your group. Then, decide which six are the most important.")

Next, we ask pupils to place the cards containing their main ideas face up on the table. If there are important relationships among some of the major ideas, they should place these cards side by side. ("Now, put the cards with your major ideas on the table. Lay them so they are facing up. If some of these ideas are closely related, put those cards close together.")

At this point, we instruct pupils to take cards from the second packet. ("All right, now I want each of you to take several of the green cards.") We ask them to look at the cards with the major ideas (the pink cards) and think about facts and other pieces of information from the reading that are related to each main idea. We have them write one fact or one item of information on each green card. ("Look at your major ideas. Your reading presented quite a bit of information about each one. I want you individually to write down some information about the major ideas on the green cards. Write only one piece of information on each green card. Also, make a note about the specific major idea it relates to.")

When this phase concludes, we give pupils time to discuss the specific information on the cards and the main idea to which it is related. Each group then arranges the cards with the specific information under the main ideas to which they refer (under the pink cards).

A graphic layout of major ideas and supporting information results from this activity, with one set of cards representing major ideas and the other representing supporting information. All groups are asked to make a chart displaying their organization, on either a large piece of paper or an overhead transparency.

The activity concludes with each group displaying its chart. A final discussion focuses on similarities and differences in major ideas and supporting information on each chart. We conclude by discussing any ideas that may have been missed by the groups.

Interaction Frames

Interaction frames help learners work with social studies content that refers to interactions among individuals or groups. For example, pupils in many fifth-grade classrooms read about the conflict between Roger Williams and the Puritan leaders of the Massachusetts Bay Colony. The interaction frame procedure is particularly useful for helping learners grasp positions of contending parties in such situations. Interaction frames are organized around four key questions:

- What were the goals of the various individuals or groups?
- What actions did they take to accomplish these goals?
- How did the individuals or groups get along?
- What happened as a result of contacts between and among these individuals or groups?

We ask pupils to think about what they have read as they respond to these questions. Then we start the interaction frame lesson by identifying the specific people or groups that will be the focus of the activity. We organize learners into groups, and each group develops answers to the four key questions. Each group shares its responses as part of a general class discussion. Pupils may construct a summary interaction frame chart based on the discussion. A model for such a chart is provided in Figure 15–4. Often it is useful for us to provide copies of this chart to the class to reinforce understanding.

Writing and the Social Studies

In recent years, concerns about pupils' writing skills have paralleled worries about their reading abilities. As with reading, teachers have been encouraged to provide opportunities for pupils to write in all of their major elementary school subjects. Social

Individual A

1. Goals of A.
(What was wanted?)

_____

_____

2. Actions of A.

_____

_____

Individual B

1. Goals of B.
(What was wanted?)

_____

_____

2. Actions of B.

_____

_____

3. How did A and B get along? (Cooperation, conflict, etc.)

_____

_____

_____

4. How did they resolve any conflicts?

_____

_____

_____

5. What happened to A?

_____

_____

_____

5. What happened to B?

_____

_____

_____

6. Summary and conclusions.

_____

_____

_____

Figure 15–4
Sample format for an interaction frame chart.

studies lessons often present an excellent context for our learners to develop and refine their writing abilities.

Researchers report that languages reflect and reinforce the cultures of their speakers (Halliday, 1973; Halliday & Hasan, 1989). One implication of this finding is that language instruction should tie clearly to pupils' use of language in natural settings (Halliday, 1973). There are many opportunities to do this in the context of social studies instruction. Halliday (1973) has identified seven basic functions of language:

- Instrumental
- Regulatory
- Interactional
- Personal
- Heuristic
- Representational
- Imaginative

These functions suggest a framework for planning writing activities that are closely tied to social studies lessons.

Instrumental Function

The instrumental function of language, sometimes referred to as the "I want" function, concerns how people use language to meet their needs. For example, people write to apply for jobs, to place orders for goods and services, and to invite people to visit. We can involve our pupils in social studies–related, instrumental function writing by having them do such things as the following:

- Writing letters requesting information from government agencies
- Writing to invite special guests to the classroom
- Writing a class request to the principal
- Completing mock job applications or loan applications
- Writing captions to accompany collages of pupil-assembled pictures illustrating personal "wants and needs"

Regulatory Function

This function concerns tasks that control behavior or that provide information about how a task should be performed. It is sometimes called the "do as I tell you" function. Road signs, directions for repairing or constructing something, and printed collections of traffic laws illustrate the regulatory function of written language. We can give pupils experience with regulatory function writing activities such as these:

- Writing to friends out of town inviting them to visit and giving them directions to the pupil's home
- Pretending that a trek over the Oregon Trail has just been completed, writing to friends in the East telling them what they should bring and providing them with other directions about "moving West"
- Writing rules for the classroom or the school, or for the care of pets or materials
- Writing suggestions to the principal about needed new rules
- Preparing written directions for such things as building a log cabin, making candies, or engaging in a traditional craft

Interactional Function

This function, sometimes labeled the "me and you" function, includes communications that seek to improve the quality of interpersonal relations. Social studies activities consistent with this function include the following:

- Writing to a friend to visit the classroom
- Preparing and sending thank you notes to special guests
- Creating personal holiday greeting cards to be sent to specific people
- Writing regularly to a pen pal in another state or country
- Playing the role of an explorer and writing an imaginary letter back home to a member of the explorer's immediate family

Personal Function

This communication type is used by people to express their personal feelings or ideas and to explore the personal meaning of something. Letters to the editor, reaction statements, and poetry are examples of writing in this general category. The personal function is sometimes called the "here I come" function. The following examples illustrate ways we can involve pupils in personal function writing:

- Writing letters to the editor in reaction to something printed in a news or editorial column
- Writing an account of a personally experienced event
- Preparing and sending a letter to a public official expressing personal opinions about a controversial issue
- Writing a poem to express feelings about something studied in a social studies lesson
- Keeping a personal diary
- Preparing a time capsule that includes items of interest to class members along with explanations of some of their personal beliefs

Heuristic Function

Sometimes referred to as the "tell me why" function, the heuristic function of language has to do with information seeking or gathering activities. People exercise this function when they take notes or develop questions they want to have answered. The following examples illustrate possible applications of heuristic function writing in the elementary social studies classroom:

- Writing down questions to be asked after study of a particular social studies topic or to be asked to a guest speaker
- Keeping note cards with information about a topic that is being studied
- Taking notes while listening to a speaker
- Keeping minutes at a meeting
- Writing down hypotheses to explain a puzzling situation after considering relevant data

Representational Function

The representational function of language concerns the use of language to transmit information. It is sometimes referred to as the "I've got something to tell you" function. The following examples suggest possible uses of representational function writing in elementary social studies classes:

- Maintaining an imaginary diary for someone who was present at an important historical event
- Writing a short history of the local community
- Preparing a classroom newspaper or newsletter
- Labeling items on a map and writing accompanying explanations
- Developing lists of major ideas to be included in oral reports

- Writing an account of a past event based on an oral history interview
- Writing a report of information learned on a field trip

Imaginative Function

This is a creative, "let's pretend" function of language. When using it, individuals allow their minds to wander in unpredictable ways. Possibilities for including imaginative function writing in the social studies program include the following:

- Writing stories to complete a "what would happen if . . . ?" statement
- Writing a play or television script about something studied in a social studies lesson
- Writing song lyrics about a topic studied in a social studies lesson
- Inventing and writing novel solutions to important social problems such as drug abuse and air pollution
- Preparing a written account describing what life might be like 50 years from now
- preparing political cartoons referring to current topics and issues

These seven functions are all part of a comprehensive writing program. Teachers too often restrict social studies writing activities to those related to the representation function. We need to encourage other kinds of writing. Over time, this kind of training improves the sophistication of pupils' writing skills. These skills make them more effective communicators, not only in their social studies classes, but in other settings as well.

KEY IDEAS IN SUMMARY

1. Integrating the curriculum so that subjects are taught in the context of learning about an important topic or theme helps pupils understand the relatedness of subjects and is more consistent with the way the world is organized.

2. Teachers have available several methods of choosing themes. One approach involves reviewing the topics normally taught at that particular grade level, identifying important topics or themes. Teachers can survey pupils for their interests and concerns and then use those issues as a focus for thematic instruction. Topics that are selected should be feasible, worthwhile, contextualized, and meaningful.

3. A useful device for identifying the ways that content can be integrated is to draw a semantic map or graphic organizer that illustrates the relationships among different topics. This graphic can then be used to guide unit development.

4. Children's literature selections are excellent sources around which to build integrated lessons. After reviewing social studies topics and identifying themes, teachers can select high-quality works of children's literature that fit the emphasized themes. Specific skills in different content areas that need to be taught can then be selected and taught in the context of the reading.

5. Social studies goals and the goals of many other curriculum areas are complementary. Learning about those subjects enhances social studies understanding and helps pupils attain objectives in that specific curricular area. Eisner (1991) makes the point that what individuals learn about a culture is influenced by the types of representations that they use when learning. Therefore, if the arts, music, math, and science are used to learn about another culture, the types of representations increase and help the individual obtain more understanding.

6. Language arts and social studies are especially compatible subjects. The goal of language arts is to develop communicative competence. Competence is enhanced when the language arts are taught in the context of meaningful and functional experiences.

7. Readers' theater is an especially strong dimension of the language arts that can be integrated with social studies. Pupils identify selected incidents from the social studies or from children's literature. They then write a script of the incident and present it to the class. This involves the four main language processes of reading, writing, speaking, and listening.

8. Reading materials are widely used as information sources in elementary social studies classes. This suggests a need for social studies teachers to be concerned about learners' reading abilities. It makes sense to integrate some reading development activities in social studies lessons.

9. Specific plans for assisting pupils to learn from prose materials can be developed for each of the three major stages of the reading process. These stages are (1) prereading, (2) during reading, and (3) postreading.

10. Teachers are concerned with developing pupils' writing as well as reading skills in social studies lessons. Writing activities can be organized under seven major language functions: (1) instrumental, (2) regulatory, (3) interactional, (4) personal, (5) heuristic, (6) representational, and (7) imaginative.

CHAPTER REFLECTIONS

Directions: Now that you have finished reading the chapter, reread the case study at the beginning. Then answer these questions.

1. How would you now respond to the question of whether writing activities should be emphasized in social studies lessons?

2. Give some examples of where you think it would be particularly appropriate to integrate the teaching of mathematics, science, and other traditional school subjects and social studies.

3. In what ways could reading and writing activities be included so that time is not taken away from more traditional social studies content?

4. What are specific examples of social studies activities consistent with each of the writing functions?

EXTENDING UNDERSTANDING AND SKILL

1. Review a chapter of a social studies text designed for use at a grade level you would like to teach. List possible themes that could be used as a focus for integrating a unit involving several different subjects.

2. Prepare a graphic organizer illustrating how several different subjects might be studied in the context of a theme or a question.

3. Read a children's literature selection. Brainstorm ways various subjects might be taught using the book as a focus.

4. Experiment with multipass reading. Choose a chapter in a book that is unfamiliar to you. Read the chapter several times using the multipass technique described in the chapter. How effective was it for you? Do you think it took a significantly longer period of time to read the material this way? Do you think it enhanced your comprehension?

5. Identify a topic you might teach to learners in the middle or upper grades. Identify appropriate writing activities that could be developed for at least three of the seven language functions discussed in the chapter.

REFERENCES

BEANE, J. A. (1992). "The Middle School: The Natural Home of Integrated Curriculum." *Educational Leadership, 49*, pp. 9–13.

BLUMENFELD, P., KRAJICK, J., MARX, R., AND SOLOWAY, E. (1994). "Lessons Learned: How Collaboration Helped Middle Grade Science Teachers Learn Project-based Instruction." *The Elementary School Journal, 94* (5), pp. 539–551.

COLLINS, E., AND CHANDLER, S. (1993). "Beyond Art as Product: Using Artistic Perspective to Understand Classroom Life." *Theory Into Practice, 32* (4), pp. 199–203.

EISNER, E. (1991). "Art, Music and Literature Within Social Studies." In J. Shaver (ed.), *Handbook of Research on Social Studies Teaching and Learning.* Englewood Cliffs, NJ: Merrill/Prentice Hall, pp. 551–558.

GIESE, J., PARISI, L., AND BYBEE, R. (1991). "The Science-Technology-Society Theme and Social Studies." In J. Shaver (ed.), *Handbook of Research on Social Studies Teaching and Learning.* Englewood Cliffs, NJ: Merrill/Prentice Hall, pp. 559–565.

HALLIDAY, M. A. K. (1973). *Explorations in the Functions of Language.* London: Edward Arnold.

HALLIDAY, M. A. K., AND HASAN, R. (1989). *Language, Context, and Text: Aspects of Language in a Social-Semiotic Perspective*. 2d ed. New York: Oxford University Press.

LAUGHLIN, M., BLACK, P., AND LOBERG, M. (1991). *Social Studies Readers' Theater for Children: Scripts and Script Development*. Englewood, CO: Teacher Ideas Press.

MARKER, G. (1992). "Integrating Science-Technology-Society Into Social Studies Education." *Theory Into Practice, 31* (1) , pp. 20–26.

MANZO, A. V. (1969). "ReQuest; A Method for Improving Reading Comprehension through Reciprocal Questioning." *Journal of Reading, 13* (2), pp. 123–126, 163.

NORTON, D. (1995). *Through the Eyes of a Child: An Introduction to Children's Literature*. Englewood Cliffs, NJ: Merrill/Prentice Hall.

RUDMAN, M. (1993). *Children's Literature: An Issues Approach*. 3d ed. New York: Longman.

SAVAGE, T., AND ARMSTRONG, D. (1992). "Were Things Really So Cheap in the 'Good Old Days'?" *The Social Studies, 83* (4), pp. 155–159.

SAVAGE, M., AND SAVAGE, T. (1993). "Children's Literature in Middle School Social Studies." *The Social Studies, 84* (1), pp. 32–36.

TOMPKINS, G., AND HOSKISSON, K. (1991). *Language Arts: Content and Teaching Strategies*. Englewood Cliffs, NJ: Merrill/Prentice Hall.

SOCIAL STUDIES FOR LIMITED ENGLISH PROFICIENT LEARNERS

CHAPTER GOALS

This chapter provides information to help the reader:

- state the need for altering social studies instruction to accommodate limited English proficient pupils,
- identify the potential problems that limited English proficient pupils have in learning social studies,
- define *sheltered instruction* in social studies,
- list principles of language development to consider when planning lessons, and
- define specific instructional approaches useful for teaching limited English proficient pupils.

CHAPTER STRUCTURE

Introduction
Potential Problems for Limited English Proficient Learners in Social Studies
 Cultural Conflict
 Lack of Social Studies Background
 Sequential Nature of the Curriculum
 Difficulty of Social Studies Materials
Sheltered Instruction in the Social Studies
Principles of Second Language Learning in Content Fields
 The Affective Filter
 Meaningful and Comprehensible Input
 Stages of Language Acquisition
 Preproduction
 Early Production
 Speech Emergence
 Intermediate Fluency
 Context and Cognitive Load
 Learning Types of Knowledge Structures
 Description
 Sequence
 Choice
 Classification
 Principles
 Evaluation
Successful Instructional Practices for Teaching Limited English Proficient Learners
 Cooperative Learning
 Multimedia and Concrete Experiences
 Language Experiences
 Semantic Mapping
 Guided Writing
Key Ideas in Summary
Chapter Reflections
Extending Understanding and Skill
References

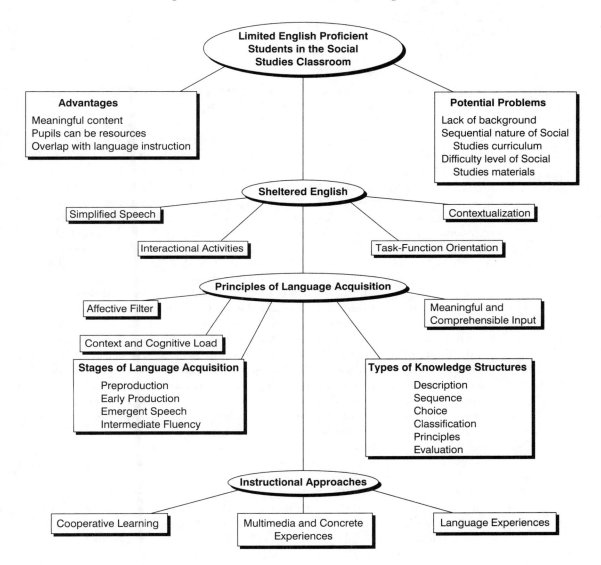

Figure 16–1
Social studies for limited English proficient students.

Chapter 16

Case Study

SHOULD YOU ALTER INSTRUCTION FOR LIMITED ENGLISH PROFICIENT PUPILS?

John Taylor wearily made his way to the Wednesday afternoon faculty meeting. The first two weeks had been busier than he could have imagined. Foremost among his concerns was how to prepare lessons that would meet the needs of the diverse group of fourth graders assigned to this, his first, class. He had pupils who had difficulty reading, those who appeared to be gifted, some mainstreamed special education pupils, and nearly 40 percent of his class had a primary language other than English. Some of them communicated quite well, while others had limited comprehension. He knew a bit of Spanish, so that helped with some of the pupils. However, he also had pupils whose primary languages were Korean and Vietnamese. He needed all the time he had to try prepare for his class. The last thing he needed was another meeting.

He settled into a seat near the rear of the library and jotted down notes as announcements were made. Mrs. Quesada, the principal, announced that the district was continuing to experience an influx of students from a variety of cultures. The newest wave appeared to be a considerable number of Romanians who were settling within the attendance boundaries of the school. As a result of these demographic shifts, and in response to pressure from the state department of education, the school board was requiring attendance of all teachers to a series of workshops focused on the topic of teaching limited English proficient pupils. Furthermore, all nontenured teachers were going to be required to obtain the bilingual teaching credential as a condition of continued employment. The district would pay the cost of obtaining the credential. The announcement precipitated a loud explosion!

"Wait a minute, I've got enough to do without attending another series of meetings!" was the retort of one veteran teacher.

"I agree," said another. "Plus, I disagree with the whole concept. Individuals who come to the United States should be prepared to learn English and to learn it quickly! We should not be required to disrupt the learning of all pupils to accommodate the language needs of these students. They should be placed in a total English immersion program until they learn English well enough to enter our classrooms!!"

"Yeah" agreed another. "If we went to another country we would not expect that they would teach us in English. We would be expected to learn the language of the host country." John noticed some nods of agreement as well as several frowns of disapproval.

"I think we are forgetting something," one teacher remarked. "Our concern ought to be providing success for all pupils. It will not do anyone any good to ignore the learning needs of these pupils so that they are hindered in their educational progress and end up dropping out or becoming alienated. We have a commitment to teach all of the pupils." John was surprised at the explosion and was confused as the debate raged around him. It was obviously a topic that evoked strong passions.

What Is Your Response?

Read this case carefully. Then respond briefly to these questions:

1. Do you think that regular classroom instruction should be altered to facilitate the learning of limited English proficient pupils?
2. Should pupils first acquire proficiency in English before studying content areas such as social studies? Why or why not?
3. Do you think that accommodating the needs of these pupils interferes with the learning of other pupils? Why or why not?
4. What specific things can be done to aid the learning of these pupils?
5. What problems do you think you might encounter in trying to teach these pupils social studies?

INTRODUCTION

The number of pupils who have a primary language other than English has increased dramatically over the past few years. These pupils are generally referred to as *limited English proficient* (LEP) learners. Some people object to the "LEP" designation as a pejorative term and prefer the term "English learner." However, since we are all lifelong English learners and because limited English proficient is a common term used by the government for classification purposes, we will use the term *LEP* in this chapter for the purpose of clarity. We by no means intend the term to imply anything negative or demeaning.

Between 1985 and 1992 the number of LEP learners enrolled in schools across the United States increased by nearly 70 percent. Somewhat over 6 percent of the total K–12 population is comprised of LEP learners (Association for Supervision and Curriculum Development, 1994). Many teachers (not just specialists in bilingual education or English as a second language [ESL] education) have responsibilities for helping these pupils learn and grow. These statistics suggests that it is probable you will have LEP pupils in your classroom. These young people will not be able to deal with social studies content in the same way as pupils with well-developed English communication skills. What problems may they experience in learning social studies content? What will you do? You cannot ignore these pupils and deliver lessons as if they were not present. That some teachers fail to respond to the needs of these young people is evident in the sad reality that children from non-English-speaking backgrounds drop out of school at nearly twice the rate of individuals with English-speaking backgrounds (Garcia, 1994).

To "catch up" and "keep up" with their peers who are native speakers of English, schools must deliver programs that assist these young people to master academic content at the same time they are learning to be more proficient users of English (Early, 1990). Their needs must be met and appropriate learning experiences provided if they are to grow toward productive citizenship. There is evidence that well-planned school programs and sensitive teachers can support the personal and academic development of language minority pupils (Garcia, 1994). For example, teaching English through content area instruction facilitates both English acquisition and academic achievement.

Pupils need two types of language proficiency to succeed in content area classes. One of these focuses on the development of *basic interpersonal communication skills*. This kind of language proficiency allows pupils to participate in everyday conversation in informal situations. This is what they use to communicate on the playground, in the store, or elsewhere to convey their needs. The second type of language proficiency is termed *cognitive/academic language proficiency*. This kind of language expertise allows pupils to understand and communicate in classroom discussions where the contextual clues are reduced and where unique terminology is used. It usually takes pupils whose first language is not English several years to acquire a cognitive/academic language proficiency as good as that of a native speaker of English. Sometimes teachers make the mistake of assuming that because a pupil has developed a fairly high degree of basic interpersonal communication skill that she also possesses a high level of cognitive/academic language proficiency.

Social studies lessons are especially useful vehicles for helping pupils develop both interpersonal communication skills and cognitive/academic language proficiency. The study of culture is a major ingredient in language acquisition programs. Those pupils who are receiving assistance in bilingual programs or English as a second language programs will have experiences that tie closely to their social studies lessons. For example, learners who spend part of the day in bilingual classrooms often are able to use content from their social studies classes in assigned conversational exercises. There are many opportunities for regular classroom teachers and bilingual teachers to engage in cooperative planning of experiences that can benefit youngsters who are working to become more proficient in English.

The social studies curriculum allows learners from different cultures the opportunity to share their native culture and history with peers. Pupils from different backgrounds become resources who can help all pupils in the class learn important social studies content and values. These pupil-to-pupil exchanges enrich content understanding and at the same time help individuals to develop self-respect and pride in their cultural heritage. This situation is very beneficial for nonnative speakers of English as they work to develop a more sophisticated cognitive/academic language proficiency in English.

Another advantage of social studies lessons for LEP pupils is the opportunity they provide for them to learn and understand basic American cultural values and beliefs. This kind of learning helps them sort through the mysterious behavior of others in the classroom and keeps them from making embarrassing mistakes. As teachers, we need to make sure that these new understandings do not come at the expense of their home culture.

POTENTIAL PROBLEMS FOR LIMITED ENGLISH PROFICIENT LEARNERS IN SOCIAL STUDIES

There are some potential problems for LEP learners in social studies classes. One is that social studies is usually a very "language bound" content area. Teachers tend to rely on written and oral language to convery concepts, ideas, and key points. For this reason, social studies can be a particularly challenging area of the curriculum for pupils and teachers. However, it is not just the amount of reading that creates problems, but also the type of reading. Much required social studies reading is expository in style and filled with abstract concepts and unfamiliar terms and names (Short, 1994).

Social studies teachers often place a great deal of emphasis on writing papers and reports. Such expectations cause problems for many learners in the classroom. They are especially troublesome for LEP pupils, many of whom still lack highly developed English-language writing skills.

Subsections that follow highlight problem areas we need to consider in planning instruction for LEP pupils.

Cultural Conflict

If we are unaware of sociocultural factors in play in our classroom, it may be difficult for our LEP pupils to succeed (Garcia, 1991). Anthropologists define *culture* as the attitudes, values, beliefs, and traditions shared by a group of people. Culture gives direction to the lives of people and helps them make sense out of their environment (Garcia, 1991). It influences how people perceive themselves and others and exerts a powerful influence on the way they behave. Initially, all pupils, regardless of race, creed, or social class, come to school as culturally whole individuals with a language, a set of values, attitudes, beliefs, and knowledge (Garcia, 1991). We need to understand the cultural heritages of our learners so we can develop activities and interaction patterns that are consistent with their values and beliefs.

LEP pupils often find the predominant classroom culture to be different and strange. They may be unaware of the rules and social conventions that guide social interactions (King, Fagan, Bratt, & Baer, 1992). For example, a Vietnamese student related to one of authors the embarrassment and confusion she felt when her teacher did not understand her name or how to pronounce it. The result was a barrier that hindered her learning and progress.

These learners may not understand how to relate to us or to others in the class. As a result, they may find themselves in a situation of cultural conflict where what they have learned in their primary culture is contrary to what we, as teachers, expect of them. They may become confused and embarrassed. A frequent response to this situation is withdrawal and a refusal to participate. This is the opposite of what they need if they are to progress in learning the language. It is imperative that we understand the cultural backgrounds of our pupils and that we use this information to plan instruction that is responsive to their needs.

Expected patterns of interaction in our classrooms often are at odds with what LEP children have experienced at home or in social settings with others from their ethnic or cultural group. For example, many classroom environments feature a rapid pace of instruction and an emphasis on individual performance and competition. This pattern may be totally unfamiliar to some LEP youngsters in our classes (Au & Kawakami, 1994).

We need to strive for *culturally congruent* instruction. This kind of instruction builds on pupils' cultural and linguistic strengths. Abundant evidence exists that learners who receive instruction consistent with the norms of their home culture will have better learning opportunities (Au & Kawakami, 1994).

Lack of Social Studies Background

What pupils already know is critical to what they can take away from a new learning situation. New knowledge must be related to previous learning if it is to be meaningful. Many LEP pupils lack the prerequisite knowledge to succeed when new lessons are introduced. For example, LEP youngsters whose families have come to the United States as immigrants may not have had previous instruction in some topics that are featured in most U.S. social studies programs. When this is the case, these young people have no conceptual base they can use as a foundation when we, as teachers, introduce new information. We need to be particularly careful to diagnose entry-level understandings of our LEP pupils.

In addition to lacking formal instruction in topics familiar to most American learners, recent immigrants to this country may know little about traditions and events that become part of the shared cultural heritage of people who have lived here for some time. For example, they may have no understanding of Thanksgiving or of the Pilgrims. In our schools, many classes from kindergarten through sixth grade include activities related to Thanksgiving. These activities may be confusing and mystifying to pupils from another culture. An example of this situation happened to one of the authors when he moved to Texas. One of his sons was enrolled in a history and geography of Texas class, and had some difficulty with this class because the teacher and the other students made assumptions about famous people and places that were familiar to native Texans but were unknown to him. Just imagine how much more difficult it would be for a pupil coming from another culture, speaking another language!

Finally, even those LEP learners who have previous experience in American schools may have difficulty because they have an inadequate understanding of central concepts taught in classes they have attended (King, Fagan, Bratt, & Baer, 1992). Research indicates that it takes from five to seven years for LEP pupils to achieve a level of language proficiency that is on a par with pupils who speak English as their first language (Short, 1994; Cummins, 1981). Because young children develop verbal fluency in social conversation fairly rapidly, we may assume that our LEP youngsters' levels of English comprehension are higher than they really are. Therefore, even when LEP pupils have been exposed to certain ideas and concepts in previous years, there is no assurance that they have been adequately understood. This point reinforces the need to monitor carefully what our LEP pupils really know. Often, we have to provide additional instruction to fill in the gaps.

Sequential Nature of the Curriculum

Social studies curriculum and social studies texts generally follow a regular sequence of topics. They assume pupils have been continuously enrolled in American schools. For example, nearly every school in the United States teaches U.S. history in the fifth grade. It is assumed that pupils have already received specific instruction about the local community and the state in previous school years. The cumulative nature of the elementary social studies curriculum often creates problems for LEP pupils (King, Fagan, Bratt, & Baer, 1992). These difficulties are especially serious for LEP pupils in middle schools and high schools.

For example, the *History-Social Science Framework for California* includes the study of United States history and geography in grades 5, 8 and 11. In grade 5, the content stops with westward expansion, with some attention to linking the past with the present. Grade 8 includes a summary of what was learned in grade 5 and expands the content to the study of industrial America up to World War I. The 11th grade curriculum then begins with the Progressive Era and moves to the present. Pupils coming into California schools from other countries who missed either the California 5th or 8th grade program not surprisingly often experience difficulty when they encounter the 11th grade program. For teachers, this suggests a need to think beyond the limits of the prescribed grade-level content when working with LEP learners. We have to be sure these young people have access to key ideas that they will need to succeed as they progress through the entire school program.

Difficulty of Social Studies Materials

Another major problem relates to the nature of the material often used in social studies classrooms. Unfortunately, many social studies classes do not include hands-on or manipulative activities that often can enhance comprehension for LEP pupils (Short, 1994). Although there are pictures in most social studies books, they tend to depict events or famous people. Typically they do not supply the concrete references helpful to LEP pupils.

In addition, social studies lessons often include specialized terminology that can create confusion. For example the term *strike* as used in a social studies lesson on labor relationships is very different from how *strike* is used in describing a battle or a baseball game. Similarly, pupils may have a different understanding of a term or an event than that assumed by the teacher. For example, a pupil coming from another country with a different form of government might have a different interpretation of the term *democracy* than United States natives.

Reading material used in social studies creates difficulties for LEP pupils. The typical expository style compresses huge volumes of information into a short selection. This results in a heavy concept load that makes comprehension difficult for pupils who do not have highly developed reading skills (Perez & Torres- Guzman, 1992). In addition, much prose material is not written in ways that stimulate high levels of interest.

In summary, LEP pupils encounter many problems as they seek success in the social studies. Most of these can be overcome if we are sensitive to their needs and work hard to judge entry-level understanding, monitor progress carefully as lessons develop, and adjust lessons to respond to special characteristics of our LEP learners.

SHELTERED INSTRUCTION IN THE SOCIAL STUDIES

LEP pupils come from enormously varied backgrounds. They trace their ancestry to different countries. Languages they speak at home are diverse. It is not uncommon for school districts to have pupils in their district with 20 or 30 different first languages. It is simply not possible for school districts to employ teachers who are proficient in all of these languages. Therefore, the idea of providing instruction in the first language until the pupil is ready to be "mainstreamed" into an all-English classroom is not feasible. One response to this situation is what has been termed *sheltered instruction*. Sheltered instruction is based on the work of Krashen (1982). It seeks to is make the content of the instruction more comprehensible to the LEP pupil. There are four basic elements of sheltered instruction:

- Simplified speech
- Contextualization
- Task-function orientation
- Interactional activities

Simplified speech means speaking clearly with controlled vocabulary and reduced syntactic complexity of sentences. *Contextualization* refers to the extensive use of visuals, body language, and other techniques that provide nonverbal clues to the learner. *Task-function orientation* refers to relating new information to everyday life and to concrete experiences. Thus, teachers use language for real communication, not just as a contrived academic exercise. This is intended to make the language useful and meaningful. *Interactional activities* provide opportunities for pupils to interact with others and use the language they are acquiring. This means placing emphasis on content rather than on correct language usage.

Sheltered instruction in social studies provides pupils with concrete examples of abstract ideas and concepts. Extensive use of realia, pictures, charts, graphs, and nonverbal behavior supplements words. The content emphasizes practical application of ideas and concepts. Numerous opportunities are provided for LEP pupils to work in groups where they have opportunities to talk and discuss. When we talk to pupils in a sheltered instructional situation, we carefully avoid overuse of unfamiliar idiomatic expressions, and we often repeat key words and ideas. We speak as clearly and slowly as possible. When preparing new prose material, we carefully control sentence length and take care to assure that other elements that can contribute to reading comprehension problems are eliminated.

The next section introduces basic principles associated with successful programs that focus on second language learning in the content areas.

PRINCIPLES OF SECOND LANGUAGE LEARNING IN CONTENT FIELDS

Understanding some of the basic principles of language acquisition can help us to create classroom learning environments where both LEP and native English-speaking pupils can be successful. Subsections that follow introduce examples of principles we can use to prepare lessons in content areas such as the social studies for classes that include LEP pupils.

The Affective Filter

A key element in providing a classroom environment where second language learning is enhanced is the social–emotional component. This is what experts in language acquisition call the *affective filter*. The affective filter refers to the combination of the affective variables of self-concept, motivation, anxiety, and fear that can facilitate or block language learning. The climate of the classroom interacts with these variables to raise or lower the affective filter. It is hypothesized that when the affective filter is high, or when there is a great deal of anxiety or threat, a pupil has trouble processing information that would be comprehensible if the affective filter were lower.

The affective filter differs from pupil to pupil. Young people who have a positive self-concept and are motivated to learn English tolerate more anxiety and generally move quite quickly through the early stages of language development. On the other hand, those filled with anxiety or fear struggle and may become frustrated as they attempt to learn the new language.

What this implies for the teacher of LEP pupils is that the classroom climate needs to be a safe and an encouraging one. We need to use positive reinforcement and to celebrate pupils' successes. We must be careful when correcting pupils so they do not develop a fear of ridicule or failure. Teachers and English proficient pupils in the classroom need to model acceptance and encourage linguistically different learners.

Meaningful and Comprehensible Input

This principle is a part of the sheltered instruction concept. It directs us to present material to LEP pupils in ways that are meaningful and comprehensible; that is, the content and presentation must be relevant and important to the pupil. Many of us recall our frustrations when we were beginning the study of a foreign language. Sometimes, instruction we received was ineffective because we were asked to learn phrases that were relatively unimportant and that we could not imagine ourselves using in the normal course of our lives. This kind of language instruction contrasts with how young children first learn a language. They begin by mastering words and phrases that are important and meaningful to them. This pattern has implications for us as we think about planning social studies lessons, particularly for classes enrolling LEP pupils. One of our major tasks is to find ways to relate social studies content to the experiences and lives of our pupils. Social studies lessons that are abstract or that deal with topics remote from their everyday lives will do little to help LEP pupils learn either English or social studies content.

In addition to being relevant to pupils lives, we also must exercise care to select learning materials that are comprehensible to LEP pupils. Language that is too abstract or too technical will not be understood and will not lead to improvement. New information that pupils can comprehend builds carefully on what they already know. This implies a need for us to carefully diagnose entry-level understandings of our learners.

Social studies material can also be made more understandable when we provide numerous clues to meaning. For example, we can use pictures, graphs, charts, and concrete objects to illustrate key points. Multiple reinforcements of information help to shore up pupil understanding.

An outline of key points helps to make lessons more comprehensible to LEP students.

Stages of Language Acquisition[*]

Understanding the stages of language development helps us plan and implement meaningful and comprehensible material. The following stages are based on what has been termed the "natural approach" to language development (Terrell, 1981):

- Preproduction
- Early production
- Speech emergence
- Intermediate fluency

Preproduction

This is the beginning stage of receptive language acquisition. This stage often is found among people from non-English-speaking countries who have recently arrived in the United States. The name of the stage is based on the idea that even though these individuals may know a few English words, they are too shy to respond and generally prefer to remain silent. They may point to items, use gestures such as nodding, or use other actions to communicate with others. Somewhat later, they may respond with "yes" or "no" or with single words in their primary language or in English. It is normal for this stage to last for six months or longer. You need to recognize that it is normal for

[*]Thanks to Carmen Zuniga-Hill, California State University, Fullerton for her assistance in outlining these developmental stages.

pupils in this stage to be reluctant to speak, and you should not place undue pressure on them to do so. Speaking will emerge naturally.

At this stage, people focus their attention almost exclusively on aural comprehension. They observe gestures and try to make sense out the input by using context clues. They guess about the meaning of vocabulary words.

We can assist pupils at this stage by using contextualized language. Gestures, realia, or pictures provide contextual clues that can help them find the meaning of what was spoken. We need to speak at a slow rate and to articulate words clearly. Short, simple directions and questions such as, "Point to the _____," or "Is this a _____?" are useful in helping determine the comprehension of pupils at this stage. It is also a good idea to write keywords on the board and to emphasize them in oral presentations.

Early Production

At this stage, individuals begin to try limited production of the language. They are starting to develop basic interpersonal communication skills. They can communicate with short verbal statements that may be memorized to fit certain contexts. The result is that these attempts to produce language contain many mistakes of pronunciation and word usage. These individuals may have a receptive vocabulary of about 1,000 words, but can produce only about 10 percent of these. This stage may last from six months to one year.

Progress of these pupils is facilitated when we introduce them to written words and phrases that they find meaningful. They should not be ridiculed because of their misuse of language. Modeling correct usage is an appropriate way to provide correction. The purpose is to help lower the affective filter of these young people so they are not afraid to attempt communication in their new language. Patterned language usage and the use of contextual language is critical. Graphic organizers, story maps, and language experience charts are all helpful to these pupils as they seek meaning in the language they hear.

Speech Emergence

At this stage, individuals begin to feel more comfortable with the language and are more willing to attempt to speak sentences and participate in conversations. There is a noticeable expansion of comprehension. They have now broadened their receptive vocabulary to about 7,000 words, with about 10 percent production. They still need help in continued vocabulary development and in the development of their basic interpersonal communication skills. This stage tends to last for about one year.

Because learners at this stage are more confident in their abilities to use the new language than at earlier stages, we have fewer worries about undermining their self-image when correcting their mistakes. At this stage, it makes sense to direct our correction efforts to improving their levels of comprehension. Some sensitivity remains regarding the ability to pronounce all words in the new language correctly, and we have to be careful about drawing too much attention to this kind of difficulty. Graphic organizers are still useful in helping pupils discover meaning in a text.

Pupils who have arrived at this stage of language proficiency can begin to participate in group writing activities and in reading self-selected literature. Our major task is to provide as many opportunities as possible for these pupils to use English in a variety of contexts. They need to be encouraged to participate in discussions and conversations, and challenged to respond to questions that require them to make fairly lengthy verbal responses.

Intermediate Fluency

It often takes pupils three or four years to arrive at intermediate fluency. At this stage, individuals engage in everyday conversations with ease. However, pupils may be reluctant to speak in front of large groups. They still make some mistakes and, although there appears to be a high degree of fluency, comprehension of content in academic areas such as social studies may be a problem. At this stage, pupils have developed a fairly high level of development in the language domains of listening and speaking. However, they still need assistance in achieving nativelike fluency in reading and writing. They can engage in extended discourse and can give oral reports. They can benefit from working with peers on activities requiring reading and writing. These pupils often enjoy using their new communication skills in small groups. We are able to challenge these youngsters with tasks requiring quite sophisticated thinking skills. Correction of mistakes can be done in a much firmer manner than in previous stages.

Even at this stage, pupils' level of language proficiency in some areas is likely to fall short of that of native speakers of English. Because many of these pupils speak the language well, sometimes there is a tendency for teachers to confuse verbal fluency with total mastery of the language. When this happens, these pupils' needs may be overlooked, and they may not get the kind of special assistance we need to give them to assure they comprehend the academic content of lessons. We need to remember that these pupils are being asked to learn content presented in a language in which many will not yet have attained native-speaker fluency.

Context and Cognitive Load

The four stages of language acquisition emphasize the importance of context in helping LEP pupils comprehend lessons presented in English. Cummins (1981) identified the *context* and the *cognitive demands* of a message as two important variables that teachers need to consider when communicating with individuals with limited language abilities. He used these two variables to construct a four-cell matrix that is useful in determining the type of tasks and instruction that can be provided to pupils (see Figure 16–2).

Quadrant A includes language that is used in a clear context and that is relatively undemanding cognitively. This includes the basic interpersonal communication skills that an individual needs for simple communication with others. Activities such as buying lunch, getting materials, following simple directions, and drawing a picture fall into this category. These would be appropriate for individuals in the early stages of language acquisition. The social studies content provided for individuals at this level would need to be very basic, concrete, and embedded in the context of classroom and school activities and should not extend much beyond comprehension of key vocabulary.

Figure 16–2

Varying context and cognitive load for LEP pupils.

Source: Cummins, J. (1981). "The Role of Primary Language Development in Promoting Educational Success for Language Minority Students." In California State Department of Education (ed.), *Schooling and Language Minority Students: Theoretical Framework.* Los Angeles: California State University, Los Angeles Evaluation and Assessment Center.

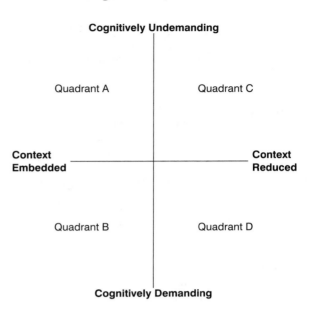

Cognitively Undemanding

Quadrant A   Quadrant C

Context Embedded — **Context Reduced**

Quadrant B   Quadrant D

Cognitively Demanding

Quadrant B of the matrix includes activities that are still very context dependent but that are more demanding cognitively. In other words, the lessons need to include many clues that are provided in a concrete manner so that pupils can comprehend the message, yet that require more sophisticated thought processes, beyond recall or repeating language patterns. Examples might include social studies lessons accompanied by concrete objects, pictures, graphs, story webs, games, dramatization, or building projects. These kinds of learning experiences are appropriate for pupils in the speech emergence phase. They need instruction provided in a fairly intellectually demanding context but where clues are present to assist their search for meaning. It is important to remember that more cognitively demanding material is generally more interesting and challenging to the pupils. Therefore, we need to try to move to this type of instruction as soon as possible. However, it is important that the cognitive demands not be so high as to raise the affective filter to a level where progress is blocked.

Quadrant C indicates those types of activities that are not too intellectually demanding and are also relatively free of context clues. A good example might be talking on the telephone. There is no context to help the individual sort out the meaning of the message even though the message might be a simple one. An example of a classroom activity might be that of following written directions. Unless accompanied by a chart or a diagram, there are few clues to help the LEP pupil sort out the meaning of the message. This type of instruction is appropriate for those pupils who have made considerable progress in the speech emergence phase and who may have reached intermediate fluency.

Quadrant D includes those types of activities and tasks that have reduced numbers of context clues and that are cognitively demanding. This includes activities such as reading the textbook, taking a test, and listening to a speaker or a lecture. Pupils who can function at this level have achieved quite a high level of literacy in English. Most of the typical social studies activities can be conducted with minimal regard for the special comprehension needs of these pupils. Individuals at this level have arrived at a level of cognitive academic language proficiency.

When designing social studies instruction, we need to diagnose the stage of language acquisition of the LEP pupils in the class. The matrix can then be used to determine the types of activities that might be most appropriate for them.

Learning Types of Knowledge Structures

Mohan (1986) proposed a framework that we can use when deciding on the types of activities we should provide for LEP pupils. His framework is based on the idea that knowledge is structured similarly from situation to situation. If pupils learn types of knowledge that apply to certain situations, then they can transfer this to different content areas to enhance their comprehension of the content. Mohan also states that these knowledge structures have certain common linguistic features that set them apart. These features facilitate transfer of learning from one language to another. Finally, Mohan points out that these distinct knowledge structures can be represented by key visual organizers that have the potential to help learners organize and simplify content.

Mohan (1986) identified six distinct types of knowledge structures. Each of these knowledge structures can be explored through a set of questions:

- Description
- Sequence
- Choice
- Classification
- Principles
- Evaluation

Description
This knowledge type requires pupils to observe, identify, locate, or describe persons, objects, settings, or events. The types of questions we can ask in this category related to issues such as, Who? What? Where? How many? Key visuals appropriate to this knowledge type are pictures, slides, diagrams, maps, and drawings.

Sequence
This knowledge type requires pupils to organize things in order, note changes over time, follow steps in directions, or note recurring cycles. Some questions in this category we might ask include, What happened first? What was next? What was the order? Key visuals that can help pupils understand issues associated with sequence are flow charts, timelines, and filmstrips.

Choice

This knowledge type requires pupils to make decisions, select from alternatives, propose alternatives, and take action. Some questions we might ask related to choice include, What are the alternatives? What would you do? What other choices could be made? What would be the consequences? This type of knowledge is consistent with the types of strategies discussed in Chapter 8, "Developing Prosocial Behavior." Key visuals for displaying the relationships in this knowledge type are flow charts and decision trees.

Classification

This knowledge type requires pupils to identify common attributes and to group and define items with common characteristics. It is very much like concept formation, described earlier. Among classification questions, we might ask, What things go together? How are these items alike? How are these items different? What other ways could these things be grouped? Key visuals for illustrating this knowledge type include charts, webs, tables, and semantic maps.

Principles

This knowledge type requires pupils to explain, predict, interpret data, formulate hypotheses, test hypotheses, apply information, and note cause and effect. This knowledge type is consistent with the interpretation of data and the inquiry approaches introduced earlier. Some questions related to principles we might ask include, How do you explain that? What caused that? Why do you think it happened that way? What do you think would happen if . . . ? How could you apply this to problems? Key visuals that can facilitate mastery of this knowledge type are Venn diagrams, cycle charts, and data retrieval charts.

Evaluation

This knowledge type requires pupils to make a judgment about the worth or relative strength of something. Questions that we might ask include, Which is the best choice? What criteria would you used to judge the worth of this? Which one is right? Key visuals useful for displaying this type of thinking are rating scales, grids, and rank ordering.

Some of these knowledge types are easier for pupils to master than others. This has implications for us as we plan learning experiences for our LEP learners. For example, content related to "description," "sequence," and "classification" often is not so complex as content related to other knowledge categories. For this reason, we might opt to focus on content of this kind when preparing lessons for pupils at the early production stage of acquiring English. Lessons focusing on more demanding content, associated with categories such as "principle formulation" and "evaluation," need to be reserved for LEP pupils who have developed fairly advanced levels of English usage and comprehension. When we take care to match knowledge types to LEP pupils' individual levels of English facility, we improve the prospects that they will master the content. This is important because every academic success learners experience has the potential for enhancing their self-image and motivating them to learn more.

SUCCESSFUL INSTRUCTIONAL PRACTICES FOR TEACHING LIMITED ENGLISH PROFICIENT LEARNERS

Researchers have identified several common characteristics of classrooms that are successful in helping LEP pupils achieve success. In these classes there is great emphasis on functional communication from teacher to learner and from learner to learner. These classrooms tend to be organized around a theme and to have an integrated curriculum. There is a great deal of pupil collaboration on almost all activities, with a minimal amount of individual work. Finally, there is an informal and almost familial atmosphere (Garcia, 1994). Instructional practices that relate to these characteristics include cooperative learning, multimedia and concrete experiences, and language experiences.

Cooperative Learning

Cooperative learning approaches are strongly recommended for LEP pupils. Cooperative learning maximizes the opportunities for pupils to interact with each other and to use language in a nonthreatening environment. Pupils who might otherwise be silent because of embarrassment are more likely to communicate in a small group. Elementary school pupils can be quite inventive in communicating with those with very limited English. In cooperative groups, they are able to help the LEP pupil comprehend

Cooperative learning approaches facilitate interaction and lead to improved language usage.

what is happening in the classroom. The group rewards serve as strong incentives for the LEP pupils. It helps them avoid the fear of failure and provides them with opportunities to succeed in spite of their language difficulties.

Multimedia and Concrete Experiences

Because many social studies ideas are communicated in written form and are abstract, concrete experiences and different types of media are important aids to pupil learning. This is particularly true when we work with LEP pupils, who often are challenged both by the difficulty of abstract content and by the necessity to learn in a language they do not yet know well.

Many social studies concepts can be conveyed through the use of pictures. A good picture file including pictures of objects and scenes is an extremely useful tool for teaching social studies to all pupils. Maps, globes, artifacts, and filmstrips are useful as well. There are particular advantages in using filmstrips with classes that include LEP pupils. The narrative that accompanies most filmstrips can be rewritten to accommodate the stage of language acquisition of the pupils. In this way pupils get pictures to accompany the English, which reinforces the content being introduced visually and provides additional practice in reading English.

It is also useful to make audiotapes of classroom discussions, and make them available to pupils. They can replay them as many times as needed to comprehend the material. Pupils can stop the tape and ask the teacher if they do not understand the meaning of a word or a phrase. Sometimes other pupils in the class can listen with them and provide clarification.

Flashcards and sentence strips are also useful supplements. Important names, dates, concepts and terms can be written on flashcards. The key vocabulary and concepts can then be previewed at the beginning of the lesson and reviewed periodically during the lesson. Sentence strips with key phrases or ideas can also be developed. For example, if we were teaching a fifth-grade class that included LEP pupils, we could prepare flashcards featuring names of various explorers. We might review these with the LEP pupils before the lesson. During the lesson, we could display appropriate flashcards when introducing each explorer, which would provide a visual reference for the spoken word and enhance comprehension.

Another activity based on flashcards is to have the pupils develop word banks of commonly used or imperfectly understood terms. These terms can then be addressed specifically in developing comprehension. As the pupils continue to develop their language fluency, they can keep adding to the word bank. Not only does this help them review and learn new terms, it provides them with a visible record of their progress.

Field trips provide pupils with concrete experiences. Visits to stores, parks, factories, and the local neighborhood forge a link between everyday tasks and language acquisition. Other concrete activities for social studies classes include construction of social studies projects such as models, dioramas, or murals. Dramatizing events and role playing represent still other approaches to embedding social studies content in contexts pupils will view as "real." For example, the principle of "taxation without representation" is commonly included in fifth-grade lessons. However, this is an abstract idea that may be difficult for a second-language learner to grasp. Acting out a dramatization where individuals are required to pay a fee with no opportunity for input or discussion can make the idea concrete and help pupils grasp the meaning.

Lesson Idea 16–1

ALTERING A LESSON TO ACCOMMODATE LEP PUPILS

ORIGINAL LESSON

Grade Level:	4
Objectives:	Pupils will use cardinal directions to indicate the relative location of places on a map.
Overview:	Understanding the cardinal directions is an important skill in helping individuals orient themselves. They are important in understanding the relative and absolute location of places.
Procedure:	***Learning Set*** Ask the class, "How many of you have asked someone for directions on how to get somewhere?" Allow them to share stories of problems with unclear directions. Tell them, "Today we are going to learn about something called 'cardinal directions.' These can help you learn how to find places on maps and help you give better directions to people."
	Presentation Show the class a compass. Ask if anyone knows what it is and how it is used. Illustrate how to find north using the compass. Inform them that north is one of the cardinal directions. Show them the compass rose on a wall map. Inform them that the compass rose tells the direction that north is on the map. Place the map on the floor of the classroom and orient to north using the compass and the compass rose. Ask the class if they know what direction is the opposite of north. Introduce them to the concept of "south." Point out the direction south on the map. Tell them there are two other cardinal directions. If they are facing north, the direction to their right is east, the direction to their left is west. Have them identify those directions on the map. For guided practice give them a few questions orally. Examples might be, What direction is Chicago from New Orleans? What direction is Los Angeles from New York?
	When it appears that they understand the concept, give them a worksheet that asks them to identify the direction one place is on the map from another.
Closure:	Ask, "What did we learn today? How is understanding cardinal directions useful?

ALTERED LESSON

Grade Level:	4
Objectives:	Pupils will use cardinal directions to indicate the relative location of places on a map.
Overview:	Understanding the cardinal directions is an important skill in helping individuals orient themselves. They are important in understanding the relative and absolute location of places.
Procedures:	***Learning Set*** Take the class outside during the middle of the day. Have them note their shadows. Show them a compass and ask if anyone knows how it is used. Use the compass to show them that at about noon their shadow points roughly to the north.
	Presentation Return to the class room and find north using the compass. Give pupils a card with *North* printed on it and have them place the card on the north wall of the classroom. Show them a wall map and point out the compass rose. Tell them that the compass rose tells the map reader which direction is north on the map. Take the map off the wall and orient it on the floor of the classroom. Ask which direction is opposite of north. Provide one of the pupils a card with *South* printed on it. Have a pupil place the card on the south wall of the classroom. With the map on the floor, call on individual pupils to stand at one place on the map and then walk either north or south. For example, "John, Where is Los Angels on our map? Please stand on Los Angeles. Now walk north from Los Angeles." "Maria, find Chicago on the map. Walk south from Chicago. Call on some of the limited English proficient pupils to perform the task. Introduce east and west by giving two students cards labeled *East* and *West*. Have the pupils place the cards on the appropriate walls. Repeat the exercise of walking from one point to either east or west. Then mix the directions and have them walk in one of the four cardinal directions.
	Have the class work in groups using a map to identify the relative locations of places listed on the map.
Closure:	Ask, "What did we learn today? How is understanding cardinal directions useful?" Call on LEP pupils and check for understanding by giving students such directions as, "Juan, point to the north."

Language Experiences

Most pupils have a natural desire to communicate. Communication is essential in building the language skills of LEP pupils. However, many LEP pupils are embarrassed and fearful about sharing. In other words, they have a high affective filter. Our lessons need to encourage communication in the classroom (King, Fagan, Bratt, & Baer, 1992). Two approaches that can foster this kind of communication are semantic mapping and guided writing.

Semantic Mapping

Semantic mapping encourages visual representation of connections among ideas. One way that semantic mapping can be used is to present the pupils with a topic or an idea. They then brainstorm to generate associations with the topic. Next, ask them to organize these associations into a graphic that serves as an advance organizer for the material presented. Once the pupils have completed their study of the content, they revise their map. The process of eliciting a visual framework that can be used in comprehending the content, the chance to participate and exchange ideas with others, and the revision of the visual framework during and after the lesson aids overall comprehension and is extremely useful to LEP pupils (Reyes & Molner, 1991).

Guided Writing

Guided writing promotes generation of ideas in an oral context and integration of reading and writing in social studies. It is a technique that appears to be effective for older elementary LEP pupils (Reyes & Molner, 1991). The procedure begins with brainstorming and a discussion of what pupils in the class already know about a topic. The outcome of this discussion is a brief outline or web of the topic. Following this discussion, assign learners to groups and ask each group to write a short piece following the outline or web. This working together allows LEP pupils the opportunity to share as well as to observe the connection between spoken and written vocabulary. After students have completed these short written assignments, quickly read and analyze these initial drafts. Then return them to the groups with a checklist containing suggestions they can incorporate into a more polished second draft.

Next, ask pupils to read material on the topic using the guides or outlines to help their comprehension. After discussing the material together in their groups, they go on to write a third draft of the paper, including the new material and ideas they learned from the reading. This helps the LEP pupils comprehend the reading and see the connection between the four language arts processes of speaking, reading, writing, and listening.

At later stages of language development, pupils can be encouraged to keep content journals, wherein they write down information and questions about the content they are learning. This helps the pupil communicate with the teacher on a one-to-one basis in written form. These journals are useful to the teacher in quickly identifying misconceptions or "fuzzy" understanding of the content.

In conclusion, you can do many things to help LEP pupils attain success in the classroom. The satisfaction of seeing the growth and learning of LEP pupils makes the additional effort worthwhile.

KEY IDEAS IN SUMMARY

1. The rapid increase in the number of limited English proficiency (LEP) pupils in the schools has increased the need for teachers who know how to meet their needs. Teaching them in content areas such as social studies allows them to

progress academically while they are acquiring a new language. Teaching content areas has been found to facilitate language acquisition.

2. Two types of language proficiency are important for pupils to succeed in content area instruction. The first is basic interpersonal communication skill. This proficiency allows pupils to interact with others and to communicate their needs, and usually develops in a relatively short time. The other type of proficiency is cognitive/academic language proficiency, which allows pupils to understand a subject when the context clues are reduced and when unique vocabulary is present. It usually takes an individual several years to reach this level.

3. Social studies is an appropriate subject for LEP pupils because it has the potential for providing meaningful learning experiences. Teaching in this area of the elementary curriculum allows these pupils to bring in their own backgrounds as resources for lessons and to engage in instructional experiences that can help them become more proficient users of English.

4. There are potential problems for LEP pupils in social studies classes. Some social studies teachers introduce print material that may be too difficult for some LEP pupils. Further, many of these youngsters lack previous background in social studies content, often because they have not attended U.S. schools in earlier years when content was introduced that teachers erroneously assume everyone in their present grade level already knows.

5. Sheltered instruction is an approach designed to make content instruction more comprehensible to LEP pupils. Sheltered instruction involves simplified speech, providing a context for the instruction, focusing on a task–function relationship, and providing for numerous interactional activities.

6. When teaching LEP pupils, teachers should attempt to reduce the anxiety and fear of the pupils and provide input that is meaningful and comprehensible.

7. The four stages of language development are (1) preproduction, (2) early production, (3) speech emergence, and (4) intermediate fluency. An understanding of the characteristics of each of these stages helps teachers design successful lessons for LEP pupils.

8. Varying the contextual clues present and the cognitive complexity of communication is important in providing comprehensible input for pupils at the different stages of language acquisition.

9. Certain knowledge structures are similar across situations. These knowledge structures have common linguistic features. Key visuals that fit with each knowledge type can be used to provide context clues for learning. Teaching these knowledge structures to LEP pupils along with the linguistic features facilitates their learning across content areas. The knowledge structures that can be taught are (1) description, (2) sequence, (3) choice, (4) classification, (5) principles, and (6) evaluation.

10. Successful instructional practices for LEP pupils involve the use of cooperative learning, multimedia and concrete experiences, and semantic mapping and guided writing procedures.

CHAPTER REFLECTIONS

Directions: Now that you have finished reading the chapter, reread the case study at the beginning. Then answer these questions.

1. How would you respond to the statements of the teachers in the faculty meeting?
2. What is your position on the inclusion of LEP pupils in social studies classes? Do you believe that altering instruction for LEP pupils interferes with the learning of non-LEP pupils?
3. What else do you think you need to learn to be able to meet the needs of LEP pupils?
4. Have your ideas about the teaching of LEP pupils changed as a result of reading this chapter? If so, what specific ideas or perspectives have changed?

EXTENDING UNDERSTANDING AND SKILL

1. Identify those elements of a classroom that have the potential for creating cultural conflict for pupils from different cultures. State how you think instruction in social studies might be made more culturally congruent for pupils from other cultures.
2. Check the credential (teacher certification) requirements for the state where you reside. Are requirements designed to prepare teachers for teaching LEP pupils? If so, what is required? If not, what do you think should be done?
3. Visit an elementary school and see what is done to provide for the learning needs of LEP pupils. Use the ideas presented in this chapter to evaluate the school you visit and to identify areas where improvement might be needed.
4. Imagine that you are teaching at the grade level of your choice and that a new pupil who speaks almost no English has been enrolled in your class. What specific things could you do to help the pupil learn the social studies content for that grade? Give specific suggestions, and provide your rationale for them.

REFERENCES

Association for Supervision and Curriculum Development (1994). *Update*. Vol. 36, No. 5. Alexandria, VA: Association for Supervision and Curriculum Development.

AU, K., AND KAWAKAMI, A. (1994). "Cultural Congruence in Instruction." In E. Hollins, J. King, and W. Hayman (eds.), *Teaching Diverse Populations: Formulating a Knowledge Base*. Albany, NY: State University of New York Press, pp. 5–23.

CUMMINS, J. (1981). "The Role of Primary Language Development in Promoting Educational Success for Language Minority Students." In California State Department of Education (ed.), *Schooling and Language Minority Students: A Theoretical Framework*. Los Angeles: California State University, Los Angeles Evaluation and Assessment Center, p. 12.

EARLY, M. (1990). "Enabling First and Second Language Learners the Classroom." *Language Arts, 67* (October), pp. 567–575.

GARCIA, E. (1994). "Attributes of Effective Schools for Language Minority Students." In E. Hollins, J. King, and W. Hayman (eds.), *Teaching Diverse Populations: Formulating a Knowledge Base*. Albany, NY: State University of New York Press, pp. 93–103.

GARCIA, R. (1991). *Teaching in a Pluralistic Society: Concepts, Models, Strategies*, 2d ed. New York: HarperCollins.

KING, M., FAGAN, B., BRATT, T., AND BAER, R. (1992). "Social Studies Instruction." In P. Richard-Amato and M. Snow (eds.), *The Multicultural Classroom*. White Plains, NY: Longman, pp. 287–299.

KRASHEN, S. (1982). *Principles and Practice in Second Language Acquisition*. Oxford: Pergamon.

MOHAN, B. (1986). *Language and Content*. Reading, MA: Addison-Wesley.

PEREZ, B., AND TORRES-GUZMAN, M. E. (1992). *Learning in Two Worlds: An Integrated Spanish/English Biliteracy Approach*. New York: Longman.

REYES, M., AND MOLNER, L. (1991). "Instructional Strategies for Second-Language Learners in the Content Areas." *Journal of Reading, 35* (2), pp. 96–103.

SHORT, P. (1994). "The Challenge of Social Studies for Limited English Proficient Students." *Social Education, 58* (1), pp. 36–38.

TERRELL, T. (1981). "The Natural Approach in Bilingual Education." In California State Department of Education (ed.), *Schooling and Language Minority Students: A Theoretical Framework*. Los Angeles: California State University, Los Angeles Evaluation and Assessment Center, pp. 117–146.

EVALUATING LEARNING

CHAPTER GOALS

This chapter provides information to help the reader:

- recognize key features of evaluation,
- describe authentic evaluation,
- explain challenges facing individuals who would like to see more authentic evaluation in the schools,
- distinguish between formal and informal evaluation procedures,
- describe procedures for using informal evaluation techniques,
- point out the strengths and weaknesses of selected formal evaluation techniques,
- suggest ways records can be kept to indicate pupil progress in elementary social studies classrooms, and
- explain how evaluation data can be used to assess an instructional program's effectiveness.

CHAPTER STRUCTURE

Introduction
Authentic Assessment
     Problems in Implementing Authentic Assessment
Informal Evaluation
     Teacher Observation
     Teacher–Pupil Discussion
     Pupil-Produced Tests
     My Favorite Idea
     Headlines
     Newspaper Articles
     Word Pairs
     Alphabet Review Game
     Mystery Word Scramble
     Anagrams
     Other Informal Techniques
     Record Keeping and Informal Evaluation
Formal Evaluation
     Rating Scales
     Learning Checklists
     Attitude Inventories
     Essay Tests
     True/False Tests
     Multiple-Choice Tests
     Matching Tests
     Completion Tests
Using Evaluation Results to Improve Instruction
Key Ideas in Summary
Chapter Reflections
Extending Understanding and Skill
References

Authentic Evaluation

— Seeks to assess learner behaviors that parallel as closely as possible how proficient adults use content in the world beyond the school

— Identifying ways in which learners should demonstrate behaviors and establishing appropriate levels of proficiency are challenges for teachers

Informal Evaluation

— Teacher observation

— Teacher–pupil discussion

— Pupil-produced tests

— My favorite idea

— Headlines

— Newspaper articles

— Word pairs

— Alphabet review game

— Mystery word scramble

— Anagrams

Formal Evaluation

— Rating scales

— Learning checklists

— Attitude inventories

— Essay tests

— True/false tests

— Multiple-choice tests

— Matching tests

— Completion tests

In addition to providing information relating to individual pupil progress, evaluation results also provide insights that are useful for assessing the overall effectiveness of instruction. This information assists teachers to reflect on what they have done. It helps them identify needed modifications in their teaching approaches.

Figure 17–1
Evaluating learning.

Chapter 17

Case Study

IF TESTING TAKES TOO MUCH TIME NOW, WON'T "BETTER" FORMS OF TESTING MAKE MATTERS EVEN WORSE?

Phillipa Grandjo, who has taught seventh graders for many years at Miles Standish Middle School, serves as her school's representative on the district's Central Social Studies Curriculum Council. She made these comments recently at a Council meeting when the issue of evaluation came up:

> As I look back over my 20 years teaching in this district, I'm struck by how much more time we are asked to spend testing learners today compared to when I started. We have standardized tests. We have some the district has devised. And, in response to some parental concerns, we have even developed a testing program in our social studies department at Miles Standish so we can gather information about content areas that are of particular interest to our own faculty.
>
> All of this testing business takes time—too much time, I think. Every time we stop teaching to administer a test, we deprive people in our classes of opportunities to engage new content. I know that we need to stop to take stock of what our people are learning, but I don't think we need to spend nearly so much time testing.
>
> I'm particularly concerned about all this talk about "authentic assessment." I applaud the intent to develop ways to assess learners that really require them to do the kinds of the things we are attempting to teach them.
>
> For example, if one of our purposes in our social studies lessons is to help our young people develop a clear-headed argument in support of a position, an evaluation that requires us to listen to them do so either orally or in writing makes sense. We certainly shouldn't be administering something like a true/false test and, based on how well a youngster does, making some kind of an inference about his or her logical reasoning powers. That requires a tremendous leap of faith—one that I think goes way beyond what results of a true/false test can tell us.
>
> But the alternative, more "authentic procedure"—I mean the oral exam or essay that calls upon pupils to lay out their logical thought processes— requires an incredible amount of time to administer. It will take even more time away from what we have available to teach new content.
>
> We seem to be caught in a dilemma. Many of us feel that testing already takes too much time. Kinds of tests that don't take too much time to administer, for example true/false and multiple-choice tests, often don't tie closely to kinds of learning we really want to emphasize. But, more "authentic tests" will add even more time to the already excessive hours already devoted to testing. All of this is very confusing, and I'm not sure what the answer is.

What Is Your Response?

Read over this teacher's comments. Then, respond briefly to these questions:

1. Ms. Grandjo suggests that teachers today spend more time testing learners than they did in previous years. What forces may have led to this change?

2. If teachers are spending more time testing than they used to, is this good or bad? Why do you think so?

3. What does Ms. Grandjo imply that good "authentic tests" can do that are beyond the capability of many more traditional types of teacher-made tests, for example, true/false and multiple-choice tests?

4. Is it possible to develop a testing program that would be "authentic" but that would not consume excessive amounts of class time? Support your response.

5. How do you suppose other members of the district's Central Social Studies Curriculum Council reacted to Ms. Grandjo's concerns? Why do you think so?

INTRODUCTION

To begin the evaluation process, we must gather information of some kind about pupil performance. Many options are available to us as we consider this task. Today, there is increasing interest in using "authentic" measures. These require pupils to engage in sophisticated demonstrations of what they have learned. They are designed to encourage development of thinking and performance skills that are similar in many ways to those characterizing proficient adults. Other, more traditional, assessments often feature the use of informal techniques (relatively open-ended exercises that can be completed successfully by pupils who have mastered the relevant content) or formal techniques (typically, structured examinations that feature multiple-choice, true/false, matching, completion, and essay items). Once we have gathered the data, we move on to make judgments about the adequacy of pupils' performances based on these results and on whatever special personal knowledge we have about the young people we teach.

All assessment approaches require us to gather information about pupils before making any judgment about their performance. In this chapter, we introduce authentic assessment approaches, and informal and formal data-gathering techniques.

AUTHENTIC ASSESSMENT

All of us have probably heard someone say that "teachers shouldn't teach to the test." The logic behind this view is that most tests sample too narrow a range of what pupils need to know. This problem has been widely recognized by people who support authentic assessment. *Authentic assessment*, also referred to as *performance assessment* (Stiggins, 1994), seeks to provide pupils opportunities to demonstrate what they have learned. That is, they are encouraged to put new knowledge to work in ways that are as similar as possible to how this information is used by proficient adults. Let's consider an example.

Imagine we are teaching social studies to a group of a sixth graders. As part of our program, we decide to supplement the regular world areas and cultures program with lessons focusing on issues facing the local community. Suppose a local zoning board is considering whether a company should be allowed to locate a new plant in an open area bordering a residential neighborhood. Some people in the community are excited about the new plant and the jobs it will bring. Others fear that it will ruin the adjacent residential neighborhood and produce environmental damage.

In a traditional class, we might assign pupils to gather information about contending positions and organize activities such as debates, discussions, and brainstorming sessions to get pupils actively involved in a consideration of these issues. Assessment probably would take the form of an essay item or a series of objective test questions (true/false, multiple choice, and so forth). Since we're interested in authentic assessment, we will do something different. We might require pupils to give testimony at a simulated hearing of a zoning board. Actual zoning board members or, at least, knowledgeable adults from the community, can be brought in to hear pupils' testimony. We would tell members of our class to organize arguments using the best evidence they can find. They might also be required to turn in a written summary of their position to the person playing the role of chairperson of the zoning board. Evaluation of individuals in this kind of a situation is based on what they are able to demonstrate in a setting that replicates many features of the world beyond the school.

Authentic assessment encourages complex pupil performance, and is thought to encourage the development of sophisticated thinking (Wiggins, 1989). Supporters of this approach believe that it can lead to a significant and relevant emphasis on learning (Spady, 1994). If this is true, pupils' motivation may well be enhanced because their learning tasks bear a real connection to what they see adults doing every day.

Problems in Implementing Authentic Assessment

Though solid logic supports the idea of authentic evaluation, implementing this approach poses certain difficulties. Spady (1994), an expert who has worked with programs featuring authentic evaluation, made these comments about one key challenge: "Reformers from coast to coast agree that measures other than student grades and Carnegie units must be used for determining student and district achievement. But what outcomes *are* and what kinds should be expected . . . are still disputed."

In a nutshell, while many people agree that pupils should be expected to demonstrate in sophisticated ways what they have learned, there is by no means widespread agreement as to what form these demonstrations should take or regarding criteria to apply in judging their adequacy. How authentic assessment procedures should be designed, how much money should be committed to their development, and what should be done to assure that they do not discriminate against certain groups are all issues that continue to be debated in the field (Baker, 1994).

Longstanding tradition also represents a challenge to those favoring more use of authentic assessment procedures. Parents and other community members have memories of school days featuring essays, short-answer quizzes, and lots of tests with true/false and multiple-choice items. They also are used to letter grades being awarded, at least in part, based on pupils' performances on these kinds of exams. Authentic assessment represents a departure from these familiar procedures. Because even supporters admit that there remains much debate about what should go into a high-quality authentic assessment program, some parents and other community people are reluctant to support efforts to move away from more traditional evaluation practices.

Despite these concerns, interest in authentic assessment remains high. Support for the idea of requiring learners to engage in more sophisticated demonstrations of learning continues to grow. Researchers are hard at work on issues associated with establishing quality standards for a variety of authentic assessment approaches (see, for example, Stiggins, 1994). For an example of how authentic assessment might be applied to a social studies assignment, see Box 17–1.

INFORMAL EVALUATION

More traditional evaluation often relies on information obtained through use of *informal* techniques. These feature teacher observation of a variety of pupil performances. We use results to identify behavior patterns that suggest whether a child has mastered a given skill or cognitive understanding. Sometimes these pupil responses cannot easily be graded "right" or "wrong." Sometimes, too, informal evaluation sheds light on pupils' attitudes.

Informal evaluation often can be accomplished quickly. For example, if we want to know whether a given pupil can get along with others (an important social skill), casual observation of the pupil's behavior in class and on the playground is usually sufficient. There is no need for a sophisticated test. A simple, dated notation can record the information ("Marta played well at recess and got along well with others in class today, 10/18/96").

Informal evaluation is nonthreatening, and provides information about pupils' "natural" behavior patterns. This is true because much of it takes place without pupils being aware that it is happening. This is a far different situation from that facing learners confronted with a formal test. Though informal evaluation is used throughout the elementary social studies program, it is used more frequently by teachers of younger elementary school pupils than by teachers of fourth, fifth, and sixth graders. One reason for this is that very young pupils lack the reading and writing skills needed to take formal tests, so their teachers must rely more on informal procedures. Additionally, the social studies program in the early grades is heavily oriented toward developing basic skills and helping pupils to get along well with others. These skills and behaviors are often more easily assessed informally.

Certain cautions must be observed when using informal evaluation techniques. Because these techniques require us to make inferences about pupils based on observing their "natural" behaviors, sufficient observations must be made to provide a sound basis for judgment. Additionally, we need a systematic scheme for recording information. Because classes often include large numbers of pupils and because many different kinds of things happen each day, we sometimes find it hard to recall important behaviors of individual pupils. We need a recordkeeping scheme that prompts us to take notes about individual behavior patterns close to the time of their occurrence. When we keep careful records and take multiple observations, informal evaluation can pro-

BOX 17–1   An Authentic Assessment Assignment

This example was developed for use in a fourth-grade class. The focus of the social studies at this grade level in this state (as in many others) is state history. Look over the following authentic assessment exercise. Think about how it differs from the kinds of things you remember being asked to do to evidence learning when you were in elementary school.

A Story Based on Our State's History

Our state today is different from what it was 50 years ago. Think about some things that have changed. Pick out one thing that is different. Here are some ideas of things that may have changed:

- Schools
- What we eat
- How we spend free time
- How towns and neighborhoods look
- How we get from place to place

Tomorrow, we will be bringing some older people to class. They are people in their 60s, 70s, and 80s. All have lived in our state for many years. Each of you will have a chance to interview these people about the subject you choose. For example, if you choose "changes in schools," you can ask these people about what schools were like when they were children. What did the buildings look like? What were classrooms like? What did people wear? What did they study? What kinds of books did they use? Did they have libraries? These are the kinds of questions a person interested in "changes in the schools" might ask. I want you to write down the ideas you get from these visitors.

On the day after tomorrow, we'll write papers, one to two pages. Each of our papers will tell a story. The story will be about how our subject has changed. A person who chooses "changes in the schools" as a topic, for example, will write a story called, "How schools have changed over the past 50 years." As you prepare to write your papers, I want you to think about two major ideas that might explain why these changes have happened. Then, I want you to develop at least two questions related to each idea. Think about possible answers to these questions and about how these answers might help explain the changes. Before we start writing the papers, I'll give you some examples of what I hope you will do. In your paper, I want to see your ideas, the questions you asked about each, and your conclusions.

Everyone also will have a chance to make an oral report. This will give all of us a chance to learn what you have learned. You will report on the same information included in your paper.

Evaluation Guidelines for the Teacher

In looking over each pupil's paper, consider whether the pupil did the following:

- Listed two ideas to explain the change
- Developed two questions for each idea
- Used information gathered from talking with the older visitors in responding to the questions
- Included information that suggested an ability to distinguish between fact and opinion
- Based conclusions on evidence that she or he gathered
- Prepared arguments using logical, point-by-point development in both the paper and the oral presentation

vide useful information about each pupil's progress (see Box 17–2). The subsections that follow introduce common informal evaluation procedures.

Teacher Observation

Teacher observation of pupils is an important informal evaluation tool. Some aims of the elementary social studies program can be assessed in no other way, such as those related to general attitudes and to interpersonal relations skills. For example, "work cooperatively with others" is an objective for kindergarten pupils found in many school districts' social studies curriculum. Obviously, a written test cannot determine how well children have mastered this objective. We must observe children directly to effectively evaluate how well they get along with each other.

Informal evaluation often prompts us to give specific directions to an individual pupil about an attitude, a skill, a desired interpersonal relations behavior, or an item of academic content. Good teacher observation looks for specific behaviors (being polite when others are speaking, sharing, and so forth). We should maintain a brief written record of pupils who are experiencing specific problems so we may note both progress and continuing areas of difficulty.

Teacher–Pupil Discussion

Personal discussions with individual pupils often provide us with insights. These conversations may reveal much about their attitudes, interests, and understandings. Dis-

---

BOX 17–2   **"I Don't Think *Good* Kindergarten Teachers Need Records."**

Recently, a prospective kindergarten teacher made these comments:

> All the kindergarten teachers I've talked to say they spend too much time keeping records. They tell me they feel they must write down "everything" about every child. It seems to me this is a big waste of time. It *has* to take valuable time away from working with children. Also, I think a really *good* kindergarten teacher should know the children so well as individuals that there is no need for a formal written record. I mean, if a youngster is slow to learn colors or something else, the teacher should know. I can't understand why so many kindergarten teachers waste so much time on recordkeeping.

Think About This

1. If many kindergarten teachers spend a great deal of time on recordkeeping, why do they do so?
2. Is time spent on recordkeeping wasted? Explain your view.
3. How might a kindergarten teacher react to this person's comments?
4. If you were to discuss this matter with this person, what would you say?

Teacher–pupil discussion is an important component in evaluating pupil understanding and progress.

cussions also help us to test the accuracy of our perceptions about how individual learners are feeling and about how well they are mastering social studies content.

There are obvious problems with this approach. Time constraints make it difficult to have long discussions with each pupil (Ebel & Frisbie, 1986). Hence, it is not possible to sample individual pupils' learning in this way with a great deal of frequency. Because of this limitation, we have to supplement this approach with other procedures.

Pupil-Produced Tests

This technique is applicable primarily to learners in grades four, five, and six. By the time pupils have progressed this far in school, they typically have taken dozens of teacher-prepared tests and are quite familiar with the common formats of basic test types, such as true/false and multiple choice.

Many teachers find that having pupils develop their own test items over studied content provides useful information about what they have learned. Typically, learners focus on what they perceive to have been most important. From this focus, we can determine what pupils have learned from a particular body of content, and can identify individuals who have developed mistaken impressions and who need additional work with the material. To make the exercise credible, many teachers incorporate a few pupil-generated items on a subsequent scheduled examination.

My Favorite Idea

A space on the chalkboard or a large sheet of butcher paper is needed for this exercise. To begin, we invite pupils to write their "favorite social studies idea" in this space once or twice each week. As a preparation for this activity, we have to provide examples of the kinds of things that pupils might write. ("I would *hate* to have my feet bound like they used to do to girls in China." "I think men here should be forced to wear pigtails like they used to wear in China.") Children should be encouraged to write about whatever has engaged their interest. To personalize the activity, we sometimes ask children to sign their names after their comments.

This exercise yields insights about the kinds of information and attitudes pupils are taking away from social studies lessons. We often learn things that are worth including in the records kept on individual class members. The technique also provides benefits for learners. It motivates them to think more seriously about their social studies lessons, knowing they will be asked to contribute a "favorite idea."

Headlines

One measure of learning is the ability to summarize accurately. If summaries are accurate, then we have grounds for concluding that pupils grasp essential features of the material on which the summary is based. We can test pupils' abilities to summarize by asking them to write or state orally possible headlines for newspaper articles about current study topics. Written headlines can be displayed on butcher paper, a bulletin board, or a chalkboard.

Pupil-produced headlines give us basic information about how each learner grasps a subject's essential features. Comments derived from examining each child's headline can be noted in a gradebook, on a progress chart, or in some other appropriate manner. Additionally, our review of all of the headlines produced by the class can pinpoint any widespread misconceptions. These can be addressed in followup work.

Newspaper Articles

With learners in grades four, five, and six, we can expand the headline activity to include actually writing a short, related newspaper article. To prepare for this activity, we introduce pupils to basic formats for newspaper articles and give them guidelines concerning length and kinds of information to include. The content of the articles provides us with a great deal of evidence about levels of understanding of each pupil, and helps identify learners who need additional help. Where large numbers of children appear confused about certain issues, the class as a whole can be involved in a clarifying discussion.

Some teachers find it useful to "publish" some of the best articles, distributing them to all class members (and perhaps to other classes), to the principal, and to parents. Copies may be displayed on a bulletin board in the class or in a display area in the hall. The possibility of becoming a "published journalist" is an incentive that motivates pupils to do good work.

Word Pairs

In a word-pairs assessment activity, we present pupils with a set of cards on which single words have been written, and ask them to find pairs of cards that go together. We check each learner's work and ask why the child thinks cards in each selected pair are associated. Help is given to individuals who are having difficulty. We maintain records of each pupil's performance. When many learners are making a similar mistake, we deal with the issue with the whole class. The activity concludes with a discussion to reinforce appropriate relationships between words in each correct pair.

As an example, a word-pairs activity focusing on naming leaders and what they lead might use cards, each containing one of the following words:

President   State
Classroom   Teacher
United States   City
Mayor   Governor

We give each learner a complete set of eight cards and ask that these cards be arranged in appropriate pairs. The completed pairs should look like this:

President–United States

Governor–State

Mayor–City

Teacher–Classroom

Alphabet Review Game

The alphabet review game can be used to assess either individuals or groups of learners. This simple exercise provides pupils with a review of basic alphabetizing skills and at the same time reviews currently studied material.

We lead a class discussion to decide what information from the current lesson is the most important. Then, we ask learners to find as many important terms as they can that begin with each letter of the alphabet. Pupils are instructed to skip letters if they cannot find any important terms that begin with them. (For example, relatively few important terms begin with "X.") We set a limit to the time spent on each letter, usually three or four minutes.

This exercise can be done by pupils working alone or in groups. When in groups, each group works together to find terms beginning with each letter. We walk around the room to monitor each pupil or group. Often it is desirable to keep records of each learner's progress. As a followup activity, lists for each letter can be shared, and pupils can review the meanings of the terms.

Mystery Word Scramble

The mystery word scramble takes advantage of children's love of puzzles. Typically, the exercise focuses on previously introduced key terms. Letters in these terms are scrambled. A definition of the unscrambled term is provided. Pupils look at the definition and try to decide what the word is. As an added feature, we may circle one space in

---

Directions (Answers are provided in parentheses)

The words at the left are real words, but the letters have been mixed up. Arrange the letters to form the correct word. Write the word in the spaces provided. The definition at the right of each mixed-up word will help you decide what the correct word should be.

Mixed-up Word	Definition	Correct Word
tedolingu	Imaginary lines on a globe used to measure distances east and west.	_ _ _Ⓞ_ _ _ _ _ (longitude)
uteltaid	Imaginary lines on a globe used to measure distances north and south.	Ⓞ_ _ _ _ _ _ (latitude)
reqtuoa	An imaginary line around the globe that separates the northern and southern hemisphere.	_ _ _ _ _ _Ⓞ (equator)
mabroteer	A device for measuring air pressure on the earth's surface.	_Ⓞ_ _ _ _ _ _ (barometer)
hehepsimer	A term that means "one half of the earth's surface."	_ _ _ _ _ _Ⓞ_ _ (hemisphere)

Mystery Word Directions

One letter in each of the above words is circled. Together, these letters form the mystery word. Write the letters in the blanks provided below. The mystery word is defined just to the right of the blanks.

_ _ _ _ _: A term used to describe a model of the earth. (globe)

Figure 17–2
Sample mystery word scramble exercise.

those provided for pupils to copy the correct term. When all terms have been properly unscrambled, the circled letters will spell out a "mystery word," usually another important social studies term.

Pupils like mystery word scrambles. The exercise provides a means for us to learn about pupils' understanding in a way that minimizes their anxiety. If many learners have problems identifying the same terms, these can be featured in a followup class discussion, We can easily keep track of each learner's success in identifying the appropriate terms. A sample format for a mystery word scramble is provided in Figure 17–2.

Anagrams

Anagrams are words created by rearranging letters of other words. For example, the word *opus* can be made by using all of the letters of the word *soup*. Anagrams can be used as a means of informal assessment. We can present the exercise to pupils as a puzzle. Many pupils will participate completely unaware that we are observing their performance.

Oral Directions (Answers are provided in parentheses)

Look at the word in capital letters. Then look at the definition. The definition describes a different word from the one at the left, but this new word uses all the letters in the word to the left. Write this new word in the blanks provided at the end of the definition.

LEAK   1.   A large body of fresh water completely surrounded by land. _____(lake)
MASTER 2.   A body of running water, such as a river or a brook. _____(stream)
FURS   3.   The name given to the waves of the sea as they crash on the shore. _____(surf)
DIET   4.   The twice-a-day rising and falling of the level of the ocean. _____(tide)
SALE   5.   A sea animal with flippers that lives along rocky coastlines. _____(seal)
LOOP   6.   A small and rather deep body of water. _____(pool)
ALIENS   7.   This refers to something, such as sea water, that contains salt. _____(saline)

Figure 17–3
Sample anagrams exercise.

In setting up an anagram exercise, we usually provide the original term plus a definition of another term that can be made using the letters of the original term. Next, we encourage pupils to look at the definition and to think of a word that fits it that uses all of the letters of the original term. The new terms should relate to content that has been recently studied. Pupil performance on the anagram exercise gives the teacher some indication of how well individual learners have mastered basic terminology.

An example of an anagram exercise for pupils who have recently studied bodies of water and marine life is provided in Figure 17–3.

Other Informal Techniques

These informal observation techniques are only a sample of the many that we can use. Among other techniques are sorting activities of all kinds, which help pupils recognize major category labels and items that belong within each category. Some teachers may ask groups of learners to debate issues. The positions introduced during the debates reveal the depth of understanding of individual participants. Crossword puzzles, hidden-word puzzles (puzzles where words are disguised in a random-seeming array of letters), and other puzzles and games are widely used. "What I Learned" diaries are favored by some teachers. The list of possibilities goes on and on.

The decision to use a given procedure should depend on whether, for the specific classroom and circumstances, the answer to this question is "yes": "Will this procedure provide sufficient information for me to judge any given pupil's performance?"

Recordkeeping and Informal Evaluation

Informal evaluation techniques generate much useful information. Good recordkeeping helps teachers make maximum use of this information. There are many ways to record data on pupil performance.

Informal evaluation techniques play a major role in assessing pupil learning in the elementary grades.

Secondary school teachers often rely exclusively on a gradebook to record information about learners' progress. This scheme does not work as well in elementary classrooms. The informal evaluation procedures widely used with younger learners do not lend themselves well to a record reflecting either a numerical score or a letter grade. Instead, much information about pupils is of a "can" or "cannot" or a "yes" or "no" nature. For example, one aim of many kindergarten programs is for pupils to know the name of their school and town. The child either does or does not know these facts.

To keep track of pupils' progress in elementary social studies classrooms, many teachers use *daily performance progress checklists.* (Despite the name, teachers do not always update these records daily. Depending on individual circumstances, several times a week may suffice.) These easy-to-use sheets allow the teacher to note quickly how each learner is faring on a limited number of focus competencies. These checklists can be tailored to fit content, and specific notations can be modified to accommodate the needs of the teacher. To record such information, the procedures must allow for frequent observation of small increments of learning that cannot necessarily be described in terms of numerical scores or letter grades. Some teachers find it convenient simply to note whether a pupil has (1) mastered the competency, (2) partially mastered the competency, or (3) not mastered even a part of the competency.

Figure 17–4 illustrates an example of such a daily performance progress checklist.

A daily performance record such as shown in Figure 17–4 is easy to use. It provides a measure of each learner's performance on every area emphasized during a day's lesson. Collectively, this information can indicate areas of strength and weakness as they exist within the class as a whole.

Periodically, teachers enter this daily information into a cumulative record. A cumulative record form typically includes all grade-level competencies. It summarizes what

Kindergarten—Mr. Bianca:
Daily Performance Progress Checklist

Today's Date: _____

FOCUS SKILLS

Member of the Class	Identifies Relative Location (near, far)	Cites the Pledge of Allegiance	Names the Days of the Week
Brenda	+	+	+
Erik	+	-	W
Gretchen	-	-	W
Howard	-	W	+
Juan	+	+	+
Karen	+	W	-
Lawrence	W	W	W
Adela	+	+	+
Paul	+	W	W
•			
•			
•			

(This same pattern follows for the rest of the class.)

Figure 17–4
Sample daily performance progress checklist.
Key: + = the pupil has mastered this competency; W = the pupil has partially mastered this competency, but more work is needed; – = the pupil has not even partially mastered this competency yet.

has been observed about an individual child over time. An example of a social studies cumulative record form for kindergarten is provided in Figure 17–5.

FORMAL EVALUATION

Formal evaluation procedures include teacher-prepared tests and standardized tests. When informal assessment techniques are used, pupils often do not know they are being evaluated. With formal evaluation techniques, learners almost always are aware they are being tested. As a result, pupils' anxiety levels often are higher during formal evaluations.

Many kinds of tests qualify as formal assessment instruments. Subsections that follow introduce several that often are prepared by elementary social studies teachers.

Rating Scales

Frequently we need to assess learning outcomes beyond those that can be tested using forced-choice examinations such as multiple-choice or true/false tests. For example, some learning objectives may call on pupils to give brief oral summaries of positions, to

Because youngsters in the early elementary grades do not take as many formal examinations (multiple choice, true/false, and so forth) as do older pupils, it is not practical to keep records in a grade book where little provision is made except for noting numerical scores and letter grades. Though grades will have to be given to youngsters (at least in most districts), the documentation of youngsters' work is often accomplished more conveniently using a cumulative record form of some kind.

A separate cumulative record form is kept for each pupil. Often, these are kept in individual file folders. Periodically, the teacher will review the information taken from less formal observations of daily performance. (See the daily performance record referenced in the material on "Recordkeeping and Informal Evaluation.") The teacher typically notes on the cumulative record form those competencies a youngster has mastered. These forms provide data that can be used to compile information to share with parents during parent-teacher conferences and during formal progress reports from the school.

Cumulative record forms vary greatly from district to district. The following one is an example of what you might expect to find in a form designed to reflect the progress of a youngster in the social studies component of the kindergarten program.

Cumulative Record: Social Studies—Kindergarten

Name of Pupil:

Directions

Place a check mark in the blank before each competency the pupil has mastered. Also note the date the check mark was entered.

Area I: History-Social Science—Knowledge, Skills, Values

_____ 1. Understands term "basic needs."
_____ 2. Tells how families meet basic needs.
_____ 3. Identifies property as his/hers/mine/ours/yours.
_____ 4. Defines work and play.
_____ 5. Names self, school, community.

Figure 17–5
Sample social studies cumulative record form for kindergarten.

build models, or to increase their frequency of participation in class discussions. A rating scale can provide information about learners' proficiencies in these areas.

Rating scale preparation begins with identifying a set of focus characteristics. The rater makes judgments about a given pupil's relative proficiency by circling or otherwise marking a point on the scale. The points on a good rating scale refer to specifically defined pupil behaviors. Some rating scales are deficient in this regard. For example, suppose we were interested in the degree to which individual pupils volunteered information during class discussion. A poorly designed rating scale to gather this information is depicted in Figure 17–6.

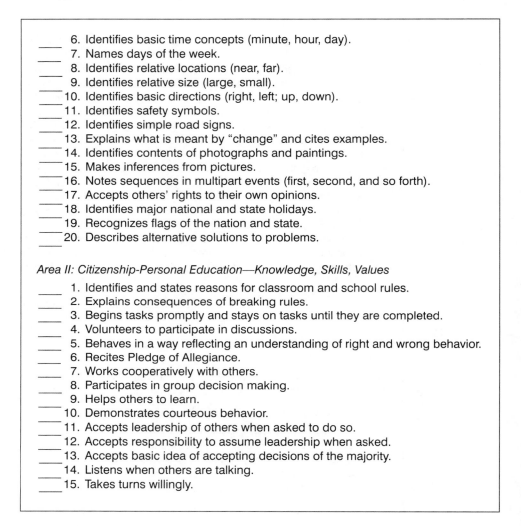

_____ 6. Identifies basic time concepts (minute, hour, day).
_____ 7. Names days of the week.
_____ 8. Identifies relative locations (near, far).
_____ 9. Identifies relative size (large, small).
_____ 10. Identifies basic directions (right, left; up, down).
_____ 11. Identifies safety symbols.
_____ 12. Identifies simple road signs.
_____ 13. Explains what is meant by "change" and cites examples.
_____ 14. Identifies contents of photographs and paintings.
_____ 15. Makes inferences from pictures.
_____ 16. Notes sequences in multipart events (first, second, and so forth).
_____ 17. Accepts others' rights to their own opinions.
_____ 18. Identifies major national and state holidays.
_____ 19. Recognizes flags of the nation and state.
_____ 20. Describes alternative solutions to problems.

Area II: Citizenship-Personal Education—Knowledge, Skills, Values

_____ 1. Identifies and states reasons for classroom and school rules.
_____ 2. Explains consequences of breaking rules.
_____ 3. Begins tasks promptly and stays on tasks until they are completed.
_____ 4. Volunteers to participate in discussions.
_____ 5. Behaves in a way reflecting an understanding of right and wrong behavior.
_____ 6. Recites Pledge of Allegiance.
_____ 7. Works cooperatively with others.
_____ 8. Participates in group decision making.
_____ 9. Helps others to learn.
_____ 10. Demonstrates courteous behavior.
_____ 11. Accepts leadership of others when asked to do so.
_____ 12. Accepts responsibility to assume leadership when asked.
_____ 13. Accepts basic idea of accepting decisions of the majority.
_____ 14. Listens when others are talking.
_____ 15. Takes turns willingly.

Figure 17–5
continued

The rating scale in Figure 17–6 provides an illusion of specificity, but it fails to indicate exactly what each rating point means. As a result, two raters who observed a given pupil might award the learner quite different ratings. In the language of test-design specialists, this rating scale lacks *reliability* (the ability to produce consistent results when applied to similar situations). A better, more reliable rating scale would be one that more specifically identified meanings of each rating point. Note the specific improvements in the rating scale shown in Figure 17–7.

Directions

Circle the appropriate number for each item. The numbers represent the following:

5 = Outstanding
4 = Above average
3 = Average
2 = Below average
1 = Unsatisfactory

How would you assess this youngster's willingness to volunteer to speak during classroom discussions?

5   4   3   2   1

Figure 17–6
Rating scale with poorly defined rating points.

The ratings in Figure 17–7 are scaled in such a way that two or more raters observing the same pupil behavior would be quite likely to award the learner a common rating. A reliable rating scale can contribute much good information about important categories of pupil behavior.

Learning Checklists

Checklists share with rating scales the characteristic of measuring behaviors that are not easily assessed through written tests. Learning checklists depend on the teacher's ability to see and record information about behaviors of interest.

Directions

Circle the appropriate number for each item. The numbers represent the values indicated.

5 = volunteers on 80–100 percent of opportunities to do so.
4 = volunteers on 60–79 percent of opportunities to do so.
3 = volunteers on 40–59 percent of opportunities to do so.
2 = volunteers on 20–39 percent of opportunities to do so.
1 = volunteers on 0–19 percent of opportunities to do so.

How often does the youngster volunteer to participate in classroom discussions?

5   4   3   2   1

Figure 17–7
Rating scale with clearly defined rating points.

Checklists are not as flexible as rating scales, which may offer a continuum that includes many rating points. For instance, the examples in Figures 17–6 and 17–7 allow a user to select one of five rating points. Most checklists, on the other hand, are designed only to note the presence or absence of a given behavior. This is not necessarily a limitation; sometimes "yes" or "no" or "present" or "absent" judgments are all we need.

Measurement specialists Gronlund and Linn (1990) have identified checklist guidelines. The following list draws upon their work:

- Identify and describe each desired pupil behavior as specifically as possible.
- Add to this list the most common incorrect, or error, behaviors.
- Arrange the list of desired behaviors and incorrect, or error, behaviors in the approximate order one might expect to see them.
- Develop a simple procedure for checking each action as it occurs.

Suppose we were interested in how individual pupils were grasping the distinctions among the concepts "county," "country," and "continent." (Many learners confuse these concepts.) By listening to pupils' oral comments or by short interviews with several class members, we could determine how learners were faring with this task, and could record this information about each pupil on a checklist. A sample checklist is shown in Figure 17–8.

All of the checklists, when completed, would provide information not only about each child but also about any misunderstandings that may be widespread throughout the class. This information would tell us to highlight certain points during class discussions.

Name of Pupil:_____

	Yes	No
Distinguishes between "county" and "country."		
Distinguishes between "county" and "continent."		
Distinguishes between "country" and "continent."		
Confuses "country" and "county," but not "country" and "continent."		
Confuses "country" and "continent," but not "country" and "county."		

Figure 17–8
Learning checklist.
To use this checklist, the teacher simply places a checkmark in the appropriate box or boxes.

Attitude Inventories

Not all assessment is directed at obtaining measures of pupils' cognitive achievement. There are times when we are interested in learners' attitudes. In such cases, we often use attitude inventories to provide this information.

Attitude inventories call on learners to rate their relative interest in subjects or topics. They are presented a list of alternatives. Directions tell them to indicate their preferences in rank order. If there are six items, they will indicate their first- through sixth-place preference.

Suppose at the beginning of the school year, we found that members of our class were not particularly looking forward to their social studies lessons. We might try to develop more positive reactions to this part of the school program by involving them in interesting social studies activities throughout the school year. To test the success of our effort, we might give the inventory on different occasions. Pupils would take it first at the beginning of the year and then again some months later, after they had been exposed to lessons designed to enhance their interest in the social studies. A sample attitude inventory is depicted in Figure 17–9.

Many pupils may rank their interest in the social studies program as relatively low when first completing the attitude inventory. Our hope is that they will rank it higher relative to other subjects later in the year after they have been exposed to lessons designed to prompt their interest. A higher average rating for the social studies on the second inventory would tell us that our plan to improve learners' attitudes is succeeding.

Essay Tests

Essay tests are much more common in the upper grades than in the middle and lower grades. Few essay tests are used at all with primary-grade learners, who lack the writ-

---

Topic: Interest in School Subjects
Directions: Listed below are some of the subjects you will be studying this year. Look at each one. Place a number "1" in the blank in front of the subject in which you have the greatest interest. Place a number "2" in the blank in front of your next favorite subject. Continue this pattern until you conclude with a number "5" in the blank in front of the subject you like least.

_____ mathematics

_____ reading

_____ science

_____ social studies

_____ physical education

Figure 17–9
Sample attitude inventory.

ing skills needed to respond properly. These skills are quite rudimentary even in middle-grade pupils.

Though not appropriate for all elementary learners, essay tests do have a place in the overall school social studies program. Quite apart from their function as an indicator of pupils' academic learning, they contribute to fluency with the written language. With respect to content, essay tests allow learners to assemble bits of information into meaningful wholes (see Box 17–3).

Essay tests are well suited for such purposes as determining pupils' abilities to interpret, compare and contrast, and generalize about given information. Essays help us to test more sophisticated kinds of pupil thinking. On the other hand, when assessment focuses on less sophisticated thinking skills (recall of specific names and places, for example), other kinds of tests, including true/false, multiple-choice, and matching, are more appropriate.

Guidelines for preparing good essay items follow:

- Write a question that focuses on a specific and somewhat limited content area. Essays take time to compose. Not too much content can be covered in the time available for pupils to respond.

BOX 17–3   **Needed: More Essay Tests**

The following comments appeared on the editorial page of a local newspaper.

Youngsters are poorer writers today than they were fifty years ago. Why? It surely cannot be that our children are not as smart. The explanation is simple. School children are no longer compelled to write essays.

Today we have schools filled with electronic scoring devices that encourage teachers to give more and more multiple-choice and true/false tests. These devices doubtless save time. But they also discourage teachers from giving essay exams which, even today, must be graded by hand. The result is that children are not asked to do much writing, and many of them never learn how.

Mastery of the written word is a hallmark of an educated adult. We support the adoption of a school policy that requires elementary teachers to give only essay examinations after grade three. This step may appear radical. However, given the lamentable decline in writing skills, it is one we should take.

Think About This

1. What problems for teachers would result from adoption of this proposal?
2. What other "causes" for a decline in pupils' writing proficiency might you suggest, other than the increasing use of objective tests in the schools?
3. Would teachers at some grade levels find implementing this proposal more difficult than teachers at other grade levels?
4. If you were asked to respond to the writer of this editorial, what would you say?

- Write questions that encourage pupils to include examples and specific details. Note the differences between items (a) and (b):
  (a) What are differences between the northern and southern hemispheres?
  (b) Discuss the weather and seasons in the northern and southern hemispheres. State the differences in (1) the months of the year when summer occurs, (2) the months of the year when winter occurs. Also, (3) tell what the relative position of the earth and sun have to do with these differences.
- Give pupils specific instruction about how much they are expected to write. Usually length expectations are best explained in terms of numbers of paragraphs desired. Even upper-grade learners may have trouble writing a full page on a given question.

Correcting essay items can pose problems. More is involved than simply comparing a pupil's response to answers on a key, as with multiple-choice or true/false tests. While it is more difficult to score essays reliably, certain procedures can make such grading more consistent.

First, we can prepare a sample response to each essay question. This procedure often will reveal potential problems with the language used in the question itself. Our completed response will also identify major points we will want to look for while grading pupil responses. Some teachers list these points separately after they have written their sample responses.

Inexperienced teachers often read one pupil's answers to all questions before going on to the next learner's paper. It is better to read every learner's response to one question at a time. This is desirable because different standards tend to be applied to different questions. If all answers to a given question are read together, there is a better chance that we will apply the same grading standard to each pupil.

Sometimes, the order in which we read essays will make a difference in how we grade them. For example, we may become frustrated when the same mistake appears on paper after paper. Unconsciously, we may grade the papers read later more harshly than those graded earlier. To guard against this possibility, it is wise to read responses several times (when this is practical) and to shuffle the papers so the order is changed with each reading.

Results of essay exams sometimes reveal that expectations for pupils have been set too high. If a review of all answers reveals that many students have missed critical material, this may indicate that they need more instructional time. Grading criteria occasionally have to be adjusted so learners are not punished for not knowing material that the whole class needs to work on.

True/False Tests

True/false tests are widely used in elementary schools. Individual questions can be prepared quickly. Pupils have little difficulty learning how to take them. Because learners can respond to a large number of questions in a limited time, a single true/false test can cover much content. The tests can be corrected quickly. Many schools have machines that electronically score them, provided that learners mark responses on special answer sheets.

Because true/false tests depend on absolute judgments (that is, the answer must actually be "true" or "false" and not something in between), we have to be careful to avoid oversimplifying complex issues.

For example, suppose we asked pupils to respond "true" or "false" to this statement: *The sun set yesterday.* Quite likely our expectation is that learners will respond "true." However, the statement really represents an irresponsible distortion of a complex issue. True, the sun did *appear* to set yesterday, but it did not actually move at all. What happened was that the earth turned, and, to someone on the earth, the sun seemed to set.

True/false tests also have been accused of encouraging guessing rather than learning. Critics argue that pupils will sometimes get a higher score than they deserve as a result. Measurement specialists doubt that this is terribly serious, stating that pupils are as likely to guess wrong as to guess right. Overall, guessing is unlikely to raise the score of a pupil who does not know the content.

The following are guidelines for preparing true/false tests:

- Avoid giving unintentional clues. These include use of words such as *all, no, never,* and so forth, that tend to prompt an answer of "false."
- Approximately half of the questions should be false. True statements are easier to construct. Learners who guess tend to mark "true" more frequently than "false."
- Every statement should be clearly true or false. "The Yankees are the best baseball team," and similar subjective statements are not appropriate for a true/false test.
- Avoid double negatives in statements. "It is never undesirable to drink milk for breakfast," is a confusing double-negative statement. "Drinking milk for breakfast is recommended by a majority of health authorities," is much less confusing.

When learners' answers are not recorded on electronic scoring sheets, several options are available. Some teachers provide blanks in front of each statement. When providing blanks, we should not allow pupils to enter "T" for "true" or "F" for "false." The printing of these letters sometimes results in a hybrid form halfway between "T" and "F," and we don't know whether the pupil really means to indicate "true" or "false." We may suspect that the pupil does not know, either.

One remedy for this problem is to require pupils to write out the words "true" and "false." Some teachers tell pupils to use a "+" sign for "true" and a "0" for "false." An even better solution is to print the words *true* and *false* to the left of each statement, then direct learners to simply circle their choice.

Better true/false tests probe for understanding. Some of the best require pupils to look at several pieces of information at the same time and to answer related questions. For example, true/false tests can be used to assess pupils' abilities to grasp information presented in graphs, tables, and charts. An example of a true/false test that directs learners' attention to a table of information is presented in Figure 17–10.

Multiple-Choice Tests

Multiple-choice tests have several advantages. Unlike true/false tests, which give learners only two answer choices, multiple-choice tests provide three, four, or even five

Name:_____

**Ages at Which the Average American Man and Woman
Married at Different Historical Times***

Year	Age of Average Man When He Married	Age of Average Woman When She Married
1890	26	24
1910	25	21
1930	24	21
1950	23	20
1970	23	21

Directions

This is a true/false test. Each statement refers to the table above. Look at the table before you decide on your answer. Circle "true" for true statements; circle "false" for false statements.

true   false   1.   In 1890, the average man was older than the average woman at the time of marriage.

true   false   2.   The smallest difference between the age of the average man and the average woman at the time of marriage was in the year 1950.

true   false   3.   In 1970, the average man was younger at the time of his marriage than the average man in 1910.

true   false   4.   The greatest difference between the age of the average man and average woman at the time of marriage occurred in the years 1930 and 1970.

true   false   5.   This chart tells us that men married in 1890 at younger average ages than in 1970.

Figure 17–10

Sample true/false test.

*Source: Data are adapted from the U.S. Bureau of the Census. *Historical Statistics of the United States, Colonial Times to 1970*, Bicentennial ed., Part I. Washington, DC: U.S. Government Printing Office, 1975, p. 19.

options. As a result, they can test pupils' abilities to recognize degrees of "correctness." Though the length of individual questions is typically longer than in true/false tests, multiple-choice questions still do not require a great deal of time to complete. Consequently, a given multiple-choice test can cover a fairly large body of content.

Multiple-choice tests reduce chances that a learner will get a high score as a result of guessing. This is true because there are many more answer options than in true/false tests. As with true/false tests, multiple-choice tests can be scored quickly. Systems are available to score such tests electronically.

There are difficulties associated with preparing and using multiple-choice tests. A good test takes time to prepare. It is not easy to think of good *distractors* (plausible incorrect answers). Also, older learners are often inclined to argue that several options may be correct. Most problems associated with multiple-choice tests can be avoided if we take care when preparing individual questions.

The part of the multiple-choice question that introduces the item is called the *stem*. The alternative answers are called the *options*. In a properly prepared multiple-choice item, the stem should provide learners with a context for answering, and should serve a focusing function. Consider these two examples:

1. Washington
   (a) is a common family name in France.
   (b) is the capital of the United States.
   (c) is a province of Canada.
   (d) is a state on the Mississippi River.
2. The capital city of the United States is called
   (a) Ottawa.
   (b) Washington.
   (c) New York.
   (d) Richmond.

The options provided should be plausible. When some options make no logical sense, pupils will respond to the correct answer as much because of the nonsensical options as because of their knowledge of the content. For example, few pupils would have difficulty responding correctly to this item:

What is the softest?
   (a) cotton candy
   (b) brick
   (c) steel
   (d) window glass

Stems and options are stated positively in good multiple-choice items. Negatives can be very confusing. Note this example:

Which is not a statement correctly describing the duties of a governor?
   (a) The job of a governor cannot be said to include the supervision of his or her staff.
   (b) The governor does not serve as a member of the state supreme court.
   (c) The governor is not uninvolved in the affairs of a political party.
   (d) The governor is not absent from ceremonial events.

When preparing multiple-choice items, we need to assure that each stem has a single correct answer. The correct answer should not be a matter of opinion or judgment. Consider this example:

The very best chili peppers are grown in the state of

(a) Arizona.
(b) Texas.
(c) New Mexico.
(d) California.

Obviously, the question of which state has the best chili peppers is a matter of opinion. It is not something that can be adequately tested by a forced-choice test. Matters of opinion and debate are much better handled in essays.

Finally, when preparing multiple-choice questions, we need to exercise care in locating the correct answer. Placement of this answer should vary. There is a tendency for some teachers to select either option (b) or (c) as the correct answer in a four-option multiple-choice item. Evidence suggests that pupils who are guessing tend to answer (b) or (c). If too many correct answers are in those two places, these learners may receive higher scores than they deserve.

Matching Tests

Matching tests are especially useful when we want to test pupils' understandings of new terms. They are easy to construct and correct. They can focus learners' attention on important vocabulary terms they will need to know as they continue to work in a given unit of study. Matching tests cannot assess as broad a range of content as either true/false or multiple-choice tests. A matching test focuses exclusively on terms associated with a limited topic area.

Matching tests consist of two columns of information, one containing the definitions, the other containing the terms. Pupils match the definition with the term it describes. Blanks occur before each numbered definition, and letters of the alphabet precede each term. Learners as asked to place the letter of the correct term in the blank before its definition.

Measurement specialists prefer to set up matching tests so that definitions are on the left and terms are on the right. This practice encourages the learner to read the definition first and then to look for the term. The definition provides specific clues and makes the search for an appropriate term a relatively focused activity. The alternative arrangement causes pupils to look at individual terms and then to look through all of the definitions. This is less efficient than the preferred format.

It is essential that there be at least 25 percent more terms in the right column than there are definitions in the left. If there are *exactly* the same number of items in each column, then a pupil who misses one item is forced to miss two. [If the answer for item 1 is (a) and item 2 is (b), and a pupil selects (b) for item 1, the student has by default also missed item 2.] Adding choices makes it possible for the student to miss only one item if one of the additional distractors is chosen.

The entire matching test should be printed on a single page. Teachers sometimes prepare a matching test in which the right-hand column of terms is so much longer than the left-hand column of definitions that the right-hand column goes over to a second page. When this happens, some pupils invariably fail to notice the terms on the second page, and consequently their scores suffer. If length of the terms column is a problem, it is better to split the matching quiz into two separate tests, each of which contains all items on a single page. A properly formatted matching test is shown in Figure 17–11.

Completion Tests

Completion tests are easy to construct. They eliminate guessing and can sample a variety of content. However, an individual completion test does not usually cover as much content as either a true/false test or a multiple-choice test. Pupils must write responses in their own handwriting, which is a slower process than noting choices on true/false or multiple-choice forms.

We have to be careful when creating completion items. Unless an item is formatted properly, more than one answer may be logically defensible. Attention to the wording of the items can greatly diminish this problem. Consider these two versions of a completion item:

- The navigator sailing for Spain who many consider to be the discoverer of America was _____
- The name by which we know the navigator who sometimes is called the discoverer of America is _____

Name: _____

Topic: Resources

Directions

This is a matching test. Look at the definitions on the left. Then look at the words on the right. Find the word on the right that matches each definition. Place the letter before the word in the blank before its definition. There is only one correct answer for each definition.

_____ 1.   Materials people take from the earth to meet needs and wants.

_____ 2.   Resources that cannot be replaced.

_____ 3.   The source of fuels such as gasoline and oil.

_____ 4.   Special skills, knowledge, and tools people use to create things to make life better.

_____ 5.   Resources that can be replaced.

_____ 6.   Known supplies of a resource that are available for use.

a. human resources
b. coal
c. natural resources
d. technology
e. petroleum
f. geology
g. renewable resources
h. nonrenewable resources
i. reserves

Figure 17–11
Sample matching test.

The first version has many logical answers. For example, pupils who answered "a man," "a native of Italy," "A Genoan," or even "a sailor" might make a case for the correctness of their answer. The second version provides a better focus. It limits the range of probable answers, as a well-written completion item should do.

There are other correction problems associated with completion items. Paramount among these is the issue of spelling. Some teachers claim that since the major concern is mastery of content, then logically little attention need be paid to spelling. However, elementary social studies teachers are charged with teaching spelling as well as social studies. They often find themselves in a quandary when dealing with completion-test responses. To take too much off for spelling tends to turn the exercise into a spelling test. To take nothing off for misspelled words may convey to pupils that spelling is only important during the spelling period. This problem can be resolved by fixing the amount to be deducted for spelling errors and informing pupils beforehand.

Another dilemma we face when correcting completion tests concerns how to handle synonyms. If the correct word for a blank is *hat*, should the word *cap* be accepted? What about *chapeau* or *bandanna*? Answers to these question are important because doubts as to what constitutes a correct answer can undermine a test's reliability.

Some problems associated with completion items can be solved when a modified version of this test type is used. It features the usual sentences and blanks to be filled

---

Name: _____

Test Topic: Climate

Directions

This is a completion test. You are to fill in each blank. Read the words at the bottom of the page, select the word that belongs in each blank, and write it there. You will not use all of the words at the bottom of the page. Every blank has a different correct word; no word at the bottom of the page will be used more than one time.

The four basic elements of climate are temperature, precipitation, air pressure, and   1   . The amount of direct sunlight a place receives depends on its   2   . Little direct sunlight is received in   3   latitudes. Places in high latitudes are generally colder than places in   4   latitudes. Most of the United States is located in the   5   latitudes. Land surfaces cool more   6   than water surfaces. Air temperatures are   7   at high elevations than at low elevations. Temperatures are too low for the air to hold much   8   in high latitudes.

Choose answers from this list.

wind	latitude	low	cooler	dusts
snow	longitude	hotter	slowly	rapidly
moisture	high	middle	clouds	

Figure 17–12
Sample completion test.

in, but, in addition, provides a list of words at the bottom of the page. This list includes both answers and distractors. Pupils are told to find the correct word at the bottom of the page and to write it in the blank where it belongs. Since the words are there for pupils to see, they can be held accountable for spelling (simply a matter of correct copying). No synonyms are accepted because learners are directed to use only the words at the bottom of the page. See Figure 17–12 for an example of such a test. General guidelines for preparing a completion test are as follows:

- Use only one blank per item.
- Place the blank at or near the end of the item. This provides pupils with context clues.
- Avoid using "a" or "an" before the blank. These words will cue pupils to look either for a word beginning with a vowel or for a word beginning with a consonant.
- Avoid placing blanks in statements that have been extracted verbatim from the textbook. Such a practice encourages pupils to focus on textbook wording rather than on textbook content.

USING EVALUATION RESULTS TO IMPROVE INSTRUCTION

Evaluation results have uses beyond the assessment of individual pupil progress. They also help us to evaluate the quality of our instruction. When evaluation results are used for this purpose, scores of all learners are viewed collectively.

Suppose we gave a group of grade-five pupils a test over the general topic of the regions of the United States. The test included 28 items. Seven items focused on each of these subtopics: (1) climate, (2) topography, (3) natural resources, and (4) population characteristics. After analyzing pupils' scores, we found that the following percentages of learners had missed three or more questions in each subtopic area:

climate—10 percent

topography—12 percent

natural resources—25 percent

population characteristics—55 percent

These figures indicate that class members experienced the most difficulty with content related to population characteristics. Many also missed items associated with natural resources. These results might lead us to provide additional instruction to clear up misunderstandings related to both these topics. Additionally, the next time we teach this content (perhaps the following year to a new class), we might consider reorganizing and improving material relating to areas that test results indicated were problems for our present group of learners.

Teachers who make systematic use of their evaluation results are in a position to refine their instructional plans rationally. These results tell them what they are doing well and what areas might be presented more effectively another time. Over a period of several years, weak spots in the instructional program can be converted to areas of strength.

KEY IDEAS IN SUMMARY

1. Authentic evaluation is designed to encourage learners to master and demonstrate content in ways that are highly similar to how this content is used by proficient adults. The idea is to get away from traditional testing techniques that reward behaviors that, sometimes, have little relevance for the world beyond the school. In using authentic assessment, teachers are challenged both to identify appropriate ways for pupils to demonstrate what they have learned and to establish appropriate standards to use in judging the adequacy of pupils' performances.

2. Informal evaluation depends on teachers' observations of many different kinds of pupil performances. Often learners do not even know they are being evaluated. Informal evaluation occurs at all grade levels. Since informal techniques do not require learners to have well-developed reading and writing skills, they are particularly favored by primary-grades teachers.

3. There are many kinds of informal evaluation techniques. Among these are teacher observations, teacher–pupil discussions, pupil-produced tests, My Favorite Idea displays, learner-produced headlines and newspaper articles, word pairs, alphabet review games, mystery word scrambles, and anagrams.

4. Good recordkeeping is essential if teachers are to derive maximum benefit from informal evaluation procedures. Daily performance checklists keep track of pupils' progress. The teacher may later transfer relevant information to a social studies cumulative record form.

5. Formal evaluation includes tests by teachers and standardized tests prepared by commercial firms. Formal evaluation techniques are more common in the middle and upper grades than in the primary grades because most such procedures require learners to have mastered basic reading and writing skills.

6. Rating scales and checklists provide information about specific pupil behaviors. Rating scales may be used to make judgments about several levels of performance quality. Most checklists only indicate whether a pupil can or cannot do something.

7. Attitude inventories can be used to provide information about learners' reactions to various school subjects and to various parts of the social studies program. They require pupils to rate their relative interest in provided alternative selections.

8. Essay tests are most common in the upper grades. They require well-developed writing skills and provide learners with opportunities to put together isolated pieces of information in a meaningful way.

9. True/false tests can cover a broad range of content. Some critics say they encourage guessing. Their use is limited to testing content that can be described in terms of absolutes (something must be clearly true or false).

10. Multiple-choice tests help eliminate pupil guessing while allowing the teacher to sample a wide selection of content. Writing good multiple-choice items, however, is a difficult task that requires considerable time and composing skill.

11. Matching tests are useful for testing pupils' grasp of associations. All material for a given matching test should be printed on a single sheet of paper. Care must be exercised to design these tests in such a way that a pupil who misses one item does not automatically miss two.

12. Completion tests pose correction problems for teachers. To what extent should synonyms be accepted? How many misspellings should be tolerated? Some teachers prefer a test type that includes a list of words from which pupils are to select their answers. This reduces correction problems.

13. The evaluation of learning has two important functions. First, it provides a basis for assessing the progress of individual learners. Second, analysis of score patterns of a class can indicate to the teacher areas where instruction was not effective, suggesting areas to cover in a class discussion reviewing content covered in the test. It can also suggest needed modifications in the teacher's instructional plan when teaching the same content to other pupils.

CHAPTER REFLECTIONS

Directions: Now that you have finished reading the chapter, reread the case study at the beginning. Then answer these questions:

1. What is meant by *authentic assessment*?

2. Describe some of the problems teachers face in implementing authentic assessment.

3. Point out examples of informal evaluation tools often used by elementary teachers to assess pupils' learning of social studies content.

4. What are at least three evaluation procedures? Describe strengths and weaknesses of each.

5. How can results of evaluation be used to improve the social studies instructional program?

EXTENDING UNDERSTANDING AND SKILL

1. Do some reading related to the general topic of authentic assessment. Be especially alert for articles dealing with its application in elementary school settings. What problems have teachers encountered in developing more "authentic" assessments? What kinds of public relations issues have arisen as a result of decisions to implement authentic assessment? What benefits are claimed for this approach?

Specifically, what might you do to incorporate authentic assessment into your elementary social studies program? Summarize your answers to these questions in a short paper.

2. Read a textbook on the evaluation of learning. Prepare note cards on three or four formal evaluation techniques not mentioned in this chapter. Orally present these to the class.

3. Review several school social studies textbooks prepared for a grade level you would like to teach. Look at the ends of the chapters. What kinds of tests are provided? Do the books contain other suggestions relating to evaluation? Summarize your findings on a chart. Present it to your instructor for review.

4. Visit someone who teaches a grade level you would like to teach. Ask about the tests used in the social studies program. If possible, bring back samples of formal tests. Present an oral report to the class, and share copies with other students who may have an interest in the same grade level. Take care to point out the numbers of items on the tests and the tests' several levels of difficulty.

5. Begin a resource file of informal assessment techniques. Gather information from interviews of teachers and professors of education, from professional journals, from evaluation textbooks, and from other sources. Do not include any of the informal techniques mentioned in this chapter. Try to find at least 10 techniques appropriate for assessing pupils' social studies learning at a grade level you would like to teach. Share this material with your instructor and with your class.

REFERENCES

BAKER, E. L. (1994). "Making Performance Assessment Work: The Road Ahead." *Educational Leadership, 51* (6), pp. 58–62.

EBEL, R. L., AND FRISBIE, D. A. (1986). *Essentials of Educational Measurement.* 4th ed. Englewood Cliffs, NJ: Prentice-Hall.

GRONLUND, N. E., AND LINN, R. L. (1990). *Measurement and Evaluation in Teaching.* 6th ed. Englewood Cliffs, NJ: Merrill/Prentice Hall.

SPADY, W. G. (1994). "Choosing Outcomes of Significance." *Educational Leadership, 51* (6), pp. 18–22

STIGGINS, R. J. (1994). *Student-Centered Classroom Assessment.* Englewood Cliffs, NJ: Merrill/Prentice Hall.

United States Bureau of the Census. (1975). *Historical Statistics of the United States, Colonial Times to 1970.* Bicentennial ed., Part 1. Washington, DC: U.S. Government Printing Office.

WIGGINS, G. (1989). "A True Test: Toward More Authentic and Equitable Measurement." *Phi Delta Kappan, 70* (9), pp. 703–713.

SUBJECT INDEX

Activity cards, 182–185, 189

Affective domain, 133, 135, 156

Aims, 128, 156

Altering the content of learning, 176, 178

Altering learning goals, 177, 178

Altering the method of learning, 177, 178

Altering the rate of learning, 175, 178

Analemma, 432

Anthropology, 102–111, 120
    archaeology, 103
    classroom activities, 106–111
    cultural conflict, 109
    culture, 104–109
    human evolution, 103
    storytelling, 111

Assigned roles group, 201–202, 223

Authentic assessment, 519–521, 545
    problems, 520

Basic interpersonal communication skills, 494, 511

Bradley Commission on History in the Schools, 39, 41, 74
    themes, 41–42

Brainstorming, 245, 255
    rules, 245

Case studies, 310–315, 323, 336

CD-ROM, 412–414, 420

Children's literature, 50, 106, 109, 317, 365, 390, 464, 485

Citizenship education, 9, 28, 29
    civic competence, 9
    emphases, 11
        knowledge, 11
        skills, 12
        values, 12

Civics. *See* Citizenship education, Law-related education

Classroom debate, 210–212, 223
    debate sequence, 211–212

Cognitive/academic language proficiency, 494, 511

Cognitive domain, 132, 134, 156

Computers, 409–418
    arguments for, 416
    cautionary arguments, 417
    curriculum integration, 416, 421

Concept attainment, 168, 188

Concept formation/diagnosis, 168–170, 188

Concepts, 25–26, 166, 187
    attributes, 26
    types of concepts, 167
        conjunctive concepts, 167, 187
        disjunctive concepts, 167, 187
        relational concepts, 167, 187

Consumer Price Index, 467, 468–469

Content analysis, 98

Cooperative learning, 217–222, 223, 506
    approaches, 218
        jigsaw, 218–220
        learning together, 220
        teams achievement divisions, 221–222
    characteristics, 217

Creative thinking, 244–245, 255

Critical thinking, 246, 255
    steps, 246

Cultural literacy, 7

Culturally congruent instruction, 495

Curriculum, 14–19
    grade 1, 16
    grade 2, 17
    grade 3, 18
    grade 4, 18
    grade 5, 18
    grade 6, 18
    grade 7, 18–19
    grade 8, 19
    kindergarten, 16
    planning, 19
        focus questions, 20–23

Curriculum standards for the social studies, 14, 15

Data retrieval chart, 107, 241–243, 255, 338–339
Databases, 411, 420
Death education. *See* Psychology
Decision making, 250–253
    steps, 250

Economics, 63–74
    classroom activities, 64–73
        choices, 66
        costs, 66
        economic systems, 70–71
        future consequences, 72–73
        handy dandy guide, 64–73, 75
        incentives, 67–69
        trade, 72
    economics systems, 63
        command economies, 64
        market economies, 64
        traditional economies, 64
    scarcity, 63
Educational software, 409, 411–412
Energy education,
    classroom activities, 395–396
    issues, 384–387
    nonrenewable resources, 384–386
Environmental education, 380–384, 397
    challenges, 381–384
    classroom activities, 387–394
    deforestation, 381–382
    global warming, 381, 397
    ozone depletion, 383, 397
    toxic waste, 382–383, 397
Equal roles group, 199–201, 223
Ethnocentric. *See* Anthropology
Evaluation results usage, 544, 546

Formal evaluation, 530–544, 545
    attitude inventories, 535, 545
    completion tests, 542, 546
    essay tests, 535–537, 545
    learning checklists, 533–534
    matching tests, 541, 546
    multiple-choice tests, 538–541, 546
    rating scales, 530–533, 545
    true/false tests, 537–538, 545

Gender equity purposes, 357–359
    monitoring teaching procedures, 359–361
    sources of information, 371–372

    teaching approach, 366–367
Generalizations, 26, 171–174
Geographic Alliance Network, 62
Geography, 52–62, 74
    classroom activities, 58–62
    curriculum, 53
    Guidelines for Geographic Education: Elementary
        and Secondary Schools, 53
    human environment interaction, 54
    investigating location, 60
    location, 53
    movement, 55
    observing human-environment interactions, 61
    place, 53
    region, 57
    spatial interaction, 61
    thinking geographically, 58–60
Global education
    case studies, 336
    characteristics, 331, 332
    contributions emphasis, 337–338, 345
    criticisms, 333, 345
    experience emphasis, 336, 345
    intercultural emphasis, 338, 345
    learning experiences, 334–344
    monocultural emphasis, 335, 345
    oral history, 336
    personal emphasis, 340–344, 345
    purposes, 332, 344
    sources of information, 334
Globes, 430–433, 450
    advantages, 430
    disadvantages, 430, 451
    elementary globes, 432, 451
    intermediate globes, 433, 451
    parts of the globe, 433
    readiness globe, 431, 451
Goals, 128, 156
Group learning
    advantages, 196
    difficulties, 197
Group types, 198

History, 38–52, 74
    classroom activities, 43–50
    curriculum, 41–42
    external validity, 50, 74
    historical inquiry, 43
    holiday observances, 50

internal validity, 51, 74
investigating artifacts, 48
local community, 48
people resources, 47
time and chronology, 45–46
History and social science education, 10
    emphases, 12
        knowledge, 12
        skills, 12
        values, 13
History-Social Science Framework for California
        Public Schools, 39
Homework Hotline, 408

Individualized instruction, 165, 175, 188
    formal approaches, 177–187
Inducing a generalization, 171
Informal evaluation, 521–530, 545
    alphabet review games, 526
    anagrams, 527–528
    headlines, 525
    my favorite idea, 524–525
    mystery word scramble, 526–527
    newspaper articles, 525
    pupil produced tests, 524
    record keeping, 528–529, 545
    teacher observation, 523
    teacher-pupil discussion, 523
    word pairs, 525–526
Inquiry, 237–244, 254, 255. See also Reflective inquiry;
        History, historical inquiry
    basic steps, 238–239
    discrepant event, 243
    focusing pupils' thinking, 243
Instructional objectives, 130, 156
    audience, 130
    behavior, 131
    conditions, 131
    degree, 131
Instructional planning, 138–141, 155
    knowledge about available resources, 140
    knowledge about content, 139
    knowledge about learners, 138
    knowledge of teaching methods, 140
    pupils' expectations and prior experience, 139
Integrated curriculum, 460, 485
    the arts, 465
    language arts, 471
    mapping the integration, 463, 485

mathematics, 466–470
music, 465–466
science and technology, 470–471
Intended learning outcomes, 129, 156
Internet, 408, 414–415, 420, 421

Joint Committee on Geographic Education, 62
Joint Council on Economic Education, 73

Knowledge structure types, 504–506, 511
    choice, 505
    classification, 505
    description, 504
    evaluation, 505
    principles, 505
    sequence, 504

Law-related education
    basic legal concepts, 304
    basic questions, 303
    community resources, 320
    Constitution and Bill of Rights, 304
    consumer law, 306
    criminal law, 306
    definition, 301
    family law, 307
    goals, 302–303, 323
    information sources, 307–310, 323
    legal system, 305
    topics, 304–307, 323
Learning activity packages, 181–182, 183, 189
Learning centers, 179–180, 188
Learning contracts, 186, 189
    closed learning contracts, 186
    open learning contracts, 186
Lesson plans, 152–155, 156
    instructional objectives, 152
    managing learners, 154
    motivating, 153
        establishing a learning set, 153
    presenting content, 154
    teaching approaches, 152
Limited English proficient learners
    cooperative learning, 506
    cultural conflict, 495
    difficulty of material, 497
    guided writing, 510
    instructional practices, 506–510
    lack of background, 496

Limited English proficient learners, *continued*
    language experiences, 509
    multimedia and concrete experiences, 507
    potential problems, 494–497, 511
    semantic mapping, 510
    sequential curriculum, 496

Map and globe skills, 437–448, 451
    absolute location, 444, 445, 446
    direction, 442, 446
    earth–sun relationships, 447, 449
    interpreting maps and globes, 447–448, 449
    relative location, 444, 446
    scale, 438, 443
    shape, 438
    symbols, 439–442, 443
    teaching map and globe skills, 448–450, 451
Maps, 433–437
    conformal maps, 435
    distortion, 435, 450
    equal area maps, 436
    projections, 435
Metacognition, 232, 254
Mock trials, 317–319, 323
Moral action, 268
Moral decision making, 268, 282, 292
    teaching, 282–291
        historical application, 286–291
        steps, 283
Moral development stages, 277–279, 292
Moral dilemmas, 279–282
Moral judgment, 267. *See also* Moral dilemmas
Moral sensitivity, 267
Morality, 266
Motivation, 27, 29
Multicultural education
    classroom approaches, 361–371
    cultural deficit, 355, 372
    emphases, 355–356, 372
    genetic deficit, 354, 372
    goals, 357–359
    monitoring teaching procedures, 359–361, 372
    multiple perspectives, 368–371
        characteristics, 368
        example, 368–371
    single group studies, 361–367
        characteristics, 361–362
        examples, 362–367
    sources of information, 371

National Center for Economic Education for Young
        Children, 73
National Commission on Social Studies in the Schools, 38
National Council for Geographic Education, 62
National Council for History Education, 51
National Council for the Social Studies, 9, 52
    Task Force on Curriculum Standards, 14
    Task Force on Scope and Sequence, 16, 17
Native Americans, 106–107
Newspapers, 98

Personal digital assistant, 419, 421
Planning
    long range. *See* Unit planning
    short term. *See* Lesson plans
Political science, 81–91, 119
    classroom activities, 85–90
    conflict resolution, 87–90
    controversial issues, 90
    curriculum, 82–85
    foundations of American government, 90
    macropolitical organization, 84–85
    micropolitical organization, 82–84
    rule making, 86
Political socialization, 81–82
Problem solving, 246, 255
    steps, 247
Prosocial behavior, 266, 291
Psychology, 111–119, 120
    aggression, 114
    classroom activities, 114–119
    death education, 119
    emotions, 118
    fears, 114
    individual differences, 112, 117
    observing people, 115–116
    perception, 112–114, 117
Psychomotor domain, 136, 137, 156
Pupil performance standards, 14

Readers' theater, 472, 486
Reading study skills, 472–481, 486
    graphic post-organizers, 480
    interaction frames, 481
    multipass reading, 478
    ReQuest, 475
    structured overview, 474
    visual frameworks, 475–478
Reflective inquiry, 7, 28, 29. *See also* Inquiry

Reflective thinking and problem-solving education, 11
    emphases, 13
        knowledge, 13
        skills, 13
        values, 13
Reliability, 532
Role playing, 212–214, 223
    goals, 212
    steps, 214

Second language learning principles, 498–499, 511
    affective filter, 499
    context and cognitive load, 502–504
    meaningful and comprehensible input, 499
Self-concept. See Psychology
Sheltered instruction, 497–498, 511
    contextualization, 498
    interactional activities, 498
    simplified speech, 498
    task-function orientation, 498
Simulations, 215–217, 223
    simulation phases, 216
Small group approaches, 203–210
    buzz session, 208–210
    inside-outside, 205
    numbered heads together, 207
    think-pair-share, 205
    two-by-two, 203–205
Social problems, 6, 28. See Sociology
Social science disciplines, 10
Sociology, 91–102, 119
    classroom activities, 95–102
    communication, 94
    community studies, 100
    group membership, 96
    institutions, 92
    investigating communication, 97
    primary groups, 92
    relationships within and among groups, 94
    secondary groups, 93
    social change, 94
    social problems, 94, 100
    stratified groups, 93
Spreadsheets, 411, 420
Stages of language acquisition, 500–504
    early production, 501
    intermediate fluency, 502

    preproduction, 500
    speech emergence, 501
Storyline, 315–316
Storytelling. See Anthropology
Structure of knowledge, 23–27, 29

Thematic units, 459
    choosing themes, 460–463, 485
    contextualized, 462
    feasible, 461
    meaningful, 462
    worthwhile, 461
Thinking aloud, 233, 254
Tutoring group, 199, 222

Unit planning, 142–152, 156
    assessment ideas, 145
    identifying grade level, 143
    identifying prerequisite knowledge, 144
    identifying a topic, 143
    including features of quality social studies, 143
    integrating content, 144
    intended learning outcomes, 144
    organizational scheme, 144
    reviewing the unit, 145
    suggested teaching approaches, 145

Values, 266
    aesthetic values, 266, 292
    clarifying values, 269, 292
    classroom approaches, 268–277
    moral values, 267
    role playing, 272–277, 292
Videocassettes, 418, 421
Videodiscs, 418–419, 421
Visualizing thinking, 234, 254

Word processing, 410–411
Writing, 481
    language functions, 482–485, 486
        heuristic, 484
        imaginative, 485
        instrumental, 483
        interactional, 483
        personal, 484
        regulatory, 483
        representational, 484

NAME INDEX

Aardema, V., 111
Adler, D., 317
Alexander, P., 254
Aliki, 119
Allen, J., 64, 76
Armstrong, D., 64, 76, 136, 157, 467, 488
Au, K., 495, 513

Baer, J., 245, 256
Baer, R., 495, 496, 510, 513
Baker, E., 520, 547
Barr, I., 315, 325
Barr, R., 9, 31
Barth, J., 9, 31
Baylor, B., 107
Beane, J., 459, 487
Begay, S., 106
Bentley, J., 464
Berelson, B., 27, 31
Berman, S., 8, 31
Beyer, B., 250, 254, 256
Black, R., 472, 488
Bloom, B., 132, 133, 157, 158
Blumenfeld, P., 461, 487
Bocanegra, F., 364
Boehm, R., 76
Borich, G., 218, 225
Bratt, T., 495, 496, 510, 513
Brophy, J., 217, 218, 225, 360, 375
Brown, L., 381, 384, 400
Bruner, J., 23, 31
Bullard, S., 317
Buscagalia, L., 119
Bybee, R., 487

Chambers, R., 357, 375
Chandler, S., 465, 487
Cheney, L., 256
Cherryholmes, C., 7, 31
Chew, G., 48
Clark, C., 127, 138, 158

Clifton, L., 119
Clinton, W., 331, 346
Cohen, E., 196, 201, 225
Collier, C., 50
Collier, J., 50
Collins, E., 465, 487
Colman, P., 333, 347
Cosby, W., 288, 289, 290, 291
Costa, A., 254
Cummins, J., 496, 502, 503, 513

Denniston, D., 383, 400
DePaola, T., 106, 365
Dewey, J., 238, 256
D'Ignazio, F., 419, 423
Doyle, W., 127, 158
Dunn, K., 246, 255, 256
Dunn, R., 246, 255, 256
Durning, A., 381, 382, 400
Dyrli, O., 414, 423

Early, M., 513
Ebel, R., 524, 547
Eisner, E., 459, 460, 463, 465, 487
Englehart, M., 132, 157
Erickson, F., 355, 375

Fagan, B., 495, 496, 510, 513
Flavin, C., 381, 384, 400
Flynn, V., 357, 375
Foster, C., 225
Fraenkel, J., 190
Franklin, P., 106
French, J., 232, 245, 256
Frieberg, J., 265, 294
Frisbie, D., 524, 547
Fritz, J., 50, 109
Furst, E., 132, 157

Gagnon, P., 76
Gallant, R., 106, 107, 121

Garcia, E., 493, 506, 513
Garcia, R., 495, 513
Garland, S., 109
Garner, R., 254
Garza, C., 147
George, J., 109
Giese, J., 487
Goble, P., 365
Good, T., 217, 218, 225, 360, 375
Grant, C., 369, 371, 375
Griffin, S., 394, 400
Grismer, L., 119, 121
Gronlund, N., 129, 158, 534, 547

Halliday, M., 482, 487, 488
Harjo, L., 106, 121
Harmin, H., 133, 158
Harvey, K., 106, 121
Hasan, R., 482, 488
Hawkins, J., 265, 294
Hayman, W., 513
Heller, C., 265, 294
Hickey, M., 317, 325
Hill, W., 132, 157
Hirsch, E., 7, 31, 232, 256
Hoffman, M., 265, 294
Hoge, J., 90, 121
Hollins, E., 513
Holobec, E., 220, 225
Horwitt, S., 10
Hoskisson, K., 471, 488
Howe, L., 269, 292, 294
Hoyt-Goldsmith, D., 106
Hunt, I., 50

Ingpen, R., 119
Ishii-Jordan, S., 355, 375

Jackson, J., 106, 121
Jacobsen, J., 381, 382, 383, 400
Jarolimek, J., 225
Johnson, D., 220, 221, 225
Johnson, R., 220, 221, 225
Joyce, B., 214, 225

Kadrmas, S., 334, 347
Kagan, S., 207, 225
Katz, W., 106

Kawakami, A., 495, 513
Keller, H., 119
King, J., 513
King, M., 495, 496, 510, 513
Kirshenbaum, H., 269, 292, 294
Kohlberg, L., 269, 277, 279, 292, 294
Kracht, J., 76
Krajick, J., 461, 487
Krashen, S., 498, 513
Krathwohl, D., 132, 133, 157, 158

Lacapa, M., 106
La Farge, P., 8, 31
Lanegran, D., 76
Laughlin, M., 472, 488
Leming, J., 10, 31
Likona, T., 265, 294
Linn, R., 534, 547
Lipman, M., 246, 257
Loberg, M., 472, 488
Lyman, F., 205, 225

MacArthur, D., 434, 435
Malotki, E., 106
Manchester, W., 434
Manzo, A., 475, 488
Marker, G., 488
Marx, R., 461, 487
Masia, B., 133, 158
McCarthy, R., 423
McGowan, T., 27, 31
McGuire, M., 315, 325
McIntyre, W., 265, 294
McNeil, K., 49
McNeil, R., 49
McTighe, J., 205, 225
Mellonie, B., 119
Miles, G., 49
Miles, M., 107, 119
Mohan, B., 504, 513
Molner, L., 510, 513
Monk, J., 76
Morrill, R., 76

Natoli, S., 53, 76
Nelson, M., 91, 103, 111, 121
Nickerson, R., 232, 257
Nixon, J., 317

Northrup, T., 411, 423
Norton, D., 464, 488
Nuno, J., 364

O'Brien, K., 390, 391, 400
O'Connor, M., 387, 400
O'Dell, S., 50, 464
Olmstead, J., 196, 225
O'Neil, J., 333, 347

Parisi, L., 487
Parker, W., 7, 31, 232, 257
Paterson, K., 119
Patrick, J., 90, 121
Perez, B., 497, 513
Perkins, D., 232, 257
Perry, C., 265, 294
Peterson, P., 127, 138, 158
Peterson, R., 355, 375
Postel, S., 381, 400
Pugnetti, G., 347

Raths, L., 133, 158
Ravitch, D., 232, 257
Rest, J., 267, 292, 294
Reyes, M., 510, 513
Rhoder, C., 232, 245, 256
Risinger, F., 37, 76
Rogers, C., 265, 294
Rogers, F., 119
Rooze, G., 411, 423
Roy, P., 220, 225
Rudman, M., 464, 488
Ruggiero, V., 244, 257

Santelesa, R., 419, 423
Savage, M., 50, 76, 464, 488
Savage, T., 50, 76, 136, 157, 464, 467, 488
Scheid, K., 232, 254, 257
Schmuck, P., 357, 375
Schmuck, R., 357, 375
Schug, M., 50, 64, 65, 76, 417, 423
Shaftel, F., 277, 294
Shaftel, G., 277, 294
Shea, C., 383, 387, 400
Shermis, S., 9, 31
Short, P., 495, 496, 497, 513

Simon, S., 133, 158, 269, 292, 294
Sisson, E., 391, 393, 400
Slabbert, J., 244, 245, 257
Slavin, R., 221, 225
Sleeter, C., 369, 371, 375
Smith, E., 232, 257
Smith, P., 27, 31
Soloway, E., 461, 487
Sorauf, F., 82, 121
Sowards, A., 395, 400
Spady, W., 520, 547
Squires, T., 48
Stahl, R., 91, 103, 111, 121
Starke, L., 400
Stearns, P., 409, 423
Steiner, G., 27, 31
Stiggins, R., 519, 521, 547
Stoner, D., 390, 391, 400
Strutchens, M., 354, 375
Suchman, J., 243, 244, 255, 257
Sunal, C., 339, 347
Sutton, A., 27, 31

Taba, H., 23, 31, 169, 190
Taylor, P., 10, 31
Terrell, T., 513
Thayer, W., 370
Thornton, S., 7, 31
Tompkins, G., 471, 488
Torres-Guzman, M., 497, 513
Tye, B., 331, 346, 347
Tye, K., 331, 346, 347

Viorst, J., 119

Wass, H., 119, 121
Wasson, D., 301, 325
Weber, P., 381, 400
Weil, M., 214, 225
Wentworth, D., 64, 65, 76
Wiggins, G., 520, 547
Wildsmith, F., 390
Williams, M., 294
Winitzky, N., 195, 196, 225

Zenger, J., 288, 289, 290, 291
Zuniga-Hill, C., 500